P9-CFI-458

WORLD BOOK COMPANY

Professional Books in Education

VAN MILLER, *Consulting Editor*

ADOLESCENT
DEVELOPMENT
in American Culture

Harold W. Bernard

GENERAL EXTENSION DIVISION
OREGON STATE SYSTEM
OF HIGHER EDUCATION

WORLD BOOK COMPANY

Yonkers-on-Hudson, New York

ADOLESCENCE is a period of development that proceeds from childhood and charts the course toward maturity. The period is characterized by a gratifyingly large number of successes in overcoming the many difficulties that are encountered. The perennial concern over the teen agers is experienced by adults who, a decade or two ago, caused their own parents and teachers to worry. These considerations form the basic framework for this book. We must know the obstacles that confront the adolescent and we must view the hazards with a perspective that permits proper evaluation. We can then reduce or avoid some of the difficulties and make the adolescent period more successful for more young persons.

The tone of this book is fundamentally optimistic. While recognizing that some adolescents fail, it is also acknowledged that most have varying degrees of success in their progress toward maturity. Emphasis is on the majority of adolescents, who are growing symmetrically, rather than on the attention-demanding, spectacular minority. Often the author has taken familiar data and given them a somewhat different interpretation. This is most frequently done by showing that not one, but many, factors produce behavior. Through the expanded interpretation the hope for better behaviors and attitudes may be perceived. Optimism leads to a greater stress on citizenship than on the more sensational subject of delinquency.

The major emphasis is on the force of culture in creating the problems of, and shaping the behavior of, adolescents. Behavior is learned; and while intelligence and physique must be considered, it is the cultural milieu—socio-economic status, the family, the community, the school, the working world—that is uppermost in shaping the direction (if not the rate) of development. The emphasis on cultural dynamics is accomplished by (1) first developing certain basic concepts—the meaning of adolescence, growth principles, the unique needs of adolescents, and by describing the features of American culture that bear most heavily on adolescents. (2) Next a number of the factors that combine to produce behavior —physical, intellectual, and emotional development, and the home, school, and socio-economic status—are discussed. (3) The next part reveals the outcome of these forces in the form of interests, moral and spiritual values, and social adjustments. Perspective is maintained by discussing some of the instances in which adolescents fail to make adjustments to the demands placed upon them. (4) The final part points to the fact that the problems of adolescence simply prepare and inoculate an individual for his next developmental tasks. In late adolescence and early maturity he must establish his own home, become a citizen, a producer, and begin to face the reality that he soon will be the leader of the following generation.

The book is addressed to parents, counselors, teachers, and those in late adolescence who will soon assume these adult roles. The materials have previously been used with such persons and a gratifying response has been obtained. Throughout, there is an attempt to show what the data presented mean in terms of guiding and helping the adolescent.

Case studies have been sparingly used despite the advice of many that they make interesting reading. The case approach has been avoided because the author believes that surveying a limited number of cases may lead to an ill-founded feeling of understanding and competence. Actually, what produces delinquency in one may produce a drive to achievement in another. A successful technique in the hands of one teacher is a failure for another. But whatever the symptom of behavior, we know that there are causes; and for each person the causes—and the remedy—are unique. Adolescents have much in common but each is a case in himself, not to be duplicated in a text.

Research materials have been studied and integrated into the entire volume. Complete coverage of research data has not been attempted, but representative sampling has been sought.

Many people have contributed to the completion of this volume. Dean J. C. Caughlan and Dean Viron A. Moore have avoided "loading" me with heavy committee and teaching responsibilities. Glenn M. Blair, Lawrence E. Cole, and Van Miller have made specific and helpful suggestions for improving the manuscript.

The photograph facing the opening page of Chapter Four is a United Press Photo. The photograph facing the opening page of Chapter Fourteen is used through the courtesy of the Chief of Police, Portland, Oregon. The photograph of the bride and groom (Chapter Fifteen) is of Hal and Sue Sloat and is used with their permission. All other photographs were provided through the courtesy of the Department of Instructional Materials, Portland Public Schools, Portland, Oregon. The authors and publishers who permitted direct quotations from their books and articles receive acknowledgment in footnotes.

My wife, Evelyn, has helped to provide the time which it takes to incubate and hatch a product of this kind. Mrs. Alta Diment typed and re-typed the manuscript many times and kept a constant check against errors in references and grammar.

HAROLD W. BERNARD

Contents

List of Figures

List of Tables

Part One

BASIC CONCEPTS IN

THE PSYCHOLOGY

OF ADOLESCENCE

ADOLESCENCE is but one stage or phase of the total life processes of continuous development. Many factors influence patterns of growth prior to adolescence, and what takes place during adolescence charts the course of subsequent development. These factors are sometimes called physiological, sociological, economic, and the like, but all must be considered as having intimate bearing on what is termed psychological.

Part One of this volume explains the interrelations of the multiple forces which influence growth and defines the particular use of recurrent terms. Psychological factors that pervade the entire course of development are described with particular reference to their impact during adolescence. Thus principles of growth and the concept of need satisfaction are discussed with special emphasis on adolescents.

The course of human development is profoundly influenced by the culture in which individuals live; hence a basic part of the orientation for this book has to do with the problems that are particularly insistent in American culture. Although physiological development and the general principles of growth will be much the same in all societies, certain problems of growth are unique in our indigenous culture. These include such things as age of marriage, work opportunities, the tradition of education for all, speed of technological change, and war and the threat of war. These receive special attention because they so profoundly affect the course of growth during adolescence.

The basic principles of growth and the uniqueness of American culture are operative in all aspects of adolescent development. These are discussed in greater detail in the remaining three parts of the book.

What are the facts about the nature of adolescence? Is the nation's future dim or will today's adolescents help build a better world? Why is an optimistic view of adolescents warranted?

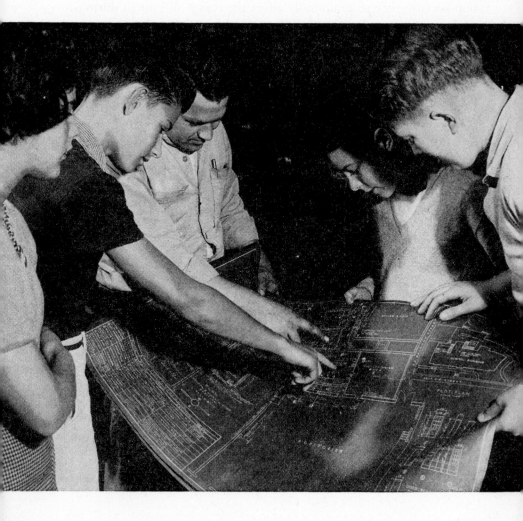

CHAPTER ONE

The Meaning of Adolescence

Adolescents are the hope and future of our nation. The study of adolescence is the despair of the psychologist. It has been said: "You can always tell an adolescent—but you can't tell him much." It may be said of the study of adolescence: Much is known about adolescence, but a great deal of it is not true. At least, many of the generalizations made about adolescents and adolescence contain only part of the truth. Since adolescents are the hope and future of our nation, it is important that the phenomena of adolescence be seen clearly. The elements of truth in current generalizations must be expanded to include the data that are less clearly recognized. When adults—parents, teachers, counselors, youth workers—see more of the whole truth, and act accordingly, the great promise of youth will be more completely fulfilled.

Points of view

The spectacular versus the statistical

A front page item of today's paper carries the headline, "RAID SNARES 13 TEEN AGERS." The details follow: "Thirteen teen-age boys and girls, many of them partly intoxicated and partly undressed, landed in police custody early Sunday when juvenile division police and a liquor agent raided a noisy beer and petting party at 4905 S. E. 84th Avenue." The last line, after more details, is (at

5

this point) of parenthetical interest: "Police reported the parents of the host teen ager were away for the week end." [253]

The spectacular attracted nation-wide headlines and was described in leading news magazines when some baby-sitters went astray. Three teen-age girls, fifteen, sixteen and seventeen years old, were caring for a doctor's children when they decided things were too dull. They hastily agreed to take a few of the mother's clothes and embark on a trip. They found not only clothes but $18,000, which they added to their loot. A little shopping enlarged their wardrobes. After cocktails and meeting some boys the remainder of their cash was gone and so was their liberty. In a few brief hours they had stolen a huge sum of money, registered as Mrs. at a hotel with boy friends, and smirked at their pictures when the police showed them the newspapers.

We are periodically dismayed by the statistics on violent crime which show that teen agers contribute to it to a degree that is out of all proportion to their numbers in the total population. These statistics could lead to the conclusion that adolescents are unstable, unpredictable, and are a burdensome—even dangerous—element in our society. The headlines are read and the conclusion is reached that the younger generation is "going to the dogs." It may be encouraging for adults to know that this conclusion is perennial. [92:2] About 2350 years ago Socrates was ready to give up hope for the coming generations. "The children now love luxury; they show disrespect for elders and love chatter in place of exercise. Children are now tyrants, not the servants of their households. They no longer rise when elders enter the room. They contradict their parents, chatter before company, gobble up dainties at the table, cross their legs, and tyrannize over their teachers." Socrates's words should help remind the adult of today that his parents probably wondered about whether or not the then younger generation would be able to make it under their own power.

An optimistic view of youth is more than a matter of blind faith. There is much evidence that young people will keep moving forward. The author examined the inside page of the same paper that carried the "RAID SNARES 13 TEEN AGERS" headline. One article indicated that close to three million students are now in college— ten times the enrollment of 1900. Moreover, these students are in large numbers earning their own way, winning scholarships in order to pay part of the costs, or promising to pay back money loaned to them. The other article, in the same issue, was headlined, "YOUTH DISAPPOINTED IN ELDERS' FAILURE TO ACHIEVE RACIAL EQUALITY IN NATION." The beginning words of the article provide grounds for the proper evaluation of the "13 TEEN AGERS" headline: "American youth are disappointed in failure of their elders to achieve racial equality in this country—and predict that the next generation will correct this situation, student panelists at the eighth annual meeting of the Portland Urban league declared Sunday. The meeting, at Benson High School auditorium, *attracted 1000 persons.* Carlos Ogimi, Reed College student body president, said mankind's biggest problem consists in helping the world's non-white peoples to find a satisfactory way of life." *

At the same time the three teen-age girls were adventuring with sex and $18,000, another less spectacular event was taking place. Forty finalists had come from all over the nation to compete at Washington, D. C. for Westinghouse's "Search for Science Talent." The first place winner won a $2,800 scholarship, and all the prizes amounted to $12,200. Bringing this down to cases, Patricia K. played an important role at the graduation exercises of her high school. (The slight newspaper mention is more a reflection of what people read than it is an indication of editorial policy.) Pat had played a difficult piano composition as a part of the graduation exercises. There she was introduced as having won a four-year scholarship to the college of her choosing as the result of her successful participation in the Westinghouse competition. She, like the three baby-sitters, had sought adventure and excitement. She had found a more real and lasting kind of adventure.

Military leaders and statesmen assert that we have much to be thankful for, in the United States, in terms of agricultural, mineral, technological, power, and transportation resources. But these men quickly add that these are not the most gratifying resources. The greatest national resource is the young men and women who transform material resources into military might. (It will be shown later in the chapter that Hitler and Mussolini recognized this resource.)

* "Youth Disappointed in Elders' Failure to Achieve Racial Equality in Nation," *The Oregonian,* April 13, 1953.

These young people are adaptable, courageous, confident, and intelligent. They are not "trained" to fight; they *are* educated for adaptability.

There are many answers to the question, "What is the typical adolescent like?" Many answers are couched in terms of instability, foolhardiness, intemperance, or delinquency. These are, however, the minority. Against thirteen "partly intoxicated" teen agers there are a thousand youth studying serious problems. Against three errant baby-sitters there are forty vying for college scholarships. Against our deplorable rate of delinquency there are thousands of youth manning the military outposts of the nation. There is a discouraging spectacular view of adolescents. There is a counterbalancing, encouraging statistical view.

The physiological view

At the beginning of the century, the work of G. Stanley Hall [127] set the theme for emphasis upon the physiology of adolescence. He performed a great service for students of behavior by pointing out ways in which the adolescent period differed from other phases of life. Much attention was devoted to the thesis that adolescence was a period of stress and strain. Hall, and the writers who studied his works, attributed many of the peculiarities of adolescence to the physical facts of puberty. Rapid growth, changes in voice, alteration of body proportion, the growth of facial and axillary hair, and the increase in size and function of the sex organs seemed to constitute the important explanatory factors for the uniqueness of adolescence.

These physiological factors must be considered in a rounded view of the phenomena of adolescence. But the physical factors must be considered in the context of the period in which one lives and in the particular cultural milieu. Further, the "unique" developments of adolescence must be studied in terms of antecedent growth. There is considerable danger of overemphasizing the physical and unique events when studying adolescence. It is taking a long time to catch up with the thinking of some pioneers in the proper assessment of physiological factors. In 1924 L. M. Terman, writing in the preface of M. A. Bigelow's book, indicated that there had been too much emphasis on the physiological aspects of adolescence. He commended Bigelow for stressing the continuity (rather than the cataclysmic nature) of growth and for showing how the social environment intensifies the normal growth processes. [24:v–vi]

Another authority to question the hypothesis that growth processes, inherent within the individual, accounted for the phenomena of adolescence was Leta S. Hollingworth. [144] She pointed out that growth, change and development are normal processes. These orderly changes would not, in most cases, explain aberrations of behavior.

The tendency to view the physiological factors as aspects of the total context in which adolescents function was given impetus by studies of comparative culture. Margaret Mead drew attention to the fact that adolescence, as a period of stress and strain, was probably the result of cultural pressures. [210] Ruth Benedict compared three distinctly different societies and showed that the behavior and adjustment of a person, at any age, can only be explained in terms of the customs, goals, personal relationships and beliefs that permeate that society. [16]

The cultural view

The lessons anticipated by Mead and Benedict have been forcefully stressed by Robert J. Havighurst in *Developmental Tasks in Education,* W. Lloyd Warner and others in *Who Shall Be Educated?* and A. B. Hollingshead in *Elmtown's Youth.* These books describe the class differences that exist in our nation and show how they markedly influence the behavior of individuals. One of the steps forward that must be taken in the study of adolescence is for us to understand the influences social class has on behavior (see Chapter Eight). If we go on thinking that the muscle and hormones of growth are what explain adolescence our conclusions will be based on partial data. The vast differences between individuals in attitudes toward and habits in education, marriage, and work may be generated by androgens and estrogens and other hormones, but those attitudes are molded by culture.

There need be no wish to "return to the good old days," in the statement that there are profoundly different influences operating today from those of five or ten decades past. These will be dealt with in later chapters, so we need only list them now.

1. Adolescents are more and more becoming a minority group. In 1800 the average age in this country was sixteen; today only about 34 per cent of the population is less than twenty. Society is increasingly being geared to the speed and orientation of chronologically mature persons.

2. The faith of Americans in the value of education still continues to be strengthened. More and more people are staying in school for longer periods. Thus, in a society where one of our first questions to a new acquaintance is "What work are you in?", opportunities for work are long delayed.

3. Youth find it increasingly difficult to be placed in remunerative work. Technological changes make more advanced working skills necessary. Older, experienced workmen are preferred over the stronger, but less skilled, youthful aspirant for a job. The coming age of "automation" threatens to magnify this problem. Getting one's first job is also made more difficult by the increasing number of older persons in our population—living longer, they hold the available positions more tenaciously. Minimum age laws for employment also tend to delay the entry of young persons into paid work. These factors force on adolescents a condition of prolonged dependency and increase the financial burden on parents—which, in some cases, generates a handicapping resentment.

4. All of the foregoing factors combine to form a sentiment against youth's getting married, even though sexual maturation has been achieved and the sex drive is at or near its peak strength.* Yet study of comparative culture and our own national history proves that the assumption of early responsibility has promoted more symmetrical progress in maturing.

5. Our society is steadily growing more complex. (This author does not, however, imply that life is more difficult—we also have more information and techniques to meet the complex problems.) Hence, prolonged education is necessary to prepare people to live in a smaller and more scientific world.

---

* The danger of generalizations about adolescence and adolescents is here illustrated. The fact is that the age of marriage has lowered in recent years due to GI assistance in prolonged education—and perhaps due to changing attitudes of some parents. Further, it must be noted that the effect of sexual maturation is conditioned by knowledge about and attitudes toward the physical aspects of sex.

The individual view

Anthropology and biology must be supplemented by the psychological data regarding individual differences. It seems that a great many of the generalizations about adolescence must have been based upon the unique and exceptional. The waywardness of youth and the awkwardness of adolescence are illustrations. Some youth are wayward and some are awkward—but neither kind represents the generality. One of the difficult problems of *some* adolescents is the matter of wide differences in which the age of puberty is reached. Some boys manifest evidences of puberty at the age of ten while others will show the same evidences as late as twenty. [255] Girls have their menarche as early as nine years and as late as twenty. [282]

An examination of the diaries of boys and girls shows vastly different experiences and values. That which is for some a major problem is not only not mentioned by others but apparently is not even of enough concern to be "covered up." Some youngsters look forward with eagerness to several post-graduate years in order to become physicists, psychologists, or physicians; others view education as an obstacle to their immediate gainful employment.

An appreciation of the differences between individuals may be stimulated by a study of the physical facts of puberty. It may be furthered by an appraisal of economic condition and social class status. William H. Sheldon's books, *The Varieties of Temperament* and *Varieties of Delinquent Youth* emphasize, if they do not explain, some facts about difference in physique and behavior. Both adults and adolescents must appreciate the fact that deviation from some hypothetical average is both normal and inevitable. Anna Freud has made a thought provoking suggestion in the conclusion that the characteristic problem of the adolescent has to do with the strength of his instincts. His anxieties are not necessarily associated with any one specific drive, such as sex. [112:168]

Those who are tempted to generalize about adolescence might do well to reconsider periodically the abundant data regarding individual differences.

The importance of a viewpoint

The significance of the point of view one takes is illustrated by the differences in data produced by various studies. The G. Stanley Hall pattern of studies emphasizes the element of stress and strain. Adolescence was to Hall and his followers a difficult period of transition from childhood to maturity. Adolescence, according to Benedict, Havighurst, Hollingshead, and Mead is simply a matter of continuous growth. It is complicated and difficult or orderly and progressive depending upon the kind of demands placed upon the adolescent in terms of his class and culture. The California Adolescent Growth Study, under the direction of Harold E. Jones, draws attention to the continuity of growth. It is apparent that adolescence should be seen in the broad setting of what has gone on before and what will follow. The physical and cultural facts must be taken into consideration.

Data such as those mentioned in the preceding paragraph may be called objective, but a rounded study of adolescence must also include certain subjective data. Adults need to know that there is a difference in the representative view that they take of events from the view taken by a representative adolescent. Adults have less appreciation for physical action than do adolescents. Adults are probably less inclined to court adventure and excitement. An evening at home may be dreaded by an effervescent youngster but eagerly anticipated by the jaded adult. These and many other differences in viewpoint must be appreciated by those adults who wish to understand the motivations and behaviors of adolescents.

Subjectivity is operative whether one's view of adolescents is fundamentally optimistic or pessimistic. Certainly, the psychology of suggestion gives a theoretical basis for adopting the optimistic view. (1) We tend to see that for which we are looking. Many deer hunters are killed or injured each year because this tendency is not considered. (2) Individuals tend to live up to the expectations established for them. Parents who expect their boys to be gentlemen often have gentlemen for sons. Parents who expect the worst from their children frequently find that their expectations are justified. (3) Attitudes are contagious. If some adults are optimistic about the place and role of adolescents they invite others to adopt the same attitude. Adolescents themselves will absorb some of the confidence.

Hal Boyle, war correspondent and columnist, reveals perspective and optimism (both worth emulating) in the following words:

America is a strange land where the old people are forgotten and the young are denounced.

Right now the scapegoat of our times is "the teen-ager." Practically everybody seems to be picking on him. But as far as I can tell his basic crime consists in the fact he is over twelve and hasn't yet reached the age of twenty. He is in his teens, and that seems automatically to make him a criminal suspect these days.

The teen-ager is a headline kind, according to the stock caricature of him now emerging. He dresses like a bum, has the manners of an ape, and if you look into one of his ears you can see daylight coming through the other ear.

He is a noisy, shiftless, full time freeloader off his parents, or else he earns his pin money selling dope to his high school buddies. He is a hot-rod driver. He and his teen-age girl friend spend their evenings seeking panic thrills. Their favorite fun: Smoking reefers, holding up filling stations, and dynamiting Sunday Schools.

It is all so familiar. Youth always seems to be going to hell in some kind of wagon, or so middle-aged people want to believe. A generation ago the devils of their day were the daring flappers. . . .

Next the rah-rah college boy . . . "What is our country coming to?"

Well, it has come to the teen-ager, and I think we are pretty lucky to have him. . . .

The teen-ager of today was born in a major economic depression and reared in an atmosphere of world war and international tension. . . .

I think one reason for the sometimes frantic criticism of the teen-ager is the realization among adults that their world may hinge in the next few years upon whether the teen-ager can stand up under strain.

He will. In Korea I met a squad who told me proudly about one of their teen-age members: "He carried and dragged a wounded buddy 40 miles across the hills."

Crossing the teens is a perilous journey for any child growing into manhood. He needs help not yelps. If I were a teen-ager today, I'd tell myself:

"Look, you middle-aged critics, it isn't my fault I'm young or that you are growing old. Go on and make a better world yourself—if you can. But be mad at time, not at me. I'm wise to you—you're just jealous of me." *

The author subscribes to this point of view because of his experience as a classification officer for the U. S. Navy and as a member of summary and general courts martial boards; both the good and the bad were seen. Thousands of teen agers were serious, stable, willing and eager to serve. Resentment at having educational careers and marriage delayed or interrupted was a minor note against the theme, "There's a job to be done. Let's get it over with."

This theme is repeated in the following words:

Young people most bitterly know the frightful cost of living to keep peace in the world, and they willingly submit to the cost, not from want of spirit, but from a knowledge that it is the best thing to do. You cannot say of them, "Youth Will Be Served," because the phrase suggests a voracious striking out from security, wealth and stability. The best you can say for this younger generation is, "Youth Will Serve." †

This article from *Time* begins with the caution that should be observed in the writing of a book on adolescence, a caution that should be adopted by every student of adolescence. It is the caution that parents, youth workers, teachers, and ministers must frequently call to mind—the difficulty of painting a portrait of an entire generation. "Each generation has a million faces and million voices. What the voices say is not necessarily what it will act on. Its motives and desires are often hidden. It is a medley of good and evil, promise and threat, hope and despair." ‡ With this warning some gen-

---

* Hal Boyle, Associated Press, June 8, 1951. Quoted by permission of Wide World Photos, Inc.

† "The Younger Generation," *Time*, 58, Nov. 5, 1951, p. 52. Courtesy *Time* Magazine; copyright Time Inc., 1951.

‡ *Ibid.*, p. 46. Courtesy *Time* Magazine; copyright Time Inc., 1951.

eralizations are made in the article: Youth are grave and fatalistic. They are conventional and gregarious. Girls want to have both a career and marriage. Youths' morals are confused. They expect disappointment. They want a faith and they will serve. They are silent—they do not make speeches, issue manifestoes or carry placards.

The necessity, and perhaps inevitability, of a viewpoint is demonstrated by Thornton Wilder's reaction to this article. He admits the element of truth in the generalizations but proposes to "read the manifestations differently." He sees youth today as trying to consolidate and stabilize a liberty that has been won and/or thrust upon them. Their apathy has been acquired from their elders who have not been sure how much authority they should use and how to use it. Their desire for security Wilder sees as a desire to avoid "false situations"—for example, incompetency and duplicity in high places. He sees youth today as being the first ones really to face the situation of international men and women. Their search for faith he sees as a manifestation of the fact that youth look around and see the failure of the faith adults profess. Their self-containment is not apathy —it is due to the fact that they cannot explain and explore their complex world at the same time. He asks those who lack faith in adolescents to visit with some of the Fulbright scholars with whom he conversed. [346]

The reader need not anticipate that this book will depend entirely upon a sentimental view of the adolescent. Research data will be used and used liberally, but there will not be solely a cataloging or summarizing of research studies. Not only must research data be collected and classified, they must also be interpreted. [344:410] Adolescents can be better understood if the data are interpreted in terms of a fundamentally optimistic viewpoint. Faith in youth is central to understanding.

Some basic concepts of adolescence

The weakness of generalizations

It should be obvious from the foregoing material that generalizations must be made with caution. Many generalizations are based upon extremely limited data. What happens during one's own youth, what one's own adolescent son or daughter does, or what is read in the paper, does not necessarily represent the generality— the norm. What may be the norm for a particular community is often not a sound basis for a generalization applied to another region. What was generally true of the adolescent of the depression days does not represent a trend when youth are living in a state of preparation for hot or cold war.

Numerous generalizations, many of which represent extant beliefs, will be examined in subsequent chapters. Those that stand the test of representing the majority of young people must still be regarded only as rough guides. In the final analysis generalizations will help to formulate inclusive programs for groups of adolescents. But these same valid generalizations may not be helpful in understanding individuals. Those who work with adolescents must do what Wilder implies—get back of the general to the causes of the particular.

The principle of multiple causation

Multiple causation must be dealt with in the study of adolescence. It has already been indicated that adolescence is more than a matter of physical and physiological growth factors. These are important but they take place in a particular historical era. Growth takes place in a particular cultural milieu (pity the teen-age girl who is too thin or too fat to fit the Hollywood mode). Physical development takes place in a family atmosphere—some fathers jest at the son's upper-lip down while some mothers help their daughters to be proud of womanhood. Some teachers willingly and objectively discuss matters of sex development while others say, "They will learn about the filthy stuff soon enough anyway." The growth and characteristics of adolescents will not be understood until appreciation is developed for the multiplicity of causes.

If this multiplicity seems so obvious as to warrant no attention, the reader might reflect on some of the questions he has asked or heard asked. "What causes delinquency?" "Why does my child suck his thumb?" "Why are youth so impolite?" or "What can I do with a pupil who is just plain lazy?" are questions that reveal a certain näiveté, which needs to be dispelled. One can pick up almost any magazine or newspaper and find the simple answer. "Waywardness of youth laid on doorstep of home," "Schools flayed for failing to meet youth needs," "Police too lax with youthful offenders," and "Community neglectful of opportunities to aid youth" are titles which *when combined* indicate the approach that must be made. Parents, teachers, civic leaders and officials, religious workers, medical doctors, heads of public amusement centers, and youth workers can as individuals take some of the forward steps in aiding adolescents. All of them *working together with* and for youth can help to realize more of the potential that is expressed by various optimists.

Adolescence and puberty

Adolescence as a social phenomenon will be better understood if there is a distinction made between it and puberty. *Puberty* refers to the beginning maturation of the physical aspects of sex. The word *pubescence* originally referred to the growth of hair in the pubic and other areas. [24:12ff.] More will be said of pubescence in the next chapter, but it should be mentioned now that the onset of puberty is rather clearly definable.

Adolescence, strictly speaking, refers simply to the process of growing up. It is a period of life set off from other periods for the sake of convenience in academic discussion. It is intimately related to what has preceded and what will ultimately develop. Adolescence begins with puberty and ends with maturity. These words are clear but the period is not. Maturity is a difficult thing to define, difficult because it is variable (see Figure 1). In some places, times, and societies one assumes adult functions at the age of sixteen years. In some instances (man studying for a medical career) one may still be dependent and consequently not an adult until the late twenties. Service in the armed forces gives some teen agers an opportunity to perform adult roles at a relatively early age.

It is at the point of distinguishing between puberty and adolescence that the assertion can be made that adolescence is a product of our times and culture. The phenomena of adolescence are firmly rooted in physical fact and cultural setting.

Adolescence is a phase of growth. There are many generalizations that can be made about growth processes. One of the more significant principles, from the standpoint of adolescence, is "Growth is continuous and gradual." R. H. Kuhlen places major emphasis on

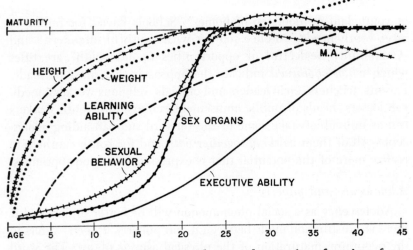

FIG. 1. **Curves representing growth toward maturity of various functions. Rationale for representative curves:**

1. Height. Probably the easiest curve to draw. In general, the child at two years of age is about half as tall as he will be as an adult.
2. Mental age. The consensus is that in terms of retentivity, plasticity and modifiability the biological basis for learning reaches its peak at about 20–25 years.
3. Weight. Increase in weight slows up in later childhood (wide individual variations) accelerates just before puberty and tapers off during adolescence. Weight often continues to increase into the middle years (and middle section).
4. Learning ability. Learning requires a brain and preparatory experience. The adult with a background of knowledge has more "appreceptive mass" with which to attack new meanings and concepts. He has an operational advantage over the "callow" youth.
5. Sex organs. Rapid growth from pubescence, but may begin as early as ten (there are cases on record when it has begun at 3 years) and as late as twenty (also exceptions which are still later).
6. Sex behavior. Perhaps the line should not go above the line of maturity. It is so drawn to show that sex activity though less vigorous in the middle years should (and often does) become an aspect of mature love. Sex behavior in early marriage is often an end in itself.
7. Executive ability. In a complex society, experience is more important than physical maturity. Professional men are reaching their peak in the forties. Statesmen and judges are beginning to reach (in their forties) the prominence they will achieve as senior citizens.

18

the idea that the study of behavior must accompany the entire life span. The kinds of adjustments the adolescent make are dependent upon his preceding experiences. The adequacy of adolescent adjustments foreshadows appropriateness of adult behavior. [179:25ff.]

But concern with preceding events should not cause one to overlook the present. Parents who regret that they did not do a better job in the first decade of their children's life should realize that "continuity" means that development does take place in the teen years. Teachers who believe that the individual's personality is formed in the first six or ten years should re-think the implications of the word continuity. The assertion that an adolescent is neither a child nor an adult—that he is neither fish nor fowl—is erroneous. The adolescent is unique but only in degree—not in kind. It would be more accurate to say that an adolescent is a person vacillating between childish and adult behavior. He is an individual who at times acts like a child and at times, when he has had appropriate preparatory experience, acts like an adult.

There are some unique phases of adolescence

That which is known of human behavior in general is also applicable to the understanding of adolescence. This is simply another way of stressing the continuity of development. However, there are differences in the kind and intensity of problems at various ages. The adolescent has the same basic needs as others, but these needs are different in insistence and intensity. [20:98ff.] In short, some aspects of growth deserve special study because the adolescent years are in certain respects unlike any other period of living. Glenn M. Blair has listed four conditions that may be considered unique problems of adolescence.

1. Adolescence is a transition period which overlaps childhood and adulthood.

   He is often treated in an ambiguous manner by his parents, teachers, and other members of society. He is told one moment by his parents, for example, that he is too young to drive the family car; the next moment he is informed that he is too old to be carrying on certain childish antics such as crying. . . . It is very probable that the vacillating and unstable behavior often attributed to adolescents is due to the fact that they find themselves in new and overlapping situations where their role is not structured.*

2. The adolescent, like all others, is profoundly affected by the culture in which he lives. The symptoms of stress that are observed in some societies are lacking in others. This is due to the length of the period which indicates the relative ease or difficulty with which the adolescent assumes an adult role.
3. Rapid biological changes sometimes impose stress, provoking psychological problems.
4. The adolescent has certain "developmental tasks" that must be accomplished in his progress toward maturity. Other "stages" (childhood, early maturity, later maturity) also have problems but they are somewhat different. It would, however, not be correct to subscribe to the notion that the problems of adolescence are more difficult. In fact, R. J. Havighurst, who has worked on the clarification of these tasks, stresses the idea that the adequacy with which tasks are accomplished at any age conditions the efficiency of doing the succeeding developmental tasks. [135]

Adolescence is unique in that the same problems are more pressing then than they seem to have been earlier. Such things as emancipation from parents, the necessity for living up to peer expectations, adjustment to strengthened sex drives, and planning for education and career are examples of some of the insistent problems.

Adolescence as the achievement of maturity

When the meaning of adolescence is discussed there will usually be some reference to the achievement of maturity. But the word "maturity" is actually of little value in clarification. The beginning of adolescence is fairly clear but the end is left vague [80] because there are so many ways in which one matures. Carl Binger suggests that "maturity" be dealt with as an undefined word, thus avoiding lists of criteria; but he indicates the need for a guiding *concept* of maturity. [25] Some of the attributes of maturity can be dealt with

---

* Glenn M. Blair, "What Teachers Should Know About the Psychology of Adolescence," *Journal of Educational Psychology*, 41, 1950, p. 357.

as goals to be achieved. This does not help to define the end of adolescence but it has practical value. It can be used in defining the processes of growth that are involved in progress toward more appropriate behavior. The concept of "maturing" as contrasted to "maturity" has the advantage of indicating the continuity of growth. We cannot, for example, say that one is mature when he has adjusted to the demands of society because one must continue to adjust even after he has been retired from his work or profession.

Examination of the chapter headings of this book will show that a pervasive factor is that of maturing. A preview of goals in the maturing process will show these areas to be predominant:

1. Emotional—one must be able to make decisions, resolve conflicts, and achieve inner balance and tranquillity.
2. Social—one must have regard for the rights, wishes, and welfare of others and must work in socially approved ways for the improvement of defects and elimination of unjust mores.
3. Vocational—one must work to support himself and his fellows at jobs that must be done. Necessity must, at times, come before preference.
4. Spiritual—one must exercise all aspects of his personality, using the spiritual facet to guide and challenge effort toward social and emotional composure.
5. Recreational—facets of personality that are not employed in one's daily work should be exercised in individually productive and socially approved manners.

As such phases of growth as these are studied it must of necessity be with the idea of taking additional steps in maturing. If a generalization can be made about adolescence, if continuity and uniqueness can both be recognized, it might be through perceiving adolescence as a period in which further and sometimes unique steps are taken to a more appropriate maturity.

Obstacles to adolescent development

Different historical periods and different cultural mores have presented varied problems to adolescents. The obstacles mentioned in this section refer to adolescents in the United States. The same statements could not be safely made of adolescents the world over.

Lack of family responsibility

One of the factors in our culture that make adjustment for some difficult during adolescence is their age at the time of marriage. Some boys and girls marry at the age of sixteen or seventeen and start having families. The responsibility thus assumed gives them an opportunity to become more independent and also to gain prestige in the eyes of their fellows. A few generations ago, if marriage were delayed until a later age the large parental families gave girls an important role to perform. The eldest girls were often caring for infant brothers and sisters. By the time these infants got to be in the teens their elder siblings were having children with whom they could help. The boys found many duties about the home to perform because many of the consumer goods were produced at home and labor-saving devices were not so prevalent.

The average age of marriage is somewhat lower today than it was in 1890 [10:108]—this despite the reduced assurance of work opportunities, which causes many youth to delay marriage until they can compete more confidently with adults for available jobs. The increasing popularity of education contributes to delaying marriage "until education is completed." Prior to marriage there is less opportunity for heavy and genuine responsibility in the home because of the small size of families and the production of goods away from the home. When couples do get married in their teens their knowledge of birth control often causes them to delay having children. This results in either having relatively small responsibility in the home or in the development of unrealistically expensive living habits. Both of these, of course, complicate personal adjustment problems.

Even those who are nostalgic about the good old days should realize that customs and mores are but little subject to logical processes. Actually there are advantages on the side of late marriage—better psychological preparation and more mature biological functioning. Since problems are to a remarkable extent dependent upon the attitude taken toward them, the role of youths' counselors is relatively clear. It is necessary to acquaint youth with the real nature of their problems and help them to take advantage of the opportunities inherent in late marriage.

Delay of work opportunities

In our society an important question is, "What do you do?" When the answer to the question is, "Nothing," there is frequently an apologetic tone. Many youth might find it easy to adjust to this because their peers do not have jobs either, but there is frequently an adult about who taunts them: "Why, when I was your age. . . ."

The availability of work opportunities is a rapidly fluctuating phenomenon. In the late twenties there was considerable work, even for youth. In the thirties there was little work, even for experienced and trained adults. During the war years there were abundant opportunities for youth to work and serve in the armed forces. But, unless war and preparation for war continue to be chronic conditions, the shrinkage of work opportunities for youth will be a problem. Those who wish to understand and help youth must see this whole problem as one of major importance.

It has been shown that the life span of animals should be about five times as great as the growing period. Dogs take two years to grow and live for ten to fifteen years. (It is doubtful if this longevity computation is reduced by puppy mortality.) Horses live to be twenty-five or thirty, taking five years to grow. Man, it has recently been shown, can and biologically should reach the age of 100 years or more. [32:45] Hence, it *may be* that the prolongation of minority for humans is a factor in increased longevity and that the possible period of adult productivity is increased by not hastening youth into maturity. Technologically, too, there is reason to avoid hastening youth into the working life. The complexity of industrial, commercial, and scientific organizations should make a period of longer preparation for work advantageous, providing better orientation and insight into overall complexities. [89:45] Again, as will be shown in Chapter Sixteen, Adjusting to the World of Work, the problem for youth leaders is to take advantage of the assets while properly evaluating the liabilities of delayed work opportunity.

Military service

Youth today, as well as formerly, will do that which they understand has to be done. Despite personal inconvenience and disruption of plans most youth do their part with remarkable willingness. This does not mean that military service does not impose difficulties in the way to adjustment. At the same time it does not seem realistic to just eliminate such service. It is difficult for a young man to look at the interruption of his educational, social, and vocational plans with equanimity and shrug it off with "C'est la guerre." It may be, however, that the most questionable feature of military service is not the service itself but the lack of certainty by which it has been characterized. A man does not know how old he must be or may become before it comes time for him to serve. He does not know how long he will be in uniform. He does not know how long he may continue in school. He has to choose among a variety of possible active-duty-plus-reserve plans. He is not sure which plan will prove best for him. Studies of mental hygiene show that uncertainty is as much a destroyer of balance as are the actual events of disappointment and frustration. Hence it would seem that one approach to the reduction of tension for some adolescents would be to place military service on a predictable basis. In the meantime, youth workers will have to aid youth to interpret this uncertainty in such a way as to help them absorb their difficulties.

Authoritarianism

Laws, customs, regulations, and authority afford children and adults part of the basis for feelings of security. Too much law and regulation was resisted by our ancestors and is resisted today. People living in a democratic society like to have a voice in their government. One of the major problems of adolescents is to outgrow the restrictive regulation of their parents, schools, and communities. (Adults who are irritated by this manifestation of adolescence should take time to consider that they would not really want adolescents to be obediently servile.) Yet many aspects of our culture are authoritarian.

H. H. Anderson points out that in spite of our democratic tradition authoritarianism is abundantly manifested. Politically there are powerful pressure groups. There is a hierarchy of authority in industry. Authoritarianism exists in colleges and universities and in the public schools. Family life is still dominated by the authoritarian role. [6:171] These factors must be recognized in any effort to improve developmental opportunities for youth. Many of the difficult problems youth encounter center around the conflict between the desire to grow up and be independent and the pervasiveness of authoritarian institutions and customs.

Adolescents are a minority group

In 1850 about 24 per cent of the population was between the age of ten and nineteen. Today only 14.7 per cent of the population is in that group. [316] It seems that increasing longevity will further reduce the percentage size of the adolescent group. F. G. Dickinson views this as the basis for a class war between youth and adults. The struggle will be manifested in heavy taxes to pay pensions, stronger bonds between employer and worker that will resist the invasion of youthful labor, and adult resistance against raises in wages from which they will not profit (in retired status). [84] Whether we agree with this view or not it might well indicate the nature of the difficulties a minority group encounters.

Where the interests of the adolescent group conflict with those of the adult group adjustment problems readily develop. Hence the desire of young people for emancipation as against the desires of adults to satisfy their wishes may cause difficulty. The desire of young people to work may interfere with adult job security. Many of the delinquencies of youth are actions sanctioned, or at least tolerated, when performed by adults. [327:128] Youth, being an identifiable minority group, is condemned for these actions. P. H. Landis likens the position of the adolescent to that of the immigrant child in that both have to bridge two cultures. He uses the term "marginal man" to describe the dilemma. [182:121] Resolution of some problems of adolescence will come about as the result of investigating such conflicts to see if there is not some ultimate identity between the desires of the dominant and the minority groups.

Contrasts between professed beliefs and actions

There are a number of contrasts between stated ideals and actual behavior which might serve as the source of confusion for some adolescents. The fact that somehow these conflicts are absorbed might well cause us to admire the stability of youth. Examination of these dichotomies can serve to stimulate adults to evaluate the consistency of their own conduct. Such examination might lead them to provide a better example for youth.

The confining of sexual relations to marriage is verbally recommended, yet newspapers and magazines report pre-marital and extra-marital episodes among people in high places. The promiscuity of persons in lower socio-economic strata may be regarded as an indication of unfortunate ignorance. Promiscuity among the prominent, however, is likely to be taken by youth as a justification for weakening their own restraints.

Honesty is endorsed as the best policy. Parents and teachers are deeply shocked by minor thefts and the cataclysmic nature of cheating, but the theft of thousands of dollars may become a matter of political and legal equivocation. High governmental officials have been continued in office long after the mist of doubt has proved to be an opaque fog. Yet youth are sometimes condemned because they do not have firm ideals.

Cooperation versus competition, lawlessness and the evasion of law against obedience to law, the equality of man versus organized intolerance, and temperance versus higher statistics on drug and alcohol addiction are other examples of the conflicting ideologies young people meet.

Two approaches to these obstacles to symmetrical growth are suggested: (1) adults should attempt to improve their own conduct, and (2) the errors of our ways should be admitted and the ultimate price of low level conduct should be pointed out to youth.

Importance of the period

Rapid growth in early years

The principle, "growth takes place most rapidly in the early years" will be discussed in the next chapter. For now, let it be said, this also means that *some* growth is taking place at all times. But adolescence is the last period when growth is taking place so rapidly that a major opportunity for big gains is present. The adolescent is still flexible and he is typically motivated to make the most of himself. [206:19] He is still engaging in the processes of exploring his world, he is seeking a place for himself, he is concerned with matters of personal and social adjustment. These processes and motivations provide fertile fields for change. A few more years will see his habits of thinking and acting more firmly set. He will be seeking to consolidate himself in a particular niche. Changes in ideals and orientations will continue, but they will be less rapid than they were in the adolescent years. We can admit that the adjustment problems of adolescence are in part due to the kind of adjustment made prior to adolescence. It must also be admitted that some conflict is dependent upon present external circumstances. [130]

The complexity of our times

We read and hear from numerous sources that the world of today is rapidly moving, quickly changing, and increasingly complex. Less frequently, but with equal justification, we hear that our resources for meeting the complexities of the world have been improved. In short, life today is more complex and more rapid but not necessarily more difficult or dangerous to live. Yet the knowledge of the nature of the world, the techniques for using the scientific methods and tools that have been accumulated, must be acquired. This is the big opportunity of the period called adolescence. It is a time of preparation for living effectively in a changed world. N. L. Bossing asserts that the increasing complexity of society demands or at least justifies the prolongation of adolescence in order to prepare for adulthood. [35]

One of the challenges for those who work with adolescents might well be to convince the young people that prolonged adolescence is an opportunity. Young people should be shown that many of the mores that shape their thinking were formed when the average age of the population was much less. They should know that the nature of adjustment has been changed; but they should also know that the future, now as earlier, depends on taking advantage of the available preparation period.

The significance of adult help

Regardless of what parents, teachers, counselors, and youth leaders do, the adolescent of today will achieve some sort of adult role. Without constructive help and guidance, assumption of that adult role might be unnecessarily delayed. Without help the degree of adulthood might be less than is theoretically possible. Without help the injuries received in adolescence might leave psychological scars that will distort the lives of adults.

The whole purpose of the study of adolescence is to make growth in the teen days more wholesome and better directed. We hope to reduce some of the hazards that lead to unnecessary failure and the consequent feelings of inadequacy. The naming of some of the adjustment problems of adolescents will indicate the potentialities inherent in guidance by informed and sympathetic adults: academic proficiency, peer relations, educational choices, occupational choice and adjustment, problems of citizenship, choice of a mate, and the forming of a set of values. The adolescent period is important because the time still available makes it possible to prepare more adequately to meet these problems.

Objectives of our study of adolescence

Prediction and control of behavior

The study of the psychology of adolescence is for the purpose of anticipating what will happen and providing a sort of inoculation for those happenings. Of course, it is realized that prediction and control of human behavior cannot be characterized by the same certainty that characterizes mechanical action. But an examination of the causes of behavior can *in general* provide the clues for anticipating the environmental changes that might improve behavior.

The study of the psychology of adolescence is directed at the discovery of growth factors that seem to be dominant. Psychology is thus a statement of probabilities. Through our understanding of the factors that contribute to a given action we hope to change that action so that the probability of satisfaction for the adolescent (and other members of his society) is enhanced.

The change of norms of conduct

The study of the psychology of adolescence should hasten the change of norms of conduct that, due to changed conditions, no longer have their former validity. Examples of such norms might be these: the belief that one should become a wage earner in his teens, the belief that teen-age girls should resemble the current

Hollywood mode, the belief that it is psychologically dangerous to delay sex experience, or the belief that youngsters are not mature enough to vote while they man the ships, guns, and planes of war.

Kingsley Davis sees the problems of adolescence, from the viewpoint of society, as the changing of anachronistic norms.

> From a societal and ultimately more significant point of view, it is how the norms themselves may be changed so as to ease this adjustment and achieve the maximum use of the adolescent age stratum. Since in our society the adolescent's status is known to involve strain and inconsistency, the norms governing it will receive their share of attempted revision. . . .*

The individual purpose

From the standpoint of the individual adolescent the purpose of the psychology of adolescence is to facilitate adjustment. This, of course, means many things. It includes adjustment to the mores of society. It must involve the choice of and adaptation to an occupational role. Adjustment to one's peers and to his mate is also included. Each of the chapters of this book contains a consideration of some area of adjustment so enumeration here is unnecessary.

Closely allied to the matter of adjustment is the problem of integration. This implies that the individual has gone a little further in his adjusting than simply resigning himself to the pressures of society. It means that he has learned to control his impulsiveness and can see that his self-control benefits both himself and others. It implies that he has reached a level of moral maturity. [266:11] Integration means that the individual has recognized his abilities and has attempted to develop them. It means that he is aware of his limitations and can refrain from "singing the blues."

Robert J. Havighurst has provided a stimulating point of departure in the study of adolescence in the concept of "developmental tasks." [136] It can be said with considerable accuracy that the study of adolescence should result, either directly, or indirectly through the education of adults, in the individual's comprehending and accomplishing his developmental tasks with greater facility.

* Kingsley Davis, "Adolescence and the Social Structure," *Annals of the American Academy of Political and Social Science*, 236, 1944, p. 8.

The objective of our study as a hope

The assertion, "He who controls the youth, controls the future," would receive the endorsement of the psychologist. Popular clichés indicate that events transpiring today condition the happenings of tomorrow. Examples of such clichés are, "Today is yesterday shaking hands with tomorrow," "You are today becoming what tomorrow you will be," "As one grows older he grows more like himself." The faith that Americans have historically had and the faith which they today manifest are indicative of the hope that rides on youth. The study of adolescence is another facet of the hope that life can be better tomorrow.

It seems unfortunate that those who have had the deepest convictions about the hope residing in youth should be dictators. Erika Mann in *School for Barbarians* describes how carefully Hitler and his cohorts planned the lives of youth. Every waking moment of boys and girls was somehow filled with an approach to strengthening their emotional (not intellectual) convictions that it was a great opportunity to serve Hitler. Home life was consciously disintegrated by having meetings for all family members on such a schedule that time together was virtually impossible. Only approved teachers were continued in their positions. The traits of humanity that are emphasized in religious tradition were consistently and systematically ridiculed. [207] This emphasis on indoctrinating youth bore results in the fanaticism of the Nazis.

Much the same thing took place in Italy. The motto of the Duce was, "In the Balilla we see the great hopes of to-morrow rising over the horizon like the dawn and sunrise of a new world." The Balilla was a youth organization that followed the childhood organization called "Sons of the Wolf." The continuous program of sports, athletics, and marching aimed to produce the hard-muscled and devoted soldier-citizen. The youth organization that carried this program up to the age of eighteen was the Avanguardistic. All of these programs were supported and buttressed by propaganda coming through the school, press, and radio. Youth was the hope of the dictator. [247] In Communist Russia there is presently a planned effort to destroy home life and convert the younger generation. [298]

No doubt the ultimate failure of the Nazi and Fascist programs was due to a multiplicity of factors. It is tempting to speculate that the failure might have been due to the lack of a durable ideal. We cannot, of course, endorse the objectives of the Nazi and Fascist Youth programs. We can, however, note that their success (in a negative direction) does indicate the pliability of youth. We can hope that surrounding youth with desirable influences and opportunities could lead to even greater results in a positive direction —a vast improvement in life. "Healthy personalities mean persons who can live and find fulfillment of their needs and aspirations as organism-personalities. The education of the emotions as resources for living more richly and fulfillingly is the great unfinished business of secondary education today." * It seems realistic to hope that healthy personalities can also be an outcome of the study of the psychology of adolescence.

Summary

Adolescence is one phase of the total continuous developmental process of the individual. It covers the period from puberty to the less clearly defined time when the person becomes an adult. Although sexual maturation is one phase of growth toward maturity, that alone is not enough to identify the end of adolescence. The assumptions of adult roles in work, family relations, social orientation, and citizenship are also indications of the end of adolescence. Since the ages at which these roles are assumed differ in various societies, the period of adolescence varies correspondingly. Another way of clarifying the meaning of adolescence is to think of it as a period of emergent independence. At puberty the dependence of childhood is continued; but various breaks with adult authority and protection are manifested, until adult independence is gradually achieved. Although this period will differ for individual adolescents, the teen years can make an acceptable distinction of the adolescent period. Some will have assumed an adult role in marriage, some in work, some in citizenship before twenty; some will be adults in all respects before twenty; the remainder will take another year or two but will be no less mature, when they have achieved independent

---

* Lawrence K. Frank, "Needs and Problems of Adolescents in the Area of Emotional Health," *High School Journal*, 35, 1951, p. 74.

adult status, than those who mature earlier. Hence in this book all those physical, emotional, intellectual, and cultural factors that determine the length and characteristics of the individual from puberty to adult functioning are matters of concern. Briefly then, adolescence may be defined as the period of emergent independence, extending to the time of assumption of responsibility in the various adult roles.

There are many ways of looking at adolescents. At times it seems that the spectacular and bizarre are predominant in the behavior of young people. But careful examination shows that by and large youth are adjusting well. Recently there has been a shift from the physiological emphasis to an emphasis on the cultural shaping of the adolescent personality. It is felt that recognizing the many-faceted nature of adolescence will finally result in a better understanding of the individual.

Generalizations about adolescence must be made with extreme caution; however, it seems safe to say that it is one phase of a continuous process of growth from conception to death. There are some unique phases of growth during adolescence but these are unique mainly in the matter of degree.

Changes in the cultural pattern which seem to impose hardships on adolescents indicate the probable fruitfulness of the cultural orientation. Examples of changes that are often obstacles to adolescent development are the following: obstacles to marriage and diminished family responsibility, reduced opportunity for work, uncertainty about military service, authoritarianism, membership in a minority group, and contrasts between professed beliefs and actual behavior.

The adolescent period is important because growth is still taking place rather rapidly, because of the complexity of our times, and because of the need for adult guidance. This important period can be capitalized upon by more accurately learning the causes of behavior, by attempting to change outmoded mores, by more intelligently assisting individuals, and by maintaining a steady hope for the future. These understandings and approaches will reduce the number of the spectacular cases of adolescent behavior. Better understanding of the nature of adolescence will warrant an optimistic view of the future.

1. Would you consider that the problems of adolescents today are different in any significant ways from those you experienced as an adolescent? (Students still in their teens can help provide the perspective needed in dealing with this question.)

2. Observe a group of adolescents at a restaurant or ball game. What generalizations can you make about them? Contrast your statements with the generalizations your classmates make on the basis of their observation of youth in a local high school.

3. Discuss with three or four of your fellow students some mores that might be changed to the advantage of youth.

4. When do you think the period of adolescence should be considered to be ended?

5. What constructive suggestions do you think can be derived from the youth programs in Fascist Italy and Nazi Germany?

6. Cite some reasons that tend to justify the assertion that cultural factors are more powerful than physiological factors in shaping the personality development of adolescents.

7. What are some of the major reasons for differences in adolescent behavior—reasons that make generalizations hazardous?

8. Formulate what you believe would be a sufficiently comprehensive concept of adolescence.

9. What advantages might accrue to the adolescent from military service?

10. In what ways might prolonged education be considered a handicap to adolescent adjustment?

11. What do you think should constitute the major objectives of the study of adolescence?

RECOMMENDED SUPPLEMENTARY READING

Bigelow, Maurice A. *Adolescence* (New York: Funk and Wagnalls Company; 1937), 99 pp.
Although the copyright date is not recent, this little book clearly presents contemporary thinking. Some persistent misconceptions are criticized. Sexual development is regarded as a part of total growth and includes emotional and intellectual phases.

Duvall, Evelyn Millis. *Keeping up with Teen-Agers*, Public Affairs Pamphlet No. 127 (New York: Public Affairs Committee; 1947).
Duvall points out the recurrent strain and suspicion that sometimes characterizes adult-adolescent relationships. Typical problems (dating, choice of career, assumption of responsibility) are used to illustrate some approaches to the dilemma. Good reading for adolescents as well as adults.

Frank, L. K., in National Society for the Study of Education, *43rd Yearbook*, Part I, *Adolescence* (Chicago: University of Chicago Press; 1944), Ch. 1.
Adolescence is regarded as a period of transition. The impact of the social milieu is stressed. Body changes and the influence of these on behavior are basic considerations. The fact that social demands are heavy is reflected in types of disease, accident, and mental illness rates during the teen years.

Goodenough, Florence L. *Developmental Psychology*, 2nd Ed. (New York: Appleton-Century-Crofts, Inc.; 1945), Ch. 18.
The chapter emphasizes the essential continuity of growth—of which adolescence is but one phase. The author criticizes the notion of adolescent awkwardness. Adolescence must be understood through the study of sex interests and development, social adaptation, and emotional emancipation.

Jones, Harold E., in Roger G. Barker, and others (Eds.) *Child Behavior and Development* (New York: McGraw-Hill Book Company, Inc.; 1943), pp. 591–606.
This reading, "Development in Adolescence: A Case Report," shows how an individual is affected by various forces—home, neighborhood, school peers, and physical and intellectual factors. The selection is particularly valuable in suggesting that we keep our attention on individuals rather than on generalities.

Wattenberg, W. A. *The Adolescent Years* (New York: Harcourt, Brace & Company, Inc.; 1955), pp. 3–22.

The chapter, "Viewpoints," indicates some of the representative behaviors of adolescents, some of the ways of studying them, and some of the cultural factors that must be considered. Interesting anecdotes are included.

Democracy (Encyclopedia Britannica Films, Inc., 342 Madison Ave., New York) 11 min., so., b. & w.

Deals with the nature and meaning of democracy. The two essential features of democracy—shared respect and shared power—are defined and illustrated.

Make Way for Youth (Association Films, 35 West 45th St., New York 19) 22 min., so., b. & w.

The citizens of a community, young and old, are shocked into action by tragedy. Together they organize a youth program to break the barriers between neighborhoods, races, and religions.

What are some common features of mental, physical, emotional and spiritual growth? Need adolescents feel odd because they do not fit the "typical" pattern? How can the "deviant grower" be helped to develop a healthy concept of self?

CHAPTER TWO

Principles of Development Related to Adolescence

The subject matter covered by adolescent psychology is not unique. All the topics in child psychology, psychology of adolescence, psychology of exceptional children, and educational psychology are found in each of the others. There is a different emphasis, there is the necessity for a varied interpretation, but the subject matter is always behavior. Hence, it is quite natural that a study of adolescence should begin where many courses in child psychology, educational psychology, and social psychology begin: that is, with the basic principles of development.

Most readers will find it unnecessary to be informed that development is more than physical.* It also involves mental, emotional, and social growth. Further, it must be understood that these phases are not disparate. Mental, emotional, and physical growth are aspects of the total development of the individual. They are separated only for the sake of discussion. Growth is an organismic process; that is,

---

* Specialized studies may make necessary a distinction between growth and development. When this is made, *growth* refers to changes due to intrinsic factors—sheer increase in size. *Development* refers to changed (improved) function, which depends upon exercise or experience as well as upon intrinsic factors. For practical purposes the two processes cannot be separated.

37

it concerns numerous interrelated phases of development: chronological age, height, weight, dental development, bone development,
intellectual, physiological, emotional, and social growth. The growth
of one part of the organism affects and is affected by the growth of
other parts and functions. This interrelatedness of development is
what makes the study of psychology so difficult—simple answers
cannot be expected. There are, obviously, many factors involved in
adolescent development.

Developmental principles and their implications for adolescents

The following paragraphs will briefly describe, and then will illustrate, *some* of the meanings and implications of growth principles
for adolescence. The principles will be found to be operative during
other phases of life—the emphasis or degree of importance will vary
somewhat for adolescence.

Growth is a product of the interaction
of the organism with its environment

At any time in life, the individual is what he is because of his responses to hereditary potential and to the conditions that surround
him. It has been demonstrated that a cell that contains the potential
for development into one part of the body may be made to develop
into another part if it is transplanted at just the right time. [126:82]
The old controversy between the hereditarians and the environmen-
talists is seen to be futile, as far as reaching a conclusion is concerned, in the light of this principle. Musical aptitude is partially
dependent upon hereditary potential, but it will never become musical ability without an environment that provides for musical instruments and some degree of encouragement or challenge. Even
these will not produce musical ability alone—there must be a person who will utilize his aptitude and environment by studying and
by practicing. Thus, three things are involved: (1) hereditary potential, (2) environmental stimulation, opportunity, or challenge,
and (3) the response of the individual to what he is and to what he
has. His growth at any time is the result of what he is (hereditary
potential) what he has (environment) and what he does (re-

sponse). It is the same way, to a greater or lesser extent, with height, weight, or intelligence. The relative predominance of any of the influences will vary with the trait concerned; for example, personality is known to have an organic basis, but an individual's pattern of traits is thought to be very much due to what the environment has caused him to be.

This principle will throw much light on the understanding of the adolescent. Recent developments in psychological theory have to a large extent been an elaboration of this principle. For example, the trend away from the belief that adolescence is a period of stress and strain shows a repudiation of the belief that this phenomenon (*sturm und drang*) is inherent in the organism. It is now recognized that more or less abrupt physical changes disturb the individual very much in proportion to the manner in which society views these changes. Further, the way the individual views these changes will vary greatly within a given society because of the responses they generate in him. Specifically, some adolescents in a particular socio-economic status in a particular city will differ widely in their behavior from others with apparently the same environmental conditions.

It was the consensus up to about 1935 that intelligence was largely an inherited capacity. There were a few individuals who did not subscribe to the notion. They took particular pains to give special training to their offspring so they would develop into highly intelligent individuals. Their success, in some instances, led others to experiment, and they were often less successful (for example, training did not greatly change the intellectual status of feeble-minded children). Careful studies began to be published in the middle and late thirties which indicated some remarkable "changes in IQ." Various interpretations were placed on these changes: (1) the tests were unreliable, (2) the tests were not valid—they were measuring education, and (3) individuals under certain conditions actually did experience an increase in intelligence. [294:427] More and more students seem to be accepting the latter point as being valid.* The current consensus, in short, is that intelligence

---

* This is not to deny that all psychologists and educators are still hoping for more valid and reliable instruments for estimating the present status of intellectual development.

is a function of the interaction of the individual's potential with his environment.

Data on the changing IQ are more susceptible to statistical treatment than are studies showing the influence of environment on personality traits. Many, including those with no background in academic psychology, realize that a person's traits are to a very large degree formed by the environment in which he lives. "He acts just exactly like his father" is a frequently heard expression. Psychologists expand and clarify this contention with elaborations of the thesis: "Child behavior reflects parental handling," and "There are no bad children—only poor parents." These observations are dangerous because an element of truth is contained therein, but not all the truth is there. Careful analysis shows that besides the environment provided by the parent, there is also the emotional and intellectual capacity of the child, which produces his responses to the environmental factors. This statement has been experimentally supported by showing that rats inherit a predisposition to normal or neurotic responses. [204]

The fact that growth is a product of the interaction of the organism with its environment establishes the framework for one of the major emphases in this book; namely, helping the adolescent will depend largely upon changing environmental conditions. He can be aided in gaining a healthful concept of self. Parents, teachers, counselors, workers in youth groups, and others (such as employers) who have contact with youth cannot do much about small stature, large stature, early maturing, late maturing, bowed legs, moles, hair color, and the like. These result largely from intrinsic growth factors. These people can do much to change some of the conditions that make adolescence the difficult period it sometimes is for some individuals. They can do a great deal in helping the adolescent to develop confidence in his abilities and to be proud of his uniqueness in physical traits. Youth can be helped to develop behaviors that will serve to make them acceptable to their peers and among larger social groups. In short, the inevitable factors involved in growth (which was the major emphasis in older adolescent psychologies) will be recognized. At the same time, stress will be placed on the individual's response and on environmental factors to the extent of overstating the case. There is merit in contending that *adolescence is to a very large extent a culturally produced phenomenon.*

Growth is continuous and gradual—it is not saltatory

The word "saltatory" comes from a French word meaning "to jump." Here the implication is that growth does not proceed by leaps and bounds. Rather its pattern—for the individual as a whole and for any part of the individual—is one of gradualness and of continuity.

Continuity means that there is a relationship in terms of growth between what is taking place now and what previously occurred. It means that new characteristics of personality do not suddenly appear. And it means that what take place today are the preliminary steps of the journeys that will take place tomorrow and the days after. The phenomenon of continuity may be exemplified by some things that many know but might not have fully appreciated. For example, it is known that an individual does not suddenly become delinquent. In most instances the young person who becomes delinquent gives indications of his potential misbehavior in what is known as pre-delinquent behavior. [181:136] Most thinking people do not readily subscribe to the parental contention, "Since he became an adolescent I just can't handle him anymore." We realize that the parent cannot handle his offspring, but we do not think the problem is something that just sprung up suddenly. Rather we are likely to wonder if the parent had previously handled that youngster as wisely as he should have. Put in a positive manner, it is accurate to say that where parents have had high rapport with their children *as children* they quite often have some rapport with their offspring during the period of adolescence.* There are instances in which an apparently well-behaved adolescent suddenly went "berserk" on being released from family restrictions. But even here development was continuous—that individual had been gradually accumulating tensions which had simply (but not suddenly) reached the breaking point.

---

* It will be shown later that some of the rapport will tend to disappear because of the praiseworthy desire of the adolescent to get rid of parental domination. There is a tendency for adolescents to feel that parental domination is thwarting development.

Full appreciation of the continuity of development will cause the adults who work with young persons to have a more realistic conception of what can be expected of them. It will be realized that since it takes a long time to develop a disapproved trait it will probably take some time to develop another trait that might be more desirable. We should not expect that just because some dynamic leader has been obtained, or because some spectacular program has been launched, there will be no further difficulties in adolescent adjustment.

The continuity of development should also be emphasized to the adolescent. It may do him some good to know that it takes many, many steps to complete a long journey and it takes many, many separate acts to acquire a physical or intellectual skill. One of the things that is noticed about adolescents is their impatience. Adults who can point out the recent gains made by the adolescent will be able to indicate the possibility of the next gains, which will continuously be made. It will certainly have *some* effect on *some* adolescents to know that other people as well as adolescents have been impatient for more rapid results. They should know that adolescents, and others, have discovered that continuity of development is inevitable.

There may be some inclination to doubt that growth during adolescence is gradual. It has frequently (and loudly) been emphasized that the adolescent growth spurt is the source of much of the "difficulty of adolescents"; but the reassessment of growth data points to continuity of development. [28:138] Several items in this connection are worth noting: (1) Some adolescents do not experience much of a spurt—they seem to grow at a rate quite like that of the years preceding and the years following. (2) The adolescent spurt means that more inches were gained this year than were gained last year—but some gain was made last year. Hence the adolescent spurt consists of a hump in the curve that is drawn to describe the total growth pattern for height. (3) The spurt in growth during adolescence is neither absolutely nor relatively so rapid as the growth made by a child in his first and second years. (4) A point of incidental interest is that the spurt is not experienced in adolescence but in the pre-pubertal period. The relatively more rapid growth occurs just prior to adolescence (see Chapter Five).

If growth is thought of as an organismic process (involving numerous aspects of the total, integrated individual) the "adolescent spurt" is completely replaced by the "gradual" concept. Height and weight do appear to have spurts. Growth of the internal organs is more continuous and gradual. A different pattern of continuity is shown in brain size—which is 90 per cent complete by the age of six. The function of intelligence, however, does not slow down until toward the end of adolescence. But knowledge is in a very rudimentary stage and in many instances will continue to grow at a gradual rate for a remarkably long period of time. [169]

A mother in one of the author's classes some years ago stayed after class and expressed her concern about the future of her daughter who was about to enter college. She had heard stories about drinking episodes and sex delinquencies and was concerned lest her daughter be misled by the more sophisticated college students. Several questions were asked about the girl's adjustment in high school and about her relationships at home. The prognosis seemed favorable and the mother was so informed. Three years later the mother appeared and made remarks about as follows: "I don't suppose you remember me but . . ." (she then recalled the foregoing conversation). She continued, "I'd just like to tell you that my worries were in vain. Sue had a wonderful time in college—made good adjustments both socially and academically. In her junior year she married a man who had graduated when she was a sophomore and who is now an engineer in the Sunshine Mines." There are of course, deviations from the general pattern. But there is a general pattern of gradualness and continuity that can serve as a warning. Adolescence is a phenomenon that has its roots in early life. This fact can, however, provide assurance for those who are satisfied with the development a particular individual has made up to the present.

Growth proceeds most rapidly in the early years

It seems as though some persons (including some psychologists) deliberately seek to misinterpret the meaning of this growth principle. These people make the statements that "It is too late now," and "The personality of the child is formed in the first six (or eight or ten) years of life." As is the case with some of the other misconceptions in psychology, the danger of these misinterpretations lies in the element of truth they contain. In some instances it really is "too late." The broad patterns of personality *probably are* laid down in outline form during the early years of life. But the whole truth of the growth principle must embrace the implication that, since growth proceeds *most* rapidly in the early years of life, there must be *some* growth in the years that succeed the early years. There have been maladjusted children and adolescents and adults who have been rehabilitated. [104] Healthy personalities are ones that grow throughout their entire life spans.*

Taking cognizance of the fact that growth is continuous and gradual (and that this continuity and gradualness continues throughout the life span of the individual) should not prevent recognition of the fact that early growth is relatively more rapid. The early health patterns, both mental and physical, are exceedingly important because they set the stage for the smaller increments of later development. The early experiences of the child in home, peer groups, school life, and wider community relationships are potent influences during later years. Early experience conditions the way in which a man establishes his own home, how he adjusts to his neighbors, how he acts in adult life upon opportunity for study, and how he takes his place as a citizen of the world; but these early influences are not the only ones. Early parental mistakes can be remedied. Poor parental influences can be counterbalanced to some extent by artful teachers. The negative attitudes some children acquire in the elementary schools can be offset by a helpful high school teacher or even by interested and understanding college professors. Scout leaders, girls' counselors, and religious advisers have at times seemed to redirect the course of development.

There are three reasons for particular interest in this growth principle from the standpoint of adolescence.

1. It is during the *very* early part of adolescence that the abrupt growth in height and weight, so frequently noted, takes place. Puberty—the onset of sexual maturation—is considered to be near

---

* Research in gerontology (study of the problems of aging) shows that the amount of personality growth that takes place during the mature years is much greater than was formerly thought possible. Such studies indicate that the amount of unused potential for intellectual, emotional, and personality growth in the later years provides much hope for richer living for those in the second forty years.

the beginning of the inexactly defined adolescent period. The period of rapid physical growth is actually a pre-pubertal phenomenon, and puberty marks the beginning of *deceleration* in the physical growth pattern. There is, therefore, an implication of this growth principle that is too little recognized. Namely, to the extent that rapid physical growth in the adolescent does constitute a problem it is one that must receive attention in the very early teen years.

2. The second implication of this growth principle extends beyond that of height and weight. It means that the more time that passes during which the adolescent is faced by perplexing and frustrating problems the less hope there is for his absorbing those difficulties with a high degree of success. It is the upper elementary and junior high school teacher who will do most to help the adolescent who is perplexed about his physical self. It will be the teachers and counselors at this age level who will do most to provide him with the ideals, interests, and skills that are developed during adolescence. It has been found, for instance, that the peak of reading interest is reached at about twelve or thirteen years of age. [308]

3. The third implication has to do with the entire life span of the individual up to the present. The period of rapid growth in pre-adolescence is not so rapid as was growth in the first year or two of life. It is then a little surprising to find that although one- or two-year-old children make remarkable gains in physical skills, motor coordination, emotional orientation, and social efficiency the adolescent is said to be awkward, emotionally unstable, and socially inept. The rapid growth of the child seems to cause no problems of adjustment, yet many problems are attributed to the rapid growth of the pre-adolescent. Actually, research data controvert this widespread and deeply rooted misconception. [87] The adolescent is progressively becoming better coordinated, he is continuing to make gains in emotional stability, and he is solidifying the kind of social responses that had their inception in the earlier years of life.

Patterns of relative growth tend to remain consistent

This principle has reference to the individual. There is an implication that there are different rates of growth for various parts of the organism and for various aspects of the total personality. The main connotation, however, is that, considering any one part or aspect of the total individual, an initially rapid rate of development fore-tokens a later relatively rapid growth in that characteristic. For ex-ample, a child who has grown rapidly in terms of mental function so that at the age of two or three he is in the ninety-fifth percentile will, as an adolescent and as an adult, *tend* to rank in a similarly high position. The child who is physically small for his age at two years will *tend* to be small for his age at sixteen or seventeen. It has been noted that it is possible to predict with a fair degree of accuracy that the adult height of an individual will be very close to twice his height at two years of age.

The consistency of the growth rate is not a law—it is simply a helpful generalization. It was noted in a preceding section that some marked changes in IQ have been reported. But in connection with these studies it is worth noting that the rate of growth might have remained steady if there had not been a marked change in the environment of the individual. Part of the consistency of the growth rate resides in the hereditary potential of the individual; but there is also the probability that for most individuals there are likely to be no changes in environment marked enough to affect the rate of in-tellectual progress. [357:356] There is also the possibility that vary-ing rates of intellectual growth may be inherent in the organism. It may, for instance, have been partially decided at the time of con-ception that a child would grow slowly for a period of time and then accelerate in terms of mental growth. Another child might have grown rapidly but have ceased growing sooner than the average; thus he might attain a relatively small intellectual stature as an adult. This possibility is, in fact, one of the explanations that is offered to explain changes in IQ.

There is a similar phenomenon in the physical growth of the ado-lescent. Thus far, no factors have been isolated that seem to ex-plain the comparatively early onset of puberty in some individuals—except the sex factor, since girls, on the average, mature at an earlier age than do boys. Race, climate, and level of culture have at times been thought to be factors associated with earlier-than-average pu-berty; however, none of these have withstood the test of repeated and prolonged investigation. (Except that there is some indication that good diet hastens puberty.) Yet the fact remains that some boys and girls mature at a much earlier age than do their age mates.

This tends to make predictions of ultimate height somewhat difficult because the early maturing boys and girls cease growing sooner than do the ones who grow for a longer period before experiencing the deceleration of growth that follows puberty.

The foregoing exceptions, because they are exceptions, serve to emphasize the generalization: growth rates tend to remain constant. This is one of the generalizations that enable psychology to be a science devoted to the prediction and control of behavior. The early growth manifestations of a child, whether they be in the areas of mental, physical, emotional, or social development give some basis for the prediction of what later behaviors in these areas will be. When some of the major contributing factors to a particular pattern of growth have been identified, then it is possible, because of the consistency of growth, to know that alteration of the contributing factors will result in a change in developmental pattern. But when "other things are equal" the consistency phenomenon enables us to make valid predictions. These reduce the range of search when seeking specific causes for an individual's behavior or misbehavior. Some of these generalizations are as follows: Delinquent patterns of conduct are foretokened by pre-delinquent behavior. The outlines of a person's emotional conduct are established in childhood. The pupil who is weak in academic work in the elementary school is unlikely to do outstanding work in high school and college. The so-called "second childhood" of the later years is simply an indication that the individual has never really been mature. A person cannot run away from his problem because he must take himself along. A girl should not marry a man to reform him. The man on the street has summarized it with the statement, "A leopard cannot change its spots."

Patterns of growth in a particular species
tend to follow an established sequence

It must be admitted that not all individuals in a given species are alike. Men are personally intrigued by the different speeds with which horses run. Dogs have been bred that are particularly adapted for hunting, running, sheep watching, and for leading the blind. But the point here is that horses are horses and dogs are dogs. Dogs walk, are weaned, attain full size, and come in heat in periods of time that are subject to rather precise prediction. The period of gestation for a horse and for a dog are different; but for the particular species it is a number of days that can be definitely counted.

In the normal human being, patterns of behavior appear in an orderly sequence and within limited spaces of time. [120] Not many children walk before the age of eight months, but most of them are walking by the age of three years. Children walk before they talk, they talk before they spell, and they spell before they write stories. Moreover, these various behaviors tend to appear within definite bands of time and should they not do so there is likely to be some concern on the part of teachers and parents.

Certain sequential patterns of behavior occur during adolescence, which, if functionally recognized, will make adolescence less troublesome than is sometimes the case at present. (There is not necessarily an implication that these sequential patterns are inherent in organic constitution. Girls give up playing with dolls at certain—but broadly described—times. Boys frequently do not play with dolls at all. Both these phenomena are intimately related to the cultural mores in which these young people are reared.) There will normally occur, along with the development of the sex organs and the appearance of the secondary sex characteristics, an interest in the other sex. Boys will take more notice of girls as girls than they formerly did. Girls will show greater interest in boys as boys. It becomes important for the adolescent to act like his peers, to dress like his peers, and even to use the same "slanguage." These matters are of extremely great (unfortunately not enough adults realize how great) importance to the adolescent. As interest in the other sex is awakened, as the social horizons of the adolescent expand, a natural growth sequence is the desire to become independent of one's parents. If parents resist this natural (and highly desirable) growth trend, the adolescent may have to go beyond the point of asserting independence to the point of repudiation of parental authority.

Some of the natural patterns of growth are the cause of some concern on the part of adults. It will help the adolescent get through these growth sequences if the adults will regard them as *passing phases of development*. Some of the stages of development that disturb the adult are discussed below.

1. Interest in face and form: The adolescent is likely to spend considerable time inspecting the moles, hair growth, pimples, and contour of his face. There may be some concern about whether he is the right height, weight, and shape.
2. Adolescent crushes: It is quite normal for girls to fall in love with some classmate or older woman and for boys to form an ardent attachment for a boy or a man. These attachments will normally wear themselves out; but it may be that they will wear out less readily if the situation is highly charged with emotion due to the rabid concern of some parent or teacher.
3. Nocturnal emissions: These are probably more disturbing to the misinformed or uninformed adolescent than to the adult; but there are some adults who evidently think that the ejaculation of semen without intercourse is in some way harmful, and they pass on their misconception to the adolescent.
4. Masturbation: Manipulation of the sex organs is described in reputable psychology books and manuals on child raising as a normal bit of conduct. [205] Parents read the comments and agree (intellectually), but they find that their emotional set is such that they think it is a morbid interest when their own child pulls his penis or opens her vulva. It is a passing phase of development and will no doubt be treated as such by more adults as the notion becomes more widespread.
5. Falling "seriously" in love: This is a grave situation—particularly for the great bulk of our population (the middle class). The adolescent thinks that he is seriously in love, but the adult who will allow himself the luxury of reflection will realize that it is a passing phase of development if it is treated as a *serious,* but not vital, question by the adult.

Each individual has his own rate of direction of growth

The fact that there are certain patterns of behavior for a species does not mean that there are no differences in the manifestation of that pattern. One of the most perplexing problems with which psychology has to deal is that of individual differences. Whether the concern be the shape and placement of the ears, the contour and proportion of the legs, the social behavior of the individual, or the magnitude of the IQ, there are differences that are clearly seen and there are differences that are obscure. Both these variations make the prediction and control of behavior difficult—but not impossible, because broad trends do still persist.

No time need be spent trying to establish the fact of individual differences. That is done in practically every general psychology, educational psychology, child psychology, and education text. The big problem is to give a functional recognition to the existence of these differences. Specifically, it must be recognized that commendable work for two different individuals may be work of a distinctly different quality and amount. It should be recognized that a child is not abnormal if he does not show an absorbing interest in the things that seem typically to interest most of his age mates. Our nation will be strengthened, our schools will be improved, and our adolescents will more frequently be mentally healthy when teachers, parents, counselors, and youth workers recognize the implications of differences. It will, for instance, help the adolescent if he is not pressured into attempting to improve his academic marks if he is already working well in terms of his indicated capacity. Such recognition would force the school to provide for a varied curriculum, which would increase the holding power of the school. A more effective school and a happier individual would strengthen our potential as a nation. [58:6]

Attempts continue to be made to correlate the easily observable differences in size and bodily shape with the less discernible differences in personality orientation. Most of these attempts have been useless, or the correlations have been so low that any predictions are worthless. A recent attempt which avoids the error of sharp categorization is that of W. H. Sheldon, who divided body types into three continuous categories. He theorized that the extremes of these types (endomorph, mesomorph and ectomorph) should have certain personality orientations. [275:11] Suffice it to say, at this point, that his theory still seems to warrant open-minded consideration. Whether or not there is a direct and discernible somatotype for basic personality trends, the fact of personality differences must be seriously considered. For example, it is quite conceivable that there may be persons who are not the outgoing, cordial personalities that the school so frequently seeks to develop. Conversely, there may be shy, reticent, aloof persons, who are in perfectly good mental health. The implication is that, just as there are differences in academic aptitude, so too there are differences in personality orientation. These should be respected as the right of the individual adolescent.* Teachers, parents, and youth workers might well recognize these differences in personality orientation by ceasing the effort to make dancers, club members, or conversationalists out of everyone. [152]

Additional force is added to the suggestion that adults need to give functional recognition to these differences because the adolescent often has trouble in facing variations. If the adult who is in close contact with the youth can really appreciate the value of differences, then the adolescent may better be able to tolerate his own differences. One of the important achievements of every individual is for him to learn to appreciate and accept himself. This is not just a lesson for those in the second decade of life. It is a problem before and after this particular period. Sometimes adolescents are bothered by their excessive tallness, excessive shortness, being overweight or underweight, their hair color, their complexion, and the like.

From recent studies it appears that there is an orderly, regular process of growth, development, maturation and aging, a sequence of changes beginning at conception through which every organism must pass. It is as if each individual must travel along the same broad highway.

But it is also clear that each individual human organism, with its specific heredity and its individual nurture and care will pass through those sequential changes, will travel along that highway, at his or her own rate of progress. Each will attain the size, shape, weight, functional capacities, will grow and mature rapidly or slowly, will begin to age, according to his or her idiomatic pattern. †

A few simple, direct and truthful words will not convince. The disturbed adolescent has spent hours brooding over his differences,

---

* It must be admitted that shyness may be a symptom of social maladjustment; but before it is classed as such, other symptoms should be found that corroborate the contention.

† Lawrence K. Frank, *Nature and Human Nature* (New Brunswick: Rutgers University Press; copyright 1951), p. 67.

and it is only by repeated reassurances that some measure of confidence in the value of his differences may be established. Further, it should hardly be necessary to mention, all disparaging and sarcastic remarks on the part of adults must be avoided. The orientation for this avoidance might be to learn that adolescents are not awkward, that they are not emotionally unstable, that they are not socially inept—NECESSARILY. Adults might also indicate that it is natural for humans to distrust the strange or unfamiliar. We are uneasy among a group of foreign-language speakers, we are ill-at-ease in a new social group, we do not know just what to say to cripples. This uneasiness makes us want to defend ourselves—which we often do by making disparaging remarks about others. This realization may help some to rationalize any disheartening remarks they hear about their own differences.

The effect of training varies with the stage of maturation

This principle is a statement related to the phenomenon of readiness. Readiness means that the organism is mature enough to profit from a given experience. Thus, *an* important factor in reading readiness is a mental age of six and a half years. The brain must have matured to a certain degree before a sense of equilibrium has been developed that will allow the child to walk. Readiness to do simple arithmetic problems is not usually achieved until some time after reading readiness has been achieved—thus the various processes of addition, subtraction, multiplication, and division are being delayed a grade or two in comparison to traditional placement. [225:18] Not much is known about readiness as a helpful phenomenon during the period of adolescence. At the present time, it seems that a study of the stage of maturation should be a fruitful field of investigation for the student of adolescence. A great deal is to be learned about "striking while the iron is hot."

One study of the stage of maturation that might well be used as a pilot study is that concerning the study of algebra. It is known that the rate of attrition in formal algebra is very high in the freshman and sophomore years. Yet these same students studying algebra in their senior year seem to grasp the concepts very well. Students of no greater intellectual ability than those who failed algebra in their freshman year were successful when they studied the subject in their senior year. Thus far there has been little tendency to put this research finding into practice; though there have been some attempts to weed out the candidates for algebra classes in the freshman year. It seems not to be fully appreciated that there is a significant difference between mental age and intelligence quotient as an indicator of the present level of mental development. For example, a pupil with an IQ of 110 as a freshman might not have the mental age to study a given subject successfully; but three years later, with the same IQ but with a higher mental age, he could conceivably be successful. [20:276]

It may be conjectured that the implications of the statement, "the effect of training varies with the stage of maturation" lie, not in waiting for additional maturation, but in teaching according to the degree of maturation that has been achieved. Several instances can serve to illustrate the problem involved.

1. Does the fact that some adolescents are deprived of making decisions, even in areas where such powers would be reasonable, render them less capable of ultimately attaining full maturity? Referring back to our first principle, "growth is the product of the interaction of the organism with its environment," is it possible that being deprived of the opportunity to develop an independence from parents until 18 to 21 years renders the individual less capable of achieving a healthy degree of independence in later years? There are instances in which parents have only reluctantly "untied the apron strings," with the result that their children have been somewhat immature all their lives. [105:76]

2. Some potentially able students in college are seemingly unable to fulfill the promise that test data indicate. The remark, "Oh, he's an intelligent person but he just has not learned to apply himself," is too frequently heard. Contributing factors to such a situation are, first, the precise, page by page, undifferentiated assignments given by some high school teachers. Second, the sudden removal of supervision in the execution of study responsibilities may inhibit growth. Although the Eight Year Study * *suggested* approaches to many questions, it indicated, among other things, that such was indeed

---

* A five volume report of this study titled *Adventure in American Education* was sponsored by the Progressive Education Association and published by Harper & Brothers.

the case. Where students in high school had had freedom and responsibility they made good adjustment in academic colleges and
improved the quality of their adjustment as the years passed. Moreover, the superiority of these students, while slight in the strictly
academic areas, was quite marked in extra-curricular and avocational pursuits. [46]

3. Capitalizing on the growth principle that "the effect of training varies with the stage of maturation" could mean many things
that would lessen the impact of our culture on adolescence. Youth
might be given more responsibility in the home rather than having
so many concessions made to them because they are teen agers.
Teachers should realize that a sense of responsibility does not come
out of maturation alone. Maturation provides the base for profitable
experience; hence, responsibility for study should be placed on the
student and the concept of "counseling with" rather than "adviser
to" should be emphasized. Particularly in the middle-class family
the adolescent might be strongly urged to get a part-time job instead
of being forced to hear his parents lamenting, "I do not want him
to suffer the hardships I had." Parents should regard the early dating experiences of adolescents as valuable social laboratories rather
than expecting young people to wait "until they are old enough."

The foregoing examples are illustrative. The growth principle
does not assert that maturation is the major factor. It plainly says
that educative experience is dependent upon the maturation factor;
but the experience is necessary.

Growth is a process of both differentiation and integration

Differentiation means that body parts and movements and intellectual meanings are becoming more and more distinct. Out of the
shape that is the embryo there develop arms and legs, and somewhat
later from the arms and legs there develop fingers and toes—complete with nails. Body parts are differentiated by the time of birth.
But differentiation of movements goes on. Out of the squirmings and
grimaces, which are not always clearly understood by adults, the
baby ultimately evolves a smile of welcome for mother, a howl of
rage at being placed back in bed, or a gurgle of contentment when
a nipple is thrust in his mouth. As differentiation continues, it is
not necessary for a young woman to stamp her feet and scream to

show anger or distaste. She can do a better job by certain inflections on the words, "You louse." A youngster playing his first ball game in the outfield will run toward the batter, then back up in a frenzy and finally lunge and miss the ball that drops five feet to the left of the spot where he originally stood. The practiced high school athlete starts with the crack of the bat runs hard for several feet then stands and lets the ball fall easily into his glove. This is an example of differentiation out of mass, extravagant (at times almost random) activity, to specialized, economical action. The single-syllabled words of the baby that mean many things to a mother may someday become the differentiated vocabulary of an orator who selects just exactly the right word to convey the clearest meaning. A man is not just a man; he is a scoundrel, a scholar, a Democrat, a gentleman, or a cad.

Integration may appear to be the opposite of differentiation but it would be more accurate to speak of the two as being complementary. Integration means that the actions, parts and functions that have become distinct and unique are welded together in a coordinated, efficient manner. The high school lad who makes the easy catch in baseball has not only differentiated the flight of the ball, but he has coordinated (integrated) visual perception with running, timing, and use of the arm. It is a highly complex combination of perceptions and movements, but because it is so well integrated it has the external appearance of such a simple thing that the spectator says, "I could do it myself." The words of the orator, to be most effective, must be more than differentiated. They must be integrated into a clear pattern. There are matters of timing, inflections, gestures, and emphases that serve to convey to the listener stimulating nuances of meaning. And again the degree of integration conveys the notion that it is all very easy to do. Swimming, golfing, painting, playing the piano, and the like all look easy when the action is executed by a well integrated performer.

These simultaneous and complementary processes of differentiation and integration operate during the period of adolescence. Numerous examples might be cited, but some representative ones are as follows: a continuing differentiation of interests, increased differentiation of the sex organs and secondary sex characteristics, further differentiation of uniqueness of personality, further differentiation of independence from parental domination and the sharpening of the differentiated sex role (male or female) one will assume in adult life. Recognition of the naturalness of differentiation as a growth phenomenon should help adults appraise what happens during adolescence; and it should help the adolescent appreciate the inevitability of the differentiation that too often causes him embarrassment.

Examples of integration will include the increasing skill of the adolescent in the performance of bodily activities. The adolescent faces the sometimes difficult problem of integrating himself into a society that has put up barriers (perhaps unwittingly) which make the integration difficult. The need to integrate himself with his peer group is a powerful one for the adolescent. Parents sometimes fail to recognize the importance of this process and prohibit or ridicule certain clothes, hair-do's, and fads approved by adolescents. Definite assistance in the many areas of integration (for example, acceptance of self) should be given by counselors and teachers because growth in so many areas is becoming slower and slower. The learning an individual does is to a very large extent a matter of differentiation, and it would be well for teachers to recognize how it operates—and therefore to work with the process.

Correlation rather than compensation is the general rule

This principle is the psychological interpretation of "To him who hath it shall be given." It is particularly important because of the widespread impression that the contrary is the rule—that a weakness in one area is made up for by a strength in another. The misconception is expressed in the apparently extensive belief in such clichés as the following: "Strong back, weak mind," "Beautiful but dumb," "The myopic Phi Beta Kappa," and the variously stated idea that a person who is weak in reading, history, arithmetic, and the like will have some sort of natural aptitude for working in mechanical or manual activities. The facts are that there is a slight tendency for the brighter children and youth to be physically stronger— taller, heavier, less likely to have sensory defects, less subject to minor illnesses, and with greater vitality—than their age mates of lesser intelligence. The better students naturally have better eyesight, but they may have put some strain on their eyes due to excessive reading. The average girl on the college campus is likely to be better looking than the average girl in an institution for the mentally defective. No study has yet been publicized proving that mechanical aptitude is based on low mentality; in fact, the higher scores on mechanical aptitude tests are earned by those with the higher IQ's.*

Correlation shows a tendency—the "general rule." A correlation is not a law; therefore, generalization for an individual on the basis of the tendency is dangerous. The correlation we have been discussing, when expressed as a coefficient, is so low that application to individual cases is unwarranted. Consequently the greatest usefulness of knowledge of the principle is to avoid subscribing to the misconceptions noted above. There are enough difficulties encountered in the process of growing up so that an additional hazard should not be introduced by giving credence to misinformation. In short, the academically slow individual should not necessarily be steered into mechanics. The studious youngster should not be excluded from social activities and dramatics.

The "general rule" of correlation should not be interpreted as the opposite extreme; that is, it should not be thought that the academically slow person has no chance of having unusual musical ability. Thus, while the best musicians will tend to have higher than average intelligence, it is entirely possible that a genuine source of satisfaction for some youth who is frustrated in academic pursuits will be found in the opportunity to exercise his unusual musical aptitude. There are mentally slow pupils who are extremely well adjusted in social activities and who have unusual aptitude for leadership.

Factors influencing development

Identifying some of the factors that influence the rate and direction of development will supplement and further illustrate the principles mentioned in the foregoing section. These factors will be

---

* There is some evidence that persons with low intelligence are less likely to have accidents when doing routine and monotonous but simple jobs than is the person with higher intelligence. This is attributed to the fact that a simple job does not utilize all of the more intelligent person's mind and that he is likely to seek diversion by wandering.

expanded in subsequent chapters. At this point the purpose is to impress the reader with the multiplicity of conditions affecting growth.

Sex

Many attempts to identify inherent sex differences have failed. It has been postulated that what appear to be sex differences are often cultural differences. The superiority of boys in mechanics and mathematics and the superiority of girls in language and expression are probably matters of cultural influence. Boy babies are slightly heavier (on the average) than girl babies and retain that superiority until the pre-pubertal period of accelerated growth. Girls then surpass boys because they experience puberty earlier. However, the earlier physical maturity of girls causes them to cease growing at an earlier age than boys, and their ultimate height and weight are less. Boys differ more widely than girls in intelligence. There are more gifted boys and more who are mentally defective. Boys suffer more physical handicaps (vision, hearing, physical deformity) than do girls. [12:150]

In evaluating sex factors it is most important to remember that these generalizations are for large groups. *Differences between the sexes are very much smaller than the differences within the sex.* That is, generalizations for individuals are likely to be erroneous.

Intelligence

Relatively high intelligence is associated with accelerated development. This statement may be deduced from the "correlation" principle and from the principle stating that growth is a product of the interaction of heredity and environment. Bright children, for example, walk and talk earlier than do the mentally defective or average. Puberty occurs somewhat earlier for the gifted individual than is the case with the generality. [309:22] Early social maturity and higher occupational status are also associated with high intelligence. It may be concluded that high intelligence enables one to profit more from his environment. To this the speculation might be added that the thus expanded "functional environment" stimulates further intellectual growth.

Endocrine glands

The glands of internal secretion have a profound effect on growth at all stages—from conception to old age. A pinch too much or too little of this or that hormone makes the difference (sometimes) between brilliance and moronity, between stability and instability, between sexual adequacy and sexual anomaly. Despite the fact that the thyroid (or parathyroid or pituitary) has been found, on medical examination, to be defective, the glands work as a total system. This total system undergoes particularly noteworthy changes during puberty and sometimes gets out of the necessary delicate balance. At times this imbalance seems to right itself—that is, other glands work to correct the imbalance caused by the hypo- or hyper-functioning of another. Lack of vitality, late (or excessively early) sexual maturation, skin disorders, and behavior disorders are some of the more frequent indications of glandular imbalance.

The import of the glandular factor is that understanding the adolescent is a joint undertaking. It involves parents, teachers, counselors, adolescents, doctors, and sometimes judges.

Nutrition

The statement has frequently been made that, as a nation, we are well fed but not necessarily well nourished. Cooking, processing, and refining foods sometimes have the effect of reducing nutritive values. Food and diet are important at all ages. During the period of adolescent development, nutrition must be considered in connection with acne (there is no implication that nutrition is the answer in all cases), lack of vitality, or dieting for an athletic event or to fit the current concept of womanliness.

There is some evidence to support the contention that, despite the need for evaluating methods of food processing, the nation *is* well nourished. One is the steadily increasing height and weight of successive generations. The other is the reported earlier onset of puberty as compared with some other cultures and regions.*

---

* A graduate student or a student desiring to make a supplemental report might try to reconcile these conflicting data. If good nourishment accelerates the onset of puberty, why is not the average size of the adult smaller? It has been indicated that early puberty is associated with a shorter over-all growth period. Thus, early puberty would deprive the individual of growing time.

Emotion

The effect of emotion upon the growth of the child is well known and the information has been widely disseminated. More than one mother has been (with justification) concerned about the effect of emotional climate on growth, sleep habits, appetite, and allergies. "Tender-loving-care" has discernible effects on physical growth as well as upon appropriate personality development. It is not enough to give academic recognition to the fact that environment conditions the extent to which one's potential is realized. It is necessary to examine the specific effects of various emotional climates. This will be done as social class is examined, when peer relationships are considered, as we study the values of adolescents, and as adjustment to society is examined.

Because behavior always has multiple causes, it is not possible to assert with finality that strong emotions create this or that condition. Suffice it to say that in such things as acne, social reticence, posture, delinquency, mental illness, and drug addiction, chronic disintegrative emotions have sometimes been playing a part. The happiness, confidence, leadership, studiousness, and ambition of adolescents are also related to emotions. The growth and development of the adolescent cannot be understood unless the factor of emotion is seen to be pervasive.

Socio-economic status

The coordinated, interdependent role of growth principles, and the factors that condition their operation, is well illustrated by analysis of socio-economic status. Low economic status is sometimes indicative of the possession of low potential for intellectual development. Studies show that even in the instances where intellectual potential is relatively high, low socio-economic status inhibits development. [334] Nutrition is frequently not so sound in the lower classes as in the higher. Similarly, it has been found that the incidence of crippling conditions is higher in the less advantageously situated families. [185:205] Different ideals and objectives motivate children and adolescents who come from different classes. These differences reveal themselves in varied responses to the opportunities provided in the school. [324]

School teachers, doctors, ministers, psychologists, and lawyers come from the middle and lower-upper classes. Since there is a tendency to think that others come from a background such as our own, the young people from the lower classes are likely to be misunderstood. Their differences, rather than being indications of orneriness, are natural and normal responses. It is particularly important that social class influences be studied when an attempt is being made to understand the personality and emotional responses of adolescents.

Other factors influencing growth principles

Moral tone of the family, parental relationships, religious orientation, membership in a minority racial group, and accident and disease are other factors that may influence personality growth. There is the possibility that geographical climate influences the direction and defines some of the limits of growth. The influence of bodily build upon interests, disposition, and personality persists as a stimulating field of investigation.

All-in-all it is safe to say that the principles of growth are valuable guides. They comprise generalizations that help in prediction and understanding. They are not laws. They do not form the basis for mathematically precise calculation. Yet all that is said in subsequent chapters would be pointless unless the principles of growth did tend to be operative.

Summary

The psychology of adolescence is like other branches of psychology, but it has a somewhat different emphasis. The principles of growth function in the adolescent years in much the same manner that they did in the pre-natal period and in early childhood. Briefly, these principles are as follows:

1. Growth is a product of the *interaction* of the *organism* with its *environment*. This involves three things—the hereditary potential of the individual, the effective environment of that individual, and the response he makes to himself and the environment.

2. Growth does not proceed by leaps and bounds—it is continuous and gradual. Slowly—day-by-day and week-by-week—the ac-

cretions that are growth accumulate. The process is gradual but nonetheless sure and continuous. However, this does not mean always at the same speed.

3. Growth proceeds most rapidly in the early years; but, it should be emphasized, it *does* proceed also in the later years. The childhood period is important to the adolescent, *and* the experiences and growth of the adolescent are important in shaping the kind of adult he will be.

4. Patterns of individual growth tend to remain consistent. For any individual, the rapid grower will tend to keep his pace and the slow grower will tend to fall further and further behind, in the particular area of growth concerned.

5. Patterns of growth in a given species tend to follow an established sequence. Although individuals must be studied as individuals, there are certain developments that take place during certain (even if not sharply defined) periods. Particular events in an individual's life may be more accurately predicted if previous (anticipatory) developments are known.

6. Each individual has his own rate of growth. Common trends in growth may be postulated; but within the broad pattern, which is characteristic of the species, there are an infinite number of variations for individuals. Psychological principles will hold for large groups of subjects, but individuals must always be studied as individuals.

7. The effect of training varies with the stage of maturation. Much instruction is relatively ineffective because the individual is not mentally or physically "ready." Some instruction is relatively ineffective because instruction is delayed beyond the point when the individual is most plastic. Empirical evidence points to the probability that the adolescent could mature more rapidly if he were given more realistic instruction and experience.

8. Growth is a process of both differentiation and integration. These two complementary phenomena characterize growth of the organism—the body parts differentiate in shape and function and then are integrated in coordinated action. They also characterize the growth of the individual into his culture. He becomes a different and distinct individual but must finally become a functioning part of the culture.

9. Correlation rather than compensation is the *general* rule. This is simply a case of "the rich become richer and the poor become poorer"—with many exceptions. Its main practical import is to warn the serious student of psychology of the inadvisability of basing predictions for individuals on generalizations. Correlation of traits is of academic interest. Knowledge of individuals is of practical importance.

A number of factors or conditions cause variations in the functioning of the foregoing principles. These are not contradictions so much as they are explanations. Sex, intelligence, functioning of endocrines, nutrition, emotional climate, and accident and disease are among the factors that must be studied when an understanding of adolescent development is sought. All behavior is caused. Principles of growth form the basis for understanding these causes.

STUDY AND REVIEW ITEMS

1. Cite a number of exceptions to the statement, "The subject matter of adolescence is not unique."

2. Describe some examples from plant and animal life illustrating that growth is a product of the interaction of heredity and environment. Does this hold for the phenomenon of height in humans?

3. What techniques would you suggest for helping the adolescent appreciate the implication of the fact that growth is continuous and gradual?

4. What approach would you suggest for the adolescent who asserts, "I've never had a chance. My parents have been too easy (or hard) on me"?

5. How would you account for the phenomenon of the changing IQ in the light of the principle that growth rates tend to remain constant?

6. Work out a table for the adolescent years that shows the approximate time and order of appearance of certain behaviors and physical features.

7. In view of the fact that the adolescent wants to be like his peers, how can we help him absorb the inevitability of the fact that each individual has his own rate of growth?

8. Can you cite some examples, other than those mentioned in the text, that illustrate the relationship of developmental level to the effectiveness of instruction?

9. Do you see anything in the phenomena of differentiation and integration that would seem to explain the reality of "adolescent awkwardness"?

10. See if you can recall any instances in which you have heard people make ill-founded remarks that could be attributed to belief in the compensation of traits.

RECOMMENDED SUPPLEMENTARY READING

Blair, Glenn M. "What Teachers Should Know About the Psychology of Adolescence," *Journal of Educational Psychology,* 41, 1950, 356–361.
   The author believes that some important aspects of the psychology of adolescence have tended to be overlooked. These are: adolescence as a transition period, the forming power of the culture, the impact of biological factors, and the necessity for achieving certain developmental tasks.

Munn, Norman L. *Psychology* (Boston: Houghton Mifflin Company; 1946), Chapter 5.
   "Factors in Psychological Growth" is a chapter in which heredity, environment, and maturation are considered. Illustrative examples are taken from cultural anthropology—the Hopis—and from controlled studies of twins. The nature of psychological experimentation is shown.

Neilon, Patricia. "Shirley's Babies After Fifteen Years," *Journal of Genetic Psychology,* 73, 1948, 175–186.
   This article describes the re-study of children at the age of seventeen who had first been studied from birth to two years. The comparative personality sketches of individuals at the two times showed a tendency for characteristics to persist. The continuity of behavior is demonstrated.

Neugarten, Bernice L. *Your Heredity,* Life Adjustment Booklet (Chicago: Science Research Associates, Inc.; 1951).

This pamphlet illustrates the kind of helpful material available for adolescents. How heredity works, the nature and extent of individual differences, and some suggestions for absorbing one's own differences are some of the topics dealt with.

Skinner, C. E. (Ed.) *Educational Psychology,* 3rd Ed. (New York: Prentice-Hall, Inc.; 1951) Chapter 2.

In this chapter T. R. McConnell shows how the principles of growth operate in the learning process. The development of personality is shown to be in accord with the basic growth principles. Examples and materials are drawn from the psychology of childhood, adolescence, and later maturity.

Zubek, J. P., and P. A. Solberg. *Human Development* (New York: McGraw-Hill Book Company, Inc.; 1954), pp. 95–130.

This selection on "physical development" is helpful in placing the period of adolescence in the total context of development. Characteristic changes in circulation, respiration, digestion, skin, body proportions, strength, and the like are described for children, adolescents, and the later years.

AUDIO-VISUAL MATERIAL

He Acts His Age (McGraw-Hill Book Company, Inc., 330 West 42nd Street, New York 36), 13 min., so., b. & w. or col.

Presents ways of meeting problems of emotional development in children so that the child will be acting in a manner appropriate for his stage of development. Phases of emotional development up to the age of fifteen are presented.

Principles of Development (McGraw-Hill Book Company, Inc.), 17 min., so., b. and w.

This shows the fundamentals of growth with emphasis on basic principles. Intelligence, sex, motivation, heredity, health, and family are shown as growth influences. Children are the subjects, but inferences may be drawn for adolescents.

What needs of adolescents are approached through engaging in significant work? What are the most pressing needs of adolescents? How does society often hamper the satisfaction of insistent needs?

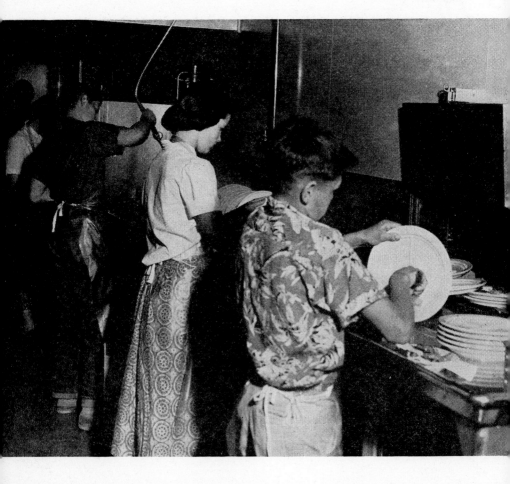

CHAPTER THREE

The Needs of Adolescents

The great need of every adolescent is to be understood and to be recognized as a worthy individual. (This, in fact, is the great need of every one of us.) Some of the needs of adolescents stem from the physical facts of puberty. A great many needs arise from the impact of cultural influences—both national culture and that provided by the immediate family and neighborhood. If the nature and origin of the needs of adolescents are recognized by parents, counselors, youth workers, and teachers, those needs have a better chance of approaching satisfaction. If the needs are not recognized, the transition period of the teen years is made more difficult. More young people will suffer, or even succumb, from the hazards of the journey through these years. When the recognition of needs is implemented through changes in society and the modification of adult attitudes, youth will be more capable of fulfilling an optimistic hope for the future. The study of needs thus provides one key to the understanding of adolescents.

The nature of needs

Definition of needs

The word "need" suggests something of importance—although, conversationally, "need" may indicate an item of relatively small import ("I need a new hat"). Psychologically, the meaning of the

67

word is in close accord with the dictionary definition. A need is something vital, imperative, indispensable, or urgently required. Some needs are so imperative that failure to satisfy them would result in death. Physical needs such as those for water, food, rest, and the maintenance of a rather uniform temperature are examples of vital needs. The need to be loved is frequently mentioned by psychologists. There are cases in which the need to be loved has been denied yet the individual has continued to live—physically. There are also cases in which the lack of love has resulted in death. It is safe to generalize that, when needs are *approaching* satisfaction, growth will be more symmetrical and realization of potentials more complete. When needs are denied, twisted lives, disappointed individuals, and frustrated personalities are likely to result. Needs may not be so imperative that their denial threatens biological life, but they are imperative enough that a full life, psychologically, is impossible unless they approach satisfaction.

Needs are dynamic in nature

The need for approval may have little effect on the infant, whose physical needs are dominant. But a mature man, who still has physical needs, may find that the desire for approval is such that he can and will starve himself. A need that is partially fulfilled may seem to lack imperiousness. For example, an adolescent who feels that he is approved by his peers gives no manifestation of the need for approval, whereas the adolescent who is shunned by his peers may find this need most imperious. The need for accomplishment may drive the young adult to work long and intensively while the octogenarian laughs at the impatience of youth. Thus, the need that is most vital at one age is only a mild motivator at another age. The need which one person has for love, or accomplishment, will differ in intensity from the need which another has for being loved. The urgency of a need will vary also with the environmental conditions of the individual. The need for independence will take markedly different forms in the youth belonging to the upper class from that shown by the youth from the lower class. The nature of needs may be generalized but, for better understanding, needs must be studied in terms of individual adolescents.

The urgency of needs varies from person to person. Individual differences in the strength of needs arise from variations in physical and mental capacity and in what one has experienced. There may be a weak drive toward the satisfaction of social needs because of low mentality. Sex drives may be weak because of underdeveloped gonads. The need to do and achieve may be feeble because of hypoactive thyroid glands. Experience also conditions the vitality of needs. Some success in the satisfaction of a need may encourage the individual to increased effort. Near fulfillment of the need may result in apparent satiation. Complete blocking of need satisfaction may not incite one to greater effort but rather devastate him so completely that he ceases all effort. Bodily build may condition the imperiousness of a need.

. . . less than ten boys out of every hundred are sufficiently mesomorphic to engage with even moderate success in the more strenuous forms of athletics, requiring great strength and physical endurance. Hence the almost criminal folly of encouraging all boys, whatever their hereditary make-up, to develop athletic ambitions. By doing this educators condemn large numbers of their pupils to an unnecessary disappointment and frustration, plant the seed of neurosis among the unsuccessful, and foster a conspicuous bumptiousness and self-conceit in the extreme mesomorph. A rational policy with regard to athletics would be to tell all boys the simple truth, which is that very few of them can expect to excel in the more violent sports, that such excellence depends primarily on a particular inheritance of size and shape, and that persons of other shapes and sizes not suited to athletic proficiency have as good a right to realize their own *natural* capacities as the extreme mesomorph and can contribute at least as much to society.*

Body build is not all there is to athletics—but there is truth in the foregoing statement. Those who work successfully with youth must understand these variations in need—at least to the extent of knowing that there are differences.

Needs are rarely, perhaps never, satisfied

The need for food, rest, and exercise is constantly changing as the individual moves about and grows. The need to be loved, or to

* Aldous Huxley, "Who Are You?" *Harpers*, 189, November, 1944, p. 515.

accomplish, or for approval, is similarly only partially fulfilled at any one time. Beneath the steady feeling of being loved there must be periodic overt manifestations of love. We should then, in order to speak accurately, say that *needs should be on the way to being satisfied.* There should be approaches to the satisfaction, even though complete fulfillment of the need is improbable or impossible. This statement should be a reassuring one to the parent, teacher, or youth counselor. It means that a robust personality is possible for the adolescent even when conditions are far from perfect. Parents need not think that the need to be loved must be satisfied every hour on the hour. There are times when they can say, "Stop bothering me now." Teachers will know that an adolescent need not succeed at every task attempted. Pressure should be brought to bear to get young people to attempt the difficult task. The need to accomplish can be partially (and adequately) satisfied by achievement in another area. The counselor can be assured that the adolescent's strong muscles or approved figure can offset the disappointment of poor complexion.

Philosophers and psychologists assert that having a goal—a purpose—provides the lure for living. Unsatisfied needs give everyone a reason for vigorous pursuit of life. If need satisfaction is completely blocked, the result is despair. If needs are on the way to being met the individual will continue to strive toward his goals. The advisers of young people and the young people themselves should know this fundamental proposition.

We may conclude that the concept of needs provides a fruitful approach to the understanding of adolescents. However, the generalities involved in the concept should not be allowed to obscure the need for attention to differences.

Basic human needs

There are many ways of expressing fundamental human needs. Percival M. Symonds lists the following needs: to be with others, to gain attention, for approval, to be a cause (to create), for mastery, for security, for affection, and to satisfy curiosity. [302] W. I. Thomas considers a similar list under the heading of wishes: for new experiences, for security, for response, and for recognition.

[310] W. C. Trow classifies needs under the following headings: bodily activity, knowledge, sensory enjoyment, security, mastery, and service. [322:134] Daniel A. Prescott, basing his conclusions on studies of children who experienced personality disturbance because of unsatisfied needs, lists three: ego, status, and integrative needs. [248:110] A careful examination of the various lists will show that they are quite similar. For convenience in discussion, the needs will here be discussed under three headings: (1) organic, (2) psychological, and (3) social.

Organic needs

Organic needs include such things as the need for rest and exercise, for protection from bodily injury, for food and water, and for the maintenance of a bodily temperature of about 98°. These needs are common to all, so ways in which they may be approached for the adolescent must be considered.

The contrast between rest and exercise makes it difficult to formulate an acceptable generalization. But it is certain that some difficulties in understanding the adolescent are due to unbalanced emphasis on one or the other. For example, the parent may be prolonging a conflict with his son or daughter regarding late hours or participation in athletics. The parent may insist that rest is necessary and therefore less tennis is in order. This stand cannot be taken on the basis of rest *or* exercise—it must be taken in terms of the entire situation. If the adolescent is thin, cross, lacks appetite, and shows other symptoms of fatigue, then more rest may be the wise course. It is possible, too, that due to the buoyancy of youth, a very little rest will serve to bring him quickly back to physical par. Insisting that he get more rest, for rest's sake, may only make his need for exercise the more insistent. Balance between rest and exercise, *in terms of the individual,* is the difficult goal for which teachers and parents must strive.

The adolescent must be protected from physical injury. Yet the provisions for such protection must be such that the desire to explore and experience (need to satisfy curiosity) are not thwarted. Squirreling in hot-rods carries the threat of injury, but a car provides an avenue to recognition for some adolescents. Recognition of the organic need for protection from injury suggests that (1) sources of need satisfaction that are not dangerous should be provided and (2) adolescents should be called into the council that discusses such problems. This is now being done more frequently in the home, in the school, and in community youth organizations.

Organic needs are not *simply* organic. Social pressures determine the way in which such needs are met. Quitting the basketball team, even if the adolescent himself feels the need for more rest, is not an easy decision. Adolescents are certainly not unaware of the dangers involved in squirreling and in experimentation with drugs. But there are times when, *for some individuals,* need denial has been so consistent that a compensation is sought.

Adults must recognize that the thwarting of organic needs is an important factor to be considered in understanding adolescents. We can expect, as parents, that too much exercise with insufficient rest (or too must rest with insufficient exercise) may contribute to irritability. We may expect, as teachers, that an improper diet may contribute to inattentiveness or listlessness. Even in our well-fed society, there are instances of malnutrition. Ill-fitting shoes, thinly clad legs, impaired hearing, defective vision, over-exertion, or physiological hunger are factors functioning in the conduct of adolescents.

Psychological needs

Psychological needs are as imperative for personality integrity as are organic needs in the maintenance of life. Different authorities state the psychological needs in various ways, but for understanding the adolescent four can be used to illustrate how behavior is influenced.

1. THE NEED TO FEEL SECURE. There is an important difference in saying the need to *feel* secure and the need to *be* secure. The difference is in the adolescent's reaction to his situation. There are some who have the material advantages, the physical attributes, the social skills, and the intelligence that would seem to make for security—yet feel insecure. Others apparently suffer many lacks—but give the appearance of feeling secure. Hence, counseling, which is designed to improve the objectivity of perception, is often an important factor in feelings of security.

The foregoing does not rule out the fact that there are situations that *contribute* to feelings of insecurity. Since descriptions of these frequently appear in psychological literature, it will probably suffice to list some of the more pervasive factors in insecurity.

a. Lack of harmony between parents
b. Competition between parents for children's love
c. Homes broken by divorce, death, separation or desertion
d. Conflict between the mores of the school or community and conduct within the home
e. Inability to "keep up" in clothes and activities because of inadequate finances
f. Major and minor differences in bodily build, weight, complexion, and the like
g. Parents' and teachers' making comparisons between individuals.

It is important, in attempting to understand adolescents, that it be realized that feelings of security are *not given* to the individual. Some literature gives the impression that feelings of security derive from being loved, from the way in which infants are fed or from being protected from hostile environments. This is partially true. Feelings of security do have their *origin* in such factors; but, in the final analysis, genuine feelings of security come from the individual's being able to "breast the current" under his own power. Parents must loosen their hold so adolescents can develop skill in solving their own problems. Teachers must provide opportunities for youth to exercise their capacity for self-direction. Community planning must include giving youth credit for a desire to be good, contributing citizens.

2. THE NEED TO MANIPULATE AND SATISFY CURIOSITY. Satisfaction of this need presents another dilemma to the adult. How does one safely allow enough freedom to satisfy the adolescent's curiosity and when does firsthand experience become too costly? Certainly we do not want every youth to learn a hate for war from direct contact. Each youth should not have to learn for himself that some drugs are quickly and dangerously habit-forming. Youth might well be told that the perfect marriage mate is not to be discovered through sexual experimentation.

There are bounds to the extent to which the direct satisfaction of curiosity should be sought. But it is probable that those bounds are much wider than the typical anxious parent or teacher thinks. There are some disappointing cases on record which show that the girl who was carefully restricted in high school dating, by her timid parents, had not learned how to conduct herself prudently in college. In fact, there are some who believe that if a youth does not go through the experience of puppy love, crushes and infatuation, he is to some extent limited in his ability to achieve mature conjugal love. Here it would appear that steps should be taken to satisfy curiosity. (This, however, does not mean that the author is recommending promiscuity. It will be made clear in a later chapter that such is distinctly *not* his recommendation.)

Situations and problems in which the need to manipulate and satisfy curiosity should be considered by parents *in council with* adolescents might include the following: when to come in at night, choice of part-time occupations, where they might go for recreation. Teachers might encourage curiosity by being cautious in the use of workbooks, by encouraging reading beyond the minimum, by respecting questions that are raised (even when apparently off the subject), and by suggesting areas of research and investigation outside the classroom.

3. THE NEED FOR ACHIEVEMENT. This need manifests itself from infancy onward. It is obvious when the infant seizes the spoon and spreads pablum on his face, when he pulls away from his parent so he can button his own clothes. The school child shows it when he grabs the pencil from the teacher to write his own name—"I can do it myself." The need is manifesting itself in many ways in the adolescent—striving to earn his own money, to decorate his own room, to govern his own affairs. In school, pupils wish to do well in the tasks that are set before them. The need for achievement does not have to be taught—though its manifestations can be obscured by continued failure in tasks that are inappropriate.

Obstacles in the way to marriage and the assumption of adult responsibilities often thwart the fulfillment of this need. Limited work opportunities threaten personality development because of the lack of achievement in the important area of *occupation*. This is a particularly difficult obstacle in a society where the mark of an individual is what he does.

The prolonging of education need not be the obstacle to achievement it sometimes is. Education can, in fact, be the compensating factor. The key to a kind of education that provides more and wider opportunities for achievement has been expressed by many writers, representative of whom is Arthur T. Jersild:

> The failures, reminders of limitations, and the rejection which children face at school are often artificial and forced. They may have the effect of humiliating the child by depreciating his worth in a manner that does no good to society and does him great harm. *Much of the failure at school is contrived.* Much of the depreciation children encounter there is based upon false evaluation. Some of it rests upon a punitive approach to education which in some schools has a savage intensity. The cards are stacked against many children. They are stacked when teachers, in league with the prevailing competitive pressures in our society, attach greater importance to certain school achievements than they merit, and apply pressures which *make the child feel that he is worthless in all respects because he does not happen to be a top performer in some respects.**

4. THE NEED TO BE INDEPENDENT. Limited work opportunity, barriers to marriage, and prolonged education (accompanied by financial dependence on parents) are obstacles to the fulfillment of this need. More will be said of the implications for parents of this need in a later chapter. Let it here be said that parents should hesitate before using the expression, "As long as I'm paying the bills, I'm going to give the orders."

Many things can be done in the school to promote a healthy fulfillment of the need for independence. It is, of course, recognized that independence is a relative matter—even the adult must be dependent to the extent of being cooperative. Hence, steps toward independence can be defined in terms of democratic functioning. Educators can check their effectiveness in implementing the fulfillment of the need for independence by using the list compiled by the United States Office of Education. Here are some illustrative questions:

---

* Arthur T. Jersild, *In Search of Self* (New York: Teachers College, Columbia University; 1952), p. 91. Italics added. Reproduced by permission of the publishers.

Do students in your classes have a voice in determining the projects or problems on which they will work?

Do students in your classes share in evaluating what they have done?

Is the slow learner in your classes given opportunities to do something important which he can do relatively well?

When your students cooperatively plan an activity, do they carry out their agreed-upon assignments and responsibilities?

Do you admit to your students that you are not an authority on all questions arising in class?

Do your students show eagerness to participate in student self-government?

Does the student editor of your school paper or magazine have the freedom of the press?

Do students have opportunities to share in group solutions of school problems?

Do students have a fair opportunity to defend themselves against a teacher's charge of misconduct?

Are opportunities provided for students to discuss student council activities? *

These and the other questions in this pamphlet may serve school workers as a guide to the progressive fulfillment of the need for independence. The list has the further advantage of placing independence in the social context of cooperativeness.

Social needs

Man, as an animal, is poorly equipped to cope with the demands of nature, *except* for his brains and his habit of living in groups. This exception makes an infinite difference, and it follows that continued mastery of the environment depends on the ability to function well in groups. No matter what profession or occupation one follows, his success is largely dependent upon his ability to get along with others. The home, government, and the school depend on the fulfillment of social needs for their value—they are institutions designed to facilitate need satisfaction.

---

* *How Democratic Is Your School?* (Federal Security Agency, Office of Education, 1949. Unnumbered).

1. THE NEED FOR BELONGING. A person's concept of himself and his attitude toward others is conditioned by his feeling of belonging—or lack of it. One of the difficulties of adolescence is that adolescents constitute a minority group. When the young person has no requisite job to perform with his mature body, his ability to achieve a feeling of belonging tends to be thwarted. When parents refer to the cost of raising children, without mentioning the compensating joys, it is difficult for the adolescent to believe that he belongs.

Like other needs, this one is not to be accomplished in a simple and specific manner. The whole regime of life is concerned; but some general recommendations can be made. Belongingness is closely allied to being recognized for what one is. This means that one is liked and respected despite his shortcomings. Youth workers must recognize some of the difficulties involved in being a member of a minority group and make due allowances. Effort must be made to give youth an opportunity to engage in at least part-time employment. Attention must be devoted to convincing youth of the ultimate value of prolonged education with its accompaniment of dependence—and parents must recognize that their older children do not enjoy this dependence.

2. THE NEED FOR LOVE AND AFFECTION. Pediatricians advise parents to administer tender-loving-care in large doses for the physical as well as the psychological well-being of children. The need for love does not diminish as one grows older, though its steady denial may cause an individual to deny its importance. Many children who have "problems" and many delinquent adolescents have had their behavior traced directly to the blocked need for love. When children are talked to, played with, cuddled, praised, and patiently taught they develop a friendliness and confidence that lay the basis for successive lessons of social adjustment. When there is little time for children, perfunctory handling, abrupt orders, and obvious impatience they probably begin to doubt and fear the world. Subsequent experiences are colored by the child's reacting in a hostile and suspicious manner.

One example might be cited to give point to the generality. Many cases of promiscuity, particularly in girls, have been attributed to the lack of parental love. Although the girl may have relatively little sex appetite she consents to intercourse because of the attention she momentarily receives. Other types of aberrant behavior have been traced to a lack of self-respect that has been derived from the child's experience of failing to find adequate satisfaction for his need to feel loved.

3. THE NEED FOR COMPANIONSHIP. One of the cruelest punishments devised by man is solitary confinement. The most confirmed criminal, who would vehemently deny his linkage with any other person, is urgently in need of companionship.

The wise parents of adolescents recognize the insistency of this demand when they permit their children freedom for selecting friends. The parents try to be patient with those occasions when the agreed-upon hours for getting home are not strictly kept. The need is recognized when criticisms of clothing, hair style, and the use of current slang expressions are withheld. These parents are giving recognition to the fact that dress, mannerisms, and vocal expressions are symbols of companionship.

It should be recognized that implementation of the need for companionship is much more than a matter of current satisfaction. Provisions for companionship also provide experience and training that will help later when the time comes for wise selection of a marriage partner.

4. THE NEED FOR UNDERSTANDING. This need overlaps the needs which have been previously mentioned. It is probably because of this duplicating feature that George D. Stoddard has said, ". . . the one great need of every adolescent—of every person— is stressed: to be understood and respected." * The whole study of adolescence is an approach to the satisfaction of this need. Let it here be said that an understanding of the adolescent will help him in achieving the social needs of (1) showing an enlightened regard for the welfare of others, (2) improving his ability and disposition to cooperate in social activities, (3) developing the ability to make and keep friends, and (4) achieving the kind of personality that will make it easier for others to love him.

---

* George D. Stoddard, in 43rd Yearbook of the National Society for the Study of Education, Part I, Adolescence (Chicago: University of Chicago Press; 1944), p. 354.

Developmental tasks of adolescence

Life is a matter of growth. No matter what the individual's age, unique developments must be accomplished if he is to handle successfully his problems of adjusting. The concept of "developmental tasks" has been formulated to describe the problems of living in each of the successive periods of life. Robert J. Havighurst has been particularly active in the description of the tasks infants, children, adolescents, adults, middle-aged, and older people must accomplish. [135] His formulation is particularly valuable because it emphasizes the influence of social class status—a factor that is all too frequently overlooked.

Developmental tasks are learnings that are requisite to effective contemporary processes of adjustment and that prepare one for the succeeding stages of growth—hence they are learnings that must be accomplished in a restricted time period. Developmental tasks arise out of the (1) psychological and (2) physiological nature of the individual as he lives in a particular (3) cultural milieu. These tasks constitute needs of the adolescent just as surely as the need for love, for food, for accomplishment, and the like form the basis for behavior.

Achieving new and more mature relations
*with age-mates of both sexes.**

This task involves learning to see girls as women and boys as men. The physiological basis is the maturing of the sex organs and their functioning. The psychological basis is the need for peer approval and companionship. In the upper and middle classes this is viewed as an important period during which adolescents should learn social skills and develop friendship and which should end in courtship and marriage. In the lower class this new relationship with age-mates often involves sexual experience and ends in comparatively early marriage.

---

* Robert J. Havighurst, *Human Development and Education* (New York: Longmans, Green and Company; 1953), pp. 111–158. Headings from here through page 85 are directly quoted by permission of the publishers.

Achieving a masculine or feminine social role

This is the problem of accepting one's sex and acting appropriately. The physiological basis is the increasing differentiation of the sexes—women develop less physical strength than men while gaining in their attractiveness to men. Psychologically, achieving a role is not difficult for the boy because society accords positions of importance more readily to the male. It may be difficult for females because of their dependence on males for support. The problem is becoming less difficult for women, as there are more opportunities for work and participation in the professions.

Accepting one's physique and using the body effectively

One should be proud of, or at least accept, his physical stature. Further, this task involves learning to use and protect one's body. The first problem, that of accepting one's size and shape, is probably the one of greatest psychological impact. Because puberty occurs at such markedly different ages in various individuals there is a difference in the time of the pre-pubertal growth spurt. This added to different inherited body framework creates differences that are particularly difficult for adolescents to accept because they are desirious of being liked and being accepted by others of their peer group. Crowded teeth, acne, moles, size and shape of nose, as well as breast development or growth in the size of male sex organs are other common causes of concern. These worries have their origin in, or at least are intensified by, the stress our society places on being good looking—in the Hollywood style.

Havighurst suggests five procedures that might help the adolescent to achieve this task efficiently. (1) Group students for physical activities on the basis of skills and the extent of physical development already achieved. (2) Teach, in biology and hygiene classes, the normality of variation in tempo of physical development. (3) Whenever possible group pupils in the junior-high-school in terms of physical status rather than solely upon the basis of age. (4) Use dancing, drawing, and painting as an approach to greater freedom and enjoyment in the use of the body. (5) Provide opportunities for adolescents to get information and assurance regarding their own physical development. [136:122]

Achieving emotional independence of parents and other adults

Sometime during life an individual must cease being dependent on older persons and at the same time develop respect and affection for them. This task has its biological origin in the growth of the body to adult size and in the development of sexual powers. Since sex gratification normally requires marriage and the establishment of a new home, the individual must become emancipated from his or her parents' home. Psychologically this task is difficult because of ambivalence on the part of both parent and adolescent. The parents want their child to grow up but they are afraid of what will happen to him because of innocence and inexperience. It is difficult for adolescents because they want freedom, yet at the same time they recognize that they do not have the ability to cope with all situations and, of necessity, do seek counsel.

In the lower social classes this task is relatively simple because young people start to work at an earlier age and the earning of money facilitates the achievement of independence. The task is not particularly difficult in the upper classes because money is not typically an insistent concern. Consequently, young people can accept financial aid without feeling that their parents are sacrificing or that they are parasites. It is a rather difficult task for adolescents of the middle class because of the insistence on prolonged education and the probability of financial difficulty for parents.

Achieving assurance of economic independence

The task of feeling that a man can earn his own living, if necessary, is particularly important in a society that places high value on productivity. Physical size is the biological basis of this task. The psychological basis is found in the delay our culture imposes on the process of growing up. Except in times of war and marked prosperity, it is difficult for youth to get the jobs and earn the money that do so much toward establishing feelings of worth. It is not necessary that boys actually earn their living—it is frequently simply a matter of earning enough so that they can feel they could make their way if necessary. This has not been such a difficult task for girls but, as more women go into business and industry, the cultural demand for independence is increasing.

Achieving a feeling of economic independence is most difficult for those in the middle class. Prolonged education diverts the youth from getting jobs. Late marriage diminishes the necessity for quitting school and going to work. As with achieving emotional independence, the task is less difficult for the upper class because of the small tendency to worry about financial matters. It is not a particularly difficult task for the lower class because of the custom of quitting school and marrying at an early age and actually getting some kind of job.

Assistance in the accomplishment of this task will probably come through providing work-study programs, planning approaches to the provision of part-time employment, encouraging capable youth from the lower classes to continue their education, and showing all youths the ultimate economic value of prolonged education.

Selecting and preparing for an occupation

This task involves selecting an occupation for which a person has ability and in which he is interested and making preparations for the pursuit of the job. Physically, the task is based on the achievement of adult body size and strength and upon the ability to develop specialized skills and dexterities. Psychologically, the task is imposed by the emphasis upon what one does as the measure of what one is.

Selecting and preparing for an occupation are most difficult for the middle-class youth. He must get a job that will make him upwardly mobile (see glossary: social mobility) or at least maintain his social status. Since the cost of education is often burdensome, fumbling in the matter of job choice must be held to a minimum. The task is somewhat less difficult for the upper-class youths because their position is somewhat more secure. The cost of education is not likely to be burdensome. The task is easily achieved by the lower-class youth who shift readily from one job to another and who are content, as are their fathers, with holding any job that pays well.

There are many difficulties in the way of achieving this task in an efficient fashion. (1) There are some 40,000 defined job titles listed in the *Dictionary of Occupational Titles*—hence finding *just* the right job is difficult on the basis of sheer magnitude. (2) We do not know enough about the unique skills needed in particular jobs—

notably the professions. (3) We do not know how to test for the traits, abilities, capacities, and the like that are thought to be important in given occupations. (4) The demand for workers of a particular kind does not correspond to the number who are capable, qualified, and interested in doing the job. (5) The need for workers in a particular area often undergoes marked change in a short period—the increased demand for elementary teachers in recent years is a well-known example.

Preparing for marriage and family life

There is a tendency to think of this task as one of particular importance to girls. Actually, both boys and girls need to develop healthy attitudes toward family life and having children since a large fraction of their time will be devoted to these activities. Boys, as well as girls, need to have knowledge about home management and the care and rearing of children.

Biologically, this task evolves from sexual maturation. Psychologically, it is a task because of the widely variant attitudes toward marriage and children. Many approach marriage or the having of children, or both, with doubt or even fear. Others look at marriage as a chance for personal fulfillment. Still others seem to regard it as a necessary or conventional thing without envisioning the possibilities it holds for the enrichment of one's total life.

The stability of marriage differs widely from one social class to another. In the upper class, marriage occurs early and is frequently unstable and lacking in real harmony. Middle-class people marry at a somewhat later age, tend to establish lasting unions and to confine sex relationships to the marriage partner (see Chapter Eight). Lower-class individuals marry early, often live with parents or in-laws, desertions and common law marriages are relatively frequent, and sex experience is not confined to the marriage partner.

Developing intellectual skills and concepts
necessary for civic competence

Civic competence refers to the ability to live and deal effectively with the problems of our democratic society. It involves the development of concepts about law, government, social, economic, and political institutions, together with the development of language and problem-solving ability.

The biological basis of this task is physical and mental maturation. Growth in ability to learn entirely new things reaches a peak in the teen years, although the ability to develop new concepts—because of experience—continues to develop in later years. Psychologically, the task varies greatly from individual to individual. Some easily grasp the concepts necessary for civic competence and find it easy to keep in functional contact with the average person. Others must strain to read even simple newspaper articles and are unable to develop either the concepts or interests that will help in the solution of democratic problems.

There are, of course, differences between individuals in the various social classes, which stem from the above-mentioned psychological and biological differences. There are also differences in the rigidity of class structure in various communities. Some upper-class persons may be complacently ignorant of civic affairs, but there are many who regard it as their responsibility to lead in community and civic affairs. They are frequently the ones who hold office and take active part in committee work. Middle-class persons have a healthy orientation toward citizenship but may find the press of vocational or professional achievement so steady as to prevent much civic activity in the early adult years. The middle adult years and later adult years are ones in which middle-class persons often become actively aware of the task of civic competence. Lower-class persons typically find little motivation toward civic participation. There often exists the feeling that they lack the power to do anything against the strength of the middle and upper classes.

Assistance in developing civic competence can be given by teachers and parents who are themselves participating citizens and who teach the concepts and knowledges necessary for understanding problems. Help can be given by community leaders who can find responsible positions for youth on playgrounds, community centers, and youth organizations. The Four-H clubs and Future Farmers are noteworthy examples of the latter. Librarians can help by making the reading of books attractive, by selecting and advertising those of appropriate level and design. The attitude toward community service expressed in the home is of primary import.

Desiring and achieving socially responsible behavior

In order to live a full life one must contribute to the welfare of others—he must recognize the values his society has established. One's concept of his own worth and the place of mankind in nature are intimately involved in this task.

There is no biological basis for this task, aside from the fact that everyone is born into society. It stems from the pressures that characterize membership in a group. The importance of the task in the life of the adolescent is clearly illustrated in the desire to be approved and accepted by one's peers. It involves the sublimation of many personal desires and wishes for the sake of approval and of earning future privileges. Many problems of adolescence—delinquency, transiency, feelings of despair—stem from conditions that deprive the individual of opportunity for earning money or assuming significant duties. This was evident during the depression years and may be contrasted with the opportunity war provides for important service.

The nature and import of this task differ widely from one social class to another. The upper-class adolescent typically develops a feeling of responsibility for carrying on social obligations and assuming responsible occupations. The task for middle-class youth is complicated by going away to college and by seeking jobs away from the childhood home. Never having formed adult ties in the home community, they find it difficult to develop abstract loyalties to larger units. Lower-class youth feel little responsibility to the community —their loyalties are confined to the smaller group of family and neighbor.

Acquiring a set of values and an ethical system
as a guide to behavior

One must acquire a set of values (conditions to be desired) that is feasible. He must be conscious of striving for those values or conditions, and they must harmonize with each other and with the values of others.

Many individuals are not interested in religious or philosophical problems. But those who are interested live more fully and effectively because their actions have the economy of purpose—rather than the aimlessness of chance. Havighurst lists six ways in which an individual comes to formulate a set of values:

1. Through satisfaction of physiological drives
2. Through satisfactory emotional experience
3. Through concrete reward and punishment
4. Through association of something with the love or approval of persons whose love and approval is desired
5. Through inculcation by someone in authority
6. Through reasoning or reflective thinking. [136:149]

Deciding on the nature of the physical world and of man often involves difficult problems for the middle- and upper-class adolescents. The scientific view of the physical world is easily accepted, but there is frequently trouble with a scientific view of the nature of man. The task is not an insistent one for lower-class youth—they simply ignore it. Some live apparently without values, while others accept authoritative religions without questions.

There are several ways in which the institutions of the home, the school, and the church may give assistance in the achievement of this task. The leaders of young persons, the teachers, should be carefully selected as persons worthy of admiration and imitation. Opportunity for autonomous activity with one's age-mates should be provided, but there should be subtle adult supervision. The direct study of morals and values through books, and the discussion of them, should be encouraged. The meaning and significance of modern science should be taught by sympathetic teachers who recognize the danger of serious conflict with authoritarian religions.

The imperative needs of youth

The study of basic needs and of developmental tasks are two approaches to a better understanding of the nature of the adolescent and his problems. A third look at some of the problems of youth is afforded in the view developed by the National Association of Secondary-School Principals, under the heading The Imperative Needs of Youth. [244]

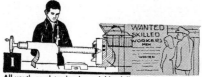

1. All youth need to develop salable skills and those understandings and attitudes that make the worker an intelligent and productive participant in economic life. To this end, most youth need supervised work experience as well as education in the skills and knowledge of their occupations.

6. All youth need to understand the methods of science, the influence of science on human life, and the main scientific facts concerning the nature of the world and of man.

2. All youth need to develop and maintain good health and physical fitness.

7. All youth need opportunities to develop their capacities to appreciate beauty in literature, art, music, and nature.

3. All youth need to understand the rights and duties of the citizen of a democratic society, and to be diligent and competent in the performance of their obligations as members of the community and citizens of the state and nation.

8. All youth need to be able to use their leisuretime well and to budget it wisely, balancing activities that yield satisfactions to the individual with those that are socially useful.

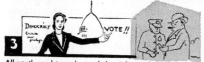

4. All youth need to understand the significance of the family for the individual and society and the conditions conducive to successful family life.

9. All youth need to develop respect for other persons, to grow in their insight into ethical values and principles, and to be able to live and work cooperatively with others.

5. All youth need to know how to purchase and use goods and services intelligently, understanding both the values received by the consumer and the economic consequences of their acts.

10. All youth need to grow in their ability to think rationally, to express their thoughts clearly, and to read and listen with understanding.

FIG. 2. **The imperative needs of youth**

Reproduced by permission from a poster prepared by the National Association of Secondary School Principals.

1. *Saleable skills*

"All youth need to develop saleable skills and those understandings and attitudes that make the worker an intelligent and productive participant in economic life. To this end, most youth need supervised work experience as well as education in the skills and knowledge of their occupation." Steps toward satisfying this need have been taken by including work-experience programs in the schools. Such programs help youth to feel that they are, or can be, significant in a culture that values a person for what he does. Work-experience tends to offset the psychological impact of delayed employment. However, these programs may not be expanded rapidly because of the influence of the academic tradition in the high school, and because of the inevitable increase of educational costs. In the meantime there is something of real significance that can be done.

Parents, teachers, and other youth leaders can stress the advantages of prolonged education. Stress can be placed upon (a) the formation of habits of punctuality, (b) thoroughness in the performance of routine, and often non-paying, jobs, (c) dependability, (d) and listening carefully to directions. Willingness to do tasks that are "beneath one's dignity," giving credit to others for their performances, and eagerness to "learn from the ground up" are attitudes that should be developed. Ability to get along with others is of primary importance; hence youngsters should be encouraged to exercise courtesy, to lend a helping hand whenever possible, to dress appropriately and neatly, and to develop skill in listening. These are only representative suggestions of general, but significant, approaches to the developing of saleable skills—which actually involves the whole field of personality development.

2. *Good health*

"All youth need to develop and maintain good health and physical fitness and mental health." Young persons must assume much responsibility for filling this need, though the advice and instruction of adults play a significant role. This need can no more easily be satisfied by one approach than can the need for developing saleable skills. Good mental and physical health depends upon a person's attitude toward himself. A man must have accepted himself as a person worthy of maximum development. The home plays its part by accepting the child and youth in such a manner as to provide opportunities for developing a sense of security. The school helps the individual to accept himself as one worth preservation and development by providing a wide variety of opportunities for challenge and for successful performance. The community must show young persons that they are an important segment of the population by playing up the positive contributions they make rather than placing undue emphasis upon the spectacular actions of a minority. In the long run, while the position of the home and school are focal, good mental and physical health is an outcome of the structure and orientation of society as a whole. Health is a problem involving the total culture.

3. *Democratic citizenship*

"All youth need to understand the rights and duties of the citizen in a democratic society, and to be diligent and competent in the performance of their obligations as members of the community and citizens of the state and nation, and to have an understanding of the nations and peoples of the world." Legally, a youth becomes a citizen when he reaches a specified chronological age. Functionally, a youth progressively takes the steps toward effective citizenship by having a stake in democratic affairs. A voice in the running of family affairs, participation in student government, responsibility in the conduct of youth organizations, school studies such as history, civics, economics, sociology, and law, and firsthand experience with civic institutions in the community are the basic factors that produce functional citizenship.

Democratic citizenship will not be encouraged by adults who use the "voice of doom." The utterances, "What's the use?" "What difference does it make?" "The forces in power are too great"—so frequently heard from adults—will not encourage diligence in the performance of citizenship. The more realistic approach is that the world is in a constant state of change and that change can be for the better when mentally healthy, intelligent, and optimistic persons pool their resources for betterment. Citizens of the state and nation must study the personal worth of individuals of minority groups, and membership in youth groups must not be based on arbitrary factors.

4. Family life

"All youth need to understand the significance of the family for the individual and society and the conditions conducive to successful family life." It is a widely recognized psychological fact that personality and behavior trends are oriented by the family group. Without the family, the human animal would lose many of his unique characteristics. Anything done to threaten the stability of the family also threatens the basic structure of our society. Divorce, separation, and sexual promiscuity are both cause and result of weak family life. Instruction in the home and school must be directed to an assessment of the disadvantages of these threats.

Several steps can be taken to improve youth's chances for the satisfactory approach to the need for appreciating the significance of the family. One of the most fundamental steps is to encourage wholesome boy-girl relationships, both in the home and in the neighborhood. This may necessitate a change in attitude of some parents and some teachers regarding the importance of play and social activities involving both sexes. Youth should have opportunities to investigate questions regarding their physical growth and social development. Leadership for such investigation must come from wholesomely oriented parents and youth leaders. Heretofore, direct study of the problems of parenthood has been largely neglected at the secondary level. Fortunately, excellent materials have been recently published that will aid the school in dealing with this common need of all youth.*

5. Consumer needs

"All youth need to know how to purchase and use goods and services intelligently, understanding both the values received by the consumer and the economic consequences of their acts." Millions of dollars are spent annually by advertisers to create wants that are

---

* National Society for the Study of Education, *52nd Yearbook, Part I, Adapting the Secondary-School Program to the Needs of Youth* (Chicago: University of Chicago Press; 1953), 316 pp.

sometimes unrelated to values. There is altogether too little understanding of the role and function of the "other fellow" in the operation of our economic system. Living from day to day, or hand to mouth, is characteristic of a large segment of the population. Certainly, the purchase and use of goods is a common and important activity. Without help this can be an extremely confusing problem. With help, adolescents will be more likely to become adults who come closer to self-realization and social effectiveness.

The persistent roles of habits, knowledges, attitudes, and skills must be recognized as psychological factors subject to control and direction. Parents and teachers must attempt to show youth what is best in terms of the present and future—values must be emphasized. It is not enough to depend on the transfer values of study and instruction; specific illustrations must point the way to the application of knowledge. Young people must be given opportunities to purchase goods and services under leadership that indicates the relative and long-term values. This may range from the purchase of school supplies and clothing to the hiring of an orchestra for the spring dance. In the home and school, youth must be given exercise in the planning and management of funds.

6. *Science and life*

"All youth need to understand the methods of science, the influence of science on human life, and the main scientific facts concerning the nature of the world and of man." This is indeed an exacting task in a world that is constantly accelerating in technological, medical, and social progress. It must be realized that scientific knowledge cannot be functionally divorced from philosophical values.

Representative suggestions for implementing this need might include the following: Formal study emphasizing the nature and worth of human life; stressing the application of science to the problems studied in the classroom; teaching and illustrating the steps used in methods of science; and illustrating the application of science through field trips, shop work, and laboratory science. Since the steps of the scientific method are common despite widely differing subjects of investigation, it is desirable that appropriately designed and written books be provided on a wide variety of subjects.

By means of such provision, differences in interest may be met while the emphasis on science remains common.

7. *Appreciate beauty*

"All youth need opportunities to develop their capacities to appreciate beauty, in literature, art, music, and nature." This need actually has two facets—appreciation and expression. However, expression will be dealt with under the next heading on leisure. Appreciation of the various art forms is a way of seeing the world in a different perspective and extending one's perception of the world. What is said of reading in the following passage might also be said of pictures, sculpture, music, and nature.

> Before I bought my first pair of glasses, I remember, the trees were only a blurred blob on the horizon. But after I put them on, I was astonished to see that they had definite shape: twigs, leaves, stumps of old branches—all the details I had missed because I didn't have the full use of my eyes.
>
> Good reading does for the mind what good glasses do for the eyes: it lets you in on the details of living. It's not unfair to say that most people go through life with their eyes closed: hundreds of things happen all about them that they never see because they have never known what to look for: good reading shows you what to look for. Good reading is like being converted, or falling in love, or getting married: the whole world has a new smell.*

There have always been those who have urged the inclusion of activities leading to the appreciation of beauty in the curriculums of the schools and colleges. Such an emphasis, however, has sometimes been weakened by the stress upon the accumulation of knowledge and preparation for the world of affairs. The knowledge that the effective life is one of considered balance must become more widely disseminated. Parents and teachers need to appreciate the fact that striving for the appreciation of beauty is much more than a constructive use of leisure time, it is a way of achieving wholesome balance in life.

---

* J. Bernard Haviland, in Alfred Stefferud (Ed.), *The Wonderful World of Books* (New York: The New American Library of World Literature; 1953), p. 71.

8. Leisure time

"All youth need to be able to use their leisure time well and to budget it wisely, balancing activities that yield satisfactions to the individual with those that are socially useful." This need is becoming increasingly important as output per man hour increases and the working day and working week become shorter and shorter. Labor saving devices in the home pass on the saving of time to the homemaker. "Stupendous spectacles" and "supercolossal productions" have been devised to capitalize on the demand for something to do. While there may be nothing harmful about movie-going, TV watching, or the filled football bowl, there is little that is psychologically constructive. Spectatorship is a passive, rather than creative, use of leisure time.

Juvenile delinquency is, in part, a problem of leisure time. The gravity of the problem is indicated in the following statement:

> Gerald was . . . a nice-looking youngster from a respectable family in the community.
>
> Jerry wanted to be a regular fellow. When his crowd in school began slipping off to side alleys for a few gulps of cheap wine— "Sneaky Pete," the boys called it—Gerald went along.
>
> After a time the wine lost its kick. Somebody in the crowd had an idea. "Hey—why not let's try reefers? I know a guy can get us all we want—cheap. He'll even give us some for nothing." To the gang it sounded like adventure.
>
> Soon Jerry was smoking four or five reefers every day.*

Excessive use of beverage alcohol, addiction to narcotics, and other forms of delinquency are much larger problems than may be embraced by stress on the wholesome use of leisure time; but teaching the socially useful employment of leisure is a tangible starting point. It should be emphasized here that constructive use of leisure is much more than an avoidance of the negative. It is a means of adding meaning and vitality to the life of the individual. The constructive use of leisure involves much more than any "pass-time."

---

* Will Oursler and Laurence D. Smith, *Narcotics: America's Peril* (Garden City, N. Y.: Doubleday and Company, Inc.; 1952), pp. 43–44.

The seriousness of the whole problem must receive the consideration of parents, teachers, youth leaders, as well as law-enforcement officials, civic leaders, publishers, and others who mold public action and opinion.

9. *Respect for others*

"All youth need to develop respect for other persons, to grow in their insight into ethical values and principles, to be able to live and work cooperatively with others, and to grow in the moral and spiritual values of life." Shakespeare stated what psychologists endorse, that the beginning point of respect for others is respect for one's self:

> This above all: to thine own self be true,
> And it must follow, as the night the day,
> Thou canst not then be false to any man.
> *(Hamlet,* Act I, Sc. 3)

Those who would help youth develop respect for others must first respect youth. Young people must build their ego status by accomplishment, being liked, being independent, and feeling secure. However, it must not be thought that ethical values are simply absorbed. It will pay to discuss these values, to encourage reading that deals with values, and to give advice and counsel. The National Association of Secondary-School Principals recommends the following as approaches to the satisfaction of this need: (1) Students and teachers planning study problems together, (2) supplementing textbooks with excursions, periodicals, and teaching aids, (3) making traditional school subjects more functional, (4) student choice of action after student-parent-teacher conferences, and (5) using parents and community agencies as aids to developing values. [244:63]

10. *Rational thought*

"All youth need to grow in their ability to think rationally, to express their thoughts clearly, and to read and listen with understanding." This need is particularly insistent in a society where citizens are called upon to make informed analyses of, and decisions on, local, state, and national problems. The need cannot be fulfilled in home and school atmospheres where the spirit of authoritarianism prevails, or where time and energy are extravagantly wasted in the attempt to answer questions that are vague and meaningless to the pupil. More stress should be placed upon the asking of questions and the search for pertinent information that will lead to *tentative* conclusions.

Thinking is based upon the possession of facts, but the facts must be regarded as means to an end. Teachers and parents should encourage youngsters to deal with problems independently of feelings or prejudices—as far as possible. The technique of listening and judging must be emphasized through exercise. Youth groups and classroom activities should use discussion techniques as a device for encouraging free expression. Grammatical form in writing and talking should be secondary to the spontaneous expression of the young person.

The individual adolescent

The section entitled "Basic human needs" shows that in some ways the adolescent is like *all* other persons; the sections called "Developmental tasks of adolescents," and "The imperative needs of youth" show that in many ways the adolescent is like *some* other persons; but in the section now starting the emphasis is on the fact that an adolescent is like *no* other person.

Intellectual differences

Psychological descriptions of human traits or groups of individuals result from averaging the entire range. The consequence is that the generalizations only approximate the uniqueness of a person. There is a tendency to lose sight of the individual. This is not to say that generalizations are of no value. Averages help us to know what to look for in specific persons or situations. But in addition to the study of adolescents as a group it is necessary, for improved understanding, to study each adolescent.

Approaches to the satisfaction of the needs of adolescents who are intellectually gifted will differ at many points from the approaches to meeting the needs of those who are mentally dull. Typically, the gifted child comes from a superior cultural and educational background. His knowledge in terms of subject matter mastery is 44 per cent beyond that of his age-mates. His interests are spontaneous and cover a wide variety of fields. He learns to read easily and spends more time at it than does the average youngster. He rates high in emotional stability and knows and readily applies ethical and moral concepts. [309:55–57]

Christine P. Ingram presents the following description of the intellectual ability of 13, 14, 15, 16 year and older mentally *retarded* individuals:

> Mental development approximates that of average children eight to ten or eleven years of age. The power of voluntary attention and concentration on a given task has increased. Rote memory is good, memory of images and logical memory are improving.
>
> Powers of comparison, generalization, and abstraction are weak or lacking. The differences from the average child are most marked in respect to these abilities. Concrete illustrations of the meaning of such words as charity, courage, or envy may be given if taught, but definitions of abstract words cannot be formulated.
>
> Language expression is still far below expectation for the average child. Descriptive and abstract terms are generally lacking. The use of adverbs is not common. The majority have probably not acquired more than 7,000 to 9,000 words, contrasting with about 15,000 or more for average children of the same age.*

It is obvious that teaching and leading individuals who represent these extremes will be a substantially different problem from that of dealing with the adolescent who is closer to the hypothetical average.

Physical differences

Three major points of difference characterize adolescents. One is the type of body build that causes marked differences in weight at any given teen age; another has to do with variations in height; and the third relates to the age of the onset of puberty. These will be dealt with in another chapter, but it is important to recognize here that variations in these three aspects create some of the problems of accepting one's self and some of the problems of peer relations.

* Christine P. Ingram, *Education of the Slow-Learning Child,* Second Edition, p. 25. Copyright 1953, The Ronald Press Company.

In addition to these three areas of difference there is the, sometimes related, problem of energy drive. Some adolescents have ample energy to support both growth and activity requirements. Others seem to have only enough energy to support growth requirements and are relatively lethargic in activity. Realistic programs for adolescents must recognize differences in activity levels. Two implications must be recognized: one is the wide range of normality, and the second has to do with what can rationally be expected of the individual within a given morphological category.

It is up to parents and teachers to initiate approaches that will make individual adolescents and their peers accept the implications of differences in body builds and energy available for activity. This can be done by stressing the value of differences to society.

Personality differences

A concomitant of differences in intelligence and body builds *plus* differences in experiences causes adolescents to be interested in different activities and to accept different values. In short, differences in personality must be recognized. Personality is here taken to mean one's predisposition to behavior. It is the tendency to act in a certain manner. The actual behavior is a symptom of the underlying personality, but the personality indicates the probability of a given behavior.

It is obvious that the interest aspect of personality is a reflection of intelligence. It is no less obvious that an individual's orientation is related to his body build and energy supply. These *may* stem primarily from innate factors, but probably most important are the general cultural factors and specific experiences a person has had. For instance, the Balinese are careful, deliberate people who regard hurry as unnecessary and stupid, while the typical American is competitive and hurried. Further, one's personality orientation is determined by his social status and the values held by parents and others in the community. The problems of adolescence would be much simpler if American culture were more homogeneous, but the fact is that differences in class values are quite marked. It is precisely at this point that the study of adolescence has been incomplete up to very recent times. It is now recognized that an understanding of the differences in values and ways of living are at least as important as is the understanding of physical and psychological differences. This point will be more specifically indicated in the following chapter.

Summary

The approach to the fulfillment of needs is urgently required for the living of an effective and satisfactory life. Some needs are characteristic of persons of all ages and cultures. Some needs are particularly urgent during the adolescent years and some are more insistent for particular individuals than for others. An understanding of adolescents is based partially upon knowledge of the nature and functioning of both the common and the unique needs.

Needs cannot be fully met, but making an approach to partial satisfaction is a continuous problem. Attempts to meet such common needs as organic, psychological, and social needs are first steps in improving adolescent adjustment. It must be realized that the classification of needs is for the sake of convenience in discussion. Functionally, any given need is organic-social-psychological in nature.

One view of the unique needs of adolescents is through the concept of developmental tasks. These tasks include: (1) improving adjustment to age-mates of both sexes, (2) accepting a masculine or feminine role, (3) accepting and using one's unique body and physique, (4) becoming emotionally independent of parents and other adults, (5) taking reassuring steps toward economic independence, (6) selecting and preparing for a vocation, (7) preparing for marriage and family responsibilities, (8) developing civic competence, (9) behaving in a socially responsible manner and (10) acquiring a guiding sense of values. To the extent that these tasks are successfully performed, the adolescent lives satisfactorily at present *and* is prepared for vigorous attack on the developmental tasks that will be met in his next stage of growth.

The National Association of Secondary-School Principals has compiled a list of Imperative Needs of Youth. Where there is an overlapping of behaviors described in developmental tasks, the repetition seems justified for the sake of emphasis. At any rate, Imperative Needs are: (1) developing saleable skills, (2) developing and maintaining good physical and mental health, (3) knowing and acting upon the rights and duties of a citizen in a democracy, (4) understanding the significance of the family, (5) knowing how to purchase and use goods and services, (6) understanding the methods and implications of science, (7) developing appreciation for beauty—art, literature, music and nature, (8) creating useful leisure time pursuits and interests, (9) developing respect for others and (10) improving ability to think, talk, read, and listen.

In addition to these common needs of humans in general and the needs of adolescents in particular, it is important to study the unique mental, physical, and personal orientation of the individual adolescent. By combining all these approaches, the great need of the adolescent—to be understood—will have greater likelihood of fulfillment.

STUDY AND REVIEW ITEMS

1. Describe some differences in the way the need "to be a cause" might be satisfied for adolescents from a low economic status and for adolescents from high economic status.

2. Select any one basic need and describe how it is a product of social, physical, and psychological forces.

3. Suggest some ways in which parents might see that approaches are made to the satisfaction of organic needs.

4. What are the really important considerations in establishing feelings of security in adolescents?

5. Evaluate the statement: It is easier for boys to accept a masculine role than it is for girls to accept a feminine role.

6. Formulate what you would consider to be a sound approach to the problems of marriage within the scope of the high school.

7. Describe some things that might be done to foster emotional independence from parents.

8. Would you agree that the practical approach to the development of saleable skills would place attitudes and work habits above training for specific skills?

9. Make a list of a dozen or so values for adolescents that you would deem to be of highest merit.

10. Describe some community program, with which you are acquainted, that serves to develop attitudes and skills of good citizenship.

11. Describe what you consider to be a workable program for encouraging good mental health.

12. Besides those listed in the text, what are some ways in which individual adolescents are unique?

RECOMMENDED SUPPLEMENTARY READING

Educating for American Citizenship, 32nd Yearbook, American Association of School Administrators (Washington, D. C.: National Education Association; 1954), pp. 146–166.

This chapter relates basic needs to the problem of developing citizenship. Do's and Don'ts for the home and school are listed as they relate to the satisfaction of needs and the development of good citizens. Special techniques for analyzing needs are briefly mentioned.

Eiserer, Paul E., and Stephen M. Corey, in National Society for the Study of Education, *52nd Yearbook,* Part I, *Adapting the Secondary-School Program to the Needs of Youth* (Chicago: University of Chicago Press; 1953), pp. 44–61.

The psychology of learning is stressed in this chapter with particular emphasis on how youth learn to meet needs. Four propositions stand out: (1) what one learns depends on his perception, (2) changed perception results in changed behavior, (3) behavior is most appropriate when perceptions are accurate, and (4) teaching is for the purpose of improving perception.

Havighurst, R. J. *Human Development and Education* (New York: Longmans, Green and Company, Inc.; 1953), pp. 111–176.

Part III is a description of the nature of developmental tasks for adolescents. Suggestions for their successful achievement are given, as well as specific recommendations for the school curriculum.

Malm, Marguerite, and Olis G. Jamison. *Adolescence* (New York: McGraw-Hill Book Company, Inc.; 1952), pp. 457–501.

This chapter begins with a statement of needs and illustrates, by means of excerpts from case studies, how individuals are satisfied or thwarted in their attempt to meet their needs.

Mikesell, William H., and Gordon Hanson. *Psychology of Adjustment* (New York: D. Van Nostrand Company, Inc.; 1952), pp. 49–67.

This chapter is not specifically related to the needs of adolescents. There, however, is a pertinent and readable presentation of bodily and learned wants. A reason for the diversity of explanation of human wants is presented.

Zachry, Caroline B. *Emotion and Conduct in Adolescence* (New York: D. Appleton-Century Company, Inc.; 1940), pp. 1–24.

The chapter "Education and the Adolescent's Tasks of Life Adjustment" develops the idea that "With recognition that emotional, physical, and intellectual functioning are together involved in social development, logic demands that the school broaden its objective to that fostering growth toward an adulthood in which both the claims of the individual and the requirements of his society may be satisfied." (Pages 26–27)

AUDIO-VISUAL MATERIAL

Children Growing up with Others (United World Films, Inc., 1445 Park Ave., New York 29, N. Y.), 30 min., so., b. & w.

Shows how youngsters grow from involuntary dependence into contributing members of their family, school, and community groups. The need for tact, discernment, and patience on the part of adults is emphasized.

Meeting the Needs of Adolescents (McGraw-Hill Book Company, Inc., 330 West 42nd St., New York 36, N. Y.), 19 min., so., b. & w.

This shows how the basic physical needs of adolescents are met in the home, how mental development is stimulated, how youth are guided in their spiritual development. It points out some of the worries of parents and how the concerns can be constructively solved.

How does the role of adolescents in American culture differ from their role in other societies? What are some of the hazards imposed by our society? How can better advantage be taken of the unique benefits provided in American culture?

CHAPTER FOUR

Special Problems of the American Adolescent

Simple but spurious explanations of man's behavior have been periodically advanced. Sex drive, physique, environment, mind, soul, and diet are among the apparently simple explanations. The truth seems to be that no simple explanation can suffice. Psychologists must deal with complicated, dependent, and changing factors. This means, among other things, that sex, physique, and brain are valid explanatory factors when considered in the milieu of physical environment and social conditions. At the time of conception the human organism is characterized by a potential for development. How development takes place depends upon the environment and the organism's reaction to the environment. It is only for the sake of convenience that the study of adolescence is divided into chapters on sex, home, school, occupation, and the like. Among the factors acting upon the organism as a potential is the culture—those aspects of the environment that are man-made. Law, custom, technology, and institutions are cultural components that influence the development of biological potential. "All human behavior is, of course, to a great extent influenced by the culture in which it is surrounded. Particularly marked, however, are the effects of the culture upon adolescent behavior. The length of the period of adolescence, for example, depends upon the way society treats the adolescent." *

The factor of culture is so pervasive that it cannot be handled as a single topic. Much that could properly be considered in this chapter must, for the sake of organization, be discussed in other chapters. The following cultural factors are omitted at this point and considered elsewhere: Sex behavior is dealt with in Chapters Five and Fourteen. Changing occupational trends are mentioned in many contexts and are treated in detail in Chapter Sixteen. The new meaning of leisure is described in Chapter Eleven. Chapters Six and Fifteen deal with the impact of changing family problems and patterns. Yet all these are integral aspects of the topic "cultural impact."

The purpose here is to describe some cultural factors that are not discussed elsewhere and to direct attention to some of the conditions that must be more clearly perceived if we are to come closer to understanding adolescents. This emphasis on the social conditions that affect behavior is probably one of the more outstanding recent developments in psychology.

Persistent factors in American culture

Rapid change

Perhaps the major characteristic of American culture is its inconsistency. From one decade to another American culture is no simple thing. The ideas, mores, customs, and institutions of Colonial America were far different from those now current. The problems of adjustment, for persons of all ages, are different in a predominately urban society from those that were faced by a rural population. The goals of individuals are different today in an industrial and commercial milieu from the goals of persons in an agrarian economy. Mankind always has faced, and always will face, problems, but the approaches to a solution of problems are different in a society in which frontiers are in the realm of intellect and ideas from the time when the frontiers were geographical.

Such changes as have been indicated have taken place in some-

---

* Glenn M. Blair, "What Teachers Should Know About the Psychology of Adolescence," *Journal of Educational Psychology*, 41, 1950, p. 358.

what less than 400 years—a short time in the history of mankind. Further, the greatest amount of change has taken place within the last 100 years. There seems to be rather general agreement in the forecast that social change will take place at an increasingly rapid rate.

Homer P. Rainey has stated that increasing tempo is one of the more outstanding characteristics of social change. This makes it increasingly difficult for citizens to get an adequate conception of their world and to adjust to it. This situation is called cultural lag. Social institutions cannot keep pace with invention and scientific knowledge. The gap between technology and social behavior constitutes one of the serious problems of our time. [254:17]

A decade later there seems no need to question the accuracy of the above statement. One example may be taken from the realm of technology:

> Another factor that confirms this belief is the steadily increasing rate of patent issuance as the result of large-scale demands on the part of industry for new technological equipment. In effect, then, this age of so-called transition will not be one between two stable periods of social change, but a transition between a slow one and an incredibly more rapid one.*

Adolescents, like all other persons, are profoundly affected by these and other cultural changes. Fluidity of mores and customs does not provide a solid base upon which to guide young people in their decisions and choice of goals. By way of contrast, Chinese adolescents are much less troubled by matters of obedience and respect for parents than are their American counterparts. The former have generations of stable custom behind them and the problem of obedience simply does not arise. The Chinese is expected to follow his father's occupation while the American is typically expected to make his own choice and rise to greater heights than his parents. In some instances, it is as though the American youth were expected to take up from where his father left off.

It has been repeatedly pointed out that in rural communities, where face-to-face relations are intimate, youth are more firmly

---

* Henry E. Stevens in Franklin R. Zeran (Ed.), *Life Adjustment Education in Action* (New York: Chartwell House, Inc.; 1953), p. 477.

bound to community expectations. In the city, where face-to-face relations are impersonal, the pressure to maintain reputation is less influential.

Generally speaking, the change in the nature of relationships and in technology makes it imperative that the period of adolescence and youth be a time of preparation—rather than simply a time of introductory participation. (1) The need to understand science is great. (2) The importance of social science is magnified. (3) There must be an emphasis upon guiding principles rather than learning temporary and specific answers. (4) The need for guidance rather than prescription is increased. The advice stemming from "When I was a boy . . ." will not, because it cannot, suffice.

The gap between generations

The bridge of communication between one generation and the next is often a frail one. This was indicated in Chapter One by a quotation from Socrates. Goodwin Watson has quoted a report of 1865 to show that the problem is persistent:

. . . for the last ten years I have been a close observer of what has passed among the rising generation in this great metropolis [New York], and I cannot suppress the humiliating conviction that even pagan Rome, in the corrupt age of Augustus, never witnessed a more rapid and frightful declension in morals, nor witnessed among certain classes of the young a more utter disregard of honor, of truth and piety, and even the commonest decencies of life.*

The gap between generations is only in part a function of rapid social change; hence, it is to be expected that communication may become increasingly difficult. The gap is in part due to different personality orientations, which are a function of age. Older people have less effervescent physical energy and often fail to appreciate the enthusiasm of youth for daring adventures and exploring activities. Older people, having lived with social taboos for a longer time, are likely to have accepted convention, while young people are striving to achieve ego status. Older people may still be impressed by the social and technological changes they have witnessed, while

---

* Reverend D. Silliman Ives in the report of the Board of Metropolitan Policy for 1864, published in *The New York Times,* January 5, 1865. Quoted in Goodwin Watson, *Youth After Conflict* (New York: Association Press; 1947), p. 3.

young people take for granted that which surrounds them. Parents have achieved an established place among their peers and seek to understand their "bewildering offspring," while young people have long been in contact with their parents and are now seeking to understand and be understood by their peers.

Blaming either the younger or older generation for the gap is not a solution. Adults must seek to understand the differences in the energy, goals, aspirations, and needs of the adolescent as contrasted to those that characterize maturity. Teachers and youth leaders (but often not parents) are in an advantageous position to encourage discussions dealing with the ideals and hopes of the older generation.

Differences between the generations will always exist. The differences are greater in a dynamic society than in a static one. However, the gravity of a problem depends on the attitude taken toward it and the data available for its solution. Improved communication can establish a strong bridge over the gap. The basic starting point for both young and old is the realization that, "The difficulty is probably not in him so much as in his world, which does not provide the easy and gradual approach to maturity that an earlier world did." * A better realization of causes will tend to avert the blame-placing behavior.

As a final word on the gap between generations, it should be observed that, statistically speaking, there is less clash between the generations than might be inferred from the foregoing. In a nationwide study, it was found that approximately 20 per cent of youth report conflict with their parents. [257] Apparently, 80 per cent encounter no notable conflict. It is evident that the gap can be spanned.

Authoritarianism

Despite the fact that we live in a society imbued with the tradition of democracy, there are many indications of authoritarian behavior. Pressure groups in politics frequently achieve results that are not synonymous with the good of all. Corporations are run by a small board of directors, which is typically guided only by token votes of stockholders. All too frequently college professors have little to say

---

* Marynia F. Farnham, *The Adolescent* (New York: Harper & Brothers; 1952), p. 107.

about policy in their institutions, and students are not asked to share in the determination of curriculums and standards. The typical public school teacher will tell you that his freedom is inhibited by the local or state course of study—handed down by higher authority. The value of the tradition of authority in the family has been questioned in recent years, but obedience to parents is still regarded as a prime virtue. Thus, authoritarianism is present in government, business, education, and the home. [6:171–181] Its presence is regarded as an unhygienic condition for the rearing of young people; and a decline of the autocratic emphasis in the home and school is a necessary step in providing more wholesome personal development.

There can be no doubt that direction and authority are necessary. It would be foolish to expect children and adolescents to discover effective ways of living entirely by direct experience. In fact, the sensible exercise of authority is essential to a feeling of security— young people would have too great a burden placed upon them if authority were removed. It is necessary to consider the extent to which authority is needed and points at which it can be diminished. A first step in this consideration is to evaluate the functions of authority.

How are we going to achieve social order and advance our human values? Are we going to continue to think in terms of increasing state control, which has been the trend since 1890? The Interstate Commerce Commission, the Federal Trade Commission, the Sherman Act, and all similar legislation and regulatory legal machinery exemplify our practice of passing a law whenever we are faced with the disorder and conflict that follow on the breakdown of older patterns and sanctions. Is the police state, controlling irresponsible citizens, to be our idea of a planned society, or are we going to try to develop and educate personalities who can and will be responsible for maintaining and advancing social order? These are the really basic questions we face in every area of group life, especially in our educational programs for children, for youths, and for adults. Here the crucial issue is whether we will seek to rear obedient, submissive individuals who will bow to authority or to foster personalities capable of self-discipline and friendly, cooperative living.*

---

* Lawrence K. Frank, *Personality and Culture* (Danville, Illinois: The Interstate Printers and Publishers; 1948), p. 18.

Once having evaluated the function of authority we will be in a better position to decide where it is necessary and where it can be diminished. Wiser decisions can be made regarding *how* authority should be exercised. Florence Goodenough asserts that, while restriction is necessary, growing individuals can be allowed much more freedom in making instructive mistakes than many nervous parents think. [126:676] If youngsters are to live in a democratic society authoritarian training will place them at the disposal of bosses—they will be unprepared for the self-direction demanded of citizens who must make decisions and assume responsibility. The issue is whether rule by authority or democratic processes is to be the accepted way of life. [208] The problem of authoritarianism is not new; it has been apparent in the United States since the days of Jefferson and Hamilton, and its roots are as old as mankind.

Hurry

Many specific traits of American culture could justifiably be selected for emphasis and analysis; one of these traits deserving mention is the tendency to hurry. William James has indicated that this is not simply a characteristic of contemporary living. He believed (looking at the nineteenth-century scene) that many Americans were sent abroad *to rest their nerves* because they worked so intensely. The mistake was not in the nature or the amount of work but rather in the absurd feelings of hurry, anxiety, tension, which so often accompanied work. The European, on the other hand, could do the same work without the breathlessness and solicitude for results that characterizes the American.

These perfectly wanton and unnecessary tricks of inner attitude and outer manner in us, caught from the social atmosphere, kept up by tradition, and idealized by many as the admirable way of life, are the last straws that break the American camel's back, the final overflowers of our measure of wear and tear and fatigue.*

The fifty and more years that have elapsed since this was written have seen no improvement.

---

* William James, *Talks to Teachers on Psychology*, New Edition (New York: Henry Holt and Company; 1899, 1939), pp. 214–215.

Psychologists and psychiatrists have pointed to the hurry that leads to tension as being an important factor in all kinds of psychosomatic illnesses. Hurry is not solely a characteristic of the adult; it is something that is felt by the very young child. Many behavior problems are traced to the hurry of parents to get their children toilet trained and to wean them from nursing or taking food from a bottle. [78:76–85] Other evidences of hurry are manifested in the pressure to get children to read in the first grade, to do arithmetic in the third grade, and to become little men and women. There is a hurry to get youngsters through high school, to pick out and select a career, and (in *selected* behaviors) to "act your age." Even in the matter of clothing haste has become evident. Willard Spalding has suggested that one source of difficulty for the adolescent is caused by the early wearing of long pants. At one time, the discarding of knee pants was an indication of maturity that gave at least some self-assurance. [289] Today, when boys put on long pants at the age of two, the opportunity for this assurance is denied. Similarly, girls felt they were grown up when they first wore silk stockings—today the mothers are wearing bobby sox and the apparel distinction between childhood and adulthood is obliterated.

These symptoms of hurry—weaning, reading, clothing habits—simply suggest the problem. It is not likely (as was indicated by William James) that the habits of society will readily be changed. But approaches to the problem can be made by stressing to young people that relaxed and organized effort toward specific goals is more effective than feverish activity. Although it is easy to catch, by contagion, the feeling of rush, many individuals keep good mental health and do effective work by heeding the advice of doctors, psychiatrists, and psychologists. There are many attractive opportunities for development, such as music lessons, dance programs, Boy Scouts, church programs, and the like that parents are likely to encourage their youngsters to enter. These are good *in moderation,* but too wide participation tends to build frustration and tension. [20:88–89] It may be up to teachers and other youth workers, who are better acquainted with the danger of tension than is the typical parent, to help adolescents make the choices that will lead to an organization of time that will foster moderation.

Variety of social patterns

There are many differences between urban and rural modes of life. Urban young people have a more pressing problem of the utilization of leisure time. A prominent contributing factor to delinquency is the lack of organized recreational activities and facilities. There is the probability that city youth find it is easier to escape the eyes of neighbors than do rural young people. Competition in educational activities is keen and there is relatively less chance for compensating activities when one cannot survive scholastic competition. Urban families tend to be somewhat smaller and the parents' occupations are more likely to take them out of the home. This has the effect of freeing young people from the home at an earlier age and reducing the amount of adult guidance available. The number and variety of social contacts may have the effect of stimulating conversational ability and elevating the verbal aspects of intelligence. [188:6] This observation is supported by the fact that rural youth are more concerned about expressing themselves than are those from other groups. [97] Farm youths have better chances to do significant work and thus enhance their feelings of individual worth. Rural young people come into contact with the realities of death, birth, sex, illness, and natural forces. Their environment is somewhat less mediated by science and invention than is that of their urban counterparts.

Differences in social patterns can be noted within the families established by foreign born parents. In these, the children are torn by the habits and expectations of their parents and what they perceive to be acceptable conduct on the part of their school peers. The confusion is magnified by the reaction of the parents who see themselves losing their children through having their prestige torn down. This phenomenon exemplifies a whole series of problems encountered by ethnic groups—Poles, Greeks, Mexicans, for example. The younger generation disdains the standards and values of the older generation, but in the process there is born a deep sense of guilt and bewilderment. [331:152]

These examples should suffice to show those who work with youth that it is dangerous to expect typical reactions from them. American cultural forces are no one thing, and wide differences in family backgrounds, personal goals, conditioning experiences, and attitudes and ideals must be reckoned with. Those who work to recognize these varieties must do a great deal of investigative work; but, in the long run, the results will be more rewarding than will be the case for those who depend upon misleading generalizations.

Population factors in American culture

Age changes

The American population today is considerably older than it was a hundred years ago. In 1850 the median age was 18.9 years while in 1950 the median was 30.1 years. In 1850, 52.5 per cent of the population was below 20 years of age, while in 1950 only 34.3 per cent was in that age bracket. [316] Figure 3 shows age components for males and females. Despite the accelerated birth rate that followed World War II, it does not appear that this trend will be more than temporarily interrupted. [96:186] One prediction is that by 1990 the age group below 20 years of age will constitute about a fourth of the total population. [312:288] This change in the composition of population creates both difficulties and opportunities for young people.

Before dealing with the implications of age changes for adolescents, it is necessary to mention that these changes are by no means uniform. Fertility is high, and consequently the proportion of young people is higher in southern states and in rural regions. Fertility is relatively higher in the low income groups. Thus, the greater burden of supporting young people falls largely on the adults who are the less able to carry it. It is, however, an obligation that falls upon our entire population since another feature of population change is intermigration—the moving of rural youth to urban centers.

One hazard of the change in proportion of young people to the total population is that the gap in understanding between generations is widened. When young people constituted half of the population their needs and wishes had to be given consideration by virtue of their numerical strength. There were automatically more frequent associations of adults with young persons. Financial independence, and frequently marital independence, was encouraged

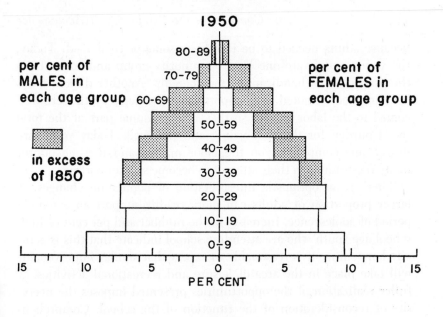

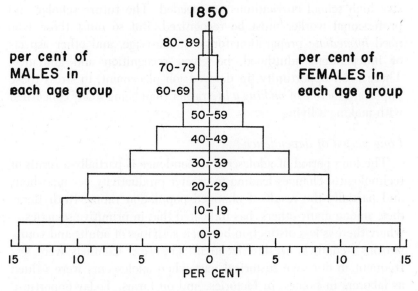

FIG. 3. **Age components of United States population, 1850 and 1950**

From Clark Tibbitts and Henry D. Sheldon, "Introduction: A Philosophy of Aging," *The Annals of the American Academy of Political and Social Science*, 279, 1952, p. 4. (Note: Read 0–9 as "zero to nine years of age." On the per cent scale the number to the left indicates the per cent of males in an age bracket; the number to the right, the per cent of females.)

because adults needed to be free from some of their load. Today, the young people are one kind of minority group and suffer from the psychological handicaps of membership. Another difficulty has been implied—limited work opportunity. Formerly youth were welcomed to the labor market so they could assume part of the total social burden for the very young and the aged. Today youth are unwelcome competitors on the labor market and they encounter many frustrations in their attempt to become self-supporting.

There is an optimistic interpretation of population changes. A larger proportion of adults can more readily support an extended period of adolescence. Increases in the number and per cent of high school age youth who are attending school indicate that this is actually happening. It is reasonable to expect that similar improvement will take place in the area of leisure and recreational activities. A fuller realization of the opportunities presented imposes the necessity of reconsideration of the function of the school. Comprehensive high school curriculums are needed. The future scholar and professional worker must be recognized. But so must those who need *immediate* preparation for jobs, marriage, and other aspects of independent adulthood, be given recognition and guidance. There is an opportunity, in delayed job placement, to stress those important factors of *making a life* rather than being solely concerned with making a living.

Long period of dependence

The long period of adolescent dependence is partially a result of technological changes leading to greater productivity per man hour and partially the result of changed population ratios. Ruth Benedict, among many others, has indicated that in primitive societies— where there is less distinction between activities of adults and young persons—conflicts are less frequent. [17:123] Conflicts were less frequent in our own historical past when adolescents were valued as laborers in homes, in factories, and on farms. Today opportunities for becoming independent are much less frequent. This problem is particularly acute in the upper years of adolescence when physical and mental maturity has virtually been reached.

Attacking the causes is not, in this case, a practical approach to the problems. We must learn to live with the situation as it is instead of longing for the good old days. As a matter of fact, society is so complex that longer periods of study are required to understand and deal intelligently with problems. Independence won slowly will be stronger than an independence thrust upon an inadequately prepared individual. Some tentative suggestions that might facilitate this progressive growth should include the following: (1) Encourage contact with peers so that the individual's voice will be heard. (2) Seek to find some significant home and community work opportunities. (3) Present facts about sex in the preadolescent period when there is less chance that the topic has become intensely personal and highly emotionally charged. (4) Devise recreational facilities that afford physical exercise and creative opportunity. (5) Provide for self-direction by including young people in the formulation of plans for them. (6) Consider the spending of an allowance as a personal matter.

Minority groups

The term *minority group* basically refers to numerical inferiority. It is the only characteristic those in such categories have in common. [83:368] It was indicated in Chapter One that some of the difficulties of adolescents stem from the fact that they are a minority group. Ethnic groups—characterized by differences in values and behavior due to cultural influences—and color castes (Negroes and Indians), as well as religious behaviors, have been classified under the heading of minority groups.

Some adolescents suffer the double handicap of being in both the adolescent category and in a religious, ethnic, or color minority. Moreover, it is easier to escape the debilitating effect of minority position due to ethnic factors than it is to escape the factor of color. Some parents teach their children to face and accept the minority position while others attempt to ignore or fight against such classification. Therefore, we must recognize that problems of minority groups are by no means uniform. Our conclusions must be tentative and suggestive rather than definitive.

Typically, membership in a minority group that suffers from discrimination has some tendency to produce questionable personality traits. Delinquency has long been noted as a symptom by sociologists. J. W. Tait studied 2000 eleven- to fifteen-year-old children of Italian-born parents, using tests and interviews, and concluded that on the average prejudice toward them tended to produce inferiority feelings, feelings of rejection, inadequate social adjustment, introversion, and emotional instability. [305] Feelings of persecution, a tendency toward ambivalence, submissiveness, and aggressiveness have also been noted as concomitants of prejudice and discrimination. [349:139]

While there are discouraging evidences of discrimination on the international scale, there are some hopeful changes in the national scene. In 1953 *Time* magazine carried a special feature entitled "The U. S. Negro, 1953: A Decade of Progress." Evidences of diminishing discrimination against the minority group that has the greatest difficulty in utilizing social mobility because of color are as follows: A greater variety and number of jobs available, substantial increases in the proportion of Negro voters, improved chances for justice in the courts. Negro college enrollment up 2500 per cent over 1930, and better standards of living indicated by marked increases in life expectancy. [326] It seems reasonable to think that a great deal of this improvement is due to what children learn in school through direct teaching and the actual practice of democratic behaviors.

The problem of prejudice is greater in extent than the size of the minority group that experiences such attitudes and behaviors. The psychological effects are even more detrimental to the wholesome development and emotional balance of the prejudiced person. [82] No doubt prejudice is, in many instances, the result of initially poor personality orientation; but it must also be recognized that, at the best, it inhibits personality growth and, at the worst, many actually contribute to deterioration.

Several things may be suggested that will serve the dual role of helping a prejudiced person improve his behavior and lessening the hazards of the persons who are the objects of discrimination. The emotional and intellectual maturity of adults is of primary importance. Through direct teaching, prejudice must be revealed as an indication of emotional immaturity—a kind of personality defense mechanism closely related to that called projection. Present the facts to young people—for example, that because of wide intragroup differences, stereotypes cannot possibly embrace all individuals. Encourage contacts between all persons, regardless of skin color, ethnic differences, and religious beliefs. While the automatic transfer of learning can be depended upon to effect some changes, it must be recognized that if maximum transfer is to occur it must be directly sought; that is, teachers must discuss the relationships.

In the final analysis, however, it must be admitted that study-discussion is only a partial approach.

It would be a mistake, however, to think that fundamental research would in itself solve the problems of how to obtain a more genuinely democratic society and how to free children from prejudice. In a basic and inescapable sense, the problem of prejudice is not only a problem of individuals but also of society. The problem of reducing prejudice and eliminating discrimination must be approached on a societal basis if it is to be dealt with successfully.*

Current influences in American culture

Control by women

One of the major needs of adolescents is to recognize and accept appropriate sex roles. Boys are expected to be aggressive, explorative, rough, strong, and to dress plainly. Girls are expected to be polite, courteous, docile, and to dress in garments adorned with ribbons and lace. The latter role is not learned without difficulty due to the increasing popularity of jobs for women outside the home; but it is the boy who experiences the greatest difficulty of assuming appropriate roles of masculinity because, to a marked extent, close association with a male model is denied.

We muffle him in feminine affection, and present his father to him as an animated whip to enforce his mother's role of affectionate ruler. All through his impressionable years he associates with women whom he can not take as models, interesting and admirable as often they are. This being so, without being able to identify with the only adults he knows, denied the stimulating companionship with men, he falls back on the age-group, that standardizing level-

---

* Helen L. Witmer and Ruth Kotinsky, *Personality in the Making* (The Fact-Finding Report of the Midcentury White House Conference on Children and Youth, New York: Harper & Brothers; 1952), p. 158.

ing influence in which all personality is subordinated to a group type.*

That the control by women does have an effect is indicated in the research of Henry Elkin, who found that soldiers attempted to live up to an idea of virility that was rooted in the psychological conditions of preadolescence. [98] There was a tendency to exaggerate and distort the manifestations of dominance and aggression.

It is probable that control by women will become progressively stronger. The father who serves only as a breadwinner teaches his son a similar attitude. The consequence is that men are more and more avoiding the role of part-time disciplinarian and seeking refuge in lodges and service clubs that meet in the evening, thus effecting a further reduction of male influence in the home.

A counterbalancing trend may be noted in the increase in the number of male school teachers in the upper elementary grades. This desirable trend can be continued only if teaching salaries are high enough to allow the man to look forward a number of years and see some assurance that he can earn enough to provide for himself and his family. However, employing more men teachers is not enough, since a teacher functions in a different role from a father. Adult education and family life education in the high school must emphasize the restricting influence of a family life that does not provide an example of functioning masculinity.

Radio, television, and movies

Mass communication and entertainment present a perplexing problem to the student of adolescent behavior. On the one hand, movies are condemned because of the large proportion of time devoted to crime, hostility, and other forms of violent emotion. Television programs are subject to the same criticisms, including the "something for nothing" scheme and devotion to the worthless if not the degrading. Little proof that these media are a direct factor in undermining adolescent character is afforded in research investigations; nevertheless, it must be admitted that as features of our total culture they do have an inevitable, cumulative effect.

* Margaret Mead, *Growing Up in New Guinea*, in *From the South Seas* (New York: William Morrow & Company, Inc.; 1939), p. 237. Copyright 1928, 1930, 1935, 1939 by Margaret Mead.

There is also something to be said on the positive side. These media are important means of presenting facts, ideas, moods, and attitudes to all of the public, including children and adolescents. Young people today have a better idea of how people in other parts of the nation and world live because of the opportunity to learn from radio, movies, and television. Certainly, there is little justification for the wholesale condemnation of aspects of our environment with which we have to live. Blaming the producers and dependence on censure and bans is no solution to the problem. The problem is neatly summarized by Arthur L. Mayer, writing about the movies:

> The shape of films to come is daily molded in the curve of yesterday's box-office window. You may deprecate that box office as a standard of merit but in the words of an insignificant writer with whom I find myself constantly in amazing agreement, "It is an unfailing barometer of what we want in our heart of hearts . . . frippery or meaning, shadow or substance. The responsibility," if I may continue to quote from Arthur Mayer in the *Theatre Arts Anthology,* "for making the motion picture a mighty instrument of mankind's hope and salvation lies not with producers, distributors, or exhibitors, not even with authors or directors, but with the audience. That audience is you and me and our relatives and our friends. If we support, not with chatter but with cash, not in the drawing room but in the theater auditorium, those films which give a true account of our honest problems and highest aspirations, we can make our motion pictures a symbol and token of all striving humanity—a living voice speaking among the people." *

Aside from the cumulative effects on personality of radio, movies, and television, the big hazard lies in overindulgence. Studies of the leisure-time activities of children and adolescents show that movies and radio rank high in terms of interest, time spent, and percentage of the total population involved.† The author's main objection to movies, radio, and television is that young people are conditioned to a desire to be entertained. They come to feel that it is somebody's

---

* Arthur L. Mayer, "Myths and Movies," *Harper's Magazine,* 202, 1951, p. 77.
　† For a summary of studies, see Marguerite Malm and Olis G. Jamison, *Adolescence* (New York: McGraw-Hill Book Company, Inc.; 1952), p. 450.

responsibility to keep them occupied—not their own obligation. The time spent in being passively entertained is too frequently time lost from activities that should be creative. Play, we are told by child psychologists, is *the* important business of childhood. From play, children gain the physical exercise that develops strength and co-ordination; moreover, they gain social experience and competence and develop varied interests. Children who have had time for creative play are likely to become adolescents who can more intelligently utilize the additional freedom that growing up affords. The cliché, "An idle mind is the devil's workshop" may be questioned. Perhaps idleness is a hazard only when it masters the individual, not when it is an opportunity for self-fulfillment.

Recommendations regarding "What to do" by Josette Frank appear to stem directly from the foregoing observations.

SUGGESTIONS FOR PARENTS:
1. Try to understand the basic needs of children.
2. Know what kind of programs your children see and hear.
3. Discuss favorite programs with them.
4. Consider their feelings—do not snap off the radio or forbid shows.
5. Point out values in order to develop critical judgment.
6. Teach them how to budget their time.
7. Suggest that upsetting programs be avoided for a time.
8. Help them find enjoyable substitute activities.

SUGGESTIONS FOR TEACHERS:
1. Do not ignore comics, movies and radio as prevalent experiences.
2. Be familiar with favorite programs so they can be discussed.
3. Occasionally conduct class discussions on these subjects.
4. Direct attention to wholesome programs and movies.
5. Seek to encourage the development of a wider range of interests.
6. Suggest that distracting comics be temporarily put aside.
7. Make use of educational movies, radio and television programs.

SUGGESTIONS FOR THE COMMUNITY:
1. Stimulate research by specialists which will reveal facts.
2. Study the recreational and cultural opportunities of the neighborhood.

3. Become familiar with what is available, on newsstands, on the air and in the movies, to young people.
4. Make these media the subject of adult discussion which calls for the observations of children and adolescents.
5. Make your approval of good and acceptable programs known to producers and distributors.
6. Express your disapproval of the harmful or unworthy.
7. Seek the cooperation of local broadcast stations and motion picture distributors.*

Movies, radio, and television are prominent features of contemporary culture. (See Figure 4) The exercise of moderation and discrimination can turn them into factors conducive to a better and fuller life.

The automobile

A glance at Figure 4 indicates that a realistic approach to the problems of adolescents must take into account the impact of the automobile on modes of living. Two decades ago, Robert S. and Helen M. Lynd reported the following comment: " 'Why on earth do you need to study what's changing this country?' said a lifelong resident and shrewd observer of the Middle West. 'I can tell you what's happening in just four letters: A–U–T–O!' " †

The Lynds further reported that, although there were some who considered a car a luxury to be bought after the budget had provided for a home and clothes, many would place a car before home ownership and the clothes budget—and some would even let the food budget suffer. N. L. Bossing and R. R. Martin have indicated that the automobile has been a factor in a number of changes in ways of living. (1) Rural disintegration has been prompted by the availability of city markets and stores. (2) Rural residences have been moved from remote or isolated areas to the side of improved highways. (3) Perishable foods have become more widely distributed by the heavy motor trucks. (4) Leisure-time activities have

---

* Josette Frank, *Comics, Radio, Movies—and Children* (Pamphlet No. 148, Public Affairs Committee, Inc., 1949), pp. 30–32.
† Robert S. Lynd and Helen M. Lynd, *Middletown* (New York: Harcourt, Brace and Company, Inc.; 1929), p. 251.

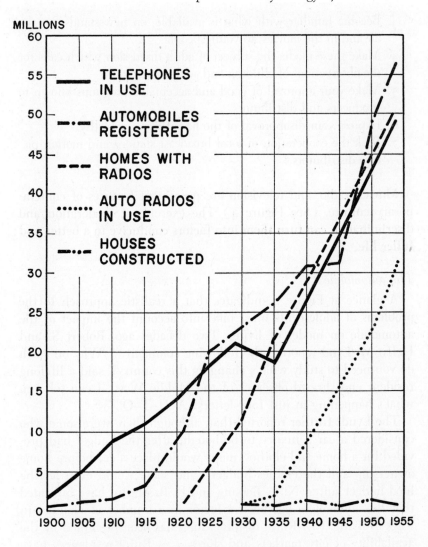

FIG. 4. **The changing nature of living**

"Houses constructed" is plotted to show that the changes are not simply a matter of population growth. (This chart should be studied in connection with the "gap between generations" as well as with "current influences.")

been changed from such things as community Fourth of July cele-brations to individual sight-seeing and picnicking jaunts. (5) The pattern of crime and delinquency has been markedly changed by the automobile. [36:258]

It is in the latter two areas that the automobile has its most direct effect upon adolescents. There is considerable dependence on the motor vehicle to take parties on skiing trips, to lakes, rivers and the ocean for swimming and boating, and simply for the sake of sight-seeing and traveling with no particular destination in mind. The popularity of dine and dance spots has been partly due to their availability as places where young persons may escape the close supervision of responsible adults. Courtney Riley Cooper has writ-ten discouragingly of motels and auto courts where one may *not* find a "vacancy" if he carries baggage and looks like a tourist—rooms are saved for those who will only stay an hour or two and thus permit several rentings during a night. [67]

It seems likely that the automobile is a factor in encouraging dis-respect for law. The stigma of a traffic ticket, if any, consists in getting caught rather than in the breaking of law. Many youngsters, with the knowledge of their parents, drive cars before they are legally licensed. The theft of autos is frequently an offense of younger persons who are looking for a thrill or who take a car on sudden impulse. New fashions in murder, robbery, kidnaping, and sex offenses are influenced by the automobile.

Another impact of the automobile is revealed in statistics of traf-fic accidents. The accident proneness of adolescents is reflected in the high insurance rates charged when a driver of the family car is below the age of twenty-five. The big cost of traffic accidents is, however, in terms of death and permanent injury. There is a ray of hope, however, in the educability of the teen-age driver. Where the adolescent has been taught to drive by driver-training teachers, rather than by parents or peers, the record for safe and *sane* driving is surprisingly good.

The automobile, like the radio, television, and movies, is some-thing we must learn to live with. It is not side-stepping the issues in-volved to say that the solution of problems presented by the auto-mobile lies in an over-all attack upon the human forces that underlie those cases in which adolescents suffer from the impact of machines of many kinds. Stability of personality, socially oriented behavior, and behavior directed by knowledge and information must be encouraged through a multi-faceted approach such as is suggested by this entire volume.

Military service

An unpleasant fact to face, for all Americans, is that we are a nation in a state of preparation for war. Calling a particular phase of this condition an armed peace does not change the dilemma presented to adolescents—particularly the males. War or the threat of war adds another uncertainty to the world of the adolescent. However, as is the case with so many other situations that contribute to confusion, the adolescent seems to take it in stride. The observation of the author was that, in World War II, most of the young men considered military service an unpleasant but essential job that should be done with as much efficiency and dispatch as possible. The same observation has been made of the Korean conflict: "But they fought, they endured, they stayed to the bitter end; they fought a war they did not particularly believe in, to the armistice they have little faith in, and they will fight again, automatically and instantly, if the armistice should fail." *

There are many points of confusion regarding the performance of military service: whether "bright" boys should be exempt so they could receive the training needed as technicians and specialists, what the proper age for service is, whether school should precede or follow military training, how the marital status of the young man should effect his obligation. A little study and a little talk will soon convince one that these questions are not easily answered, but there are some aspects of the problem that seem to be somewhat more amenable to a solution. One is that training for armed service should be an accepted part of living in a democracy. The other is that a definite policy should be formulated so that the young man may know what to expect. These two items are interrelated.

Despite our traditional objection to a standing army and our fears of a military dictatorship, war and preparation for war have characterized our national history. Kallen states a sound case:

---

* Eric Sevareid, "Why Did They Fight?" *Harper's,* 207, October, 1953, p. 25.

On the record, that military education should be universal, and universal as an organic part of general education, is as necessary to the democratic way as that education in general should be universal. In a democracy, the trained and armed volunteer possesses a dangerous advantage in just that kind of knowledge and skill that could render him a menace to the democratic way. It is by means of such educational inequalities that minorities usually overpower majorities and retain the power they seize. This has been the record throughout history. . . . Only the equal distribution of the science and art of arms can provide any reliable offset to this monopoly of an aggressor minority.*

Certainly it would seem that the wise course for parents and teachers would be to point out the advantages of military service, which has become a part of our way of life, instead of bewailing the time as being lost. The record of the GI in college has demonstrated that military service may contribute to an intellectual maturity that makes study more profitable. The social horizons of service personnel have been broadened. [213] Some youth find, in the military, a kind of life they like and welcome as a career. There is an opportunity for "youth to serve," which has been frequently mentioned as one of the needs of adolescents.

Regarding the second aspect of the problem—there are, of course, difficulties in the way of establishing a settled policy for length, time for beginning, and conditions of military service. But it seems that youth should be considered as well as the national exigencies. If such a view were taken, it would be possible to state a minimum (and inescapable) period of service. If war were not an immediate threat the battle could be fought—as in the early 1930's in the Civilian Conservation Corps—against flood, wind, and forest fires. As yet untried fields, such as responsibilities in civic offices, might also be included in the area of national service.

Like other problems being faced by the adolescent, that of military service has many facets. The production of *good* democratic soldiers should be an outcome of our national mores. An orientation

---

* Horace M. Kallen in H. Gordon Hullfish (Ed.), *Educational Freedom in an Age of Anxiety*, 12th Yearbook of the John Dewey Society (New York: Harper & Brothers; 1953), pp. 178–179.

supported by history might include the following items: Military preparation reduces an aggressor's initial advantage. Training for all would avert the danger of a huge standing army. Free men have in the past supported, and must be able to support in the future, their freedom by means of fighting. No fighting unit can be better than the men who compose it:

> For commitment of the self, intellectual realization is more important than fire power. . . . For obviously, no gun, no plane, no tank, no ship, no bomb can be any better than the human being whose weapon it is. . . . Man power is the energy of a faith, illumined by understanding, on which the man is ready to bet his life and which he would rather die for than yield.

> If the nation's schools were to develop the liberal education as a discipline of freedom which includes the knowledge and skills of the citizen-soldier as a phase of its consummation, the schools would become what they of right should be—the meetinghouses of the religion of democracy.*

Dealing with cultural factors

Conflict between ideals and reality

A frequently mentioned source of difficulty for adolescents is the discrepancy between ideals and reality. This difference is, however, one that persons of all ages face continuously. It is faced, *and withstood,* by the child when he discovers that his dad cannot lick all other dads, when he finds that his dad does not boss all others at the plant, office, or store, and when he discovers that there is no corporeal Santa Claus. The incidence of trauma accompanying such discoveries has been successfully reduced by parents who have anticipated the difficulty and by fathers who have admitted to their offspring that they are neither omnipotent nor omniscient. The gap between ideals and reality can be anticipated by adults who have the faith to teach that the width of a chasm depends partially upon a man's point of view and his equipment for spanning it.

The conflict between ideals and practice has been written and talked about in such areas as sex activities, conduct of business, the

---

* Kallen, *op. cit.,* pp. 183–184.

description and practice of democracy, and the home and professional life of the churchgoer. The danger of the conflict is that some youth may develop an attitude of cynicism or defeat. When they see that the ideal is not achieved, they assume a "don't care" attitude and behavior. On the other hand, they may adopt militant, aggressive, and offensive behavior in an effort to eliminate the imperfect situation. [81] Either of these extremes is short of the characteristics desired in mature citizens—those who would keep striving toward an ideal and in so doing would get at causes instead of attacking symptoms. Since maladjusted people are frequently thwarted idealists, it is important that adolescents be led to consider the normality of conflict between that which should be hoped and striven for and current practice.

An ideal is a mental image of something perfect—a standard for beauty or excellence. As such, it serves the important function of a goal toward which to grow. It is desirable that adolescents understand ideals as stimuli to directed effort rather than things that should be immediately achieved. The following considerations may provide fruitful points of departure for putting across the notion that ideals are normally ahead of practice.

1. Man's imperfection is a challenge to continuous growth. The greatest psychological gift any of us possess is a realization of our own shortcomings and a desire to improve. Without this we should soon become static and maladjusted individuals.

2. The discrepancy is sometimes a result of the adolescent's own lack of perception. A concept or generalization takes on more meaning and more ramifications as one grows in experience. The lack of experience of an adolescent leads him to interpret a generalization narrowly and literally, while additional knowledge will place the idea in a wider context.

3. The discrepancy is often magnified by the emphases made in radio or TV reports and in newspapers and magazines. Chicanery in politics receives much attention, yet the fact is that chicanery is the exceptional thing. T. V. Smith, speaking before a group at Northwestern University, said in effect:

I thought, with my experience and training, as a professor of political science that I should immediately be able to make a contribution to the people of Illinois as a legislator. I found instead, that I listened with admiration, to the wisdom which was revealed in legislative sessions. I admired the honesty of the typical representative of the people.

That there have been small and mean men in politics there is no denying. But they are the minority. The greatest number must be sincere, intelligent, and honest or our nation could not have proven itself to be an international power. The same thing must be said with regard to honesty in business. If the great bulk of business men were not honest our whole economy would quickly break down.

4. The *status quo* does not always represent what people want. Few people want war, but the problem of how to avoid it has not yet been solved. Alfred Kinsey's statistics on the promiscuity of both men and women do not prove that promiscuous behavior contributes to wholesome personality development or the welfare of American society.

The gap between ideals and reality provides challenges and opportunities for youth who see the futility of cynicism.

Social drift and social planning

In current psychological theory the concept of animism has been discarded. We do not believe in evil forces or evil spirits or even evil machines. We do believe that there are evil men—intelligent but ruthless and selfish. There are no inescapable and inevitable negative results that *must* accrue for adolescents from population trends, the existence of minority groups, the automobile, radio, television, or control by women. It is man's servile resignation to problems that makes it seem that a particular phenomenon (for example, the automobile) must have a particular social result (for example, removal from supervision by adults).

There are three ways in which the historical tendency to permit social drift may be transformed to a psychologically sound, purposeful behavior. (1) Individuals must be led to think through their own purposes. It would seem to be particularly important that the tension-producing, and progressively demanding, pursuit of material goods be made subservient to self-fulfillment and social service. The latter orientation is not a twentieth-century discovery—

it is ages old but has perhaps been temporarily transcended by the thinking that has accompanied the industrial revolution. (2) Community study and planning should be correlated with and serve as a supplement to the subject matter of the schools. This would serve the double purpose of making education more meaningful (purposeful rather than purposive) and help induct young people into a participating citizenship. (3) National planning for the welfare of all has been a matter of increasing political concern for the past two or three decades. Many specific mistakes occurred as choices between individual and collective welfare have been made, but it would seem fair to say that the course has been one of general improvement. Two features in national planning stand out from a psychological viewpoint. One, the long term welfare of the majority must take precedence over the interests of pressure groups —only in this way can man's faith in himself survive. Two, the preventive and therapeutic values of creative work must be safeguarded for every individual. The "something for nothing" orientation must be continuously and systematically debunked.

Opportunity for adolescents

The outlook for adolescents is not a gloomy one. In almost every persistent and current influence that bears upon the developing individual there are advantages as well as disadvantages. There may be discerned, by an examination of the historical past, an encouraging ability on the part of adolescents and youth to make admirable adjustments to what appear to be overwhelming situations. One might even go so far as to say that conflict may be needed in order to stimulate optimum development. (We have seen that growth is the product of the *interaction* of the *organism* with its *environment*.) But, it should hurriedly be added, there are enough obstacles to growth so that hazards need not be intentionally sought, or left remaining, when they could be removed. There are many adolescents who break under the burdens imposed upon them. There are others who have been so weakened by teen-age experiences that they do not have the vitality to live a productive adulthood. If more attention could be diverted from defensive fighting to creative endeavor, the life of the adolescent *and society* could be greatly improved.

Summary

As the concept of instinct has declined in popularity as a psychological explanation of behavior, the role of cultural causation has been recognized more clearly. The impact of culture must of necessity be described in many different chapters in this volume. The present chapter deals with the phenomenon of rapid change which makes it necessary for young people to question prescription and to seek new answers. The gap between the generations is widened by the rapidity of change—though it must be recognized that the gap is bridged more often than not. Authoritarianism is widely extant but is out of harmony with our personal and political philosophy. Our hurry to get things done also characterizes our haste to have adolescents act the part of adults and adds confusion to their already perplexing world. Our difficulty in understanding these factors is increased because they are by no means uniform influences in all social sub-groups.

Population changes have marked influence on adolescents because (1) they are becoming a smaller portion of the total population, (2) the changes have tended to lengthen the period of dependence on older persons, (3) many adolescents are members of ethnic, religious, and color minority groups and consequently are vulnerable to the cruelty of discrimination and prejudice.

Some other current influences on the adolescent include: the prolonged control by women which increases the difficulty of learning an appropriate male sex role; the stimulation of radio, television, and movies; the geographical mobility made possible by the automobile; and the uncertainty connected with a vaguely defined period of military service.

There are ways out of the difficulties adolescents face but the ways, obviously, are not simple or widely accepted. For the present, we must say that personal and group planning must characterize any fruitful approach to the problems. Optimism, which is warranted on the basis of past successes, must be maintained. Simple but spurious explanations of human behavior cannot be depended upon. Many factors must be recognized in the genesis of adolescent personality, and one of the factors is that of cultural influence.

1. Cite, from reading or travel experiences, some behaviors of people from other lands that contrast sharply with our own culturally imposed behaviors.
2. Do you think that the rate of social and technological change will decrease, settle at the present pace, or increase? Give your reasons.
3. What would you consider to be some effective approaches to the reduction of authoritarianism?
4. Besides those effects on adolescents, what are some of the probable effects of changing population ratios?
5. Suggest ways in which the prolonged period of adolescent dependence might be converted into opportunities for development.
6. Why do you, or do you not, consider that the most serious feature of prejudice is its effect upon the prejudiced person?
7. Present some arguments against the proposition that control by women is a hazard for male adolescents.
8. Discuss the techniques that might be used in a high school class devoted to evaluating radio or TV programs. Do the same for a class that is analyzing movies.
9. What are some of the reasons why driver training classes have resulted in a lowering of accident rates?
10. Try to decide upon a sound military service policy; present it to your classmates for evaluation.
11. What are some general policies you think should be included in a plan for social engineering?

RECOMMENDED SUPPLEMENTARY READING

Josselyn, Irene M. *The Adolescent and His World* (New York: Family Service Association of America; 1952), pp. 26–55.
   These chapters deal with (1) social pressures affecting adolescents and (2) ways in which the contradictory demands for dependence and independence cause difficulty and create opportunity.

Kuhlen, Raymond G. *The Psychology of Adolescent Development* (New York: Harper & Brothers; 1952), pp. 146–189.
   In this chapter Professor Kuhlen discusses the relation of culture to personality and then gives details of the impact of rural or urban residence

and social class status on adolescents. Sex roles, income of parents, social change, and economic structure illustrate the impact of culture.

Landis, Paul H. *Adolescence and Youth,* 2nd Edition (New York: Mc-Graw-Hill Book Company, Inc.; 1952), pp. 51–72.

Professor Landis asserts that our industrial society is a major force in creating problems for adolescents. Age changes in society, changing mores, horizontal mobility (moving from place to place) and vertical mobility (change in social status), and urbanization are discussed.

Parsons, Talcott, in Clyde Kluckhohn and Henry A. Murray (Eds.) *Personality—in Nature, Society, and Culture* (New York: Alfred A. Knopf, Inc.; 1953), pp. 363–375.

The adolescent can most profitably be studied in his total life role; that is, from infancy through adulthood. This chapter provides such a discussion under the heading, "Age and Sex in the Social Structure of the United States."

Seidman, Jerome M. (Ed.) *The Adolescent: A Book of Readings* (New York: The Dryden Press; 1953), pp. 2–60.

These five chapters by various authors deal with adolescence of the Hopi Indians, contrasts between German and American Youths, and problems of adolescents in modern American society.

Watson, Goodwin. *Youth after Conflict* (New York: Association Press; 1947), pp. 195–298.

The whole book could be read with interest and profit. It serves to show the continuity of adolescent problems from the time of the Civil War. The two chapters indicated (pp. 195–298) describe youth after World War II and make some challenging predictions.

AUDIO-VISUAL MATERIAL

Experimental Studies of Social Climate of Groups (State University of Iowa, Iowa City, Iowa), 30 min., so., b. & w.

Shows the behavior of groups of boys in organized clubs run on democratic, laissez-faire, and autocratic principles. Behavior varies as membership is transferred from one type of leadership to another. An excellent portrayal of an aspect of culture.

High Wall (McGraw-Hill Book Company, Inc., 330 West 42nd Street, New York 36), 32 min., so., b. & w.

Shows how environment and training produce a young bigot. Discussion of the film may point out ways to combat prejudice and discrimination in our schools and communities.

Part Two

THE DYNAMICS OF ADOLESCENT DEVELOPMENT

PART TWO is a discussion of six major forces that shape the course of development during adolescence. If these forces can be made to work in the same direction, rather than as conflicting vectors, there is greater likelihood of harmonious, straightforward progress. The coordination of forces will result in more complete realization of social and individual potential.

Physical factors are of incontestable significance. The age at which puberty is achieved, the health of the individual, physical stature, and motor skills are considered. These are of particular significance because of their bearing on the individual's concept of self. Attitudes toward self in turn condition the ways in which each one works toward realization of his potential and his adjustment to society.

Recognition is given to the primary place of the *home* in shaping behavior habits and attitudes. Discussion of favorable and unfavorable home conditions point the way to making them more constructive.

Schools supplement the work of the home in forming the adolescent personality. Opportunities and achievements of the school are weighed against the existence of defects. These defects are portrayed as evidences of failure to recognize factors that are inherent in physical growth and parental conditioning.

Adolescents are by no means a homogeneous group. If teachers, parents, and other youth workers are to achieve optimum results, they must recognize the differences in conditioning which stem from varied *social status.*

Differences in *intelligence* must also be recognized. In this text two items are uppermost: (1) the age at which intellectual growth ceases and (2) the intrapersonal variability of intelligence—that is, the necessity for recognizing individual talents.

Since what a man loves, is interested in, does, aspires to be, are as important as what he knows, *emotional growth* is important in the dynamics of adolescence. Suggestions for improving emotional stability are based on an understanding of emotional development during adolescence.

What problems are created by the differential growth patterns of boys and girls? Do adolescents grow too fast, eat too much, sleep too little? What is the source of the notion that adolescents are awkward?

CHAPTER FIVE

Physical Factors in Development

The emphasis placed on cultural factors should not prevent an appreciation of the dynamic import of physical factors. What an individual inherits broadly determines the kind of adolescent and adult he will be. The germ cells set the limits beyond which environmental factors cannot induce growth. The endocrine system must be taken into account when studying the energy an individual has available for reaching the innate potential that external factors encourage and/or allow. There is an inherited potential for the development of intelligence beyond which cultural stimulation will be ineffective and often irritating. No matter what phases of adolescence we may be studying—intelligence, character and personality, heterosexual adjustments, interests, emotional behavior, socialization—the physical and physiological factors are contributing aspects.

The roles of culture and physical factors are a part of the heredity and environment problem. Psychologists are little concerned about how much of the person is due to heredity and how much is due to environment; but they are greatly concerned about integrated growth processes, which have inseparable internal and external facets. In addition, there is a third facet, which has to do with the individual's *response* to his inherited physical and intellectual po-

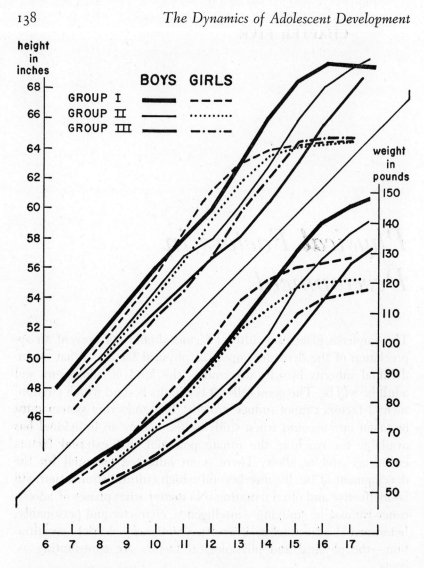

FIG. 5. **Growth trends**

Average height and weight of boys and girls of early, middle, and late maturing groups. From F. K. Shuttleworth, *The Adolescent Period: A Graphic Atlas*, Evanston, Illinois: Child Development Publications, 1951, Fig. 152.

Features to note:

1. Girls at the age of ten plus to eleven plus tend to exceed boys in weight (when they are about 57 to 64 inches tall).

tential as it is influenced by environment. In this chapter we are concerned with physical growth factors and the individual's response to them in our culture.

Height and weight changes in adolescence

The growth spurt

Probably one of the most widely, but not necessarily accurately, known features of adolescence is the so-called growth spurt. If you talk to some adults on this subject, they are likely to report that they or their children grew from six to seven inches in about a year at about the fourteenth year. The young people quickly outgrew outfit after outfit, and the arms and legs grew so rapidly that stumbling and awkwardness were continually noticed. Research data do not support such popular views. There is an increase in the rate of growth but it occurs in the pre-pubertal period, *just before the phase known as adolescence begins.* Figure 5 shows that the "spurt" begins on the average at about nine to eleven years. This increased rate of growth lasts from about two to four years, and the average gain in height for boys *during the period* is about eight inches—varying from about four to twelve inches. [295:83]

Probably a few adolescents do outgrow their clothes; and since approval of the peer group is so important, a slight misfit becomes a real tragedy (and the author sincerely means *real*). However, most

2. Girls at the age of 9 plus to 14 plus tend to exceed boys in weight (when they weigh about 70 to 120 pounds). This temporary superiority is associated with the girls' average earlier pubescence.

3. The yearly increments of height and weight increase more rapidly beginning at about the tenth year (the curves bend slightly upward).

4. The growth spurt covers a span of about two to four years. The longer periods of accelerated growth are experienced by those who mature at the higher ages.

5. The early maturing groups tend to retain their superiority in height and weight, though the differences between early and late maturers tend to be lessened by the time maturity is reached. (The Curves GI, GII, GIII especially tend to be further apart at 11 to 13 years than they are at the age of 17.)

discarded clothes will show signs of having been well used. Infants, babies, and pre-school children are the ones who outgrow their clothes and shoes. Their spurt in growth is much more pronounced than is that of the typical adolescent. As for adolescent awkwardness, it is difficult to determine where the misconception arose— except from the tendency to generalize from specific instances. The infant grows, percentagewise and absolutely, more than does the adolescent—yet he is constantly gaining in grace, skill, and coordination. The adolescent is not growing so rapidly that he does not know where the ends of his extremities are—he too is growing in coordination, though he may not have achieved an adult level in spite of being almost as large. It is in comparison with adults that the fallacy of awkwardness probably arose. The statement that adolescents are awkward is not footnoted in texts—the statement that they are gaining in skill can be footnoted. [87, 101] Growth is continuous and gradual, though this does not mean uniform, throughout the years.

Differences in early and late maturers

Differences in height and weight are often troublesome to the teen agers who are concerned about being like their peers. Those who experience early puberty tend, temporarily, to exceed their agemates *and* their accelerated rate of growth is concentrated in a shorter period of months. This group of boys and girls will achieve physical maturity and cease growing sooner than will the late maturers. It should be noted (see Figure 5) that the differences between early and later maturers tend to be lessened by the time of maturity for both groups. [15] It is important that parents and teachers appreciate these differences so that young people can be helped in accepting the normality of marked differences in the early teen years. The early maturer can be comforted by telling him that he is now becoming an adult, and the late maturer may be assured by pointing out that the chance of later reaching maturity with less difficulty is the probable reward for later development. However, it will also be well to indicate that the potential each one inherits from ancestors must also be considered.

The average girl experiences the pre-pubertal spurt about two years earlier than does the average boy. Girls begin their accelerated growth between the ages of 8.5 and 11.5 years, reaching the high point of acceleration about 12.5 years and achieving adult stature between 15 and 18 years. Boys begin their increased growth between 10 and 15 years, reaching the high point of acceleration at about 14 years and achieving maturity between 17 and 20. These physical changes, as will be shown later, are accompanied by differences in interests and behavior, thus creating quite a disparity of personality orientation between boys and girls and among boys and among girls. This has led some writers to criticize the fact that different provisions in education and other experiences are not provided for boys and girls.* Doubt is cast on the validity of the recommendation that differential experiences for the sexes be provided by the fact that an average is a point, whereas normality is a range. Specifically, *some* boys are reaching physical maturity at the age of 17 while some girls are still not physically mature at 18; or some boys are beginning their accelerated growth at 10 years while some girls do not reach that point until the age of 12. The differences *between* the sexes are much less than are the differences *within* a sex. Blanket provisions for sex differences would serve to place additional problems of adjustment on those at the extreme ends of the normal range. It would seem to be the part of wisdom to help young people, through guidance, to meet and absorb the differences that will exist whether or not there are any artificial arrangements; however, it cannot be denied that the relatively earlier maturation of girls is a persistent problem in the study of adolescence.

The wide range of normality

One of the difficulties psychologists and educators continually face is that of applying the generalizations that come from averages to the specific instance of a unique individual. Some teachers have been so surprised by the author's statement that "50 per cent of our population is below average" that they have said, "That just isn't so!" These are the teachers who strive futilely to bring all children up to grade average in comprehension of subject matter. In the matter of physical growth, as in intelligence, the adult's problem is to help the individual, who is not average, appreciate his normality. For

---

* See J. S. Plant, "Social Significance of War Impact on Adolescents," *The Annals of the American Academy of Political and Social Science*, 235, 1944, pp. 1–7, and Paul H. Landis, *Adolescence and Youth,* Second Edition (New York: McGraw-Hill Book Company, Inc.; 1952), p. 40.

instance, the average age of girls at the first menstruation (menarche) is 13 years, yet a girl may be quite normal and have her menarche at 11 years or at 17 years. After the menstruation period has become regular or stabilized, the average number of days between periods is 28 days, but a girl may be normal and have up to 40 days without menstrual flow. The average age of the maximally accelerated growth period of 12.5 years for girls and 14 years for boys must not lead teen agers, teachers, or parents to doubt the normality of variations as wide as four years on either side of the numerical average.

If "to be forewarned is to be forearmed," then it will help the tall thirteen-year-old girl who is dancing with the short thirteen-year-old boy to know that she is quite normal. It will help the short lad to know that he is not necessarily going to turn out to be a runt. The forewarning should be *before* the problem has been encountered and before the idea that one is abnormal has become a conviction. Advice given contemporaneously with the problem is often not satisfying. Further, teen-age group discussions will help. While Sally is concerned with her tallness, Jane is concerned with her plumpness, and Mary is bothered by her moles . . . and so on. Teachers and club leaders find that a boy who is concerned about his normality feels less sorry for himself when he discovers that others are concerned about other things that *to him* are rather absurd.

Evaluating height-weight changes

The normal differences in body build, due largely to inherited predisposition, have tended to discredit the once popular height-weight tables—which are based upon averages. It is now recognized that individual patterns of development may vary widely without warranting the concern of adults or the worry of adolescents. The words underweight or overweight take on justifiable significance only when the uniqueness of the individual is considered.

An encouraging approach to the evaluation of height-weight differences has been developed by Dr. Norman C. Wetzel, who emphasizes the need for comparing the individual with himself. [341] As Figure 6 shows, seven channels for normal development are provided, A_3 through B_3. The areas outside the "physique channels," A_4 (obese) and B_4 (extreme thinness or poor), are considered to be worthy of immediate investigation. Otherwise, concern is held chiefly for those subjects who shift more than one half of one "physique channel" in ten levels of forward progress (isodevelopmental lines) and for those who advance less than ten to eleven levels per year.

It may at first seem that the Wetzel Grid is so complicated as to be discouraging. However, some teachers who make use of the grids have the pupils record the data. The teachers and administrators feel that the graph of growth serves as a motivating device to get adequate sleep and rest and to give the matter of proper diet functional consideration. Anne M. Clemmons and Harriet Williams used the device with eighty boys and girls from 13 to 18 years in a unit dealing with nutrition. In six weeks time those showing satisfactory growth changed from 28.75 per cent to 50 per cent. Discussion of the grids was part of the class work and some valuable pupil insights were achieved.

> . . . one girl could not gain on the amount and quality of food she ate in relation to her outside activities of cheerleading and dancing; another girl's late hours due to working as a baby sitter and social activities such as dancing kept her from gaining; and a boy gained in spite of the same work he had carried on during the former period when he had shown a downward trend. His reason was that he had improved his nutrition enough to care for the extra activity. [His is the record plotted on Fig. 6.] *

This quotation serves to emphasize that growth is a product of the interaction (pupil's response to his knowledge) of the organism (body-build) with its environment (nutrition and rest).

Sexual development

Endocrine factors

The changes in growth patterns, described in the foregoing section, are initiated and influenced by the smooth, or ductless, glands of internal secretion—called the endocrine system. Each endocrine gland produces a hormone that is secreted directly into the blood

---

* Anne M. Clemmons and Harriet Williams, "Motivating Adolescents to Optimum Growth with the Wetzel Grid," *Journal of Home Economics*, 44, 1952, 192–194.

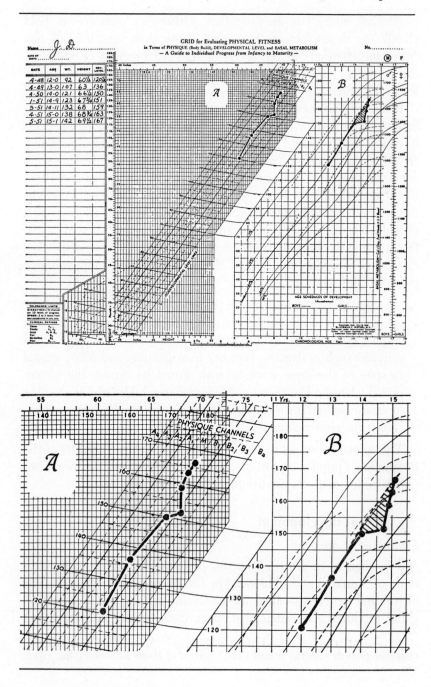

stream and performs some rather specific function in the "wisdom of the body." Hereditary factors, sunlight, and psychological factors also play a part in growth; but since the endocrines produce marked effects in the chemical balance of the body they are of special interest in the study of adolescence.

Various glands seem to have predominating functions in growth, metabolism, and activity; but the outstanding fact is that the glands act as a closely integrated, cooperating, *and antagonistic,* finely balanced system. Since these glands influence growth, intelligence, physical energy, interests, emotionality, health, and longevity it is inevitable that they play an important role in the behavior of adolescents. There is no hope that the science of psychology will be reduced to the test tube containing hormones (the products of the smooth glands) but the endocrines cannot be ignored as factors contributing to personality and behavior.

Little is known about the *pineal* gland, a tiny body located near the brain. It seems to function mainly during childhood and probably retards sexual development. The *thymus,* located in the chest, is relatively large during childhood and atrophies in late childhood and adolescence. It too, is presumed to function as an inhibitor of precocious sexual development. The *pituitary,* located at the base

---

FIG. 6. **The Wetzel Grid**

Each individual is weighed and measured periodically and the course of development is plotted on the Grid Panel, A (the middle and broadest section of the grid). The points plotted—weight on the vertical scale on the left and height on the horizontal scale at the top—are extended to the Auxodrome Panel, B (the right hand section, "Age Schedules of Development") and marked at the lines indicating the subject's age. (This has been done for a boy, twelve years old at the first measurement. The deviation from his normal progress channel was due to a heavy work load. He was brought back to normal by eating five daily meals of good quality food.) Thus, by plotting the height-weight intersections of A, the Grid Panel, and extending them to B, the Auxodrome Panel, a curve is developed which compares the individual's growth with the norm for his channel (body type). This reproduction of the front side of the Grid is by permission of Dr. Wetzel and NEA Service, Inc.

of the brain, is called the master gland because of its intimate relationship to the functioning of other glands. Its most notable function has to do with bodily and sexual growth. The *parathyroids,* located in the lower throat region, control the metabolism of calcium. The *thyroids,* also located in the lower throat region, control oxygen metabolism. The *islands of Langerhans,* located in the pancreas, control sugar metabolism. The *adrenal* glands, located near the pancreas, produce the hormone known as adrenin or adrenalin and work with the nervous system to produce vascular and respiratory changes that prepare one for the emergency of violent emotions. It also functions less violently in the milder emotions. The *ovaries* produce the germ cells which, when fertilized by the products of the *testes,* the spermatozoa, become the embryo. The glands that are of special interest in the development of adolescents are the pituitary and the gonads.

The anterior lobe of the pituitary produces the (1) gonadotropic hormone, which stimulates the development of sex organs and sex characteristics, and (2) the growth hormone, which stimulates body development: height, weight, musculature, and fusing of the epiphyses. There are two gonadotropic hormones: (1) The male hormone, testicular hormone, which stimulates growth of the prostate gland, the seminal vesicles, penis, and the secondary sex characteristics. (2) The female sex hormone, estrogen, contributes to the production of germ cells and causes ovulation. After the pituitary has aroused the sex glands from the dormant period of little development during childhood the reciprocal, or antagonistic, role of the glands is noted; that is, the gonadotropic hormones inhibit the activity of the pituitary in its production of growth hormones. Normally, the increased activity of the pituitary begins about the age of ten or eleven years, just preceding the "growth spurt" mentioned earlier. Inadequate amounts of the growth hormone produce dwarfism, excessive amounts produce pituitary gigantism; inadequate amounts of the gonadotropic hormone result in a hypogonadal or hypogenital condition (sex organs are immature and secondary sex characteristics fail to appear) while excessive amounts result in precocious sexual development and the appearance of male characteristics in the female.

Not only are the gonads stimulated at puberty by the hormones from the pituitary but the gonads seem to become increasingly responsive to the gonadotropic hormones. Further, the gonads begin to produce their own hormones and cooperate in the development of the sex organs and the secondary sex characteristics. The ovaries (female) produce, among other things, ovarian hormones, and the testes (male) produce testicular hormones which influence behavior, interests, and growth. If the ovarian and testicular hormones are not produced early enough, growth continues for too long a period and the broad hips, long legs, and narrow shoulders of the eunuch are the result. At the age of about twelve the ovaries are about 40 per cent of mature size, they grow rapidly and by the age of 20 are full size. In comparison to skeletal growth the male sex organs grow little in the first ten years, but by thirteen are about two-thirds adult size and by fifteen are 90 per cent adult size. The organs are fully developed functionally by 20 years though the testes may continue to grow slightly. [9:82] Other functions and relationships are indicated in Table 1, page 148.

Before describing more of the physical changes of adolescence it may be well to indicate that these physiological alterations must have an influence on behavior and its motivation.

. . . What part the specific hormones play is still conjectural, although there can be little doubt that the gonads provide an important source for sex drive. If the sex hormones are essential factors in sexual instigation, as these studies seem to indicate, then an increase in the amount of hormones present in the organism at pubescence should result in a change of behavior. Psychological examinations of a number of pubescent and post-pubescent boys have revealed that the quantity of hormone output apparently had a significantly greater effect upon the interests, attitudes, and stimulus-susceptibility of the boys than did either chronological age or physical status. Other investigators have found that in two groups of girls who were equated for age, one group being post-menarchal and the other pre-menarchal, the sexually mature group more nearly approached the adult norms of interests than did those who were sexually immature.*

---

* John Dollard, Neal E. Miller, Leonard W. Doob, O. H. Mowrer, Robert Sears, *Frustration and Aggression* (New Haven: Yale University Press; 1939), p. 93.

TABLE I **Glandular Aspects of Sex Development and Function**

	GLAND PRODUCT (most frequently a hormone)	FUNCTION *
PITUITARY (anterior lobe)	Growth hormones	Stimulate growth, gonad activity, fusing of epiphyses
	Gonadotropic hormones androgen (male hormone present in both male and female)	Growth of prostate, seminal vesicles, penis, etc. Produces secondary sex characteristics
	estrogen (female hormone present in both sexes) Progestogen	Inhibits action of pituitary Stimulates growth of breasts, mammary glands, uterus, Fallopian tubes, vagina
GONADS ovaries	Theelin Follicular hormone	Stimulates secretion of estrogen
	Germ cells	Causes ovulation
	Corpus luteum	Broadening of hips
	Estrogens (ovarian hormones)	Growth of pubic hair Changed musculature
testes	Androgens (testicular hormones)	Lowering of voice pitch
	Spermatozoa	Broadening of shoulders

* Although primary or predominant functions are indicated, it is important to remember that the *entire* glandular system acts as a unit. The brackets suggest the comprehensiveness of function.

There are cases of abnormality and growth caused by the malfunctioning of the endocrine system—dwarfism, gigantism, eunuchism, maleness in the female and femaleness in the male. More and more of these exceptional cases are being successfully treated by operations, glandular therapy (the administration of hormones), and by the use of radio-active isotopes. However, these are medical questions. It is important for both doctors and others who work with young people to realize that there is a wide range of normality. Many apparent deviations from normality are the results of genetic and extrinsic factors rather than hormones. Furthermore, some of the deviations are transitory imbalances, which occur with the changes of adolescence, and will correct themselves without treatment. [100] The endocrine system has its own capacity for self-correction. To begin tampering with the system may cause other malfunctionings to occur at a later time.

Male sex organs and their functions

After the period of latency in childhood the sex organs grow rapidly and become capable of serving their reproductive function. The male's contribution to reproduction is sperm cells or spermatozoa. These are produced in organs called the testes, which are a pair of compactly coiled tubules, about an eighth of a mile in length, which are kept at a constant temperature by the scrotum's drawing away from the body when the male is warm and drawing closer when cold. The sperm are produced by division of the cells that line the tubes of the testes. Hundreds of sperm could be placed on a space the size of the period at the end of this sentence; they are shaped like tadpoles with a rounded head and a thin tail that aids in propelling them on their passage through the epididymis, vas deferens, seminal vesicle and finally through the urethra. The penis, a muscular, external organ, becomes rigid due to constriction of its blood flow during sexual excitation, so that it can more easily be received by the female vagina, which is prepared for the entry by fluids that lubricate the inner walls during sexual excitation. Further excitement, through pressure, warmth, and motion, causes the prostate gland to expel (ejaculate) semen through the urethra, thus facilitating the passage of the sperm into the vagina. The sperm then travel through the womb to the Fallopian tube where one sperm finally fertilizes the ripened egg. Millions of sperm are released at each ejaculation, even though only one is required for fertilization.*

* Diagrams of the male and female reproductive systems can be found in many physiology and hygiene textbooks. Excellent illustrations are on pages 111 and 133 of Scheinfeld, *Women and Men* (Harcourt, Brace & Company, 1943).

It should be noted that although adolescents may be physically capable of performing sexual intercourse, functional maturity is not achieved immediately with the first menstruation. That is, after puberty there is a sterile period of from a month to several years before the hormones are produced with sufficient intensity to make the complete reproductive process possible.

Normally, the first ejaculation does not occur during intercourse. Rather the penis becomes erect through sexual excitation (conversation, erotic pictures, movie love scenes), bodily warmth and movement—car or horseback riding—and by rubbing with the hands (masturbation) until ejaculation results. Nocturnal emissions (seminal discharge during sleep) are also normal and boys should know in advance that they might occur. Sex education can be given before puberty on a much less personal and emotionally disturbing basis than it can be after puberty. [28:96] It is important that boys should be in rapport with their parents and have confidence in them so that problems can be discussed and worry allayed.

Despite the fact that physicians have for years stressed that masturbation is a normal phase of growing up, the belief is widely extant that it will lead to impaired health, insanity, and lack of masculinity. The fact is that masturbation—in both boys and girls—is a normal phase of growing up.

> Actually, masturbation is part of man's *Via Sacra* to adult living, and a nearly inevitable part of his growing up. It has its purpose. It solves a problem, or part of one, for a while. It postpones the necessity to cope with the ultimate, for it is beyond the power of the youngster to proceed at once to a full sexual expression.*

Adolescents are advised to avoid *excessive* masturbation, because as a *phase* of growing up, psychological development should not be arrested at this infantile and adolescent level. The psychological effects—worry, shame, feelings of baseness and inferiority, and fear—are the big dangers. Yet all too often the advice given to teen agers tends to intensify the feelings of guilt, remorse, fear, and inferiority. The more masturbation is stressed, the more compulsive the thoughts about sex become. [361:213] Despite the youngster's

---

* Marynia Farnham, *The Adolescent* (New York: Harper & Brothers; 1952), pp. 25–26.

desire to avoid masturbation his thoughts about it are a source of psychological stimulation. This suggests that the more effective approach would be to frankly state, to the adolescent, that it is a passing phase of normal conduct and then: (1) encourage adolescents to maintain good health practices, (2) encourage participation in appropriate physical exercise—this may mean the avoidance of vigorous exercise for some, (3) aid them in achieving success and satisfaction in school work, (4) help them create a variety of interests, (5) promote opportunities for participation in group heterosexual relationships, and (6) manifest confidence in them and hope for them. In these and other ways, which the reader may suggest, we can encourage the process of sublimation. Sound sex education cannot be restricted to the physical aspects of sex—the effective program is one that recognizes the multiple facets of adolescent personality.

Female sex organs and their functions

The sex organs are stimulated to accelerated growth at puberty before skeletal growth is completed. Since the sex organs of girls are mainly within the body, there is an enlargement and paunchiness of the abdomen. This may cause embarrassment unless it is understood that the hips will naturally broaden and the abdomen will flatten as growth proceeds—the paunchiness is another passing phase of development which the pubescent girl must appreciate.

The main female sex organs, the ovaries (about the size of almonds), are lined with follicles containing thousands of microscopic egg cells. At the time of puberty the eggs begin to ripen and the follicle bursts and a ripe egg is periodically discharged into the Fallopian tubes (about five inches in length and the diameter of a pencil). The discharge of the egg occurs about midway between the periods of menstrual flow (on the average, about fourteen days after the preceding menstrual cycle). The egg remains in the tube from two to five days, where it must be fertilized by a sperm cell if reproduction is to occur. If the egg is fertilized, hormones from the ovaries prepare the uterus (a hollow, pear-shaped, organ about three inches long) to receive and nourish the egg, by causing the endometrium (the lining of the uterus) to become a thick, plush bed. The egg becomes attached to the walls of the uterus, extracts nourishment, and develops into the embryo and later the fetus. After approximately nine months of intrauterine development the cervix and vagina are relaxed and muscular contractions push the baby out of the mother's body.

Most of the ova are not fertilized and soon come to the end of their life cycle. The enriched lining of the uterus sloughs off and is discarded through the vagina by means of periodic menstrual flow.

> And now that there's no further need for the enriched lining of the uterus, it breaks down—and in a few days, it flows through the uterus-opening into the vagina and is discarded. This flow has no more significance than many other excess materials that the body discards. Items like fingernails, or eyelashes, or hair—that fall out or are snipped off.*

With such a background of understanding as is indicated by the foregoing the young girl can be assured that the menstrual flow is an indication of normal progress toward maturity and she can more accurately assess such superstitions as the following:

> The loss of menstrual blood weakens you.
> Cold drinks give you cramps.
> A pain between periods means something's wrong.
> If the dentist puts in a filling it won't stay.
> It's dangerous to take baths or showers during your period.
> It's risky to shampoo your hair at this time.
> Stay in bed the first day.
> Exercise is bad for you.
> ALL SUPERSTITION! ALL NONSENSE! †

On the positive side, girls can be helped by parents who refrain from building psychological hazards, who avoid the terms "the curse" and "the sick time" when referring to menstruation. Some discomfort may accompany the physiological processes described above, *but most of the pain during menstruation is psychological—* caused by fear, embarrassment, and suspicion of abnormality—and can be avoided through proper instruction. The advisable approach

---

* *Very Personally Yours,* p. 5. (A pamphlet for young girls.) Copyright 1946, 1953—Kimberley-Clark Corporation.
    † *Ibid.,* p. 6. Copyright 1946, 1953—Kimberley-Clark Corporation.

is through over-all attention to physical and mental health. Some things that can be recommended to decrease physical discomfort are:

Partake of a good diet which will prevent constipation and provide adequate nourishment.

Develop good posture through alertness, self-confidence, and exercise.

Provide for adequate amounts of regular sleep.

Take specially designed exercises to strengthen abdominal walls and maintain suppleness.

Avoid extremely hot or cold baths—but not warm baths.

Keep clean so that embarrassment is avoided.

Other physical changes in adolescence

The fact that body temperature in children may vary more widely than that of an adult without its being a matter of gravity, is well known. Adolescence is a period of physiological learning and such things as temperature, elimination, and menstruation become more regular and stabilized as maturity is achieved. Some of the difficulties stem from the adolescent's attempt to adapt to an adult world while his internal environment is still in a state of flux. [279:57] An understanding of sex and other physical changes of adolescence will help us to appreciate the nature of these adjustments.

Secondary sex characteristics

The changed balance of endocrine functioning that occurs at puberty and stimulates growth of the gonads also results in a number of other changes, known as secondary sex characteristics. Among these are growth of the female breasts, deepening of the voice, appearance of facial and axillary (arm pits) hair, and some changes in the sweat glands. These changes are of some significance because they aid in the assessment of developmental status. It has been shown that there are marked deviations in the normal pattern of growth. Size and age are not reliable, and may even be misleading, indications of functional maturity. Thus, we may be expecting more in the way of mature behavior from a large fifteen-year-old boy, who is pre-pubescent and growing rapidly but is actually immature in stability and kind of interests, than from a smaller fourteen-year-old boy who, despite his size, has achieved some of the stability and interests of those closer to maturity. Even if the mental age of the larger boy were higher the developmental and behaviorial status of the smaller boy might be nearer to maturity. Not only can we understand the adolescent better for knowing some of these secondary sex characteristics but we can help the adolescent to understand himself.

An early manifestation of maturation in girls is the development of their breasts, which usually undergo four rather distinct stages. In infancy the papilla, or nipple, does not project above the surrounding surface but in early childhood becomes slightly elevated. Then at the age of about eleven the nipple and surrounding areola become slightly elevated. Next the primary breast develops, largely an increase in the amount of fatty tissue underlying and surrounding the nipple and areola. The final stage, called the mature breast, may never be achieved by some women; but there seems to be no concern for worry because the primary breast functions as well as the mature ones. While breasts are an indication of maturity, there is a great variation in their mature size; hence, it is the stage rather than the size that affords the clue to development. One might judge from reading the older literature on adolescents that there are indications of a healthy change in the attitudes of girls regarding their maturity. We have read that girls were ashamed of their breasts and tried to hide them with tight binding or loose fitting clothes. Today they seem to indicate that they are justifiably proud of their development by wearing sweaters that tend to reveal their womanhood; they may go so far as deliberately to exaggerate.

Another clue to maturity is the deepening of the voice; though, like breast development, it is not thoroughly reliable. Due to the lengthening of the vocal cords and the increased rate of growth of the larynx both the boy's and the girl's voice pitch lowers about an octave. The boy's voice particularly becomes somewhat unreliable for a period of time and may cause him some embarrassment if adults afford themselves the luxury of thinking it is funny. The normality of the occurrence, and its indication of approaching maturity, should be stressed. The voice change normally occurs some years after the onset of puberty, and there is great variability in the time of the change. Hence, it is not a thoroughly reliable indicator of the time of puberty but is nevertheless *an* indication of progress toward maturity. It should further be noted that there is no relationship between pitch (bass or tenor) and degree of masculinity. Hence, in a society where maleness is valued, the late voice changing lad or the one who turns out to be a tenor need feel no inferiority simply because his is a different pattern of growth.

Some time after the age of puberty (about fourteen years in boys) pubic hair begins to appear. It grows at the base of the penis and as it grows heavier and thicker usually takes a diamond shaped pattern—that is, grows up to a tip on the median line of the belly. The pubic hair of girls first appears on the outer lips of the vulva and in about 90 per cent of the cases assumes an inverted triangular pattern—a horizontal upper edge. Some girls have hair that grows upward toward the umbilicus—as well as considerable hair on the face and limbs. This hirsutism, while not an average development, is not an abnormality. Many girls who have an excessive amount of body and facial hair are just as feminine as are those whose hair growth is average. Axillary (under the arms) hair begins to appear somewhat later than does pubic hair.

Facial hair is particularly notable on the post-pubertal boy. Down appears on the upper lip, becomes darker and heavier, extends outward toward the corners of the mouth, appears on the chin and upper cheeks—continually becoming more deeply pigmented and heavier. Heaviness of the beard is no indication of degree of masculinity. There is a change in the shape of the hair line of the male adolescent from the crescent shape over the forehead (which is characteristic of boys, girls, and women) to one in which there are wedge shaped indentations of the hair line at the sides of the forehead. This receding of the hair line at the corners of the forehead, the *calvities frontalis adolescentium,* is a later-appearing characteristic. It, like many other secondary sex characteristics, is subject to wide individual differences. It is poorly developed in quite normal men and must be regarded simply as one clue in judging maturity.

Just before puberty there is an increase in the number of skin disorders—the incidence of which drops rapidly in the teen years. The disorders are associated with changes in the duct glands of the skin. There are three types of these glands: (1) The meocrine sweat glands, which cover most of the body, open directly on the surface of the skin, and secrete a slightly acid product. (2) The apocrine sweat glands, which become more active before and during puberty, are larger than the meocrine glands, open into the upper portions of hair follicles, and secrete an alkaline product that has a distinctive odor. These glands are located in the axillae and in the mammary, genital, and anal regions. (3) The sebaceous glands are closely associated with hair follicles, secrete a fatty substance and serve the function of keeping the skin moist and pliable.

Since the increased functioning of these glands begins at such widely varying times, it frequently causes adolescents some embarrassment. Adolescents should know that, due to the increased activity of the sweat glands and the differences in products secreted, odors are much more noticeable than they were in childhood. Hence, it will be necessary to take more frequent baths to control unpleasant odors. This is particularly important for girls during the menstrual period, when there is an increase in activity of the apocrine glands. Both the apocrine and sebaceous glands become easily clogged and are thought to give rise to pimples and acne. These disturb the individual and frequently much time is spent before the mirror pressing and squeezing the pores in order to remove blackheads and pimples. Usually physicians advise balanced diet, the avoidance of excessive sweets, and careful and regular washing— but not scrubbing—as the best means of having a clear skin. Some do, however, advise washing and the removal of large blackheads by squeezing, being careful to do the squeezing with clean fingers. Since the apocrine glands are closely associated with the functioning of the reproductive system, it is not surprising that some stubborn cases of acne have been successfully treated with the administration of estrogenic hormones. Girls may avoid some embarrassment arising from skin disorders by the judicious use of cosmetics. This may serve the double purpose of camouflaging blemishes and giving them the feeling of being grown up. Much skin disorder can be regarded simply as a passing phase of normal development; and though the adolescent may be able to see many of his peers who have a clear skin at a given time, he may be assured to know that at some time during development others will have some of the difficulty he is experiencing at the moment.

The import of these secondary sex characteristics—breast development, deepening of the voice, the growth of pubic, facial and axillary hair, and changes in the functioning of the skin glands—is that each affords some clue to the degree of maturity achieved by an individual. Attention given to these details will help the adult to understand variations in behavior that are not explicable in terms of size and age alone. Knowledge of these indicators of maturity can also be an important aspect of the adolescent's understanding of himself.

Physiological changes

The idea that the adolescent's heart is too small to support both rapid growth and strenuous physical exercise is a persistent one. Current studies indicate that the great danger of overexertion is in the latter part of the first decade of life. [219:90] Between the ages of four and ten the heart, in comparison with the rest of the body, grows relatively slowly, the lag being greatest at about the age of seven. By the time of puberty, the heart growth more closely parallels growth of the rest of the body. It is true that the heart has not reached adult proportions in adolescence, but it pumps blood into an arterial system that is small and is quite able to do its job. Of course, there are some dangers of overexertion, but the danger lessens rapidly each year after puberty. It has, for example, been recommended that the term "athlete's heart" be abandoned because even strenuous exercise will not damage normal hearts. Nevertheless, young athletes should have close medical supervision because strenuous exercise may harm a heart that is already weakened by other causes. [317] Probably more harm is done by parental anxiety that is passed on to the adolescent than by prestige-seeking basketball coaches who overwork their star players by long hours of practice and refrain from putting the second-rate substitute into a close game.

Blood pressure is a function of age, weight, and maturity. Blood pressure rises just before puberty; and, for a time, the average blood pressure of girls exceeds that of boys. After thirteen years of age the blood pressure of boys increases more rapidly and by sixteen exceeds that of the average girl. As blood pressure increases the pulse rate slows but the heart drives blood with greater force. The trends based on ages are less distinctive than the changes that take place in relation to physiological maturity. For example, when the reference point for girls is the menarche, pulse rate, blood pressure, and oxygen consumption decline steadily [278]—some of these girls are, of course, eleven years old while others are fifteen. Incidentally, these changes are offered as a partial explanation of the reduced vigor and activity of girls in their post-pubertal years. The pulse of children and adolescents responds quickly to exercise and recovery is rapid. The pulse of an older person responds less rapidly to exercise and return to normal takes place more slowly. The contrast is an illustration of the tendency of the more mature organism to be functionally stable. The adaptive capacity of the circulatory system is one explanation of the relatively high level of physical drive in adolescence.

Important implications stem from these developmental trends. Adults must know the developmental level of *an* adolescent before they can properly assess activity, fatigue, drive, and attitudes toward these items. "All such studies present a physiological dilemma, since if a constant amount of work at a constant rate is used in a developmental study, the exercise which may be maximal for the 12-year-old boy becomes mere child's play for the same boy when he reaches the age of 17." *

The digestive system undergoes a number of significant changes during adolescence. The stomach becomes larger and less tubular than in childhood; the walls of the stomach and intestines become thicker and stronger and peristaltic movements are more vigorous. Thus the adolescent can assimilate more food and of greater variety than formerly. These are helpful changes because during the period of accelerated physical growth, when all the physiological alterations that have been described are taking place, there is an increase in food requirements. Some adolescents, particularly those who are relatively free from chronic emotional disturbances, are likely to develop voracious appetites. This need not be alarming if activity levels are high, though there are some difficulties involved when the young person suddenly shifts from vigorous physical exercise to a relatively quiet academic milieu. Another hazard of the demanding appetite of the adolescent is that of between meal snacks. Actually,

---

* Nathan W. Shock, in National Society for the Study of Education, 43rd *Yearbook, Part I, Adolescence* (Chicago: University of Chicago Press; 1944), p. 67.

a snack may be needed. Hot dogs, hamburgers, and milk shakes (soft drinks are currently being seriously questioned because of their relation to dental caries) may be helpful if they are not taken just before a meal where a balanced diet could have been obtained if the appetite had not been just previously satisfied. The tendency of college girls to skip breakfast and have a doughnut and coffee at 10:00, thus taking the edge off appetite for the noon dormitory or sorority meal (where balance is provided by a dietitian) is noteworthy as an example of the harmful practices adolescents may adopt.

Other physiological developments during adolescence include the eruption of more permanent teeth, further progress in the ossification of the bones—in fact, ossification is sometimes used as a measure of maturity—and changes in skeletal structure. The broadening of the hips of girls, to provide for enlarging sex organs, has been noted. In boys there is a broadening of the shoulders and a deepening of the chest with a concomitant increase in lung capacity.

Somatic variations

The fallacy of types

There is a widespread tendency to attempt to classify people into distinct categories. Thus there are saints and sinners, fat and lean men, optimistic and pessimistic, mature and immature, children and adolescents, fifth graders and seventh graders. Actually, these and similar categories tend to confuse rather than to clarify. One person may have in mind a fifth grader who is quite mature while another thinks of a seventh grader who is immature—the two being quite alike in terms of interest and behavior. The man who is pessimistic about his business prospects may be quite optimistic about his children's future. In short, there is a continuousness of differences in any one respect that makes it fallacious to classify people into types.

Psychologists have attempted to classify people on the basis of body build—hoping to discover some predictable personality traits that accompany physique. One of the more notable early attempts was that of E. Kretschmer who divided physique into three categories: (1) asthenic—thin, underdeveloped body, (2) pyknic—

heavy, thickset body, (3) athletic—well-developed, muscular body. [177] The difficulty of classifying people into these types is indicated by the fact that Kretschmer had to add a fourth category, the dysplastic, which is a mixture—pyknic legs and asthenic trunk, for example. Kretschmer did find some relation between body build and the type of mental illness a person would have if he broke down. The asthenic was more likely to have schizophrenia and the pyknic was more likely to suffer from manic-depressive psychoses. The relationship between body build and normal personality was less susceptible to prediction.

Varieties of physique

The fact that body types cannot be sharply differentiated does not mean that there is no relation between physique and personality. The search for relationships is continuing under the leadership of William H. Sheldon, who hopes to provide a new framework for psychology: "It has been growing increasingly plain that the situation [interpretations of human life] calls for a biologically oriented psychology, or one taking for its operational frame of reference a scientifically defensible description of the *structure* (together with the behavior) of the human organism itself." * His study avoids the error of discrete types by providing for continuity of measurement. Three focal types are postulated: endomorph—abdominal predominance (fat men, relatively little skin in proportion to bulk covered); mesomorph—predominance of bone and muscle (athletic type); and ectomorph—lean body, delicate bones, large skin surface in proportion to bulk. The measurements of a person's build are summarized in a three digit number, 7 indicating the maximum of that type and 1 indicating the minimum. Thus an extreme endomorph would be coded as 7–1–1, an extreme mesomorph as 1–7–1, and one who was predominantly ectomorph would be 1–1–7. Such extremes occur very rarely, combinations such as 4–3–4, 2–5–2, or 4–4–4 are more likely to be found (the sum of the digits does not

---

* William H. Sheldon, *The Varieties of Temperament* (New York: Harper & Brothers; 1949), p. xv. See also Sheldon and Others, *The Varieties of Human Physique*, 1940, and *The Varieties of Temperament*, 1942, both published by Harper & Brothers. Material quoted above is used by permission of Dr. Sheldon and the publishers.

have to be nine). With this flexible system Sheldon has studied at least seventy-six different combinations in terms of degree of the focal type possessed. In addition to the purely bodily differences Sheldon sometimes found it necessary to refer to such "secondary" features as hirsutism, texture of the skin, and the possession of sex characteristics typical of the opposite sex. Thus there is considerable flexibility in his approach.

Physique and personality

The relationship between somatotype and personality is of particular interest in the psychology of adolescence.

Names have been given to the three correlated groups of traits. *Viscerotonia,* the first component, in its extreme manifestations is characterized by general relaxation, love of comfort, sociability, conviviality, gluttony for food, for people, and for affection. The viscerotonic extremes are people who "suck hard at the breast of mother earth" and love physical proximity with others. The motivational organization is dominated by the gut and by the function of anabolism. The personality seems to center around the viscera. The digestive tract is king, and its welfare appears to define the primary purpose of life.

Somatotonia, the second component, is roughly a predominance of muscular activity and of vigorous bodily assertiveness. The motivational organization seems dominated by the soma. These people have vigor and push. The executive department of their internal economy is strongly vested in their somatic muscular systems. Action and power define life's primary purpose.

Cerebrotonia, the third component, is roughly a predominance of the element of restraint, inhibition, and of the desire for concealment. Cerebrotonic people shrink away from sociality as from too strong a light. They "repress" somatic and visceral expression, are hyperattentional, and sedulously avoid attracting attention to themselves. Their behavior seems dominated by the inhibitory and attentional functions of the cerebrum, and their motivational hierarchy appears to define an antithesis to both of the other extremes.*

---

* William H. Sheldon, *The Varieties of Temperament* (New York: Harper & Brothers; 1942), p. 10–11. Quoted by permission of Dr. Sheldon and the publishers.

Of course, we are all acquainted with individuals whose body types would not seem to accord with the kind of personality revealed in their daily lives. There are tall, thin boys who seem to enjoy the vigorous pursuit of athletics that is purportedly more natural to the mesomorph. Some heavy-set, chunky individuals are interested in scholarly pursuits and engage in contemplative behavior. There are athletic-looking persons who enjoy eating and fellowship and who love comfort. No doubt the kind of culture in which an individual has lived, especially the tone and interest of family life, does much to shape these personality orientations. The fact of differences in personality cannot be ignored, however, and it is entirely possible that bodily structure plays a part in the *tendencies* to develop in a given direction. Certainly, those who attempt to interpret the behavior of adolescents cannot blithely endorse the behavioristic tendency to explain everything on the basis of education, environment, and experience.

"But," runs the argument, "how does one explain the fact that the athletic-appearing (mesomorph) individual does become a scholar?" Environment is the answer. Another question must be asked: "Does the development of a personality that is not in accord with a person's body type predispose him to mental breakdown?" For example, will forcing young persons into athletics, dancing, intense scholarship also force them toward emotional instability? Even if body-type is discredited as a cause, parents and teachers well might ask themselves if in their attempt to make boys and girls into musicians, serious students, competitive individuals, or social "butterflies" they do not cause an otherwise adequately adjusting person to become tense, uncertain, and unhappy. Some youngsters can be happy sitting and watching others dance, compete, and carry off scholarship awards.

There is another unanswered question: Does not the growth of some adolescents tend to change their body build—though Sheldon believes a child can be accurately somatotyped by the age of six? Despite the question, the following conclusions seem to be warranted: (1) Sheldon's morphology should be viewed with an open mind because it provides for continuous variation of differences rather than discrete types. (2) Personality must be interpreted on the basis of inherent factors as well as environmental influences.

(3) Young persons may be presently well adjusted and still not fit some popular stereotype. (4) Those who work with young persons should respect their socially acceptable inclinations (whether innate or acquired).

Strength and skills in adolescence

Strength

Physical strength increases rather steadily during the first twenty years of life, with periods of acceleration at about the age of six and again at puberty. In a study of six thousand boys and girls it has been found that up to the age of about thirteen the sexes are about even in manual strength but after that boys are markedly superior. Manual strength increases markedly for boys in the teen years—they double their strength from six to eleven and double it again by the age of sixteen. Since the most marked increases in physical strength take place after about the age of fifteen it is felt that strength may be a rather sensitive indicator of phases of maturity. [165:101] However, strength in general does not follow a uniform pattern. There are marked differences in the ages at which specific increases, such as grip, shoulder thrust, shoulder pull, high jump, broad jump, chinning, and push-ups, occur. However, in every measure of strength it is found that typically the post-pubescent individual is measurably superior to the pre-pubescent subject. Exceptions to the generality are those that might be expected in terms of individual variations in body build—the mesomorphic individual tends to be superior to his ectomorphic peer who is in the same phase of physiological development. There are a number of measures of physical development, but no one of them has proven to be entirely reliable in measuring strength. [147:365] A combination of measures provides the best index to physical fitness.

Sex differences in strength are quite variable. Boys excel girls of the same age in strength of grip, but girls are less likely to be surpassed in leg strength. One measure in which girls are superior is in inward thrust (clasping), a measure in which they achieve practically adult status at the age of about thirteen. It has been speculated that this is a true sex difference based upon the muscular development supporting the breasts. [165:106] In other measures girls have their accelerated growth earlier than do boys but quickly lose their approximately equal status as boys reach their puberty. It is the consensus of those who have studied this phase of adolescence that, aside from the earlier onset of acceleration of gain in strength, the differences between boys and girls are largely ones of cultural influence. Girls need strength in order to function efficiently, but beyond a variable minimum there is no expectation or prestige pressure which encourages a girl to the activity and exercise that will develop into an *ability* the potential she has in the form of capacity. In fact, the development of strength in a girl may lead to problems of adjustment because she may be called a tomboy. Finally, in regard to sex differences in strength, it should again be observed that the differences between the sexes are less than the differences within a sex. Because heredity, diet, relative frequency of disease, and opportunity for and encouragement of exercise are all conditioning factors in strength, there are wide individual differences and some girls will exceed some normal boys.

Contrary to the popular cliche, "Strong back—weak mind," there appears to be little correlation between strength and intelligence. At the extremes of intelligence, however, there are some noticeable differences. Feeble-minded children as a group tend to be relatively weak, and L. M. Terman found that gifted children were above the generality in many physical measurements, including that of strength. [309:20] This finding accords with other factors in development—namely, that taller, heavier and earlier maturing adolescents tend to have greater strength than those who are shorter, lighter, and develop at a later chronological age.

Motor performance

Motor performance has to do with deftness and accuracy of coordinated movements. Motor skills, like strength, play an important part in the adjustment of the individual and, especially for boys, are vital factors in the establishment of self-esteem. Attempts have been made to find a central factor of motor ability, or general motor capacity, but these endeavors have failed because there is great variability among the various measures. Superiority in one skill does not uniformly, or even usually, accompany superiority in another. John E. Horrocks, after analyzing a number of studies, concludes that there is neither a general motor ability nor is there complete specificity of skills; that is, some measures do show a moderate correlation. [147:356] (See Glossary.) There is a regular increase in motor skills with advancing age despite accelerated growth in skeleton, height, and weight. Thus there is no foundation for the popular notion that adolescents are awkward because they are adolescents. Such awkwardness as exists must be attributed to criticism and ridicule of more advanced peers and adults, which results in cumulative embarrassment. "It is obvious that neither an ashamed self-consciousness nor an attempt to hide a lack of skill by withdrawing from any practice of it will have a favorable effect upon further development in this area." *

Sex differences in skills are quite informative since girls tend to be about equal to boys in such things as the 50 yard dash, jump and reach, broad jump, distance throw, and the Brace test † at the age of twelve. After this age the differences become more marked in favor of the boys. Since skills depend not only upon innate capacity but also upon extrinsic factors such as motivation, exercise, diet, and health it is to be expected that at least part of the boys' superiority is due to cultural influences rather than sex *per se*. This same generalization will hold for the differences existing among boys— which are far greater than the differences between the average boy and the average girl. Hence it is important that plans for young people take into consideration the factors that enhance or inhibit the optimum development of innate capacity.

Implications of the development of strength and skills

As was indicated earlier, the possession of strength and skills beyond a variable minimum is relatively unimportant for girls; but for boys muscles and motor performance are of an importance hardly to be underestimated. [131] The adolescent boy is expected (and he expects) to be manly, athletic, rugged, and sportsmanlike. If he can live up to expectations he has gone a long way toward social acceptance and the development of a mentally healthful self-

* Harold E. Jones and Robert H. Seashore, in National Society for the Study of Education, *43rd Yearbook, Part I, Adolescence* (Chicago: University of Chicago Press; 1944). p. 124.

† A widely used test of motor performance, which includes a variety of tests of bodily coordination and acrobatic agility.

assurance. If he fails to satisfy himself and to earn prestige by virtue of some degree of athletic proficiency, he may have to seek compensation in other ways—sometimes ways that are subject to strong adult disapproval.

The importance of strength and motor performance in a boy's adjustment are demonstrated in a study made by H. E. Jones. [164:157] It was found, in ten cases, that those who possessed strength, good physique, and physical fitness tended to have social prestige, popularity, and satisfactory personal adjustment. Nine of these boys were above average in height and weight, eight of them were above the average of their classmates in physical ability, and eight of them were advanced in skeletal maturation. Of ten boys in the group of low physical strength, eight were below average in weight though their height was about average. Their health history and present health records were poor; nine of them had marked susceptibility to illness. These ten low-strength boys were not necessarily disliked by classmates but there was a tendency for them to be ignored. Six of them were shy and retiring. Their lack of popularity was reflected in, or at least accompanied by, poor scores on personal adjustment inventories—six of them were considered to be definitely maladjusted by the end of adolescence. These findings corroborate an earlier study by F. M. Thrasher of Chicago gangs, in which it was found that athletic skill, gameness, and daring were necessary for the boys who hoped to be leaders of their peers. [315:345] It has been found that improvement of poise and confidence results from the development of skills. Training in motor skills lessens the prevalence of fears and makes it less probable that a child will resign himself to "taking a back seat." [161:7] Inasmuch as health and physique are a part of personality it is to be expected that the approximation of mature size, strength, and skills would be assets to the individuals who are seeking prestige, approval, and independence. However, the reader must be cautioned against deciding that maturity is all there is to leadership and popularity. In a study of pubertal status and leadership, A. J. Latham found that only in athletic leadership was there a statistically significant superiority of mature over immature boys. In elective and appointive positions biological maturity does not seem to be a significant influence. [184]

Minimum implications of these data include two items. First, it is important that adolescents be led to make comparisons with themselves. They should evaluate growth in terms of where they are now in contrast to what they were six months or a year ago. The Wetzel Grid is a step in this direction in terms of height and weight. Physical education programs in the school should be so designed as to provide for the exercise of varied skills which will meet individual differences. Thus, instead of simply providing for athletics there should be opportunities for acrobatic skills, dancing, posture exercises, and even instruction in how to walk. Girls as well as boys will gain from dancing activities that include folk dancing, ballroom dancing, and creative dancing. Manual training and work in the household arts can be included in a comprehensive approach to the teaching of skills.

Second, guidance should promote the development of indirect compensatory activities—which would not exclude direct attempts to develop skills like those mentioned in the preceding paragraph. Indirect compensation would mean instruction in music, hobbies, school clubs, dramatics, and reading—activities that would provide satisfactions for those who did not make the school team. The adolescent's evaluation of physical prowess is not an inherent tendency. It is a cultural imposition and can be modified by guidance that stresses other kinds of values. Compensating activities are not frills in education, they are considerations designed to promote the rounded development of efficient adulthood.

A big handicap to the implementing of these two minimum considerations is overemphasis on athletics. For at least three decades educators have been criticizing the stress placed on interscholastic activities with the goal of championships; but in many instances the situation shows little improvement. It is still true that the development of "first" teams curtails the intramural program. "There are promising developments in the eradication of bad educational practices. Secondary schools, through their national, regional, state and local organizations, have an important role to play with colleges and universities in the elimination of current abuses in our athletic programs . . ." * These activities deserve the strong support of those

---

* Lloyd S. Michael, "What's the Score in Athletics?—In Secondary Education," *National Education Association Journal*, 42:16, 1953.

who are interested in the all-round development of all adolescents. The arguments that interscholastic games build sportsmanship, that they support the activities that do not pay, that they build stadiums and gymnasiums, are frequently reiterated and must be met in terms of sound educational objectives. It must be admitted that the local citizens are enthusiastic about championships, but it is equally obvious that these citizens have been financially responsive to public relations programs that have soundly presented the facts concerning the proper and expanding functions of education.

A third possible implication of strength and skills considerations has to do with the fact that we live today more or less in a state of preparation for war. In World War II there were 1,250,000 medical discharges for men between the ages of 18 and 37 (presumably in the prime of life physically), about two-thirds of which were for physical disability. [264] Since only a small proportion of physical defects are congenital, it seems evident that schools should carry on both a remedial and preventive physical education program. An athletic program that helps every boy to achieve near his potential thus has its place not only in optimum development of the individual but in the nature of our national life. Personal satisfaction and health must be the objectives of such a program rather than the enhancement of the reputation of a coach.

The health of the adolescent

Diet

"You are what you eat" is not quite an accurate expression but diet does have marked influences upon growth, bone development, muscular tonus, vitality, intellectual functioning, and health. Despite the fact that nutrition plays a large role in the present height and weight superiority of the average individual of today over the average a few decades ago, the perfect diet has not been defined or utilized. Since adolescents are justifiably concerned about health and physique, it is important that their leaders apply some of the knowledge extant about diet.

James Rorty, reporting on experiments taking place at Cornell University, states that the tendency to overeat and to consume high caloric foods leads to obesity, lack of vigor, shortened life, and susceptibility to disease. [261] The fact that the experiments were conducted on rats should not dim the observations that are made in parallel human activities. The use of white bread, refined sugar, and prepared foods are dietary habits that American people are loathe to break. [260] On the other hand, there are assets in the category of diet in the form of rapid transportation that makes perishable foods marketable, techniques for freezing foods, and the variety of palatable foods offered for sale. The liabilities can be off-set by educating people to demand the good foods that *could* be available and to *use* those that are now available.

Milk is a good food at all ages and is needed in the development of strong bones and teeth. It has been shown that addition of milk to the diet of school children improved their physique, their general health, *and* their mental alertness. [39:141] A striking example of the important role of milk is afforded in the case of "The Red-Headed Africans," a deficiency disorder of certain African Negroes. Goats are almost unknown in this region and cows cannot survive because of the prevalence of sleeping sickness. After children are displaced from the mother's breast their hair often becomes pre-maturely white or reddish, tissues are waterlogged, fatty degeneration of the liver ensues, and there is a characteristic skin rash. Fortunately, the condition can often be cured in a few weeks by sup-plying dry skimmed milk reconstituted with water. [45] Adolescent boys and girls who avoid milk because they fear that they will be-come fat should know that excessive caloric intake is the main factor causing obesity and that milk is an all-round food that performs many valuable functions in body economy.

The role of milk in the diet is simply illustrative of the necessity of giving attention to nutritional requirements. Muscular develop-ment requires proteins, inorganic salts are needed for the nerves, and calcium is necessary for the normal functioning of the heart. Vitamins of various types are essential to vision, glandular func-tioning, dental development, mineralization of the bones, intellec-tual development, and resistance to disease. These vitamins seem to be best provided in the regular diet because in pill form there are frquently some unpleasant results from overdosage. Carbohydrates and fats are required for the energy adolescents sometimes use ex-travagantly in order to keep up with their own demands for acting grown-up. Recommended daily dietary allowances for adolescents are listed in Table 2, page 170.

TABLE 2   **Dietary Allowances for Adolescents** *

DIETARY FACTOR	GIRLS 13–15 YEARS 108 POUNDS	GIRLS 16–20 YEARS 119 POUNDS	BOYS 13–15 YEARS 103 POUNDS	BOYS 16–20 YEARS 141 POUNDS
Calories	2600	2400	3200	3800
Protein, grams	80	75	85	100
Calcium, grams	1.3	1.0	1.4	1.4
Iron, mg.	15	15	15	15
Vitamin A, IU	5000	5000	5000	5000
Thiamine, mg.	1.3	1.2	1.5	1.8
Riboflavin, mg.	2	1.8	2.5	2.5
Niacin, mg.	13	12	15	18
Ascorbic acid, mg.	80	80	90	100
Vitamin D, IU	400	400	400	400

* Recommended Dietary Allowances, Revised 1945, Food and Nutrition Board, National Research Council, Circular Series, No. 122, Washington, D. C., 1945.

Caloric needs will, however, vary with height and weight (see subsection, "Evaluating height-weight changes") and activity. Boys participating in interscholastic athletics can eat, and they need, substantially larger than average amounts of food. A high school coach, himself overweight, warned his players that "people dig their graves with their forks." Some of his boys lost weight, becoming markedly more irritable and less efficient as performers, in their attempt to heed his advice. After vacations, when activity levels have been high, and a return to the quieter regime of school work it may be advisable to cut the amount of food consumed. Another danger point in diet, mentioned above, is the tendency of hungry adolescents to eat unwisely between regular meals. The excessive consumption of candies can be condemned for the same reasons as well as for the threat to good dental hygiene.

Sleep

The old Puritan statement, "Six hours of sleep for a man, seven for a woman, and eight for a fool," is not an adequate standard. There are individual differences in sleep requirements. The youngster and his parents should study their unique individual needs and see that each one's schedule provides for plenty.

If a person can answer "No" to the following questions he is probably getting sufficient sleep: Do I get drowsy during the day? Do I sleep so deeply that it is difficult to awake? Do I fall asleep immediately on "hitting the pillow?" Am I still drowsy after arising? If the answer to these questions is "Yes" it may be desirable to provide for a longer sleeping period.

If young people could be persuaded to take cat naps during the day they could replenish their bodies and energy before rapid rates of fatigue had begun. Since it is improbable that they will be persuaded to do this, at least they might be taught how to relax physically during those moments when they are waiting for a bus, for a class to start, or for a meal.*

Accidents

The second greatest cause of death among adolescent boys comes under the heading of accidents. From the age of fifteen to nineteen there is a marked increase in the accident rate. This is probably due to the larger sphere of activities and the need to be daring and adventuresome. Automobile accidents are the most prevalent and are of particular interest because they illustrate the discrepancy in growth rates of various traits and functions. Although the reaction time of adolescents is at or near its peak and strength and coordination are nearing their maxims, their judgment and reason are far from mature. Physically their ability to drive is more than adequate, but the accident rates show that psychologically they are (as a group) poor drivers. Fortunately, psychological readiness for driving can be improved by instruction. Youngsters who have learned to drive from trained instructors, who supplement teaching with

---

* Edmund Jacobson, *You Must Relax,* Third Edition (New York: Whittlesey House; 1948, 304 pp.) gives a detailed description of how to learn to relax mentally and physically.

safety education, have excellent records for safe operation of vehicles. Those interested in the welfare of youth will do well to
support and encourage driver training classes in our schools. (See
Chapter Thirteen.)

School athletic programs are a source of injury. The danger to the
heart has been mentioned; there is also danger to the joints and
catilaginous structure. [194] The threat is greatest during the
periods of rapid growth and it is therefore important that physical
education programs be planned to avoid blows, shocks, and excessive
strain.

Disease.

The greatest single cause of death in adolescence, in the 15–19
age bracket, is tuberculosis. In the 10–14 age group it is also the
greatest cause of female deaths—automobile accidents take the
greatest toll among boys at these ages. Appendicitis, pneumonia, and
endocarditis are among the high-ranking causes of death during all
the teen years. Venereal disease, while not a high ranking cause of
death, deserves attention because 25 per cent of all cases are in the
age group below twenty. Many of the recorded cases in the age
groups above twenty are of long standing, the venereal disease having
been acquired earlier. [153]

Sex differences in health and hygiene

Girls have less energy and muscular development than do their
male peers. This is *partially* explicable in terms of the higher protein
metabolism of boys, who have a smaller tendency to generate fatty
tissue. In part, these differences may be due to the lack of social pressures which promote physical activity. Thus girls between the 7th
and 12th grades sometimes seek to be excused from their physical
education classes. Their lack of desire to participate reinforces the
natural tendency to an increase of fatty deposits. [195] Here is an
excellent example of the interaction between innate and cultural
factors in the development of the individual.

Girls, it has been shown, are quite susceptible to tuberculosis. This
is probably due to a combination of factors, among which might be
included (1) their lack of participation in outdoor sports, (2) the
physical drain of puberty, which is relatively more rapid than it is

in boys, and (3) the expectation that they will work in the home—after a full day at school. It is important for all adolescents, and especially for girls, to have emphatic lessons in health and hygiene that stress the importance of well-balanced diet, regular rest and sleep, and appropriate regimes of exercise.

Approaches to better health

Teachers are in a better position to teach the lessons of health and hygiene than are parents. Many adolescents have the feeling that their parents' concern is just a way to restrict their liberty and independence; yet, because they are not completely ready for independence, they turn to another adult whom they know well—their teacher. A program of health and hygiene might well include the items dealt with in the schools of Arlington County, Virginia: [108]

Knowing your body
American Red Cross junior first-aid course
Contributions of posture, exercise, nutrition, rest, and sleep to personal fitness
Mental health, heredity, and current research on health
Dating and boy-girl relationships
Reproduction—with a view to eradicating erroneous beliefs
Polio, cancer, and wonder drugs
Narcotics and alcohol
Driver education—with emphasis on attitudes
Disease, community health, health agencies, and preparation for marriage

These topics are guides; no two classes are alike because each class is tailored to the members' needs and interests. Field trips, group research, panel discussions, moving pictures, and outside speakers are used to supplement and complement text books and references.

It should not be difficult to motivate effective instruction in health and physical fitness. Adolescents are, as a group, interested in their bodies and their approach to maturity. They are interested in the approval of their peers—boys know the importance of health and skills. Girls *should* know that their popularity among both boys and girls will depend more on their vitality and good humor than it does on figure and size. The unity of mind and body should be appreciated by the adolescent—and by teachers. Whatever can be done to improve the health and hygiene of the adolescent is an integral part of the approach to the totality of optimum development during adolescence.

Summary

Physical development is the result of environmental pressures playing upon inherent potentials. The adolescent's attitude toward himself and his development should be conditioned by a knowledge of the wide variations of normality in size and in time of accelerated development and the consequent necessity for making comparisons with his former status. Changes in endocrine functioning form the basis of changes in body economy and functioning that condition energy supply, personal interests, and social activities. The secondary sex characteristics—changes in voice, body proportions, growth of hair, and musculature—are often quite perplexing because individual variations are so noticeable. Differences in secondary sex characteristics have a noticeable parallel in body types— which may possibly have intimate relationships to basic personality trends. Both adolescents and their counselors should recognize differing orientations and avoid the temptation to make everyone conform to "the average."

Strength and skills are important, particularly to the adolescent boy, because his prestige and popularity are intimately related to his status in these areas. Skills and posture are important to girls not only from the standpoint of prestige but because they constitute a reflection of the individual's concept of self. It is incumbent upon leaders of adolescents to provide for the variety of interests and potentialities that will enable each one to come closer to the realization of his potential. Furthermore, compensating activities should be planned for those whose potential is so low that there is little likelihood of their receiving direct satisfaction from strength and skills.

No realistic program for the physical health of adolescents could be complete without consideration of the factors of diet, sleep, rest, and recreation. Direct instruction in these areas is needed so that the adolescent can appreciate his own responsibility and assume increasing degrees of self-direction. Instruction dealing with accident and disease has proven to be highly effective, but present statistics show that there is still a long way to go. The phenomena of psychosomatic illness and accident proneness show that there is an inevitable mind-body unity. A knowledge of physical factors in adolescence is an essential facet in a complete understanding of the maturing individual.

STUDY AND REVIEW ITEMS

1. What difficulties, related to physical development, did you have in your adolescent years? Could these be considered as typical?

2. What could you say to reassure the adolescent who is a late maturer? To reassure the early maturer?

3. Do you think that there is any more, or less, reason for the adolescent to be disturbed by endocrine changes than for the woman who is experiencing the menopause?

4. How much, and in what way, should boys and girls, aged twelve or thirteen, be instructed in sex development and function?

5. Assume that you are a teacher of teen-age boys, describing secondary sex characteristics, and the boys begin to giggle. How would you handle the situation?

6. Do you believe that there is a basic relation between fundamental personality trends and body build?

7. How much of the differences in strength, skill, and health between boys and girls do you think is cultural and how much is physiological?

8. What compensating activities might be suggested for a mature but physically weak fifteen-year-old boy of normal intelligence?

9. Do you think that preparation for military service should be an objective of a physical education program?

10. What do you believe would be an adequate program of physical education for girls from the age of twelve to eighteen?

11. What important factors in health do you think have been omitted from this chapter?

12. Describe some approaches to health education that you think would be most impressive to adolescents.

RECOMMENDED SUPPLEMENTARY READING

Bernard, Harold W. *Toward Better Personal Adjustment* (New York: McGraw-Hill Book Company, Inc.; 1951), pp. 46–79.
Some details of physical health, of particular interest and importance to high school and college students, are described. Mind-body relationships, sleep, diet, the need for exercise and play, and the proper use of drugs are discussed in terms of immediate application.

Diehl, Harold S. *Textbook of Healthful Living,* 5th Edition (New York: McGraw-Hill Book Company, Inc.; 1955), Chapter 1.
"The Possibilities of Longer Life and Better Health" depend on our application of knowledge since the limits of life have not changed since antiquity. The major causes of death in recent years, health in the armed forces, and preventable causes of death are among the topics considered.

Gallagher, J. Roswell. *You and Your Health* (Chicago: Science Research Associates, Inc.; 1950), 48 pp.
This readable booklet, addressed to teen agers, presents sound facts regarding normality, attitudes, diet, physical fitness, the avoidance of disease, and the prevention of accidents. Some questions frequently asked by adolescents are answered.

National Society for the Study of Education, 43rd Yearbook, Part I, *Adolescence* (Chicago: University of Chicago Press; 1944), pp. 8–142.
These six chapters, by outstanding authorities, deal with facts (and their interpretation) about physical changes, body build, physiological changes, development of strength, and the nature and role of motor and mechanical skills. Each chapter is richly documented.

Seidman, Jerome M. (Ed.) *The Adolescent—A Book of Readings* (New York: The Dryden Press; 1953), pp. 88–138.
The three recommended chapters deal with (1) the characteristics and variations of normal adolescent growth, (2) metabolism, respiration, and

endocrine changes, and (3) the relation of nutrition to rounded development.

Sollenberger, Richard T., in R. G. Kuhlen and G. G. Thompson (Eds.) *Psychological Studies of Human Development* (New York: Appleton-Century-Crofts, Inc.; 1952), pp. 34–40.

Endocrine factors play some role in personality development, but what that role is is not clearly known. Sollenberger finds some correlation of behavior with the changed endocrine functioning at adolescence but indicates that the relationships are complex and not due to hormonal changes alone.

AUDIO-VISUAL MATERIAL

Heredity and Pre-Natal Development (McGraw-Hill Book Company, Inc., 330 W. 42nd St., New York 36), 21 min., so., b. & w.

A step-by-step picture of growth, division, and eventual union of male and female sex cells. Heredity, development of the fetus, delivery, and some of the early activity of the neonate are other aspects shown.

Human Reproduction (McGraw-Hill Book Company, Inc.), 21 min., so., b. & w.

Models and realistic drawings are used to show sex functions and anatomy of both sexes. Conception and birth are shown in a factual and technical manner. Suitable for college but of questionable value for high school.

The Story of Menstruation (International Cellucotton Products Company, 919 N. Michigan Ave., Chicago 11), 10 min., so., color.

This free film is a Walt Disney animated production which shows just why and how menstruation takes place. It gives authentic advice on how girls should care for themselves, emphasizing the desirability of healthy everyday living. A teaching guide is available.

What are the characteristics of good parents for adolescents? Why must youth-parent conflict be regarded as normal? What are the problems faced by the parents of adolescents?

CHAPTER SIX

The Adolescent and His Parental Home

All of the wide differences in the personality and behavior of adolescents cannot be attributed to varied rates and potentials of physical growth. An extremely potent force in the life of the growing individual is his home—the prevailing tone of parent relationships, parent-child and sibling relationships, and the material status of the home. The infant is born a plastic, pliable, permeable being who immediately begins to absorb feelings about himself and his world—this is reflected in the present belief that mothers should sleep with, feed, and cuddle their newborn babies while still in the hopital. The constancy of home and parental influences is reflected in the speed with which we say of a delinquent, "It's his home—his parents are at fault." Not only does child behavior reflect parental behavior but the influence continues into the adult years. L. M. Terman has found that the most important single predictive factor in happiness in marriage is the happiness of the parental home. [307:370] Sometimes the reflection is distorted. The individual, instead of copying his parents, repudiates them and acts in a directly opposite manner. That is, the aggressive parent rears a submissive child, kindly and friendly parents may have selfish and seclusive children. [304]

The student of adolescence must, however, avoid the temptation of ascribing too much to family influence. Besides the physical and physiological factors there are community influences, school influences, and the unique reaction that each individual spins for himself out of the environmental pressures that stimulate potential. The developmental task (see Chapter Three) of emancipation from the parental home is, for example, dependent upon parent personality, physical, intellectual, and emotional factors and upon education and community behavior patterns.

Basic considerations

No typical home

There is no such thing as a typical home. In every phase of the home that we could name there are countless variations in quality and amount. In some homes parents live in a cheerful, cooperative, mutually helpful, and respectful relationship; in another there is tolerance, indifference, but peace; in still another there is open hostility. One home may have a mentally healthy, happy, and confident divorcee as the sole adult while another has both parents and a set of grandparents who are loved and appreciated by all. Again there may be one parent (who has proven himself difficult to live with) or two parents and one grandparent who are at odds with one another and who alternately and unpredictably attack or abet the actions of the adolescent. The home may be a two-room affair down by the river with no yard and no paint, or it may be a twelve-room brick Colonial with large rooms and four baths—with quarters for the maid over the brick garage. The income may be such that the adolescent cannot dress "fit for school" or such that the seventeen-year-old son not only has access to the new Cadillac but also owns his own Chevrolet. There may be only one child—who is wisely treated by his parents, or badly spoiled. There may be twelve children who are studious, neat, industrious, and respected; or there may be twelve—every one of whom is a menace to the community. Thus differences in family income, material aspects of the house itself, and varied psychological relationships prevail in different homes.

The adult who seeks to understand adolescents must take care to know the home as it really exists rather than to yield to the temptation of thinking that his own home was representative. It is particularly important for teachers, who are predominately of middle-class origin, to realize that the majority of their pupils homes will tend to be, in material aspects, considerably below the level of the teacher's parental home. Of course, some schools in large communities draw pupils largely from homes better than those enjoyed by the teacher.

Still another imponderable in the adolescent's home is too frequently overlooked—namely, his reaction. A case met by the author illustrates the importance of the adolescent's response. Ralph was a seventeen-year-old junior, of athletic build, large but not so far above average as to be disconcerting, good looking, and in excellent health. He had an IQ of about 115 on the Otis Quick Scoring Test, he did good school work and was well liked by his teachers. A variety of hobby and reading interests made it possible for him to contribute soundly to class activities. There was no football in his high school but he was a good first-string performer on the baseball and basketball teams. He was popular with both the boys and girls in the school; he could dance well; he was neither a leader nor was he withdrawn. His fifteen-year-old sister admired him and he saw to it that she had a good time at parties and dances. His middle-class home was as good as the average in the community. His home, as seen by his classmates and teachers, was superior in a psychological sense. His parents liked young people and made them welcome guests when they came to play games, visit, and play the phonograph. He had boxing gloves, skis, skates, baseball equipment, boys' books, and a subscription to *Boys' Life*. He had an allowance and, because of his maturity, was able to earn good money at part-time jobs. Yet, despite his advantages, his behavior became increasingly troublesome. He kept late hours, was reported drunk on several occasions, and visited brothels in a neighboring community. He was finally apprehended by the authorities for having been involved in a brawl with the "bouncer" in the local pool hall—a place forbidden to adolescents. Oddly, it was the untrained sheriff, not Ralph's teachers, who discovered the cause of his deviant behavior. His father, in order to supplement his income as a carpenter, took a part-time position as the pastor of one of the three local churches.

Ralph felt that this was a rather sissy thing to do and in order to prove that he was a man among men and not a "Preach" as his classmates called him, played the part of the big man about town. It is gratifying to report that his sound background and understanding parents, coupled with his own fundamental worth, easily straightened him out. Apparently his one encounter with the law was sufficient to bring him to his senses. After the brief flurry of gossip, he again assumed his place in school and among his age mates.*

The normality of conflict

It is a popular notion that "the course of love never runs smoothly." Psychologists are currently stressing a parallel theme, "Conflict in adjustment is normal." We can go further and say that conflict is not only normal, it is desirable. In a way of life in which freedom of choice and action is both a characteristic and an ideal, it is inevitable that there are going to be alternatives both of which are attractive. Selecting one is perplexing, and after the choice some element of disappointment ensues. An important lesson of life is to learn to make choices and to stop ruing what might have been. Thus, experience that gives exercise in the making of choices, and involves conflict, is a desirable aspect of healthful living. The thing we wish to avoid is continued and unresolved conflict that leads to chronic frustration and personality disintegration. Seeds for the continuation of conflict are sown by the extremes of (1) asking children to make choices for which they are unprepared and (2) making decisions for children that are chronically at odds with their own wishes and orientations.

Even in the best of family situations for the adolescent, it must be expected that there will be some conflict—between siblings and between children and their parents. If there is no conflict it is probable that an unhealthy situation exists. Either the youngster is so

---

* It is the author's conviction that the individual's response is often slighted in case studies. The investigator is advised to obtain health data, psychological data, information about the home, siblings, parents, school history, and the like— all of which are important. But a detailed analysis of the individual's feelings is also of basic importance. This can be obtained by teachers through free writing, observation, and, after the establishment of sound rapport, formal and informal interviews.

cowed that he does not resist parental edict and authority, or the parent is so lacking in authority that he offers no resistance to the wishes and whims of the adolescent. In either case the absence of overt conflict is no guarantee that internal conflict has not reached the unhealthy state of frustration.

Parents, though sometimes superficially disturbed by the revolt of their children, should appreciate opposition as a healthy indication of approach to maturity. Parental consistency is desirable, but it might be well if parents would occasionally say "No" when they actually hoped that the child or adolescent would keep pressing until a "Yes" was elicited. Too often parents hope to see their children persevere in the face of difficulties—yet the same parents feel ineffective unless they win on every occasion of conflict.

Parents who recognize the normality of conflict should be not just comforted and reassured; they should see in child-parent conflict healthy progress toward the independence of maturity and be gratified. J. R. Gallagher has provided a helpful summarization:

> When understood as a manifestation of thwarted attempts at independence, adolescent rebellion is easier to tolerate. You also find it easier to sit by and see mistakes being made when you know that mistakes today mean fewer in the future. The errors in choice of friends, the poor planning, the low grade in subjects you could have helped your children with, are hard to take—much harder to take than the falls that accompanied those first halting steps. But even as they learned to walk smoothly by being allowed to try, so will they become mature only if you let them do for themselves.
>
> It does not always require restraint to produce signs of rebellion. These young people are less confident than they care to admit; their show of defiance is balanced precariously. Angrily protesting that they are no longer babies, they fear independence and may tomorrow seek the very help they reject today. Small wonder that, being confused and anxious, they behave childishly at times.
>
> Ironically, those adolescents who find the leaving of their parents and the acquisition of independence most difficult may treat their parents the most cruelly. The more the breaking away disturbs them, the more fierce and childish will be their outbursts.*

* J. Roswell Gallagher, "Why They Rebel," *The Atlantic*, June, 1953, 70.

Adult authority and youthful independence

There is definitely a place for adult authority—the right and power to command and decide—in the home life of the adolescent. For one thing, there are the customs and mores of society to which he must learn to adjust and with which he must learn to live. His need to conform to the demands and expectations of society will more easily be realized if he has had appropriate preparatory experiences in the home. There can be no doubt that many of those for whom authority takes the form of iron bars and stone walls once lived in homes where patterns of authority were inappropriate. In the second place, authority helps to build the feelings of security that are so essential to the psychological well-being of an individual. Rather than frustrating the normal individual, authority provides him guides for conduct, without which he would be carrying too big a load in decision making. Motorists do not use the safety rails on mountain highways, or on precipices overhanging the ocean, but the presence of the rails makes them feel comfortable. Authority performs a parallel service for the adolescent. It helps to make him feel comfortable in a situation that might easily become distressing.

The issues at stake in the problem of authority are more easily stated than are the answers. Parents and teachers both ask the question, "When should I state firmly what should or should not be done?" The old answer, equivocal as it is, must be given: "It depends." Some adolescents, because their parents have given them preliminary preparation in making choices and decisions, can be given greater freedom from authority than can others. It depends upon how many people will be affected if a mistake is made. It depends on expenses, the pattern of community life, the security of the parents, on intelligence, and similar factors. But of this we can be sure—that adolescents are capable of acting wisely in a far greater number of situations than anxious parents give them credit for.

Some guiding principles in the exercise of authority that has for an ultimate goal the intelligent self-direction of the individual might well include the following:

1. Firmness is necessary when the whims of the adolescent conflict with the good of the family or with his own ultimate welfare.

2. Adults should learn to yield when the issues at stake are inconsequential; they should not insist on "showing who is boss."

3. A good example should be set. Admonitions regarding speeding, courteous driving, late hours, and smoking are less effective when adults do not observe the behaviors being recommended.

4. The processes of reasoning should be used. Even when the adult must enforce his authority, it is advisable to explain the reasons and listen to counter arguments. M. Farnham describes cases where the adolescent has continued to argue even after he has been convinced of the adult's correctness. [105:83]

5. Look for suitable substitute behaviors. This need not mean sending the daughter to Europe in order to let her forget her love for a certain boy, but it does mean providing some alternatives of choice that will help the adolescent to save face.

6. Use democratic procedures—shared responsibility and shared power. Let the adolescent have a "listened to" voice in the counsels that are to guide his behavior. The late Kurt Lewin and his associates have shown experimentally that such procedures result in pride in workmanship, better personal adjustment, and more wholesome social relationships than do *laissez faire* or autocratic procedures. [190]

The reader who is desirous of seeing a more definitive set of rules to guide the parent of adolescents might reflect that rules pave the way for a type of authoritarian control that is today questioned. Guiding principles which pave the way to the dynamic solution of unique difficulties are helpful in achieving the democratic ideal of authority which is our national ideal. Adults must ask themselves what they are trying to achieve. If the desire is to produce strong, courageous, independent, and self-reliant young people then there must be a progressive loosening of imposed authority. If the goal is to protect the children and make them obedient, then autocratic discipline can and will extend the period of emotional and social infancy. [146:85]

The role of parents: a balanced perspective

Authorities in the field of child and adolescent psychology have so long and so consistently emphasized the role of parents and the home in personality formation that some parents have been over-impressed. If it were true that personality were formed in the first six years of life then there would be little use for the school and no hope for the rehabilitation of the errant. The fact is that growth is a continuous process (see Chapter Two); and contemporary psychologists are finding and reporting more and more evidence that growth, especially in mental and emotional spheres, continues well into the later years—certainly far beyond adolescence. "Behavioral growth in adulthood is often blocked by the confusion with physical growth, which definitely stops in adulthood. Not believing in further personal growth in adulthood, many men do not seek models of maturity beyond their own parents whose level they have already reached." * Such a, now typical, observation should give parents the needed reassurance that if they themselves can grow and change, the errors of the past need not be fatal. It is not too late to provide altered and wiser guidance and support for the probing adolescent. A standard joke regarding adolescents contains an element of truth and hope for parents: Adolescents are frequently surprised to find how much smarter parents have become between the adolescent's fifteenth and twentieth birthdays.

Parents should realize that although the home factors are important they are only some among many factors that must be taken into account. Such a realization will help the parent to assume a more relaxed role. He will then be able to be more calm in the face of conflict and to exercise the necessary authority with improved perspective. Knowledge of the continuity of growth should help the adult achieve perspective. He will realize that, despite the temporary readjustments and rebellion—these are essential parts of growing up—the love and confidence he has given his offspring will become manifest in a wholesomely developing youngster.

Negative home influences

It is unlikely that any home is wholly bad in its effect upon the lives of adolescents, and probably few homes are entirely free from defects. Judging from the large numbers of adolescents who are making wholesome adjustments to their many problems, it is probably accurate to state that the majority of homes should be evalu-

* Ian Stevenson, "Why People Change," *Harpers,* 207, December 1953, 59.

ated as good ones. However, in order to remedy the poor and improve the good, it is pertinent to indicate some of the existing negative home influences.

Abnormal attachments

It happens frequently that when a young person is brought to a psychologist or psychiatrist and contributing factors have been studied, the expert will say, "It is the parent who needs help." Abnormal attachments of the parent for the child may take the form of excessive domination, overprotection, substituting love for the youngster for the love of one's mate, or failing to permit emancipation of the adolescent. All of these are evidences of immaturity on the part of the parent involved, and each will have a unique set of influences. Among the possible etiological factors the following might be found: factors inhibiting growth during the parent's own childhood and adolescence, unsatisfactory marital adjustment, or absence of personal goals that would divert time and energy from preoccupation with parental responsibility. Our concern, however, is with the effect of these attachments on the adolescent. He may react (1) by being openly rebellious and defiant, (2) by passively submitting and remaining childishly dependent, or (3) by developing neurotic tendencies.

An example of the childish, dependent reaction is afforded in the case of Louis C. Louis was a large, good-looking lad, with above-average intelligence, who had flunked out of three different colleges in as many terms. Because his aptitude tests were so promising, the author decided that Louis might be salvageable. Consultation with his high school principal and one of his college advisers revealed that there had been a steady pattern of interference by the mother. In high school she had been present during his registrations, seeing to it that he got the "best teachers" and the right courses; and instructors were informed of Louis's likes and dislikes. Interviews revealed that she had flown across the country three times during one term to consult with his college instructors and advisers. Louis probably could have been popular with the girls, but his mother's concern about having the "right" girl quickly discouraged any female hopefuls.

It was decided that if Louis were to be admitted to a fourth try in college the mother would need some instruction. She readily came to a conference and the situation was brutally revealed to her. Overprotection and maternal domination were explained and the advice was given, "Let Louis make up his own mind if he should try college again, where he should try and what courses should be taken." The advice was futile. Her parting words were, "I'll talk with him and see if I cannot convince him that he should try again." As far as Louis was concerned he was evidently past the point of caring. He seemed perfectly satisfied with things as they were. He did not care whether he went to college or stayed at home and drove about in his convertible. He had no thoughts of going to work. As was the case when he was in high school, he was almost completely indifferent.

We most frequently see these attachments as inhibitions of the adolescent's heterosexual development. The mother who is jealous of the boy friends of her daughter [105:76], the father who thinks his daughter is too good for the boy friends who make themselves available, are inhibiting the development of their youngsters. The sad part of these abnormal attachments is that if the steps toward maturity are not taken at the appropriate time for them it is probable that they can never, without expert aid, be taken. Certainly, the longer the delay the less likelihood there is that the stunting of growth during a particular phase of development will ever be completely compensated for.

The climacteric as a factor in adolescence

It has been noted that at the age of puberty there are a number of marked changes in physiological and endocrine functioning. These changes, at the beginning of the reproductive period, are matched by endocrine and physiological changes at the decline of the reproductive period. The decline is more noticeable in women since menstruation ceases at about the age of forty to fifty years. As the ovaries become less active they fail to produce enough ovarian hormones to counteract the production of gonadotropic hormones by the pituitary and a temporary imbalance of the endocrine system results. "There are many general symptoms, including crises of vasodilatation (hot flashes) in the skin of the head, neck, and upper part of the chest, together with a sensation of suffocation and sweating. Frequently a tendency to obesity appears and sometimes there are signs of virilization (hair growth . . .)." * However, like the onset of puberty, the climacteric is a normal phase of the total developmental process and it is the consensus of authorities that the disturbances of the menopause also stem from tradition. That is, women become depressed because they feel, in a society where their sex role plays a large place in their status, that their period of social and biological usefulness is over. [272:231] Still another parallel between puberty and the climacteric is to be noted: namely, generally good adjustment renders one less susceptible to the trauma of temporary endocrine imbalance.

There is no sharply defined time for the male climacteric, rather there is a steady decline in sexual virility. A. C. Kinsey reports that the decline is partly the result of general physical and psychological fatigue. [173:227] This view is supported by the observation that males in the middle forties sometimes "go astray" as they seek erotic stimulation in a new and younger partner. It is apparently difficult for a man to accept the fact of his declining sexual power; and, blaming his wife for the inadequacy, he seeks and receives a temporary stimulation in new sexual outlets. After a period of such activity he begins to accept the facts and is often ready to "return to the fold" if his wife is sympathetic and tolerant.

These data are presented, not as being of importance *per se* but because of their bearing on the family life of the adolescent. The mother and father both are undergoing personal problems of adjustment that make it somewhat more difficult to understand and withstand some of the marked changes in their adolescent's behavior. The difficulties can best be approached by added efforts on the part of both the younger and older generation to understand and tolerate the behavior of the other. The adolescent should realize that his parents are having some difficulties and attempt to diminish their perplexity by less antagonist resistance to parental suggestions and authority. He must try to realize that the irritability of his mother and the waywardness of his father are not so much fundamental personality orientations as they are manifestations of a passing phase of adjustment. The adults should realize that a part of

* By permission from *Human Physiology* by Bernardo A. Houssay and others. Copyright 1951, McGraw-Hill Book Company, Inc. Pp. 645–646.

the problems of adolescents is dependent upon the view taken of them; that is, parents may be somewhat hypersensitive and hyper-critical because of their own psychological insecurity. Let it be repeated, these are not necessarily characteristics of the family. The observations, however, do hold for *some* adolescents and their parents; and teachers would be well advised to try to clarify the problem by showing adolescents that they have a responsibility to parents.

Indebtedness of the adolescent

A technique used to enforce a parent-adolescent attachment as well as a symptom of strained relations is the feeling that the young person is in debt to his parents. Financially, of course, it must be admitted that young people are liabilities. A few decades ago children and adolescents were of immense value in terms of material well-being. They could help with household chores, perform profitable duties on the farm, and even hire out at an early age as farm, factory, or mine laborers. The changes (mentioned earlier) in household appliances, urbanization and industrialization, changed labor laws, and the extension of education have markedly changed the position of adolescents. That the burden on parents is a real one is shown by the fact that, despite our ideal of education for *all* American youth, there are many who cannot or will not go to school because of the expense of books, clothes and, at the college level, of nominal tuition fees.*

The idea of indebtedness is expressed by reminding the adolescent of the expenses he involves, by suggesting that he get a job "like I did when I was a boy," or by attempting to supervise the spending of an allowance. While it may be admitted that there is some merit in these ideas their expression, like the matter of autocratic authority, can often lead to a heightening of normal conflict. There are several things that can be said in defense of the adolescent. He did not create the contributing conditions and, in all probability, he would cherish a greater degree of financial inde-

---

* In a study of Syracuse High School drop-outs, "lack of personal funds" was second only to the general complaint, "Dissatisfaction with school." Harry P. Smith (Research Director), *Syracuse Youth Who Did Not Graduate* (Syracuse, New York: Board of Education; 1950), pp. 23–25.

pendence. There is the possibility that the desire for ego gratification prompts the parent to prolong the dependence of his offspring. [88:97] He is willing to bear the burden, but he also wants to be sure his efforts are appreciated.

It is equally hazardous to supply freely all the wants and desires of the adolescent. The parents recall their own earlier frustrations— limited wardrobe, restricted leisure activities, curtailed schooling, and tightened budget. They want their offspring to have the best, often not stopping to realize that overcoming obstacles was the very thing that provided them with many satisfactions. Despite their good intentions it is easy, in moments of irritation, to remind the adolescent of what a burden he is. Frequently the adolescent does realize his dependence, and because of his inability to change the situation is all the more resentful when he is reminded of it.

The remedy does not lie in going to work at an early age, nor in leaving home—a common occurrence during the depression years. [201] The solution lies more in the change of attitudes than it does in the change of conditions. Parents must achieve the "developmental task" of adulthood having to do with rearing children. [136:262] This involves taking satisfaction from successful daily living in the home and in work life—satisfaction that will be reflected in the young person's warmth of personality, security, and eagerness for life. The child and the adolescent *owes* his parents nothing—parents must even earn the respect of their children. Parents should develop the emotional maturity that will permit them complete satisfaction at the psychological level of seeing their children make steady progress toward maturity.

Low income

A major factor in a good home for adolescents is the security and maturity of the parents. Certainly in a society where individual worth is to a marked degree judged by material possessions, it is to be expected that the competence and self-respect of parents will be both a cause and outcome of family income. The occupational frustrations of parents must inevitably be reflected in their family life. Statistics would indicate that low income could very probably be the source of considerable difficulty in the typical American family. The United States Bureau of Labor Statistics indicated that an income of from $2,734 to $3,111 a year was needed by a family of four in the thirty-four largest American cities, if prevailing standards were to be met for health efficiency, nurture of children, social participation, and the maintenance of self-respect and the respect of others. [61] Yet over a quarter of all U. S. families in 1950 had incomes of less than $2,000, and about half the families had under $3,000 per year [216:23]

The importance of health, strength, and vigor to the adolescent has been noted. Inasmuch as there is a discernible relation between health status and freedom from physical defects, low income is a contributing factor in some of the physical and personality problems of the adolescent. Actually, the relation between income and health is circular—both are causes and effects—but some of the concomitants of low income, such as occupational hazards, poor housing, inadequate nutrition, and poor medical care limit the realization of the potentiality of some adolescents. [44]

The tendency for traits to be correlated (see Chapter Two) is illustrated by the fact that personality development parallels the above data on health.

Lack of funds is a high ranking reason for not attending school. The problem is particularly acute for low income families. Again, there is a vicious circular relationship. Low income families often live in communities and regions where schools are inadequate for ordinary classroom instruction, yet the highest incidence of disabilities that call for special attention occurs in this category. Moreover, irregular attendance caused by migratory living causes pupils to be retarded and underrated on aptitude tests—this underrating tends to result in further deprivation of opportunity. "The U. S. Wage and Hour Regional Office Division of the Department of Labor found over 480 children under sixteen at work during school hours in New Jersey fields between the beginning of 1951 and November 1952." * In 1950 the Bureau of the Census estimated that over 300,000 children between ten and sixteen were working for wages in agriculture. [217:161] Fortunately, steps are being taken to remedy these conditions—houses and schools for migratory

* Mary H. Vorse, "America's Submerged Class: The Migrants," *Harper's Magazine*, 206, February 1953, 26.

workers are being provided in some states and localities—but much remains to be done before the discouraging circle can be broken. [329]

The usual correlation of traits is reversed when it comes to the matter of personality disturbance. Despite the fact that larger families tend to have the lower incomes, it is the smaller family that experiences the greater number of severe disturbances. It is in the smaller family that broken homes or family tensions most frequently result in poor school achievement (intelligence being equal) and emotional disturbances in youngsters. [99] This observation suggests the cheerful note that the handicap of low income may, at least in some aspects, be compensated for by mature attitudes and behaviors of parents.

High parental expectations

There are three major causes of high parental expectations: (1) a sincere, if over-enthusiastic, desire to have their children have a better chance than the parents had, (2) a feeling that their own worth is judged by the status of their children in competition with those of neighbors, and (3) a compensatory device by which the parent makes up for his own failure by seeing his offspring win honor and prestige.

The middle-class desire to have children "have the advantages" results in pushing them into dancing classes, music lessons, book clubs, athletics, attendance at concerts, extra classes, and youth organizations. In moderation these are commendable activities—in mass they are likely to be disconcerting, if not devastating. Young people need some free-time activities in which they will have to make decisions about the use of their time. If some person or organization constantly supplies activities for them they are deprived of an opportunity to develop initiative.

Evaluating the adolescent solely on the basis of comparison with his relations or neighborhood peers does violence to the need to be deemed a worthy person for himself alone. It is a fundamental of mental hygiene that a person must be accepted for what he *uniquely* is. Actually, comparisons are likely to entail two hazards. First, one may develop feelings of inferiority because some one trait is emphasized at the same time that another trait, equally important, is ignored. Second, comparisons may lead to a state of self-satisfaction when, as a matter of fact, achievement is less than capability. An example of the first and an illustration of how easily and unintentionally damage may be done, is afforded in the case of a high school senior girl. This girl actually was near the head of her class in academic work; she was mature, pretty, and had an enviable figure. Yet one of her teachers discerned that she had hampering feelings of inferiority. The parents knew better than to make direct references to her achievement—but in family discussion and in conversation with friends it was always a cousin, the same age, who was then doing honor work in his sophomore year in engineering school, who received the plaudits. The girl's ordinarily enviable accomplishments were quite overshadowed by the praise received by her cousin.

Some parents attempt to compensate for their own real or imagined failures through stressing the necessity for a certain kind of achievement on the part of their sons or daughters. [330:386] Fathers sometimes attempt to make their sons big league baseball players or star basketball players because, in their youth, they failed to fulfill their aspirations. Sometimes these efforts are successful; sometimes the boy is quite unfitted to fulfill the expectation and failure is magnified because of the frustrated hopes of the parents. Frustration—or victory achieved at too great a price in terms of lop-sided development—may occur when the goal is for the son or daughter to become a musician, doctor, lawyer, or professor. The ambition of the parent may conflict with the aspirations of the young person; for example, the father may wish to have his son succeed him as a business executive while the son desires to become a concert singer or violinist. Whatever the specifics of the high parental expectations might be the basic remedy is clear. Parents must develop enough maturity to focus mainly on their own goals, and adolescents must be permitted to live their own lives without excessive domination. Thus, the aspirations of the adolescent will come to coincide with reasonable parental ambitions, and a wholesome team relationship will fortify the youngster's endeavors.

Better homes for the adolescent

Parental role in time of stress

Even in the best of homes, it is inevitable that the adolescent will make mistakes. It is at this point that the good home is clearly manifested. Instead of blaming the adolescent and stating, "It would not have happened if you had just heeded my advice," wholehearted support should be evidenced. Unless this support is given, the youngster may develop feelings of guilt out of all proportion to the misdeed—certainly the feeling of guilt will only prevent his making wholesome compensation for his misdeeds. He may, on the other hand, only rationalize his error because of the criticism and leave home or become more resistant to guidance.

A sixteen-year-old girl who became pregnant by her high school sweetheart finally had to tell her parents of her condition. They ordered her to quit seeing her boy friend, demanded an abortion— despite the fact that the young people wanted to get married—and let her know in no uncertain terms that she had betrayed her parents and their trust in her. This treatment contrasts markedly with the attitude of a mother, who had been a girls' adviser in high school, who said: "I advise strongly against premarital sex relations; but, if you do get in trouble, please remember that you can count on me in any and all circumstances." Such an attitude, in a crucial situation, serves to illustrate the possibility of a tolerance for errors that might be allowed in less critical situations.

Although the author does not generally agree with the pessimistic thesis that "today is a time of stress and strain," it seems to be an inescapable conclusion that living in a "state of war or preparation for war" complicates problems of adjustment. J. H. S. Bossard points out that war aggravates adolescent-parent conflict in several ways. First, war creates excitement, which in turn fosters adolescent activity that is frequently at odds with the conduct that parents approve. Second, it stimulates the development of self-reliance and independence, which deprive parents of some of their economic advantage. Third, war accelerates cultural change, which widens the gap between the generations so that understanding is more than usually difficult. The cultural continuities are broken, with an inevitable increase of conflict between adolescents and their parents. [34] These conditions are not of the adolescent's making, yet he is inevitably caught in the stresses that are created. Instead of repudiating the adolescent for his manifesting the symptoms these stresses create, the parent has the unenviable task of striving all the more staunchly to give him the emotional support he so much needs. "War or preparation for war" is only illustrative of the stresses with which the adolescent must deal. The aid of parents is probably most necessary when it is most difficult to give.

Choice of friendships

Because parents are aware of the influence of peers on the behavior of their sons and daughters, they are likely to be concerned about some of the companions selected. This problem becomes more acute when adolescents widen the range of their activities and associate with those outside of their immediate neighborhood. There can be no doubt that the concern of parents is justifiable, since the way an adolescent dresses, the way he talks, and the activities he pursues are markedly influenced by what his friends are doing. C. M. Tyron has shown that as a student progresses through school, to the twelfth grade parents are *less* frequently and friends *more* frequently mentioned as the individual with whom they would talk in response to the question, "What would you do if you were worried about something?" [325] This is probably less an indication of lack of parental prestige or erroneous treatment than it is an indication of the commendable desire to be weaned from parental dependence. Whatever it is it does serve to show that friendships are a behavior influence.

Parents do not need to be convinced of the role of friendship in the development of personality. What they do need is to realize that direct interference and attempts to dominate selection of friends will often lead to tensions that will make wise guidance more difficult. They need to know that ultimately, if independence is to be achieved, the young persons will make their own selections. The experience adolescents gain in the early years will be a factor leading to mature judgments. Hence some parents have solved the problem by outwardly accepting all choices—but when a tacitly disapproved friend is selected they attempt to show the discrepancy between the family attitudes and ideals and that of the new friend. This they do by inviting the friend into the home, taking him into the family circle, and thus showing the contrasts. Another approach is to depend upon the early training of healthy interests. Since many friendships are based upon mutual interests the young person will be less likely to form a lasting friendship with those who differ markedly. Such approaches are much more likely to succeed than is interference, which is likely to make the adolescent stick to his choice because he rebels against having his independence threatened.

As in the case of situations involving stress, the fundamental thing is a feeling of personal security—a security built through the continuing influence of parents:

> How is the adolescent to be given this sense of personal security? To answer this question we must consider the basic ingredients of personal security and match them against the qualities of an ordinary home. The adolescent needs a stable base from which he can practice his developing powers; he needs freedom from ridicule and sarcasm, and he needs a long background of training in independence and responsibility which gradually increase as his strength increases. The ordinary family is the most stable unit. It is the unit in which the adolescent most naturally expects to find affection, sympathy and understanding because these are the ties which hold families together. . . . The very fact of family name and family tradition helps to give the adolescent that sense of belonging which is so useful during periods of stress.*

The family council

The foregoing material on situations of stress and the selection of friends suggests an approach to similar problems such as allowances, late hours, choice of activities, academic problems, and work around the home. This approach is the family council in which the adolescent and his parents discuss, on a truly give-and-take basis, the many problems that arise. Studies show that there is a high incidence of problems in vocational, educational, recreational, and social choices. [31] This does not mean that conflict is the typical

---

* George H. Preston, *The Substance of Mental Health* (New York: Rinehart and Company, Inc.; 1943), pp. 109–110.

relation between parents and adolescents, but conflict does occur in about 20 per cent of the cases. Common adolescent reactions are that they cannot discuss personal things with their parents, that they are afraid to tell when they have done something wrong, and that they feel there is a barrier between them and their parents. They feel that things would be better if they were told *why* rather than simply being told "No." [257]

Holding a family council would be a step toward the satisfaction of the psychological needs for belonging, for love and affection, and for recognition and understanding. It would aid in the achievement of the developmental tasks of emancipating oneself from parental domination, selecting an occupation, preparing for marriage and family life, achieving socially responsible behavior, and developing a system of values. It would also facilitate the satisfaction of several of the "Imperative Needs of Youth." (See Chapter Three.)

The inception of a family council cannot be left until the adolescent is questing for independence. It must begin early and consist in progressive steps toward the adolescent's actually making the decisions and adjusting to the difficulty—with the advice and counsel of the parents. Specific ages cannot be cited at which the adolescent should be making his own decisions; some are ready at thirteen or fourteen while others are not prepared until several years later. There is, however, a point of consolation for apprehensive parents in the fact that adolescents tend to think about problems in much the same manner as those about them. [256:43] It will aid parents if they let the younger generation know how they think in a manner that makes adult ideas palatable—that is, as ideas shared with co-workers. This will occur more readily when each person is encouraged to speak his mind and is listened to by others. It is a two-way process in which the parent recognizes the individuality of the adolescent and the adolescent appreciates the good intention of his parents. Evelyn M. Duvall, Executive Secretary of the National Council on Family Affairs, states: "Mutual respect and genuine affection are needed for understanding each other. The process is long. When the gap between the generations is as great as it is today, it takes a while for each to understand the other." *

---

* Evelyn Millis Duvall, *Keeping Up With Teen Agers*, Public Affairs Pamphlet No. 127 (New York: Public Affairs Committee, Inc.; 1947), p. 27.

Parental maturity

Advice on the parental role in time of stress—recommending adolescent freedom of choice in friends and activities and the formation of a family council—is probably a prescription for an attack on symptoms only. The really basic problem is one of parental maturity and all that the term implies. In this particular context two aspects of maturity are outstanding: (1) the desirability of the parent's accepting his age and ceasing to try to artificially preserve his youth, (2) the necessity for establishing new tasks and goals for *himself*.

There seems to be a reluctance on the part of some, if not many, middle-aged persons to admit their age. Some even seek to recover their youth. There is an effort to restore youth with the help of physicians, beauticians, and health "experts." Cosmetics, hair restorers, vitamins, "falsies," and girdles are used to delude others into thinking the user much younger. Of course, there are some justifications for this attitude. The reluctance to hire older people and the emphasis in advertising on the importance of youthfulness are examples of the pressures to avoid aging.* Whatever the causes, it seems that the prestige of adults in the eyes of adolescents could be increased if adults admitted their age and acted accordingly. The author disagrees with the contention that parents should be their sons' and daughters' pals. It seems somewhat ludicrous that a mother should pride herself in the remark, "You're her mother! I thought you were sisters." This does not mean that parents should not be interested in the activities of youngsters or that there should be no family picnics, excursions, or joint undertakings. It does mean that the adolescent will also receive impetus toward maturity by being released from some of the intimacies of mother-daughter and father-son companionships and stimulated to make peer contacts. When adolescents ". . . see older persons acting kittenishly or childishly; vaguely, they resent the loss of the comforting parental stereotype." †

---

* It is possible that the popularity of this attitude may decline as adolescents become increasingly a minority group and as more adults achieve greater ages.

† James H. S. Bossard, "Family Background of Wartime Adolescents," *Annals of the American Academy of Political and Social Science,* 236, 1944, 39.

Asking parents to act their age is perhaps like asking them to lift themselves by their bootstraps. As in the case of changing the behavior of children and adolescents the remedy probably lies in the substitution of new activities and interests. One of the developmental tasks of middle age is to develop new leisure-time activities. At this time the demands of the growing family are lessened, and there is less pressure to get established in one's occupational life. [136:271] Unless some of this leisure time is taken up in civic activities, the more vigorous pursuit of hobbies, travel, or the like, there is some likelihood that the temptation will become great for the parent to project himself into the life of his adolescent. Pertinent suggestions for developing a life of one's own might well include the following:

Examine work satisfactions.

Review youthful interests.

Explore unfamiliar fields.

Develop husband-wife hobbies.

Be socially useful. [121:13]

There are many aspects of growth toward maturity—physical and physiological, psychological factors, group mores—but a very significant one is the progressive establishment of currently important goals. Only adults who are themselves growing intellectually and emotionally can provide the morale, support, and example that will have the maximum salutary effect upon adolescents.

A study which revealed that significant and desirable changes in attitudes toward children resulted from a planned program of training indicates that help is available through education. [297] The steadily increasing interest in adult education, the formation of study groups in clubs, and the variety of publications dealing with geriatrics and gerontology indicate that help is available for the parent who wants to grow. However, as is the case in psychiatric treatment, the first essential is an individual who wants to change.

Helping the adolescent evaluate his home

Throughout this chapter there has been an implied or stated emphasis on the importance of mutual understanding. The parent has certain responsibilities, but so does the adolescent. It is necessary that young people get into their heads the notion that their parents have the best of intentions for them and their welfare. Underlying the hesitancy of parents to grant freedom and independence of action is a love for their children that leads to a genuine concern about their safety—physical and moral.

Teachers and leaders of youth groups are in an advantageous position to give guidance leading to the adolescent's appreciation of his parents' attitudes. The same information or advice coming from parents would be likely to fall on deaf ears because of two factors: First, the adolescent is often trying to outgrow his parent and does not want to heed the admonitions. Second, the professing of parental sincerity is too likely to be occurring during a time of stress—when emotions are at a pitch that is not conducive to receptivity. These two points turn to advantages for the teacher: First, as the adolescent attempts to be freed of his parents he is still not ready for complete independence, so he turns for advice to the only other adult with whom he is well acquainted. Second, the teacher is not involved in the parent-adolescent conflict.

Some of the points of understanding that the teacher or youth leader should emphasize are the ones mentioned in this chapter. All parties must realize that conflict is normal and, while they will attempt to reduce it, should not have exaggerated feelings of guilt when it occurs. There is some logic to the belief that when the parent pays the bills and assumes the responsibility he should have some voice in the conduct of affairs. If there are abnormal attachments the youngster should see his parent as a sick person and treat him accordingly—at the same time that he fights the more steadily for independence. The climacteric imposes difficulties on adjustment of parents, and they can be helped to solve some of the psychological difficulties by adolescents who exercise patience. Teachers had best contact the parent when ambitions for the adolescent are unrealistically high—but in the meantime it may help the adolescent to appreciate the sincerity of his parent's hopes. If the adolescent can get his parents to hold a family council he should attempt to make it a cooperative search for answers rather than an opportunity to state demands. Finally, it might be indicated that floating in an easy current does not build strength. Adolescents who have to work for independence are receiving an innoculation for the more healthy pursuit of adult life in which independence must be ethically and morally oriented. The sagacity with which they conduct their present affairs is a foretoken of the kind of approach they will make to their own adult problems.

Such points as these can be put across in personal interviews. Better yet would be an informal contact in which the teacher and adolescent meet on an informal base—the five minutes before, after, or between classes, or when the student comes early or stays late to carry out some plan. But probably the best approach is when adolescents meet together and, under the guidance of the teacher, discuss with each other these and similar problems. They will, in such council, have two real advantages. First, they will discover that their problems are not unique—other adolescents are not having the same problems but they are enough alike so that similarity can be recognized. Second, there is a motivating factor inherent in the fact that the adolescent has evolved his own answers rather than having had them given by an adult. The youth council provides an opportunity to exercise the independence that is being sought.

Summary

Adolescent behavior is conditioned by national events, by wider cultural processes, by intelligence, physique, and the like. But even with this reservation there is no doubt that the parents of adolescents occupy a strategic position. If their position is a sound one and is wisely held, they can give much help to the young person. If the position is indefensible or equivocal, the adolescent is faced with an additional hazard to harmonious development.

Generalizations are made with the knowledge that there are many exceptions; there are no typical homes—each is, in its way, unique. There is probably some conflict in each home, but it need not lead to the abnormal situation—frustration. Autocratic authority is a thing of the past for the healthy home. Authority based on understanding, authority that is gradually released and that will lead to socially oriented independence is the goal. To reach this goal experience must be available at early ages. Parents can trust the functioning of democratic authority when they come to appreciate the gradualness and continuity of behavior. Truly, today is yesterday shaking hands with tomorrow.

There are, inevitably, some negative home conditions that need the attention of parents, teachers and counselors, and adolescents. One negative home condition is abnormal attachment of parents for their children—an inability to free them for independent action. Another hazard lies in the physiological and psychological disturbances that sometimes accompany the climacteric. The feeling that the adolescent should be indebted to his parents must be replaced with the parental conviction that the opportunity for raising healthy young men and women is its own reward. Low income and high parental expectations constitute difficulties for some young persons.

There are several characteristics of a good home for adolescents, toward which parents should strive. One is the parental determination to stand by the adolescent when he has made an error. This does not mean that the parent must approve delinquent actions. A stand should be taken, but not the "Don't darken my door again" one. Free choice of friends should be permitted, even when the parent disapproves. The parent must trust that his emphasis over the years on moral and ethical living will have a persisting influence. Family councils are being revived as an effective approach to the solution of parent-adolescent problems. Parental maturity must be sought through the formulation of progressive goals that accord with the inevitable changes in the nature of adult responsibility and developmental tasks.

The problem of a good home for adolescents is also a responsibility of adolescents. Teachers can help youth to see this responsibility. However, probably the best approach is for youth to meet with one another and formulate their own answers.

STUDY AND REVIEW ITEMS

1. What do you think of the policy of some judges of demanding the presence of parents when adolescents have been apprehended in delinquent acts?
2. In the case study cited, do you think Ralph was responsible for his behavior or was he simply the victim of circumstances not included in the description?
3. If it is true that authoritarian discipline is on the decline, do you think, in view of delinquency rates, that it is a good thing?

4. What do you consider to be some of the typical difficulties that the adolescent encounters in his parental home?
5. Do you feel that the adolescent should repay his parents for the expenses they have incurred for the young person's education?
6. What do you think would be an effective approach to parents who have too high expectations for their children's achievement?
7. What do you think the role of parents should be when their son has been apprehended for drunkenness?
8. What would be a good approach to formulating a sensible hour at which young people should be home after a date? What do you think the answer should be?
9. What books have you read that might help parents to continue their *maturing processes*? What are some other things you would suggest to prompt continued maturing?
10. How might a woman of 45 years, who has spent her life in the home, become a "socially useful" person?
11. What do you think can be done to help the young person appreciate some of the difficulties which parents are experiencing?

RECOMMENDED SUPPLEMENTARY READING

Farnham, Marynia F. *The Adolescent* (New York: Harper & Brothers; 1952), 243 pp.

Direct, clear, and sometimes difficult to accept advice is given to parents in this book. There is considerable emphasis on the parents' role in helping adolescents to make adequate sex adjustments. Personal experience and training as a psychiatrist are evidenced by the author.

Jenkins, Gladys G. *How To Live with Parents* (Chicago: Science Research Associates, Inc.; 1948) 48 pp. (pamphlet).

Although addressed to adolescents, this will also enlighten the older generation. The fluctuating roles of dependence and independence are discussed, typical arguments are outlined, and suggestions are given for resolving difficulties.

Preston, George H. *The Substance of Mental Health* (New York: Rinehart and Company, Inc.; 1943), 147 pp.

This is a psychiatrist's presentation of the factors in family life that are detrimental to, and those that are conducive to, mental health. Parents will find the material of direct help, and students will find that it is psychologically sound. It is far above average in readability.

Reynolds, Martha M. *Children from Seed to Saplings,* 2nd Edition (New York: McGraw-Hill Book Company, Inc.; 1951), pp. 239–273.

Some of the essential similarities and differences of 15- 16- and 17-year-olds are dealt with in this chapter. Part of the material will be a review, but the remainder tells of some of the implications for parents that arise from this stage of development.

Seidman, Jerome M. *The Adolescent: A Book of Readings* (New York: The Dryden Press; 1953), pp. 524–575.

These chapters include one by Margaret Mead dealing with the contemporary family from an anthropological view; one by Kingsley Davis on parent-youth conflict; one by John Levy and Ruth Monroe on the adolescent's family; and one by L. M. Terman and others on marriage prediction tests.

Witmer, Helen Leland, and Ruth Kotinsky (Eds.) *Personality in the Making* (New York: Harper & Brothers; 1952) Chapters 4, 5, 9.

These chapters are "the product of many minds and hands" and may therefore be somewhat more reliable than a report written by an individual. The chapters indicated expand and clarify some of the problems just touched on in this book. Family life factors that need additional study are mentioned.

AUDIO-VISUAL MATERIAL

Heredity and Family Environment (McGraw-Hill Book Company, Inc., 330 W. 42nd St., New York 36), 9 min., so., b. & w.

The film depicts a high school psychology class studying the development of one of its members. Physical, emotional, and mental foundations are inherited but environment develops the potential. The home as a factor in this development is illustrated.

Overdependency (McGraw-Hill Book Company, Inc.), 32 min., so., b. & w.

This is the story of a young man whose life is crippled by behavior carried over from a too dependent childhood. He has difficulty in facing everyday problems and seeks refuge in illness and the solicitude of his mother, sister, and wife. Treatment by a general practitioner helps him face his problems.

What must be done to make the school an agency to meet the needs of ALL youth? What kind of teachers are needed? What must be the characteristics of functional curriculums?

CHAPTER SEVEN

Adolescents and Their Schools

There can be no doubt that family life, from infancy on, is a powerful factor in the dynamics of adolescence. But, as has just been indicated, the healthy adolescent is engaged in a struggle to outgrow
his family and create a life that is uniquely his own. Among the
cultural influences, including community factors and the family,
the schools are a significant element in the dynamics of adolescence.
Without engaging in a debate as to whether the home or the school
is the more important, it is safe to say that schools are a factor of
prime importance in many, and could be in more, adolescent lives.
There are several reasons why schools *might* be more important
than the home during the years of adolescence. Obviously, one of
them is the normal repudiation of the parent by the adolescent. Another is the fact that schools provide a readily available refuge for
the adolescent as he leaves his family. Finally, because parents have
less opportunity and incentive than do teachers to keep abreast of
the times and to be acquainted with the psychological phenomena of
adolescence, some of the shortcomings of the home can be compensated for in school.

Schools open doors for adolescents; but for many adolescents the
school doors are not open. It is true that none are arbitrarily denied
admission; but, for many, school is so disagreeable that they, and
their teachers, sigh with relief when they do not attend. In opposition to the statement that schools are created to serve children
and youth, there is the widespread conviction (rarely admitted)

that if young people do not fit the Procrustean Bed of the curriculum they should not be allowed to clutter up smooth educational routines for those who learn academic knowledge readily. It has often, and truthfully, been said that adolescents with below-average intelligence, and many of those from lower socio-economic strata, find little to fit their needs in secondary schools. It is evident that if schools for *all* American youth are to become a reality some changes in thinking and practice must take place. This chapter (1) describes some of the advantages and disadvantages for adolescents of schools as they now are and (2) suggests some ways to improve them.

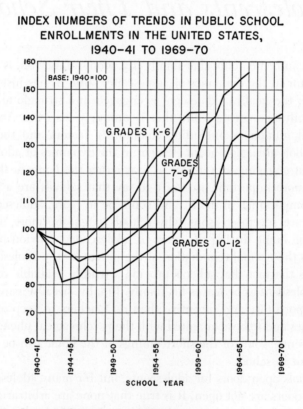

INDEX NUMBERS OF TRENDS IN PUBLIC SCHOOL
ENROLLMENTS IN THE UNITED STATES,
1940–41 TO 1969–70

FIG. 7. **Trends in public school enrollments**

From N. L. Engelhardt, Jr. *School Enrollment Begins Long Climb,* A Research Report of Engelhardt, Englehardt and Leggett, Educational Consultants, New York, 1952.

Basic considerations

Status of the secondary school

Historically, education in American Democracy has been a persisting ideal. The basic concerns of early settlers and of succeeding generations were homes, churches, and schools. Only recently, however, has secondary education been legally admitted to be a public concern. The famous Kalamazoo decision in 1874 established the now accepted principle that public education need not be restricted to the elementary schools. Since 1890 the percentage increase in secondary school enrollments has been much greater than the increase in the elementary school. This increase was somewhat slower from 1900 to 1910 but has averaged a doubling each decade from 1890 to 1930. From 1941 through 1944 enrollments decreased, due to the number of boys who were accepting employment, but since 1945 enrollments have again increased and the rise is now increasing in speed.

The unprecedentedly high birth rates, which began in 1947 and reached an all-time, and unexpected, high in 1952, coupled with low child mortality rates are creating staggering problems for those working in secondary education. Enrollment in senior high schools, now climbing slowly, will increase sharply in 1961 and the years following. It is estimated that enrollment in the senior high schools in 1969–70 will be 40 per cent above the enrollment of 1956–57. This trend is graphically presented in Figure 7.* Larger school enrollments are due only in part to population growth. A greater portion of the adolescent population is attending school. Educators must face the problem of meeting an increasingly large diversification of adolescent needs, interests, abilities, and problems. It is apparent that schools play a large part in the lives of adolescents—a part that is becoming steadily larger.

The increasing popularity of secondary education is changing the educational status of the population as a whole. Less than forty years ago only four out of every 100 boys and girls who entered

---

* These trends indicate that, for the student now in college, secondary education will provide a wide open field of opportunity for engaging in significant professional work.

high school were graduated. Today approximately thirty-five out of
100 who enter are being graduated. In 1953 the number of adults
who had a full high school education was four and a half times as
great as in 1930 and 80 per cent greater than in 1940. The changing educational status of the population is shown in Figure 8.

This figure shows that there was little rise in the average educational level of white persons in the forty-year period from 1880 to
1920, but following World War I there was a rise of three years in
a period of only fifteen years. This means, among other things, that
a high school education is no longer the comparative advantage it
was—it is *essential* for those who wish to compete on a basis of
equality. Two questions must be asked: How many pupils remained
in school to approximate the reaching of the limits of their educa-

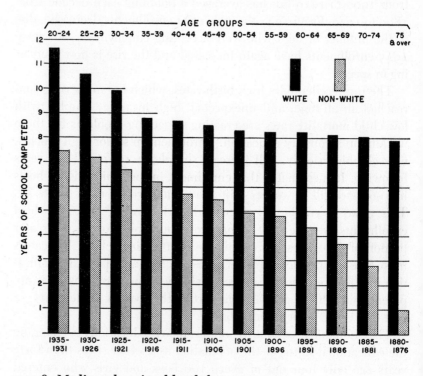

FIG. 8. **Median educational levels by age groups**

From *Education—an Investment in People* (U. S. Chamber of Commerce, Committee on Education, 1945–46), p. 31.

tional capacity? What educational changes must be made in order to reduce the number of drop-outs? Young people must be convinced that they too must be active in the opening of educational doors.

Despite the fact that the holding power of the school has increased markedly in recent years, educators are more than ever aware of the large numbers of youth that are not being served in schools. [339] In 1900 11 per cent of youth from 14–17 years of age were enrolled in school—in 1950 73 per cent of this age group were enrolled. [268] But drop-outs occur with increasing frequency after the age of fourteen. The 9th and 10th grades and the age of sixteen years are the most critical points at which decisions are made as to whether or not to continue school. Approximately 50 per cent of sixteen-year-olds have left school before the 10th grade. [86:7] Drop-outs begin, however, long before the sixteenth year. Ten per cent of children from five to seventeen are not in school. And the important thing to remember is that these are children— not just statistics. If schools are to be for all American youth, it is necessary that the schools be made to fit the needs of youngsters, and the glib answer "They can't get anything out of school" will have to be repudiated.

Figure 8 shows that one reason for non-attendance at school is related to skin color. Since the measurement of intelligence shows that colored people are potentially just as educable as other persons, it seems evident that either custom, or schools which do not fit the needs of some groups, are at fault. Perhaps there is some fault on both sides. Studies of social strata show a similar tendency: Tradition, and schools that do not fill needs, result in low attendance of those from lower socio-economic strata. Table 3 shows school attendance by social strata. The figure 100 means that the same proportion of children are represented in the educational category as they represent in the population. An index of less than 100 indicates disproportionately fewer, and more than 100 represents disproportionately more, cases than one would expect to find in terms of the average.

One reason for failing to hold some youngsters in school is monetary. School board members must convince voters that it takes financial support to provide varied courses of study, adequate plant and

TABLE 3   **Quota Fulfillment Indices** *

CLASS	NON-ATTENDANT	TRADE SCHOOL	HIGH SCHOOL	PRIVATE SCHOOL	LIBERAL ARTS COLLEGE	HIGHER VOCATIONAL SCHOOL
I	6	70	79	348	494	155
II	39	24	110	168	303	132
III	60	79	106	162	164	119
IV	92	76	110	96	61	90
V	105	100	106	66	55	100
VI	151	159	82	62	18	77

* James S. Davie, "Social Class Factors and School Attendance," *Harvard Educational Review*, 24, 1953, 178.

equipment, and talented, compassionate teachers. Most people feel that education is a sound investment; and rare, indeed is the *individual* who feels that his own education could profitably have been shortened. Another reason for drop-outs points to shortcomings of the school staff. Teachers and administrators often disapprove of pupils who are not enthusiastic about school. They forget individuality of personality and stress academic achievement. They feel that a student must pass his courses before he is permitted to engage in very educative "extra-curricular" activities. Slow learners, teachers often feel, should not be retained in school. † A third reason for drop-outs is the local and family custom of school attendance. Personal philosophy, accidents, and proximity of schools are other factors influencing the holding power of the school. Most of these factors require long-time attention. But an immediate solution lies in teachers who will study their own unintentional class bias and review their educational philosophy and then remove some of the inadvertently placed, but unnecessary, obstacles. With automation

† Harold Hand remarks that those pupils who show themselves to be least competent in meeting school tasks are the ones who are most quickly released to face adult problems. See William O. Stanley and others (Eds.) *Social Foundations of Education* (New York: The Dryden Press, Inc.: 1956), p. 236.

(as one example) demanding more and better-educated workers, loss of able students is not just a personal disadvantage—it is a loss of national human resources.

The function of the secondary school

Many statements of the functions of secondary education have been made, from the "Seven Cardinal Principles of Education" to recent statements centering about the needs of youth. The Cardinal Principles stated that the purpose of education was to promote the well-being of individuals and their fellows. The school ". . . should develop in each individual the knowledge, interests, ideals, habits, and powers whereby he will find his place and use that place to shape both himself and society toward ever nobler ends . . ." Hence, the main objectives of education are "1. Health. 2. Command of fundamental processes. 3. Worthy home-membership. 4. Vocation. 5. Citizenship. 6. Worthy use of leisure. 7. Ethical character." *

The statement of purposes is both a goal, and a reflection, of changes in our way of life. The first high schools and their forerunners, the academies, were available only to the small portion of individuals who were going to continue on to college. These early schools were strongly influenced by their European models and the consequence was that only those who showed themselves to be scholars were given much encouragement. Even today the curriculum is dominated by the college preparatory function, and teachers with their cry of "If we don't demand scholarship how will they get along in college?" reflect the preoccupation with the traditional academic approach to education. An examination of the Cardinal Principles indicates that educational leaders were concerned with a much broader concept of education—only one of the principles emphasized the academic: Command of the fundamental processes. Fortunately, research shows that young people are being prepared for college in large numbers despite a broadening of the purposes of high school education. [46]

It is probable that the many restatements of the aims of education

---

* Report of the Commission on the Reorganization of Secondary Education, "Cardinal Principles of Secondary Education," U. S. Department of the Interior, Bureau of Education Bulletin 35, 1918, pp. 9–11.

are in part due to the failure of educators and citizens to realize the import of *all of the principles*. Recent restatements have centered around the concept of needs (See Chapter Three) and have been directed to the goal of making education serve a greater and greater proportion of our youth.

A function of secondary education that is only infrequently discussed in print is that called the "custodial function." In addition to the idealistic aim of making better citizens through more complete self-realization, there is the fact that without schools many youth would have little to do. Except in times of war and unusual prosperity these youth would, or at least could, become idle wanderers if the schools did not provide them with something to do. Keeping young people off the street is an important function. However, it is to be hoped that the schools can be more significant than simply being providers of "busy work." The function of delaying the adolescent's competing on the labor market can be served at the same time that the possibilities for his living a more effective life are enhanced.

The value of schooling

One way of keeping youth in school is to show them that American's esteem for education is more than an idealistic notion. Statistical studies corroborate opinions regarding the value of schooling. The following figures relating to the money value of an education must be viewed critically—the fact that those who are more intellectually able *tend* to be the ones who continue in school must be considered. Averages do not account for the individuals who have much education and receive low income, nor for those with low education whose income is in the higher brackets. But, other things being equal, the income *probabilities seem to favor* those who are relatively more educated. U. S. Bureau of The Census figures, released in 1955, give the estimated life income for males as follows:

A person who has been graduated from elementary
school starts work at about age 16, 17, or 18 and,
working for a lifetime earns $116,000
1–3 years of high school 135,000
A high school graduate begins work at about the age
of 18 and earns in a lifetime 165,000

1–3 years of college 190,000
A college graduate begins work in his early twenties
    and earns in a lifetime 268,000

The difference between the high school and college graduate is $103,000 and four years of school attendance. Another recent estimate sets the difference in income at $100,000. [69] College education, on the average, pays off in terms of additional lifetime earnings at the rate of $25,000 per year in school. Even recalling that statistics are sometimes classified with lies, it seems safe to conclude: There will be many individual exceptions to the individual data that make up the average; but education tends to produce, and/or select, the kind of people who earn a relatively high income. The monetary value of education is not uniform or automatic. The relation of scholarship and success indicates that for an individual to get value out of an education he must put effort into his school work. Parents and teachers should make early and continuous effort to instill the conviction in adolescents that scholarship has real merit.

Table 4 shows that among those who earn $5000 or more per year about 50 per cent attended or were graduated from college, about 40 per cent had attended or were graduated from high school, and about 11 per cent had eight or fewer years of schooling. Adoles-

TABLE 4   **Median Income by Age and Years of School Completed** *

AGE	ELEMENTARY SCHOOL (8 YEARS)	HIGH SCHOOL (1–3 YEARS)	HIGH SCHOOL (4 YEARS)	COLLEGE (1–3 YEARS)	COLLEGE (4 OR MORE YEARS)
25–29	$2,255	$2,573	$2,892	$2,764	$2,928
30–34	$2,557	$2,922	$3,308	$3,591	$4,227
34–44	$2,803	$3,178	$3,523	$3,962	$5,142
45–54	$2,912	$3,209	$3,687	$4,099	$5,549

* Data are for males. Source: Department of Commerce, Bureau of the Census; *U. S. Census of Population*, 1950, Vol. IV, Part 5B.

cents might well get educational motivation from such figures—which show that society values the contribution of the educated person. Their desire to earn pocket money today must be weighed against the educational investment in their, and the nation's, future.

The relations of income to education are indications, not invariables. It becomes even more difficult to *prove* the value of education in terms of intangibles—but the indications are there. Statistics on the incidence of divorce tend to show that schooling pays off with marital happiness. In 1950 there were 11 marriages for each 1000 of the population and 2.5 divorces for each 1000. This, in round numbers, amounts to one divorce in every four marriages. Broken down into groups classified by educational achievement, it is found that when a college person marries a non-college person, the incidence of divorce is one in eleven marriages. When a college person marries a college person the incidence is further reduced to one divorce in thirty-three marriages. Undoubtedly there are other factors than education at work. Marital happiness of parents is an important correlate of marital satisfaction of the younger generation. It may be that this stability on the part of parents contributed simultaneously to extended education *and* stable marriage. Further, the stable personality that contributes to happy marriage may also be the kind of personality that enables one to stick to the arduous task of education. Finally, it is possible that the person who has the intelligence for continued education also has the intelligence required to solve the problems that inevitably arise in marriage. Age at the time of marriage must also be considered. It does, however, seem reasonable to credit education *with part* of the understanding and appreciation of differences that contribute to the adequate adjusting of persons in various situations. No doubt experience is a good teacher, but education is the social institution for selecting and directing experience.

There are some who believe that richness of living may be partially indicated by the quality of one's leisure-time activities. It has been discovered that the circulation of some of the nationally known magazines (*Harper's, Atlantic Monthly, Saturday Review of Literature,* for example) is greater in communities where average educational attainment is high. A line graph showing the circulation of these magazines follows the same line as does that showing average grade achievement in the community concerned. [94:47] There are those who say that the pulp magazines do no harm and that if a person likes them he is entitled to them. However, pulp magazines can be criticized, not that they are dangerous, but because they do not add anything to one's life. The better magazines may assist a man in living a creative life by causing him to think, by informing him of what is going on in the world, and by presenting the viewpoint of those who do think.

The creation of interests in music, art, literature, and drama is another indication of the value of education in the enrichment of life. Studies of the relation of education to civic participation are not particularly impressive. College graduates, for instance—though well informed, aware of issues, and conscientious about voting—do not exert the political influence that their role in life justifies. They seem, like so many less educated persons, to leave politics to the professional and content themselves with complaining about conditions. [134:125] It is apparent that educators cannot assume that education will automatically transfer to functional citizenship. Specific plans and procedures must be designed to accomplish this outcome (see Chapter Seventeen).

The big argument, of course, in a democracy is that education contributes to more effective citizenship. The role of education in this respect is reflected in the words in the Preamble to the Constitution of the United Nations Educational, Scientific and Cultural Organization: "The Governments of the States parties to this Constitution, on behalf of their peoples, declare that since wars begin in the minds of men it is in the minds of men that the defenses of peace must be constructed. . . ."

Education is an investment in people. The investment can be enriched by (1) seeing that its benefits accrue to a greater proportion of the population and (2) by seeing that it serves better the needs of the individuals in the population. American high schools must be designed and operated with these goals in mind for adolescents. Barriers to school attendance must be reduced by devising programs to meet the needs, the interests, and the differing orientations of adolescents who come to school from varied social backgrounds, with varied objectives, and with varied abilities. Approaches to these goals are suggested in the two following sections.

Educational problems of adolescents

Youth and today's schools

The continuing high respect that people have for education, the increasingly large numbers who attend high school, and the effect of schooling on effective living all attest to what is good in American high schools. An observer has only to take an objective look at youth to see that there is much to be proud of in the nature, extent of, and availability of education. It is no accident that the mother of two preadolescents and leader of a group of teen-age girls said, "I'm amazed at what I see in young people today. At the city council meeting, yesterday, the most vocal *and logical* of those present were the high school youngsters. They got to the floor and spoke directly, clearly and pertinently on the question [civil liberties legislation]. In my day there was not a one of my high school group who could do what many were doing at the council meeting yesterday." This statement is not just a local opinion. While it may not represent a consensus, it is certain that many hold much the same view. Phyllis Battelle, Woman's Editor for International News Service, asserts that children are getting older faster. Youngsters feel, with justification, that they know more than their parents about some things. [360]

Our high schools are as good as they are because they have been constantly changing to meet current needs. Further changes are needed to preserve the vitality of the school. An examination of some of the shortcomings of the school will serve to direct attention to some of the factors that will preserve dynamic schools. Many shortcomings become apparent when studied in relation to the student who drops out of school.

Youths' view of their schools *

It is gratifying to note that 79 per cent of a large sample of teen agers admit that they like school. Over half of them, however, admit that they have difficulty with their studies and wish they knew more about how to study. (Those who know what the average level of

* Data in this section are from the Purdue Opinion Poll, a survey of 15,000 young people between the ages of 12 and 20. H. H. Remmers and C. G. Hackett, *Let's Listen to Youth* (Chicago: Science Research Associates; 1950), 49 pp.

intelligence is in the high school and how much intelligence is required to do school work of the traditional kind simply do not make the unguarded statement that youth shrink from challenges and hard work.) Despite the fact that they buckle down to their work

21% said they doubt the value of the things they study
10% said their courses are too far removed from everyday life
35% would like to take courses not offered in their school
33% would like to take more vocational courses
49% would like to get some practical work experience
25% said they need advice in choosing courses
50% wondered what courses would be of most value to them in later life. [256:22]

The relationship between teachers and pupils is generally good. However, about a fifth of the students think teachers play favorites. A few complaints (4 to 14%) mentioned that teachers offered no encouragement, were not interested in the same things, used ridicule, were too strict or too impersonal. These opinions and criticisms of the school expressed by youth warrant more respect because the things the students mention are precisely the factors that are discovered when studies of drop-outs are made.

Adolescents and their teachers

Teachers have several advantages over parents in their influence over adolescents. They have been specially trained for their work. They deal with many youngsters and have better chances to develop perspective. They are less emotionally involved and can maintain objectivity. The young person who is attempting to outgrow his parents turns to another adult—the teacher—for guidance. The actual clock hours spent with teachers often exceed those spent with parents. For such reasons as these continued efforts must be made to improve teacher-pupil relations.

Many lists of the qualities of good teachers have been compiled. The characteristics most often mentioned include: friendliness, fairness, knowledge of subject matter, personal appearance, cheerfulness, and respect for individuals. Actually there are many different "personality types" that are successful because there are many different adolescents to whom appeal must be made. The young person aspiring to be a teacher need not feel that he *must* have a given set of characteristics and qualifications. There are, however, some bits of advice that will enhance the efforts of the teacher to work effectively with adolescents.

1. The feeling that pupils and teachers are members of hostile camps should be avoided. On the other hand, the teacher should not attempt to become a buddy of the adolescent—the pupil needs leadership and will be bewildered by an adult's attempt to be a buddy.

2. Differences between pupil ability and interest must be recognized. Grading pupils on achievement regardless of where the pupil stood initially will often cause able students to be satisfied with less than commendable effort and will result in feelings of frustration and futility on the part of those who achieve less rapidly.

3. Assigning uniform home work in the attempt to prepare for college will impose handicaps on those who live in crowded homes, who must work after school, who travel long distances by bus, who have healthy outside school interests, and whose parents do not have the "middle class" veneration for education that probably prevailed in the teacher's home.

4. While teachers should be enthusiastic about what they teach they should not be disappointed if they do not make disciples of their pupils. They must bear in mind that adolescence is an exploratory period, that different orientations exist, and that other teachers too are making demands on the pupils' time.

5. It will be well to bear in mind that the social life of the school is important. Attempts should be made to encourage all pupils to participate actively in some of these social activities. Tying the academic to the social life has been found to be quite effective.

6. Young teachers should be aware of the existence of adolescent attachments to teachers and avoid encouraging those who are apparently susceptible.

7. Whether they wish it or not, teachers become models. They must therefore attempt to live the kind of life that will afford them maximum lasting satisfaction as well as to provide a good example for adolescents.

Curriculums for adolescents

Studies of the effect of certain courses on pupil behavior and intellectual functioning have for generations shown no striking differences. A shop course, a home economics class, a course in life adjustment problems can with exemplary teaching be as effective in improving thinking, social behavior, and preparation for college as the traditional classes in English, mathematics, and science. These studies do not, however, daunt the subject-matter enthusiast. [336:429] There is a place for the traditional academic courses and for the more novel courses. Pupils who have not yet developed the habits of application or respect for chemistry that will lead to success may develop the necessary interest through success in a shop course. Pupils who do not have the mental ability to succeed in algebra may learn habits of confidence and self-respect through efforts in "social living" or dramatics.

Curriculums for adolescents should, in short, be characterized by variety. While interests are created by contact, familiarity, and success it must be remembered that pupils are, at the beginning of a class, at different stages of development. Trying to force an interest, trying to force successful participation, will more often lead to pupil maladjustment than to pupil enthusiasm. The need for variety in the curriculum is also indicated by the fact that specific sub-abilities in intelligence begin to emerge from general intelligence during the adolescent years. Variety will increase the probability that these sub-abilities (see Chapter Nine) will have a chance to be expressed and developed. Variety will also increase the likelihood that the different ways in which adolescents perceive their needs will be recognized.

There are many ways in which the variety needed to meet the needs of youth can be recognized. It but remains for educational leaders to put into practice what is known about the characteristics, problems, and needs of youth.

It must be evident to the reader that only a relatively few schools have departed from the traditional subject-centered program that has been under attack for a long time. The senior high schools have changed their basic design hardly at all in the past three decades.

Only a handful have revised their programs in terms of the needs or problems approach—and this in the face of significant research in the area of adolescent needs and problems and of considerable experience in curriculum reorganization.*

Truancy: a symptom of inadequate schools

Some young people are not strong enough to withstand the failure and frustration they find in school; others are too strong to submit to the imposition of teachers and courses they dislike. For one of these reasons they begin to slack off in school attendance. Occasional truancy may be regarded as a manifestation of youth's drive for independence; but frequent truancy must be regarded as a symptom of a school that is ill-fitted to meet the needs of individuals. Truancy is a forewarning of the probability that the individual will soon become a drop-out and deprive himself and his society of the advantages that accrue from extended education.

Teachers who read the symptom of truancy counsel with the student. They seek to get across an explanation of the function of the school and the individual courses within it. They draw up a new and more suitable program of studies. They offer their friendship and support. They show by word and action that they realize two psychological facts (1) that behavior is caused and (2) that truancy is one way of an adolescent's saying, "I'm hurt. I'm sick. I need help and understanding." L. K. Frank, speaking of adolescents in general, asserts:

> It is to be noted that during these years of readjustment and more or less painful growing up, teachers have a large opportunity to help adolescents, not by playing amateur psychiatrists and inviting confidences which they are often incapable of handling wisely, but by exhibiting a friendly understanding and, above all, a respect for the man or woman who is struggling to emerge from the confused adult.*

---

* Harold Alberty in National Society for the Study of Education, *52nd Yearbook, Part I, Adapting the Secondary School Program to the Needs of Youth* (Chicago: University of Chicago Press; 1953), p. 139.

† L. K. Frank in National Society for the Study of Education, *43rd Yearbook, Part I, Adolescence* (Chicago: University of Chicago Press; 1944), pp. 252–253.

Factors contributing to school leaving

Retardation in grade level or repetition of subjects is a rather reliable clue to potential drop-outs. Failure can be due to wrong choice of program, to not spending sufficient time on preparation and getting behind, or to lack of motivation; but we most frequently think of the intelligence handicap. It is true that the average intelligence of the stay-in is higher than that of the drop-out. One study found the difference to be between 95 IQ for the latter and 105 for the former. [229] But the fallacy of the average again asserts itself. *Many of the pupils are quite capable* of doing acceptable work if they but had the right direction and inclination. It has been estimated by teachers that a successful high school career would have been possible for 40 per cent of drop-outs; almost 20 per cent had intelligence for college work. [277] Another study reported that 12

TABLE 5   **Outstanding Element in Reasons for Leaving School as Given by 209 Non-Graduates** *

NATURE OF DISSATISFACTION	STUDENTS WHO GAVE DISSATISFACTION WITH SCHOOL AS		
	Principal reason for leaving	Contributory reason for leaving	Either principal or contributory
Failing grades, discouraged	38	22	60
Dissatisfied with courses	29	25	54
Disliked teachers or methods	25	40	65
Disliked social relations	13	23	36
Unable to adjust after transfer	8	2	10
Thought discipline severe	5	4	9
Miscellaneous reasons	17	16	33
Disliked school generally	74	33	107

* Elizabeth S. Johnson and Caroline E. Legg, "Why Young People Leave School," *Bulletin of the National Association of Secondary School Principals,* 32, November, 1948, 18.

TABLE 6   **Percentage of drop-outs giving each reason** *

	PERCENTAGE OF BOYS GIVING EACH REASON	PERCENTAGE OF GIRLS GIVING EACH REASON
1. Dissatisfaction with school	34	40
2. Lack of personal funds	26	31
3. Lure of a job	27	28
4. Family support	18	31
5. Inability to see relation between school subjects taken and future work	31	16
6. Felt self too old for grade	18	16
7. Inability to get along with teacher(s)	23	8
8. Inability to learn	10	17
9. School did not offer suitable subjects	13	10
10. Illness	6	12
11. Insufficient credits for graduation	9	7
12. Felt self too poor in comparison with others in class	2	7
13. Inability to get along with principal	6	1
14. Other	13	18

* Harry P. Smith, *Syracuse Youth Who Did Not Graduate* (Syracuse, New York: Board of Education; 1950), p. 24.

per cent had IQ's above 108 and, of these, 5 per cent were above 114. [86:34] Data on Syracuse, New York, drop-outs revealed that more than half had the intelligence to do satisfactory school work of the kind now offered. "Of the others it may reasonably be asked whether, with adjustment of curriculum and teaching methods, practically all of them could not have completed their secondary school work satisfactorily." † Teachers have the responsibility for

† Harry P. Smith (Research Director), *Syracuse Youth Who Did Not Graduate* (Syracuse, New York: Board of Education; 1950), p. 33.

challenging *all* adolescents, regardless of their unique make-up, to capitalize upon their abilities.

For many, school must be made easier—or better suited to the kind of intelligence the students possess—in order to keep them happy in school; but the solution of the problem is not watering down the curriculum. There are other reasons for drop-outs besides failure, and some failures are not due to lack of ability. Table 5 presents data representative of studies of drop-outs.

Lack of adequate financial resources is another high-ranking cause of leaving school. This is shown in Table 6—which repeats some of the factors listed in the Johnson and Legg report.

The data in Table 6 should be compared with those in Table 3 relating to social class and school attendance. Items 2, 3, 4, and 12 show that despite the ideal of universal education some young people cannot bear the nominal fees that are required in many schools—or, just as serious, they *feel* that their finances are inadequate. For many the costs are more than a feeling. Paul B. Jacobson has estimated that the cash cost per high school pupil averaged about $150 in 1950—a real burden for the two-fifths of American families that earned less than $3000 per year, especially if more than one in the family were attending school. [156:102] Even in schools where books and school supplies are free there are costs that tend to keep some pupils from participating in student activities and thus gaining maximum satisfaction from school attendance. Some of the activities and their costs to senior high school pupils are listed here [128:28]:

Golf	$50.00	Band	$3.50	Annual	$2.25
Tennis	15.00	Basketball	2.80	Football	2.10
Class rings	13.00	Track	2.70	Intramural	
Baseball	12.25	Orchestra	2.25	(girls)	2.05
				Swimming	1.50

It is possible that an example of the effect of these costs is reflected in the suggestion of youths in the Syracuse study that sororities and fraternities be eliminated. They felt that these resulted in class distinctions and consequent heartache and resentment which accompanied the feeling of not belonging. [286:48] Any activity that creates one of these "hidden" costs of education must be examined carefully: Do the benefits the activity provides for some students outweigh the problems it creates for students with less money to spend?

The President's Commission on Higher Education [140] reported that the outstanding factors in college attendance were: finances, propinquity to college, college tradition in the family (one or both parents attended), and ability to do college work. Examination of the data on high school attendance shows that financial reasons are also at work on the secondary level. Propinquity is probably less of a factor at the high school level, though some pupils do have to pay bus fares. It is interesting to note that ability to do college work is not the factor of first importance—and this condition is seen to exist also at the high school level, since many drop-outs have the ability to do secondary school work.

These items are of parenthetical interest. The point the author wishes to emphasize is that of family tradition for education. In the Syracuse study approximately two-thirds of the parents of drop-outs had completed nine or fewer grades. Only twelve fathers and twelve mothers of 264 drop-outs had any schooling beyond high school level. It was concluded that ". . . any inspiration which a child might have from the educational background of his parents is almost nil." * It must not be assumed, however, that the parents were unconcerned about their sons' or daughters' education—that they did not share the American's traditional respect for education. Of 211 drop-outs, in only 20 cases did the parents make the decision or not care about it. The parents of 64 acquiesced while, of the 211, there were 113 whose family disapproved of the decision to quit. [286:29] It is evident that the parent's admonition must be supported by a good example. Teachers can make a significant contribution by acceptance of, and interest in, those adolescents whose attitude is apparently poor. Wise teachers will recognize the "recalcitrance" and "laziness" of some pupils as symptoms of environmental forces. They can then counsel with the student who has problems in the attempt to get him to take a different view of his situation and future.

---

* Harry P. Smith, *op. cit.,* p. 22.

The attitude of the drop-out

It has been shown that both the individual and his environment must be taken into account when behavior is interpreted. The adolescent himself must assume some of the responsibility for leaving school before he has derived an approximation of its benefit to him. Some people chronically run away from difficult or unpleasant situations—and some no doubt are running away from themselves. It can safely be assumed that some of the adolescent's dissatisfaction with school is another manifestation of the natural and normal revolt against authority—but the drop-out has carried the conflict further than most of his peers. This observation is supported by follow-up studies of the drop-out in his job experience. The degree of job-satisfaction, the number of promotions or raises, the length of periods of employment, and the ability to hold on to one job are all less for the average drop-out than for those who continue their schooling until graduation. [323:6] Since many of the jobs taken by the early drop-out are ones that require little or no special training it must be assumed that personality inadequacy (for example, inability to get along with others or to take directions) rather than educational lack often explains their job dissatisfaction. In fact, the reasons for changing or leaving a job bear a striking resemblance to the reasons given for leaving school: disliked the work, work too strenuous, disliked employer, poor or low pay, discipline too strict, and work monotonous. [286:53]

Psychologically, the explanation that leaving school is contributed to by personality defect is insufficient. There must be reasons for the lack of adequate personality development. These reasons will, of course, reside to some extent in economic conditions, varied ability, parental influence, and previous school experiences—the same reasons as those given for leaving school. This may appear to be arguing in a circle, but it actually suggests one of the most practical solutions to the problem of making secondary education more widely available. If school teachers, principals, and counselors will become aware of the symptoms of dissatisfaction with school (low grades, subject failures, rebellion against authority, and truancy) and attempt to get at the causes, *for individuals,* many cases of dropping out can be prevented. Further, it must be realized that this is not a job for those in secondary education only. Teachers in the elementary school must do their part to prevent dissatisfaction before it becomes chronic. Parents must assume some of the blame for the personality inadequacy of their offspring. Community organization must be such that the child experiences a predominance of satisfactions over dissatisfactions. Happiness is to some extent a habit, and education at all levels must find ways to strengthen that habit.

All the blame for drop-outs can be placed neither on personality defects in the individual nor on curriculums, methods, or teachers. However, the logical starting point for improvement *is* the school. [155:18] Teachers, counselors, administrators, and the taxpayers who support the schools have the opportunity to change the financial status and educational tradition of our schools so as to bring us closer to realizing the dream, EDUCATION FOR ALL AMERICAN YOUTH.

Toward better schools

Recommendations of the Canadian Research Committee on Practical Education

A four-year study of Canadian schools and their products, conducted by representatives from the fields of agriculture, commerce, education, industry, labor, and the home, concludes (from data similar to those cited above) that secondary education can and should be the right and privilege of every child. The recommendations of this committee are so pertinent, conclusive, inclusive, and terse that the author feels he can do no better than to quote them at length.*

WE RECOMMEND

TEACHERS

1. that education authorities take steps to raise the status of the teaching profession along the lines suggested above (i.e., (a) higher qualifications for teachers; (b) remuneration commensurate with the training, responsibility, and significance of the teacher's func-

---

* *Better Schooling for Canadian Youth*, Final Report, The Canadian Research Committee on Practical Education, Toronto, Canada, 1951, 26 pp. (The quotation from this report continues on pages 229–233.)

tion in our society; (c) longer periods of education and training; (d) better methods of teacher selection; (e) recognition of work experience as a part of the qualifications for teaching.)

RETENTION IN SCHOOL

2. that education authorities provide educational programs which, by their availability to all pupils, however economically or geographically situated, by the quality of the instruction and supervision, by the variety of courses, by the adequacy of the accommodation and equipment, and by the atmosphere of democratic freedom under wise authority, will be conducive to retaining pupils until the completion of the secondary school course of study . . .

3. that the legal school leaving age should be 16, subject only to certain specified exemptions; and that there should be no differential between urban and rural areas;

4. that school administrators and teachers be more vigilant to recognize promptly any sign that a pupil is failing to make progress in any of his subjects, to discover the reason for such weakness, and to take steps to remedy it;

5. that education authorities be ever mindful of the effect of the "lack of income" factor on withdrawal from school; and minimize the influence of this factor by; (a) keeping to a minimum the "hidden costs" which sometimes make it unnecessarily difficult for students to continue at school . . . (b) recognizing the value of part-time work not only as a means of income, but as providing training and experience, and also as assisting the student to make his choice of occupations; * trying to secure more financial assistance for deserving students in the form of school bursaries, scholarships, and student loan funds, not only through federal, provincial, and municipal sources, but also through community organizations;

6. that school authorities strive for a closer contact between the school and the home through such media as parent-teacher consultations, visitations, parents' group meetings, and informative progress reports;

7. that school authorities undertake a well-planned program of public

---

* Further discussion of part-time work and work experience education is contained in Chapter Sixteen, "Adjusting to the World of Work."

relations to make known the objectives and opportunities offered in local schools, and to impress upon parents, pupils, and the community the benefits to be derived from better education.

COURSES OF STUDY

8. that schools offer a variety of courses to suit the varied interests and aptitudes of the pupils and make provision for the ready transfer of pupils from one course to another;

9. that all courses have a core of common subjects that will assist in developing those understandings, attitudes, habits, and skills that make for well-integrated, socially responsible citizens who can think critically and independently;

10. that courses be planned with the special employment opportunities of the local community in mind, and that educators consult leaders in the community in adapting the curriculum to local needs;

11. that special courses be provided for pupils who will not complete a regular secondary school course, and that, in these special courses (a) the development of good citizenship in its broadest meaning be the main objective; (b) this general objective, which is possible of attainment through many features of school organization and administration and instruction methods, be used to develop in the students a real love of learning, a sense of achievement, and a desire to continue to develop proficiency in their vocations in after-school years;

12. that universities broaden their admission requirements still further;

13. that education authorities periodically determine the effectiveness of the various courses in meeting the objectives of secondary school education.

GUIDANCE AND PLACEMENT

14. that the general principles of guidance be included in all teacher-training programs;

15. that special training be required of teachers assigned specific guidance duties, and that business and industry cooperate with education authorities to assist these teachers in securing first-hand knowledge of the various types of employment opportunities and job requirements;

16. that all secondary schools provide pupils with available up-to-date educational and occupational information;

17. that all secondary schools provide a guidance service to assist pupils; (a) to become oriented to the program, activities, resources and regulations of the school; (b) to identify educational needs and plan appropriate programs of studies and activities; (c) to identify difficulties in school progress and plan appropriate remedial steps; (d) to identify occupational interests by planning appropriate investigations, studies, or work experience;

18. that the school maintain complete cumulative pupil records in order that principals, counsellors, and teachers may better understand their pupils; and that these records be transferable between schools;

19. that all secondary schools take a definite interest in job placement so that, through direct contact with employers and in co-operation with employment agencies, the pupils will receive assistance, if needed and desired, in securing suitable employment;

20. that the school maintain a "follow-up" of pupils after placement to help them, when necessary, through the adjustment period, and to secure information which will be of great value in planning and evaluating school programs;

21. that the school co-operate with other community agencies which are interested in guidance such as Children's Aid Societies, Y. M. C. A., Y. W. C. A., Big Brothers, Big Sisters, local health units, and personnel organizations.

CITIZENSHIP

22. that the content of courses, the methods of teaching, and the organization of special activities all have as a primary aim the development of good citizens;

23. that the teaching methods be such as to develop in pupils the ability to use the scientific method of enquiry in order that they may learn to weigh issues and arrive at logical conclusions on the basis of sound and reliable evidence;

24. that school programs, curricular and extra-curricular, be conducted in such a manner that pupils will have ample opportunity to make group decisions, to participate in policy formation, to assume responsibility, and to work co-operatively.

25. that the school should exemplify democracy in its own life and work—that is, teachers and administrators should embody the best practices of democratic living both in their relations with pupils and in their relations with one another.

BASIC EDUCATION

26. that all teachers strive to develop clear and logical thinking by their pupils;
27. that all teachers insist on high standards in oral and written expression;
28. that, as one method of obtaining better oral and written expression and clear and logical thinking, greater use be made of oral and written reports based on assigned tasks and projects, both group and individual;
29. that more emphasis be placed on the fundamentals of arithmetic computation and every-day arithmetic problems, and that short daily periods of drill in these fundamentals be continued through the secondary school grades.

OCCUPATIONAL COMPETENCE

30. that, in order to provide more time for general education, specific training of the individual pupil for particular occupations be deferred as long as possible;
31. that the emphasis in vocational training be on the development of basic skills and sound work habits, rather than on the development of highly-specialized skills;
32. that general education programs include adequate prevocational exploratory courses designed to assist in the selection of areas of specialization;
33. that work experience be utilized to provide practical experience and to give students an opportunity to explore various avenues of work, and that business and industry co-operate to this end;
34. that teachers of practical subjects have a thorough knowledge of their trade and have training as teachers;
35. that home economics be offered in all secondary schools and that more girls be encouraged to enroll in these courses;
36. that courses in business education be extended to include training for workers in the distributive trades as well as for office workers;

37. that courses in industrial arts be offered in all secondary schools and include, where required, specialized courses designed to develop specific skills needed in industry;
38. that agriculture be offered in all secondary schools in rural areas and include, where possible, practical courses such as farm mechanics, farm management, soil conservation, and marketing.

FURTHER EDUCATION

39. that steps be taken to strengthen further the concept that education is a continuing process that does not terminate upon leaving school;
40. that part-time education between the ages of 16 and 18 be extended as rapidly as possible;
41. that community institutes be established to provide training in part-time education in daytime and adult education in the evenings;
42. that community institutes provide vocational training courses as well as cultural and avocational subjects, and that their facilities be available for community recreational services in order that they may become centres of community life;
43. that, in order to develop an effective community institutes' program, a greater degree of co-ordination be effected within the provincial government service so that the programs of high schools, apprenticeship training, university extension, and various other organizations may be more effective;
44. that the administration of the community institutes be vested in municipalities or school districts and the members of the administrative body be representative of industry, agriculture, labour, and education;
45. that financial support for community institutes be provided by federal, provincial, and local authorities.

Factors in changing educational concepts

The recommendations of the Canadian Committee (which have been cited above, beginning on page 228) are derived from a study of actual conditions. It will be informative to examine a few of these recommendations in the light of the psychological characteristics and needs of adolescents and to see how the recommendations fit in with psychological theory.

1. TEACHERS. The importance of good models, after whom adolescents may pattern their conduct, is recognized in the theory of learning. Good salaries for teachers constitute a sound investment in young people. In a capitalistic society, salaries must be such that able people are attracted to teaching, that experienced teachers may be retained, that prolonged education is justified, and that feelings of security may be fostered. As the adolescent grows away from his parents it is necessary that he be able to turn to another *mature* adult because he is not quite ready to proceed entirely on his own. Teachers occupy a strategic position in the development of adolescents that society cannot afford to overlook.

2. RETENTION IN SCHOOL. The importance of feelings of success in motivating school work is stressed in all educational psychologies. A variety of courses, which will permit each pupil *some success and some challenge,* is a prerequisite to sound education. When mass education fails to provide for both challenge and success many pupils will stay away or fail to approximate maximum advantage from the school. [239:87] The school has no right to engender in young people feelings of inadequacy by making the concept of success so nearly synonymous with academic success—one ability among many that contribute to success in life.

3. PARENTS. The way in which parent-teacher groups are organized must be carefully analyzed. The adolescent's need for independence indicates that his school problems should not be *solved* by his parents. It might be better to have the young person work with teachers rather than with parents *and* teachers. Because he is resisting his parents he might feel that both parents and teachers are in league against him in his growing up. For this reason, the author has in another place [20:101] recommended that parent-teacher associations at the high school level not be encouraged. However, Dr. S. R. Laycock has pointed out some dangers:

> The basic reason why I am interested in P.-T. A. work is that I have a conviction that a school or a school system cannot be much better than the public opinion on which it rests. At least that seems to me to be true in a democracy. If a school happens to have a good principal or if a school system has the leadership of a good superintendent of public instruction, then the school can go a little ahead

of public opinion. This, however, has limits and the school which moves too far ahead of public opinion will soon find itself pulled up short. It seems to me that only as our parents and other citizens study the problems of developing children and youth can we, as educators, expect intelligent support from them. This is as true of the secondary school as of the elementary school. Citizens are bound to have *some* views regarding the school's purpose, curricula, methods of discipline, and equipment. I would much prefer to have an intelligent opinion which is based on careful study than an uninformed one. My conception of the P.-T. A. has always been that it is a study-and-action group which discusses and deals with three main topics: (1) What schools are for (2) What children and adolescents are like and (3) How children and adolescents can best be helped to develop in home, school and community.*

The public relations aspect certainly has real merit at any time and particularly when the demand for salaries, buildings, equipment, and extended services is as it is. This compromise might be suggested: that the parent study groups become Parent-Pupil-Teacher Associations—this will help to give youth the voice in the conduct of his affairs that he needs and wants.

4. READING. Much more emphasis should be placed on reading as a skill that is vital to continuing education—whether in college, on the job, at home, or as a citizen. Unfortunately, reading is too often only incidental to the performance of high school work. Since there is the psychological phenomenon of functional autonomy (an activity carried on because of its own motivating power—reading because one can do it well), it seems that direct instruction in improved reading skills is a simple and fundamental approach to better education. Fortunately, brief periods of direct instruction for older pupils bring about marked changes in reading skill. Many students have doubled their rate and improved their comprehension in practice periods as short as four weeks. [22:113] Special reading classes—and not just for those who are below average—will result in improved academic work as well as better all-round development. Over half the adolescents in the Purdue Opinion Panel indicated

---

* Personal letter from S. R. Laycock, formerly Dean of Education, University of Saskatchewan, Saskatoon, Canada, November 25, 1952.

that they wished they knew how to study better. [256:19] The study of Syracuse drop-outs also indicated that young people feel the need for instruction in how to study. [286:47] California graduates have stressed the same need. [197]

5. PREPARATION FOR COLLEGE. Despite years of study and volumes of reports, the *ideal* college preparatory course has not yet been formulated. Students with many different backgrounds succeed in college courses. Reading skill is accepted as being of prime importance. A love for learning and good work habits are significant. These can be acquired by means of *many* different approaches. Experimental evidence indicates that much more freedom might profitably be allowed by both secondary and collegiate institutions. A study carried on in thirty schools for eight years indicated that students who went to "progressive" high schools (and were freed from conventional college entrance requirements) suffered no handicap in comparison with graduates of the subject-matter-set-out-to-be-learned curriculums. Specifically, there were 24.7 per cent college drop-outs among the progressives and 28.2 per cent drop-outs among the pupils who had been graduated from conventional schools. The grade point average of "progressives" was .04 higher but they averaged .02 points lower in foreign language—of no significance except as indicating that no great disadvantage was suffered. Seventy-five per cent of the progressives were judged by their teachers to be more capable of carrying on independent work. The progressives voluntarily listened to more speeches and music on the radio, attended more lectures and concerts. They read more books besides textbooks, and they participated in more cultural pursuits. They took more active part in student activities with the exception of athletics. [46] It seems, from such evidence, that education for life and preparation for college are not antithetical.

Matched person for person, the graduates of the progressive schools were more competent, more creative, more alert and intelligent after four years of the new type of high school education than their mates in the conventional schools. They won more academic honors, they had more intellectual skill and information, they were more systematic and objective in their thinking, knew more about the meaning of life and education, and had a deeper and more active intellectual curiosity. They were markedly more concerned about the life of their own community and of the crucial affairs of the world outside. They had more resourcefulness. They won more honors in student organizations, athletic teams, music, the theater and the dance and the other creative arts. When left to their own resources they initiated more important and stimulating nonacademic activities.*

6. GUIDANCE. The author wishes to protest against the haste to get adolescents to make a vocational selection. We do not yet know enough about testing for aptitudes *or* analyzing jobs for the skills and knowledges needed to perform them well to make accurate predictions at an early time. More will be said of this in a later chapter; let it suffice to say, at this point, that guidance should be personal rather than vocational—that emphasis should be on work and study habits, getting along with others, developing a respect for the dignity of labor, taking directions, becoming dependable, and fostering adaptability. These are the qualities that will, to a marked extent, determine success in any endeavor.

7. COMMUNITY AGENCIES. Cooperation between schools and community agencies is essential to a balanced approach to the improvement of the lot of adolescents. Their lives are lived both inside and outside the school. They bring their out-of-school experiences into the school as a part of their background for responding and understanding. To think that the school can operate independently of other agencies is to emphasize the "ivory tower" concept of education. It is no wonder that the Canadian Committee recommends work experience as a prerequisite for all teachers.

8. CITIZENSHIP. Full living today is the best preparation for sound citizenship tomorrow. The continuity of growth is an inescapable principle of psychology. We will fill the present needs of adolescents today and the wider citizenship needs of tomorrow by giving students a chance to have a part in the decisions that affect them, by allowing them experience in making choices,† by per-

---

* Harold Rugg, *Foundations for American Education* (Yonkers: World Book Company; 1947), p. 601.

† A concept of the underlying purpose of education is that it should help individuals to make appropriate choices. Van Miller and Willard B. Spalding, *The Public Administration of American Schools* (Yonkers: World Book Company; 1952), pp. 3–16.

mitting them to think, and by giving them opportunities to make mistakes.

9. FAMILY LIFE EDUCATION. Most pupils now in high school will become wives, mothers, husbands, and fathers within a period of five or six years. [197:10] Family life is a social institution, not an animal instinct; and it can hardly be stated too emphatically that specific instruction should help young people to get a good start in solving the problems of family life they will inevitably meet. It is a sad commentary on our educational system that this responsibility finds so little emphasis in the school.

10. FURTHER EDUCATION. Growth is a steady process continuing throughout each human's lifetime. It was indicated in Chapter Five that even physical growth is taking place in the fourth decade of life. The unique human characteristic of intellect has been shown to be capable of more and longer growth than are physical traits. The schools have a profound responsibility and a remarkable opportunity for establishing the habit of intellectual development. This can best be done by relating school work intimately to the needs of adolescents and by giving *all* young people the thrill of success and achievement.

Summary

Schools are the formalized institutions for inducting the young into wider horizons of life and for the improvement of that life. Though our ideal is "Education for All American Youth" there are evidences that many young people do not approximate the reaching of maximum benefits from school.

The problem of making schools more effective is complicated by the constantly increasing enrollments in the secondary schools and by the expanding demands made on the schools. This problem involves our entire social structure and the philosophy of individuals as well as school workers. Approaches to the solution of the dilemma involve thinking through the purposes of the school and attempting to make those purposes more functional. Outstanding among the statements of the functions of the school are the "Seven Cardinal Principles of Secondary Education," the "Developmental Tasks of Adolescents" (Chapter Three), and the "Imperative Needs of

Youth" (Chapter Three). That these aims have been realized to some extent is shown by the statistics on the monetary value of education, the continuing faith of people in education, and its value in enriching the social and cultural life of individuals.

That we have fallen short of our stated aims is shown by studies of drop-outs. Studies of those who have quit school prematurely reveal that there are many factors at work. A sign of dissatisfaction on the part of youth is truancy—which indicates frustration, boredom, and discouragement. Back of this symptom are such things as grade failure, lack of finances, inappropriate curriculums, personality inadequacy, and ineffective teaching. While the attitude of parents is generally favorable to the continuation of education, their example and tradition are often not such as to encourage the young person to continue an education that does not always seem to satisfy his needs.

The logical starting point for educational improvement is a broader concept of educators' roles—though they are not alone to blame. Problems that must be studied include: better training and pay for teachers, *functional* curriculums, reduction of hidden costs, improved understanding of the role of the school by citizens, improved pupil guidance, instilling a continuing love of learning in pupils. Suggested approaches to solution of these problems include: selection of stable teachers, providing more varied curriculums, teamwork by parents, teachers, *and* young people, and emphasis on reading skill, family life education, and personal mental health. These are not easily achieved goals; but good schools open doors to youth which lead to happiness and effectiveness.

STUDY AND REVIEW ITEMS

1. Prepare a statement, which might be presented to adolescents, concerning the importance of schooling—utilizing the data on enrollment trends.

2. Do you feel that preparation for college and the approach to adolescent needs can be met in one given high school?

3. Do you think it is likely that some of the support organized labor gives to schools is motivated by the desire to avoid competition?

4. Besides improved stability in marriage, what are some indications that improved personal adjustment is gained through education?

5. Would you agree that the average high school pupil today is better informed (or intellectually more mature) than the high school student of twenty years ago?

6. Prepare a statement to the effect that youth are in error when they feel that they should have more vocational courses.

7. What steps might be taken to encourage the able student to do the kind of academic work that would lead to greater personal satisfaction?

8. Suggest some ways in which the pupil who is not backed by adequate finances might be encouraged to stay in school.

9. What, in addition to salary, are some compensations that might be listed for high school teachers?

10. Which of the recommendations of the Canadian Research Committee do you consider to be of greatest importance?

11. Discuss, pro and con, the place of P.T.A. in high school.

12. Defend or attack the proposition that all boys and all girls should have a course in family life education.

RECOMMENDED SUPPLEMENTARY READING

Jacobson, Paul B. (Ed.) *The American Secondary School* (New York: Prentice-Hall, Inc.; 1952), pp. 70–133.

   The place of education in American democracy and the changing nature of the school's function, making schools effectively free, and steps in providing education for all American youth are discussed in these three distinctive chapters.

Kettelkamp, Gilbert C. *Teaching Adolescents* (Boston: D. C. Heath and Company; 1954).

   This book is addressed to prospective high school teachers. It contains a description of the problems to be met, the characteristics and preparation of teachers, and the needs and nature of adolescents—so that they may be more wisely guided in their educational and vocational careers.

National Society for the Study of Education, *52nd Yearbook, Part I,*
   Adapting the Secondary-School Program to the Needs of Youth (Chicago: University of Chicago Press; 1953), Chapters 7 and 15.
   Chapter 7 describes a number of core programs designed to meet the
   needs of youth and concludes with a shocking summary of the reasons we
   fail to do the job that is clearly charted. Chapter 15 makes some suggestions as to how more effective high school teachers might be secured and
   prepared for their work.

Rugg, Harold. *Foundations for American Education* (Yonkers: World
   Book Company; 1947), pp. 571–604.
   One of the great scholars of American education reviews some of the
   recent problems and developments in secondary schools in this chapter. He
   describes briefly the eight year study of secondary schools under the
   heading "Loosening the stranglehold of the college on the high school."

Zeran, Franklin R. (Ed.) *Life Adjustment Education in Action* (New
   York: Chartwell House, Inc.; 1952), Chapters 3, 7, 18.
   These three chapters deal, respectively, with the meaning, objectives,
   and criteria of life adjustment education; with the kind of curricular experiences designed for life adjustment; and the place of student activities
   in such a program of education.

AUDIO-VISUAL MATERIAL

Problem of Pupil Adjustment, Part I, "The Drop-Out" (McGraw-Hill
   Book Company, Inc.; 330 West 42nd St., New York, 36), 20 min.,
   so., b. and w.
   Steve quit school after his freshman year and has since drifted from
   one job to another. He was eager to begin school but, because his class
   work was unrelated to his outside life, he lost interest and incentive.

Problem of Pupil Adjustment, Part II, "The Stay-In" (McGraw-Hill
   Book Company, Inc.), 19 min., so., b. and w.
   An actual school program where individual needs are met is shown.
   Not only in vocational courses—poultry raising, driving, etc., which are
   taught—but in academic classes as well, values are in terms of pupil experience and need. Under this program "drop-outs" are less than 5 per
   cent of the total student enrollment.

Why do some adolescents encounter more difficulty than others in being accepted? Are pupils from all social classes given a real chance in the life of the school? Should an attempt to raise the social class status of those in the lower categories be made?

CHAPTER EIGHT

Social Status Influences

Our respect for American Democracy—our ideal of equality of treatment for all persons—renders the concept of social stratification somewhat unpalatable. But ignoring socio-economic differences does not alter the fact of their existence. Facing and studying the situation will provide clues for eliminating some of the existing injustices. Thus will another obstacle to the symmetrical development of adolescents be made more surmountable.

It was made clear in the previous chapter that the school was not a factor of equal importance in the lives of all adolescents. Some dropped out of school early and received few of the possible benefits, while many found the school an extremely dynamic factor in their development. In some states education is much more popular than in others—more youth receive the benefit of a high school education in Wyoming (over 60 per cent) than in Kentucky (less than 30 per cent). Similarly, the influence of social stratification is by no means a uniform one. It is the consensus of scholars on this subject that social classes (this term is frowned upon because it suggests rigidity) are relatively well defined in older, medium-sized cities of the northeastern United States; that social class is somewhat less perceptible in younger cities of the same size on the west coast and in great cities. Thus, some youngsters may grow up acutely aware of social standing while others feel little personal experience with the phenomenon.

Differences in the dynamics of social class do not erase the fact

243

that, for some, family, school, and community activities and experiences are strongly conditioned by their status. For example, it was shown in Table 3 (above, page 212) that class VI youngsters were much overrepresented in the "non-attendant" category while class I youngsters were overrepresented in the category of liberal arts college attendance. Not only is school attendance conditioned by class standing but the attitudes and ideals that are absorbed in the family and taken to school are also conditioned by these influences. The problems and behavior of adolescents will be better understood after examining some of the data on social stratification.

Basic concepts

The meaning of class

The word *class* refers to the differentiation of individuals in a society into higher and lower prestige strata. As members of the various strata, individuals have varied privileges, prestige, and opportunities. In some societies an individual's position in the class hierarchy is determined by birth—he holds or inherits the rank of his parents. In other situations his position may be determined by the particular skill or skills he possesses. In the United States the prime factor seems to be the ability to make money. There are other factors, such as family and tradition, but these can often ultimately be traced to the economic factors. Possession of wealth does not *guarantee* a high position on the social scale—another item of importance is that known as social participation. [335:81] A person must have the ability to act in a manner acceptable to the group concerned.

Many writers have used a six-fold categorization of social class. The percentages in each class are not equal because the evaluation of class is on behavior—manner of living—rather than being an arbitrary division. A. B. Hollingshead [143] uses the five-class categorization shown on page 245.

It is probable that in various communities the numbers would differ markedly from those shown. Further, the distinction between the classes must not be thought to be sharp. A given person might think himself to be in class III while another would judge him to be class IV—each having valid reasons for his evaluation.

CLASS I	Upper-uppers⎫ Lower-uppers⎭	approximately 3 per cent
CLASS II CLASS III	Upper-middle class⎫ Lower-middle class⎭	approximately 38 per cent
CLASS IV CLASS V	Upper-lower class⎫ Lower-lower class⎭	approximately 58 per cent

Social mobility

This term refers to the fact that a given person may take on the behaviors of, and be accepted by, a higher or lower class. He is not, as in the caste system of India,* in a rigidly defined group from which he may not escape. Although upward mobility is possible it is not always easy. The idea of class becomes most repugnant when situations are perceived in which those from a higher class discriminate against lower class individuals *because* they are "not the right sort." That is, intelligent, well-behaved, good-looking individuals are sometimes viewed with disdain because of who they are rather than what they are. Sometimes it is the upwardly mobile person himself who inflicts pain—it may be necessary for him to repudiate his family, friends, and neighbors before he can be accepted in the next higher level. On the other hand, upward mobility is sometimes accomplished with no apparent difficulty. Those who are in the lower group wish their upwardly mobile friend the best of luck in his new experiences, and the upper group welcomes him.

The factors that condition mobility are of particular interest because it is through these that some of the cruelties of social class may be obliterated. Beauty may serve as the key. A beautiful girl may capture or be captured by a man in a higher class. If she has been educated it may be easy for her to appreciate some of the modifications of dress and behavior that must accompany her rise in status. Some girls have set out deliberately to study the mores of the higher class to which they wish to rise so that they are prepared

---

* The past half century, under British rule and Western influence, has somewhat weakened the caste system in India; but it still has a powerful hold and the essential principle has been little weakened. T. Walter Wallbank, *India in the New Era* (Chicago: Scott, Foresman and Company; 1951), pp. 23–25.

for the change when the opportunity occurs. Unusual success in making money may be the key to higher social status. The success must, however, be accompanied by the desire to be upwardly mobile. Some who achieve success are so sure of themselves that they feel no need to make the effort to dress and behave in the approved manner. Others may not feel secure but still will not permit themselves the luxury of change for fear that someone will accuse them of being socially ambitious. Unusual talent in a field such as music, painting, writing, acting, or singing may give the possessor the prestige that will enable him to reach a higher social level. [334:34] The special talent does not always need to be accompanied by a large income, though earning ability usually helps if skill in social participation is present.

The strongest and most readily available factor in social mobility is education. Many teachers come from the upper-lower or lower-middle classes and are upwardly mobile to the upper-middle or even the lower-upper classes. The education acquired for qualifying as teachers also prepares them to dress, talk, act, and think in ways that are acceptable to the higher status groups. Education is a factor for those who are upwardly mobile from the lower three categories —especially since the form and content of education are so largely determined by those in groups II and III. Things other than education account for mobility from class II to class I—in fact, class II people are on the average better educated than those in class I. Preparation for and participation in the professions of medicine, law, dentistry, and the like are, as is the case with teaching, factors in upward social mobility for many persons.

Elmtown's Youth

A number of studies have been made of the functioning of social class structure in various communities. These particularized community case studies yield insights that are in some ways superior to the results of studying phenomena in general; that is, the study of delinquency in city A causes the observer to focus on details that are often different from those cited in the general study of delinquency. If the reader will bear in mind that the operation of class structure will be much different in another town, it might prove advantageous to examine one situation rather than to generalize. Data in this section are taken from A. B. Hollingshead's book, *Elmtown's Youth* * and illustrate a typical functioning of social class structure in a small midwestern town. Older towns of similar size are perhaps also illustrated by the Elmtown data.

The class structure of Elmtown

It is necessary to be born into the 3 per cent of the population that constitutes class I. Families are small, divorce is rare, and there is much emphasis on "good blood." Typical incomes (as of 1941) are $5,000 yearly with a few ranging up to $30,000. Cadillacs and Buicks are popular cars, and adolescents often have a late model coupé or convertible. Property ownership is high and so is interest in low taxation rates. (A very much needed high school building did not become a reality because of the influence of this small group of persons—who most often send their secondary school youngsters away to private schools.) Hired help in both the home and office frees class I adults for travel, shooting, and country club activities. Most of the young people go to college (see Table 3) but relatively few take graduate work leading to the professions. Membership in church is imperative but attendance is sporadic. Tailormade and "exclusive" model clothes are a vital part of maintaining the status code. High moral standards are outwardly endorsed but there is some discreet drinking and gambling—even when the law is broken there are no arrests. [143:89]

About half the families in class II have their position by inheritance and the rest have won their place. They identify with class I but have little chance of gaining such status. They gain their living as lawyers, doctors, dentists, engineers, business owners, and from salaried positions—earning from $3,000 to $10,000 in 1941. Ownership of a late model car is deemed essential, but two-car families are rare. Nine-tenths of them own homes in the best residential sections. Both men and women are very active in community and political affairs and some hired help is available to free the wife for her civic duties. Education is a vital (some writers say "obsessive") concern and this group is, on the average, better educated

---

* (New York: John Wiley & Sons, Inc.; 1949.) All quotations are used by permission of the publisher.

than is class I. Boys accept the vocational aim of business and the professions while girls are educated for a good marriage—though there is no attempt to marry them off. Marriages are contracted at a relatively late date, in terms of the national average, and are comparatively stable with their two or three children. Travel is limited but membership in the country club and church are concomitants of class II status. This is the group that contributes school board members, church workers, and civic leaders.

Class III persons envy those who are higher and look down upon but do not scorn those in class IV. They believe that class IV people do not have the ingredients for success but feel that their own position is due to the efforts of those above to keep them where they are. Income varies from $2,000 to $4,000, with one-sixth of the wives working as teachers, secretaries, and bookkeepers to supplement their income. "These families most nearly fit the typical American stereotype represented in popular magazines." * Two-thirds of them own their own homes and a quarter of them reside in the best districts. As a group, they are the best church attenders. Their relatively stable marriages are contracted somewhat earlier than is the case in class II and they average 3.6 children—wives are faithful but an occasional husband goes astray. Education is a highly desired goal but achievement of a college degree is rare—1 per cent of the fathers and 10 per cent of the mothers reach the goal. They join clubs, lodges, and societies, a few belong to the country club, and they advertise their doings in the local papers. Law is violated more frequently than is the case with class I and II, but there are no arrests of I's and II's and few of class III persons.

Class IV members, acknowledging their inferior status, resent the attitudes of the higher classes and avoid contact with those who are lower. They are regarded by others as being poor but honest, hard workers who try hard but are unsuccessful. Family incomes average about $1,500 annually and there is no chance to save, even when patronizing their favorite stores—mail order and chain stores. Seventy-five per cent of them have cars, but only a third own, or are buying, their homes. One-third of the families are broken by separation, divorce, or death but even so they average 4.3 children.

---

* Hollingshead, *op. cit.*, p. 97.

One-third of the mothers work in addition to doing their household work with few helpful appliances. Women accept the idea that their place is in the home; the men are not joiners though they do gather in pool halls and on the streets with other men. One-third of the men and one-fifth of the women have not completed the eighth grade; one out of twenty men and one of eleven women have been graduated from the secondary school. Religion is either systematically shunned or enthusiastically accepted. Leisure time is occupied with radio and movies; there is little reading of magazines, books, or newspapers other than the local papers. Baseball is popular but there is practically no traveling. Periodically, a class IV person gets the attention of the community by virtue of having committed a crime.

Class V persons are regarded by others as delinquent, immoral, slovenly, shiftless, and troublesome. They ". . . give the impression of being resigned to a life of frustration and defeat in a community that despises them for their disregard of morals, lack of 'success' goals, and dire poverty." * More than half of the wives work as waitresses, dish-washers, and domestic helpers to supplement the yearly incomes which average about $850. While they do not actually beg for furniture and clothing they know how to make their wants known to charitable people. Banks do not loan these people money, and even the loan companies exercise extreme care in lending them money. Many of them are undependable workers because they will and do leave jobs without notice. They are excluded from the better residential areas of Elmtown, living in a swampy region across the tracks. Their homes are small, run-down, box-like structures, heated by coal or wood stoves. The furniture is in poor repair, wardrobes are nothing but nails in the wall. Privacy, which psychologists say is a necessary ingredient of wholesome personality development, is virtually unknown—children (averaging 5.6 per mother), parents, and other relatives live together in two or three rooms. It is small wonder that the fathers, after a day's work, have a strong desire to get out of the house—there seems to be little concern about the mothers' feelings. Here the broken home statistics are built up: half the homes are upset by divorce, separation, deser-

---

* Hollingshead, *op. cit.,* p. 111.

tion, or death. The casualness of marriage leads Hollingshead to call the family pattern one of "serial monogamy." [143:116] Twenty to twenty-five per cent of the births are illegitimate. Education and religion are also weak institutions. Five out of 230 adults have been graduated from high school. Gambling, gossip, drinking (beer), and seeing cheap movies are the major leisure-time activities, and these are not pursued as family units. Four-fifths of the women have been in trouble with legal authorities—mostly for drinking and sex offenses—and half the men had, between 1934 and 1941, been convicted for drunkenness, sex crimes, and offenses against property.

Elmtown adolescents in school

The study of class structure in Elmtown was made ". . . to test the hypothesis that the social behavior of adolescents is related functionally to the position their families occupy in the social structure of the community." * Some of the disappointing concomitants of class are to be observed in the functioning of the school. If the reader feels that these concomitants are too definitive he should know that for another community he might be right; still we have such statistics as are given in Table 3 (page 212).

Upper-class pupils choose the high prestige college preparatory course (64 per cent) and shun the low-ranking commerical curriculum. Half the class III pupils take the general course and the rest divide equally between the college preparatory and commercial choices. Class IV pupils take the general and commercial course, with only 9 per cent electing the college preparatory. Class V's are virtually the same as IV's in choice except that only 4 per cent take the college preparatory curriculum.

It is disappointing to report that grades received seem to reflect class status. "Although intelligence was associated significantly with class position, the degree of association was not high enough to account for the concentration of failures in class V. Neither was it great enough to attribute the high grades in classes I and II to the intellectual capacity of this prestige level." † Since education is an important factor in upward mobility it will be well for teach-

---

* Hollingshead, *op. cit.,* p. 439.
† Hollingshead, *op. cit.,* p. 175.

ers to examine some of the probable causes of this inequitable situation: (1) the low regard for education that some pupils bring from their home, (2) the possibility of worry, strain, and failure in the home creating a disorganized emotional condition in the pupil, (3) the teacher's taking as a personal affront the inevitable fact that pupils from the lower class cannot have the same values as are prized by the teacher, and (4) the possibility that a low grade for an upper class pupil is withheld because it might have unpleasant consequences for the teacher. Despite the low grades of class IV and V pupils, most of the conferences between their parents and teachers are concerned with matters of discipline. Conferences between upper-class parents and teachers are more likely to deal with academic work.

Student activities hold, for the most part, little attraction for class V pupils—though boys from all strata participate in sports in equal proportions. In fact, in another study, cases are described in which the course of upward mobility was initiated by athletic competence. [334:11] However, when it comes to attending games class V pupils are underrepresented. This is not entirely a cost factor (see Chapter Seven); these children do attend movies for which the admission price is about the same. School dancing is the least popular of all student activities and practically no class IV or V pupils attend. One class V girl is reported who went to a dance with a class IV boy but had such a miserable time that she did not try it again. (Upperclass pupils do dance at the country club and a few from the lower classes dance at the dine and dance houses.) Participation in any student activity ranges from 27 per cent in class V to 100 per cent in class I. A class IV girl summarized the situation by saying, "Frankly, for a lot of us there is nothing here, but just going to classes, listening to the teacher, reciting, studying, and going home again. We are pushed out of things. There is a group of girls here who think they are higher than us. They look down on us." *

Elmtowners believe that the school's holding power is a matter of whether the pupil lives in the city or on the farm—they think school leavers are farm youth. Actually, three-quarters of the school leavers live in town. From 100 per cent of class I and II youths

---

* Hollingshead, *op. cit.*, p. 202.

of high school age who attend the figure drops to 58 per cent of class IV and 11 per cent of class V who attend. As is seen from the data on mothers and fathers who stayed in school, there is a tend-ency for girls to stay longer than boys. School attendance follows a family pattern—the time youngsters stay in school approximates the time the parents stayed.

> . . . we are convinced that this pattern has been handed down in many cases from the grandparents to the parents, and on to the ado-lescent's generation. We shall go one step further and say the adoles-cents may be expected to transmit it to their children through the subtle process of social learning in the family and the community, *not* through the germ plasm.*

Hollingshead, in these words, shows both the magnitude of the task and an approach to its successful accomplishment.

Those who work with youth must change the community influ-ences and the attitudes of youth toward them so that youth may use the school in the struggle to improve their status. That the school must bear some of the responsibility is shown by the fact that seasonal employment does not seem to explain the break with school—the first six weeks of a term is the crucial period. Those who drop out have poor attendance records and low scholarship rec-ords, but *there is no significant difference in the intelligence of the class V's who stay and those who quit school.* Other factors in school leaving include economic pressures, peer relationships (the attitude of a youth's clique toward school is a powerful factor in staying or leaving), and the attitude of teachers. The sentiment was often ex-pressed by teachers that withdrawal constituted good riddance. Teachers recalled not only individual cases of withdrawal but also remembered that the leaver's brothers and sisters had caused trouble. A class IV girl reported that the dirtiest thing she knew of was when a doctor's daughter was made salutatorian when it was her sister who, on the basis of grades, deserved the honor.

Social and recreational behavior

The belief that friendships are formed on the basis of likenesses in age, interest, and intelligence is not supported by Hollingshead's

---

* Hollingshead, *op. cit.,* p. 337.

data. Clique formation follows definite class lines; if girls from different strata become friends, former friends show their disapproval and the girl must drop her new friend or her old clique. Half the boy and girl cliques are within a given status level; one-third cross one class line, and 4 per cent include three levels. An individual's reputation is largely derived from the clique with which he is associated.

The majority of dates are within one class but occasionally spread across four classes; that is, a class IV individual may date in any other social status, but only 3 or 4 per cent of dates are with class I and 6 or 7 per cent with class V. Note that there is a tendency for all those above to avoid class V's.

The sex taboo is operative in all class levels but is violated more often by those in class IV and V. Hollingshead is cautious in his generalizations regarding sex behavior because of the need for interviewers to exercise reticence (because of community mores) in asking questions, but he does say,

> No case was found in which the boy [admitting sex relations] belonged to a lower class than the girl. Clearly in this small sample there was a strong tendency for young Elmtown males to exploit lower class females sexually. . . . Irrespective of the number of cases, the available figures throw a narrow beam of light on the question of whom young males in our society seek out for sex thrills.*

Hollingshead finds in dating, cliques, and sex behavior the clearest evidence in his study that the behavior of adolescents largely reflects the adult class structure.

Analysis of recreational pursuits is made difficult because some kinds of pleasure—drinking, gambling, and sex activities—are not freely talked about. Although these are not frankly discussed, both adults and youngsters recognize them as a part of the culture. Drinking differs from one class to another mainly in terms of place and what is drunk rather than in amount or frequency. Drinking is associated with age so that by the senior year in high school two-fifths of the boys and a fifth of the girls have experimented. Excessive drinking by girls causes them to be avoided by others in their clique at all class levels. Boys in general approve of drinking if it is not

---

* Hollingshead, *op. cit.*, p. 240.

done at school or at the church. It is part of the mores not to talk about drinking around teachers, preachers, or parents. If questions are asked they make it a rule not to admit anything. "Nevertheless, some students talk from time to time about certain students' drinking, often only after the person gossiped about has drunk to excess. But if adults try to track these stories down they invariably encounter denial after denial; no one knows anything." *

Boy Scout groups are mainly for class III and above—1 out of 116 class V boys was in scouts while 13 out of 21 class II boys belonged. Camp Fire Girls were also organized for, and by, the right people, and no class V girls belonged. While Girl Scouts are less exclusive the fact seems to mean that girls in the upper classes are less interested. Less than a third of Elmtown's youth are involved in these formal organizations.

Most recreation is informal; visiting, following clique groups, is a popular activity at all social class levels except V, where each individual tends to go his way alone. Motion picture attendance attracts over 90 per cent of Elmtown's youth, the higher classes attending more frequently. The feature film is less important than the theater where a person's friends attend. Class IV and V youngsters attend the "Bright Star" and "Silver Bell," where the cowboy and second run films are shown; the rest attend the "Elmtown" to see the first run pictures.

Clique groups dominate the issue of invitations to the frequent dancing parties held for class II's and the less frequent dances of class III and IV. No dances are held for the V's. Public dances are held at "Morrow's" which are attended by class V girls but not by class II's. "The net effect is the segregation of the young people along class lines at the private, semi-public, and public dances." †

Reading is not a popular pastime and those who do read some are looked down upon. There is some reading of slicks but book reading is confined to those that supplement school work in class II. It seems that some girls from class V use reading as an escape. Bowling is popular in the upper classes but attracts no class V's. Class V youngsters (50 per cent) frequent the roller skating rink, but

---

* Hollingshead, *op. cit.,* p. 320.
† Hollingshead, *op. cit.,* p. 306.

fewer than 10 per cent of the class I and II young persons participate. Girls who attend the skating rink have shady reputations—all of a group of five skating girls was said by one of them to have had sex relations with the "right fella."

Hunting and fishing are popular with all boys, but class V's cannot get permission to hunt posted areas. Trapping is enjoyed by class V boys but the smell, added to his social class, makes the trapper difficult to accept at school. The pool hall is a respectable place but women avoid it and class V boys are excluded. Although men and boys from all other classes play pool there is no increase of social interaction because playing is restricted to an individual's clique mates.

The young Elmtowner's religion

Young people learn the attitudes and acquire the religion of their parents much as they do their other behaviors and attitudes. Devout parents raise reverent children. Lax parents raise children who have little regard for religion. The lower the class level the lower is the percentage of affiliation with a church. Churches for the higher social classes have the greater number of youth organizations designed to meet the needs of young persons—but the needs are social rather than religious. Membership in church youth groups follows the same pattern of exclusion and inclusion that is found in cliques and dating patterns. Although some ministers frown upon movies, dancing, and card playing the young people follow the standards approved by their group. If their behaviors are disapproved by the ministers they are likely to withdraw from active participation in church sponsored activities. One situation (reminding us of the fact that teachers are influenced in their grading by class status) is that ministers find working with class IV's and V's non-rewarding. Four ministers ". . . frankly stated that these people are beyond help, as far as the ministers are concerned, and they do not try to reach them in any way. Seven reported that they officiate at funerals, weddings, and baptisms if they are asked; two refuse to perform these rites on religious grounds." * It is discouraging to find that if ministers work with those at the lower social levels they lose their

---

* Hollingshead, *op. cit.*, p. 117.

grasp on those in the higher strata. It is to be hoped that the Elmtown religious situation represents a minority of cities—but a look around is disheartening.

Work experiences

The dilemma of occupational orientation (see Chapter Sixteen) is complicated by the influences of social class. Elmtown gives some evidence that job selection is as much a matter of family background as it is a matter of interest and aptitude. Class I and II youth work, if at all, as clerks in the better stores and offices; having a part-time job is a part of the mores for class III and below; and many young people from class IV and V work to help support their families. The jobs open to students have prestige values related to the adult work world. Office work in stores and the "Mill" and for professional workers is rated highest, clerical work in locally owned stores is next, followed by clerical work in chain stores and those owned by Jews. Work in service stations and theaters is respectable but lacks prestige value. Waiting on table or washing dishes is menial labor, viewed with disfavor by adolescents, and is only slightly higher than janitorial work and garbage and ash hauling.

If a class II parent, who usually makes the job contact, allows his son or daughter to work at a job below his class he is frowned upon by his peers and condemned as "hogging" jobs by those in lower classes. Being a waitress has caused a class IV girl to be dropped by her clique mates. A class II boy was dropped by his clique mates when he became a fry cook; with his new friends in class III and IV he learned to drink and became a "common bum." Class II youth and some of the class III, if their parents have "pull," get desirable jobs—the rest take what they can get.

Vocational interests of adolescents follow their family patterns. Three-quarters of class II and a third of class III youth choose the professions. Class III and IV youth choose sales and clerical work. Class V's have quite diversified interests—they may ". . . list highly dramatic, romantic, and freak jobs, such as wild animal trainer, bareback rider in a circus, six-day bicycle racer, juggler in a carnival, which we placed in the miscellaneous group (25 per cent)." *

---

* Hollingshead, op. cit., p. 284.

Elmtown's youth do not believe the myth that anyone may become a millionaire or a president or can readily climb the economic and social ladder to success. This is reflected in the fact that a given pupil's occupational aim accords rather well with the promise that class status holds for him. W. L. Warner and others also point out the fallacy of believing that ambition, hard work, and ability will take a young person to the top of the socio-economic heap. [334:51] The social class with which a person identifies himself is just as intimately related to plans to attend college as is his ability to do college work. [283]

Persistency of status mores

Social conditioning

During his pre-school years, a child necessarily receives the majority of his experiences from within his home and from his immediate neighbors. Culture, for the child, is vested predominately in his parents, and their way of meeting his needs constitutes his direct contact with the social milieu. Throughout the individual's life, these early patterns remain as the essential matrix for his subsequent cultural accommodation. It is important for those who work with adolescents to realize that the young person who has different ideals, ambitions, concepts of right and wrong, and habits from those of the teacher or counselor has an extensive background which has formed the differences. The worker must realize that it is not laziness or recalcitrance that causes some youngsters to sneer at academic school work. It must further be realized that no momentous changes will be wrought because of a few words of wisdom uttered by the adult. The item of promise is a revamping of educational practices that will encourage handicapped youngsters to continue their educations. Acceptance by the teacher may do much to help the young person live with his difficulties.

Contrasting methods of child rearing

Most social scientists accept the notion of social stratification in the United States. Whether it be the five-fold classification used by Hollingshead or Warner's six categories, whether it be merely upper, middle, and lower, or whether we simply say that people are different, the fact of varied motivations and behavior remains. Eleanor E. Maccoby and Patricia K. Gibbs studied the attitudes of parents from the middle and from the lower class on the assumption that adult personality has its basis in child rearing practices. [196] Their study of Boston metropolitan families reveals some consistent differences, which indicate the difficulty an adolescent might later have in the struggle for upward mobility.

1. The two classes do not differ significantly in infant feeding practices, but the upper-middle class mothers do schedule feedings somewhat more rigidly.
2. The upper-lower class mothers are more severe in approaches to toilet training. They scold more often and use more punishment when there are toilet accidents.
3. Mothers of the upper-lower class are more severe in sex training—they have higher standards of and stress earlier the matter of modesty. They react emotionally and use punishment when children masturbate while mothers of the upper-middle class either ignore, or seek to distract children from, masturbation.
4. Children can more freely show aggressiveness toward their upper-middle class parents than can those who are upper-lower class.
5. Parents of the upper-lower class, with some inconsistencies in comparisons, tend to use more punishment, deprivation of privileges, and ridicule in controlling children than do the upper-middle class parents. The latter use more praise and reasoning to accomplish their purposes.
6. Upper-middle class mothers are warmer and somewhat more demonstrative to their young children than are mothers of the upper-lower group.
7. Husband-wife relationships are characterized by more mutual respect and affection in the upper-middle class, while in the upper-lower group there is more criticism of the husband and there are more differences of opinions regarding methods of child rearing.
8. The extent of father involvement in child rearing does not differ in the two groups.
9. The authors wondered if the differences might be a reflection of education rather than class so they compared the answers of

mothers from both classes who had equal amounts of education. They concluded that the differences really were those of class conditioning, "The tendency for the upper-middle mothers to be more permissive and less severe in their child training than the upper-lower mothers holds up when the mothers' education, age or ethnic origin are held constant." *

Aggressiveness and placidity

Claudia Lewis has described the contrast of her experiences in a Greenwich Village nursery school with those in a Cumberland Mountain village in Tennessee. [188] She admits the fallacy of the average or typical child but does note some differences. In Greenwich Village families were small, more than half of the mothers worked outside the home, incomes were sufficient for healthful but not spacious living. The children were strong and vigorous. They were active both physically and verbally. They lived intensively— in their play, in their enthusiasms, in their work, and in their frustrations. Their appearance of intellectual giftedness was corroborated by intelligence tests. Teaching them required ingenuity, patience, and skill in understanding individuals. All-in-all the children were creative, aggressive, and vociferous.

Children in the Summerville Nursery were shy and quiet, they were happy and *interested in what the teacher was doing.* There was much less shouting and interpersonal aggression as well as less exercise and development of speech functions. Baby talk at the age of four or five was difficult to understand. Their Stanford-Binet scores were lower than those of the average child in Greenwich Village, especially on the verbal portions of the test. The differences, which Lewis admits to be matters of degree, were probably due to differences in the mode of life. In Summerville 60 per cent of the population was dependent upon some degree of relief. The parents looked and acted old for their chronological age. All of them were kind to their children. They spent practically all of their time with their children—at work, at home, and even at the dances held for recreation. Everyone went to bed and got up at the same time—ob-

---

* Eleanor E. Maccoby and Patricia K. Gibbs, in William E. Martin and Celia B. Stendler (Eds.) *Readings in Child Development* (New York: Harcourt, Brace & Company; 1954), p. 395.

viously, there were no baby sitters. The children were placid and carefree. There was no pressure to make them go to school if they happened to feel like staying away.

Lewis does not conclude that children are better off in one community than in another, but she does ask a question. Are high intelligence, drive and persistence, and creativeness purchased at the price of conflict, thwarting, and strong stimulation? The question need not be answered prior to formulating the conclusion that there are marked differences in personality due to the contrasting social milieu in which the child develops. Neither can we avoid the conclusion that adolescents who grow up in one kind of culture will have a difficult time accepting and being accepted in a culture that is markedly different. It should not be thought that social intercourse between various social strata is deliberately or maliciously avoided. It is simply a matter of being more comfortable among one's kind. A step toward the solution of the problem of discrimination is made when the problem is called to mind and deliberately studied. This is certainly the case in the improved status of the American Negro in the past decade, though the problem is by no means solved. [209] As more and more people become aware of the psychological and social factors at work in preventing mobility, and thus denying our democratic ideal, the better the chance will be that mobility will be based on ability.

Rural-urban differences

Values in contrasting communities

Paul H. Landis asserts that the basic values in rural communities center about (1) work for work's sake, (2) the goal of ownership of land, and (3) family life that centers about the children and their roles. [183:352] The farmer takes pride in toil and in the visible products of his manual labor. He teaches his children to get ahead by devotion to consistent work and faithful diligence. Children are valued because they can help in the performance of the tasks that are the primary concerns of the rural world. In contrast, Landis points out, the city dweller (1) orients his life about the pleasure motive—work is performed because it is a means to the end of living a life geared to the achievement of happiness. (2) Conspicuous consumption seems to transcend the motive of production.

(3) Marriage is often a matter of personal convenience and satisfaction rather than primarily an institution devoted to the care and welfare of children. In the city, the worker does not usually see the product of his labor in concrete form so he gets recognition by buying pleasure and possessions. Children are taught that outward appearances, proper dress, knowing the "right" people, and "having pull" are more important in getting ahead than are ability and hard work—the virtues taught by the rural parents.

Some of the differences between rural and urban life are disappearing with improved transportation and communication. Farm youth are more and more becoming acquainted with the stimulation of urban life and there has been a rising conflict in the rural home as the youngsters seek to emulate the pleasure-seeking life of their city peers. This is thought to be one of the factors in increasing migration to the city—though technological advances in farming methods must also be taken into account.

In summarizing the differences Landis states that while urban youth lack the core values that prompt a person toward admirable life goals, their less rigid system of values, and their greater breadth of experience, give them help in the transition to adulthood. Rural youth, on the other hand, are more introverted, less adaptable, and have narrower interests. Stable values help them in adaptation to their accustomed environment but may handicap them in making a transition to another situation. [183:93]

Family life in contrasting communities

Ray E. Baber states that it is doubtful if any aspect of social change in the past century has had more effect than the shift of a population that was in 1900 about 40 per cent urban to one that, in 1952, was 63.7 per cent urban. [10:8] He notes some of the factors that are mentioned by both Landis and Lewis in their contrasts of rural and urban families.

1. The city family has been subjected to a housing system that entails crowding, discomfort, and irritation of emotional poise. This overcrowding fosters immorality and ill-health and, it might be added, deprives the adolescent of the privacy he so much needs.

2. The cohesive nature of the rural family disappears in the city. Neighborhood contacts are, with the possible exception of a

next-door friend, impersonal and casual. There is little sharing of whole family friendships of the kind found in the country.

3. The city family is composed of individuals each of whom tends to go in his own direction. The country family, it has been noted, shares the common task of making a living.

4. Living within the family's means is a difficult task in the city where advertising appeals are insistent and the necessity of keeping up a good front is felt.

5. Much of the fun in the country is spontaneous and homemade. In the city, commercialized recreation is much more alluring than the pallid but more permanent enjoyments of the rural home. Youngsters learn to depend on others for the supplying of their desires for pleasure and entertainment.

6. Contrary to some popular conceptions, it is easier to find a suitable marriage partner in the country than it is in the city. Whole families are known to one another in the country, but it may be quite difficult for boys and girls to meet in the city.

7. "Furthermore, the anonymity of the city is an invitation to prostitution and illicit unions that offer temporary, and sometimes permanent, substitutes for marriage and family life." *

Youth workers should become aware of the influence of these varied family patterns because it is so easy to fall into the error of thinking of Americans as a homogeneous population. Ours is probably one of the more heterogeneous nations. Generalizations regarding adolescents must be cautiously drawn because (1) the psychological or sociological study may have been made on a unique group, (2) the experience of the "generalizer" may have been limited, and (3) the observer's own adolescent experience, particularly in home and community life, is unlike that of many adolescents. Teachers, especially, must become aware of the fact that their attitudes and practices reflect the values of their earlier life while their pupils may come from quite different backgrounds.

Adolescent adjustment in contrasting communities

A number of contrasts in behavior have been noted in the behavior of rural and urban youth. For example, rural youth experi-

---

* By permission from *Marriage and the Family,* 2nd Edition, by Ray E. Baber. Copyright 1953, McGraw-Hill Book Company, Inc. P. 9.

ence greater conflict with their parents—there is less conflict between members of families in small towns and still less in city
families. [296] This is probably due to the greater freedom in the
city, the lack of recreation that holds different ages together, and
the rural adolescent's knowledge that his urban peer has fewer obligations. There is a less mature and varied interest in play activities
in the country, due to the fact that children of all ages must often
play together. Hence, the progression to more grown-up activities
by older pupils is prevented. This difference is tending to disappear as more schools are consolidated. [147:389] There is a difference in the occupational choices of rural and urban youth. Rural
boys tend to choose agriculture and engineering while urban youth
choose the professions and commercial activities. Almost half the
rural girls choose to be teachers while city girls choose commercial
and secretarial careers almost as frequently as they do teaching—
teaching being the most frequently chosen occupation for city,
town, and farm girls. [284] Work opportunities are more readily
available for farm youth—thus giving them a chance to gain the
significance and recognition that go a long way toward offsetting
some of the handicaps of varied experience. City youth suffer the
double handicap of difficulty in finding any work at all plus the fact
(see Chapter Sixteen) that the work they do find is often the
blind alley type—this, of course, does not refer to the work found
after adolescence has been spent in going to school. The large number of men who were found to be physically unfit for military service
has led to the conclusion that urbanization, with its dependence on
mechanization, indoor work, and lack of hard physical work is resulting in a less sturdy population. [73] This fact, or even this
ground for suspicion, suggests the importance of having physical
education programs that meet the needs of many students (see
Chapter Five).

Whatever the cause of typical personality differences between
adolescents living in varied regions and circumstances, it seems that
the conditions, as such, should not be allowed to interfere with the
mobility that is a part of our national heritage. We turn now to what
is the greatest factor in upward mobility—education.

Implications of social strata for schools

The educational challenge

Social status, it has been indicated, is a matter of social participation (behavior) and wealth. Chapter Seven has described the relationship between education and income and between education and behavior. The most readily available factor in upward mobility is education. The extent to which education makes it possible for each individual to achieve the status to which his total ability entitles him is the extent to which we achieve our ideal of respect for the individual. To the extent that any man is denied higher status or avoids lower status because of his initial position on the social hierarchy, we must admit failure to achieve the goal of mankind's brotherhood.

Fortunately, dreams of reaching this goal are not entirely ethereal. The elementary school a hundred years ago was faced with much the same sort of problem that the secondary schools are faced with today. The elementary school workers have faced and resolved the challenge. Today the holding power of the common school is such that the great majority of elementary school pupils are staying in school. Individual differences are quite effectively met. Teachers in any given grade vary their approaches, vary the level of instruction and the materials to meet individual and small groups of individuals. Provisions are increasingly being made for the partially seeing, the hard of hearing, the delicate, the deformed, and the child of retarded mental development. Perfection has not been reached. Problems have not been finally solved. But the progress is commendable.

The struggle to respect the individual has begun at the secondary level. The fact that this aim has not been successfully achieved is manifested in the average educational achievement of our citizenry and by the study of school drop-outs. There is no clear consensus regarding the function of the secondary school in relation to social stratification. There are, on the one hand, those who believe that the school should cater to the needs of the intellectually elite; there is much talk of maintaining standards and passing courses. These people, it seems, tend to overlook the possibility of the existence of valuable abilities other than those that underly academic superiority. It is these who criticize compulsory attendance to the age of eighteen because there are so many of these late teen-age youngsters who do not fit the mold that is so comfortable for the teacher. On the other hand, there are those who strive for equality of opportunity and who see in education the most powerful factor in implementing this equality. These people see in the increasing tendency of business leaders and professional men to be drawn from families of the same class a threat to the vitality of our country. [47] They would seem to agree with Oliver Goldsmith, who wrote in "The Deserted Village":

> Ill fares the land, to hastening ills a prey,
> Where wealth accumulates, and men decay;
> Princes and lords may flourish or may fade;
> A breath can make them, as a breath has made;
> But a bold peasantry, their country's pride,
> When once destroy'd, can never be supplied.

It is here assumed that there is general agreement on the belief that our best workers at any level should be allowed to assume their deserved place on the basis of ability rather than ancestry.

What can be done in the schools

The problems created by class structure are society-made. But steps toward improvement, like the reduction of delinquency, must begin at some point. There is reason to believe that those who work in the schools are in the most strategic position to effect improvement.

1. Teachers must understand *social status differences*. Teachers should develop a perspective that recognizes that each person sees the world from a different vantage point. The experiences of a teacher's own childhood and adolescence must not be considered typical. Clinical psychologists stress the importance of not showing shock at the most surprising revelations of a client—and teachers must avoid showing shock when they encounter widely different ideals, mores, thoughts, and behaviors. Such understanding, of course, is not to be achieved by a process of lifting oneself by the bootstraps. There are some things that can be done.

Teachers might well make a rather detailed study of such reports as those on "Elmtown," "Yankee City," "Old Town," or "Summerville." These need be considered neither representative nor typical but illustrative of a situation in some places and perhaps indicative of events that take place to a lesser degree elsewhere. Teachers should more actively participate in the life of the community—not just by teaching Sunday school or by joining a bridge club but by visiting all kinds of homes, getting acquainted with many of the local businesses and industries, gaining membership on civic boards and commissions, and keeping informed on contemporary events.

2. *Different kinds of intelligence* must be recognized. Intelligence tests yield indications of the individual's capacity for dealing with the kinds of tasks traditionally performed in school. This is an important capacity and is positively correlated with other kinds of successful functioning. But it is not the only kind of intelligence. Musical capacity, social intelligence, motor functioning, appreciation of, and ability to function in the realm of, aesthetic and mechanical pursuits are sometimes found to be only slightly correlated with test intelligence.

Teachers must recognize that intelligence is "measured" only indirectly. Innate intelligence is inferred from developed, or operative intelligence. Hence, experience conditions the amount of innate intelligence that is indicated in an intelligence quotient or a mental age score. Davis and Eells have recognized this in their "Davis-Eells Games" [77]—an intelligence test designed to impose less of a handicap on children from the lower socio-economic levels (see Chapter Fifteen). Some psychologists, recognizing that children from the lower social strata are handicapped in the development of their verbal intelligence, recommend that a scale of correction (adding points) be adopted.

The teacher has two problems relating to intelligence. One is to be sure that an intelligence test is an accurate indicator of intellectual potential, and the other is to recognize that even if a pupil's intelligence is sufficient to do good school work his motivation (without being mean or recalcitrant) might be inadequate.

3. *Educational goals* must be broadened. The study of those who drop out of school indicates that high schools are not filling the needs of many youth. The prevalence of the college preparatory

emphasis verifies this criticism. However, it must be admitted that the problem is recognized, attempts are being made to broaden goals, and considerable progress is being made—witness the increased holding power of the school. Our schools are by no means on the "brink of collapse." What is needed is not a new set of goals but an attempt at the more complete implementation of the goals that have already been formulated. A study of the "Imperative Needs" of youth or of the "Developmental Tasks" of adolescence provides abundant clues as to how broadened educational goals may be realized.

4. *Methods and materials* must be diversified. Children from middle-class homes have been, for their entire lives, living in an atmosphere in which education is highly regarded. This experience creates in them a compulsive attitude toward the school. It is *highly* important that they succeed; it is shameful to have conflict with the teachers; it is a blot on the family record to be truant. With such powerful motivation the job of the teacher is greatly simplified. But there is another, and large, group of pupils who have no such compulsive attitudes. Their parents have little education and, though fathers and mothers give lip service to education, the constant pressure described above is lacking. Especially in the upper grades many youngsters are only marking time until they can quit school and find a job. Many of these feel that school is not opportunity, it is interference with opportunity. The problem of motivation is staggering.

Methods of instruction that give all pupils a chance to perform and to be recognized are steps in the direction of developing interest. Employing discussion procedures, as contrasted to assign-study-recite procedures, allows all pupils to make a contribution and fosters feelings of worth. The creation of numerous offices and functions in which pupils of varied interests and abilities may perform will contribute to feelings of significance. Methods involving the study of the immediate community will give youngsters from the lower strata a chance to describe the things they have experienced—which are just as much a part of the total life of the community as are those that are more commonly studied. In short, these pupils need methods that will permit them emotional satisfactions derived from contributing, from being liked and accepted, and from being valued for the unique contributions they can make. In the long run such methods constitute more than a contribution to individuals. They represent a contribution to society, because it is almost certain that the harsh and unsympathetic treatment some youngsters get in school creates tensions that are a factor in delinquency. [55] Improving methods will ease the job of the teacher because it will reduce the problems of classroom control.

Materials in the classroom should be broadened so that the great bulk of study is not some form of verbalization. In addition to books, references, lectures, and written reports use should be made of field trips, work experience, movies, film strips, models, and replicas. Further, it is to be hoped that in the social studies there will be more materials dealing with the life of people in the lower classes. Even a cursory examination of these materials will show that a large segment of life is rather blithely overlooked. Fortunately, there is now beginning to appear good material that describes and illustrates life in the lower social strata. This material has the double advantage of making the pupils from the lower classes feel more comfortable while broadening the understanding of the pupils from the higher classes.

5. The *struggle of lower class pupils to stay in school* should be eased. The struggle to stay in school will be eased when broader goals and varied methods are introduced. There will then be a chance for a pupil to be recognized for talents and interests other than the academic (and sometimes athletic) talent that receives the major attention at present.

Teachers can ease the struggle by accepting children as they are. This means that some who have low motivation for academic work will be forgiven for their "inadequacy." It means that greater tolerance must be granted the slow learner—since lower class children are, *on the average,* lower in test intelligence than are pupils from higher classes. This also means that the teacher will take pains to recognize and encourage talent when it is encountered in the socially less fortunate. *On the average,* pupils from the lower classes can be expected to be a year or two behind their peers in scores on achievement tests that cover the fundamentals.

An attempt must be made to eliminate the extra costs of education. Special fees for books, materials, football shoes, gym towels, club membership, school paper, and annuals should be eliminated. Individually these fees are small; collectively they may be so large as to cause some pupils to believe they cannot keep up with their peers. Probably the matter of costs should go even further to include providing a part-time job for needy pupils so that they may have enough cash for carfare or a sundae.

Attempts should be made to facilitate a pupil's acceptance by his classmates. This might be approached by (1) descriptions and discussion of the processes of socialization, (2) the teacher's asking the aid of well-adjusted pupils, who can act as big brothers or sponsors of the socially reticent, and (3) the use of sociometric groupings to capitalize upon natural attractions as well as to detect more rapidly those who need help (this technique will also help locate those most capable of giving help).

6. Pupils should *study the class status system*. Adolescent pupils are capable of understanding and tolerance but they need to be directed because of their lack of experience. They are not innately cruel or prejudiced but they are products of their life history. Studies of the nature and operation of class hierarchies might well be considered an integral part of social studies courses or personal development classes. Celia B. Stendler suggests a high school course that would include a systematic study of class structure, using such materials as are produced by the University of Chicago's Committee on Human Development—"Yankee City" and "Elmtown." [292] Such procedures would give the student a perspective from which to formulate goals, free from the limitations of prejudice. The study should reveal the phenomenon of mobility, the part status plays in school life and the selection of occupational goals, and should provide for discussion of ways to improve the situation.

W. Lloyd Warner and Mildred H. Warner have outlined a study of social class for adolescents using the following topics, "You and social class," "Learning about social class," "How you can determine your social class," "Friendship and social class," "Social class and your future," and "Where do we go from here?" [333] Neither those in the upper classes nor those in the lower classes can afford to lose the talent that is wasted through needless discrimination. Yet much talent is lost annually because of our inability to assess it and because of our apparent reluctance to use it. [76] It seems odd that such a phenomenon as class status, which so profoundly affects thinking, overt behavior, emotional responses, and health, would not be the subject of direct study.

7. *Public relations programs* are needed. Data presented thus far in this book indicate a fact to which we all give lip service: society is in an everlasting state of flux. One of the changes, of which note should be taken, is that social mobility is becoming increasingly difficult. [332] If this and other challenges are to be met in the school it is inevitable that the schools will also change. Suitable changes can most readily be effected if the public understands and favors the changes. But too often the citizens do not know the aims and problems involved in changes and remark, "It's not what it used to be." It is up to those in the school to interpret their work by reports issued at intervals, by campaigns (though interpretation is needed in other than emergency times), by newspaper and magazine articles, and through the impressions that youngsters take home to their parents.

However, the task is not one-sided. No problem as big as education or youth problems can be the responsibility of one group. Citizens have some responsibility for searching for information. They should ask questions and they need not place blind reliance on authority—though experts should not be ignored. Public relations are a phase of the give and take process of democracy.

Summary

The idea of social classes is repugnant to those who cherish the democratic ideal. However, it is recognized that people do have different talents and different contributions to make to the general welfare. The undemocratic aspect of this is that everyone is not permitted an equal chance to realize his potential. Thought and study must be given to the equalization of opportunity.

"Class" in the United States does not mean caste—which involves hereditary status more than individual ability. Class is simply one means of identifying the *average* differences between groups of people. Status is to a large extent determined by social participation and family income. Transition, known as mobility, from one group to another is possible, though frequently difficult.

There are varying degrees of distinctiveness of class lines. Older and slowly changing communities have clearer lines. Newer communities, rapidly growing ones, and large cities where interpersonal knowledge is relatively small have less-distinctly defined classes. An example of the older city where lines are clear is Elmtown. Study of this community shows that adolescents are affected in terms of in-school behavior, staying in or leaving school, and attitudes toward education. Social and recreational behavior shows consistent, though not always sharp, differences between classes. The type of religion and devotion to it reveal the impact of class conditioning. In their teen years as well as in their work later, the pressure of social class is shaping the goals, aspirations, and achievements of individuals.

Social class does not wait to begin its directive influence on growth until the young person is making social contacts outside his family. It begins in the home—where the parents have already been shaped into patterned behavior. The pervasiveness of home and community influences is illustrated in the average differences of behavior existing between rural and urban youth.

Increasing the possibility of mobility, and thus better capitalizing on our human resources, is to a marked extent dependent upon those who work in the schools. Things that might be done include better understanding by teachers of class structure, recognition of different kinds of intelligence, broader educational goals and methods, encouraging lower class youth to stay in school, direct study of class structure by high school pupils, and improved interpretation of the job of the school in facilitation of mobility. Of course, in the final analysis providing equal opportunities for all to fulfill their potential is a problem involving all of society.

STUDY AND REVIEW ITEMS

1. What experience have your classmates had with social class? Did they feel it acutely or were they largely unaware of it? How does the reaction vary with the locality of their adolescent home?

2. Why is it that progress from class II to class I is so little affected by education? Why have class I people, on the average, fewer years of schooling than class II?

3. How do you account for the fact that, although class I parents educate daughters for marriage, their average age at marriage is higher than the national average?

4. What do you think should be a core curriculum for all secondary school pupils? (Select five subjects and compare the list with that of a classmate.)

5. What would you suggest doing in the dilemma of a minister's losing his congregation if he serves those from lower social strata?

6. What are some specific behaviors you might expect in adolescence that stem from different child rearing concepts?

7. Does it seem to you that the urban values, as described by Landis, are superior or inferior to those of the rural areas?

8. How would you account for the fact that an Elmtown girl from an upper class received honors that, on the basis of academic record, had actually been earned by a lower class girl?

9. Discuss the relative advantages and disadvantages of living, through adolescence, in the country and in the large city.

10. What educational problem is presented by the fact that lower class pupils who drop out of school have just about the same average intelligence as lower class pupils who stay in school?

11. What are some suggestions for helping the lower class youngster to stay in school, other than those mentioned in the text?

RECOMMENDED SUPPLEMENTARY READING

Davis, Allison, in Guy E. Swanson and Others (Eds.) *Readings in Social Psychology* (New York: Henry Holt & Company, Inc.; 1952), pp. 531–539. (Also in National Society for the Study of Education, 43rd Yearbook, Part I, 1944, pp. 198–214.)
    This selection is a description of the ways in which levels of aspiration, behavior orientation, sex attitudes, and socialization processes are influenced by social class conditioning.

Hollingshead, August B. *Elmtown's Youth; The Impact of Social Classes on Adolescents* (New York: John Wiley & Sons, Inc.; 1949), 480 pp.

This study by the University of Chicago's Committee on Human Development is one of many. It is of particular interest because it focusses upon the effect of social class upon the behavior of adolescents.

Seidman, Jerome M. (Ed.) *The Adolescent: A Book of Readings* (New York: The Dryden Press; 1953), pp. 465–491.

Professor Seidman has selected three readings dealing with adolescents and social class. Ruth Benedict deals with cultural conditioning. A. B. Hollingshead contrasts the behavior of upper-class adolescents with that of class V adolescents. Allison Davis and John Dollard tell how it feels to be in the lower social strata.

"Social Class Structure and American Education," *Harvard Educational Review*, 23, 1953, pp. 149–338.

The summer and fall issues of this periodical contain articles by various scholars dealing with criticisms and evaluations of previous studies and also has some suggestive implications for current educational practice.

Warner, W. Lloyd; R. J. Havighurst; and Martin B. Loeb. *Who Shall Be Educated?* (New York: Harper & Brothers; 1944), 190 pp.

An excellent, brief account of the influence of social class on the educational aspirations and experiences of typical individuals from various class origins. Factors in social mobility are described. Proposals for improvement of conditions are suggested.

AUDIO-VISUAL MATERIAL

Feeling Left Out? (Coronet Films, Coronet Building, Chicago 1), 16 min., so., b. & w. or col.

This shows the snow-balling effect of a boy's being left out of group activities. The dangers of clique formation are portrayed.

The Quiet One (Athena Films, 165 W. 46th St., New York 19), 70 min., so., b. and w.

This remarkable document about an unwanted child of Harlem, who is sent to Wiltwick School for treatment, shows the environmental and psychological factors that drive him toward delinquent behavior.

How does the course of intellectual development of a baby differ from that of an adolescent? How can we capitalize on varying types of intelligence? When does intellectual development cease?

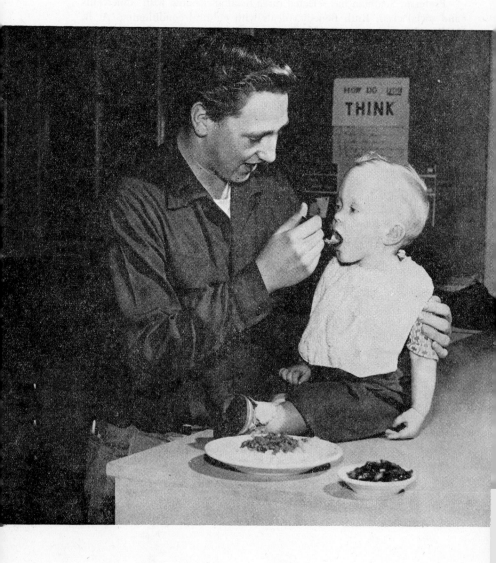

CHAPTER NINE

Intellectual Development

Man's distinctiveness as a superior creature is attributed to the ability to talk, the ability to oppose thumb and forefinger, and the level of his intelligence. Much has been said in the past half century about the nature, meaning, and measurement of intelligence. However, the continued flow of literature and the continued pursuit of research relating to intelligence indicate that we are perhaps only on the frontiers of understanding.

Two rather recent emphases indicate that the study of intelligence during adolescence, as a somewhat unique development, may be quite fruitful. One is the increasing emphasis upon the concept of "intelligences" rather than upon intelligence. It is being more and more widely recognized that the academic intelligence usually assessed through tests is not sufficiently inclusive or discriminating. The second emphasis is the amount of research devoted to the nature of adult intelligence—and the discovery that, while the test intelligence of a person in his later maturity may not be relatively high, his performance in most kinds of work is such that he competes well with younger persons. The major exception to this is in tasks requiring speed and strength—though accuracy may compensate for some of the loss in agility and power. This research indicates too that the adolescent's intelligence is somewhat different from the child's—on whom a great deal of the basic research in intelligence testing has been done.

The need for the study of intelligence during adolescence is further indicated by two, somewhat contradictory, interpretations of what is known. One of these interpretations is that adolescence represents the *last* stage of rapid learning and that we therefore must be sure to seize the waning opportunity. Of course, it is important to take advantage of this opportunity but *it may not be the last.* Interpretation number two is that even though an individual has reached the limit of mental capacity during adolescence his knowledge, judgment, insight, and independence will go on increasing for some ten, twenty, or thirty years.

Basic considerations

Varied meanings of intelligence

Concepts of intelligence vary from "Intelligence is what intelligence does" and "Intelligence is what intelligence tests measure" to the idea that it is not a noun but an adverb—one behaves intelligently. Some authorities recommend a simple definition such as the ability to do abstract thinking—to use symbols as vehicles for problem solving. George D. Stoddard states:

> Intelligence is the ability to undertake activities that are characterized by (1) difficulty, (2) complexity, (3) abstractness, (4) economy, (5) adaptiveness to a goal, (6) social value, and (7) the emergence of originals, and to maintain such activities under conditions that demand a concentration of energy and a resistance to emotional forces.*

Some object to such a shotgun approach, stating that it can hardly fail to hit the target at some point but what point is not clear. [114]

It would be nice to report that back of the varied definitions there appears to be a basic agreement, but this does not seem to be the case. Some believe that intelligence is inborn and that intelligence testing is simply an attempt to estimate what an individual's innate capacity is. Others incline toward the belief that inborn capacity is realized only through the operation of environmental conditions. This view recognizes the operation of the growth principle, "Growth

---

* George D. Stoddard, "On the Meaning of Intelligence," *Psychological Review*, 48, 1941, 250–260.

is the product of the interaction of the organism with its environ-ment" (see Chapter Two). A person is intelligent to the extent that he uses his capacity by taking advantage of environmental oppor-tunities to function effectively.

Paul L. Boynton, after evaluating nine definitions of intelligence, concludes that no satisfactory definition can be given and suggests that it might be better to use some other term. Nevertheless, the term is used and he defines it as "an inherited capacity of the in-dividual which is manifested through his ability to adapt to and re-construct the factors of his environment in accordance with the most fundamental needs of himself and his group." * This defini-tion, by using the word "manifested," agrees with the author's con-tention that the organism interacting *with* its environment is in-volved in the concept of intelligence.

Difficulties in evaluating intelligence

We shall have to wait for further research to clarify the meaning of intelligence and how it can best be evaluated. In the meantime, let it be stated that the view taken here is one of "operational in-telligence"; that is, intelligence is a function of capacity plus the nurture provided by environment. Furthermore, the view is ac-cepted that intelligence consists of many varied, even if interre-lated, kinds of adaptive behavior. To the extent that a person lives in an environment that does not stimulate the development of in-nate capacity in any, or all, of these varied areas of functioning he is to that degree unintelligent. It is as though a child with tall ances-tors and immediate parents had the capacity of being six feet tall (a potential we cannot at present assess) but due to lack of exer-cise and proper food or prolonged illness finally grew to be five feet six inches tall. At any time he is only as tall as linear measurements indicate. Unfortunately, linear measurement is superior to psycho-logical measurement. The potential for tallness cannot be meas-ured. Psychological tests can *measure* neither the potential nor the extent of developed capacity. This does not mean that mental meas-urements have no utility. They are extremely valuable devices for *estimating* both capacity and present level of functioning.

---

* Paul L. Boynton in Walter S. Monroe (Ed.), *Encyclopedia of Educational Research*, Revised Edition (New York: The Macmillan Company; 1950), p. 601.

Constancy of the IQ

If intelligence tests were accurate and if mental growth took place at the same rate as chronological growth the ratio between the two measures would remain constant. This relation could be plotted as a straight diagonal line from top to bottom of a graphical representation of mental growth (see Figure 9). In general, the rate of mental growth does tend to remain steady and successive measurements tend to be very much alike; and rate of growth has value as a predictive device in estimating what later intellectual status will be. However, since the very beginning of mental testing, variations in successive IQ scores have been noted. For a long time this variation was (1) attributed to the inaccuracy of tests. Later the idea was postulated that the changing IQ might sometimes (2) be attributed to variability of the developmental pattern but that intelligence was nevertheless an innate function. Still another view

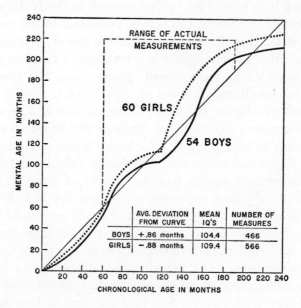

FIG. 9. **Trends of mental growth**

Mean curve of constants of mental growth for selected boys and girls. From Cecil V. Millard, *Child Growth and Development* (Boston: D. C. Heath and Company; 1951), p. 131.

is that the changing IQ may (3) be attributed to marked changes in the intellectual stimulation value of the environment. Ordinarily a growing individual remains in a relatively stable environment, so little change in IQ could be expected. Whether or not this latter view is becoming a consensus there are some who feel that ". . . we can no longer be confident that the IQ will remain approximately constant when the environment is radically improved." *

C.V. Millard lends support to the idea that test intelligence varies because of innate growth factors. He holds that there is a two-cycle characteristic of growth (Figure 9). Of particular interest to the student of adolescence is the fact that there is a slowing down of the rate of mental growth just prior to the time of puberty. After puberty there is a marked acceleration of the curve. It should be noted that, if IQ's were computed from this growth curve, boys at the age of 130 months have a mental age of 110 months and average about 85 IQ; but at age 180 months they have a mental age of about 195 months with an approximate IQ of 108. These data are corroborated by an earlier study of Harold E. Jones and Herbert S. Conrad, indicating that a slower growth period precedes a large increment between the ages of twelve and fourteen. [166:151]

It is evident that there is a very strong probability that mental tests given in the early years of adolescence are not sufficiently reliable to predict later mental status. Even more emphatically, it must be stressed that the tests of early and later childhood must not be viewed as indicative of intellectual functioning during adolescence. This is portrayed in Figure 10, page 280. Five boys with equal MA's at the age of seven have mental ages almost five years apart at the age of seventeen. Figure 11 shows two children of the same age who have the same mental age at six years but are two years apart in mental age at the age of sixteen. These data suggest that teachers must view intelligence test data as being tentative, that slow learners in elementary school need not always be kept in substandard curriculums in high school, and that individual guidance may help pupils capitalize on abilities that were not prominent at younger ages.

---

* H. B. English and C. D. Killian, "The Constancy of the IQ at Different Age Levels," *Journal of Consulting Psychology*, 3, 1939, 30–32. Used by permission of the *Journal* and the American Psychological Association.

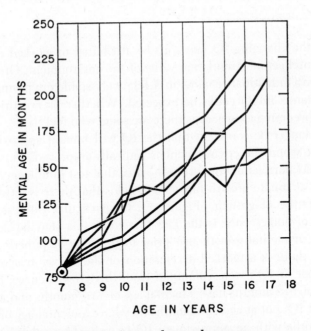

FIG. 10. **Diverging individual mental growth curves**

Source: Harold E. Jones and Herbert S. Conrad in National Society for the Study of Education, *43rd Yearbook, Part I, Adolescence* (Chicago: University of Chicago Press; 1944), p. 159.

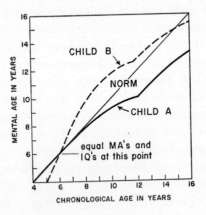

FIG. 11. **Shift in homogeneity of mental age**

MA's of two children with equal chronological ages. Source: Cecil V. Millard, *Child Growth and Development* (Boston: D. C. Heath and Company; 1951), p. 137.

The changing IQ and the environment

A number of studies made at the University of Iowa, Child Welfare Research Station, indicated that under the influence of marked changes in environment marked changes in IQ took place. This was particularly true of children of preschool age. Of particular interest to the student of adolescence is that follow-up studies showed that the increases tended to persist in the high school and college years, [340] indicating that the effects were more or less permanent. Despite individual exceptions (due to unknown factors) it is generally true that growth is continuous: childhood paves the way to adolescence and adolescence charts progress toward adulthood.

Other studies support the belief that marked changes in environment may have the effect of bringing the individual nearer to the realization of innate capacity for the development of intelligence during the adolescent years. Otto Klineberg summarized six studies, involving change of residence of Negro twelve-year-olds, and found significant improvement of intelligence test scores. [175:384] He found that the amount of change was proportional to the length of time spent in an urban environment after previous residence in a rural setting. Controls were exercised to eliminate the possible explanation that the change was due to selective migration—that is, better stock moving to the city. Improvement was definite and rapid and was attributed to the cumulative influence of a more intellectually stimulating environment.

A study of intellectual improvement during later adolescence is of particular interest to the student now in college. Robert L. Thorndike studied 1000 college students who took the American Council on Education Psychological Examination at various intervals from the age of thirteen to twenty and found, taking into account practice effects, that there was an average improvement of 34.5 standard score points. [314] He cautions that inferences should be carefully drawn from these data because the subjects were an intellectually superior group; but he goes on to say that mental growth probably continues for a longer period than has been previously thought. Mental growth probably reaches the point of zero growth sometime between the ages of twenty-one and twenty-five.

These data on the mental growth of college students are corroborated by numerous studies on the scholastic achievement of veterans after World War II. In study after study, it was found that veterans (who, typically, were older) made better scholastic records than did non-veterans who were equated on the basis of high school records and psychological examinations taken in high school. That is, though both groups were the same in test intelligence and scholastic marks in high school (hence similar achievements for both groups were predicted for college) the veterans consistently excelled. The number of veterans who dropped out of college was less than the mortality of non-veterans. [318] There are probably many factors that explain the relative superiority of the veteran as a student—greater sincerity of purpose, progress toward personal and social maturity, threat of loss of support if scholarship slumped, and the imminence of taking a job. But there is also the possibility that the good performance was in part due to increased mental capacity. Certainly the variability of test intelligence is great enough that senior high school and college advisers must be sure to evaluate intelligence test data in the light of the student's past academic history, his present attitudes and emotional status, and his very recent accomplishments. The longer the elapsed time from the taking of the test to the present, the greater should be the skepticism regarding its reliability.

The role of the environment in the realization of intellectual potential may be one of depressing the IQ. Apparently an environment that was sufficiently stimulating to the callow child may later leave him with so little stimulation that his mental growth is prematurely decelerated. Mandel Sherman and Cora B. Key studied the mental ability of children in various areas characterized by varying degrees of isolation from other communities, and found that the older the children, from eight to sixteen years, the lower was their average score on different intelligence tests. The factor of selective migration was discounted as an explanation of the lower test scores of the children in the most isolated regions. The authors offer as the "only plausible explanation" the fact that intelligence develops only as the environment makes demands. [276:345]

The environment is recognized as such a potent factor in the manifestation of intelligence in terms of current tests that an attempt has been made to build a test of problem-solving ability that minimizes social class differences—the *Davis-Eells Games.* [77] In standardizing the test the makers eliminated items that seemed to be easier for those in the more favored socio-economic group and retained those on which the lower class children could do as well. Scores on the *Davis-Eells Games* are less correlated with school achievement than are other mental tests; but the authors are not concerned because they feel that problem-solving is not solely dependent upon ability but also upon experience. This is a contention with which we can readily agree. Unfortunately, for the student of adolescence, the test is standardized only up to the age of thirteen. However, this study encourages the hope that we are coming closer to the determination of intellectual potential instead of inferring potential from academic learning.

Physical status and intelligence

Correlations between intelligence and physical status are low but positive. Predictions for individuals on the basis of these low correlations would be inane, but there is a general trend toward good health and high intelligence and superior physique and high intelligence. Various authorities have found that gifted children have slightly better health and slightly superior physiques than do average children. [350:91] Studies of handicapped children—the partially sighted, the acoustically handicapped, and the crippled—generally show less than average mental status. On the other hand, some handicapped individuals apparently compensate for physical defects by developing their mental capacities with determination. However, the experts on handicapped children take as their first step, not the theory of compensation, but the correction of remediable defects. In practice the truth of a sound mind in a sound body is recognized.

Of course, improvement of physical status is not a panacea. But enough is known about motivation and intellectual functioning so that attention to health and sensory acuity must be highly recommended. Health factors should be given as much attention in the home and the school as is given to them in schools for the handicapped and in institutions for delinquents. Rest, exercise, and diet—as suggested in Chapter Five—are of vital concern in the intellectual functioning of the adolescent.

Intellectual changes during adolescence

General mental growth

It has been widely believed that mental ability ceases to increase as early as fifteen or at least not much later than twenty years. Because of this view, it will be well to introduce the discussion of mental growth during adolescence with an apparent digression. Oscar J. Kaplan, on reviewing a number of studies of learning ability in the later years, concludes that there is much reason to revise some of our concepts regarding mental development. [169] The evidence indicates that those who exercise their learning capacity do not suffer the loss experienced by those who do not engage in learning activities. Memory, such as is called for on some intelligence tests, declines in the later years, but memory for complex tasks does not seem to suffer so much as was thought. Middle-aged subjects, when tested with the same devices that were used on them in college, showed no appreciable change after an interval of thirty-two years. There were, in fact, gains based on items involving general information, opposites, disarranged sentences, and common sense. In short, verbal intelligence apparently continues to increase.

Those who write confidently about the relationship between age and intelligence may some day have a rude awakening . . . findings do not dispose of such possibilities as the following: (1) some maintain their mental abilities into advanced later maturity without appreciable loss; (2) losses that occur are due largely to disuse or lack of appropriate training; (3) the test instruments and procedures are unsuited to older persons; (4) motivational factors differ at various ages.*

Present-day intelligence tests do not measure capacities; capacities are inferred from developed abilities. Hence intelligence as a capacity is inseparable from mental functioning. This is graphically represented in Figure 12, which shows that intelligence might well be considered an area of development rather than simply a level of response. An average twenty-five-year-old individual is capable of making more appropriate responses (one definition of intelligence)

---

* Oscar J. Kaplan, "Psychological Aspects of Aging," *The Annals of the American Academy of Political and Social Science*, 279, 1952, 36.

to his environment than is a typical fifteen-year-old. Thus, the study of mental growth in college by R. L. Thorndike (cited earlier) is confirmed by a study of A. M. Shuey which showed an average gain from the freshman to senior year in college of about thirty score points on the American Council Psychological examination. [281] Bruce Bliven, Jr., after reviewing a number of studies on learning ability in late adolescence and early adulthood, asserts that "The Learning Time of Your Life" is from about the age of twenty-three to thirty-three. [30] That is, the peak of learning ability is reached in the early twenties and continues with no, or slight, diminution until the early thirties (see Figure 12). The definition of adolescence as a period of growth toward maturity holds for mental growth as well as for other characteristics.

The clear implication of data on prolonged mental growth is that continued development should be stimulated by the persistent offering of opportunities and challenges during late adolescence. Hope for the improvement of the mental status of our nation resides in the perseverance of exercise. Furthermore, it is suggested by Kaplan

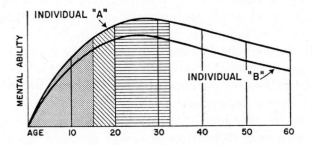

FIG. 12. **Curves representing (1) growth and (2) peak of mental ability**

1. If the altitude of the curve were all there is to mental functioning— sheer retentivity and plasticity—the individual represented by curve A would be as intelligent at age 15 as B is at the age of 20. However, if area (stippled plus slanted crosshatching) is important— level of intelligence plus time to assimilate meanings and concepts —then B at 20 is *more* intelligent than is A at 15, though both get the same score on a mental test. The element of truth in the second postulation is suggested by the fact that individuals at 40 or 50 are achieving much more substantially than are youths of 20.
2. Peak learning years are represented by the horizontal crosshatching.

(see above) and Davis that changes in the methods of mental testing may be desirable. These changes should seek to probe the kinds of intelligence that are required in adult adaptation and in functioning in the lower socio-economic levels.

Half the ability in this country goes down the drain because of the failure of intelligence tests to measure the real mental ability of the children from the lower socio-economic groups, and because of the failure of schools to recognize and train the ability. This country cannot survive as the leading world power unless we learn how to discover, recruit, and train more of the brains in the lower-income groups.*

Variation of ability

It is a well-established fact that individuals differ widely in the possession of various traits—height, weight, intelligence, and even in degree of masculinity and femininity. If an unselected group is measured for some trait and the scores are plotted in a vertical bar graph form, the ends of the bars may be joined to make what is known as the normal curve of distribution—a symmetrical bell-shaped curve. However, such a result depends upon the type of measure used as well as on the actual distribution of traits. If, for example, the measure does not give those at the upper end of the range a good chance to reveal their trait the curve is shortened at one end and loses its symmetrical form. This actually happens in some intelligence tests where some subjects finish all the items of a test before the time limit is up—they could have answered more, and perhaps more difficult, items if they had been provided. For example, some tests are apparently devised to approximate the sixth grade as a mean for the range of mental development. [166:147]

Besides the level of difficulty, another feature of intelligence tests that will affect the plotted distribution of test scores is the kinds of items used. Some tests depend upon problem solving, some largely on differentiation of perceptual patterns, and some on verbal facility. The particular aspect of intelligence that is emphasized in the test will influence the scores of the various subjects and result in a different kind of distribution curve. Intelligence is by no means such a unitary thing as is height—though it should be remarked that even

* Allison Davis, "Poor People Have Brains, Too," *Phi Delta Kappan*, 30, 1949, 294–295.

for height the relative contribution of body length and leg length will differ from one person to another.

At any rate, if a group of sixteen-year-olds were given an intelligence test the scores for mental age might vary from ten to twenty years. Thus, those who work in schools are faced not only with different kinds of intelligence but also with a wide range of differences in a single kind of intelligence. Some youngsters readily grasp the concepts that are aimed at in the schools while others encounter continual frustration in their attempt to do so.

The differentiation of abilities

It was noted in the chapter on the principles of growth (Chapter Two) that differentiation is a characteristic of development. Smiling, the display of temper, the use of fingers, and the use of arms and legs are manifested without the involvement of gross bodily movements. The baby's use of "doggie" to connote all animals comes specifically to mean dogs; and then later Dalmatians, German Shepherds, and Pekingese are distinguished as specific animals. All this is evidence of differentiation.

One of the distinguishing features of mental growth during adolescence is that intellectual traits become progressively differentiated.

It is believed that intelligence is of a very generalized character in the young child and that as he grows, specialization and localization of movement appear. This process of differentiation of responses continues throughout the life of the individual—at first on the basis of hereditary potentiality of the individual and the environment and later largely on the basis of his environment. In the first decade of life the type of intelligence itself changes—at first very fast, but more slowly toward the end of this period. For example, . . . the development of space-perception undergoes a change from very young age groups until about the age of 13. The change consisted of a shift from a tactual-visual type of localization to a visual plan of localization.*

It appears that intellectual growth during the first decade of life is of a general nature but in the second decade specialized abilities

---

* David Segel, *Intellectual Abilities in the Adolescent Period* (Washington, D. C.: Federal Security Agency, Bulletin 1948, No. 6), p. 2.

become increasingly independent. One study of the intercorrela-
tions of subtests on an intelligence test showed a correlation of .31
at age 9, .21 at age 12 but at age 15 only .18, for boy subjects. For
girls at these same ages the correlations were, respectively, .37, .30,
.10. [115] Scores on three Stanford-Binet test items—vocabulary,
dissected sentences, and arithmetical reasoning—show much the
same trend toward increasing differentiation of abilities. At the ages
of 8, 9, and 10 the percentage of subjects passing each item is about
the same—approximately one-fifth. But by age 17, while five-sixths
of the subjects pass the dissected sentences and practically all pass
the vocabulary test, only two-thirds pass the arithmetical reasoning
tests. [202:82] While it is probable that there are more likenesses
than there are differences in adolescent intelligence, such studies
as these indicate that the differentiation of mental traits increases
with progress through the years of adolescence.

H. S. Conrad and others conclude that some of the mental functions that are measured by mental tests tend to level off during adolescence but that other functions continue to improve until the end
of the college period. The possibility is suggested that some functions (memory, for example) mature early while others (such as
comprehension of abstract discipline) mature later. Another possibility is that some functions depend more on organic growth while
others are more dependent on the exercise of ability through experience. [166:178] Whatever the explanation, it is clear that growth
in general intelligence does not cease in the middle teen years.
Furthermore, the attempt to measure general intelligence probably
hides the more important thing about mental growth during adolescence—the increasing differentiation of specific aspects of intelligence. It is possible that the second greatest import of knowledge
about mental growth during adolescence resides in discovering and
capitalizing upon the uniqueness of the individual—the item of
first import is the advisability of continuing schooling through the
teen years because intelligence is still increasing.

Differences between rapid and slow learners

If the IQ of a given individual remains constant, then the older
the individuals the wider the mental difference between them becomes. That is, the person who scores above IQ 100 makes more
than 12 months' gain in mental age for each year of his life; the per-

son below IQ 100 makes less than a year's mental gain per calendar year; and thus the difference between their mental ages becomes greater. This is, in fact, what happens in the majority of cases for the typical subject. Typically, during the adolescent period individuals will *tend* to hold their positions, relative to others, in terms of general intelligence; but it must be remembered that the further an individual is from an early test score the lower the coefficient correlation becomes. (362:383)

It has sometimes been stated that not only do the dull persons grow more slowly but they grow for a shorter period of time before reaching their mental peak. This has caused some people to be only slightly concerned if slow learners tended to drop out of school at an early age—in fact relief has sometimes been expressed by teachers and administrators because the slow student, bored because of his lack of academic success, was often a trouble-maker. Recent studies confirm the statement made earlier that mental age continues to increase during the teen years—including that of individuals of lower mental ability. David Segel reports:

> The growth curves for the bright and dull show in general the same characteristics as are shown for all youth of this age with this important difference: During the first half of this growth the bright group, although beginning at a higher level, tends to grow at a faster rate than the low group, but during the last half, this trend is reversed so that the difference between the two groups is decreased.[*]

Although most studies do not agree that the differences between the bright and the dull become smaller with increase in age there is an important implication. Slow learners, like their brighter age mates, should be kept in school at least until the late teen years. There seems to be some consensus that eighteen would be a compulsory school attendance age that would allow us to capitalize more fully on the unique mental growth processes of adolescence.

Sex differences in mental development

The most important conclusion that can be drawn from study of the comparative intelligence of boys and girls is that the differences within the sex are much greater than those between the sexes. One boy differs more from another boy more than boys in general

---

[*] Segel, *op. cit.*, p. 8.

differ from typical girls. Those who recommend that girls be advanced in school over boys because they are accelerated in their growth overlook this important fact.

The range of differences for boys is greater than it is for girls. There are more feeble-minded boys than there are feeble-minded girls, but there are also more boys who are intellectually gifted. It is probable that the more frequent occurrence of giftedness among boys is due to cultural expectation and opportunity rather than being a function of sex. Girls are not expected to be superior to boys—in fact some older girls feel it a handicap to excel in academic work and find it convenient to disguise their superiority. Boys, on the other hand, are expected to excel and are given a range of freedom and a stimulus of encouragement to do the best they possibly can. It is fortunate, in the comparison of the sexes, that men have the evidence of superiority in test intelligence since in most other comparisons they suffer. Male babies die more frequently than do females. Sensory and mental defect is more common among males. Men suffer more from extremes of heat and are said to respond more readily to pain. Women suffer less frequently from psychosomatic disorders and contribute fewer numbers to the statistics on insanity. The general superiority of women over men is also indicated by their greater longevity.

Not only does the female live longer and thus get in the last word but she also gets in the first word. In every comparative study it has been indicated that girls, on the average, talk somewhat earlier than do boys. Their vocal superiority is still maintained during adolescence when their vocabulary scores on subtests of intelligence tests are higher than those of boys. They also show superiority over boys in memory and clerical ability. At the age of eight, girls do better in arithmetic, but boys catch up and excel in this activity by the time they are fifteen. Boys are also superior in subtests that probe space relations and mechanical reasoning.

It appears from these data that sex differences might well be attributed to differences in interests and activities of the sexes rather than to some direct outcome of biological predisposition. At any rate, even the consistent differences that have been noted are small and the inevitable conclusion is that the data do not support differential treatment in regard to intellectual pursuits.

Implications of intellectual development

Personal adjustment and intelligence

The relationship between level of intelligence and adequacy of personal adjustment is not direct enough to allow for any far-reaching conclusions. Gifted children show some superiority in adjustment inventories over their intellectually average peers. It is certain that giftedness and oddness are not highly correlated—as is erroneously believed by some. Feeble-minded children show a higher incidence of problem behavior than does the general child population. But, aside from the extremes of the intellectual variation of individuals, the relationship of intelligence and adjustment seems slight. Other factors seem to be more important.

A person's level of aspiration is more important than is his level of intelligence in the matter of adequacy of adjustment. What he aspires to is more important than what he has potential for. A slow learning child who is accomplishing much more than might typically be expected may still be unhappy because he does not top the class. A bright youngster may be happily oblivious to his potential and be content to rank with the average achievers. The important thing about a level of aspiration is not the degree of difficulty involved but the appropriateness of the goal for the individual, *and* where that appropriate goal originates. The goals an individual selects are more realistic when that person has had some experience with both success and failure. Pupils in school who have consistently failed go to extremes—they may not aspire even to the things they could accomplish, or they may aim for things that will almost certainly lead to defeat. Pupils who uniformly accomplish easily may similarly have inappropriate goals—failing to accept the challenge of a goal that would cause them exertion. The pupils who have been challenged to work for that which can be accomplished with effort and who have sometimes failed are the ones who have satisfactory levels of aspiration. These are the ones who effect good personal adjustment, despite their absolute level of intelligence.

The demands of society are also a factor in the relationship of intelligence and adjustment. Now that more and more youth of high school age are being enrolled in school there are more of them who are relatively incapable of achieving the satisfaction of their need for recognition through academic work. Studies of the worries of young people show that concern over school work and getting along with teachers ranks high. In a survey of 15,000 students, from one-fifth to over half of them report they are concerned with some aspect of academic achievement. [256:18] In fact, wanting to know how to study better is just as great a concern as is worry over health and as great as concern over having people like them— yet, in the study of adolescence the latter two concerns are considered to be major and relatively little is said of the former. The need for special curricular provision to suit the slow learner is indicated in Oregon's Pilot Program—a plan to make special provisions for the mentally retarded and the gifted children in selected experimental communities. There was some parental reaction to the gifted program—some parents thought that their child had been slighted. But the program for the retarded was so enthusiastically received that it surprised even those in charge. Parents, after living with the failure in the traditional program of their youngsters for years, seemed to feel no slight or shame because of their child's identification as a slow learner. The youngsters themselves began to enjoy school. Mason McQuiston, in charge of the Pilot Program reported: "The most amazing thing is the enthusiasm these kids now have for school. Youngsters who formerly hated school are now asking why they have to go home." * It is evident that personal adjustment can be improved by scaling society's demands to the indicated ability of the individual.

The author has emphasized, and will continue to emphasize, the importance of the development of skills as a basic element in the adolescent's achieving a sense of security. If those who work with youth will help find a capacity and encourage its development, they will be taking a major step in improving the lot of the adolescent. It makes little difference what that skill might be—dancing, swimming, playing cards, winning academic honors, building a racing car, performing on the ocarina, or kicking field goals—its existence and recognition by others make it more likely that that person will

---

* Mason McQuiston, "Progress in the Pilot Program," Fifty-first Oregon Educational Association Convention, Portland. March 18, 1954.

be able to live with his felt inadequacies. Thus, the experiments on many kinds of intelligences as well as evidence from empirical observations indicate the advisability of providing a greater range of activities for adolescents. This will mean that in the school a greater variety of activities must be regarded as respectable and, in the wider community, the unique offerings of different organizations must be capitalized upon to provide a variety of experiences. As a wider variety of actual achievement is regarded as commendable there will be a proportional rise in the adequacy of personal adjustment.

Intelligence and academic success

If we pause to apply what we know, we realize that intelligence is only one factor in academic success. There are also the factors of effective study habits, strong motivation, good physical health, and emotional maturity. But, in spite of this knowledge, we are sometimes astonished to learn of the superior accomplishment of some person with mediocre test intelligence. Disgust has sometimes been expressed because of the relatively low accomplishment of persons with apparently high intelligence. Both the astonishment and the disgust are evidences that we expect intelligence and academic achievement to be highly correlated. Certainly, the relationship is high, yet L. M. Terman found that 7 per cent of the children he studied with IQ's over 135 (Stanford-Binet) flunked out of college or were disqualified in their graduate years. [309:156] Intelligence tests are better predictors for some kinds of school work than for others. The correlation between reading and intelligence is .73 to .79, between intelligence and mathematics from .48 to .55, and between manual skills and intelligence from .15 to .21. [64:150] The relationship between intelligence and marks assigned by teachers is even lower than is indicated above by scores on achievement tests. It has been noted, for instance, that pupils from the lower socio-economic classes, even when equated in terms of ability with higher class pupils, receive a disproportionately large number of unsatisfactory grades (see Chapter Eight). William A. Bradley found that while it is true that about three-quarters of the A grades in high school go to youngsters with IQ's above 110 it should be noted that the other one-quarter of A grades goes to those with lower IQ's. All D grades, in this study, go to pupils with IQ's below 110 with none going to pupils with IQ's above 110. [38]

Several important conclusions may be derived from the data relating intelligence test scores to academic success in high school.

1. The tests are only approximations of the aptitudes they are designed to measure. Teachers and counselors should regard them as supplementary and fallible sources of information. Except in extreme cases, it would be unwise to make long-time predictions as to choice of school courses or vocational careers without due regard to many other kinds of corroborative data.

2. Test intelligence is only one of the factors—though admittedly an important one—that determine academic success. Low vitality, sensory defect, or too little rest and sleep, may explain some cases of apparent under-achievement. Worries over peer-relationships, physique and facial appearance, about conditions in the home, and the like may point to the lack of proper motivation as the cause of poor accomplishment. It is also possible that achievement is sometimes purchased at the cost of a well-balanced program of social and physical activity.

3. A wider range of school subjects should be classified as being academically respectable. This would give those whose interests have not developed along academic lines—including those gifted children in Terman's study who flunked out of college—a chance to gain the success and skill that contribute so much to the psychological feeling of security. Art, music, athletics, manual arts, homemaking, crafts, and various hobbies are representative of the kinds of activities that might enable school workers to capitalize more fully on the uniqueness of the individual.

4. There is a suggestion that some aspects of intelligence are favored over others in general intelligence tests—note the higher correlation between reading and intelligence than between mathematics and intelligence. Further refinement of intelligence tests may have the very practical results of opening our eyes to wider opportunities for recognition both in school and in adult life.

5. The marks awarded by teachers are unreliable. This suggests two items for consideration: (a) reducing the use of grades and increasing the use of teacher-pupil evaluation conferences, and (b) broadening the basis for judgment of pupil accomplishment.

Vocational selection and intelligence

Several considerations in this chapter suggest that the selection of a specific vocation on the basis of the adolescent's contemporary test data is wide open to criticism. For one thing, intelligence test scores do sometimes change. Whether the change is due to an actual change of intelligence or to change of emotional factors makes little difference—the test is not sufficiently reliable to peg a person's life to it. Second, the continued growth of intelligence throughout the high school and college years suggests that, at least as far as the typical student is concerned, steady progress toward maturity may result in the making up of what was apparently an intellectual shortage in the earlier years. The achievement of laudable success by pupils of a wide variety of intellectual status suggests that clear-cut lines of demarcation cannot be safely drawn.

This does not mean that young persons should be counseled not to make a vocational choice. The youngster who states that he wants to be a teacher, lawyer, or aerologist should be encouraged to study, explore, and plan his courses for such a career. He should, how-ever, also be told that it is perfectly normal and desirable that he should change his mind, *perhaps a number of times,* as he pursues that interest which predominates at a particular time. The value of supporting, corroborative, general courses should also be emphasized so that shift into another occupational category is held as an open possibility. While it is utterly foolish to repeat the cliché that a per-son can be anything he wants to be if he just works hard enough and long enough, adolescents should also know that competence is the result of the *consistent* application of industry plus intelligence.

The premature selection of a vocation, basing a large part of the choice on intelligence test data, may also have the effect of hiding a potential. It has been seen that special capacities, which are not always highly correlated with general intelligence, begin to be more prominent in the early teen years. These abilities become more dis-parate as a person matures. The early selection of, and concentra-tion on, a particular line of endeavor will limit the exploration of a variety of fields, one of which might serve the function of develop-ing a hitherto unknown capacity. In addition, the continuation of general education, instead of specializing in a narrow field, may have the effect of capitalizing on the potential for growth in general intelligence through the early twenties.

Prolonged education

This chapter has been pointed toward what has earlier been intimated, that the study of mental development during adolescence clearly indicates the desirability of continued general education for the great majority of young people through at least eighteen years of age. David Segel states two important implications arising from the nature of adolescents' intelligence.

> One is that since the growth of both physical and intellectual powers does not decelerate very fast until about the age of 18, it would seem that education for everyone up to that age might be considered the responsibility of society. This is because (1) it is an economical procedure to educate individuals before they have attained full productive capacity and (2) the right kind of education during these formative years is the only insurance of a proper development of the abilities of youth. In our complex society, it becomes important to have some control over the development of the abilities of individuals in all the formative years. Acceptance of this conclusion means (1) that worth-while educational experiences of a normal nature should be sought for all youth to the age of 18; (2) that compulsory school attendance should be extended in many States; and (3) that vocational training may be postponed until the latter part of the period—preferably to the year or two before the youth is to leave school.
>
> The other implication arising partly from the evidence presented and partly from general considerations, concerns the amount of time which youth should spend in school. The professions now require from 1 to 5 years beyond the A.B. degree and these training periods are still on the increase. This tendency when compared with the curve of learning and accomplishments during life brings up the question of a balance between such preparation and the life work in the profession. One important implication seems clear: Students in high school destined for the professions should in general not mark time, but should finish high school as early as possible.[*]

---

[*] Segel, *op. cit.*, pp. 22–23.

It should be noted too that the student who is not destined for the professions should not mark time. Unless courses and methods are changed from the academic approach, *which is justifiable for many adolescents,* to fit the needs of students for whom school at present has little appeal, this recommendation lacks validity. Fortunately, the various studies of the needs of adolescents suggest approaches to making prolonged schooling into an opportunity for intellectual development rather than a period for "marking time." Harold Alberty has suggested a number of problem areas that are wide enough in scope to provide an approach to the common needs of adolescents. He recommends [2:128] that the following areas constitute a core program, which would take from one-third to two-thirds of the school day:

Orientation in the school
Home and family life
Community life
Contemporary cultures
Contemporary America among the nations
Political, social, and economic ideologies
Personal value systems
World religions
Communication

Resource development
Human relations
Physical and mental health
Planning
Science and technology
Vocational orientation
Hobbies and interests
Public opinion
Education
War and peace

Summary

The study of intelligence continues to be engrossing for psychologists, and their interest pays off in terms of steadily increasing knowledge about the nature and functioning of intelligence. There are many definitions of intelligence with perhaps some consensus on the idea that it is the ability to make adequate adjustments to the environment. The ability to solve problems and to use abstract symbols, including language, is also frequently mentioned.

Indecision as to whether intelligence is a capacity or a developed function has contributed to the dilemma known as the constancy of the IQ versus variability of intelligence. Actually the IQ does change, but whether this indicates change in intelligence is a moot question. It is probable that as a capacity there is little if any change; but, as a function, intelligence very definitely does change. It is known that intelligence grows and develops during adolescence and that the development is reflected in test scores. Generally speaking the tests give an approximation of what the individual probably will become if he remains in the same environment. If the environment is markedly changed, however, there seems to be some possibility of an operational change in mental functioning—for normal individuals.

General mental growth continues throughout the teen years and into the middle twenties. This research finding indicates that all of adolescence is a period of steady progress in mental development. Not only are there differences in the absolute level of intelligence of different adolescents but there are also differences in the developmental patterns. The hope is justified that an adolescent who is behind his peers in mental development in his early teens may make up some of his deficit in the later teen years. There is some evidence that slow learners continue to grow for as long a time as do those who are intellectually superior. A second encouraging aspect of mental development during adolescence is the sharper differentiation of special capacities. Intelligence, even if slowing up in general growth, is developing in the direction of distinct areas.

Girls develop somewhat more rapidly in the verbal aspects of intelligence than do boys. Boys develop somewhat more rapidly in the area of space relations and mechanical reasoning. Perhaps the most significant thing about sex differences is that (1) they are slight, (2) they are probably culturally modified, and (3) the differences between the sexes are less than the differences within the sex.

Some important implications come from the data on the nature of development of intelligence during adolescence, and it is easy to agree with the concern expressed over the hesitancy to put into practice in the schools the things we know. [347] It would seem that desirable emphasis would be the following: One, personal adjustment and intelligence are not perfectly correlated. Hence, the school must emphasize personal adjustment along with the utilization of intelligence in academic pursuits. Two, the low correlation between academic success and intelligence indicates that more study should be made of the motivation of individual students. Such study should aim at more appropriate levels of aspiration of individuals so that some avoidable prolonged tensions will be reduced. Three, the growth of general intelligence and the differentiation of abilities indicate that the early selection of a vocation is a questionable practice for many, if not the majority of, adolescents. Four, the differentiation of capacities plus the continued growth of general intelligence suggests the desirability of keeping youngsters in school as long as possible during their teen years. Application of our knowledge of the growth of adolescent intelligence can further enhance mankind's distinctiveness.

STUDY AND REVIEW ITEMS

1. Prepare an argument in defense of the proposition: Intelligence is what intelligence tests measure.

2. Suppose the emotional situation, physical conditions, rapport with examiner, and the like, were held constant but that, after a year in a psychologically "good" home, a teen ager gained fifteen points on an intelligence test—would you think there had been a change in intelligence (not IQ)?

3. What advice regarding physical health would you give a teen ager who was strongly motivated to do superior high school work, in preparation for college, but who was merely "above average" in intelligence?

4. Assuming that you are in your early twenties, is there anything you can do to enhance the possibility of continued mental growth?

5. Prepare arguments for and against the proposition that girls should receive different treatment and opportunity from boys because of different patterns of mental development.

6. Do you think that pupils in the lowest quartile of intelligence should get a different approach to personal adjustment problems from those in the highest quartile?

7. What are some specific things a student might do to improve his work when he is in the middle group academically but in the upper 10 per cent intellectually?

8. What implications for school practice derive from the fact that some who are below average in their early teens tend to catch up to their intellectual superiors in their later teens?

9. Should slow learning (not mentally defective) teen agers be compelled to stay in school as long as the adolescent of average or above intelligence?

10. Is general education as important for pupils who will probably be day laborers as it is for those who will probably go into the professions?

RECOMMENDED SUPPLEMENTARY READING

Davis, Allison. *Social Class Influences upon Learning* (Cambridge: Harvard University Press; 1950), 100 pp.
   The author discusses the influence of socio-economic status on the subject's performance on intelligence tests. He feels that some present tests handicap those of lower social status and suggests that tests be designed to probe problem-solving ability.

Garrett, Henry, in Jerome M. Seidman. *The Adolescent: A Book of Readings* (New York: The Dryden Press; 1953), p. 202.
   Garrett discusses the implications of various definitions of intelligence. The intrapersonal differences in aspects of intelligence are used as the basis for recommending provisions for differential treatment. The hope for improved "measurement" devices is indicated.

Ingram, Christine P. *Education of the Slow-Learning Child*, 2nd Ed. (New York: The Ronald Press; 1953), pp. 315–335.
   This chapter contains suggestions for dealing with the slow learners in high school. It is important not only for the specific information on mental retardation but also for the implications for varied practices for "typical" adolescents.

Segel, David. *Intellectual Abilities in the Adolescent Period* (Washington, D. C., Federal Security Agency, Bulletin 1948, No. 6), 41 pp.
   This pamphlet states some general principles of growth and relates them to development of intelligence during adolescence. Specific implications

for school practice are suggested. Sixty-eight books and articles listed in the bibliography point the way to further study.

Skodak, Marie, and Harold M. Skeels, in R. G. Kuhlen and G. G. Thompson (Eds.) *Psychological Studies of Human Development* (New York: Appleton-Century-Crofts, Inc.; 1952), pp. 158–164.

"The Intellectual Growth of Adopted Children" suggests the possibility of improving the realization of potential through favorable environment. Earlier studies on this subject were viewed with much skepticism. Since the skepticism has not been entirely dispelled, the student will do well to become acquainted with the problem.

AUDIO-VISUAL MATERIAL

How We Learn (Coronet Films, Coronet Building, Chicago 1), 11 min., so., b. and w. or color.

The individual can capitalize more effectively on his mental ability by developing a system for learning: being eager to learn, using appropriate learning aids, setting goals, working with others, and seeking to know *why* things are studied.

Making the Most of School (Coronet Films), 11 min., so., b. and w. or color.

This film is designed to show high school pupils the significance of taking advantage of their school opportunities. School can be made more interesting by participating in class activities, by doing some supplementary work, and by maintaining a well-rounded program of activities.

Are the emotions of adolescents uncontrollable or is approved emotional expression possible? What are the facts regarding adolescents fears, insecurity, tension, and uncertainty? Whose is the responsibility for the emotional guidance of youth?

CHAPTER TEN

Emotional Factors in Adolescence

There is some truth in the statement "Man's intellect is but a speck afloat upon a sea of feeling." The preceding chapter showed that intelligence has much to do with adjusting, but *sometimes* it seems that how an individual uses his intelligence is more important than the absolute mental level. No choice need be made between the relative value of these two aspects. We simply need to recognize that emotion in the life of any individual—child, adolescent, or adult—is an integral phase of every activity.

While the author does not share the belief, now declining, that adolescence is a time of unique stress, strain, and emotional upheaval, the fact remains that emotional arousal and responses are an integral part of our study. Earlier chapters and those to follow demonstrate that an effective approach to understanding and helping adolescents is to comprehend the nature of emotion. Lawrence K. Frank asserts that the great potential resources for living more richly are in the education of the emotions. He regards such education as the great unfinished business of present-day secondary education. [110]

It is probable that the key to better understanding of individuals and of groups is to understand emotions. Those who work with adolescents—parents, teachers, youth leaders—must realize that the individual experiences intrinsic responses to both thwartings and satisfactions as he strives toward his goals (Figure 13). However, these intrinsic responses do not dictate specific extrinsic responses. That is, while the experience of emotion is almost automatic the overt emotional response is subject to control. Emotional behaviors are *learned*. The burden of this chapter is to show how emotional behaviors can be directed into socially and individually advantageous responses.

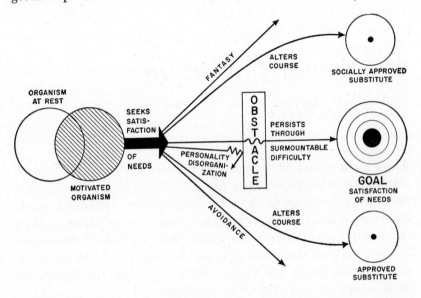

FIG. 13. **Schematic representation of arousal of and response to emotion**

As the individual develops and as organic and social situations change, basic needs motivate him toward his particular goals. These goals include both conscious and unconscious aims. Inevitably, obstacles thwart immediate satisfaction of some needs. Various individuals, depending on health, intelligence, past experience, learnings, and other factors, react to the obstacles in different ways. There are *shades* of differences between good and poor adjustment, rather than sharp lines; for example, daydreaming may lead to satisfactory substitute satisfactions and avoidance may, at times, be a wise course to take.

The nature of emotions

The meaning of emotion

Certain concepts in psychology have been so unfruitful that they have gradually been dropped. It has been said, for instance, that psychology first lost its soul, then it lost its consciousness, and now it is losing its mind. Semantic difficulty has been encountered with these words. "Instinct" is another word now only infrequently found in psychological discussion, because it meant so many things that one never knew exactly what another meant by the word. The word "emotion" has been criticized for the same reason—it covers so much ground that it is difficult for the reader of a text or article to know just what the author means. Emotions will be more amenable to study, and more effective results will be obtained, when emotions are described in more finely calibrated and differentiated terms. [203] However, there is no consensus on a terminology that has more precise meaning, so emotion is a word that must be used, albeit cautiously.

The word "emotion" embraces a number of perplexing situations. One, an emotion may be mild and constructively stimulating—as when an adolescent seeks the excitement of accomplishment in school or at home. Two, it may be mild yet tend to be destructive because it persists over a period of time—as when one is concerned about his parents' love or worried over his physical appearance. Three, it may be strong and continuing yet constructive—as when one is in love or arduously pursing some highly desired goal. Four, it may be strong, short in time, yet markedly debilitative—as when one is carried away in the mass emotion of a crowd or is involved in a panic. Five, it may originally be mild and constructive and later evolve into a strong and destructive emotion—as when one plays a good basketball game because of the competitive spirit but later loses coordination as anger and anxiety make him miss what are apparently easy shots. Some excitement coordinates and too much excitement creates tension. Six, the emotion may originally be one that is typically regarded as undesirable—hate—but may come, through constructive channeling, to be constructively dynamic—as when a citizen crusades to remove such an injustice as racial prejudice.

These contradictory and yet supplementary conditions lead to the definition of emotion as an upset condition of the organism. This definition, however, is hardly satisfactory because the upset may be only enough to initiate some constructive action—taking an interest in school work. The word "stimulated," instead of upset, seems more satisfactory. In fact, Luella Cole suggests that an emotion is a response of the total organism to some stimulus. [65:116] This definition would be further improved if, instead of stimulus, the terminology were as follows: *Emotion is the response of the total organism (physically, mentally, and affectively) to a set of stimuli or to a total situation.* That is, a person must have a given mental and physical set in order to respond. A teacher may not react negatively to a pupil's discourtesy if he is well rested or if he is saying to himself, "This pupil has a problem with which I may be able to help." The external situation is important, too. He may not ordinarily be aroused by discourtesy in the class but if two or three parents are visiting, or if the principal is present when the discourtesy is shown, his reaction will be considerably different. A. A. Schneiders covers these conditions in his definition of emotion: Psycho-physical responses to meaningful situations, which involve feeling states and certain intraorganic conditions. [266:216] At any rate, enough has been said to show clearly that emotion is discussed in a separate chapter only for sake of academic convenience. Actually, emotion is involved in topics like physical growth, the satisfaction of needs, the home, the school, and in all the other chapters in this book.

The physiological basis of emotion

There is no need here to describe the endocrine changes that occur during an emotional experience. If the reader does not have these in mind he should consult some text on general or educational psychology. It is sufficient to say that physiological conditions do not cause the emotion—a situation must also be experienced. Subjects injected with adrenalin—a secretion of the adrenal glands—report that they feel as if they were going to experience an emotion but that the expectation is not realized. [59] In short, the physiological condition or response is only part of the total situation involved in emotion.

The second important physiological aspect of emotion is that emotions are very real. They cannot be ignored, or dismissed as being figments of the imagination. Ways must be found to release the energy that is made available through the physiology of emotions.

Theories of emotion

William James and Carl Lange concurrently, but independently, formulated what is now called the James-Lange theory of emotions. It was held that emotions are the result, rather than the cause, of organic sensations that are generated by a specific situation. James said that common sense says you see a bear, you become afraid, and you run; but he believed that the order of events was see bear, run, become afraid. In short, it is the response to the emotion-evoking situation that generates the emotion itself. There is more to emotion than is expressed in this abbreviated explanation but the important practical implication is clear. Certainly there is some truth in the observation that giving way to an emotion tends to build it up. If a teacher becomes angry with a pupil and berates him or administers physical punishment his anger is likely to mount. Running from a pursuer on Halloween may cause a child to experience fright in what had started out as fun. Kissing a girl may cause a boy to feel that he is in love with her.

Adolescents, and older people too, should be told that giving vent to anger, resentment, jealousy will probably result in intensified feelings that will be increasingly difficult to manage. The tendency works in the other direction also. If a man practices courtesy he will begin to feel the emotion of sympathy. If he practices cooperation he will experience empathy. If he attends church and participates in religious study he will probably experience the feelings of reverence. The pleasant, constructive emotions can be made to play a more dynamic part in life if the first faint indications of the emotion are given exercise.

However, in dealing with the negative emotions it is not enough to refuse to express the emotion—hate, anger, jealousy, worry, resentment. Psychologists warn, with real justification, of the danger of "bottling up" emotions. W. B. Cannon's emergency theory of emotions explains why the effort to contain emotional expression may lead to difficulties in adjustment. The physiological changes that are a part of emotion—increased rate of heart beat, changes in the vascular system, release of adrenalin into the blood stream, and the like—prepare the body for a state of emergency. If increased physical activity does not burn up the extra energy made available the physical changes act as a kind of poison to the bodily system. Digestion is slowed, appetite is diminished, sleep is disturbed, movement may become uncoordinated. It has been said that one of the prices of civilization is the necessity of man's curbing his emotional expression rather than to engage in fight or flight.

Fortunately, there is a way to reconcile the apparent disparity between the James-Lange and the Cannon theories (one theory says that physical activity generates the emotion while the other says that inhibiting the physical expression of feelings results in storing up the "poisons" generated by negative emotions). *Indirect expression* of the physical energy can dissipate the product of negative emotions, but the *indirect* expression does not continue to stimulate the physiological accompaniments. If a person gets angry he can take a vigorous walk, play a game of handball or tennis, or beat a punching bag. Some housewives, when they get angry with their husbands, beat the carpet instead of the irritating spouse. One point of caution is fundamental—one must *seek* release from the emotion. If the carpet were beaten and the punching bag punched with the thought, "Here's one where it will do that guy the most good," the emotion of anger or resentment would be magnified. Calling a person names instead of hitting him does not dispel the emotion. The energy must be released in some *neutral* situation so it is necessary to alter the view of circumstances. The upset person should say, "I'm doing this to get rid of emotional tension." William James reported that emotions were not subject to introspection because as soon as an individual became studious about them the emotion tended to disappear. Adolescents who are given practice in trying to analyze the feelings of others and who seek neutral release will find that their own negative feelings diminish.

Another approach to the study of emotions is that formulated by K. M. B. Bridges. [41] She believed that emotions evolve from an undifferentiated response in the infant to more specific responses as development takes place. That is, the infant responds to emotion evoking situations by general activity and excitement. This general state next develops into distress and delight. In the next steps distress becomes differentiated into anger, fear, fright, jealousy, and the like; and delight evolves into affection, joy, elation, and so on. Bridges' view is of interest because of the emphasis upon the developmental processes involved in emotion. No doubt there must be a readiness for emotional development, but it is also clear that emotional responses are learned.

Feelings have a history. The feelings of any individual or group can be accounted for if we can get an adequate description of the situation out of which they developed and of the individual and groups who hold them. Thus in order to shift attitudes we need more ways of recognizing feelings. We need more techniques to diagnose their causes.*

The remainder of this chapter will deal with (1) factors involved in the genesis of emotional responses, (2) techniques by which emotions can be understood and modified, and (3) some of the implications arising out of these conditions for those who work with adolescents. This approach is in accord with an observation made by O. H. Mowrer; namely, psychologists have, traditionally and relatively unfruitfully, been concerned with conditions within the organism. Today the emphasis is on the external events of stimulation and overt response. [227]

Factors in emotional responses

Concept of self

A dynamic factor in the shaping of emotional responses is the conception of self an individual has evolved. If he feels secure, loved, and worthy—if his basic needs are on the way to being met —his emotional reactions are more likely to be what we call constructive. If the individual's needs are thwarted his emotions are negative—he becomes "disintegrated" or seeks refuge in flight or fantasy (see Figure 13). Feelings of security or of being thwarted

---

* Margaret M. Heaton, *Feelings Are Facts* (New York: The National Conference of Christians and Jews; 1952), p. 12.

do not, however, depend entirely upon external conditions. The self concept influences what a person psychologically perceives. This conception consists in his system of ideas and values, of his attitudes and desires, and of his commitments to himself. [162:475] The genesis of the self-concept is thus of focal interest in the study of adolescence.

From the very beginning of his post-natal existence, the individual begins to formulate his idea of himself and of the world. L. K. Frank suggests that if a child is fed when he is hungry he develops the feelings that his needs will be met and that the world is friendly. But if he is fed on a rigid schedule, left hungry and thwarted, he may feel that the world is hostile; thus fear and doubt are generated. Parental insistence on premature development of toilet habits may have the effect of causing the child to feel that he is unworthy. What the child hears, understands, and believes enters into the building of his "private frame of reference." [111:7] The individual spends the rest of his life attempting to fit his behavior into the framework that was outlined in the childhood years.

It is clear, then, that an individual's concept of self is a rather direct reflection of what others think of him. If he is loved he will find it easy to express love for others. If adult expectations do not exceed his maturing ability to fulfill those expectations, he gains confidence in himself. If he is regarded as being a worthy individual, he begins to feel that he is a person of merit. If he is praised, he seeks to continue to perform acts that will warrant commendation. If adults take time to talk and play with him, he maintains a basic confidence in his present status.

The implication of all this for adolescents has been pointed out, and will continue to be indicated, in various places in the present volume. Adults must tell the girl that she is attractive. This can be true—if the attitude has continually been expressed by others—even when the girl is not physically attractive. Girls with pleasing personalities are not uniformly those who are the prettiest. Boys should be commended for their strength, stature, or athletic prowess; or if this cannot be done, for their social, academic, or leadership skills. We must stop telling young people that they are awkward, that they are socially inept, or that they are lacking in judgment. Even on the occasions when such observations might seem to be temporarily justified, such evaluations do not serve the purpose of building a confident concept of self. Less emphasis should be placed on the moral deviations of some youth and more stress should be placed on the great majority who make praiseworthy moral decisions. Less frequent mention should be made of the financial burden of rearing adolescents and more opportunities should be provided for part-time work. In the school, varied opportunities, which are recognized as worthy, must be provided so that each unique individual has a chance to achieve, to gain approval, and to experience the satisfaction of curiosity.

Two other observations regarding the development of the self concept deserve mention. One is that teachers and parents must personally seek the mental health—feelings of security, confidence, worth, and the like—that will enable them to view differences in others with healthy perspective. Both good mental health and poor mental health are influential in the view that is taken of others. This view, it has been seen, becomes the pattern for the view that the child and adolescent takes of himself. Second, adolescents have some capacity for understanding themselves—perhaps more than we give them credit for. Practical lessons in psychology should be taught in the junior and senior high school; or, at least, be incorporated into their classes. H. E. Bullis and Emily E. O'Malley have developed a set of lessons for seventh and eighth graders designed to help in the solving of emotional problems of daily living. While the authors do not believe that these lessons constitute a panacea, they are convinced that an early start on such a study will materially aid in developing emotional maturity. [50, I:217]

Emotions and physical health

It is obvious that the attitude of adults toward young people and the demands of the particular culture in which they live (Chapters Four and Eight) are not the only factors involved in concepts of self and emotional expression. Another important influence is physical health. Individuals in poor health are, to some extent, subjected to denial of organic needs. The person with low vitality is somewhat more likely to be irritable, to become angry, and to have low levels of aspiration. Adolescents who overdo, because of the demands of competitive athletics or because of their own demands to participate in a wide variety of activities, are hard to get along with in the home and in the school. Chronic illness predisposes a person to a pessimistic attitude. Individual glands and the endocrine system as a whole must be considered as elements that predispose the individual to various kinds of emotional expression. [330:6] One of the first things that is done in studying an adolescent with problems is to have a physical examination to see if there are anomalies that might be contributing factors to his difficulties. The health of an individual is not something that can easily be isolated, it is a part of his total functioning self.

It must be observed, however, that there is a trend away from the purely medical approach to the study of emotion and behavior. Increasingly, the emphasis is on the social causation of problems. This does not eliminate the physical factors. It is simply a recognition of the fact that the view a person takes of his health and/or disabilities must be considered *along with* the physical condition itself. Studies of physically handicapped children do not show any uniform trend toward the development of specific emotional responses, though it may be that handicapped children *as a group* show more emotional disturbances than their physically sound peers. [118:363] But these differences must be, to some degree, attributed to the reaction of others and the individual to the physical condition involved. Wise parents, who accept the child, can help him to accept and live with the handicap or even regard it as a challenge to concentration upon the assets he does possess.

The relation of health and emotion is reciprocal. While health factors condition emotional responses, so too do emotional reactions condition physical health status. Ulcers of the stomach are at least in part due to chronic temper, resentment, and anxiety. Animosity can retard the digestion of food. Disgust with, and loathing for, another may give rise to skin rashes. Feelings of guilt may cause tremors and sleeplessness. These physical manifestations of emotional disturbances, in their turn, make it difficult to achieve emotional poise. One conclusion seems inevitable: seeking to achieve and maintain good physical health is a sound, though partial, approach to improved emotional response.

The possibility of bodily build being a factor in the shaping of emotional responses must also be considered (see Chapter Five).

The role of skills

A great deal is said and written about the need for the development of feelings of security in connection with emotional responses. Unfortunately, some of the discussion gives the impression that a feeling of security is something that is *given* to the individual by virtue of his being loved, being given attention, and being accepted and approved. True, these are important elements—perhaps even *the* important elements *during childhood*. But as the individual grows older, as he becomes an adolescent and adult, feelings of security are something that must be *earned*. It is a false sense of security, in the older person, that depends upon the adoration and protection of others. A genuine and sound sense of security must depend upon the individual's being able to solve his own problems— on his being able to maintain his equilibrium in "the shifting sands of time." A sense of security during adolescence depends on the development of intellectual, social, and physical skills. The love of others, their protection and guidance, are important to the extent that they serve as encouragement to the building of such skills on the part of the individual.

It has been found, for instance, that when ninth grade pupils were rated by their peers and by themselves on acceptability, those who were more acceptable were more active in social participation. Those who ranked in the upper quartile of acceptability, as compared with those in the lower quartile, were slightly, but significantly, higher in the amount of participation in dancing, tennis, playing cards, or conversing. Solitary activities ranked somewhat higher for those who were rated as being less acceptable. [40]

It has been indicated by John Dollard and his colleagues that a strong source of aggressive tendencies in adolescence is that society does not accept the teen-ager as an adult even though he may be mature or nearing maturity of body. Some of the obstacles to acceptance are technological unemployment, authoritarianism, prolonged education, and being a member of a minority group (see Chapter Four). Dollard indicates that aggressive tendencies are stronger when the individual sees his own inadequacy than when the source of frustration is some external situation. [88:48] While it is readily admitted that hurrying the adolescent to achieve adult status may result in the addition of frustrating situations, it is apparent that the adolescent must be freed from unnecessary adult domination so that he can develop the skills that will lead to the fulfillment of basic needs.

The role of skill in developing acceptable emotional behavior has been repeatedly demonstrated in studies of school adjustment. The youngster who is unable to keep up with his peers in academic achievement develops feelings of inferiority which place his emotions in a hair-trigger condition. He responds quickly and explosively to ordinary demands of the teacher. He is easily irritated by his fellow students. Or, he may reveal his emotions less ostensibly, but nevertheless surely, by retreating into seclusiveness or even by physically absenting himself from the school and the frustrating demands that accompany attendance.

As teachers tend to become proficient in cooperative planning procedures, in techniques for determining life needs of youth, in techniques for cooperative evaluation, in procedures aimed at clarifying purposes to be achieved and at procedures for fulfilling purposes, *security is fostered.*

The notion that such a system of teaching is easy, soft, or catering to "low" standards is an entirely false one. Students work diligently on problems which seem important to them; they make fundamental progress as emphasis is placed on clarification of ideas and on effective problem procedures.*

Encouraging the adolescent to build the skills that will help him to avoid the negative emotions also helps to generate positive feelings. As skills give him self-confidence he finds it easier to feel optimism, to show friendliness, to reveal courage in the face of obstacles, and to be patient with the disagreeable. It is encouraging to know that skills do not have to be specific to a situation in order to build positive affective states. The confidence a boy gains on the football field can help him live with a relatively low degree of skill in communication. The ability of a girl to play the piano will help her to overcome feelings of embarrassment over her more than average tallness. Many lower-class youngsters have overcome the handicap

---

* Robert S. Fleming, "Problems of Emotional Health in the Program of the High School," *The High School Journal,* 35, 1951, 74–79.

of being inadequately dressed by the status they have achieved in academic pursuits. Hence anything that can be done by teachers or parents to encourage the development of *some kind of skill* may have the effect of avoiding negative emotions or of fostering the pleasant and constructive ones. "May have the effect . . ."—this means that skills are not a panacea. It does happen that the skilled pianist is sometimes self-conscious about complexion, physique, or facial appearance. Not all athletes are emotionally well adjusted. It is necessary, in such exceptional cases, to try, by counseling processes or by group therapy, to get the adolescent to revise his evaluation of himself and his situation. While such processes may not be uniformly successful, at times they may be enough to tip the balance favorably.

Age and sex

As might be expected from reflecting upon basic growth principles, increase in age inevitably effects changes in emotional behavior. The total and general response of the infant to an emotion-evoking situation changes to a more localized behavior—or even to the point of no outward manifestation of the emotion whatever. In anger, for example, an infant kicks, waves his arms, arches his back, cries, gets red in the face, and tosses his head about; typically, the adolescent may give an angry retort or may walk away or even seem to ignore the incident. In short, increase in age does and should result in the inhibition of emotional response. Another change concerns that which generates emotional responses at various ages. Numerous studies indicate that those things that are regarded as wrong by children, the things they worry about, the things they fear, become matters of little concern in the adolescent years. But new concepts of wrong, new and different worries, and different fears rank high in the adolescent years. Children, for instance, are anxious and worried about improbable things—murders, holdups, wild animals, and violent deaths. In adolescence worries center about social and economic matters—concern over appearance, life work, examinations, money, and personal adequacy.

The foregoing does not mean there should be no concern about emotional responses because children and adolescents are "merely passing through stages." Although the specific thing that causes anxiety or fear may change, the pattern of anxiousness or fearfulness tends to persist. The anxious child is more likely to be an anxious adolescent than is the one confident and secure. Things that can be done to foster wholesome emotional development include the following: (1) Set a good example. Teachers and parents must outgrow their own fears and anxieties, control their tempers, and manifest their friendliness. (2) Help the child and adolescent to build the skills and knowledges that will increase his understanding and competence. (3) Encourage the maintenance of good physical health that will set a cheerful tone for daily living. (4) Be liberal with praise, and avoid criticism and ridicule. (5) Do not depend upon an intellectual approach. Emotions do not respond to reason, even in adulthood. The expression of reassurance is helpful but real progress is made when a young person experiences the feared or worrisome situation in the company of someone in whom he has confidence.

The evidence on the relative emotional stability of boys and girls is contradictory. R. G. Kuhlen cites a number of studies indicating that girls are more emotional than are boys. They react emotionally to more situations than do boys. Girls seem to be more introverted, and less confident, dominant, and self-sufficient than boys. [179:274] David Ausubel cites studies indicating that girls reveal greater emotional instability than do boys, but he indicates that the differences are, at least in part, a reflection of cultural influences and expectations. [9:147] On the other hand, statistics show that girls less frequently commit suicide and are less frequently placed in a hospital for mental illness than are boys. Boys more frequently than girls are reported to be problem children—85 per cent against 15 per cent. [12:352] Boys more frequently than girls are apprehended for delinquent activities. Perhaps the discrepancy between these two points of view lies in the difference in the ways of obtaining data. Girls seem to be more emotional when they are asked how they feel about various problems and situations. Boys are apparently more emotionally disturbed when the data come from objective measures.

There is considerable consensus on the idea that these "sex differences" are to a large extent cultural rather than biological. Certainly there are no sound recommendations for differential treatment of boys and girls on the basis of sex differences. Differences in cultural expectations afford an adequate explanation for behavior variations. Girls are expected to be docile, courteous, home loving, more affectionate, and more dependent. Boys are expected to be aggressive, rough, more adventurous, and more independent. But that which has been frequently said before still pertains: differences within the sexes are greater than the differences between the sexes. It is sometimes pointed out that the bio-chemical changes during menstruation may account for the alleged greater emotionality of girls; but, even here, there is a growing consensus that perhaps 90 per cent of such difficulty is psychological—hence, externally caused. Pursuing this line of thought, it seems reasonable to attribute the more frequent delinquency of boys and their more frequent commitment to mental institutions to cultural factors.

Emotions during adolescence

The relative difficulty of adjustment in the teen years is shown by statistics on first admissions to mental hospitals by age groups. The number of commitments in the age group 15–19 are six to eight times as numerous as in the age group below 15. However, this does not indicate that the teen years are a unique period of stress and strain because the number doubles again in the age group 20–24. From then on, for each age group of five years, there is steady increase in the number of commitments per 100,000 of the population of the age group concerned up to 85 years. [291] It seems pertinent to conclude that all of life is a period of stress and strain and that adolescence simply represents the first open exposure to the difficulties of living.

R. G. Kuhlen has done a commendable service in presenting arguments for and against the idea that adolescence is a time of unusual stress. [179:276] Data supporting the belief that stress is greater during adolescence are as follows: (1) The incidence of nail biting is greatest at the age of puberty for both boys and girls. After puberty there is a drop in incidence which suggests that tension decreases or that pride in personal grooming eliminates the symptom. (2) Ninth- and twelfth-graders, as contrasted to sixth-graders, report fewer pleasant and more unpleasant objects and situations. (3) In a group of subjects under fifteen and a group over fifteen, the older subjects revealed, in a projective test involving story writing, more themes revealing discouragement, disappointment, anxiety, dread, and the like. [303] (4) The rates of suicide and mental illness are greater during the adolescent years than in childhood; though Kuhlen points out that the rates during adolescence are lower than in the adult years. (5) A study of eighth-graders showed that girls at about the age of thirteen revealed behavior indicative of emotional disturbance but that a year or so later most of the subjects were acting in a rather adult manner. Boys did not show a comparable period of disturbance.

Other data support the thesis that adolescence is not an unduly stressful period: (1) In the same study as number five above, a series of questions related to anxieties, moods, and tensions, showed no clear age trend of increased stress. In fact, boys, as they grew older gave fewer answers indicating emotional stress. (2) The number of worries and personal problems shows a steady decrease, or at worst no substantial change, from the sixth grade through the end of public school. (3) Rates of suicide and commitment to mental hospitals are lower during the teen years than they are for the adult years that follow. (4) Teachers report that the incidence of behavior problems is greater in the junior high school than in the grades, but Kuhlen asserts that statistical studies do not support the impression that teachers report. (5) In a study Kuhlen himself made, he found that the period of the twenties was more productive of tension than were the teen years. This is about what might be expected since it is during the early adult years that major decisions of marriage and occupation are made and the initial adjustment to these choices must be made. (6) There is greater stability of friendships with advance of age through the sixth to the twelfth grades. Vacillation and "mercurical" changes become less evident.

Kuhlen's evaluation of these data leads to the conclusion that adolescence is not a particularly stormy or stressful period. Rather, it is evident that the American culture imposes a number of problems on the growing individual that must be faced. These many "first experiences" may tend to produce conflict. On the other hand, the large number of individuals who do make good adjustment suggests that preliminary help, the aid and guidance of adults, the modification of some of the less inevitable aspects of culture, and the development of appropriate "emotional maturity" at any given age, may do much to reduce the pertinency of the storm and stress concept.

Experimental modification of emotions

The study of the experimental modification of emotional responses is of interest for two reasons. First, many of the experiments suggest some practical implications for those who work with the growing individual. Second, hope for the improvement of behavior is generated in the face of the widespread belief that personality is formed in the first half dozen years of life. In this section three kinds of experimental studies that seem to have particular pertinence for adolescence are reviewed.

Frustration and regression

Roger G. Barker and his associates conducted an experiment designed to test the hypothesis that frustration leads to the de-differentiation of the person and hence to regression. [14:441] Although the study was made on preschool children it has pertinence for the study of adolescence because it suggests a theoretical explanation of non-constructive emotional responses. Further, it has been pointed out in many places, including various parts of this book, that adolescents encounter many frustrations—especially those imposed by culture—which complicate their problems of adjustment.

The experiment consisted of three parts. First, there was a pre-frustration period, which consisted of the subject's being placed in a playroom containing a wide variety of attractive toys. He was allowed to play freely but was encouraged to explore all of the toys through demonstrations by the experimenter. A point was made of showing the subject all of the toys so that interest would be developed that would later serve as a goal. Next, there was a frustration period which consisted of the dividing of the room by means of a wire screen, behind which most of the toys were kept. The child was allowed access to a limited number of simple toys in the other part of the divided room. The experimenter answered any questions but otherwise remained aloof from the play situation.

Thirty minutes later it was suggested that they leave the room—the subjects were generally quite anxious to comply. Finally, there was a post-frustration period in which the experimenter suggested to the child that they play with the interesting toys and the screen was raised. Usually the child was pleasantly surprised and returned to the toys with alacrity. He was allowed to play until he was ready to leave. This third part was not a part of the experiment; it was simply to allow the subject to satisfy his desire to play with the toys.

Two kinds of behavior appeared in the frustration period. One was termed free activities—play with the accessible toys, activities with the experimenter, looking out the window, finding other objects in the room with which to play, wandering about and giving attention to lights and noises. The other was barrier and escape behavior—physical approach to the barrier, social attempts on the experimenter, looking and talking about the toys behind the barrier and emotional expressions of whimpering and whining. Since growth consists, among other things, of a process of differentiation, regression was judged in terms of the level of differentiation expected of a child in accordance with his life age and mental age. Based on a point scale from 2 to 8, in terms of constructiveness, the children regressed from a mean of 4.99 in constructiveness to a level of 3.94 in the frustration period. This consisted of a regression of 17.3 months of mental age. Conceptually, the interruption of elaborate play and the substitution of barren, uninteresting toys caused the following: There was a decrease in the freedom of expression of the child. There was a decrease in the mood of happiness. There was an increase in restlessness and hypertension. And there was an increase in aggressive behavior—biting, kicking, and the tendency to break and destroy.

A number of thought-provoking probabilities stem from the experiment. Living continuously with a frustration may inhibit growth toward more mature emotional expression; or, if higher levels have once been obtained, the continued frustration may produce a chronic evidence of regressive behavior. It seems probable that an increasing variety of behavioral situations would foster continued differentiation of response. Frustration decreases the constructiveness of behavior. This certainly seems to appeal to those who attempt to explain delinquent behavior. Finally, and the authors point this out, the total situation must be taken into account—the physical situation, the other persons present, and the individual himself. It is also safe to say that those who are concerned about adolescents who reveal immature emotional responses would do well to see if any frustrating situation in the adolescents' lives can be located.

Autocratic-democratic social atmosphere

In the study of adolescent psychology it is important to study the processes by which an individual absorbs or rejects the ideology that predominates in his social group. An experiment by Kurt Lewin and his associates throws light upon the factors that create status and security within a group. [190] The investigation was designed to evaluate the effect of artificially created social climates on the behavior of ten- and eleven-year-old boys. By means of the Moreno test, subjects were equated for qualities of leadership and interpersonal relations. They were then divided into autocratic, democratic, and *laissez-faire* groups, each of which had distinctive character.

In the autocratic group all determination of policy was made by the leader; techniques for attaining the goal (making paper and clay masks) were dictated by the leader so that the future steps were uncertain; the leader determined the subjects who should work together. The leader criticized and praised individuals without giving reasons but was impersonal rather than hostile. In short, the leader purposely put up barriers to the free movement of the individuals in the autocratic group.

In the democratic group, policies were a matter of group determination; steps in the pursuit of the goal were discussed and explained and alternatives were suggested; members were allowed to choose the others with whom they would work; the leader attempted to be a member of the group in spirit but did not do the actual work; he gave praise and criticism on an objective basis.

In the *laissez-faire* group, complete freedom for group and personal decision was encouraged, but the leader stated that he would help when and if help were desired. The leader was friendly when he was approached but tended to remain aloof, groupings were determined by the subjects, and comments on the work were infrequent with no attempt made at interference.

After a period of six weeks of membership in these groups a number of characteristic behaviors became evident. For the *laissez-faire* group, the number of aggressive actions per meeting averaged thirty-eight, for the autocratic group there were thirty such actions, and for the democratic group, twenty. There was thirty times as much hostile domination in the autocratic group as in the democratic. In the autocratic atmosphere there was more demand for attention and more hostile subject-subject criticism, while in the democratic group there was an atmosphere of cooperation and appreciation of others. More constructive criticisms were made in the democratic atmosphere. Observers noted that boys in the autocratic group became dull, lifeless, and apathetic in actions that were not of the aggressive type. In contrast, the democratic members were more spontaneous, friendly, and fact minded. The evaluation of the boys themselves showed a dislike for the autocratic leader but they directed their animosity to their peers. They appreciated and liked the democratic leader but felt they should have more help and direction from the *laissez-faire* leader. When the leaders left the room (which they did as a part of the experiment) constructive activities broke down almost immediately and there was a marked rise in aggressiveness in the autocratic group. But in the democratic group normal activities continued for a longer period of time. One of the interesting phenomena of the autocratic group was the creation of a "scapegoat"—a boy who was picked on by his peers. Life was made so miserable for two of the boys that they dropped out. No such occurrences were noted in the democratic group. Thus, hostility against the autocratic leader gave rise to the psychological defense mechanism of displacement. The treatment of the finished product was also noteworthy. Those in the autocratic group destroyed the product of their work, in one case using the masks for weapons of "warfare." The democratic group discussed the matter and decided to leave their masks as models for other groups. There was a much greater manifestation of a "we" feeling in the democratic group than in the other.

It was anticipated that these manifestations might be due to the impact of the personality of the leader rather than an outcome of the artificially created climate. Hence, leaders were shifted. The autocratic leader of one trial was made the leader in a democratic atmosphere on another trial, the *laissez-faire* leader assumed the role of autocratic leader, and so on. However, the outcome remained consistent and the experimenters concluded that it *was* the atmosphere and not the leader that set the tone. A few boys were also shifted from one group to another. Those shifted from the democratic to the autocratic group quickly adopted the behaviors described above. The autocratic members less quickly shifted to the democratic group—causing the experimenters to decide that autocracy may be imposed while democracy must be learned.

The late Kurt Lewin, evaluating this and other similar experiments, summarized as follows:

> These experiments as a whole, then, bear out the observations of cultural anthropology and are well in line with other experiments on the effect of the situation as a whole. The social climate in which a child lives is for the child as important as the air it breathes. The group to which a child belongs is the ground on which he stands. His relation to this group and his status in it are the most important factors for his feeling of security or insecurity. No wonder that the group the person is a part of, and the culture in which he lives, determine to a very high degree his behavior and character. These social factors determine what space of free movement he has, and how far he can look ahead with some clarity into the future. In other words, they determine to a large degree his personal style of living and the direction and productivity of his planning.*

The study of social atmospheres has particular pertinence to teachers and group leaders of young people. It seems highly probable that many "disciplinary" problems stem from the climate that prevails. Teachers might save considerable time and energy if some initial time were devoted to the group determination of goals and methods. It might be that the time saved by dictating purposes is later lost in the handling of problem behavior. The possible implications for treatment of adolescents in general is also noteworthy. Perhaps greater freedom should be allowed for the growing individuals to reach toward their own goals in their own manner. The need for "loosening the reins" on adolescents has been suggested at numerous

---

* Kurt Lewin, "Experiments in Social Space," *Harvard Educational Review*, 9, 1939, 21–32.

points in this volume. Philip Wylie has observed that perhaps some of the trouble that stems from adolescents today is that too much attention is given to them, too much concern is shown. When he was a teen-ager no one gave adolescents much heed. They did, unnoticed and unpunished, things that today make headlines, call forth the police, and set social workers on missions. He feels that greater freedom in the process of growing up might be a fruitful approach to some of the present problems. [358:18]

Experimental practices in the schools

H. Edmund Bullis and Emily O'Malley have designed three sets of lessons on personal problems and mental hygiene, for use in the upper elementary grades. The technique is simple, economical, and effective. The teacher outlines some ordinary, everyday problem and then reads a short story from one of the three courses, *Human Relations in the Classroom* [50]. Students are then led to discuss the characters in the story; next they are asked if they have ever known anyone who encountered similar problems. As the lesson progresses they are asked if they have had similar problems themselves. After a few lessons it has been found that the pupils readily discuss their own problems and receive some relief from discovering that their peers have related problems. Further, they get light on how they might solve some of their difficulties. Bullis states, and his observations have been confirmed by psychiatrists and psychologists who have watched the lessons, that this approach has five advantages: (1) teachers can, and do, perform the job effectively—experts are not required, (2) the lessons do not interfere with regular curricular pursuits—the work is typically done once a week in social studies or English classes, (3) teachers gain insights that improve the effectiveness of their teaching, (4) students enjoy the classes, (5) teachers and students gain a better understanding of unique personality orientations. [50, I:14] Typical topics include how personality develops, the nature of human drives, the effects of emotions, the nature of conflict, problems arising in the home, overcoming handicaps, establishing goals, getting along together. Such an approach certainly accords with the belief of A. T. Jersild that young people have a capacity for understanding their own problems and should be given a greater chance to study them. [162:478]

An experiment in the Los Angeles City Schools involved parents, teachers *and* children in the planning of objectives and techniques for improving emotional stability. [192] The study of each school subject is planned in such a way as to make contributions to such goals as appreciation, faith, good will, kindness, generosity, and respect for others. For example, the study of science is made to contribute to reverence for the wonders of the universe. Commercial studies contribute to accuracy, responsibility, and pride in workmanship. Mathematics work stresses the need for accuracy and adherence to principles. Physical education is expected to make contributions to cooperation and teamwork. English, art, social studies are also planned in such a way as to make specific contributions to the improvement of human values. Obviously, this requires meticulous planning and this is just what is done in the form of suggested materials and activities.

Coronet Films has a number of short moving pictures (some have been cited in the "Audio-Visual Material" sections of the present volume) which are designed to bring to the attention of teen-agers some of their problems and provide the basis for fruitful discussion. [70:35] Major headings are guidance, personal, academic, and vocational; dating and family living; pre-military orientation; and health and safety. Under each heading a number of titles are listed. The films, like the Bullis materials, provide a neutral approach to intimate problems and are designed to pave the way for discussion and further study.

Each month Science Research Associates publish another booklet in their "Life Adjustment Series." There are at present well over sixty booklets in the series, which parents and teachers find helpful in counseling with teen-agers. Each booklet, of about fifty pages, is written by some person of national reputation or by some other person particularly well qualified in the area concerned. The readability is suited to high school age pupils, and booklets are interestingly illustrated. Even if the study of these booklets is not incorporated into the regular curriculum, it seems that they should be displayed prominently where they are readily accessible to pupils for their free reading activities. Teachers who have used the booklets as incidental, supplementary, or basic material are enthusiastic about student response to them.

Douglas F. Parry has studied and evaluated such experiments and materials as those described in the foregoing pages. He concluded that the results have been gratifying even if not spectacular. His conclusions are summarized under six headings: (1) Emotional control and the solution of problems of living are influenced by the situation, usable skills *and* by understanding of self and the world. (2) Facts having immediate psychological reference are more significant than those that have no personal implications. (3) Those individuals who are most efficient plan the improvement of personal, social, and occupational efficiency. (4) There are numerous ways in which the study of emotional control can be infused in the regular curriculum. (5) Some people seem to encounter few problems, but where there is contact with that which is contagious (including mental ill health), inoculation and vaccination are significant aspects of living. (6) There is much that is unknown about the universe of the human mind, but what is known can be more effectively applied. Application of even our limited knowledge will improve both personal and social living. [237]

Implications for leaders of adolescents

The implications of our knowledge of emotions for leaders of adolescents has been an integral part of the foregoing discussion. However, some additional observations about the functioning and evaluation of emotions should be considered.

The normality of conflict

Conflict occurs when an individual is faced with the necessity of making a choice. It may be a matter of choosing between two attractive alternatives or of being forced, by physical or social power, to do something unpleasant. Anyone who lives a vigorous life must inevitably encounter a number of conflict situations each day. The establishment of dynamic goals, the formulation of a life philosophy, the building of habits, are helpful in reducing the frequency of conflict situations. But the conflict aroused by novel situations is only partially resolved by objectives, habits, and points of view. Normally, most conflicts are quickly resolved by deciding upon a course of action. But it also frequently happens that after a decision is made and a course of action initiated, the individual harbors the wish that things could be different. This is the aspect of conflict that is destructive and tends to produce abnormality of behavior and emotion.

It is the continuing state of conflict, not the quickly resolved one, that gives the psychologist concern. Frustration—the persistent existence of conflict—is the thing to be avoided. There are three major approaches to the resolution of daily conflicts and the avoidance of chronic conflicts that lead to frustration.

1. THE SITUATION. Facing conflict situations at any age tends to prepare the individual for making the choices he will have to make in succeeding years. These preliminary experiences inoculate the individual against the more insidious problems that will occur in later years. This does not mean, however, that obstacles should deliberately be left in the path of the individual. Much of this book is devoted to the proposition that hazards to the development of the adolescent should be removed or reduced. If the individual is permitted an appropriate degree of freedom, he will inevitably meet numerous situations that give rise to conflict. Some obstacles to adolescent development, at present, seem to be rather inescapable —so there is no point in deliberately constructing barriers. The point is that if there are too many problems, the immature individual is inadequately prepared to meet them and will become frustrated and defeated.

2. THE INDIVIDUAL. Some people are apparently capable of meeting and dealing effectively with more conflict than are others. They have greater tension tolerance—an ability to withstand pressure. These individuals can "take it." Higher tension tolerance stems from good physical health, the feeling of security generated by being loved, the feeling of security generated by possessing skills and knowledges, and from the toughness created by having previously, and successfully, dealt with conflict. Obviously, teachers and parents should have, and verbally express, their faith in the ability and worthiness of the individual. They should encourage the development of skills and knowledges that are of immediate practical import to the adolescent. They should permit the individual a degree of freedom, appropriate to his age, that allows him to come in vigor-

ous contact with his environment—short of encountering actual danger. This cannot be categorically defined because it is an evolving concept. The entire emphasis must be upon helping the adolescent to learn to stand on his own feet.

3. THE POINT OF VIEW. Not only must an individual's skills be considered, when dealing with conflict, but the view that is taken of problems is basic. Some individuals appear to be easily discouraged in the face of problems, while others attack them confidently. The difference in attitude is dependent upon such factors as the concept of self a person holds, the degree of success he has experienced in the past, the goals he has set for himself, and upon his perception of his environment. Each of these factors suggests implications for those who work with adolescents; in general, it will be helpful to counsel with young people in an attempt to help them develop perspective. This kind of counseling requires the establishment of friendliness so that the pupil feels that problems are shared in common. It requires time so that the pupil may adequately verbalize and describe his problem and, in so doing, revise his conception of it. It requires patience so that gradually the adolescent creates his own answer or approach to the situation. [176:55] Revision of a viewpoint is an individual accomplishment, not a revelation by the counselor.

Measurement of emotional responses

A number of personality tests, emotional maturity scales, or adjustment inventories are available to teachers and counselors. The manuals accompanying these devices contain alluring statistics regarding their validity and reliability. Writers of textbooks on guidance and teaching often recommend that these tests be regarded as vital to a well-rounded testing and counseling program. Yet there is considerable consensus that these instruments are worth little and may even be harmful.

L. F. Shaffer, in evaluating one such test, asserts that its faults are those of personality tests in general. Teachers and counselors are tempted to use such devices because of their very great need to do something about personality and emotional responses. Their search for the "pot of gold at the foot of the rainbow" leads them to accept instruments of low objective value. [273:56] G. G. Thompson, after describing and evaluating a number of group personality inventories and rating schedules, expresses surprise at the continued use of these instruments in schools and youth-guidance organizations despite the negative research findings regarding their value. [311:614] H. C. Lindgren asserts that intelligence tests are at best approximations and indications and must be used with due regard for their limitations, but he feels that comparable confidence should not be placed in personality inventories. [191:483]

There are a number of reasons why personality inventories should be viewed with skepticism. One is that the words of the author of the test do not mean the same thing to him as they do to the respondent. He has in mind one situation while the question recalls another affair to the subject. Another is that the mood of the respondent varies from day to day. If his general feeling is good he will give more optimistic answers, but if an unpleasant incident has occurred just prior to the taking of the test he may be inclined to give predominately negative answers. Still another defect is that the individual does not know himself and would be loath to reveal it to another if he did. The late J. S. Plant has called this a psychosomatic envelope. [246:2] The inner self is held unconsciously inviolate from the probings of others and may even be misinterpreted to the consciousness. Finally, there is the possibility that the subject may inadvertently, or sometimes intentionally, deceive the administrator of the test.

Having said these things, by way of precaution, it can now be said that there may be times when an inventory can be used as a source of supplementary data. The counselor can ignore the score and the percentile rank achieved on the test and he can avoid labeling the subject on the basis of the results; he can then use the questions as a point of departure for an interview. He can use the atypically answered items as a starting point for getting at crucial areas of adjustment. Thus the inventory can serve as a sort of controlled counseling session. Actually, it is not the atypically answered question that is the significant matter anyway—it is the reason for the response that the counselor wants to understand. This can be done by using the schedule as a focal point in counseling.

Formal projective techniques

A projective technique may be defined as an unstructured situation to which the subject gives structure. That is, an ambiguous, amorphous, or neutral situation is described and evaluated by the subject in terms of the meaning *he* perceives. What he sees is not determined by the external situation but by what his own meanings and feelings permit him to see. He projects himself into the test situation. The Rorschach ink blots may serve as an example. A blot on the order of the ten used in the Rorschach technique may be made by dropping a blob of ink on paper and folding the paper so that a symmetrical pattern appears. The subject is then asked to tell what he sees in the blot (as the reader probably did when he reclined on his back and told himself, or a companion, what he saw in the fluffy, cumulus clouds floating overhead). Although there is something present nothing is *intended* there, so what is seen is that which is projected by the respondent.

Some advantages of the formal projective technique are the following: (1) It requires a specially trained individual to interpret the results—and the layman readily recognizes the need for expertness. This may not be so easily recognized in using the personality inventory. (2) There are no clues in the ink blot (or picture, or whatever is used in the technique) by which the subject may guess "what the examiner wants." (3) The response is unique to the individual—he is not "led" into a situation by stereotyped questions. (4) Because of the elusive nature of the technique the user is encouraged to use supplementary data in drawing conclusions.

Informal projective techniques

With the above described limitations in mind, the teacher is in an advantageous position to make use of informal projective techniques. *Clues* to the emotional responses of individuals may be inferred from the ways an adolescent plays—the degree of aggressiveness displayed, the humor revealed, the freedom of activity, and the words that accompany his play. *Clues* may be derived from the way he uses art materials—paints, finger painting, clay—as well as from characteristic themes repeated in various productions. Many art teachers use various media simply for the sake of catharsis—they do not make a serious attempt to diagnose from the way in which materials are used or from the themes which are followed. Their aim is merely to permit the student to express himself freely and "get things off his chest." It is an attempt to help the student to live with the feelings he has by reducing the weight of the feelings.

An informal projective technique that is readily available to all teachers, but especially to social studies and English teachers, is that of free, or creative, writing. The student is encouraged to write stories, poems, self-portraits, themes, or expositions—whatever his interests might be—and criticism of the content and structure is kept at a minimum. It is worth noting that if stress is early placed on form and content the originality and creativeness of the piece are stifled. When sound pupil-teacher rapport has been established, through sympathy, praise, and encouragement, it will be noticed that recurrent threads begin to be expressed. These may serve, when used in connection with supplementary data, as clues to the better understanding of pupils. As in the case of art work, there need be no great emphasis on diagnosis. The aim can profitably consist in affording the pupil an opportunity for cathartic activity. A high school teacher who made a special project of exploring the possibilities of creative writing in high school reported that she would never want to return to her former way of teaching composition. She said that while writing is not a cure-all, it is a helpful approach to the understanding of pupils. Not only is therapy provided through the cathartic experiences but better rapport is established between pupil and teacher. [269:64]

Informal projective techniques, like formal ones, have the limitations of being approximations, clue-providers, and of being suggestive. Other data—observations, standardized test results, past records, reports from other teachers—must be used to supplement and corroborate any conclusions derived from the projective methods.

Role of the school in emotional maturing

Probably the most readily accessible approach to the fostering of constructive emotional behavior in adolescents is through what is done in the school. Therefore, at the expense of some repetition, several areas of responsibility are briefly described in this section.

1. Provision for the *more equitable distribution of success and*

failure. Since negative emotions are engendered by the blocking of needs and goals and since constructive emotions arise from the satisfaction of needs and the achievement of goals, more attention must be given to the much-mouthed phrase, individual differences. Typically, some students chronically experience success—these are deprived of the wholesome experience of being inoculated with occasional failure. Others chronically fail their academic work. These have generated in them feelings of inadequacy and inferiority—which are often not entirely warranted. Suffice it to say that academic goals must be adjusted to individuals and that a wider variety of worthwhile goals or activities must be provided in the high school that enrolls a heterogeneous adolescent population.

2. Attention to *peer adjustment.* The quality of the adolescent's social relationships constitutes a significant aspect of adolescent development. [234] Three implications for teachers stand out. One, they must realize how important it is to the adolescent to fit into his group. An attempt must be made to help him to see his likenesses to others and to change traits that set him off sharply from his peers. Two, teachers must avoid the temptation to request loyalties to adults that might require the violation of a loyalty to peers (for example, expecting a pupil to report cheaters or those who violate school rules). Three, adolescents who are observed to be isolated should be studied to see if their adjustments cannot be facilitated. Perhaps taking some of the more secure adolescents into confidence and reposing in them some responsibility for a "big-brother" relationship with the isolate will help. Whatever the approach, some aid should be given.

3. Providing for *catharsis.* Some pent-up feelings can be dissipated by encouraging the pupil to participate in athletic activities, in musical pursuits, in dramatics, or in school improvement projects. As suggested earlier, art work, manual activities, and creative writing can serve as avenues of catharsis for many youngsters.

4. *Direct teaching.* Direct study and discussion of emotional and social problems should be a planned part of the curriculum. This study should be directed to the modification of the adolescents' view of their problems. The assumption is that the view a person takes of his problems is a part of the threefold approach: changing the situation, developing skills to overcome problems, and altering his view

when skills are inadequate and when the situation cannot be changed.

5. A *mature example* should be set. The emotionally mature adult should be able to see through the manifestation of behavior to the nature of the individual. There should be a realization that behavior is *caused*. Among the more important characteristics of a teacher who provides a good example are these: respect for individual worth, confidence in the democratic approach, the absence of racial and religious prejudices, sympathetic understanding, respect for the values of work, and a faith in the improvability of behavior.

Summary

The word "emotions" covers a wide range of psycho-physical conditions from constructive, invigorating feelings states to destructive, disorganizing states. These conditions have their basis in past experiences and present conditions, in physical conditions, and in the nature of external events. Our concern is with how to build the constructive emotions and live with or diminish the negative ones. We are often faced with the dilemma of repressing the direct expression of an emotion while engaging in the physical activity that will dissipate the energy made available by emotion.

Factors in improving emotional responses are numerous and varied. It is important that the individual have a high and confident concept of self. Since this concept comes partially from the view others hold of the individual, teachers and parents must learn to express praise, confidence, and respect for the growing individual. Sound physical health provides a basis for the relatively easy expression of the positive emotions and the control of negative feelings, but habit also must be considered. Skills are particularly important in achieving better emotional control since it is the blocking of goals and approaches to goals that gives rise to negative emotions. Further, positive emotions are generated by the achievement of objectives. Generally speaking, improved emotional response comes with increased age, but chronological maturing is no panacea. Sex seems to play no definitive part in the mode of emotional response. There are a few differences between the sexes that appear to stem from cultural expectations, but the differences between the sexes are less than the differences within a sex. An evaluation of studies of emotion during adolescence indicates that there is reason to believe that there is continual, if sporadic, improvement of emotional responses during this period.

Experimental studies of the modification of emotional responses give reason to hope that much more can be done to apply, more effectively, our knowledge of the nature and expression of emotion. School workers have made an attempt to apply the knowledge of emotions by teaching courses on personal adjustment, by encouraging study and discussion groups, and by providing informative material which appeals to the adolescent. The results have been gratifying and those who have experimented recommend the expansion of such programs.

Workers with adolescents should realize the normality of conflict. They should distrust the tantalizing data that seem to be offered by personality inventories and rely more on their own observations—keeping in mind the tentative and subjective nature of such observations. Informal projective techniques provide valuable, tentative suggestions when used with due caution. It is suggested that those in the school should provide for the more equitable distribution of success and failure so that feelings of confidence will be more widely felt and so that occasional frustration is experienced. Teachers should be alert to detect adolescents who may be in need of assistance in their peer adjustment. Emotional catharsis should be provided through athletics, drama, art, and various kinds of craft work. Promising results have been obtained from the adolescents' direct study of their own emotional problems. Finally, it is vital that a mature example be provided for the growing individual. In such ways as these it is felt that adolescents can realize more symmetrical processes of emotional maturing. Intelligence and emotion will thus be made to team up in the production of a secure and integrated adolescent.

STUDY AND REVIEW ITEMS

1. Examine Figure 13 and suggest some specific ways in which avoidance is used as a defense against the blocking of progress toward a goal.

2. What might you say to a group of adolescents regarding the James-Lange theory of emotions that could improve their emotional adjustment?

3. It is often suggested that growing individuals be given "deserved" praise. In view of the importance of the concept of self, what are some defects in the recommendation?

4. Name some skills, which every adolescent might be encouraged to develop, that should make contributions to his emotional stability.

5. Do you feel that there are any consistent differences in the emotionality of boys and girls?

6. Do you think adolescence is characterized by more or less emotional instability than preceding and succeeding periods of life?

7. What are some specific implications for adolescents of the frustration-regression experiment?

8. Do you agree with Philip Wylie's contention that adolescents would be less of a problem if less attention were given to them?

9. Realizing that the addition of a new high school subject would entail the dropping of another, would you recommend the establishment of a class in personal problems?

10. How might a teacher proceed to build the rapport which would be fundamental to getting pupils to express their feelings in creative writing?

11. Suggest some other things that might be done in the school to improve emotional behavior, besides those mentioned under "Role of the school in emotional maturing."

RECOMMENDED SUPPLEMENTARY READING

Ausubel, David P. *Ego Development and the Personality Disorders* (New York: Grune & Stratton, Inc.; 1952), pp. 84–102.

The author takes some of the concepts that are current in the study of adolescence and critically evaluates them—for example, the absence of "adolescence" in primitive societies, the strain and stress concept, and the effect of biological and physical changes.

English, O. Spurgeon, and Gerald H. J. Pearson. *Emotional Problems of Living* (New York: W. W. Norton & Company, Inc.; 1945), pp. 270–322.

These three chapters describe the development of personality during puberty and adolescence. Some of the perplexing situations encountered and their probable results are described. The treatment of the role of work and marriage in emotional satisfaction is valuable.

Jersild, Arthur T. *In Search of Self* (New York: Bureau of Publications, Teachers College, Columbia University; 1952), 148 pp.

The thesis is developed that young persons have much more capacity for understanding themselves than has previously been realized. Suggestions are made for developing this understanding so a healthy concept of self will result.

Kuhlen, R. G. *The Psychology of Adolescent Development* (New York: Harper & Brothers; 1952), pp. 238–288.

A well-documented and thorough study of the needs, motivations, adjustments, and maladjustments of the adolescent years. The chapter begins with "the nature of adjustments," then surveys some of the problems, and ends with a discussion of wholesome adjustment for teen agers.

Seidman, Jerome M. (Ed.) *The Adolescent: A Book of Readings* (New York: The Dryden Press; 1953), pp. 139–177.

Adolescent concerns with physique are described by A. Frazier and L. K. Lisonbee. Mary C. Jones and Nancy Bayley discuss the relationship of physical maturity to social and emotional behavior. Ruth Strang tells how emotional disturbance may interfere with reading skills.

Symonds, Percival M. *Adolescent Fantasy* (New York: Columbia University Press; 1949), 397 pp.

The major in psychology will find this to be a constructive contribution to his understanding of projective techniques as well as a means of improving his understanding of emotions during adolescence.

AUDIO-VISUAL MATERIAL

Age of Turmoil (McGraw-Hill Book Company, Inc., 330 West 42nd St., New York 36), 20 min., so., b. and w.

The film focusses upon the emotional responses of thirteen- to fifteen-year-olds—giggling, criticalness, lack of realism, random activity are among the behaviors pictured. The scenes are set in the home and show parents making both wise and unwise responses.

Understand Your Emotions (Coronet Films, Coronet Building, Chicago 1), 14 min., so., b. and w. or color.

This shows the effect of emotions on the body and upon voluntary and involuntary behavior. Conditioning is portrayed as playing an important part in the development of emotions. The aim is to show adolescents how emotional development may be fostered.

Part Three

ASPECTS

OF DEVELOPMENT

IN ADOLESCENCE

THE RESULTS of the dynamic forces operative during adolescence are best perceived by examining their influence on specific aspects of development. Part Three is a detailing of some of these independently discussed, but certainly not discrete, phases of growth.

The interests of adolescents are detailed because they are so powerful in shaping the course of development and adjustment. If we understand the variability of interests instead of accepting the lists of "typical interests" so often cited, we have useful clues to understanding individuals. Fallacious notions of interest are outlined together with suggestions for intensification and better direction of profitable interests.

Moral and spiritual values are at the core of an integrated personality. Issues the adolescent has to face in our culture are described, and suggestions are made as to how these issues may be resolved.

How and why some adolescents fail might well have been the final chapter of this section; but the close relation of some "pathology" to morality, as well as the relation of socialization to the first chapter in the next section, indicated the sequence used. If we understand the pathology of adolescence we have not only an understanding that will be therapeutic for some but we have perceptions that will help the healthy adolescent continue his good adjustment.

338

A major developmental problem of adolescence pertains to each youth's acceptance of self and his integration with those around him. Home, school, intelligence, emotion, and physique are all at work shaping his effectiveness as a social person. Heterosexual adjustment may be regarded as an integration of other aspects of development during adolescence.

When does the young person form his lasting interests? How can new interests be fostered? Is there a typical interest pattern for adolescents?

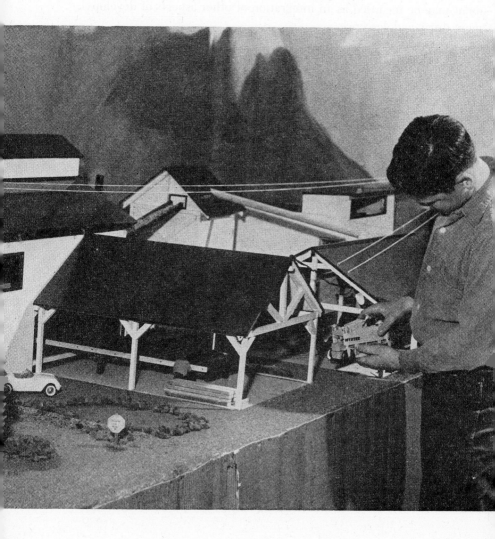

CHAPTER ELEVEN

Expansion and Integration of Interests

The interests of adolescents are the really important focal points of development in the teen years. The problem of interests is a vital one for education. The interests of boys and girls determine whether young people will be a source of worry in the community or a source of pride. The interests an individual forms determine whether he will live in conflict with society or will live harmoniously with others. The interests formed in adolescence lay the groundwork for continuing development in the adult years.

A quarter of a century ago, F. E. Bolton asserted that what a boy likes is vastly more important than what he knows. The companions he chooses, the books he reads, the ideals he holds, the things he enjoys, and his attitudes toward religion, duties, society, are the vitally significant characteristics of his life's career. "His spontaneous likes and dislikes, his loves and his hates, his longings and aversions, will really determine what manner of man he shall be." * The passage of years has not been accompanied by the accumulation of knowledge that should alter Bolton's conclusions.

Much that has been said about the characteristics and problems of adolescents is intimately related to the formation of interests.

---

* F. E. Bolton, *Adolescent Education* (New York: The Macmillan Company; 1931), p. 175.

341

Part Two, in particular, might be regarded as an exposition of interests. Adolescents and those who work with them should know how interests are evolved, how they shape personal and social adjustment, and what some of the more constructive interests might be. The interest patterns of adolescents provide part of the basis for adult insight into the motivations and personality of youth. Misconceptions regarding the nature of interests should be removed or minimized. Both young and old must give attention to the shaping of interests that have value for the here and now as well as for the future.

Basic concept of interest

The meaning of interest

The word *interest* can be better understood by analyzing its two roots—*inter* and *esse*. *Inter* means *between* and *esse* is a form of the Latin verb *to be*. Hence interest is that which exists between the individual and some event, person, or thing. It is a feeling of identity between the individual and some condition, thing, or person. This definition focuses upon the individual and immediately suggests that interest cannot be forced. Interest is a condition or feeling that occurs when a person sees the identity or meaning of some situation to his own wants or needs. He sees, in the thing in which he is interested, some personal significance—some answer to his needs. Interest is, to an extent, the result of changed or developing perception.

The role of interest in life

When an individual is preoccupied with a given series of activities time speeds by. Prolonged work and difficult obstacles are tackled eagerly and with total (mental, physical, and emotional) vigor. Everyone wants to enjoy life; and if a person can perform the obligations that are forced upon him by nature and society as the result of developed interests, his enjoyment of life can be greatly enhanced. There can be little doubt that the submissive performance of obligatory tasks contributes greatly to the high incidence of mental ill-health. "Some groups swelter at their tasks in the heavy, humid oppressiveness of obligatory functioning, like a sea-level metropolis in midsummer. Others buoyantly undertake common responsibilities with the light, stimulating freshness of the autumn in high altitude dryness." *

It is a trite statement in education and psychology that individuals differ widely from one another in physique, personality, intelligence, and experience. Many educational practices point to the reduction of these differences—for example, the attempt to have everyone conform to the same social mores. To an extent this is a commendable objective. On the other hand, our democratic society is postulated upon the worth of the unique individual and upon the special contribution he can make to the welfare of others. This, too, is a commendable objective. However, differences in physique, intelligence, and the like, are reflected in different kinds of interests. Hence, the welfare of society and of the individual is reflected in the fostering of common interests and in the expansion of different interests.

The importance of the study of interests in adolescence is emphasized by the fact that interests have a marked tendency to persist. It is true that some interests are ephemeral and transitory but, in the main, interests become more stable and enduring. This apparent contrast is due to the fact that interests in specifics, in minutiae, are more readily satiated while interests in broader fields of related activities are more stable. [133:425] Hence it is the obvious obligation of those who work with adolescents to work toward those activities that have future references as well as contemporary appeal.

The role of attitudes

Closely allied to interests are attitudes. Attitudes are less specific than are interests and are less overt. An attitude is a predisposition to act or think in a certain way, while interests are likely to be characterized by active participation. Dale B. Harris defines attitude as "a system of ideas with an emotionally toned content"—a definition that seems to find favor with psychologists. [132:129] Both interests and attitudes serve to direct motives (for example, the satisfaction of needs) as well as to act as motives in and of themselves. That is, interests and attitudes become self-generating as they result in the acquisition of skills and knowledges.

---

* Daniel A. Prescott, "Emotional Weather," *The Educational Record*, 20, 1938, 96.

Timothy, a talented youngster, received grades in English that did not reflect his ability. His teacher penned some remarks on his report concerning indifference and uncooperative attitudes. However, the teacher later discovered that Timothy was interested in tennis and invited the lad to his home to see his son's tennis trophies. Timothy borrowed some books on tennis and frequently stayed after school to talk tennis with the teacher. He wrote several papers on tennis ethics and finally did a piece on tennis for the school magazine. Timothy worked hard and long on compositions dealing with tennis. At the end of the grading period the teacher noted that Timothy had made rapid gains as an English student. [259] This is an example of interests and attitudes serving as a motive power. Sometimes, and perhaps Timothy might have been such a case if further study had been reported, the increased skill in the use of books and in writing causes the individual to want to exercise that skill. In short, competence in writing, reading, or tennis becomes the motive. Interests arise from satisfaction of the need for accomplishment.

Besides knowing that interests and attitudes are motives as well as that they serve to direct motives, those who work with adolescents should know that they are learned rather than being hereditary. The sanctions of home, community, school, and church all have a share in the formation of attitudes. Hence, no cataclysmic changes can be expected as the result of changing the situation in one aspect of the individual's total environment. However, change does take place, slowly and steadily, and it is necessary that we maintain faith in the improvability of human response. "With optimism we overhaul our school curricula, launch publicity campaigns, and march forth to slay any attitudinal dragon that we decide to eradicate. I am not saying that all this optimism is justified. But our faith in environmentalism itself is a factor of prime importance." *

The genesis of interests and attitudes

It would seem that some persons think that interests arise from some spontaneous process within the individual, though when queried they would admit the real facts. Interests evolve out of the

* Gordon W. Allport, *The Resolution of Intergroup Tensions* (New York: The National Conference of Christians and Jews; 1952), p. 7.

experience that breeds familiarity. They result from the acquisition of information and skill. Further, this information or skill must have some personal reference—hence the earlier observation that interests are the results of changed or improved perception of some thing or situation. Several implications for the development of interests during adolescence may be derived from these general observations.

It is true that, to some extent, we should begin with an existing interest and attempt to show relationships to other phenomena so that the interest will expand. This is what happened in the case of Timothy. His interest in tennis was expanded to include an interest in clearly written communication. However, this does not mean that force or pressure should never be used in getting the young person to participate in some relatively novel activity. It is quite possible that interest may develop as the result of being "pressured" into some activity and then, after gaining some information and acquiring some skill, a real identification of the individual with the activity results. There can be little doubt that each of you has developed an interest in something in which you were originally forced to engage—Latin translations, algebraic computation, handball, or playing a musical instrument. The author has tried to "sell" naval recruits on the desirability of taking training as hospital corpsmen. Many recruits protested that they were not interested; but quotas—the needs of the Navy—had to be filled and the best that could be done was to say, "We hope that you will become interested." Many of them *did become interested* after they decided that if the job had to be done it might just as well be done willingly. Ego satisfaction and recognition resulted from achievement.

It is not the force, *per se,* that stimulates the interest—it is the result of experience and success. Hence a responsibility of the leader is to set up conditions that will lead to successful performance. This means that the task to be performed must be within the ability of the individual. If a child is to be forced to practice the piano, we should know that he has some aptitude for music. This might be partially determined by giving a musical aptitude test or by studying the progress that is made in the initial period of trial.

Sometimes the desire to accomplish in a given area might profitably be reinforced by what are known as secondary incentives. The pupil is given some reward for success—a new baseball glove may reward the playing of a certain musical selection. There is a danger, however, that the secondary incentive may remain the reason for the participation in a given activity. Unfortunately, this seems to be the case in our schools when pupils have worked mainly for grades—and only so hard as they felt was necessary to get the grade they deemed desirable. This is a manifestation of the fact that the symbols of learning are frequently confused with the outcomes of learning. [54:52] It is clear that those who make use of secondary incentives must take steps to insure that this is simply a passing phase of development. Teachers who approve the pupil as a person and emphasize his progress rather than the grade he has earned are contributing to the development of lasting interests.

The role of success indicates that another factor in the development of interest is ability. The present interests of the adolescent, at which point teachers are advised to begin, are to some extent dependent upon ability. The strong, agile individual is interested in athletics. The dexterous lad is likely to be interested in manual construction. The young person with musical talent is more easily interested in playing musical instruments. Those who have developed skills in social relations are somewhat more interested in working and playing with others.

Studies that compare the bright individual with the dull show definite trends related to ability. The bright boy may become engrossed in chess while the dull one may be satisfactorily occupied with routine performances. Those with higher intelligence reveal a greater capacity and interest in self-amusement. [179:220] R. L. Thorndike found that there was some similarity in the reading interests of bright children (IQ about 123) and slow children (IQ about 92), but the degree of similarity was substantially greater if the bright children were compared with slow children who were about two years older in terms of life age. [313]

Changes in interest with age

It has been frequently noted that the individual's interest in social affairs and peer adjustment become more marked during adolescence. This is clearly shown by Figure 14 by the lines indicating the increase in interest in dancing, clothes, and social affairs,

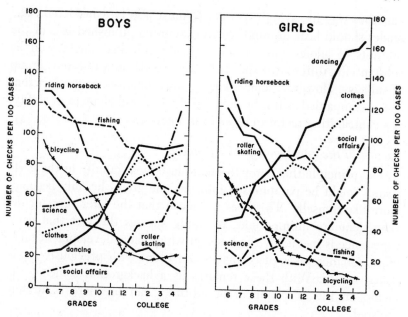

FIG. 14. **Changing interest patterns through adolescence**
Patterns shown by interests prevalent at various grade levels. From
Raymond G. Kuhlen, *The Psychology of Adolescent Development*
(New York: Harper & Brothers, 1952), p. 193.

for both boys and girls. In contrast it may be noted that activities
that may be carried on alone—horseback riding, bicycling, and
fishing—decline rapidly as a person grows older. This is in part a
result of the adolescents' burgeoning need for peer companionship.
However, these changing interest patterns must be considered representative or illustrative, rather than typical. For instance, Hollingshead has noted that roller skating is much more popular
among young people in the lower socio-economic strata than with
those from the upper classes. Dancing is somewhat less available
to those in the lower social groups and is therefore less popular.
[143:306] Similarly, it is probable that the popularity of horseback
riding would depend upon the availability of horses and upon the
number of companions who followed the same activity. It is apparent that the changes in interests, such as are depicted in Figure 14, are not simply a function of age but that availability

(another way of saying experience) must also be considered. The reader should bear in mind, when examining published lists of the interests of adolescents, that the trends indicated might well be substantially different if the study were made on a different group of subjects. However, some credence must be given to the fact that age, accompanied as it is by pubertal changes and changes in ability, *is* a contributing factor to changes in interest.

Factors in the development of attitudes

The principle that "growth takes place most rapidly in the early years," might be paraphrased into, "as one grows he only becomes more like himself." This does not mean that the later years of development are unimportant, it simply stresses the fact that early experience is inevitably the basis on which later development takes place. Change takes place that is consistent with previously established trends. With these remarks as a background some of the factors in the development of attitudes can be more accurately assessed.

Gordon W. Allport has noted four sources of attitudes. [3:810]

1. Attitudes result from the integration of many specific responses to similar situations. Thus high school pupils will develop attitudes toward self-government from the experiences of having their voices listened to in the home, from participation on committees directed to social affairs, from reading about historical events in self-determination, from reading current newspapers and periodicals, from their participation in pupil government, from experiences of self-direction in routine classwork, and from what they hear others say about it.

2. Attitudes originate in terms of specifics from general approach or withdrawal tendencies. Thus the tendency to shy away from those of another skin color may develop into a distrust or hate. It has been said, with some justification, that people tend to confirm their prejudices rather than to think. It has been implied earlier that negative attitudes may be averted by increasing familiarity. It has been found, for instance, that low racial attitude scores are related to high and low bilingual scores—students with much knowledge and with no knowledge of other cultures scored lower in prejudice than those with a little knowledge. [163] With no knowl-

edge a person would have neither a withdrawal or approach tendency while much acquaintance could be expected to result in greater objectivity.

3. This expectation might not be realized because of another factor; that is, attitudes may be taken over, ready made, from others—parents, teachers, peers. Thus a different attitude toward Negroes would tend to be generated in the South (where there is considerable acquaintance with Negroes) more easily than in some other sections of the nation. Absorption from others is probably one of the more important sources of attitudes; and is a factor that adults might gravely consider when indulging in censure of adolescent behavior.

4. Attitudes might arise from a single remarkable experience. Antipathy and disgust for sex have been reported as the result of vindictive punishment resulting from what was actually childish sex play or exploration. Cruelty from maladjusted teachers has resulted in an antipathy for school on the part of some children.

Some interests of adolescents

Personal grooming

Physical changes *contribute* to changed ability and changed perception, which mark the evolution of new interests. As adolescents approach the physical stature of adulthood they make both conscious and unconscious efforts to act and be like adults. Cultural expectations, plus physical changes, participate in the intensification of social orientation. Pubertal development stimulates the drive toward heterosexual experiences; and the need to be approved in terms of local and current modes of dress and manner is increased.

Boys are accorded prestige for physical size and prowess (Chapter Five). Hence there is an increased interest in games involving athletic skills, in the maintenance of good health which will allow them to perform satisfactorily, in "physical culture" courses which will develop corded muscles and, they hope, broad shoulders. Reading interests are frequently developed in sports, body development, and outdoor life. There is frequently some concern with what they consider to be abnormalities of face or form. Being too short, and less frequently being too tall, often tends to generate self-concepts that influence the development of interests. Sometimes the boy may react by developing compensations for the "abnormality" he feels, or he may tend to shy away from activities that he thinks will call attention to his height. Unfavorable attitudes are generated by being humiliated or being made to feel worthless.

Prior to the time of puberty body perspiration produces little odor, but after puberty the odor of perspiration is marked. In the locker room this causes no difficulty, but on the dance floor or in class after a play period the odor may cause the boy some embarrassment. Girls are sometimes concerned about the odors noticed during the menstrual period. However, both the boy and girl are typically enough concerned about the matter so that they take the necessary steps to keep clean. Changes in glandular activity sometimes cause acne. This may result in the adolescent's locking himself in the bathroom and spending several minutes in an effort to squeeze and steam out the offensive particles. Unfortunately his eighteen-inch perspective, reflected in the mirror, is likely to affect him much more emphatically than it does the individual who views him from a distance of three feet or more. Adults should be aware of these attitudes and problems so they may assist in the adolescent's developmental tasks of peer acceptance and accepting his physique.

There is the possibility that odors and acne are magnified into larger problems than they need be by the advertising in magazines. Some of the advertisements are specifically directed to adolescents. It would seem desirable for teachers and group leaders to promote discussions among young persons that might serve to properly evaluate the normality of these difficulties. The wisdom each adolescent brings from his home would help others solve their problems.

Girls have a little advantage in the matter of personal grooming in that (1) the use of cosmetics is sanctioned—thus blemishes may be covered or features enhanced—and (2) their past history has emphasized the desirability of feminine neatness and cleanliness— the boys have previously been expected to be careless and dirty. Even so, both boys and girls can be expected to spend considerable time in brushing hair, bathing, cleaning nails, and the like.

The matter of clothing is psychologically important. The young person *must* wear what he deems proper. Girls must have the proper dresses, blouses, sweaters, and skirts. Boys must have the proper trousers, shirts, and shoes. Brilliant socks, ties, vests, may be desirable to add an element of startlingness to the outfit. Parents, who bear all or part of the expense of the wardrobe, must bear in mind the importance to the adolescent of his fitting into the group —of avoiding ridicule from his peers. To rail against the idiosyncrasies of youth will most probably erect unnecessary barriers to communication. The approach to this matter should begin prior to adolescence when the middle- and upper-grade youngsters are allowed to participate in the selection of their clothes. Gradually they should learn to use some of their own money to buy clothes, and by adolescence they might well be expected to bear a substantial part of the clothes budget—how substantial a part will depend on the finances of the family, the prosperity of the era, and the availability of part-time work.

Vocational selection

In the days when the son typically followed the career of his father and when little work outside the home and farm was available to daughters, the selection of a vocation was relatively simple. Today with prestige and status so intimately dependent on the work one does and the wide variety of jobs performed, choosing an occupation is a difficult task. These difficulties are dealt with in detail in Chapter Seventeen, so only those phases that relate specifically to interest will be dealt with at this point.

The number of interests the early adolescent has will probably increase, and only in later adolescence will the number decrease and interest in one area be intensified (see Figure 19). This is not only natural and normal but is a tendency that should be encouraged. Those who recommend the early selection of a career should probably be challenged at some points. For one thing, it has been seen that interests change with the development of new skills and knowledges and with changes in capacity. Interest in a variety of things will give the individual a broader basis for later competence in a specialized field and will enhance his understanding of the relationships and ramifications of a particular job. Further, what appears to be an important and available occupation today may prove to be a rapidly declining job area in another five or ten years. Of course, early selection need not be criticized—the point is that undue adult anxiety should not be revealed even if final selection of a vocation has not been made by the completion of college.

Interest inventories have been increasingly used in recent years as a basis for vocational selection. Unfortunately, some of the users have been somewhat too enthusiastic about the reliability and validity of these instruments. No doubt they can serve as guides and as supplementary information; but the adviser who says, "You should be a teacher," or a salesman, or a mechanic is overemphasizing the importance of inventories. For one thing, interests do not indicate an ability—though there is some relationship. It has been noted that interests develop as the result of successful experience. Hence one may develop an interest, particularly if he has the attitude of wanting to do so, as the result of acquaintanceship. H. A. Toops indicates this deficiency of interest tests by asserting that the function of education and guidance programs is to remove the deficiencies and inequities of earlier experience and to provide the basis for making further progress. It is questionable whether we can assume that academic and vocational interests are unchangeable. [320:653] Certainly it seems safe to conclude that we need not be alarmed if the adolescent rapidly shifts interests to several successive vocations.

Social activities

Processes of socialization are dealt with in detail in Chapter 14, "Peer Culture and Heterosexual Adjustments," but as one of the burgeoning interests of adolescence they cannot be ignored at this point. A major social interest is the adolescent's need to become independent of his parents. Adults in the community could take a big step in avoiding the frustration that accompanies the blocking of this need and also provide an approach to the developmental task of vocational selection by establishing systematic work opportunities for youth. There is so much that could be done that would be socially constructive that it seems odd that such arrangements are not universal. A youth employment bureau could be established for prospective baby-sitters, part-time household help, grass mowers, errand boys, stock clerks, deliverymen, furnace stokers, car washers, and so on. Constructive jobs could be created by adults who would assemble with such an aim in mind. Playgrounds could be cleared, adolescent directors of children's activities could be trained, community beautification projects could be initiated with nominal wages coming from The Lions, Kiwanis, Rotary, or Council of Churches. Several significant outcomes would be realized: (1) Youngsters could have the social satisfaction of having their own money in their pockets—an important consideration in our society. (2) Youngsters would have the satisfaction of gaining the social approval that comes from engaging in significant work. (3) Training and exploration in various fields of occupational activity would be provided. (4) Associations with adults and with peers would give young people experience in effective social functioning. This is both a social and vocational advantage because success in any line of work depends to a remarkable extent upon ability to get along with others. (5) Valuable training in the use of leisure time would be provided. (6) Early participation in civic functioning would provide an orientation to participating citizenship that is otherwise frequently lacking. In all these ways the meeting of adolescent needs contributes to the development of salutary interests.

Largely because of the importance of the social interests of adolescents, the author is firmly opposed to the uniform assignment of homework by teachers. There are several reasons for this attitude: such assignments tend to widen the pupil differences that already make teaching difficult (the best students generally have the best situation for the advantageous pursuit of homework); parents, because they are emotionally involved, are frequently the poorest kind of teachers; students who can depend on catching up with homework have time to waste at school; some students have to work in order to help support their family and do not have time—they are thus unjustifiably handicapped; students who do not engage in athletic activities need some time for physical exercise—walking, informal games, and the like. But the main reason why homework should be regarded as a questionable practice is that the time outside of school is needed for social experiencing. Boys need time to engage in long conversations with their boy friends, girls need time to discuss affairs of love and life with their pals, time is needed for dating activities. Time should be available for those long and frequent (pity the long-suffering parent) telephone conversations.

Dancing is an important social activity. Fortunately, many school programs now have included in them planned periods for instruction and practice. Parents have mentioned numerous situations in which some adolescent professed a lack of interest in dating and dancing only to have, apparently, his whole orientation changed by the parent's insistence on his attending a dancing class. The adolescent's reluctance was simply a defense against the fear of revealing his lack of skill. A principal related the story of a fourteen-year-old girl whose personality was transformed from a quiet, lonesome, and scholastically ineffective person into a happy and able student by learning to do square dancing. However, for religious reasons the parents forbade further participation. Rapidly the girl withdrew from others and became gloomy. The principal went to the parents and talked the matter over with them. Since they had noted the girl's changed behavior, they decided that they might better set aside their religious objections. There is probably much more to this case than simply learning the skill of dancing. Social approval, the release of emotions through whole body activity, the development of feelings of confidence also probably played a part.

Adolescents have a strong interest in friendships, which will be discussed in a later chapter. Let it be said here that these friendships are transitory and educative. Parents should trust the wisdom of their earlier training, when and if they see their children forming friendships that are deemed undesirable. It is doubtful that a categorical demand will stop a friendship. There are cases, however, in which the adolescent seems to make a demand or behave in a way that he knows is unreasonable; when stopped he "rants and rails" but inwardly feels a satisfaction that his parents are concerned about his welfare. [187:547] Marynia Farnham suggests a number of roles for parents in the area of adolescent's interests in friends:

1. Don't expect your youngsters to follow your own likes and dislikes so far as people are concerned.
2. Respect their right to make their own choices as far as possible.
3. Know their friends by making them your friends.
4. Reserve your judgments until you are absolutely sure you are right and have evidence of it.
5. Talk things over with the youngster reasonably, objectively and without prejudice, and listen to their opinions, which are valuable.
6. If, after all this, you still feel that you must interfere with some

association of theirs, give your reasons and be sure to make it clear that you are interfering because you are certain that it is necessary for the youngster's welfare.

7. Having made a decision, stick to it, and see that it is carried out. Flabbiness and indolence won't earn the respect of these teenagers.

8. Always, all the time, keep the door open for discussion and communication.

These rules are tough to follow but they will work. Parents who have built a relationship with their children which makes this procedure natural won't have any trouble anyway.*

Recreational interests

The use of leisure time is one of the more pressing of the problems of adolescence. It is made more important because of the future implications of the present use of leisure time. The drift toward spectator and listening activities should be checked. It is not that listening and looking are necessarily dangerous—but they are not creative. Thus the individual is kept from coming closer to the realization of the potential he has for mental, emotional, physical, and spiritual growth. The negative side, of course, is that unless he does find and develop worthy leisure-time activities, there is some danger that conflict within himself or with society may develop.

Adolescents should be encouraged to take responsibility in the development of their leisure-time pursuits. But too often there seems to be some inclination for them to expect that someone will provide them with entertainment or activity. The things said earlier about the development of interests are apropos. Interests are not discovered, they are created. Each person, because of his unique capacities and experiences, has the potential for developing differing interests. The exploratory activities in which he might engage may serve to develop interest. The thing to do is to *try* the things he thinks, or has thought, he might like. Painting, building a radio or midget racer, growing and arranging flowers, playing an instrument or singing, working with children, are just a few suggestions

---

* Marynia F. Farnham, *The Adolescent* (New York: Harper & Brothers; 1952), pp. 98–99.

of the multiple activities that are readily available. The adolescent should know that he really can't know what his interests are unless he gives various pursuits a try. [178:29]

The importance of recreational interests is reflected in the behavior of delinquents as contrasted to non-delinquents. According to one study delinquents sought adventure through stealing, gambling, destroying property, while non-delinquents found excitement through competition and achievement. Four times as many delinquents smoked as did the non-delinquents; more delinquents attended movies as frequently as three times a week; but it should be noted that non-delinquents did smoke and attend movies frequently. Non-delinquents made use of playgrounds where they were available. Generally speaking, the contrast resides in the fact that delinquents tended to engage in recreations and activities that brought them into conflict with others. [124:160]

Roy Sorenson asserts that adolescents are a neglected age-group and that the neglect is most apparent in the area of recreations. This was most obvious during wartime, and he feels that wartime youth may have made a permanent contribution by calling our attention so graphically to the need for youth centers and constructive activities. There is need for making the activities inclusive enough to provide a variety of interests rather than to have one or two major activities. Incidentally, Sorenson calls attention to a factor mentioned frequently in this book—the need for adult leadership that is not domineering and dictatorial. Skillful leaders of adolescence must know how to exert leadership from an apparent background position. [287]

As this kind of leadership is exerted two considerations should be kept in mind. One is the increasing amount of leisure time available to the modern man. The other is the reputed stress, uncertainty, and pressure of modern life. The resulting tension can to some extent be repressed by refusing to think of problems—by immersing oneself in radio, television, watching ball games, or drinking to some degree of oblivion. It is agreed that repression is of doubtful and temporary benefit. The preferable courses would be to lay the groundwork, in childhood and adolescence, for a creative pursuit of leisure time that replaces worry with something positive. Because of the rapid development of our society, this task of developing wholesome recreational interests itself is a creative thing—old ways only suggest the direction of progress. A. T. Jersild indicates that the interests children and adolescents form are often superficial and stereotyped. They fail to lead the individual to a facing of his own problems. [162:474] The approach to creative recreational pursuits might well begin with a study of the needs and developmental tasks of adolescents that can be approached through recreation.

Reading interests and the adolescent

Reading ability of adolescents

Up to the time of entering high school the average adolescent has probably continued to make progress in reading skills. Unfortunately, it seems then to be taken for granted that mature skill has been achieved and no further instruction is given in reading as a tool subject. Some gain in speed will be achieved as understanding increases and, of course, comprehension improves as knowledge expands; but this improvement is incidental and fortuitous. This is the more disconcerting because the improvement of more mature students, under systematically planned instruction, is likely to be more rapid than in the case of the less mature pupil. The superior learner, to say nothing of the slower pupil, will continue to improve throughout high school and college. (Most of the readers of this book could make substantial progress, in short periods of time, through the persistent application of a plan for improving reading.) It is a mistake to assume that the able student is necessarily a good reader and will become an even better reader. [116:15]

Many studies indicate that the rate and comprehension of high school *and college* students can be bettered up to 100 per cent in short periods devoted to improved techniques. One such study showed that college freshmen could double their reading speed without lowering comprehension. [33] Military officers have doubled their reading rates without impairment of comprehension in a period of six weeks training. [68] However, it is probably well not to expect uniformly spectacular results but to be assured that *some*

improvement will probably take place as the result of planned practice—and to hope that continued practice will result in continued
improvement.

Inasmuch as interests are in part a function of ability, there is
the possibility of getting the adolescent to expand and integrate his
interests by fostering the improvement of reading skills. Reading
can provide the adolescent suggestions for self-help in meeting his
developmental tasks and satisfying his imperative needs.

Reading and adjustment

Books afford an opportunity to gain information, sublimation,
or inspiration. Through them we are linked with the past and are
given a better perspective for the future. Civilization and the progress of mankind is, to a remarkable extent, made possible by writing
and reading. Those who would argue that experience (meaning
direct experience) is the best teacher might well consider the implications of the following:

> All the wisdom of the ages, all the stories that have delighted
> mankind for centuries, are available at negligible cost to all of us
> within the covers of books. . . .
>   . . . Although they [books] are separate, together they all add up
> to something; they are connected with each other and with other
> cities. The same ideas, or related ones, turn up in different places;
> the human problems that repeat themselves in life repeat them-
> selves in literature, but with different solutions according to differ-
> ent authors who wrote at different times. Books influence each
> other; they link the past and the present and the future and have
> their own generations, like families. Wherever you start reading
> you connect yourself with one of the families of ideas, and, in the
> long run, you not only find out about the world and the people in
> it: you find out about yourself, too.*

Almost without question, reading is the most important skill in
academic adjustment. Research has, in fact, demonstrated that
there is a higher correlation between scholastic accomplishment

---

* Bennett Cerf, "It's Fun to Read," in Alfred Stefferud (Ed)., *The Wonderful
World of Books* (New York: The New American Library of World Literature,
Inc.; 1953), pp. 24–25.

and reading and vocabulary than there is between scholarship and tests of general intelligence. [22:113] Psychologists have not been so bold as to say that superior reading skills and habits of reading will raise the level of intelligence; but there can be little doubt that reading skill and wide reading interests can help the individual to use more effectively the potential he has for developing intelligent responses (see Chapter 9). It must be admitted that the relationship between reading and intelligence is reciprocal, or reversible. Higher intelligence contributes to more skill and interest in reading. Skill in reading helps an individual come closer to the realization of his intellectual potential. However, few authorities would deny that average reading skills are much lower than they need to be. The ease with which the reading efficiency of adults can be improved clearly indicates that direct attention to reading skill is highly merited—and probably will result in concomitant gains in adjusting to life's many problems.

Development of skill in reading

It is the consensus that the improvement of reading skills is the responsibility of every teacher—including the subject-matter teacher in high school. [351:171] Probably the best way to prepare teachers for this responsibility would be to have them participate in reading improvement classes or clinics in college. If this is not possible, the way is still open for some personal experimentation. Practical suggestions for self-help in effective reading have been made by M. E. Bennett [18:144], H. W. Bernard [22:106], and Charles and Dorothy Bird [27:62]. The following are some suggestions the reader can use in his own self-help program as well as points that can be emphasized as a teacher.

1. Practice daily for short periods. Disturbing one's habits is uncomfortable and the uneasiness should not be concentrated in large doses.
2. Practice on easy, interesting materials—on which one will not be tested for purposes of grading. An immediate check on comprehension of material is highly desirable.
3. Make a deliberate attempt to read faster. Use the sweep second hand of a wrist watch or a stop watch to check rates on similar material; i.e., different selections from one book by one author.

4. Adapt reading rate to kind of material and to the purpose for which it is being read.
5. Pay only minor attention to vocalization and regressive eye movements. These are symptoms of poor reading and will tend to disappear as skills are improved.
6. Try to develop, or at least assume, an interest in what is read.
7. Remember that interest in reading will increase as skill is achieved and as more reading broadens the background for understanding.
8. Be active in the reading process; ask, "What message will this selection convey?" and then "What are the outstanding points of the material I have just read?"
9. Develop vocabulary through some systematic plan.
10. Keep a record of progress—speed trials on similar material, regularity of practice, progress in vocabulary, decrease in number of regressive eye movements, and the like.
11. Be patient with slow progress. It takes time to build the familiarity with knowledge that contributes to efficient perception of it. It takes time to reconstruct habits.

Some suggestions for the guidance of teachers in their attempts to help the adolescent improve his reading abilities are:

1. Book make-up is important; recommend books that generally appeal to students of a particular age.
2. Your preferences may validly serve as a guide to pupil selection of reading material.
3. Remember that preferences in reading are subject to change. Stress, through direct teaching, standards for selection of worthwhile material.
4. Availability of books is an important factor in influencing reading habits. Have a circulating library in the room, see that books are displayed on open shelves in the library, encourage organizations to give books as awards. However, the verbal encouragement of teachers is also necessary.
5. Book selections, in terms of difficulty, should be guided by the pupil's present ability.
6. Book selections, in terms of interest, should be guided by the individual pupil's interests.

The reading interests of adolescents

It is the author's belief that there are few areas where it is so vital to "strike while the iron is hot" as in the matter of reading. Reading interests reach their peak around the age of twelve or thirteen years, and there is a decline in leisure-time reading up to the age of twenty. [93] Many factors would serve to explain this decline: the heavier press of required school work, the competition of part-time jobs, an increase in duties about the home, greater freedom to be absent from home, expanding interest in activities with peer groups. But some of the decline is due to factors that can be removed (with a concomitant lessening of the decline). It has been shown that interests depend somewhat on skill—hence improved reading skill through continued emphasis on it in the high school years would be helpful. It has been shown that interests depend upon opportunity—hence some decline could be prevented by having suitable books readily available to the adolescent. Interests depend upon the individual's unique experience and abilities— hence a wide variety of books should be available so that each could be more likely to find the book that would have maximum appeal.

It is difficult to evaluate the existing patterns of reading interests. Some studies show continuous changes in interests. Over half the books liked by boys from nine to eleven years are classed as "adventure," with "juvenile fiction" and "miscellaneous" constituting the bulk of the remainder. At the age of twenty, "adventure" has declined and constitutes a quarter of the books liked, interest in "juvenile fiction" has almost disappeared, and "miscellaneous" and "adult fiction" are by far the predominant items in reading interests. Girls show a shift from below ten years to twenty years in that "adult fiction" becomes about 65 per cent of the fare liked while "juvenile fiction" was most popular at the earlier age. Interests in "adventure" and "miscellaneous" show little change (Figure 15). Another study shows that not a single one of the ten books most liked by high school freshmen was on the list of ten most liked by seniors. The senior list was made up of the current best-selling adult novels while the freshman choices were stereotyped juvenile fiction. [42] This disparity in research results, showing both differences and likenesses as individuals pass through the teen years, indi-

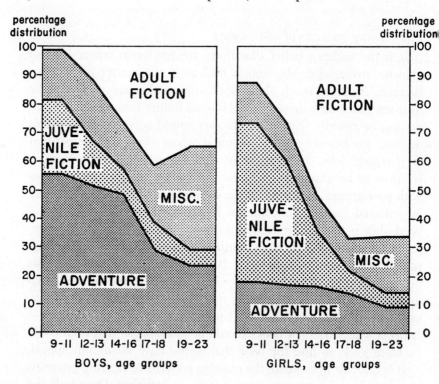

FIG. 15. **Best-liked books**

Percentage distribution of best-liked books classified according to type, by age groups and sex. Note the marked changes with age and the striking sex differences. Based on Jordan, A. M. "Children's Interests in Reading," *Teachers College Contributions to Education,* 1921, No. 107.

cates the item of real significance. Mass approaches to the reading interests of adolescents will be less effective than attempting to provide a varied diet of reading that will appeal to pupils of different levels of intelligence, different socio-economic levels, different community backgrounds (for example, industrial, business, agricultural), and different experiences.

Karl Garrison and Luella Cole have prepared lists of novels and popular literature that will be helpful to those who have the opportunity to guide adolescents in their choice of readings. Cole has titles appealing to youngsters [65:679] while Garrison [117:485] has an annotated list of popular books about adolescents that will both interest the older person and provide the adolescent reader with some ideas and insights. Also readily available is a book edited by Alfred Stefferud containing a chapter on the reading interests of adolescents, which divides the recommended titles into categories. The following are random examples:

ADVENTURE—WITH WILD ANIMALS: Raymond Ditmars, *Strange Animals I Have Known* (Harcourt, Brace); Jim Corbett, *Man-Eaters of Kumaon* (Oxford).

ADVENTURE—WITH DOGS AND HORSES: Walter Farley, *Black Stallion* (Random House); Albert Payson Terhune, *Lad: A Dog* (Harper); Jack London, *Call of the Wild* (Macmillan).

ADVENTURE—SEA: Howard Pease, *Shanghai Passage* (Doubleday); Charles Nordhoff and James Norman Hall, *Mutiny on the Bounty* (Little, Brown); Thor Heyerdahl, *Kon-Tiki* (Rand-McNally).

SCIENCE FICTION: Jules Verne, *Trip from the Earth to the Moon* (Lippincott); H. G. Wells, *First Men in the Moon* (Macmillan); Groff Conklin (Ed.), *Big Book of Science Fiction* (Crown).

SPORTS: Joe DiMaggio, *Baseball for Everyone* (McGraw-Hill); Bob Feller, *How to Pitch* (A. S. Barnes).

GIRLS' STORIES: Maureen Daly, *Seventeenth Summer* (Dodd, Mead); Helen Dore Boyleston, *Sue Barton, Student Nurse* (Little, Brown).

MANNERS AND PERSONALITY: Betty Betz, *Your Manners Are Showing* (Grosset); Maureen Daly, *Smarter and Smoother* (Dodd, Mead); Norton H. Jonathan, *Guide Book for the Young Man About Town* (Winston); Bryan Ivens (Ed.), *The Seventeenth Reader* (Lippincott). [270:53]

Probably the most complete book dealing with the specific reading interests of adolescents is Lenrow's *Reader's Guide to Prose Fiction* [186] which is designed to help teachers and pupils satisfy individual preferences and deal with unique problems. Each book is classified under one of the following major headings: The Individual's Need for Entertainment, The Individual and His Personal Environment, The Individual and His Social Environment. The latter heading includes sub-heads of social conditions, political conditions, economic and industrial conditions, professions and vocations, religion, and philosophy. The book itself is one of those prepared by the Commission on Secondary Education, which made extensive studies of the problems, goals, and interests of adolescents.

Approaches to the stimulation and utilization of adolescents' reading interests such as these (Lenrow and Scoggin) appear to be much more fruitful than those studies that show general changes in interest patterns with advance in age. Different individuals mature at various rates, they have different stimulations, and too frequently the generalization does not fit. When the approach is through individuals, there will be a much greater chance that we will capitalize upon the opportunity for wholesome development of interests—particularly in reading—that is present in the adolescent years.

Summary

The interests that adolescents form constitute important focal points in their development. It is important for adults and adolescents to understand that interests are the outcome of familiarity, experience, skill, and aptitude—they do not arise by some fortuitous condition of spontaneous combustion. Attitudes are predispositions to behave in a certain way while interests are manifested through behavior—both, however, have their origins in experience, developing capacities, and social contacts.

Adolescents are generally interested in personal grooming, and their attitude toward self is to a degree dependent upon fitting their concept of what others think is desirable. As they approach maturity, there is a growing concern with the matter of vocational selection. But the selections change with increasing age, and adults should regard this vacillation as a normal phase of maturing. Also, since interests change with age, it should be noted that findings of interest inventories should be regarded as indicative and transitory rather than as conclusive and permanent. Social interests are a major area for adolescents, and adults should be sure to accord these social affairs a proper place in the total developmental program. While complete freedom may not be warranted, it is necessary for the adult to avoid being dogmatic with regard to social activities and companions. Recreational interests show typical shifts with age, suggesting an opportunity for those who work with youth; that is, now is the time to lay the groundwork for creative and significant leisure activities. Helping adolescents find challenging recreational activities, in a world where adolescents are increasingly becoming a minority group and where time for leisure is growing, is one *positive* way in which the delinquencies of youth may be averted.

Special attention has been given to the reading interests of adolescents because it is in the early teen years that voluntary reading interests reach their peak. Two challenges arise from the study of adolescents' reading interests: one, the desirability of continuing reading instruction in high school; two, the desirability of making specific study of, and specific recommendations for, individual adolescents—in terms of each one's ability, experience, and developmental level.

Interests are susceptible to change, development, and adult influence. The direction of these interests is the central problem for youth workers. The attitudes and interests of the adolescent are determining the kind of adult he will be.

STUDY AND REVIEW ITEMS

1. Can you give some reasons for disagreeing with the contention that interests are the focal points of an adolescent's development?

2. Cite some instance in which you have developed, or some adolescent you have known has developed, an interest in something he was under compulsion to do. Have you seen instances in which force has weakened an interest?

3. What generalizations or beliefs about adolescence are confirmed or questioned by the data in Figure 14?

4. What advertising appeals might have a tendency to create anxiety in adolescents regarding their personal grooming?

5. Do you think that a boy of seventeen should have more or less definitely decided on his future occupation? Why or why not?

6. How important do you consider the recommendation that formal community agencies be organized to provide part-time work for adolescents?

7. Do you feel that there are instances in which an adolescent forms friendships largely to challenge his parents rather than as a result of interest in the friend?

8. Make a list of the major recreational interests of adolescents in your community and compare it with the list made by a classmate. How do you account for the differences?

9. It has been reported that the reading rate of college sophomores is higher than that of seniors. How would you account for this apparent decline?

10. What would be the advantages of carrying on a planned recreational reading program while you are still in college?

11. What could you do, as a high school teacher, to expand and integrate the reading interests of your pupils?

RECOMMENDED SUPPLEMENTARY READING

Christensen, Thomas E. *Getting Job Experience* (Chicago: Science Research Associates, Inc.; 1949), 48 pp.
This booklet, designed for adolescents, stresses the importance of work experience as a phase of education. It shows how experience can help form interests and discover talents, shape the formation of good work habits and attitudes, and be of later value as a source of recommendation.

Gilchrist, Robert S., and Robert J. Forbes, in National Society for the Study of Education, *52nd Yearbook, Part I, Adapting the Secondary-School Program to the Needs of Youth* (Chicago: University of Chicago Press; 1953), pp. 141–159.
This chapter contains a discussion of the responsibility of the school in providing for the unique needs of adolescents. The common needs of all adolescents receive consideration (earning a living, leisure time, and so on) but attention is also devoted to the varied ways these are approached for adolescents of different abilities and interests.

Lenrow, Elbert. *Reader's Guide to Prose Fiction* (New York: Appleton-Century-Crofts, Inc.; 1940), 371 pp.

A discussion of the place and use of fiction in the education of adolescents (50 pages) is followed by an annotated bibliography of selected novels. The titles are classified by the major theme of each novel, and the annotation suggests specific needs that might be approached by reading each book. Highly recommended for teachers and parents.

Seidman, Jerome (Ed.) *The Adolescent, A Book of Readings* (New York: The Dryden Press; 1953), pp. 230–255.

Paul Witty discusses "Television and the High School Student," Sylvia Silverman describes the adolescent's interests in clothing and appearance and Stuart Stoke and Elmer West contrast the interests of boys and girls as revealed in their spontaneous conversations.

Warters, Jane. *Achieving Maturity* (New York: McGraw-Hill Book Company, Inc.; 1949), pp. 93–113.

Several fundamental attitudes and interests of the adolescent—accepting reality, becoming independent, and assuming responsibility—are dealt with in this chapter. Although addressed to adolescents the contents are such as to improve the understanding of adults who work with them.

AUDIO-VISUAL MATERIAL

How to Develop Interest (Coronet Films, Coronet Building, Chicago 1), 11 min., so., b. and w. or col.

The film centers on the proposition that interest is an attitude that leads to willingness to focus attention on some particular thing. Three items are involved in developing interest: "How much do I know?" "What should I know?" and "How can I find out?"

Motivating the Class (McGraw-Hill Book Company, Inc., 330 W. 42nd St., New York 36), 18 min., so., b. and w.

This shows how one teacher learned from his mistakes that it is necessary for the teacher to know something of students' immediate interests if they are to engage wholeheartedly in learning activities.

Can the church effectively bolster the moral concepts of youth? What are some of the moral hazards of religion? What other agencies must join with the church to keep youth on a high moral level? What are the values we hold?

CHAPTER TWELVE

Moral and Spiritual Values

Morality is not a spontaneous outcropping of the human individual. Adherence to a moral code and belief in religion are—like the interests discussed in the preceding chapter—the result of experience and learning. Those who criticize the immorality of youths and their irreligious conduct might well reflect upon their own orientation. It is quite possible that their own behavior has been lax and that their own convictions have not been deeply anchored. Or, it could be that their convictions have been concreted, rather than anchored, so that there could be no tolerance for shifting currents of thought and manner. The guidance of youngsters into the realm of moral maturity demands, first of all, environmental stimulation and opportunity that points in the desired direction.

Each generation, as has been pointed out, seems to feel that the succeeding one is not quite so good. The rate of delinquency, reports on teen-age drug addiction, the per capita consumption of beverage alcohol, the reports on the incidence of premarital intercourse, are symptoms that the older generation views with alarm. Certainly, these problems—whether they are growing in size or not—are worthy of serious consideration. A continued search must be conducted to find the major contributing factors that create the symptom of moral laxity. Moreover, it must be realized that these problems cannot be solved with finality. The actions that are the

369

major contributors to delinquency rates today are not the same as the delinquent acts that were most frequent a hundred years ago— nor will the factors of morality today be the same one hundred years hence.

Morality and religious convictions are subject to direction and control in the same manner as are interests and attitudes. In fact, they are special instances of interests and attitudes—and they are no less important than interests in directing the course of the individual's life. This chapter deals with some of the factors that shape the moral and religious character of the adolescent, with a particular view to implications for adult leadership.

Meaning and status of morality

The concept of morality

The word "moral" is related to one much used by sociologists— mores, which is defined as the customs, folkways, and conventions that have ethical significance. A man is moral when he believes and acts according to what his society deems right; he is immoral when he does that which is judged wrong. The virtuous or moral individual does things that his culture, a part of which is religion, sanctions. Thus morality is relative in the sense that it varies from one social group to another and from one era to another. Contemporary variations are easily perceived in comparative cultural studies. It is more difficult to perceive that many and varied mores are in operation within our nation. The great bulk of our population, the middle class, must come to appreciate that the mores of the lower social strata differ markedly in some details from the dominant pattern. For instance, some delinquents are actually being moral (in a certain sense) when they do things that are approved by their families and peers but are abhorred by "outsiders."

It is apparent that morality is derived from the social group in which one lives. Hence, the degree to which moral maturity is being successfully achieved is an index of the adjustment of the individual to his group. However, adjustment as a passive adaptation may at times be immoral because of conflicting or evolving moral tenets; for example, there is evidence that the person who tacitly approves racial discrimination is judged by many to be unethical.

The widening use of alcoholic beverages is accompanied by a smaller tendency to brand the user as immoral. Generally speaking, however, it is safe to say that the adolescent who observes the rights, shoulds, and musts of dominant society is making wholesome growth and adjustment.

Adolescent disillusionment

The equivocal nature of morality is well illustrated in the conflict between morality and legality. One of the disillusioning experiences of the adolescent, as his realization grows of what actually goes on in the world, is to see deceit, selfishness, egotism, avarice, gluttony, and nepotism go unpunished. Senator Fulbright has expressed this in the following passage:

> Much of the evil of the world is beyond the reach of the law. The law cannot prevent gossip. It cannot prevent men from bearing false witness against their neighbors. It cannot restrain a man from avarice and gluttony. It cannot restrain a man from betraying his friend. The law being inadequate, men long ago supplemented the law courts with courts of equity, where the spirit of the law, rather than its letter, is paramount. Underlying the law are the codes of ethics promulgated by the great religions and recognized by all civilized men as being essential to a humane and enlightened existence.
>
> What should be done about men who do not directly and blatantly sell the favors of their offices for money and so place themselves within the penalties of the law? How do we deal with those who, under the guise of friendship, accept favors which offend the spirit of the law, but do not violate its letter? . . . We are certainly in a tragic plight if the acceptable standard by which we measure the integrity of a man in public life is that he keep within the letter of the law.*

This disillusioning process starts in late childhood when parents are perceived to be less than perfect and not totally omniscient or omnipotent. Extreme reactions to this perception may take the form of (1) deep feelings of insecurity resulting in retreat reactions—

---

* Senator J. William Fulbright, Address to the Senate as chairman of the committee investigating the Reconstruction Finance Corporation, March 27, 1951.

shyness, withdrawal, lassitude, or despair, or (2) a sort of declaration of independence characterized by revolt against authority and mores. The disillusioning is perhaps inevitable and even actually desirable. The problem is to foster a healthy attitude and approach to imperfections and inequities.

Suggestions for inoculation against disillusionment might include the following. Parents should avoid reference to the good old days and "when I was young" preachments. This argument may seem to be hypocrisy in view of prevalent injustices and conflicts in the adult world. Parents should, even during their offsprings' childhood, occasionally admit errors and false judgments. This will tend to promote growth toward mature thinking rather than permitting the discovery of the fallibility of parents to be a climactic disillusionment. Adults, instead of being dogmatic and positive in their judgments, should admit that their views often conflict with those of others. Further, they should admit that others may be right and they be wrong. This does not mean, however, that adults cannot say, "It is my strong conviction that (worship of God, the Golden Rule, abstinence from drugs and drinks, or the like) will in the long run pay you highly valuable dividends." Errors committed by the adolescent should be regarded as learning experiences instead of being condemned as indications of depraved personality. Faith in adolescents is a strong incentive to the pursuit of continued improvement. Adolescents should be allowed to make some of their own decisions so that blame for consequences cannot be uniformly attributed to adult miscalculations. It has been found that a major want of adolescents is for confidence and companionship of parents combined with a greater amount of social freedom. [11]

Antidotes for disillusionment at the school level might take the form of admitting that our ancestors might have practiced injustices, that they acted selfishly, that they made errors in judgment, and that selfishness and greed are not just contemporary problems. When the ruthlessness of some industrial and business tycoons is admitted, the charitable activities of big business can be noted. There are many heartening parallels—which can be pointed out to adolescents—to the case of the boxmaker, John F. Connelly, whose factory was burned and who was helped back into business by his workmen, competitors, and labor unions not directly involved. The words of Mr. Connelly, "I didn't know there were so many unselfish souls in one country," are worthy of repetition. [139] The young will then know that in the midst of the shady and disreputable there is also to be found the admirable and encouraging. It might be well to indicate that neither today is nor yesterday was, nor will tomorrow be, perfect. The challenge to improvement is one of mankind's greatest psychological gifts.

Some of the disillusionment of adolescents springs from the specificity of their earlier beliefs. The child's lack of experience and maturity makes it necessary for precepts and practices in the moral realm to be couched in terms of particular situations. But as development progresses there is a natural tendency for concepts to become more abstract and general and for behavior to become more consistent. [179:434] It is therefore safe to say that disillusionment is a passing phase of development. Adults should concern themselves with seeing to it that the state of doubt and uncertainty does not become chronic.

Contemporary status of morality

For the welfare of youth, adults must embrace the conviction that the moral tone of youth today is good and improving. The psychology of suggestion dictates this view. A person tends to see what he looks for, and others tend to behave in the manner expected of them. There is no organic or constitutional reason why red-haired people should have explosive tempers. Yet on seeing a red-haired person lose his temper, there is a tendency to say, "Just what you'd expect of 'Red.'" "Red" on the other hand finds it less necessary to control his temper because people do not expect him to. Similarly, if young persons hear adults emphasizing the cases of delinquency and speaking as though hardly anything else could be expected, young persons more readily take delinquent steps. The validity of this hypothesis may be inferred from its similarity to the findings of F. Harold Giedt regarding the effect of the first Kinsey report on sex attitudes and behaviors. Actual behavior showed little difference—this may be due to the immediacy of the follow-up study—but a marked change toward a freer attitude was manifested.

Though these results do not indicate that studying Kinsey's book is followed by significant changes in sexual behavior during the brief period covered by the questionnaire, the very marked changes toward much greater personal acceptance of most sexual outlets and a more liberal view toward several questions of sex mores and education show there were very definite changes in expressed attitudes. If these expressed attitude changes represent real changes, the implications are quite important, for behavior changes are very likely to follow attitude changes at a respectable temporal distance.*

The author is assuming that the young person feels the compulsion to behave on no higher level than seems to be that of the actual mores of his peers and the previous generation. The young person feels that he would not be expected to behave differently from the average person in Kinsey's statistics.

Fortunately, there is some justification for thinking that youth will act on a high moral plane—and we can therefore expect them to do so. Students in one college changed "Hell Week" to "Help Week" by repairing, renovating, and tidying up churches, hospitals, and parks in their city. Old shrubs were trimmed, new ones were planted, lawns were spaded, windows were washed; the girls helped with tools as well as with coffee and sandwiches. [235] Students from another college devoted their "Help Week" to assisting with the actual building of a church—and drew the job of laying pipe lines and digging sewers. [236] High school pupils, under competent and confident leadership, have engaged in activities leading to the reduction of traffic hazards, planning for zoning and municipal organization, cutting down on Halloween vandalism, and aiding in civic campaigns. [4:256]

No decline in morality was noted by Ira Wolfert as he praised the courage, devotion, perseverance, as well as intelligence and originality, of young men in World War II. [353] Wolfert's voice was but one of many who praised the admirable qualities of youth in a time of real stress, strain, and uncertainty. In Korea, alongside the belligerent qualities a soldier needs, kindness and self-

---

* F. Harold Giedt, "Changes in Sexual Behavior and Attitudes Following Class Study of the Kinsey Report," *Journal of Social Psychology*, 33, 1951, 131–141.

sacrifice were common. In fact, the sturdiness and stability of people, in spite of many adverse influences, is the thing that can and does incite wonder. [113:x]

Many people point to the consumption of alcoholic beverages as an indication of the moral decline of the population. The fact is that the per capita consumption of liquor in 1850 was 2.07 gallons while in 1950 it was 2.04 gallons per capita. But the percentage of users was greater in 1950, indicating that drinking has become more widespread but more moderate. [300:23] It is interesting to note that parental behavior is a discernable factor in the use of beverage alcohol by the younger generation. Of college students who drink, 89 per cent are from families in which the parents use alcohol; while 54 per cent of those who abstain come from homes where the parents abstain. And it is the behavior, rather than the advice, that counts. "Regardless of the advice factor, students are much more apt to abstain if both parents are abstainers than if one or both parents drink." *

The "causes" of deviation from mores and religious tenets

George H. Preston has stated that you cannot stop "boys" from stealing—but it is possible to stop *a particular boy* from stealing. [250:19] It is probably accurate to state, in a parallel manner, that there is no single cause or unique combination of causes for moral or religious deviation. Each person must of necessity be considered as a particular case, and generalizations only serve the purpose of suggesting probable areas of explanation. One girl may become promiscuous because she so greatly feels the need to be loved; another because she sees her mother engage in promiscuity; another because, with an adult body, she lacks the intelligence for exercising discrimination [212:49]; still another because it appears to be the thing that is being done by her crowd and she lacks the fortitude to stand by her own convictions.

This viewpoint is presented to forestall the tendency to accept the easy and simple answers that are periodically forwarded—for example, prohibit the use of beverage alcohol, see that the Bible is

---

* Robert Straus and Selden D. Bacon, *Drinking in College* (New Haven: Yale University Press; 1953), p. 76.

read every evening in the family circle, separate first offenders in custodial institutions from the chronic delinquents, give youth purposeful work to do. These approaches may have value but no one of them can be a panacea. It will take many successive steps to reach the goal of moral maturity.

There can be little equivocation over the proposition that the strength of the moral codes of one generation is strongly influenced by the codes held by the preceding generations. Whether moral tenets spring from religion or from scientific examination the fact remains that a faith in those tenets is necessary. Priscilla Robertson, who was raised and is raising her children without a belief in God, states:

> The first thing I desire for my children is a kind of openness to experience. I hardly know whether to call this openness the ability to love or the ability to perceive truth, for it is both. Perhaps the name depends on whether you open up to human beings or to abstractions, whether you think of what is going out or what is coming in. The great lesson of the new sciences of the mind, as I understand them, is that loving and the perception of truth are inseparable. Both well up from the same depths of the spirit, both are interfered with by the same psychological defenses; and among these defenses, of course, is a process called intellectualizing, a turning-away from the feelings that belong to things. In other words, the ability to see things straight is more emotional than intellectual, in my view, and the kind of emotion you need in order to perceive truth is love.*

This sounds much like the teachings of Jesus who stated the commandment and spread the gospel of love and loving. Some of us may doubt that the love stimulated by science will have the vitality of love stimulated by religion, but the fact remains that the conviction is there—in both instances—for the guidance and anchoring of youth. Adults have the obligation to tell youth what they believe, though it would be unwise to demand acceptance of the belief. Open-mindedness should be endorsed, but immature persons should not have imposed upon them the necessity for mak-

---

* Priscilla Robertson, "What Shall I Tell My Children," *Harper's Magazine*, 205, No. 5, 1952, pp. 22–23.

ing decisions before they have been prepared to make them. The adult as well as the adolescent needs the courage of his convictions.

Representative moral issues

The values we hold

It sometimes appears, from conversations and speeches, that there is a question as to whether or not our population does hold firmly to any values. A very little reflection will reveal that we do hold firmly and persistently to many ideals. Few people doubt that the strength of our nation is due to the moral and spiritual values that permeate the American way of life. Further, it is recognized that the successful solution of our contemporary problems—honest and efficient government, patterns of home and family life, accord among nations, satisfaction of personal needs, and economic efficiency—demands that continued attention be given to moral and spiritual values. There is no more pressing problem facing the youth of this or any other generation than this specific phase of emotions and interests.

The Educational Policies Commission of the National Education Association has published a statement of a set of values that appears to be agreed upon by American people. These are paraphrased in the following ten items: [95:18]

1. The individual personality is deemed to be of supreme importance. The individual is capable of making moral judgments and assuming moral responsibility and must base those judgments on social relationships such as are exemplified in the basic teachings of Christianity. It is the objective of education to explore and develop the creative powers of unique individuals without oppression or despotism.

2. Feeling responsible for one's own conduct is a mark of moral maturity. Formalized codes and the dictates and advice of parents, teachers, or clergymen must be regarded only as steps toward the goal of self-reliance tempered with social conscience. Moral maturity is revealed when a person deals firmly with himself and gently with others.

3. Institutions are designed to be the servants of man. The home, the school, and government deserve veneration only as they serve

the moral and spiritual values of human life. Devotion to community well-being should be the goal of moral teachings in the home and school.

4. Common consent and voluntary cooperation are held to be superior to the idea of survival of the fittest and rule by violence. Group decisions should be made and enforced by mutual consent. But this does not mean that if one individual does not agree he may go his own way. The schools have been designed to produce an informed citizenry, capable of making informed decisions and of choosing delegates who are prepared to make decisions for the welfare of the group.

5. Intellectual honesty and devotion to truth are opportunities and obligations of free men. In a large portion of the world these ideals are not practiced. Here, the right to speak and think independently is part of our integrity. Public schools should be institutions in which young people practice the search for truth, exchange opinions, and apply reason to the solution of disputes.

6. Excellence in intellect, character, and creativity should be fostered since the individual personality is supreme. Belief in the equality of man does not deny the fact that men differ greatly in abilities and aptitudes. The uniqueness of the individual is held to be one of the strengths of our nation. Those who work with young people should seek to inventory the useful abilities of their charges and to direct those abilities into channels that will be of maximum personal and social usefulness. Excellence in every sphere of life must be the continuing goal of the youth of our nation.

7. All persons must be judged by the same moral standards. No man has the right to harm, persecute, dominate, or exploit others. Christianity, Buddhism, Confucianism, Hinduism, and Judaism, all emphasize in some way that a man should treat others as he wishes to be treated. "The American character is typically marked by an earnest search for justice and fair play and by a quick hostility toward obsequiousness and arrogance alike." * These ideals, it is felt, should consistently be held before young people.

8. We hold that the concept of brotherhood should be held above

---

* Educational Policies Commission, *Moral and Spiritual Values in the Public Schools* (Washington, D. C.: National Education Association; 1951), p. 26.

selfish interests. The care of those who are unfortunate enough to be unable to care for themselves is an inescapable responsibility of more fortunate citizens. This implies not only a willingness to share but a determination to attack the causes of want and suffering. This imposes on those in the school the job of inculcating feelings of responsibility for self *and* others.

9. Each individual has the right to the pursuit of happiness as long as that pursuit does not interfere with the happiness of others. Adults must teach young people that there is an inescapable difference between the pursuit of happiness and the excitement and exuberance of temporary pleasures. ". . . the discipline of the young should make clear, at promising opportunities, that in foregoing a momentary pleasure one may often develop resources of mind and spirit which will in the future bring a more complete happiness." *

10. Each person should be exposed to the emotional and spiritual experiences that complement the materialistic phases of life. The Commission states that moral values are chiefly concerned with social relations while spiritual values take effect in inner emotions and sentiments. However, the entire life of the individual is affected by spiritual feelings. While denominational creeds may not be taught in school, emphasis should be placed on such spiritual values as beauty, creativity, and morality.

While it is recognized that conduct sometimes falls short of verbally expressed ideals there is little doubt that Americans do endorse the values described by the Commission. Such traits as honesty, truthfulness, integrity, compassion, cooperativeness, and reliability are highly valued in our society, and the opposites are disapproved. The psychology of prestige and suggestion makes it quite clear that adults have the unequivocal obligation of expressing their conviction regarding these values to young people. The discrepancy between the ideal and the common practice must be regarded as a challenge to growth and development rather than as an excuse of moral laxity. Boys' gangs are in part caused by the felt lack of aims and ideals. The gang is the evidence of the search for values and objectives. Young people need to have some dependable guidance

---

* *Ibid.*, p. 29.

in their search for relationships between man and man and between man and things. [226] Young people should be surrounded by adults who are ready to share their present, mature convictions regarding moral problems.

Youth and freedom

A survey of the opinions of 15,000 teen agers, conducted by the Purdue Opinion Poll, shows that mores relating to the concept of freedom are in need of examination and attention. [149] Three discouraging conclusions are to be noted. (1) There is a tendency for many high school students to reject the implications of the concept of freedom when that freedom seems to conflict with previously established notions. (2) There is a great need for helping students think through the implications of their attitudes and responses. (3) Some teachers and administrators appear to be afraid to deal with issues that are of a controversial nature. One encouraging conclusion points to the hope that if the moral issue of freedom is faced it can be fruitfully resolved; that is, the older and better educated pupils were discernably more democratic in their concepts of freedom.

The rejection of freedom is indicated in the fact that 33 per cent felt that a person who refuses to testify against himself should be forced to talk or be severely punished. About half of the students felt that large masses of people are not capable of deciding what is good for them. Fifty-six per cent said that large unused and idle estates should be divided up among the poor. Seventy-five per cent stated that obedience to and respect for authority are the *most* important virtues that young persons should learn—a response that verifies L. K. Frank's statement that we must face the crucial issue of whether we wish to rear obedient and submissive personalities or ones capable of self-discipline and friendly and cooperative living. [111:18]

The students' need for help in thinking through the implications of their answers is shown by the fact that responses were motivated by what they thought to be the protection of our way of life. Thirty-eight per cent felt that foreign visitors to the United States should not be allowed to criticize our government. Two-thirds of them thought that conscientious objectors should be deprived of their vote. Of those who had heard of Senator Joseph McCarthy, about half approved of his methods. All in all, there was no indication that the respondents were rejecting the Bill of Rights—they simply revealed that their thought processes had stopped short of generalizing the specific conclusions that had been reached.

The trepidation of school workers was revealed in the fact that three former participants in the poll returned the questions and canceled their order for subsequent polls. Six other schools apparently did not answer the questions. This situation is the more distressing when one stops to realize that it is *only* through dealing with controversial issues that any genuine opportunity for thinking is afforded. Schools will fail to prepare adequately for adult life as long as teachers feel that such issues can be ignored. [355:300]

The possibility of improvement through direct instruction is particularly encouraging. When responses of the students were roughly divided into the classifications of democratic and authoritarian thinking, it was found that the answers tended toward the democratic view among the older students and those who were in their senior year. The teen-ager who is well informed does not so easily fall under the sway of "canned thinking" and categorical answers. But the shift is not necessarily automatic. Those who lead young people should appreciate their opportunity and responsibility.

Sex morality of teen-agers

A major concern in the area of moral issues is that of the teen-ager's beliefs and behavior relating to sex. Since this topic is dealt with in detail in Chapter 14, "Socialization and Heterosexual Adjustments," specific discussion will be omitted at this point. It should be noted, however, that sex morality is derived from the sources and factors described in the present chapter.

Social class and moral values

It is important for those who work with adolescents to realize that there are continuous, if not sharply defined, differences in the values held by young people of different social strata. This is particularly important for teachers since they come predominately from the middle social groups and are likely to feel that moral beliefs and practices different from their own are indications of depravity.

Several students of class structure agree that middle-class people regard man's duty to God and to the community as being paramount. Upper-class individuals pass on to youth the idea that family history is of great significance and family prestige ranks high. Lower-class persons are likely to feel that the community as a whole (particularly the middle class) is opposed to their welfare; hence, their feelings of civic responsibility are not highly developed. They do verbally stress such things as personal respectability, thrift, responsibility to the family and church, and fidelity in marriage. The contrasts between the middle class and the lower-lower social class are more marked. There is more sex immorality among the latter; their values tend to center about food, leisure, and personal defensiveness—if not aggressiveness. Stealing is overlooked and even tacitly condoned—since there is a feeling that they are not being fairly treated. The influence of the church is absent or weak. [9:268]

A realization that there are variable class mores in the ways children are raised is a first step toward the respect for all that is necessary on the part of the leader of adolescents. Unless the teachers and counselors of the young know and respect the differences that exist, their conviction of the absolute rightness of their own beliefs will constitute a barrier to the giving of help to those who are most in need of it. Adolescents of all social strata must have basic feelings of worth.

Religion for adolescents

The religious inclinations of adolescents

It seems to be popularly, and perhaps even commonly, believed that adolescence is a period of religious awakening. There is an element of truth in this belief in that, in the period of advancing mental maturity, the individual may question beliefs with which he has been surrounded. He may begin to have some doubts about former convictions because of the knowledge and attitudes absorbed from wider and more varied experiences. But there is no statistical evidence that the adolescent period is a time of religious awakening. There is no evidence that adolescence is the time of "ripeness" for religious instruction. [137:131] In fact, it seems more probable that spontaneous concern about religion is a characteristic of those in the early and middle adult period. They are the ones who have weathered some of the crises of selecting a mate, choosing and preparing for a vocation, raising children, and now have the time, inclination, and experience to consider on a systematic basis the matter of values and religion. R. J. Havighurst postulates the idea that not until a man has growing children is he inclined to see that he has a stake in the civic, religious, and political aspects of community life. [136:264] It appears that there is more to support the belief that adulthood is the time of religious interest than to sustain the idea that there is something in the nature of pubescence that generates a search for dynamic relations with a higher being.

Devotion to and concern for religious matters are functions of the social milieu in which a child has been raised. If a child has had continuous and enjoyable contacts with the church and religious beliefs he will more easily become enthusiastic about religion as a normal phase of well-rounded living. If he sees his parents accept religion as a firm spoke in the wheel of life, he will regard religion as an integral part of a balanced existence. Parents who think that they will wait until the youngster is old enough to make up his own mind about religion and morality are deluding themselves (perhaps they are rationalizing their own indifference). Religion—like knowledge, social adaptability, interest in a vocation, and being able to love others—is an outcome of sequential growth processes. "Being saved" or "accepting God" many come to a *few* as a brilliant revelation, but for most it will continue to be a matter of the final step of many steps toward a goal.

Authoritarian religion presents problems to adolescents

The author shares Elizabeth Hurlock's conviction that adolescents need religion but not theology or dogma. [151:333] It has been noted in many contexts that the adolescent is seeking to become independent, he is desirous of being self-directing. A religion posited on authority and prohibitions will lack appeal for a healthy adolescent. Unless he has been cowed into submissiveness he wants to perceive the relation of religion to his personal and social problems *now*.

Studies of mental hygiene show that fear is a powerful threat to the development of a healthy personality. Some authorities hold that fear is a deterrent to rash action and is, therefore, at times commendable. If the reader would call such fear caution or prudence, and there is justification for such terminology, then it could be recommended that fear has no justifiable place in healthy existence. Certainly, religions that stress hell-fire and damnation, eternal punishment, and inevitable retribution for sins are of doubtful value as directives for living a moral life.

There are several reasons why the authoritative, dogmatic religion must be questioned as a mentally hygienic force in the life of the adolescent.

1. It is the consensus of psychologists and clergymen of certain denominations that the good life must be the result of inner conviction rather than imposed authority.

2. Moral conduct is the capacity and desire to seek the good for its own sake rather than because of compulsion. It is a matter of acting on ideals that give enduring satisfaction rather than immediate gratification. [266:361] Hence morality consists in the application of wide principles as contrasted to the adherence to specific rules and dictates. A dogmatic religion lacks both the vitality for change and the elasticity for giving guidance in varied situations.

3. Research indicates that knowledge of Biblical information and of moral rules and principles is insufficient to insure ethical behavior. P. R. Hightower found that in about twelve thousand adolescents there was *no* relationship between knowledge of right and wrong and actual cheating, lying, loyalty, and altruism. [141] It is evident that motivation or conviction on the part of the individual is a *sine qua non* of moral conduct.

4. Studies of delinquency, crime, alcoholism, children's misconduct, and the like, agree on indicating that something positive rather than negative is advantageous. Delinquency is better approached through constructive activities than through punishment. Crime is prevented by abilities and skills that allow the accomplishment of goals. Some alcoholism is prevented by having altruistic purposes that transcend the negative tendency to self-destruction. A functional religion must be one that emphasizes the positives of love, brotherhood, and opportunities for self-realization.

A religion for adolescents must have balance. An overemphasis on spirituality and morality will produce a disturbed individual. A well-balanced life demands physical exercise, intellectual experiences, and social contacts. If playing games and having fun are regarded as sinful, then the adolescents will be deprived of developmental opportunities. If prayers and Bible reading are used as substitutes for social visiting, picnics, and dancing then well-rounded development is thwarted. (Let it be clear that the author *believes* that prayer and Bible reading are important as a phase of total and rich living; but he feels that overemphasis on the spiritual denies the physical nature of man.) If preparation for an after life overlooks the problems of present-day living, the religion lacks balance —there are individuals who have spent so much time in their devotions that they have failed to execute their earthly responsibilities.

Religion that is an asset to adolescents

Religion can, and does, serve as an integrative force in the lives of some individuals. It provides a locus that is beneficial in the resolution of conflicts and confusions. It provides help in the making of choices. It provides a dependable guide for daily living. In order to serve these functions a religion should have certain emphases.

One emphasis is that of love. As the individual grows, and especially as he grows into adolescence, he normally becomes less egocentric and more sociocentric. Earlier, being loved may have satisfied his need. In adolescence he must not only be loved but have the opportunity to love others. He is old enough, and wants, to assume responsibilities. Yet it is not always easy to be self-effacing. It is helpful to have a religion that preaches the doctrine of love, that states that loving others is a human as well as a divine behavior. Psychologists as well as religionists recognize the importance of love in the balanced life.

In some respects, the most audacious of all the great insights that have come into the world was the apparently absurd conviction of Jesus of Nazareth that men must love one another. "A new commandment I give unto you that ye love one another." We can easily imagine the bewilderment—even the ribald laughter—of his hearers. A world that was still very far from reaching the level of universal justice could scarcely rise to the level of universal love.

In reality, this "new commandment" was not an absurd and arbitrary rule laid upon man from the outside. It was, rather, the most profound insight into man's nature that had yet been achieved. Today every psychiatrist would affirm its truth. Man is sound in psychological health to the degree that he relates himself affirmatively to his fellow men. To hate and to fear is to be psychologically ill.*

Moreover the effective religion for adolescents, or for anyone, must emphasize the outgoing as well as the receiving aspects of love. Erich Fromm characterizes the person who develops the capacity for outgoing love as the "productive person" and asserts that productive love is characterized by care, responsibility, respect, and knowledge. [113:98] Religions that stress such an orientation serve the dual purpose of aiding social orientation and adding to lasting personal satisfactions.

Another vital emphasis is that of forgiveness. The lost soul concept will not bolster the adolescent in time of trouble. A mortal living in a mortal world is going to have some immoral thoughts and perform some acts that are short of perfect. A religion that promises pain and suffering as the result of imperfection will probably have one of two effects. Either the individual will close his eyes to religion and deny the existence of any higher being, or he will live with an ever deepening sense of his own inadequacy. Symptoms of the latter may be either neuroses or psychoses. Inevitably the adolescent is going to think some licentious thoughts, he is sometimes resentful toward and rebels against his parents, he does some things that violate the mores of his society. Unless he is taught the normality of such things by a religion in which forgiveness is fundamental, the seeds of maladjustment are germinated.

A continuation of the foregoing point is that the adolescent needs a religion that emphasizes the personal worth of the individual. Just as the child's concept of self is a direct reflection of the view that his parents take of him, the adolescent who is seeking to understand religion will have his concept of self influenced by the concept he forms of God. A loving, considerate God, who is concerned with

---

* H. A. Overstreet, *The Mature Mind* (New York: W. W. Norton & Company, Inc.; 1949), pp. 101–102.

the welfare of each human, is a factor in an individual's feelings of security. A jealous, demanding deity who loses sight of the individual in the concern for all mankind is not likely to add force to personal morality. An adolescent must feel that he is significant enough to receive some consideration—he must have help in solving his problems. In fact, one of the reasons given for the alleged failure of religion in the lives of young people is that it has not met their temporary and immediate needs. [338] Some may decry the current emphasis on man's comfort that is evidenced in some religions, at the cost of spiritual aspects, [129] but if religion is to appeal to adolescents it must recognize the unity of body and spirit.

A study of the characteristics and traits of adolescents would indicate that a religion that emphasizes personal choice would have appeal. Since the adolescent wants to be independent and self-directive a religion that denies the making of choices violates an important need. If religion gives a person the idea that he is simply a pawn in the hand of an all-powerful, all-seeing, all-pervasive deity there is no need for personal responsibility in choice. If, on the other hand, the deity is conceived as allowing humans to make choices and exercise independence of action, then there is a challenge to intelligent, socially oriented behavior. Only when the lesson of freedom of choice is emphasized will the individual accept the greatest challenge of life—that of continuous self-improvement. The need for freedom of choice may be discerned in the following passage from the late Joshua Liebman.

> To accept ourselves with our limitations means also that we will recognize how variable and flexible our lives can be. The great thing about life is that as long as we live we have the privilege of growing. We can learn new skills, engage in new kinds of work, devote ourselves to new causes, make new friends, if only we will exercise a little initiative and refuse to become fixed, rigid, and psychologically arteriosclerotic before our time. Let us, then, learn how to accept ourselves—accept the truth that we are capable in some directions and limited in others, that genius is rare, that mediocrity is the portion of almost all of us, but that all of us can contribute from the storehouse of our skills to the enrichment of our common life. . . .

Not only must we accept ourselves, but we must also *change our-selves.* Until the day of our death we can change, we can tap hidden resources in our make-up. We can discipline ourselves to turn from the morbid circle of useless self-pity or enslavement to childish frustrations and begin to give of our energy to other people, to a cause, a movement, a great enterprise. In such service we can find freedom from ourselves and liberty from our fears.*

Belief in the freedom to choose between identification with some cause of social significance or personal drifting or degradation would appear to be an essential part of an adolescent's healthful background.

Adolescents and the functions of religion

Religion may be defined as the relationships existing between man and a higher, a divine, being. "Religion," as used in this discussion, does not refer to any particular sect, denomination, or to belief in a deity of any specific name. The word refers to Christianity, Judaism, Confucianism, or Mohammedanism—or, within Christianity, to Presbyterianism, Catholicism, Unitarianism, or the beliefs of the Latter Day Saints. Paul Weaver states that regardless of what particular type of religion is referred to, it is characterized by the following three functions. [338]

1. Religion places priority on selected ethical values. Of all the choices one might make, some are regarded as relatively more worth-while. Guidance in making these choices is given by the law or principles stated by the higher being one reveres—the one who is wholly wise and good. These values become the nucleus of values in living. "In Christianity there are at least three such assumptions: that persons are more important than any other objects of interest, that motives are more important in persons than other facts about them, and that love is the most important motive to have." †

2. Religion consists in a change in the individual's mode of living. To some this change is a sudden conversion and to others it is

---

* Joshua Liebman, *Peace of Mind* (New York: Simon and Schuster; 1946), pp. 97–98.
† Paul Weaver, "Youth and Religion," *The Annals of the American Academy of Political and Social Science,* 236, 1944, p. 152.

a matter of growth stimulated by religious milieus. In either event, life becomes different because life is related to preferred values. Thus there is a reduction of value conflicts and the individual becomes more capable of living in harmony with himself and others— he becomes a better integrated person.

3. The function of religion is to remind persons that they must act in accordance with the tenets of the religion. What is believed should be manifested in what is done. A man must act in the light of his religious faith or ask forgiveness if he fails. Thus there is practical direction in problems of daily living. Religion should be lived rather than argued or defended.

Weaver next shows that adolescents have, in addition to many other needs, some needs that are most effectively approached through religion.

1. Youth, because of increasing capacity for generalization, need to have a clear outlook on life. They should have help in determining the ultimate purposes of life. This need is particularly insistent in a world characterized by war and political unrest, in a time when science and traditional religion may seem to be in conflict. Weaver admits that some may disagree about the importance of ultimate personal destiny, but ". . . intelligent living presupposes a clear and accurate appreciation of the universe, its laws, and the opportunities they permit men and the limitations they impose on man." *

2. At a time when the mores of society are in a state of rapid flux, youth need a conception of ethical clarity and ethical conviction. Science, for example, does not provide an unequivocal basis for convictions about sex morality, the use of alcoholic beverages, and orientation toward money. The intellectually and emotionally mature individual may be able to make wise decisions on such matters; but the majority of adolescents can use the support of religion —especially when certain adults have not shown the desired maturity.

3. Youth need emotional sensitivity and creativity. There has recently developed in American culture a concept of "fun morality." [352:3] Having fun has become almost obligatory. Instead of feeling guilty about having fun there is a tendency to feel guilty if

---

* *Ibid.*, p. 154.

fun is not predominant in work and life. In such a milieu, youth deserve help in finding things that make more lasting contributions to happiness, as contrasted to clutching at transitory pleasures. Inhibitions are necessary. "Loyalty to higher claims than chance impulses is one of the strengths of all sincere religions. This need of youth for rich emotional sensitivity is a religious need." *

Religion in the public schools

The question of teaching religion in the public schools is highly debatable. There are those who feel that, since the various churches are reaching an inadequate number of young persons and since the faith of many parents appears to be weak, the schools must assume part of the responsibility for religious training. It is felt that there is enough in common among the Catholics and the Protestants and the Jews that religion can be taught by the proper persons without violating the rights of any one group. It is easy to agree with the statement of the American Council on Education that the majority of people hold to the brotherhood of man, to respect for the individual, to the value of mercy, and to the worth of love. [5:46] We can agree that these concepts can be effectively stressed by sincere, reverent, and tolerant individuals. We can agree that dynamic religion possesses virtues that are great enough so that they should be stressed from many angles—from the home, from the church and synagogue, and from the school. We can agree that the omission of religion from the curriculum is a form of teaching in and of itself—an implication that religion does not matter.

But the principles on which our nation was founded and which have continued to be clarified throughout the years cannot be summarily dismissed. The late Ellwood Cubberley lists the struggle to free the schools from sectarianism as one of the seven major battles fought to establish and maintain free public schools. [72:171] Because of the differences in opinion regarding the proper nature of religious instruction, sects set up their own schools. They fought for public monies and in so doing weakened the effectiveness of the public schools. Those who held to the basic nature of the role of education in a democracy saw a threat to both education and society as a whole. The outcome was that gradually, from 1844 on,

---

* Weaver, *op. cit.,* p. 155.

various states adopted constitutional provisions that forbade the division of funds among church supported schools. The "field of battle" is not entirely cleared and attempts are still being made to get public money for the support of church schools. Enthusiasts for religious teaching in the schools might well examine the past.

Released time (freeing pupils for certain periods of the week to receive religious instruction either in the school or in the church) has been tried but without startling success. Some churches do not have the time, facilities, or inclination to take advantage of the opportunity. Some children are without religious affiliation; there is a feeling that they miss something other pupils are getting, through no fault of their own. Hence released time does not solve the problem. "Above all, and aside from questions of expediency, as a matter of principle released time in actual practice, if not in theory, comes dangerously close to weakening or even breaching the wall that in democratic America should always separate church and state." * This wall is the principle that each individual shall be entirely free to worship as, where, and if, he chooses.

All this is not to say that spiritual values cannot be stressed in the schools. Mentally healthy, mature, and reverent teachers can manifest the values stressed by the major religions. But the teaching should be by example rather than by precept.

A functional approach to religion for adolescents

A religious program for youth that is recognized as being more than ordinarily effective has been in operation in Beaverton, Oregon, since 1948. No claim is made that the church, by itself, has built better character or produced more religious adults. Few if any religions or churches can make such claims. But psychologists recognize the cumulative effect of exposure to good influences as well as the cumulative effect of exposure to negative influences. Hence, the accolade of a successful program resides in the following characteristics: (1) About 80 per cent of the teen-agers in the church begin their active identification with the Pilgrim Fellowship in their first year of high school. Between 65 and 75 per cent are still active when they are seniors. (2) After a slow start there

* Leo Pfeffer, *Religion and the Public Schools,* Jewish Affairs Pamphlet, 2:No.3. (New York: American Jewish Congress; 1947), p. 22.

has been a steady increase in membership. There are no noticeable ebbs and flows of interest. (3) Youth from other churches are not recruited but many have come as guests and all are welcomed. Their parents may belong to another church of the same denomination or to another denomination, but all are eligible for office. From 20 to 25 per cent of the members of the Pilgrim Fellowship are children of non-members of the church.

The guiding principles of this organization are of special interest. They reflect a sound knowledge and active use of facts and feelings about adolescents on the part of the minister, Albert F. King, and his adult co-workers. (1) The youth program is viewed as an integral part of the church—not an extension, or arm, but as one of the facets of the unified whole. (2) There is no soft-pedaling of religious teachings. The Bible and religious literature are regularly studied, but there is a consistent attempt to relate these teachings to full, enjoyable living. It is felt that religious convictions must come as the result of improved satisfaction with daily living rather than argumentation. (3) Literal dogma is subordinate to emphasis on the underlying attitudes implied by the religious teachings. (4) Extensive use is made of committees that have real power in the determining of policies and practice. But the power is shared. Guidance and assistance by adults are characteristic. The leaders do not hold back opinions when they feel that unwise decisions might be made. (5) Every new member is put on a committee the first time he attends. It is felt that his opinion, as yet uncolored by group membership, does much to keep the program fresh and vital. (6) Committee membership is not limited to youth activities. There are youth representatives on building, membership, and finance committees for the church as a whole. (7) The minister calls on the parents of every youngster who attends—regardless of the parents' religious affiliation. (8) Parents are regularly called on to participate in the work involved in keeping the Pilgrim Fellowship dynamic. The expert and willing cake-maker or turkey-roaster is not repeatedly called upon because it is felt that *all* parents profit from the sharing of their services. Mr. King is convinced that parents are better parents because they realize that what they do is affecting not only their own child but that they have a responsibility for other young people. (9) Regularly scheduled leadership training programs are conducted within the church with the assistance of outside experts. Leaders are picked by the young persons for their ready acceptance by those young persons. But in addition the leaders have to be individuals who are worthy of emulation and who can give positive guidance without dictating.*

The program of the Pilgrim Fellowship was planned to include equally business meetings, recreation sessions, discussions, and lectures by selected experts and authorities. None of these is presently neglected, but it is gratifying to note that the lectures and discussions, dealing with both personal and religious questions, are gaining strength. The guess might be hazarded that this is because the answers are not given but techniques for arriving at the answers *are* given.

Summary

The morality of adolescents is invariably and inevitably rooted in the behaviors and beliefs of the adult community. Those who condemn the shortcomings of youth should be sure their own lives are in order. A dynamic and heterogeneous society creates a continuous shifting in the interpretation of values. This poses problems for everyone; but the adolescent, particularly, is likely to become perplexed. This perplexity is increased by his growing perception of inequities and inconsistencies. As he grows he realizes that there is often a wide gap between professed ideals and practices. While disillusionment is inevitable, it can be prevented from becoming chronic. Parents and teachers who admit their fallibility but who will nevertheless state their contemporary convictions, who maintain faith in youth, who permit some opportunity for errors, can help in the course of moral maturing.

There is much to praise in the contemporary status of adolescent morality, though the need for progress can be admitted. More emphasis should be placed on the good things adolescents do. This will have the effect of indicating possible modes of constructive behavior as well as implementing the faith in youth that is a stimulus to improvement.

---

* Personal interview, Albert F. King, Minister, Bethel Congregational Church, Beaverton, Oregon, October 13, 1954.

It cannot safely be claimed that there are no widely held values in our society. Among values that are clear-cut are belief in the worth of the individual, personal responsibility, the supremacy of man over man-made institutions, the supremacy of the group over the individual, honesty and devotion to truth, the right to and need for personal fulfillment, the universality of moral standards, the brotherhood of man, the right to happiness, and the worth of spiritual experience. In a democracy the concept of freedom needs continuing study and evaluation, but freedom itself is a permanent value.

Many wise and thoughtful persons believe that if religion is neglected the life of the individual cannot be so strong and symmetrical as it might otherwise be. Unfortunately, there is no evidence that adolescence is a time of ripeness for religious awakening. Readiness for religion is an outgrowth of the kind, rather than the amount, of experience. Some religion lacks appeal for adolescents because it is dogmatic, it invokes fear, and it undermines feelings of worth by emphasizing sin rather than love. To have appeal for adolescents a religion should emphasize its present value in daily living. It should stress the importance of loving and being loved. Giving and growing as means to personal and spiritual fulfillment should be stressed. The forgiveness of sin is important because the adolescent will inevitably see in himself disobedience, selfishness, jealousy, and sexual desire. The worth of the individual should be a steady emphasis.

The role of religion in adolescence is that of giving aid in the acceptance of persistent values, improving daily living, and thus establishing a clearer outlook on life. It would be gratifying if religion could be taught in public schools; but lack of homogeneity of doctrine, and adult disagreement on religious tenets, make this currently impractical. Fortunately, there is uniformity within religions regarding basic values. Hence teachers can teach religion in terms of ideals, morality, brotherhood, and love without the mention of sectarian beliefs.

Churches whose leaders recognize the needs of adolescents for self-direction, for significant tasks, for adult counsel (not demands), and for enjoyable living today, can be powerful factors in moral maturing. But there is no panacea for avoiding moral bewilderment. *All* the factors that produce the adolescent personality simply lay the foundation for approaching the moral and spiritual issues of a lifetime.

STUDY AND REVIEW ITEMS

1. What distinction do you think is implied in the wording: an anchored *versus* a concreted conviction?

2. Can you think of some contradictions or occurrences in our society that might cause disillusionment for the adolescent?

3. What are some evidences of striving for a higher morality on the part of society as a whole? on the part of adolescents?

4. Do you think that health and physique play a causative role in the moral status of the individual?

5. Does changing morality mean primarily a change in values or does it consist mainly in a changed interpretation of values?

6. What do you think would be the result if teachers were consistently to avoid the discussion of controversial issues?

7. Name a number of contrasts in the values held by lower-status adolescents and those held by middle-class adolescents.

8. Cite some reasons for and against the contention that adolescence is a time of religious awakening.

9. In what ways may religion serve as an integrative force in the life of an adolescent?

10. In what ways may religion function as a negative factor in wholesome personality development?

11. Discuss the wisdom of having religious instruction included as a public school curricular offering.

12. What characteristics of adolescence should be considered in church sponsored youth programs?

RECOMMENDED SUPPLEMENTARY READING

Blair, Arthur W. and William H. Burton. *Growth and Development of the Preadolescent* (New York: Appleton-Century-Crofts, Inc.; 1951), pp. 23–102.

This chapter deals only in part with moral development, *per se*. But the characteristic changes in preadolescence and the typical difficulties encountered are also implicated in moral development. Opportunities for desirable social development can easily be translated into assets for moral growth.

Educational Policies Commission. *Moral and Spiritual Values in the Public Schools* (Washington, D. C.: National Education Association; 1951), 100 pp.

This booklet is based on the conviction that moral and spiritual values are essential to the survival of our nation. The schools must teach certain values and sanction certain institutional ideals. Suggested programs for achieving these ends are described. Ways of cooperating with other agencies involved in ideology are emphasized.

Kuhlen, Raymond G. *The Psychology of Adolescent Development* (New York: Harper & Brothers; 1952), pp. 399–460.

Professor Kuhlen's discussion of "Adolescent Ideology" is based on pertinent research studies. The implications of these studies for the moral guidance of adolescents are indicated. An eighty-five item bibliography will be of particular interest to students doing research in the area of moral and religious development of adolescents.

Seidman, Jerome M. (Ed.) *The Adolescent* (New York: The Dryden Press, Inc.; 1953), pp. 286–318.

Several authors discuss various aspects of moral development in these three readings. The pioneer studies of H. Hartshorne and Mark A. May are summarized. The role of the concept of self is discussed by R. J. Havighurst and others. Hilda Taba describes the moral beliefs of sixteen-year-olds.

Thompson, George G. *Child Psychology* (Boston: Houghton Mifflin Company; 1952), pp. 552–589.

Though this chapter is in a child psychology book, the data on values, morality, and social growth deal with the adolescent and college years as well as earlier ages. The material is soundly based on research studies and is practical and interesting.

Developing Your Character (Coronet Films, Coronet Building, Chicago 1), 11 min., so., b. and w. or col.

What good character is and how it can be achieved provide the emphasis in this film. Home, church, school, and peer groups are among the influences pictured as forces in moral development.

Power of God (Evangelical Lutheran Synod of Missouri, 3558 S. Jefferson, St. Louis, Mo.), 56 min., so., b. and w.

This film shows how the word of God may help in the approach to the problems of modern life. Everyday Christians speak their beliefs through their actions.

What can be done to check this greatest killer of adolescents? Are accidents indicative of personal maladjustment? Can other causes of illness and death in adolescence be reduced?

CHAPTER THIRTEEN

The Pathology of Adolescence

Throughout this book an attempt has been made to take a realistic but optimistic view of the adolescent. A confident attitude has the double advantage of encouraging the adolescent to live up to a high expectation and prompting adults to work with greater enthusiasm. An examination of some of the negative aspects of adolescence can, however, serve two functions. One is to get a sounder perspective of the factors that influence development and thus enable us to help more effectively both the normal and deviant adolescent. Pathological reactions are often exaggerations or distortions of everyday behavior. [57:3] The other is to emphasize some of the hazards of adolescence and work toward their diminution or elimination.

There are three major ways in which the strains of growing up are manifested. One is in the incidence of death and physical disease. A second is in the nature and extent of mental illness. A third is the occurrence of breaks with society—that is, the development of habits and characteristics that isolate or alienate the adolescent from the society in which he lives. These three categories are designed simply for the sake of discussion. In actuality it is quite possible for one cause to have a different manifestation in three individuals. For example, a poor home and community environment might cause one person to commit suicide and thus classify him with the mortality statistics. In the same situation, another might become mentally unbalanced and be committed to an institution for the mentally ill. A third might be driven by his experiences into homosexuality or to murderous violence. Another way of indicating the inseparability of these three categories is to imagine an adolescent who develops deviant sex behavior—which in turn causes, or is accompanied by, emotional instability—which manifests itself in accident proneness and finally results in his death or that of some of his peers. Several symptoms may be traced to common causes.

Thus it can be seen that though we recognize that behavior is caused, we cannot always tell what the specific cause might be because *a* cause may be manifested in so many different ways. Our interest must remain focused upon some of the things that do cause difficulty in adolescence for some individuals; and we must seek, through the improvement of society in general, to reduce or remove those causes.

Diseases and mortality of adolescence

The health of teen-agers

A report of the Metropolitan Life Insurance Company states, "The teens are the healthiest years of life. During those years the frequency of disabling diseases and the time lost because of illness are at a minimum. The teen ages follow close after the age of lowest mortality, and the death rate remains relatively low, though rising steadily." * The death rate between the years of thirteen and nineteen doubles for boys but for girls the increase is only 50 per cent. The major causes of death are cancer and malignant tumors (Figure 16). Next in importance is heart disease, including rheumatic fever. Tuberculosis is relatively unimportant as a current cause of death among adolescents, being outranked by acute poliomyelitis, except among girls 18 to 19 years of age. Early marriage and parenthood increase the problems of family health, and 6 per cent of the deaths of 18- to 19-year-old girls are due to complications of pregnancy and childbirth. [215]

Many of the threats from diseases of adolescents have been di-

_____

* Metropolitan Life Insurance Company, "Statistical Bulletin," V. 34, No. 8, August, 1953, p. 1.

minished. But the threat of emotional disorder is still a large problem, which will be discussed in the following section. An attack on both physical and mental health problems can be made by giving attention to the practice of good health habits. This should include dental examination and care, treatment of sensory defects, and stress upon proper diet. The importance of dental and visual care is emphasized by the fact that about 20 per cent of the rejections of young men called for military service in World War II were due to mental defects and 13 per cent to visual defects. [195] It is estimated that approximately 62 per cent of senior high school pupils have uncared-for dental caries. Girls are particularly likely to violate good dietary practices—probably in an attempt to possess the "ideal" form. The high incidence of cancer as a cause of death calls attention to the need for regular physical examinations and the need for giving attention to any chronic symptoms that may appear.

The conclusion that adolescence is a time of stress and strain—that ill health is caused by the rapid physiological changes of puberty—does not seem to be warranted in terms of the low incidence of morbidity and mortality during this period. Of course, improvement is still needed, but the stressful aspects are due more to social structure than to the faults of adolescents in general. Both illness rates and accident rates are much higher in congested living areas. Illness occurs most frequently in those homes that are least likely to be able to bear the expenses involved in care and treatment. [43]

The likelihood of overexertion in adolescence is indicated by many authorities. Young people tend to have irregular hours of sleep, to "be on the go" too much even in terms of their good health, and to eat unwisely. These problems can be approached in the schools by teaching that relates to individual needs. [62] Stress might well be placed upon health and vigor as factors in popularity. But probably the most effective approach is social change in terms of providing youth opportunities for being significant and respected through having jobs and responsibility. The greater pride in self thus engendered will make less likely the need for defying adult advice and admonitions. It must be concluded that improvement of the health of adolescents is a matter of broad social responsibility supplemented by attention to specific individual and personal problems.

The obese adolescent

The relationship of physical and social factors in the health of the adolescent is well illustrated by the occasional obese individual. There is an increasing tendency to regard excessive weight as a physical problem complicated by psychological factors. Overweight boys and girls have a greater tendency to worry and be afraid than do those who are of normal weight. Their poundage may be considered a form of withdrawal. Being apprehensive of social contact they take refuge in the pleasures of eating. Overeating, combined with the lack of exercise that accompanies their retreat from active play with peers, results in the accumulation of fat. Contrary to popular belief, then, these individuals are not the cheerful personalities ordinarily associated with plumpness. Their quiescence and weak interest precede rather than follow their obesity.

While there are instances of obesity that are due to physiological factors, it would be well for those who work with adolescents to regard excessive weight as a possible symptom of social or emotional immaturity. This may be caused by overprotection or rejection in the home (often the obese child has a domineering mother and a submissive father) [39:29], a lack of skill in establishing close ties with peers, and feelings of general inadequacy. Like so many defense mechanisms, obesity further complicates problems of adjustment. The adolescent finds it difficult to obtain prestige from athletic pursuits and suffers from the feeling that he does not fit the physical pattern of our society.

Whether obesity hastens or delays puberty is equivocal. Good nutrition is thought to be a factor that hastens puberty, and obese girls experience the menarche somewhat earlier than their peers. Nonetheless, there is evidence that the changes of puberty will proceed more wholesomely if obese children lose some of their excess weight. [49]

Accidents in adolescence

Figures 16 and 17 (pages 404–405) show that accidents are the biggest cause of death for boys during adolescence. In the 13 to 14 age bracket boys die more frequently from violence (accidents, suicide, and homicide) than from disease; 80 per cent of the deaths of girls at this age are caused by disease. Accidents gain for both girls and boys in the age bracket 15 to 17. Disease increases as a cause of death for girls in the 18 to 19 age range, but violence increases to account for two-thirds of the deaths of boys. [215] Particularly for boys, then, accidents are the big problem in the disability and mortality of adolescents.

Motor vehicle accidents are important in all adolescent years. The proportion of motor vehicle deaths rises steadily throughout each age bracket and accounts for four-fifths of the accidental deaths of girls. The seriousness of accidents is indicated by some comparative figures. It has been said that ". . . one out of every twenty of us is, or has been, or will be, in a hospital for mental illness . . ." * The National Association for Mental Health has indicated that one out of every twelve children born each year will *at some time* require hospitalization for mental illness. [103] We are greatly concerned about these rather alarming figures (from five to eight individuals out of a hundred are included) yet they cover a wide range of causes and symptoms. Attention should also be directed to automobile accidents, which will kill, or permanently injure, twelve out of every 100 students now in high school before they are sixty-five years old. [319]

Automobile accidents are recognized as a problem of adolescence. Many insurance companies charge higher rates on cars driven by anyone below twenty-five years of age. The differential in rate is less than the actual cost to the insurers but they find it politic to spread the cost over a greater age range. One insurance company reported that 23.5 per cent of all accidents involved

AGE OF DRIVER	RATIO OF ACCIDENTS TO EXPECTANCY
0–20 years	+45.6 per cent
21–24	+88.8
25–49	−17.6
50–64	− 1.8
65+	−11.6

* Karl Menninger, *The Human Mind,* 3rd Ed. (New York: Alfred A. Knopf, Inc.; 1953), p. 3.

DEATHS FROM DISEASE

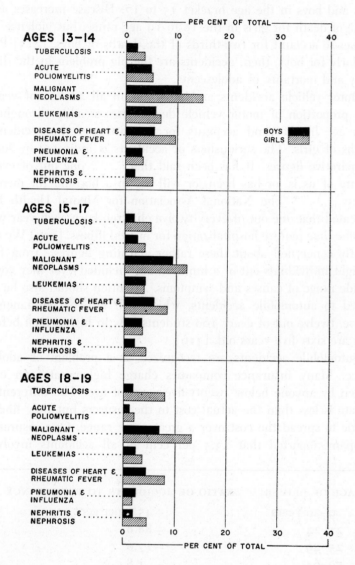

FIGS. 16 AND 17. Deaths from selected causes among adolescents

The graph on this page shows deaths caused by some of the more frequent diseases. The graph on the facing page—drawn to the same scale—shows accidental deaths. Data from Metropolitan Life Insurance Company, "Statistical Bulletin," Vol. 34, August 1953, p. 3.

DEATHS FROM ACCIDENTAL CAUSES

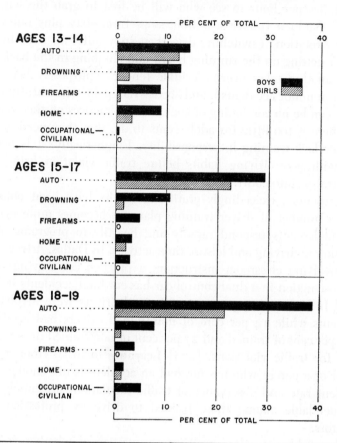

drivers under twenty-one years of age but that these drivers represented only about 15 per cent of all licensed drivers. In 1949 for every 100 fatal accidents for drivers over twenty-five years of age there were 210 fatal accidents for drivers under twenty-five. The ratio of accidents to what might be expected in terms of registrations by age groups worked out as shown in the list on page 403.*

Lack of prudence and appropriate instruction must be blamed for the high accident rate of adolescence and early adulthood since reflexes and coordination are at or near their lifetime peak during this time. It is small wonder that fatalities are high when such prac-

* "General Letter," Farmers Insurance Exchange, December 26, 1950.

tices prevail as "chicken" (taking the hands off the steering wheel at
sixty miles per hour to see who will be first to grab the wheel),
"burn" (sudden rubber scorching stops from sixty plus miles per
hour), "rotation" (switching drivers at sixty miles an hour by the
driver's getting on the running board and climbing in the back seat
while another takes over), "crinkle fender" (purposely being involved in minor accidents), and "pedestrian polo" (just brush 'em).
There can be no condoning of such insane practices on the grounds
that there is too little for adolescents to do, that they need adventure, or lack training in responsibility. Emphatically, it is best to
deal with poor driving habits before traffic violation brings the
transgressor into court.

Fortunately, exceedingly gratifying results have been obtained
from a number of driver training plans. It becomes quite evident
that adolescents respond rapidly and heartily to programs of instruction in driving and leisure-time activity. In Dallas, driver training involving classroom instruction, a practice car driving room,
and instruction in a dual control car has cut fatal accidents in half.
[224] In Delaware 3 per cent of trained drivers were involved in
accidents while 14 per cent of non-trained drivers had accidents.
Four per cent of trained and 27 per cent of non-trained drivers were
cited for traffic violations. [274] Learning to drive from a good
driver or a parent who has not had an accident is not enough. The
accident rate and observance of traffic regulations are much more
commendable among those trained to drive by professional instructors.

The problem resolves itself into a question of whether or not a
community will assume the cost of driver training. "The best way
to do this work is through regularly scheduled driver training classes
involving classroom work and behind-the-wheel experience. Such
programs are quite costly and most districts do not feel able to support them. One soon arrives at the point of deciding what should be
taken out of the school offering to make room for driver training—
from the standpoint of hours and finances." * Fortunately, improvement is rapidly taking place. In 1936 the first driver education
course was given at Pennsylvania State College; 200 colleges now

---

* Laurence E. Winter, Director of Secondary Education, Portland (Oregon)
Public Schools, February 22, 1951.

give such courses. Of the 20,000 U. S. high schools, 6000 have training cars and complete driver education programs; 850,000 teen agers are enrolled and an increase of fifteen per cent in 1953–54 has been recorded. [170] The question might well be asked, "In our culture today, is it more important to be able to conjugate a Latin verb than to be able to drive a car properly?" Until driver training programs are universal the only palliative is adults who will make the contribution of setting good examples of driving courtesy and caution.

Accident proneness

In both traffic and industrial situations a few individuals contribute vastly more than their share of accidents. In a Connecticut study it was found that 4 per cent of the drivers were involved in 36 per cent of the accidents. Other studies reported that 5 to 10 per cent of all drivers caused almost half the accidents. One hundred accident repeaters in Michigan have been arrested 769 times for traffic violations and have had 528 accidents. [222] A traffic safety engineer asserted that if the licenses of 10 per cent of drivers could be revoked the accident rate could be reduced by 90 per cent. Parallel data have been collected on industrial workers—a few accident-prone individuals keep the safety record from being better. [218:171] Similarly, in the adolescent years, a few individuals contribute disproportionately to the generally poor reputation of adolescent drivers.

The hazards to life during adolescence are approximately twice as great as during preadolescence and about twice as severe for males as for females. This is despite the fact that neither the incidence of nor the mortality from disease increases during adolescence. The greatest single cause for increased mortality rate is the spectacular rise in the number of fatal accidents. The big problem in adolescent health is to reduce accidents and rehabilitate the accident-prone person—the emotionally immature, frustrated, and impulsive youngster. Obviously, no blanket remedy can be prescribed for the many and varied conditions of immaturity. Individuals and their needs must be studied and society as a whole must be improved.

Mental disorders of adolescence

Not all those who are mentally ill are institutionalized, but an indication of the incidence of mental disease may be obtained from available statistics on mental hospital admissions. Figures from Pennsylvania and Oregon, which may be considered to be somewhat representative, are presented in the following tables.

TABLE 7   **First Admissions to State Mental Hospital (Pennsylvania) by Age Groups up to 40 years ***

AGE GROUP	FIRST ADMISSION RATE PER 100,000 OF GENERAL POPULATION	PER CENT OF TOTAL POPULATION	PER CENT OF TOTAL COMMITMENTS
15–19	42	.42	5.5
20–29	79	.79	9.5
30–39	102	1.02	12.2

* Nelson A. Johnson, "The Growing Problem of Old-Age Psychoses," *Mental Hygiene*, 30:436, 1946.

TABLE 8   **First Admissions to State Mental Hospital (Oregon) by Age Groups up to 40 Years ***

AGE GROUP	FIRST ADMISSION FROM TOTAL OF 1,888	PER CENT OF ALL ADMISSIONS
Below 15	9	.4
15–19	77	4.0
20–24	120	6.4
25–29	123	6.5
30–34	181	9.6
35–39	213	11.3

* Oregon State Board of Control, "Nineteenth Biennial Report," Salem, Oregon, June, 1950, p. 47.

These tables show that relatively few adolescents are committed to mental institutions. It is noteworthy that the age bracket 15–19 sees a tenfold increase over the preceding years. The ratio to all commitments is approximately doubled in Pennsylvania and tripled in Oregon in the next decade—20–29 years. For those who might exclaim that this is proof that adolescence is uniquely a time of stress and strain, further data indicate the rate of commitments continues to rise in Pennsylvania through the sixty-ninth year. In Oregon the rate stays about the same as the 35–39 age bracket for each five years through the sixty-ninth year. It should also be considered that as a child who suffers from mental disorder grows older (and as his parents become older) he is harder to handle and a point is reached when parents give up, after doing all they could, and have him institutionalized. Even considering this possibility, it is evident that the middle years and old age are also times of stress and uncertainty. However, the point of basic interest is the thesis, reflected in the National Mental Health Act of 1946, that much mental illness is preventable.

Neuroses in adolescence

The term "neurosis" applies to one of the major classifications of mental disorder. It is a milder form of emotional illness than the second major classification, called psychoses. While the neuroses may merge and develop into psychoses, a further distinction, beyond degree, is that neuroses are functional disorders—that is, the nervous and emotional instability is not dependent upon clearly distinguished defect of the nervous system, as psychoses often, though not always, are. [330: 48n] A neurosis does not generally result in the victim's being committed to an institution. It does tend to keep him from functioning in an efficient fashion in social and occupational activities. The disorder keeps the individual from the best realization of himself.

Neurotic traits or behaviors are said to operate in the great majority, perhaps all, of us. [105:191] Though this be true, it might be well to think of the neurotic as one whose deviant behavior is chronic rather than transitory. Certainly, all who live vigorously suffer from conflict that might result in neurosis; but the majority resolve the conflict before it results in the frustration that leads some to chronic mental illness. Karen Horney makes the important point that neuroses may be generated *both* by incidental individual experiences *and* by cultural conditions that produce anxiety and uncertainty. [146:viii] What is neurotic in one culture is normal in another.

The study of neuroses is significant to the student of adolescence because (1) the contributing factors are often similar or identical to the ones that cause normal youngsters to have difficulty in the processes of adjusting and (2) the symptoms of neuroticism have begun, or are beginning, to show in adolescence while there may still be time to render effective assistance.

Many neuroses seem to be traceable to inadequate home environments. A feeling of insecurity may be generated by the birth of a sibling who is given more attention and *appears* to be getting more love. Comparisons between siblings may undermine healthy ego development. Some parents manifestly reject the child; others may reject covertly while manifesting love. Either situation is incipiently dangerous. Too high a level of parental expectation may produce anxiety for the growing individual. Overprotection is frequently cited as a contributing factor. The child's or adolescent's opportunity for developing social, play, athletic, or academic skills—which would foster feelings of independence—is restricted by an overprotective parent. Consequently the youngster develops anxiety about and tends to withdraw from social contact with his peers. A domineering parent may have much the same effect, with possibly more fear existing in the latter case.

Disorganization in the community may be a factor in the development of neuroses. Poor living conditions, accompanied by various forms of deprivation, are held accountable for some neuroses. Racial or religious conflict or persecution must be blamed for the precipitation of some neuroticism. Much of the neurotic behavior of adolescents is attributed to the intensification of sex drives caused by the altered endocrine functioning of puberty. Fear created by menstruation and masturbation has been traced as the cause of some adolescent neuroses. Traumatic sexual experiences or promiscuity can be held accountable for other cases. (Promiscuity may also be the apparent symptom of neuroticism caused by other factors).

On the whole, however, it is misleading to represent that the adolescent battles his way to sexual adjustment through a solid phalanx of cultural prohibitions. The adjustment is inherently difficult, and cultural pressures may be out of step with bodily development, but there are considerable forces working on the side of learning.*

The fact that some neurotic behavior aroused by fear of the menses or of masturbation has been dispelled by counseling indicates that the individual's view of his problems must be considered along with the actual physical conditions that precipitate the behavior. Hence there can be no categorical listing of the causes of neuroses. Conditions that for most persons are simply conflict are for others frustration.

Symptoms of neuroses

The display of a neurotic symtom should not lead to the conclusion that the individual has a neurosis. But the chronic manifestation of symptoms does indicate that a person's hold on reality may be weakening. Early diagnosis and help may result in an individual's making more effective adjustments to the buffetings to which all of us are subject. Incidentally, there are those who recommend that teachers should not meddle in mental health problems. The answer to this argument is that if teachers do not help, many who need help will never get it from anyone. There are simply not enough psychiatrists and psychologists to do the job. Dr. Marynia Farnham states that it is dangerous to believe and hope that the youngster will outgrow his difficulties. Help given that might not have been needed is harmless. But failure to help when it is really needed will have serious consequences. [105:203] Of course, when it is at all possible the teacher should refer mental health problems to a specialist. The advice of a psychologist or psychiatrist may be available even though direct services are not. Teachers can also get considerable aid from their teaching colleagues through discussion.

Withdrawal from the companionship of others, especially from peers, is one of the more common symptoms of the basic anxiety

---

* Robert W. White, *The Abnormal Personality,* p. 122. Copyright 1948, The Ronald Press Company.

that underlies all neuroses. The youngster who walks alone, is shy in class discussions and recitations, who belongs to no organizations, and does not attend parties and dances may warrant further observation. Some youngsters are, of course, quiet and unassuming but still they do not purposely avoid contacts with others.

Chronic daydreaming that does not result in action may justifiably cause suspicion. All of us daydream, but this is the precursor of action that seeks the fulfillment of the dream. The pathological individual gets to the point that the dream becomes real enough so that it results in a kind of satisfaction. The fat, carelessly dressed and groomed little girl who impresses her peers with the tales of her conquest of imaginary boy friends is an example. Amnesia and somnambulism are more advanced forms of withdrawal tendencies.

Phobias are abnormal fears, which may be distinguished from normal fears by the fact that phobias refer to something that is actually harmless. The threat to security is in the individual's attitude rather than in the object feared. There are long lists of the names of phobias; these are rather meaningless because morbid fears may be attached to anything by some neurotic individual. [343:287]

Hysteria is an inclusive term for a large number of behaviors caused by conflict and anxiety and manifested in bodily symptoms. Dysfunction of a limb, paralysis, is a common form of hysteria. Anaesthesias, lack of feeling in a finger, arm, or some other part of the body, or lack of vision in part of the eye, are also included. Bizarre posture, excessive and uncontrollable weeping, as well as high blood pressure and heart disorders may be types of hysteria. These psychosomatic disorders are often called conversion reactions or conversion hysteria. This group of symptoms is more frequently found among females and among those who are energetic and extroverted. [65:209]

Many apparently somatic disorders are in reality psychogenic in nature. It is estimated that as high as 95 per cent of digestive disorders are manifestations of emotional conflict. Vomiting, headaches, and rashes and eczema are sometimes symptoms of neuroses. Increasingly it is being recognized that many cases of allergy are the result of anxiety. The newspaper recently carried the report of a woman who broke into a rash at the sight of her husband. A study of sixty-three allergic children showed that 98 per cent of them were rejected. In the control group of thirty-seven who were patients but non-allergic, the per cent of rejection was 24. [220] The psycho-somatic disorder is often a subconscious attempt to get the love, sympathy, and attention of which one might otherwise be deprived.

Obsessive and compulsive behaviors are other ways the individual may use to manifest his anxiety. Obsessions refer to the existence of persistent ideas in which there looms an element of fear. It is thought that obsessions have their origin in ideas or experiences the individual is attempting to repress. Compulsive behaviors are automatic reactions over which the individual has no control. They often take the form of complicated ceremonials—the need to touch the corners of a table, to count various items, to wash frequently and thoroughly.

Hypochondria is the enjoyment of illness. The hypochondriac makes the most of minor aches or injuries by describing vividly to others the suffering he experiences. The assertion that a hypochondriac is a person who, when you say, "How are you?" tells you, is an accurate one. The search for sympathy and compassion leads him to exaggerate the physical pains that the normal individual would dismiss with slight or no mention.

Depression or moodiness is another common neurotic symptom. All of us have days during which we are less enthusiastic and energetic than on others—but usually the reason for the feeling is fairly clear. The neurotic individual is moody for prolonged periods and for no apparent reason. The depressed individual is slow of movement and speech. There is often a feeling of sinfulness and worthlessness. His outlook is one of chronic pessimism.

There is no great advantage in naming and classifying the symptoms of neuroses. It is far more helpful to look back of the behaviors to the causes of them. It must be remembered that one cause does not result in a given symptom nor does one symptom in different individuals point back to similar causes. In short each individual must be studied, since one person may become compulsive due to over-strict parents while another manifests similar behavior because of conflict generated by worry about masturbation.

When a parent or teacher sees behaviors that seem to be serious— and amnesia, phobias, hysteria, obsessions, compulsions should immediately be judged as such—expert help should be sought or advised. On the other hand, shyness, some withdrawal, reverie, mild somatic disorders may respond to friendly and understanding counsel. Unless the response to the counseling is immediate in some slight degree the teacher should be quick to seek professional advice. However, since expert help is not always and everywhere readily available, teachers might well bear in mind that the "hands off" policy may in some instances actually amount to an additional push to the brink of unreality.

Some children are caught in a "vicious cycle of neurosis." Parents who are neurotic tend to make the children become neurotic. The teacher may be able to interrupt this cycle. "Since children inevitably pattern themselves on their inner picture of a precious person, one mentally healthy parent, teacher, nurse, or friend can often break into this vicious cycle and change its direction—toward mental health." *

The line between normality and abnormality is a tenuous one. Sometimes the slight help that a teacher, counselor, or youth leader can give is enough to enable the adolescent to face successfully the conflict situation that might otherwise overwhelm him.

Psychoses in adolescence

Psychoses, which constitute the second major division of mental diseases, are more serious than neuroses. Many psychoses are thought to be organogenic in nature. Deficiencies in the nervous structure, or crippling or disfigurement, render the individual more susceptible to the dangers imposed by environmental threats, and thus it may appear that the situational aspects are the causes of the difficulties. But, just as the distinction between normal and neurotic is difficult to establish, so is the distinction between neurotic and psychotic hard to define. Practically all articles and texts dealing with normal and abnormal behavior emphasize the unity of mind-body. Bodily conditions affect the functioning of the mind; and the thoughts, feelings, and attitudes of the mind influence the functioning of the body. The close relationships of the mind and the body and of normal, neurotic, and psychotic behavior will probably continue to baffle attempts to make definitive distinctions.

* June Bingham, *Do Cows Have Neuroses?* (White Plains, New York: The Westchester Mental Hygiene Association; 1948), p. 14.

Schizophrenia is the most common form of psychosis (other forms are discussed below). It often starts in adolescence and in the decades of the twenties—in fact, dementia praecox, a synonym for schizophrenia, means the early onset of mental abnormality. Defensive withdrawal is one of the first noticeable symptoms. The individual typically seems to devise behaviors of protective avoidance of his surroundings—particularly his human surroundings. Timidity, shyness, and a tendency to cling to a protective parent are examples. Often the youngster seems to prefer to play with older children (whom he can follow with no shame) or with younger children (whom he can lead without challenge) rather than with his peers, where competition might call for a stiffer battle. The subject is often successful in school and develops strong interest in his studies. White points out that this interest may not appear to be morbid but that underneath there is evidence of anxiety. Sometimes the individual develops a protected but productive life. But frequently the interests may become less numerous and less intense. There is less attempt to make friends even among older or younger children at the time of puberty. Fantasy and listlessness become more and more apparent. No one pattern of family life can be located in the genesis of schizophrenia, but maternal overprotection or unloving parents may constitute precipitating elements. Many schizophrenic adolescents have been known to worry excessively over menstruation and masturbation. [343:530]

Illustrative symptoms of psychoses

Chronic, or occasional, complete dissociation with reality is the major characteristic of the psychoses. Impossible ideas and beliefs are common. June Bingham illustrates by stating that the normal person checks to see if a cigarette is out, the neurotic goes back repeatedly to see if it is out, and the psychotic claims he never smokes —that "they will get you if you do." Some psychotics may believe that they are Napoleon, that they will write a hundred books today, that their food is poisoned, that there are snakes on the wall. [26:6] These manifestations have been given names that, like the names of neuroses, are of little value unless treatment is to get at the causes in individual cases.

Delusions of persecution, or paranoia, are manifested when one feels that everyone is against him, that they are jealous of his success, that they would like to do him harm, that no one loves him.

Obsessions and compulsions are sometimes so bizarre that they are included in the psychoses. [240:233]

Mania is a term covering actions that are typically elated and overactive. The patient is distractable, overconfident, and continually talkative. The elation may shift to explosive anger, destructiveness, and militant aggressiveness. These symptoms are easily recognized by the layman as being pathological. [57:875]

Depression, or hypomania, refers to a condition in which the subject is melancholy, discouraged, and inactive. Symptoms include sleeplessness, lack of appetite, and many real and imagined illnesses. Speech is slow and cumbersome and suicide is frequent. Often depression and mania occur in cycles, in which case the disease is called a manic-depressive psychosis. Clifford Beers, the founder of the mental hygiene movement, was a manic-depressive whose illness was cured, or cured itself, and who lived to make a significant contribution to society.

Other symptoms are delusions (false ideas) of grandeur, paralyses, phobias, and illusions (false perceptions). Whatever form the symptoms take it is necessary to remember that they are flight reactions of some sort and it is necessary to penetrate to the causes. The symptoms are but evidences that the subject, whether neurotic or psychotic, finds life too hard to face.

The layman's role with psychoses is easy to define: *Hands off* — these serious illnesses are in the province of psychiatrists.

Environmental and organic factors in mental illness

Whether or not the idea is gaining that serious mental illness is caused by constitutional factors, it is well to note that there are those who believe that medicine rather than environmental reconstruction is the important remedy.

It is certain that many other major types of mental disorder will eventually be found to have a physical basis. Schizophrenia or "split mind" also used to be explained to me as being due to a subconsciously motivated withdrawal from reality, and states of depression are still taught by some as being the late results of breast frustration in infancy. But up to 70 per cent of patients treated in the first three months of an attack of schizophrenia can now have their symptoms relieved by a series of insulin comas, and a few electrically induced epileptic fits can quickly remedy a severe state of mental depression. . . .

Epilepsy, also previously treated by attempted exorcism of the Devil, is now being controlled by ever more efficient chemical anticonvulsant drugs, and sometimes by operations on the brain to cut out small damaged areas where abnormal electrical discharges are occurring, which may fire off a major fit. . . .

As only one example of future possibilities, it is now known that crimes of impulsive violence are not only committed mostly by young persons, but by those whose electrical brain waves show a defect in normal brain maturation for their particular age. The broken and violent childhood home from which they so often come may not be the cause but often only evidence that this particular brain defect is an inherited abnormality from one or both parents. The abnormality generally rights itself by the age of forty, and impulsive violence then dies down for no other apparent reason. . . .

Today too many psychiatrists are neglecting the brain itself and trying to interfere in functions outside the proper province of medicine; while men of God, philosophers, and politicians are working on the theory that better religion, better houses, or larger prisons can remedy the badly functioning brain.*

Such a viewpoint may give some comfort to the ones who love a psychotic. They might, with such an orientation, be relieved of the feeling that something they have done or have not done precipitated the illness. If the basic cause of the illness was physical, very probably any one of a number of situations would have occasioned the crisis of an illness that was inevitable—if therapy did not prevent it. The major hope for the serious illnesses called psychoses, the above quotation indicates, resides in medical rather than psychological approaches. This view, however, is not universally accepted.

---

* Anonymous, "A Psychiatrist's Choice," *The Atlantic*, 194, July, 1954, 44–46.

The psychopathic personality

The term "psychopathic personality" is difficult to define because there are varied statements as to what it means or should mean. At present it appears to be a catch-all term [251:936] indicating that we do not know what is wrong with the person who is so designated. The individual lacks the symptoms and the causes that would earn him the designation neurotic or psychotic. Yet there is no doubt that he is an extreme deviate.

There are some general features, which in individual cases might take quite varied manifestations:

1. The psychopath is an individual without conscience. He can do the most dastardly deeds without any feeling of remorse. In fact, he often blames the victims of his misdeeds for their dumbness in allowing him to victimize them. Why he is without conscience is hard to tell. He may come from a family with high social ideals and genuine love for him; but some psychopaths seem to originate from a disorganized home in which no love or concern may be manifest. It appears that in many cases there is some defect, present from birth, which keeps him from being responsive to social demands for honesty, decency, and considerateness for others [301:496] but this defect is not lack of intelligence.

2. He is an individual with no, or very little, capacity for positive emotional response. He establishes no close emotional ties, he engages in sex activities with apparently little enjoyment. He seems to suffer from no conflict or frustration—though some reports indicate that he has fits of rage and may engage in vindictive retribution for real or imagined wrongs. [65:216]

3. He is a person who has no goals and is asocial or antisocial. Hence he feels no disappointment at being isolated and has no explanation for his antisocial activities. He can lie with fluent ease and is not bothered by indications that his stories contain many contradictions. He may admit his misdeeds, promise to do better, and promptly repeat the act or perform another that is still more despicable.

4. He is a person with normal, sometimes exceptionally high, intelligence. He can, when he desires, present a very charming social personality and thus his violations of mores and laws are unbelievable to those who know him.

The layman should use the label "psychopath" only after the designation has been deemed correct by a psychiatrist. The layman's role lies in referral to those competent to diagnose. What appears to be psychopathic may be neurotic or psychotic and hence susceptible to treatment by those trained for that work.

Suicide in adolescence

The mortality statistics reported for adolescents show that suicide accounts for somewhat over 2 per cent of the deaths of boys 13–19 and about 1 per cent of the deaths of girls. Some claim that suicide is more common among girls [265:399] while others seem to think the experience reported by the Metropolitan Life Insurance Company is representative—that is, suicide is resorted to more frequently by boys. [241:231] Studies show suicide to be about equal to tuberculosis as a cause of death in adolescence. It is more common than murder, but Karl Menninger points out that it is really murder of oneself. [211:24]

The cause of suicide is deceptively simple—the victim simply cannot go on facing what to him is an intolerable situation. Actually, it is often the quiet, shut-in, highly intelligent but sensitive individual who commits suicide. These occurrences cannot be attributed to overwork, too much study, or limited interests. They are more likely the result of cumulative experiences that are brought to crisis by some acutely disturbing experience. [109:252] There is evidence of a correlation between social disorganization and suicide. Where there are few friendships, weak family ties, and a lack of intimacy, the rates of self-destruction are high. [183:190] This indicates that suicidal tendencies are a long time in the making and that few suicides are "spur of the moment" decisions. Karl Menninger seems to support such a belief by analyzing the motives for suicide. He asserts that there are aggressive impulses taking the form of the wish to kill, the wish to be killed, and the wish to die. These motives are extreme forms of aggressiveness and submissiveness.* In summary he states:

> . . . the close scrutiny of the deeper motives for suicide would confirm this hypothesis in that there appear regularly to be elements

---

* The reader will recognize in these statements the fundamental polarity existing in the Freudian point of view: ego *versus* id, love *versus* hate, life *versus* death, conscious *versus* unconscious, and so on.

from at least two and possibly three sources. These are, (1) impulses derived from the primary aggressiveness crystallized as a wish to be killed, (2) impulses derived from a modification of primitive aggressiveness, the conscience, crystallized as the wish to be killed, and (3) I believe there is evidence that some of the original primary self-directed aggressiveness, the wish to die, joins hands with the more sophisticated motives and adds to the total vectorial force which impels the precipitate self-destruction.*

Those who work with adolescents might well look beyond the precipitating causes to the contributing factors if they would understand suicide in the second decade. Disappointment in school work, in love affairs, in occupational aspirations, or any other of the many sources of frustration, such as have been mentioned in this book, would seem to be simply the "straw that broke the camel's back." While efforts should be made to eliminate or reduce educational anxiety (which is particularly great in the middle class), arbitrary opposition to love affairs, prevention of occupational placement, and the like, the reduction of suicide is an over-all matter. As with the prevention of neuroses and functional psychoses, the basic factors are the general improvement of society and the building of mentally healthy attitudes and habits from early infancy. A good family, a comfortable home, friends, and a healthy community so the adolescent has a place, feels loved, and has someone to love are among the essentials for healthy personality development. Lacking these, some will resort to suicide, others will use milder forms of self-destruction like alcoholism, drug addiction, or accident-proneness. Still others will be aggressive and become delinquents. Many will use non-adjustive mechanisms that are called neuroses and psychoses. Probably the great majority will muddle through their problems unhappily and inefficiently.

Only one specific recommendation seems warranted in view of the deep-seated causes of suicide. We must not treat lightly the threats of suicide that the adolescent—or anyone else—utters. Since so often suicide comes as a surprise to those who thought they knew a healthy, sane, productive individual such threats must be taken

---

* Karl Menninger, *Man Against Himself* (New York: Harcourt, Brace and Company, Inc.; 1938), p. 82.

seriously. Taking these utterances seriously means attempting to understand the feelings of the individual and seeking the counsel of psychiatrists.

Social disorders in adolescence

The relationship of physical and mental disease is reflected in the word psychosomatic. Some mental disorder is manifested in anti-social conduct. Hence, as stated earlier, the divisions of this chapter are made simply for convenience. Varied manifestations of pathology may spring from quite similar causes. It should be noted, too, that delinquency is a form of the pathology of adolescence and could justifiably be considered in this section on social disorder; but it is dealt with in another chapter. The four topics of this section—crimes of violence, homosexuality, drug addiction, and alcoholic indulgence—are representative rather than inclusive of the pathology of adolescence expressed in social disorder.

Crimes of violence

In 1950, every five minutes around the clock a violent crime of murder, manslaughter, rape or assault with intent to kill was committed. Youths play a large role in the commission of crime—the average age of arrests for all crime is twenty-one years. Twenty-nine per cent of the crimes against property were committed by individuals less than twenty-one years of age. [145:440] When it is considered that the age group to twenty-one years, in such reports, stands in opposition to the rest of the span of life and that youth's reputation is protected by the practice of some juvenile courts' not reporting youthful crime, it becomes evident that crime is a significant problem in adolescence.

The majority of youthful crimes are stealing, traffic violations, and sex offenses. Injury to others is relatively infrequent but it is expensive in terms of money, happiness, and human life. Occasionally we are shocked by the murders committed by some adolescent or by accounts of raping and assault. Sometimes the crime is inexplicable, as in the murder of nurse Pauline Campbell, of Ann Arbor, by three youths on September 15, 1951, or the more recent episode in which four Brooklyn youths murdered, burned, and beat

various victims whom they did not know. Some of the usual excuses
—poverty, disorganized homes, ignorance, or organized crime—did
not seem to be factors. [271] At other times partial explanations
appear in the form of frustration aroused by disorganized homes,
impoverished living, or by body malformation and defect or facial
disfigurement. From the cases that do appear to be explicable, certain observations and recommendations may be made.

Generally speaking, it is not discreet to point to one thing as the
cause of criminal conduct. More typically, a number of vectors
converge to produce the frustration that leads to crime. Both psychogenic and organogenic explanations are valid. The individual's personal reaction to environmental and inherent factors is also significant. H. A. Murray and C. Kluckhohn state that the processes
creating individual personality are "often excessively complex."
When impulses remain unchecked the individual is anti-social or
criminal. If a person is unusually inhibited and has an exaggerated
need for dependence and approval he is often termed neurotic.
But if biological and cultural factors are integrated the result is a
normal or rational individual. [228:47]

John Dollard and others point out that several authorities attribute criminal behavior to psychological mechanisms that are basically
similar to neuroses and functional psychoses. [88:138] Some crime
can, no doubt, be partially explained on the basis of personal susceptibility created by abnormal brain waves or endocrine imbalance. However, crime is defined as a socially prohibited act by a
mentally and morally responsible person. Thus the following recommendations assume that the individual concerned has been examined and found to be organically and psychologically normal:

1. Attempts at rehabilitation of the criminal adolescent should
be consistent with the protection of the general public. If the
criminality cannot be explained, then sympathy should not prevent
the insurance of society's safety. Quarantine for some illnesses does
not mean that we lack sympathy for the patient.

2. Removal or reduction of environmental frustrations should be
accompanied by decisive handling designed to impress the adolescent with his responsibility. While we can understand his frustrations we can coldly tell him that his attitude is also important.

3. Punishments should be severe enough and immediate enough

to become a deterrent to crime despite frustration. Dollard indicates the possibility that crime is a function of disparity between frustration and anticipated punishment: low frustration plus low anticipation of punishment—no crime; high frustration plus low anticipation of punishment—crime; high frustration plus high anticipation of punishment—no crime. [88:141]

4. The high rate of recidivism and the frequency of commission of violent crimes by persons with previous records indicates that tenderness and coddling may not by synonymous with kindness either to the adolescent or his victim. While we do not like the idea of retribution it has the effect of being functional.

The author recognizes that these recommendations may be unpopular. It is recognized that they are examples of attacking the symptom. But it is to be hoped that the reader will carefully marshal his evidence before summarily discarding them.

The adolescent homosexual

Homosexuality refers to a retardation or arresting of normal sexual development in which feelings of sexual love are fastened on one's own sex. Such trends when transitory are a normal phase of development, as may be seen in the phenomena of crushes and hero worship. It is the cessation of progress toward continuing development of heterosexuality that is the concern of parents, teachers, and counselors. Usually the homosexual constitutes no great danger to society and for this reason he often feels that society is unjustified in its attempt to put barriers in the way of his expression of his feelings. There is some danger in the fact that the homosexual is likely to make converts of some who might otherwise develop normally. There is danger to themselves in that they must make adjustments to a heterosexual world. As a consequence the condition renders a person lonely, unhappy, and often miserable. He may have to live without the security of family love. However, despite personal misery the homosexual may live in a socially productive manner.

Many factors seem to contribute to homosexuality; but as with suicide, neuroses, and other forms of pathology, the causes and precipitating factors vary in individual cases.

It seems likely that some tendency to homosexuality must be due to endocrine balance. As has been shown earlier (Chapter Five) some males may have some feminine characteristics, interests, and modes of behavior. Some females have masculine builds, interests, and masculine secondary sex characteristics. Rapid development of sex maturity is reported to be a factor in the development of homosexuality in boys. Twice as many early maturing boys of college age were homosexuals as compared with others. The peak of incidence of male homosexuality is in the 10–15 year age group, with some decline in frequency to age twenty and a continuing decline in subsequent years. [173:315, 658] Age at puberty bears no such relationship to homosexual practices of women. The incidence of this behavior among women continues to rise slightly even after the age of twenty-five years and is more frequent among those with higher education. [172:462] Thus, it appears that physical factors may constitute a cause more frequently in the male than in the female.

Most explanations of the causes of homosexuality stress the environmental or psychological causes. Georgene H. Seward has reviewed studies showing that adult sex aggressions do not predispose the pubertal child to mental disorders; however, such acts may produce unfavorable attitudes toward sex, which in some cases may lead to homosexuality. [272:152] Homosexual trends are typically found in the individual with overdeveloped self-love—which, if repressed, according to psychoanalytic views, may cause paranoid delusions. [8:24] Data on homosexual adolescents suggest that these trends are more often due to lack of opportunity for heterosexual companionship than to deeply ingrained personality traits. Inhibitions produced by negative attitudes, conflict of ethical and moral ideals with sexual drives, may turn the individual from heterosexuality to substitute behaviors such as prolonged masturbation or homosexuality. [29:694]

More specific explanations of homosexuality are discussed by Marynia Farnham. She admits that the causes are extraordinarily complex, but all of them point to the disordered nature of the phenomenon. (1) Many cases can be traced to having been seduced at an early age by some person of the same sex. (2) Brutality of a sexual nature is a factor in some cases. (3) Parents who are unhappy in their own sex role make it difficult for some youngsters to establish their heterosexuality. (4) Parents who wish their child were the other sex are providing barriers to the happy acceptance of a natural sex role. (5) Prolonged cases of hero worship or crushes may become habitual and thus forestall further development. Farnham warns against believing these factors are causes. The important thing is that they may become precipitating factors due to the impressionableness of youth when an untoward circumstance may tip the balance toward homosexual gratification. [105:165]

The prevention of this unhappy occurrence is the important consideration. Social and emotional maturity appropriate to the individual's age must be the inclusive goal. Besides working for the strengthening of all those influences that foster sound personality development—mentioned throughout this book—the following specifics can be recommended: (1) Parents should encourage masculine interests, dress, and behaviors in boys and should encourage feminine interests, dress, and behaviors in girls. (2) Parents must study their own acceptance of their sex role and seek personal help if they are dissatisfied. A frequent symptom of this dissatisfaction is inability to get along with the spouse. (3) Without jumping to the conclusion that abnormality exists, the crushes and hero worship episodes of adolescence should be watched to see that they are not prolonged. (4) Opportunities for normal contacts with the other sex should be provided and encouraged when interest in such is manifested. When this interest does not appear shortly after puberty more positive steps (training in social skills *plus* encouragement) should be provided, including the assistance of experts.

Drug addiction in adolescence

Frightening statistics are presented regarding the decadence of youth reflected in drug addiction. It has been reported that at the Federal Narcotics Hospital in Lexington, Kentucky, there were three patients below twenty-one years of age in 1946 but there were 766 such patients in 1950. [342] It was estimated that there are 15,000 juvenile addicts in New York City in 1951 [328:44] and the Superintendent of New York City Schools estimated that 1500 (of 300,000) high school students were users. [90:230] It seems that adolescents are the not-too-unwilling victims of numerous and ubiquitous pushers.

It is a relief to find that some of the apparent spectacular increase in youthful drug addiction *might* be a matter of adult mass hysteria.

Lincoln Steffens once said that a newspaper reporter could create a "crime wave" at any time by detailed reporting of every crime. Perhaps somewhat the same thing has occurred with youthful drug addiction. Perhaps adults, surfeited with their failure to solve national and world problems, have sought relief by pointing to the ruination of youth. Facts on addition are equivocal. Other reports than the above indicate that the number of youthful drug addicts increased from 22 (not 3) in 1946 to 440 (not 766) in *two* Federal hospitals by 1951. [328:44] H. J. Anslinger, U. S. Narcotics Commission, reported that there were 50,000 to 60,000 addicts in the United States, in contrast to the New York Mayor's Committee which announced that there were 90,000 addicts in metropolitan New York. The report of 15,000 juvenile addicts in New York would make them one-sixth of the total of all U. S. addicts. However, the national rate of addiction of one out of 3000 would indicate that there would be 100 addicts among New York City high school students. Actually the rate in many areas is one out of 25,000. However, it should be stated that Anslinger claims that nearly all high school addicts are in New York and Chicago. In Washington 15,000 public and parochial high school students were tested and three addicts were found (1 out of 5000). [119] It becomes evident that some statistics do not support the conviction that drugs constitute a national menace to youth; nor does drug addiction point to a lost generation.

The fact is that there is today less drug addiction than there was a generation ago. In World War I, one draftee out of 1500 was rejected as an addict; in World War II one out of 10,000 was rejected. [119] Drugs, being so carefully controlled, are exceedingly expensive in illegitimate traffic. The cost of providing free drugs to prospective high school addicts, plus the danger of detection in the face of public sentiment, makes the youthful market unattractive—when known addicts will steal, embezzle, kill, pander, and resort to prostitution in order to obtain a supply.

However, one youthful addict out of 3000 to 5000 and a total of 440 of them in two Federal hospitals should be a matter of concern. Youth should be warned of the danger involved in hot-headed experimentation. They should be warned that drugs will only increase the most perplexing emotional problems. The following data might be an incentive to youth to exercise the caution most of them are quite intellectually capable of using.

1. Some addicts are "accidental" cases. They are not neurotics or psychotics who are seeking escape but simply normal youngsters who have sought a thrill or "lift" or who have been kidded by miserable creatures who want company.
2. Neurotic and psychotic individuals are addiction-prone. They might more readily submit to the temptation of seeking release from tension. It should be observed that drug addiction is at the low end of the scale in defense mechanisms because it adds so many more problems to the already overburdened individual.
3. The drug addict has a craving that is incomprehensible to the average person. He will steal from and lie to his family. He will commit burglaries and hold-ups. Girls often turn prostitute in order to obtain a temporary supply.
4. Drug addiction is confined mostly to urban areas. Unstable home life, congested living areas, racial discrimination, seem to be strong contributing factors.
5. The ease and rapidity with which a person becomes an addict should constitute a strong barrier against experimentation.
6. It is worth considering that *some regard sleeping pills as a more serious menace than marijuana, cocaine, and heroine.* Sleeping pills are deemed more habit forming and more destructive to nerve tissue than the more widely heralded drugs. Withdrawal illnesses are said to be more severe with barbiturates than with the opiates. [243]
7. The widespread report that marijuana is not habit-forming should be discredited. While it does not set up a physiological craving it is a destroyer of moral defenses and it makes addiction to other drugs easier. Many addicts got their start with "harmless" marijuana.

An intelligent approach to the drug problem seems to be the two-fold one recommended for so many of the other symptoms of pathology. One is the building of skills, confidence, and sound personal philosophy in individuals that will make purposeful use of drugs unnecessary and diminish the probability of accidental addiction. Two is to work for the removal of inadequate living conditions in both a physical sense (for example, better housing) and in a psychological sense (for example, reduction of racial and religious discrimination). Such approaches will reduce the drug hazard as well as weaken some of the other threats to youths' optimum adjustment.

Use of beverage alcohol by adolescents

If morality is defined as adherence to the mores of a group, then adult use of alcohol is moral because a substantial portion of the population (about half of the drinking age group) does use alcoholic beverages. [157:23] There are some localities in which the use of some form of beverage alcohol is low and others where it is high. More Americans are drinking less than was the case 100 years ago. The number of people who drink is steadily increasing, but the per capita consumption is declining. A hundred years ago it seemed plausible that 300 out of 1000 drinkers became alcoholics; today about 10 out of 1000 adults become alcoholics [51]—or 20 out of 1000 drinkers if the proportion of drinkers to drinking-age population cited above is valid. Moderation is prevalent and possible.

Youth are in an equivocal position respecting alcohol. Its use is moral from the standpoint of social practice and immoral because for them it violates law. Another point of equivocation lies in the fact that while adults may use alcohol without disapproval its use when driving an automobile is vigorously disapproved. Drinking while driving is immoral. With this background we may perhaps come to a better evaluation of drinking among adolescents.

One of the more extensive studies of youth and alcohol was made by the Psychological Division of the Hofstra Research Bureau, Hofstra College, in Hempstead, New York. It was found, as many other studies have also found, that the use of alcohol goes up sharply from the freshman year in high school (about age 14) to the senior year (about age 18). There are more male users than there are female users. About nine-tenths of the 18-year-olds have at some time consumed some alcoholic beverage—at home, on religious occasions, or for social activity. The importance of family background is vividly reflected in the fact that 95 per cent of the parents of this group (Nassau County, Long Island) use alcohol and 93 per cent keep it in the home. Only 15 per cent of the high school users do not use it with their families. Most of the drinking is of wine and beer—4 per cent drink whiskey frequently, but 42 per cent have tried it. [142:5]

The importance or parental example is also shown in a study of college drinking, in which it was found that 89 per cent of college drinkers come from homes where both parents drink and 54 per cent of abstainers come from homes where both parents are abstainers. Depending on the kind of college, 79 to 92 per cent of men students drink and 39 to 89 per cent of women have used alcohol. Drinking is much more prevalent among parents and students who have the advantages of high income [300:46, 76] a factor that may account for the prevalence of drinking in the high school group of the Hofstra study.

In view of the adult usage, it becomes a somewhat precarious problem as to what we should tell youth about alcohol. There seems to be some consensus on the following points: We cannot say that only degraded, discouraged, disillusioned adults use liquor since the youngster can so frequently look at his parents and adult acquaintances and see that it is not the truth. We cannot say that drinking hastens death because the statistics do not bear out the point—moderate drinkers live as long as do non-drinkers. We cannot say that it makes the drinker susceptible to disease—though alcoholics who abstain from food and hence do not get vitamins may be more prone to illnesses. It causes no permanent impairment of the brain or nervous tissue—though the temporary effects may be quite devastating.

Carlton Brown has summarized many studies by stating that alcohol *does not* increase efficiency, act as a stimulant, serve as an aphrodisiac (though it lowers inhibitions), cause insanity, epilepsy or glandular disturbance, injure the heart, kidneys or circulatory system, cause cirrhosis of the liver, cause ulcers, make the drinker fat, or cure colds. Alcohol *does* enter the blood stream rapidly, slows down brain processes and retards the functioning of the central nervous system, *temporarily* provides relief for some physical and psychological pain, reduces anxiety and tension through its anaesthetic action, in moderation increases the flow of gastric juices but in large quantities stops digestion, provides calories but not vitamins, minerals, and proteins. [48]

It is widely believed that adolescents resort to alcoholic beverages to offset feelings of insecurity or because they are emotionally unstable. One often hears that adolescents smoke because it makes them feel a little grown up and drink because they can then feel very grown up. The Hofstra study shows no such relationship. The users of alcohol are just as prominent in school activities and leadership as are the non-users, but no more so. Students generally do not feel that drinking aids social relationships—31 per cent of boys say "Yes" it helps, while 54 per cent say "No"; 19 per cent of the girls say "Yes" it helps, while 67 per cent say "No." Most pupils do not feel that the non-drinkers are frowned on for their decision to abstain—84 per cent believe the non-drinkers are "regular guys and gals." [142:26] The factors most closely related to adolescent drinking are, therefore, age and parental example. These are the focal points in the matter of presenting the problem of alcohol.

The old "scare" approach on the use of alcoholic beverages has proven to be ineffectual. Youth can and do understand such data as the following: Alcohol is a depressant. It reduces coordination and is a hazard of great magnitude when combined with driving. It reduces tensions and may become an habitual crutch for neurotics or those faced by chronically difficult problems. There is the danger of alcohol addiction—particularly for the individual who has not learned to face and solve his problems. Alcohol may reduce inhibitions and thus contribute to actions that may be regretted—this is particularly dangerous for the adolescent who does not have the years of firm habit to guide him that the adult has. [288:191]

Since there are many conflicting views on the use of alcohol, teachers might be wise to present the problem *as a problem* and refrain from giving THE answer. Let the area be one of discussion based on facts and the testing of divergent opinions. Along with the important decisions the adolescent must make regarding education, career, and marriage let him decide what his position regarding drink will be. He must learn to be tolerant of others' views on the subject and to exercise moderation if his decision is to drink. In these choices he will be influenced by the teachings of the home and the school and the church. He must learn to analyze his own motives as they influence his decisions. The conviction that this approach can be successful is indicated by the fact that few adolescents use alcohol to an extent that makes it pathological. Adolescents are a temperate group. [142:38] But it is still true that alcoholics begin with their first drink.

A high school senior once gave what the author is inclined to believe is the best argument regarding the role of alcohol for adolescents. This lad was an honor student in the science curriculum, class president, and a part-time worker who planned on taking medicine in college. He came from a home where the parents were divorced and where there was liquor which he had permission to use. "Alcohol is a depressant. While it may do little harm it does not do any evident good. If I want to be the best I can, I must learn to face all my problems—social, academic, and vocational—without depending on the temporary reduction of tension which alcohol effects. I need *all* my physical and mental abilities at full capacity to meet the competition."

Summary

Most young persons pass through the adolescent years with eagerness and justified confidence. Circumstances for some are, however, too trying. Either the environment is too harsh or the individual is too weak for adequate adjustments to be made. This chapter concerns those who fail and who might possibly need more help than is routinely given to the adolescent. This study should also make us more aware of the hazards the healthy adolescents encounter.

Mortality from natural causes is lowest during the adolescent years. Girls in the teen years die mainly from various diseases (cancer and malignant tumors rank highest), but accidents account for 20 to 30 per cent of all female deaths. Boys in the teen years die mainly from accidents, with steady increases up to 70 per cent at ages 18–19. It is evident that lessons in health must be supplemented by lessons in safety. Hopeful results in safety education are indicated by the remarkable success of driver training classes. Inasmuch as both physical disease and accidents are linked to emotional instability and immaturity, there must be continuing emphasis on lessons in mental hygiene.

Approximately 5 per cent of those admitted to mental hospitals are teen agers. Many who suffer from mental and emotional disorders are not committed to institutions—they are the neurotics who struggle, stumble, and wail their way through daily pursuits. Many factors contribute to neuroticism; lack of love and failure to establish feelings of security rank high. Teachers and counselors should be aware of the symptoms of maladjustment—shyness, fears, daydreaming, truancy, to name only a few—and attempt to determine the causal factors. If this seems to be the least bit baffling, expert aid should be secured; but such aid is so limited that unless teachers and counselors give some assistance most of those who need help will never get it. Psychoses are more serious and often have an organic basis. However, when it is a functional psychosis the approach is the same as for the neuroses—seek causes, get help, and realize that recovery is usually slow.

Some failure to adjust is manifested in social disorder. Many (in numbers but not in per cent) adolescents show their failure to accomplish the tasks of adolescence by resorting to crime. A large portion of violent crimes and crimes against property is committed by youths who have not learned to abide by the restraints imposed by society. Other failures are indicated by the development of homosexuality—or perhaps it might be said, "failure to outgrow homosexuality." Typically this behavior is not a threat to society but it promises a life of ostracism and disdain for the victim. Much has been said about the widespread use of drugs by adolescents. Statistics are equivocal but it seems that youth do not reveal themselves as the easy prey of drug peddlers. While many adolescents have experimented with some form of alcoholic beverage, they are on the whole a temperate group. Few of them use alcohol without the consent or knowledge of their parents. Some, possibly 2 per cent, are emotionally unstable and become the pathological group who learn to depend on the evanescent support of alcoholic beverages.

Our examination of the pathology of adolescence can be interpreted in an encouraging manner. Few succumb to mental illness, crime, drugs, or the excessive use of alcohol. Driver training promises to reduce the biggest threat to the health and safety of adolescents. Effective education in other areas might well effect similar reduction of other hazards.

STUDY AND REVIEW ITEMS

1. Which figures do you think are most noteworthy in the tables showing mortality rates among adolescents? (See above: Table 16, page 404, and Table 17, page 405.)

2. What, if anything, do you think should be done for and with the obese adolescent?

3. What are some of the basic features in an effective driver training program?

4. What are some of the implications of accident proneness for the guidance of adolescents?

5. What are some of the major factors contributing to neuroses in adolescents?

6. What evaluation would you put on the contention that organic bases of mental illness have been neglected?

7. In what ways are the causes of suicide in adolescence apparently oversimplified?

8. What does the amount of recidivism in adolescent crime suggest to you?

9. Do you think more or fewer youths will be tempted to experiment with drugs if data show that there are relatively few youthful addicts?

10. Do you feel that discussion of the use of beverage alcohol by adolescents should be included in the chapter on pathology?

11. Analyze your own position with regard to the use of beverage alcohol. To what extent is this position a matter of emotion and to what extent is it based on scientific data?

RECOMMENDED SUPPLEMENTARY READING

Farnham, Marynia. *The Adolescent* (New York: Harper & Brothers; 1951), pp. 165–203.

Two chapters deal with "Homosexuality" and "Psychosis and Neurosis." The author gives practical considerations for dealing with these problems but indicates that there is no great cause for alarm while we work to reduce hazards.

Hofstra Research Bureau, Psychological Division, (Hofstra College, Hempstead, N. Y.), *Use of Alcoholic Beverages Among High School Students* (New York: Mrs. John S. Sheppard Foundation, Inc.; 1953), 88 pp.

It is stated in this report that the statistics cited should not be generalized for the nation as a whole, but insight is provided into the factors underlying drinking by adolescents. The investigators feel that the alarm about adolescents' drinking is caused by an intemperate 2 to 5 per cent.

National Education Association, "The Status of Driver Education in Public High Schools," *N.E.A. Research Bulletin*, 32, No. 2, April, 1954, 99 pp.

Encouraging progress has been made in driver education but much remains to be done. This bulletin deals with costs, programs, personnel, needs, and organizational practices. A short bibliography contains suggestions for further reading.

Seidman, Jerome S. (Ed.) *The Adolescent: A Book of Readings* (New York: The Dryden Press; 1953), pp. 649–659.

Harrison G. Gough and Donald R. Peterson discuss "The Identification and Measurement of Predispositional Factors in Crime and Delinquency." They have assembled data indicating that significant differentiations can be made between delinquent and control groups.

Wattenberg, William W. *The Adolescent Years* (New York: Harcourt, Brace and Company; 1955), pp. 373–390.

Personality troubles of adolescents are grouped under three headings: neuroses, psychoses, and character disorders. Understanding their nature and contributing factors may aid in preventing some of the difficulties of youth. Illustrative examples are cited.

Feeling of Rejection (McGraw-Hill Book Company, Inc., 330 West 42nd St., New York 36), 20 min., so., b. & w.

A young socially maladjusted woman, feeling she is not wanted, suffers from severe headaches. The history of her childhood and adolescence shows the development of her emotional disturbance.

Last Date (Lumberman's Mutual Casualty Co., 4750 Sheridan Road, Chicago 40), 29 min., so., b. & w.

Four teen agers portray the consequences of reckless driving by irresponsible drivers. Many lives are affected by one boy's disregard for safety rules.

How can adolescents best be helped to happily accept their appropriate sex roles? What kind of heterosexual relations should be encouraged? What is the role of adult leadership in adolescents' social contacts?

CHAPTER FOURTEEN

Socialization and Heterosexual Adjustment

Much of the literature on and conversation about adolescence centers about the topic of sex maturation and activity. Such aspects of development as peer relationships, dating, necking, occupational orientation, acceptance of self, and personal beliefs are all influenced by sex factors. Thus the conversational as well as the academic interest in sex is warranted by the natural sequences of growth. It seems, however, that an approach to adolescence that is characterized by too much emphasis on sex may hamper the rounded development that society *and the adolescent* desire. The parents, teachers, and counselors of adolescents have the task of helping youngsters to view sex wholesomely, as a major aspect but only one aspect of their total development.

Heterosexual development is much more than the maturation of the sex organs, more than passing through various forms of sex play and experimentation which finally merge into the union of man and wife. This development is these things plus a great deal more. It seems safe to say that heterosexual adjustment is the outcome, or symptom, of successful socialization. The individual must have learned to relate himself positively to and with others. But in order to accept others he must first have learned to accept himself. He

must have the social poise and mental health that lead to a confident attack on the successive problems that life inevitably brings.

An area so significant and comprehensive as socialization and
heterosexual adjustment cannot be delimited within a chapter. Suggestions for more effective socialization are given, but the burden
of the chapter is to show the symptomatic nature of adjustments
between and within the sexes. If the reader realizes that such things
as hormonal balance, sexual experimentation, or sex instruction are
not the answers to heterosexual adjustment—but rather that these
things plus good home relations, effective school curriculums, and
a community organized to give wholesome work and play experiences to adolescents are the proper approaches—then the function
of the chapter has been realized. Good heterosexual adjustment is
the outcome of an integrated approach that involves many sets of
influences.

Socialization

Significance of socialization

A hasty glance at the reports of world scenes is enough to convince an observer that the need for getting along with others is
great. It is small wonder that The Great Teacher said, "This commandment I give you, that you love one another." In occupational
life, in community affairs, in personal matters, the need for effective
social relationships is paramount. Man is a social creature. His
characteristics are molded by his group membership. For all of us,
quite as much as the adolescent, the supreme task seems to be to
live happily with others—not just among others.

The significance of socialization is reflected in the definition of
the word: "Socialization is the process of presenting alternate channels for individual behavior together with positive and negative
sanctions which will lead to acceptance of some and rejection of
others. It emphasizes the influence of social groups, formal and
informal, upon the personality of the individual." * This means
that the individual must learn to avoid a number of things toward
which his impulses drive him and to do things he does not particu-

---

* Carson McGuire and Robert J. Havighurst, "Social Development," *Review
of Educational Research,* 17, December, 1947, 345.

larly care to do. It involves respecting the rights of others even when this means the denial of some of his own desires. Socialization is a developmental task at all ages, but it is particularly acute during the adolescent years.

Parental role in socialization

The process of socialization certainly does not begin with adolescence. The child from birth onward has been exposed to the influences that bear on the process, and all this while parental example has been a most potent teaching technique. But during adolescence the young person becomes acutely conscious of the process of adapting himself to wider social demands. While heretofore attitudes and feelings have been absorbed from parents rather unconsciously, the adolescent now becomes aware of social behavior—especially the learning of the appropriate sex role. In the ideal situation, and probably in the majority of cases, the girl attempts to emulate her mother and the boy accepts his father as model. This is true despite the tendency to repudiate parental domination.

A recent cultural shift affecting the feminine sex role is the increase in the numbers of women who work outside the home. Many of them are in rather direct competition with men and dislike the handicaps their sex imposes. This shift in women's occupational role is reflected in matters of smoking, use of cosmetics, and in modern versions of women's clothing. [238] A second element in the feminine role has been mentioned earlier; that is, the fact of continuous variation between the sexes—some men are womanly and some women are manly. If as the result of one or both of these factors a mother tends to reject her sex role a handicap is placed upon her daughter. Shirley Hamrin and Blanche Paulson suggest the possible effects: "A mother can begin to retard her daughter's development in heterosexual interests by teaching her that all men are cruel or unfaithful or beneath notice. She can, in fact, even without saying anything, impart wrong attitudes to her daughter by her own attitude toward her husband." *

Adolescents have an advantageous start toward socialization

* *Counseling Adolescents* by Shirley A. Hamrin and Blanche P. Paulson, page 44. Copyright 1951 by Science Research Associates. Quoted by permission of the publisher.

when the mother joyfully and proudly accepts her feminine sex role and when the father gladly accepts his role of breadwinner and counselor.

The role of the school in socialization

The part played by school experiences in development during adolescence has been touched upon in many places. Suffice it to say here that successful socialization is the result of multiple factors, which at first thought may not appear to be socializing—examples are as follows:

1. Every youngster must have the opportunity for successful participation in some phase of school life. This must be done through varied curricular and co-curricular provisions. In this way feelings of security and competence are engendered, which in turn prompt the individual to enter social groups with confidence.

2. An attempt must be made to keep at a minimum the barriers between social classes. Youngsters should not be barred from school sponsored groups, courses, or school attendance because of their social class membership. A step in the right direction will be taken when teachers and administrators admit that such barriers exist and are on the lookout for signs of them.

3. Provision must be made for the actual functioning of student councils, student government *and* student participation in curriculum building, evaluation and in formulating school policy. These experiences will provide some of the self-determination that is essential to wholesome development during adolescence.

4. Teachers might use such a device as sociometry * as a starting point for the formation of congenial groups. As pupils develop ease and confidence in a particular group they should be grouped so that experiences will become wider.

5. Discussion groups should be formed that center around the problems of personal adjustment. These discussions have the

---

* Sociometry is so frequently discussed in other texts that extended treatment seems unnecessary here. See, for instance, American Council on Education, *Sociometry in Group Relations* (Washington, D. C.: American Council on Education; 1948) for an explanation.

dual purpose of relieving feelings and of promoting the understanding that differences are normal—and that other adolescents have similar feelings of differences and doubts.

6. Attention should be given to direct instruction regarding sex and sex adjustment. While it seems desirable that this instruction be incorporated into the content of other classes, care must be taken that it is taught somewhere. Too often what is everybody's business becomes nobody's business.

The above suggestions do not exhaust the potentialities of the school for fostering wholesome socialization; * they are items that are sometimes overlooked. The rapport existing between pupils and teachers, the pride of pupils in the physical plant and the traditions of the school, the democratic qualities of administration, the nature and quality of the curriculum, are also important. These latter elements are so widely known and so uniformly sought that discussion here would simply be repetitious. Discussion of the role of the school might be concluded by hazarding the guess that the school, for those who continue to attend, begins to be more important than the home. R. J. Havighurst states that teachers often ". . . do not know how important their influence is, but they are the most effective guides for youth at the crossroads of life, more effective in some ways than parents are for this age group." †

The self-concept in socialization

It is apparent from much of the foregoing that successful socialization depends heavily upon the individual's having a healthy self-concept. He must feel that he is a worthwhile person in his own eyes as well as in the eyes of others. This involves having a moral code to which he is able to adhere. He must accept his limitations and take proper pride in his assets. In early adolescence a healthy self-concept involves acceptance by peers of the same sex, and in later adolescence it involves the feeling that the young person is not

---

* The school as a social system for teachers and other personnel, as well as for pupils, is described by Gale E. Jensen, "The School as a Social System," *Educational Research Bulletin*, 32, February 10, 1954, 38–46.

† Robert J. Havighurst, "Poised at the Crossroads of Life: Suggestions to Parents and Teachers of Young Adolescents," *School Review*, 61, 1953, 334.

entirely undesirable to those of the other sex. A healthy concept of self is essentially a matter of an individual's feeling that he is the kind of person who is accepted by those with whom he lives. Such feelings, it can readily be seen, make it possible to accept the commandment, "Love thy neighbor as thyself"—and thus are pervasive factors in socialization. [160:11]

The self-concept is of social origin. From childhood onward the person's feelings about himself are the reflections of what others think of him. Thus the heavy stress in the psychology of childhood upon the need for parental acceptance of the child. The whole tone of this book may be said to focus on the need of approving the adolescent. The reader has noted the repudiation of the concept of adolescent awkwardness as a helpful orientation. It is recommended that greater stress be placed on the concept of adolescent citizenship than upon juvenile delinquency, and Chapter Seventeen (on Citizenship—Delinquency) accords with this view. Since the young person's concept of self mirrors the evaluation of his parents, it is recommended that parents express confidence in, and be proud of, their offspring. Teachers should be mature enough to grant adolescents a large measure of self-determination.

Phases of adolescent socialization

Several purposes will be served by describing the approximate phases of development in socialization during adolescence: (1) Description of these phases will show parents and teachers what can be expected and thus indicate how the roles described above can be more effectively played. (2) It will provide rough criteria for judging the level of development achieved by a given adolescent. (3) It will show the normality of varied patterns of development—since the stages outlined are approximations for any given age. (See Figure 18 for an illustrative example.) (4) It reveals the differences in interests and values that separate pre-adolescents and adolescents from adults. Thus the gap between the ages, which narrows the "bridge of communication," may be more clearly perceived.

Some precautions should be observed in interpreting the schedule of development. Girls will go through these stages on an average of eighteen months to two years earlier than do boys—though it must be remembered that the differences within the sex are greater than

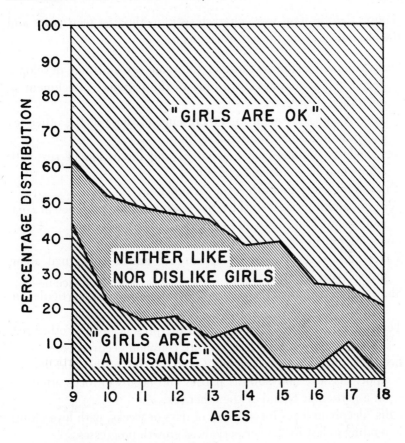

FIG. 18. **Attitudes of boys toward girls**

Anonymous reactions of 700 boys age 9 to 18 to a question concerning their attitude toward girls. At age nine 43 per cent said "Girls are a nuisance." (Based on unpublished data of R. T. Sollenberger, from Frank K. Shuttleworth, *The Adolescent Period: A Graphic Atlas*, Monograph of the Society for Research in Child Development, V. 14, Evanston, Illinois: Child Development Publications, 1951, Fig. 339.)

the average differences between the sexes. The order may not be exact—some youngsters will manifest a particular behavior before they do the one that precedes it in the listing.

With these precautions in mind the listing below may be read as though the top item were characteristic in the first teen years and the last one at about the age of eighteen:

Seeks companionship of those of the same sex and may develop a deep (and sometimes disturbing to the parents) attachment to one other of that sex.

Manifests embarrassment in the presence of those of the other sex except in highly conventional settings.

Sex modesty becomes more apparent and discussion of sex with adults may be somewhat difficult.

Talks to his peers about those of the other sex.

Will not admit interest in the other sex but, in the presence of companions, will joke with and tease those of the other sex.

Loses interest in the manifestation of adult affection.

Takes more care of personal appearance and is concerned about proper wearing apparel.

Shows interest in the other sex in general but not in a particular individual.

Tends to be loud and to show off in the presence of the other sex. Tittering and raucous laughter are common occurrences.

Becomes interested in dancing (particularly in the middle and upper classes) and boy-girl parties and begins to focus attention on a particular friend of the other sex.

Falls "deeply in love" for a period of days or weeks, with love affairs tending to last for longer periods as growth progresses.

The implication of the foregoing schedule is that adults must learn to *work with* the normal and natural developmental processes. They must avoid the tendency to hurry the growth and the temptation to poke fun at the "immature" behaviors. The assertion of F. E. Williams, written a quarter of a century ago, gains added force because it demonstrates the slowness with which sound teachings are applied.

If hetero-sexuality is not accomplished in these four or five years it never will be accomplished in a *normal* way. It may be accomplished later by some technical interference, but then only after much conflict, failure and illness. These four or five years hold the only chance the average boy and girl will have to establish heterosexuality. Once prevented, it can never come naturally and normally again.*

Substantial help will be given the adolescent in his maturing if he is free to progress through the normal stages without the feelings of guilt, shame, and embarrassment that are engendered by being kidded, laughed at, and even shamed by unthinking adults. Judging from the number of failures, socialization is at best a difficult process. The adolescent needs the support of wise and considerate adults.

Peer relationships

Adolescent friendships

There is an increasing stability of friendships with higher chronological age and grade placement. When subjects were asked, at two week intervals, who their best friends were, there was a marked tendency for more of the older respondents to name the same individual. It is to be noted, however, as with most human behaviors and traits, that there are marked individual differences in the stability of friendships at any given age. [148] It is worth noting that the instability attributed to youth is, in the matter of friendship at least, apparently a function of age rather than a characteristic of adolescents.

The sexual nature of friendships should be recognized by adults who deal with adolescents. In early adolescence it is quite natural for girls to form deep attachments for other girls and for boys to have friends to whom they "swear undying fealty." It will do more harm than good to view these as symptoms of latent homosexuality. By and large this is a passing phase of development; if there is unwise interference this phase will frequently give way to something that may be even more disturbing.

Following the attachments to the same sex there often develops the "love" of the adolescent for an older person of the same sex. Most frequently this will be discouraged by the older person, but it may be dangerous if that older person has homosexual trends.

---

* Frankwood E. Williams, *Adolescence* (New York: Farrar and Rinehart, Inc.; 1930), pp. 112–113.

Crushes on an older person of the other sex are especially dangerous because the older person may be one who is not completely satisfied with his or her own marriage. Consequently a state of affairs may be reached in which a poorly-adjusted adult takes advantage of the naive adolescent. The wise counsel of a mature adult is needed; but it must be counsel, not militant demand or carping criticisms. Teachers just out of college are often the subject of such crushes. These young teachers should realize that the admiration and devotion of the adolescent of the other sex does not indicate that the teacher has suddenly become a "lover's dream." He or she is simply the focus of a stage of development which, if not regarded in this light, may lead to undesirable consequences for both parties. Crushes, like the boy-boy and girl-girl friendships, are passing phases of development. The major defense against unpleasant consequences is the maturity of the adults who happen to be the objects of the affair.

A further step in socialization and heterosexual development is a series of puppy-love affairs. Each time, there is a tendency for the adolescent to feel that his case is different and that the "true love" has been found. Normally, there are about five or six such episodes prior to the love affair that results in marriage. The value of these experiences is reflected in the fact that boys and girls who have had five or six "serious" love affairs (serious to them, and these affairs should ostensibly be so regarded by the adult) establish better marriages than the average of those who have fewer love affairs.

Parents play an admirable role if they avoid jesting and criticism during these developmental experiences. Joking and criticism may make the process more difficult by turning the youngster away from a possible source of counsel. [199] There can be no doubt that some hasty and unwise marriages are precipitated by adults who deliver an either-or dictum in the matter of friendships and love affairs.

The nature of peer groups

The changing patterns of conduct described above, which contribute to the lack of understanding between persons of various ages, also contribute to the formation of various kinds of groups of adolescents. The greater strength and skill that accompany growth are other factors in pushing the adolescent from his family to the companionship he finds in peer groups. The desire to be grown up and to make his own way is still another force tending to the formation of peer groups.

The form a group takes depends in large measure upon the particular social environment of the adolescent, but the factor of age or maturity must also be considered. Following closely in the wake of loosely formed and transient friendships, a characteristic peer group is the crowd. This is a loosely formed group of youngsters of about the same age (middle adolescence). Both boys and girls are members and friendships within the group are of varying strengths. Some boys and girls will "pair off." There is a community of feeling within the crowd. Interests of the individual are somewhat similar. (However, it is important to realize that the crowd is more than the sum of its parts. Things will be done in the group that no member of the crowd would do by himself.) Thus crowds form more easily in communities where there is a large degree of population homogeneity than when there are marked differences in status within a small area. Not all the adolescents in a community are included in the crowd, and unless there is another such group some individuals will feel the pain of not belonging.

When there is a lack of homogeneity the peer group may be the clique—which is smaller and more purposefully organized than is the group. Exclusion of those who do not belong is an express purpose of the clique. Hollingshead found that cliques were a powerful and pervasive feature of the social and school life of Elmtown's adolescents. [143:202] Dating, membership in organizations, kinds of activities available, and even membership in school activities were strongly influenced by cliques that were largely formed within class status lines. There is in cliques a much stronger emotional involvement than there is in the crowd. Membership in cliques is for some difficult to obtain, and because of the emotion involved non-membership is therefore the more difficult to bear. However, the student of adolescence must not conclude that the clique is the cause of hardships and disappointments for the adolescent. It is more likely that the clique is the outward manifestation of tension and differences between the various social classes. The clique is a natural manifestation of the adolescent's desire to identify with his peers, and valuable lessons in socialization are learned from this sort of group. The undesirable features of the clique must be attacked through the over-all reconstruction of cultural mores which will make discrimination a widely disapproved kind of conduct.

The gang is a third kind of adolescent grouping. It is more highly structured than the clique. A primary characteristic of the gang is that of conflict. It originates and is integrated by the existence of conflicts, which may stem from race, religion, or nationality (for example the conflict encountered by the children of immigrants).

Probably the most extensive source of conflict giving rise to the gang is the need for boys to gain independence from adult direction. The gang affords an opportunity for exercising freedom, which often takes the direction of activities judged "subversive" by adult standards. Socially approved behaviors are by no means totally rejected, but the gang code is likely to reject values that are judged old-fashioned. Thus studying may be regarded as sissy, but stealing may be approved as demonstrating cunning. Daring, resourcefulness, self-reliance, and initiative are highly valued.

Gangs are widespread but probably gain most notoriety in metropolitan areas where many sources of conflict converge to accentuate gang activities. When racial and religious prejudices are rampant, where the characteristics of inhabitants of a given living section are being changed, where newcomers are competing for available jobs, there is more likelihood of gangs' breaking out into delinquency and violence.

The negative outcomes of gang formation are not inevitable. In numerous cases adults unobtrusively work *with* gangs. They counsel rather than advise, they suggest rather than dictate. They depend on youth to lead. They recognize that the function of the gang is to give exercise to the need for independence.

The pursuit of personality growth through participation in gangs obviously needs the attention of wise adults. The search for peer relationships, when it takes such forms as are described above, obviously needs the direction of wise adults. The youthful energies expended in conflict could be directed into constructive activities for the community. More will be said about such an orientation in the chapter on citizenship and delinquency (Chapter Seventeen). The concern here is to recognize the gang as an educative (or miseducative) influence and to utilize the socialization processes more constructively.

Importance of peer groups

Some crowds (which the adolescent may call "the gang") and some cliques provide valuable learning activities. Good peer relationships indicate the probability of later adequate socialization as well as providing present satisfactions. A simple way to evaluate the importance of peer groups is to examine some of the developmental tasks of the adolescent and reflect upon ways in which peer groups facilitate the accomplishment of the tasks.* Four out of nine developmental tasks of early adolescence, as listed by Lilienthal and Tyron, directly depend for their fulfillment on participation in peer groups: establishing independence from adults in all areas of behavior; behaving according to a shifting peer code; establishing strong identification with sex mates; learning a role in heterosexual relationships. Four others of the nine developmental tasks of late adolescence depend upon peer group membership for their accomplishment: building a strong mutual affectional bond with a possible marriage partner; adopting an adult-patterned set of social values by learning a new peer code; exploring possibilities for a future mate and acquiring "desirability"; learning appropriate outlets for sexual drives.

Certainly the freedom of the adolescent to function in peer groups, or even the encouragement of adults to participate, will not alone solve all the developmental problems of the adolescent. But a glance at the tasks listed reveals that peer groups may make some contribution to each and is essential for many.

Since the peer society is such an important, though unofficial, agency in the education of children in our society, it is time we scrutinized our relations with it. Very few adults have entree there, and often we do not even know that we are excluded. If we are going to use this social organization, if we wish to enrich its culture, we, not the children, are going to have to change. It means that we will have to understand and accept much more of the value systems that are operative in the children's groups. By "accept," we mean accept these codes and behavior patterns as appropriate for them,

---

* The headings listed were formulated by Jesse W. Lilienthal III and Caroline Tyron for the Association for Supervision and Curriculum Development, *1950 Yearbook, Fostering Mental Health in Our Schools* (Washington, D. C.: National Education Association; 1950), pp. 90–128.

not for us; certain children eye askance the adult who tries to *be* a child.*

The adult and adolescent peer groups

The foregoing passage advises that *we,* not the children, are going to have to change. Adults would do well to recall quite consciously their own feelings of the teen years. The desire for group approval becomes one of the strongest drives during adolescence. Parents must avoid an either-or attitude or they are likely to force decisions in favor of the peer group—this situation may arise in regard to dress, hours the adolescent keeps, where he goes for recreation, or what activities he pursues. One perplexed father said: "What do I do now? I told him that if he went to Rigdee for the dance, I guessed I would have to whip him. He said, 'Well, I might as well take my whipping now. I'm going.'" A thirteen-year-old boy who was to replace a hired baby-sitter for his younger brothers at 9:00 p.m. was told to walk home (not more than a block) with the girl sitter, refused flatly because "people might get the wrong idea." Threats, cajolery, and autocratic commands would not move him. In such cases it seems that the parents might well retreat while they can do so in good grace. This certainly does not mean that parents should relinquish all authority at the first signs of rebellion. Indeed, as is pointed out in Chapter Six, "The Adolescent and His Parental Home," the young person needs and depends on authority and would cry out if none were exercised. The point for parents is that they should save adamancy for crucial situations. If the boy described above who was going to the dance were doing so in the company of a small clique with an established poor reputation, the father should maintain his stand. If it were with the high school crowd in general the father could well say, "OK, son. In this case you win."

The pressure of peer groups is powerful, and whether parents or offspring win the conflict the adolescent is hurt to some degree. Parents should know that the conflict is normal. It may be inevitable in our culture where there are barriers to maturity. The problem becomes one of avoiding conflict on unimportant issues

---

* *Fostering Mental Health in Our Schools,* p. 128.

and in resolving it quickly when it is encountered. Those who "sagely" observe that if child rearing has been successful there will be no conflict, just have not yet gone through the experience of living with an adolescent. These advisers do harm because they make the parents who are doing good jobs feel that the existence of normal conflict is an indication of their failure.

The most difficult area of peer adjustments, asserts Paul H. Landis in summarizing a number of studies, arises out of economic and cultural differences rather than a conflict of peer group versus parental morals and ethics. [183:378] As the ring of acquaintances and friends expands with increasing age there is greater likelihood of forming enjoyable contacts before family background is known. There then arise problems of attempting to conceal family background, abandoning the friendships, or attempting to hold the friends despite background. There can be no "pat" solution to such difficulties. But close rapport between parents and youngsters will help. Discussion of such problems in social studies in the classroom will help, and teachers, *as counselors,* can help the perplexed adolescent achieve greater objectivity. Mature persons judge others on the basis of what they are—not who their parents are. The general principle is one of finding ways to hasten the achievement of this maturity. The fact that this can be accomplished is attested to by the growing consensus that in many respects the average high school youngster of today is markedly advanced over the students of two or three decades ago. [150]

The personnel of our schools have long been aware of the importance of peer relationships and have been making advances toward implementing their knowledge. Probably the most outstanding of these advances is the increase of classes called "Personal Adjustment" or "Human Relations" and similar titles—all of which recognize the need for autonomy in the adolescents' decisions and evaluations. [237] Another school emphasis is the establishment of personnel and guidance programs—which deal with peer relations and other problems of adolescence. The emphasis in this program is on getting the pupil to see ways of solving his own problems himself. Continued emphasis on the cocurricular activities of the school as an integral part of the educative process is another evidence of the recognition of the role of peer relationships.

Whatever the approach of adults—parents, teachers or counselors—it would be well to bear in mind that school courses, clubs, athletic programs, community youth centers and the like, must contribute to the following needs: (1) The need for belongingness—each individual must be accepted by some of his peers and by understanding adults. (2) The need for approval—parents and teachers must be careful not to erect barriers by ignoring the *current* mores of youth. (3) The need for success—each individual in some way should be led to develop a skill or knowledge or to have acknowledged a skill or knowledge that gives him a feeling of worth. (4) The need for security—this is a *feeling* not the result of a status. Belongingness, approval, and success are items which lead to the feeling. But discussion and study can benefit by helping the adolescent come to an appropriate evaluation of his status. (5) The need for companionship tends to separate the youth from his parents—increase in age brings about divergence of interests. He needs the support, approval, and proximity of his age mates in order to satisfy the need for companionship.

Popularity of adolescents

Anyone in a new situation is likely to be awkward and fumbling in his attempt to adjust. The adolescent in his desire to make an impression on his peers and others in his growing social world sometimes makes errors that hamper rather than facilitate his social adaptation. This is seen in tittering, loud talk, raucous laughter, and showing off. It will be noted later in this chapter that the attempt to gain popularity sometimes leads to excessive petting or submitting to premarital intercourse. Hence young people should know the factors that are of *real* importance in popularity.

Youth of both high school and college age rank the following qualities high among the characteristics they admire in the other sex: real brains, good health, dependability, considerateness, sex purity, cleanliness, and being a hard worker. Dependability and considerateness receive consideration mostly by older adolescents. Lower ranking characteristics are being a good dancer, having a clever line, and spending money freely. Boys look for good looks in girls, but girls seem to be less concerned about facial characteristics of boys. [158:195]

Concentrating upon the positive aspects of effective social personality will, in the long run, be more fruitful than attempting to remedy specific defects such as exhibitionism, excessive petting, and premarital intercourse. The positive qualities can be emphasized by teachers, but probably the most effective approach would be through group discussion. Boys and girls should be led to analyze their own friendships to see the extent to which they themselves value the qualities mentioned. There is little doubt that their conclusions will be in close accord with practices approved by adults; thus they will have an incentive to seek the development of traits that will be of permanent value.

Sexual problems and adjustments

Physical and cultural factors in sex drives

It was indicated in the chapter on Physical Factors in Development that changes in endocrine balance beginning in pre-adolescence result in development of the sex organs and secondary sex characteristics. These changes are accompanied by a series of changes in the behavior orientation of individuals. It has been noted that boys increasingly seek to impress girls with their prowess and manliness. Girls become increasingly concerned with being attractive to boys. Earlier in this chapter it was indicated that there is an increased ratio of heterosexual friendships as a youth progresses through adolescence. Finally, there typically develops a rather deep attachment between pairs of boys and girls—which in some instances culminates in marriage.

Although sex drive and sex prowess reach their high points in the late teen years it may be some years before sex satisfaction is achieved through marriage. Many young people successfully sublimate the sex drive and delay intercourse until the time of marriage. Others yield to their impulses and engage in premarital intercourse from the early teen years on. Still another group avoids intercourse but resorts to the socially disapproved techniques of homosexual contacts.

The ways in which sex drives are handled and the psychological response to the manner of handling are strongly conditioned by cultural factors. It must be further indicated that the physical drive and the cultural expectation are *reacted to by an individual.* It is almost trite to point out that in some societies premarital sexual experience is not frowned upon. In others a girl is not even considered marriageable until after she has had sex experience. In the United States two or three decades ago a girl who had premarital coitus was considered a fallen woman. Today such a girl is neither universally discredited nor admired. These generalizations are supported by the following illustrations. Mothers in some societies stroke the baby's genitals in order to quiet him, while some American mothers are manifestly shocked to see a baby boy pinching his penis or a girl rubbing her pubic region. In the lower social classes adolescents may be verbally adjured to remain continent, but if he or she does not do so there is no great concern about it. Children thus grow up with profoundly different attitudes toward sex. Some adolescents may seek and gain satisfaction of a sort from premarital intercourse. Others may obtain physical release but suffer from emotional turmoil that persists long after the temporary satisfaction. Hence we may safely say that the individual's response to cultural factors must be considered along with the physical factors *per se.* The fact is that despite the proponents of sexual freedom, there are substantial numbers of adolescents growing to maturity who suffer no ill effects from delayed sexual satisfaction. While Kinsey's data show that almost 50 per cent of his sample of American women had premarital intercourse [172:286] it is important to recognize that over 50 per cent of his sample did *not* have such experience. Leaders and teachers in certain religious orders remain continent for a lifetime and render great service to mankind. There are no statistics to prove that they suffer any more frustration than those who live licentiously. In fact, the latter are the ones who are judged to be maladjusted. There is the possibility that for some the physical drive is too strong to be controlled; but the comparative studies of society show that it is the physical drive plus the psychological response that must be reckoned with.

It is assumed, in the remainder of this chapter, that it is important to the adolescent to observe the verbally expressed mores of our society and that this can be successfully done by building attitudes that point to the control and delay of sexual appetites.

Dating

Dating may begin as early as thirteen years for girls and thirteen or fourteen for boys. Early dating may be a somewhat informal matter of pairing off within larger groups so that the boy or girl has the "moral" support of other boys or girls in the group. Shortly, however, the desire to be "alone together" asserts itself and one boy will date one girl with the intention of spending time with her. At first the dates will be spread far apart—awaiting the opportune event for securing the date. At the upper ages, however, the being together transcends the importance of the event attended and the dating becomes more regular and frequent. The age at which dating first occurs and the particular events attended will vary with the particular community and social class observed. However, the general pattern is similar and begins to culminate in going steady; for a great many couples the pattern culminates in marriage.

There are some conventions in dating that the adolescent should know and observe. One is that the boy must be the pursuer. Girls should know that their tendency toward more rapid social maturity makes them conscious of dating problems before the boy is much concerned. Because of this, if a girl becomes aggressive she may frighten the inexperienced and not too greatly interested boy. But she cannot afford to be the shy "wallflower." The boy needs the help she can render by giving him a smile and by her appearing in halls and at ball games, and so on, *without* constantly having a girl friend by her side. When a group of boys whistle at her (one alone would not have the courage to whistle) she should neither "stick her nose in the air" nor make some smart retort. A smile will convey the message that she is neither unapproachable nor an "easy mark." When the boy does ask for the date he should appear at the house (a girl loses prestige and respect when she races at the sound of the horn) and say hello to the parents. The fact that the parents expect the boy to exercise courtesy protects both the boy and the girl. It gives her the prestige that may delay or offset the seeking of intimacies, and it gives him the security of knowing that he acts in accordance with the social mores of adult groups.

"Going steady" is a term that eludes definition. For some, going steady means that a boy or girl has gone three times with the same partner—and does not mean that any mutual understanding has been reached. For others, going steady does imply a mutual understanding that movies, parties, dances, and evenings out will be spent together. This understanding may be achieved early by discussion or may be the tacit result of having had a number of satisfactory dates. There are both advantages and disadvantages in going steady that should be understood by the adolescent. This understanding can best be achieved by peer group discussion so that young people do not feel that there is an imposition of adult views.

Adolescents have advanced the following arguments for going steady: It provides a chance to get acquainted thoroughly with another person—more and varied contacts enable each to see the other person in various situations. It gives some assurance of having a date when parties and dances are scheduled. It puts a person at ease—lets him act himself instead of having to make a good first impression. Adolescents, however, recognize the following hazards: Going steady may lead a young person to get careless in matters of dress and personal grooming. It may keep one partner from going to a social event because the other partner is not then in town. It limits opportunities to get closely acquainted with a number and variety of personalities. It may keep a boy or girl from developing the variety of interests that tend to make a dynamically stimulating individual.

The significance of dating lies in the provision of social experience. It is a phase of the preparation for wholesome and enjoyable marriage. It will usually progress through the stages of group, double, and single dating. As the adolescent grows older there will be more of a tendency to "go steady" and the periods of going steady will become longer and longer. Finally, experience and age results in the development of personalities that are pliable enough, tolerant enough, and considerate enough to hazard an attack upon the progressive problems that marriage will entail.

Petting

Petting consists of the deep kissing (tongue kissing) and caressing of body parts that is definitely of a sexually exciting nature. In marriage it is the prelude to intercourse. Before marriage it may be an end in itself, it may have the purpose of petting to climax, or it may be an attempt on the part of one partner or the other to arouse the other to the point where the avoidance of intercourse is impossible.

Kinsey found that in his sample 40 per cent of the girls had petting experience by the age of fifteen, and 90 per cent had petted prior to marriage.* These findings would make it seem that petting is a normal phase of growing up, and many who have written on this problem seem to agree that this is so. Nevertheless, the advice to teen agers is to avoid excessive petting. [9:167 and 174:36] The problem for teen agers and their counselors is to determine what is excessive, since some occasional petting provides the experience in love-making that will serve to make marriage more mutually satisfactory. Group discussion will help to determine the point of excess. Girls will bring to the discussion the counsel of their mothers, and it is likely that the conclusion will be about like this: Excess is beginning when petting and the prospects of petting blot out other interests. Petting has become excessive when the stopping point leaves a feeling of disappointment and incompleteness. (Many of the boys and girls will recall that the short light kiss allowed them to go home with a smile of satisfaction, while the deep kiss and erotic movements left them with a feeling of disgust or incompleteness.) Petting is excessive when each date finds a couple going just a little further than on the preceding date. It is excessive when young people feel that their conduct has not been in accord with their own beliefs as to what is right and correct. It is excessive when the boy's hand perspiration, rapid breathing, and rigid erection (of which the girl is often aware) indicate that the activity is largely physical.

Several dangers involved in petting should be considered by the adolescent: (1) Petting is often the forerunner of unanticipated (except momentarily) and undesired intercourse. (2) It leads to the blotting out of other interests. Hence petting limits the opportunities for building the interesting and stimulating personality

---

* Alfred C. Kinsey, Wardell B. Pomeroy, Clyde E. Martin, and Paul H. Gebhard, *Sexual Behavior in the Human Female* (Philadelphia: W. B. Saunders Company; 1953), p. 233. It is the author's feeling that despite the many critics of the Kinsey reports who say that the sample is not balanced, that it represents the unconventional woman, that certain religious groups and educational strata are not properly represented, his study is the best thing we have to date and cannot be ignored. However, it is felt (1) that there are different ways of interpreting the data and (2) that interpretation is as vital a part of research as is discovery.

that will be an asset to pleasant dating days as well as a fundamental in the establishment and maintenance of a successful marriage. (3) Petting, when it stops short of intercourse, creates tension and frustration that may ultimately lead to disharmony between an otherwise well-adjusted couple. The difficult situation makes both so irritable that they imagine personality defects that do not exist or magnify out of true proportion those shortcomings everyone has. (4) Petting involves the stirring of strong emotions which might lead a young person to feel that he is in love. As is repeatedly pointed out, in this book as well as in other sources, the physical aspects of love are important but they are far from being the whole thing. Hence petting may lead to a premature marriage when other aspects of personal compatibility are lacking. (5) Excessive petting may give the girl the reputation of being an easy mark and thereby limit her opportunities to be dated by the boys whom she considers the most desirable acquaintances. Girls should know that a boy prizes the companion whom he feels is not common property but someone who has reserved her charm especially for him.

Boys should share responsibility for limiting the extent of petting and they sometimes do this competently. However, it is highly probable that the girl must assume the major responsibility for moderation. Mrs. Duvall suggests some techniques that could be helpful. One is to squeeze the boy's hands firmly and with a smile thank him for a wonderful evening, and skip home. Another is to give a little caress; one girl just before she went inside pressed her finger on her friend's chin and said, "You're swell." Mrs. Duvall suggests that the manner of showing reluctance to pet is as important as is the disapproval itself. Humor may be helpful. One girl said, as she took her friend's hands away from her breasts, "This isn't Tuesday, is it?" Mrs. Duvall says it's corny but it works. Humor was displayed by the girl who turned on the ignition and said, "Will you drive, or shall I?" These techniques demonstrate that a girl's skill in conducting herself in a way that will give more enduring satisfaction to both parties to the date may be a much greater asset than a readiness to submit to petting.*

---

* Evelyn Millis Duvall, *Facts of Life and Love for Teen-Agers* (New York: Popular Library; 1953), p. 177. This book was originally published (and is copyrighted) by Association Press.

Premarital sex relations

About 50 per cent of the females studied by Kinsey and his associates had experienced coitus prior to marriage. The incidence is much less in the early teen years—3 per cent of unmarried females by the age of fifteen had had coitus. The figure rises to 26 per cent for all those under twenty, with a continued increase to over 40 per cent in the mid-forties. [172:286] These data show that female sexual license in the teen years is not part of the practiced mores of our society any more than it is the verbally expressed ideal. Moreover, it is to be noted that the recording of coitus may be the result of one experience and that with a girl's fiancé just prior to marriage. Thus, for the 3 per cent who had coitus before fifteen and the 26 per cent who had such experience prior to age twenty it cannot be said that promiscuity was an accepted practice. This is not to excuse or condone those who violate the mores. The point is noted for the benefit of parents and counselors who may have to meet the argument, "Everybody's doing it."

A different situation is encountered where males are concerned. Here, the practiced mores do contradict the verbally expressed mores, although the double standard must be considered a part of the societal expectation. Premarital coitus begins in the early teens and by the middle forties it includes two-thirds of the total male population. In some communities and in the lower educational and social strata there is much less constraint and the incidence reaches to over 90 per cent. There are distinct differences between those with some college education and those who have less than eight years of education. While 73 per cent with the least education have coitus by the age of twenty, 44 per cent have such experience in the group with thirteen-plus years of education. As is the case with women, individual variations are wide. Some are included in the statistics on the basis of one experience and others are included when they have had limited experience with their fiancée. [174:549] The higher statistical incidence for men than for women is influenced by the tendency of the male to exploit the promiscuous female and by the profession of prostitution.

It is easier to define what the situation is than to state, with the hope of a wide degree of acceptance, what the situation should be. Kinsey introduced the latter problem with the following words:

It does not suffice to show that the persons who have had or who have not had premarital experience are the ones who make the best or do not make the best adjustments after marriage. For premarital intercourse is always a complexity of things. It is, in part, a question of the sort of individual who has the intercourse and the degree to which the premarital activity is acceptable or unacceptable in the individual's whole pattern of behavior. It depends upon the extent of the psychic conflict which may be evoked for an individual who transgresses the ideals and philosophies by which he has been raised, and to which he may still subconsciously adhere. For a person who believes that premarital intercourse is morally wrong there may be, as the specific histories show, conflicts which can do damage not only to marital adjustments, but to the entire personality of the individual. For a person who really accepts premarital intercourse, and who in actuality is not in conflict with himself when he engages in such behavior, the outcome may be totally different! *

This supports the author's thesis that sex is at least partially a matter of psychological orientation. However, it must be stated that this orientation is more than an individual matter. The adolescent may argue (perhaps a better word would be rationalize) that it is his business whether he is continent, cautiously experimental, or promiscuous. The fact is that society makes it society's business, and penalties of varying degrees of severity are imposed for violation of the laws and mores. [23:136] Next to penalties for murder some of the heaviest legal penalties are demanded for statutory rape—intercourse with a consenting girl below a stated age. [174:287n] Another point to consider is that the lower social classes may not frown upon premarital coitus, but neither does a boy or girl lose face if he or she does not participate. In fact, the lower-class girls who remain continent are taking steps toward upward social mobility.

Even if studies show that intercourse had most frequently occurred prior to satisfactory marriage it would not *per se* be an argument for changing the mores. The satisfaction from marriage might simply be a matter of a more relaxed and wholesomely acceptive

---

* Alfred C. Kinsey, Wardell B. Pomeroy, and Clyde E. Martin, *Sexual Behavior in the Human Male* (Philadelphia: W. B. Saunders Company; 1948), p. 561.

attitude toward sex that would function even though one had pre-viously decided upon the course of continence. However, the fact is that greater marital happiness is typically achieved by those whose experience is limited to marriage coitus. [10:600] Young persons as well as married adults should know that mutual sexual satisfac-tion must be mutually learned. A technique learned with a prosti-tute or a promiscuous girl does not necessarily have anything to do with the technique that will bring mutual satisfaction to a married couple.

Some attempt to justify their illicit contact on the grounds that they want to see if they are mutually adapted sexually. What they can mean by this is difficult to understand because the satisfying sex act is psychological as well as physical. A couple cannot *dis-cover* sexual adaptation in a car, motel, or roadside park where fear and haste destroy the trust and tenderness that are character-istic of the marital union. It seems that Kinsey has been most appro-priate in his appellation, "Sexual outlet."

Numerous arguments have been used in defense of chastity. Despite penicillin and other drugs the danger of disease still exists—though certainly not to the extent of two decades ago. There is the danger of unwanted pregnancy—it is judged that contraceptives are only a partial defense. Strong douches are judged to be only about 10 per cent effective, suppositories about 50 per cent, vaginal jelly about 60 per cent, and rubber condoms about 75 per cent. [13] Abortions are a threat to psychological and physical security, both present and future. The "fear" approach is frowned upon by many authorities—though it must be admitted that it seems to have worked in the past, for premarital coitus has increased since the discovery of drugs that control much venereal disease. Fear will not work with many youth because they have a desire to display their fearlessness and perhaps to defy adult rulings.

There are arguments for chastity that do not stress fear. One is that the unchaste girl is often betraying her own moral code, with a resultant undermining of a healthy concept of self. Another is that she lowers herself in the eyes of many men (often including her sexual partners) and thereby makes herself less desirable. Even lads in the slum areas desire to protect the virgin (unless she is a teaser). One boy said that if you go with a girl too long you will get to like her and get too deeply involved; he had been "banging" his girl on about every date and was getting to like her so he just dropped her. Promiscuous girls are considered to be "lays" and boys willingly share their enjoyment. The one-man "lay" he tries to keep to himself, but after he discovers that she has been with another man he boasts that he had her first. The "good girl" is the one who is known to be inaccessible; she is deemed to be more desirable as a companion and is the kind of girl a man would want to marry. On the basis of these and similar findings, William F. Whyte recommends that middle-class people become aware of the existence of definite moral-sexual codes in the lower social strata. [345] Differences lie in the extent of violation rather than in the fundamental attitude. The author has empirically observed the same attitudes as those reported by Whyte among the day laborers in mining and lumbering communities. The girls who maintain their own self-respect are the ones who earn the respect of even the exploitative male.

The discussion thus far has centered about a condition and possible approaches to it. But before the condition can be understood and before a completely satisfactory solution can be achieved the causes must be investigated. It is doubtful if all the causes for premarital coitus are known, but among some of the more important are the following: (1) Rebellion against parents, (2) a search for a sense of being loved, (3) a desire to act in accord with the rest of the crowd, (4) lack of inclination to delay sex gratification, (5) a lowering of inhibitions concomitant to the use of beverage alcohol, and (6) a lack of personality resources.

Sexual experimentation as a symptom of rebellion against parents is more of an adult problem than one of adolescence. Parents can do their part by yielding in those numerous predicaments where the adult's winning the argument is of no consequence. When the adolescent wins occasionally he can with grace admit defeat on another occasion. There should be an interest in adolescent activities without jeering and without excessive displays of authority. There should be an indication that even in the face of grave errors the parents will stand by their children. (These and other suggestions have been expanded in Chapter Six, "The Adolescent and His Parental Home.")

It is felt that a great number of girls who have premarital intercourse do so in a search for love rather than because of an overpowering sex urge. Caresses, devotion, and attention as preliminaries to intercourse are a lure to which they are susceptible because they feel they are not loved at home—especially by their fathers. The antidote for this cause is twofold. First, parents should reveal the affection they have for their children; second, the adolescent must know that a transitory physical relationship cannot fill a psychological void.

Examination of data presented earlier shows that, at least for girls, and for boys in the upper and middle class, the idea that "everybody's doing it" is erroneous. It seems that the impression is created by a vociferous minority, abetted by a number of boastful but insecure individuals who do not want others to think they are inexperienced. Actually a youth is more likely to be with the crowd when he observes premarital chastity; in any event, neither boys nor girls lose any prestige when they demonstrate that they conduct themselves on the level of accepted morality.

The lack of inclination to delay sex gratification is a crucial cause. It has been shown that for the male the sex drive reaches its peak in late adolescence, although the girl may not reach her highest level of desire until the late twenties. Furthermore, it must be admitted that the pleasures of sex are intense and worthy of being highly prized. Youth might well be informed that (1) illicit sex experiences are more likely to be "outlets" than they are to be representative of sex relations in marriage, [240:267] (2) sex urges need no more be fully and immediately gratified than the desires for food, play, or money—in fact, the control of the sex urge seems to contribute to its ultimately greater enjoyment.

Alcohol is not in any way a stimulant and consequently does not stimulate sex desire or sex power. As a depressant it does lower the inhibitions. A drinker may become reckless when he would otherwise be cautious; he may do things that under normal conditions his moral reserves would prohibit his doing. Alcohol weakens defenses that might otherwise be adequate. The ease of defying moral conventions is increased by automobiles that make it possible to put miles between youth and their possible censors. The automobile plus alcoholic indulgence make a dangerous combination for youth who under normal circumstances wish to act in accord with our established mores.

It has been indicated that many youth feel varying degrees of insecurity as they widen their geographical and social horizons with their increasing age. Girls who wish to attract and hold boy friends but feel that their beauty, conversational ability, or interests and skills are inadequate may consent to intercourse in an attempt to achieve popularity. Once having undertaken this course it becomes increasingly difficult for them to devote time to the fundamentals of popularity because they have the additional handicap of a poor reputation to overcome. They should know that any popularity they achieve through their sex alone is transitory. Boys do not like to and will not be encumbered with an easy mark. Actually, this point goes much further than constituting a recommendation that girls be aware of the inadequacy of sex activity as a way to popularity. It is a suggestion that all of the aspects of adolescent development bear upon the ability to remain continent. The home, the school, the community, must all combine their resources to build the strength and stability of personality that provide the best defense against any deviation from desirable adolescent behavior. Personality development, it has been seen, is a continuous process that is influenced by all aspects of living.

Summary

Man is a social creature, and each child must learn the techniques of adaptation which, in our society, are most advantageous for the total life span. Socialization of the adolescent is a significant area because of expanding social horizons and because the final steps of basic personality are being taken. An important step in socialization is learning to accept, and act according, to a masculine or feminine sex role. Parents help by setting a good example, by manifesting happiness in their own sex role, and by their acceptance of their children. School workers can help by providing youth more autonomy, by guiding the discussion of problems of personal and sex adjustment, by providing pupils with a variety of social activities, by teaching respect for differences, and by devising tasks that are significant to adolescents. Socialization is strengthened by healthy concepts of self—which are reflections of what others think of the individual. Parents, teachers, and counselors must show that they have confidence in adolescents' ability to make wise decisions. Socialization is a developmental process that consists of phases of development—interest in friends of the same sex, avoidance of the other sex, teasing those of the other sex, and finally experiencing various degrees of "falling in love."

Peer relationships are an avenue for achieving socialization. Friendships, cliques, crowds, and gangs are teaching-learning situations that cannot be ignored. Adults must learn to work with these peer groups to strengthen the positive aspects and to diminish the negative features. Many of the developmental tasks of adolescents are contributed to by wholesome peer relationships. Hence adequate peer relationships pave the way to adult socialization. A number of school techniques for capitalizing on the wisdom of the peer group have been developed. Among these are effective cocurricular programs, personal adjustment classes, and guidance programs.

Sex behavior and adjustment are often vexatious aspects of socialization. The sex urge, with its physical and psychological aspects, is denied immediate gratification by our moral code. Most adolescents observe the moral code and suffer no negative consequences in so doing. This is particularly true of the upper educational and social classes. Heterosexual activity becomes quite apparent in dating activities. Here boys and girls continue the lessons relating to their sex role and appropriate behavior. Petting is an almost inevitable aspect of dating in the later teen years. It, *per se,* is not dangerous but it may and sometimes does lead to unwanted intercourse. For the most part girls have the responsibility of seeing that petting is neither habitual nor prolonged. They must realize that petting is most effective in attracting and holding boy friends when it is rationed with extreme care.

The practice of premarital intercourse receives sanction from those who seek to rationalize their own deviant conduct. While large numbers of teen agers do have premarital intercourse, the norm and mores call for continence. Many seem to escape the danger involved in premarital coitus, but many do not. Since there are no proven advantages and many disadvantages—including the fact that premarital coitus is morally wrong—adults have the responsibility of presenting the hazards of violating the mores. Among the disadvantages are the danger of disease, pregnancy, and abortion; the establishment of habits and attitudes inimical to marital adjustment; the disintegration of personality; and the fact that it violates the code of our major religions—Protestantism, Catholicism, and Judaism. The major defenses of chastity are the steps leading to the fulfillment of other phases of healthy socialization. Friendships, peer adjustments, and premarital continence are symptoms of the wholesome personality development of adolescents.

STUDY AND REVIEW ITEMS

1. In what ways have the changing concepts of the feminine role made additional problems for adolescents?

2. What might be done in the school, that is not now being done or is being done inadequately, to facilitate socialization during the adolescent period?

3. Think of some adolescent you have known for some time and discuss the extent to which he or she approximates the phases of socialization described in the text.

4. Do you, or do you not, agree with F. E. Williams' statement that if heterosexuality is not established in the adolescent years it will never be normally achieved.

5. How do you think parents and teachers should react to "puppy love" affairs in order to be the greatest aid to the adolescent?

6. How do you think parents should act in the face of the prestige accorded to peer groups by their children?

7. What differences do you think should prevail in the dating practices of early adolescence as contrasted to later adolescence?

8. Discuss with your classmates the attitudes that should prevail toward petting. How could your conclusions and recommendations be most effectively presented to high school groups?

9. What is the consensus of ten of your classmates (not in the adolescence class with you) regarding premarital sex relations?

10. Do you think it is possible to separate enjoyable sex relations from affection? What would be the result of such separation for the girl? for the boy?

11. If some of your acquaintances have had premarital sexual relationships, what factors do you think contributed to their actions?

RECOMMENDED SUPPLEMENTARY READING

Fields, Morey R.; Goldberg, Jacob A.; and Kilander, Holger F. *Youth Grows into Adulthood* (New York: Chartwell House, Inc.; 1951).
    This book is addressed to adolescents and offers sound suggestions for social development, heterosexual adjustment, and selection of a marriage partner. Teachers and counselors will find practical help in the book.

Havighurst, Robert J., and Taba, Hilda. *Adolescent Character and Personality* (New York: John Wiley and Sons, Inc.; 1949), pp. 70–81.
    This selection describes how adolescents shape their hopes and goals on the basis of adult types in the community. In addition to citing the data from certain studies, it shows how the process of socialization can be studied.

Hollingshead, A. B. *Elmtown's Youth* (New York: John Wiley and Sons, Inc.; 1949), pp. 148–162, 204–243.
    These chapters show how social classes and the varied values held by the classes shape the friendships and dating practices of adolescents. Answers to dilemmas are not given, but teachers and counselors may become more aware of the problems they face by reading Hollingshead.

Kuhlen, Raymond G., and Lee, Beatrice J. "Personality Characteristics and Social Acceptability in Adolescence," *Journal of Educational Psychology*, 34; 1943, 321–340.
    This article describes the emerging adolescent interest in the other sex. The problems which this interest, and others, present are described. Personality traits of popular and unpopular individuals are presented. Changes of personality and interest with increasing age are charted.

Seidman, Jerome M. (Ed.) *The Adolescent: A Book of Readings* (New York: The Dryden Press, Inc.; 1953), pp. 492–522.

Four selections deal with (1) The Sex Information of Younger Boys, (2) How to Be a Woman, (3) Dating Behavior of College Students, and (4) A Slum Sex Code. All are substantial contributions to understanding adolescents' knowledge of and attitudes toward sex and sex activity.

AUDIO-VISUAL MATERIAL

How To Be Well Groomed (Coronet Films, Coronet Building, Chicago 1), 10 min., so., b. and w. or color.

The film demonstrates how favorable impressions are created by good health, good posture, personal cleanliness, and neatness. Implications for personal and vocational success are depicted.

Social-Sex Attitudes in Adolescence (McGraw-Hill Book Company, Inc., 330 West 42nd Street, New York 36), 22 min., so., b. and w.

A boy and girl are followed through their early education in sex, their first awareness of the other sex, dating behavior, and finally mate selection and marriage. There are excellent suggestions for adolescents regarding their heterosexual problems.

Part Four

CONTINUATION OF THE
MATURING PROCESSES

ADOLESCENCE has been defined as growth toward maturity. The time at which maturity is reached has not been, and probably cannot be, precisely located. Hence it is to be expected that in a sequential study of adolescence, a point will be reached when mature behaviors begin to overrule adolescent behaviors. Part Four of this book considers some of the points at which adolescence and adulthood most obviously overlap. It is included here (1) because those working with adolescents need to see maturing as a continuous process and (2) because the material represents goals for directing the help given to adolescents.

The average age at the time of marriage is steadily decreasing and now stands at about twenty-three years for men and twenty years for women. Many are being married at still younger ages. These younger persons need help in marital adjustment, and older persons could profit from it. Chapter Fifteen presents some data on, and some suggestions for improving, the institution of marriage. Stress is placed on the fact that marital maturing continues after the marriage ceremony.

Vocational adjustment begins early in the adolescent years—very early for some. In an area as important as life work, it is disheartening to know that so few people give consideration to *work as a way of life*. More abundant maturing will result if more persons navigate, rather than drift, through their occupational life. Chapter Sixteen presents some guiding concepts in the realm of vocational orientation.

The great aim of life in a democracy is to produce citizens who contribute to the welfare of their fellows and in so doing enrich their own lives. Chapter Seventeen shows how the goal of citizenship can more frequently be achieved. Failures do occur, however. The opposite of citizenship—delinquency—is studied to get further light on processes of cultural maturing.

The final chapter selects from the entire book those suggestions that have bearing not only upon the adolescent's present adjustment but also upon his future. Successful adolescence is a preface to continuing processes of maturing.

CHAPTER FIFTEEN

Establishing Their Own Homes

Many people still in their teen years get married. They begin one of the most difficult and intimate of relationships with relatively little preparation. The fact that marriage is an ancient institution does not endow successive generations with the wisdom of the ages. The study of marriage should be as integral a part of the study of adolescence as is the study of vocational adjustment or citizenship. Even though many people are not married during their second decade, the dreams, ideals, and attitudes that will condition the success or failure of their marriages are being formed. These young men and women too need to contemplate the problems of marriage.

The earlier an individual leaves school the greater is his chance for early marriage. In fact many youngsters leave school so they can get married—or because they did get married. Those who leave school to work gain the feeling of independence that leads them to consider the possibility of assuming family responsibilities. Hence, if wise counsel is to be afforded many young people it must be in

---

What can be done to prepare youth for successful marriage? Can falling in love be done intelligently? What factors make one a desirable "risk" in marriage?

the early years of the secondary school. Some adults object to such study because they fear it will "put ideas" into the heads of adolescents. It is to be hoped that the study of marriage will do just that— but that the ideas will be correct and sound, rather than the type that are permeated by misconceptions. If by "ideas" the apprehensive ones mean early marriage, they might be reassured to learn that those who have the greatest amount of formal education about marriage probably get married at a higher average age. This chapter deals with some of the considerations that may serve to enhance the probability of happy adjustment to family life.

It should be recognized that marriage is more than a private contract between two individuals. The customs of society and economic conditions also play significant roles. Ultimately, happier marriages depend upon the over-all improvement of our culture. However, problems are conditioned by the attitude that is taken toward them. The building of more constructive attitudes is the major concern at this point.

The marital situation

Fundamentally, marriage is the union of husband and wife. The word usually calls to mind the social sanction of such a union by the church or civil authorities. Common law marriages, after the passage of time, are also recognized despite not having been sanctioned through any formal ceremony. Marriages also differ in the strength of the union. Some people marry with the idea that their relationship can and must endure all hazards. Other marriages are contracted with the idea that if blazing romance does not continue the union will be dissolved. This latter attitude has led to the term "tandem marriage." Further complexity might be introduced by studying marriage institutions outside our own country, but the ramifications will be great enough if confined to marriage in the United States.

Ideally, marriage can be an institution for the enrichment and fulfillment of the human personality. It can help to satisfy the fundamental needs for security and significance, the needs to love and be loved, as well as to satisfy physiological drives. A successful marriage is positively correlated with success in a profession or occupation. It is the usual accompaniment of productive citizenship (there

is a disproportionately large number of bachelors in penitentiaries).
Married people live longer—some wags say it just seems longer, but
statistics support the contention. All in all, marriage is an institution
that holds great potentialities for the enrichment of the human personality. However, these rewards, like other important values, are
enhanced by study, preparation, and devoted work.

The popularity of marriage

A great deal is written about the decay and breakdown of the
family. In fact, some have become so alarmed that they have suggested some substitutes for monogamous marriage—trial marriages,
companionate marriages, and (in Russia) the abolition of marriage.* These suggestions call to mind the alarmist crys about adolescents going to the dogs, mentioned in earlier chapters. The fact
is that more and more people are getting married. In 1890 about
54 per cent of the males over fifteen years of age were married.
In 1950 68 per cent of the males in this age bracket were married.
In 1890 57 per cent of the women were married but in 1950 over
67 per cent were married. [10:17] Furthermore, the average age at
the time of marriage is dropping. Thus marriage, in spite of the
fears for it, is becoming increasingly popular.

It must be admitted, however, that there are some soiled spots
on the marital record. The large number of divorces indicates that
all is not well; but even here something seems to be attractive about
marriage since three-fourths of those who get divorces remarry
within a period of five years.

Age at the time of marriage

Girls are permitted, in some states, to marry at the age of twelve
and boys at the age of fourteen if they have their parents' consent.
The highest specified age for the male's marrying in any state is
eighteen and for girls it is sixteen. Not only is early marriage permitted but the permission is used—in 1950 there were over
250,000 boys and girls between the ages of fourteen and seventeen
who were, or had been, married. Since 1890 the average age of marriage has dropped four years to 22.8 years for men and has dropped

---

* A few years of experimentation have convinced the Russian leaders that the
state may not be the best institution for child rearing, and they have lately stressed
the restitution of marriage.

two years to 20.3 for women. In other words, more than half the men who ever marry do so before they are twenty-three and more than half the women do so before the age of twenty-one. However, the wide prevalence and increasing popularity of early marriage does not indicate that it is a wise procedure.

Of course, it cannot be stated categorically that it is disadvantageous to marry early. Someone will pertinently remark that it depends upon the individuals who are doing the marrying. Generally speaking, though, more marriages contracted before the age of twenty are broken by divorce and separation than when the marriage is consummated after the age of twenty. There are proportionally five times as many mothers who die in childbirth between the ages of ten and fourteen as between twenty and twenty-four. Again, generally speaking, it would seem wise to advise young people to delay the gratification of their sex desires and spend their teen years in the heterosexual social contacts that foster a more mature personality. It seems to be a matter of "Do you want a dime today or a dollar a month from now?" Presumably the mature person chooses time and the bigger dividend.

Since individuals and circumstances differ, it is not possible to prescribe an optimum age for marriage. It can be stated that too long a delay of marriage entails certain hazards. Marriages contracted after the age of thirty, for either spouse, tend to be somewhat less stable than those occurring while the couples are in their twenties. [306] Furthermore, the longer a person delays marriage after the middle twenties the less chance there is of ever getting married.

The breakdown of marriage

The perennial cry of "the breakdown of civilization" is sounded again when statistics on divorce are studied. The popularity of divorce is increasing more rapidly than is the popularity of marriage. In 1890 there were 6.5 divorces per 100 marriages while in 1950 there were 22.1 divorces per 100 marriages. [60] The ratio of one divorce out of every four marriages is widely accepted. The usual reaction to this statistic is that something should be done about it: tighten marriage laws, tighten divorce laws, enact uniform legislation. No doubt there are some inconsistencies and absurdities in present statutes, but the real problem is one of doing something in terms of better preparation for marriage. No one has proven that marriages are less happy or less satisfactory today than they were in 1890. Today people are less inclined, because of changed attitudes toward the role of women and the greater emphasis upon the pursuit of happiness, to live with their mistakes. In 1890 divorce was disgraceful; today it is regarded as disappointing. Smaller divorce statistics do not indicate that the marriages of 1890 were more successful than are contemporary marriages.

There are gold diggers for whom divorce is the culmination of a successful campaign and alimony is a one-man war debt. But for most couples divorce means heartache and frustration. Statistics are often people, and we might well heed the roadside sign, "Slow down before you become a statistic." Some of the problems and frustrations that accompany divorce (and other forms of broken marriage) are the heartbreak of losing someone for whom deep attachment has been formed, the feeling of failure in one of the major activities of life, the cessation of sex gratification (or often the substitution of sex activities that are much less satisfying), financial cost, including the cost of the divorce and the breaking up of a household, the burden of alimony if it is awarded, and the loss of mutual friends. Without doubt the greatest cost, and the one that most concerns society, is the effect upon children. Ideally a child should have, in order to be conditioned to his own sex role, the guidance of two parents. The emotional strain attendant upon the preliminaries of the divorce as well as the actual breakup is acutely felt by children. It is small wonder that children with problems at school, truants, and delinquents so frequently come from broken homes.

As is the case with delinquency, there are no readily isolated causes for divorce but there are many contributing factors. An examination of some of the factors which seem to impel couples toward divorce and separation might help some young people be less precipitous in their marital decisions.

Each state has a long list of grounds for divorce, and no doubt the items listed are frequently contributing factors. But the most important item is not named; that is, personality inadequacy or personality immaturity. Some of the grounds—infidelity, incompatability, cruelty, alcoholism, act of felony, indignity, and the like

—suggest this important factor. The study of psychology and mental hygiene should warn us that the grounds mentioned are not fortuitous or accidental; they are simply identifiable steps along the path of general personal inadequacy. Love is not blind; rather the lover sees things in the loved one that are not easily perceived by others. Young people might well use their acute vision to see in their dates the qualities that are symptoms of inadequacy: jealousy, resentment against parents, excessive rationalization of defects, projection, absence of goals, disdain for law and authority, lack of confidence. They should seek such qualities as respect of peers, respect for the wisdom of adults, adherence to law and authority, ambition, ability to shoulder blame and responsibility, and reverence.* The prevalence of the personality factor is indicated by Dr. Emily H. Mudd's list of six reasons why marriages fail: (1) Overdependence on parents. (2) Failure to achieve personal independence. (3) Inability to give as well as to take. (4) Ignoring the partner's needs and feelings. (5) Failure to talk things over. (6) Major differences in attitudes toward religion, children, finances, sex, and jobs. [285]

"Failure to provide" is grounds for, and in some cases cause for, divorce or separation. Contrary to popular belief, however, the lack of finances is not a major cause for divorce or of unhappiness in marriage. True, there are more broken homes in the lower socio-economic brackets, and inadequate funds do break some homes; but in most instances the home is also plagued by many other problems, including the personality inadequacy of one or both of the spouses. After a minimum income has been provided there is no increase in either the stability or happiness of the home as the higher income levels are reached. This leads to the justifiable statement of Ray E. Baber that it is not the income so much as the attitude toward money that counts. [10:228] Love does not conquer all; and prospective couples must steer their way between the extremes (1) of thinking that the bride must live in the manner to which she has become accustomed (a twenty-some year struggle by her parents), and (2) of thinking that people can change the habits and desires that have been forming for twenty years.

---

* A number of behaviors that may be used as a preliminary check list are contained in Lewis M. Terman, *Psychological Factors in Marital Happiness* (New York: McGraw-Hill Book Company, Inc.; 1938), pp. 96–100.

Young people should give serious thought to differences in background. Differences in religion, in ideals, in socio-economic background, have contributed to the breakup of many homes. Despite having talked things over—church attendance and support, children's choice of attendance—many couples have found the barriers between Catholics, Protestants, and Jews too great. Many have solved, and very successfully, the problems of inter-faith marriage, but it is still wise to recommend that young people give themselves the chance to fall in love with someone who shares their own faith. The situation is similar with regard to socio-economic differences. With all the problems that must be daily and perennially solved to gain optimum satisfaction from marriage, it is highly questionable to deliberately add problems of religion, race, and wide socio-economic differences.

The need for instruction

Young people should know that marriages are not made in heaven. Satisfactory marriage is the result of a continuous process of adaptation. It is a creation rather than a discovery. That the "made in heaven" concept is extant is indicated by the frequently asked question, "How do I know when I'm really in love?" and the answer, "You'll know when you find *the* right one." Both question and answer are based on false premises. In successful marriage each partner "falls" progressively more in love with the passage of years, until thoughts, plans, ideals, work, and recreation automatically include the spouse. The "right one" concept must be inadequate on the basis of statistics. There are probably dozens of men or women, out of even the limited number a young person is likely to meet, with whom happiness could be achieved if he or she did not think that the first clash of interest was an indication of not yet having found the "right one."

Another misconception has to do with the idea that the woman should be younger than or about the same age as the man. Studies show that there is some tendency for the marriage to be more stable when the wife is older. [122] Why the wife who is older than her husband should be happier and have a happier husband is somewhat puzzling. Perhaps it is because women reach the peak of sexual desires at a later age than do men. [172:353] Hence the marriage of an older woman to a younger man may mean the closer matching of sexual desires. On the other hand, it may simply be a matter of the greater maturity of both mates—since a woman in her twenties would be unlikely to marry a teen-age boy.

There is much discussion as to whether marriage mates should have the same traits (supplementary) or opposite traits (complementary). "Experts" line up on both sides. The consequence is that the young persons are bewildered since this seems to be a point of real importance. They may be reassured to know that both groups of experts have research data to support their contention. The answer depends upon what the spouses want and need. Some may want an intimate companionship and moral support for word and action. Others may want to maintain independence of action and choice of goals but may want to share the joy of knowing that there is someone who loves and cares. However, the answer can be still more definitive. Whether the couple has traits that are supplementary or complementary is probably much less important than the fact that the traits should be ones that indicate maturity of personality.

The need for instruction is especially evident in the matter of sex adjustments. Some women have been married for years without knowing that women can and do experience orgasm. Some people believe that women can keep from becoming pregnant if they do not respond erotically during coitus. Baber relates a case in which a college girl, attending a class in which sex and intercourse were described, became hysterical and cried, "My parents never did that!" [10:243] She, however, was no more ignorant than the woman who went to a doctor to find why she did not get pregnant; and the doctor found that her hymen was not ruptured. The wisdom of the street is evidently not sufficiently accurate, thorough, or extensive.

Courtship

Being the right mate

While the bulk of the work involved in making marriage a success will come in the years after the performance of the ceremony, the work could be lightened and some failure averted if advantage were taken of the courtship period. It seems unfortunate to the author that so much of the literature is devoted to finding the right mate. Articles and textbooks emphasize the qualities to search for in the prospective spouse. It would be more fruitful, because something can be done about it now, if more attention were directed to *being* the right person. A man might be successful in finding the dream mate only to discover, after prolonged endeavor, that he is vying with a more competent pursuer. If he had developed the characteristics that would make a good marriage mate, those qualities would still be present even after a normal two or three heartbreaks. Furthermore, the emphasis on *finding* the right mate is fundamentally selfish—a quality that is deemed hazardous to marriage. The emphasis on *being* the right one is altruistically oriented—an asset to marriage felicity.

It would be difficult to list the personality qualities that should be developed in order to be a good marriage risk, but some of the things that might be emphasized to high school and college youth will include the following: ability to get along with parents; ability to get along with peers of the same sex; the habit of listening to the counsel of others; adherence to ethical, legal, and moral codes; a well defined system of values (industry, concern for others, faith, and the like); varied interests in both work and play; varied acquaintanceship with persons of the other sex; a healthy interest in, and attitude toward, sex; the ability to recover from disappointment; good physical health habits; active participation in religion; and the enjoyment of daily living. [22:395] These are suggestive, not inclusive, and each individual should add to the list in terms of his experience and needs.

Avoidance of major differences

Adolescents will always be able to point out instances in which major differences—race, religion, and social level—have been successfully reconciled. But the fact that love does not conquer all is indicated by the ratio of divorce when attempts to span the differences have been made. Mention has already been made of marriage of persons of different faiths and socio-economic class which present difficulties because of life-long habits of thinking and acting that cannot be dispelled by discussion. The situation is similar with persons of different races. However, race differences are often rather superficial ones of color or texture of hair. Some Negroes and Japanese, for example, have the same thoughts, ideals, and habits of whites of the same socio-economic status. Intermarriage could be satisfactory (and actually has advantages biologically) if it were not for the attitude of society. Men and women must continue to live in society and the prejudices that are held by both white people and those with pigmented skin must be taken into account. A complete marriage will result in children and the children will very probably suffer, even if both parents are emotionally mature enough to forgive others for their lack of compassion. These generalizations hold particularly for the conditions prevailing in the United States. For a resident of Argentina, France, or Hawaii (for example) race differences would not need to be considered major.

Length of courtship

There are two schools of thought regarding the length of courtship, with research to support both sides. L. M. Terman found that there is little relationship between marital happiness and length of premarital acquaintance. E. W. Burgess and L. S. Cottrell found that the proportion of well adjusted marriages increased with the length of premarital acquaintance up to ten years as contrasted with couples who had known each other six months or less. [52:164]

The statistical evidence favoring long courtship must be based on some factual advantages.* Among those commonly listed is time to get to know the other's interests, personality traits, and health. But since the longer one person knows another the more likely he is to overlook deficiencies it becomes difficult to understand why this factor works as it does. Probably a major advantage of prolonged courtship lies in the fact that both persons are growing older and will usually be gaining in personality stability. Probably the greatest advantage of the prolonged period of courtship is that one partner can get to know the parents of the other. If the parents are happy in marriage there is a good chance that the attitudes and habits of the prospective spouse will favor marital felicity. All in all it seems that the prolonged courtship period is based on the premise that each man or woman must find the right mate. If the emphasis is on

---

* The reader is advised to beware of the author's bias in favor of early marriage (that is, in the early twenties) and minimum courtships.

being the right mate, another evaluation of the long courtship seems in order.

The statistics that show the advantage of long courtship do not tell how many engagements that might have become happy marriages have been broken off. It is probable that many couples "break up" because of frustration that is the fault of neither. While sex is far from being everything in a happy marriage, it must still be admitted that sex, and the gratification of sex desires, is a very integral part of the relationships of man and woman. This is particularly true in the early years of maturity. It is difficult to imagine that two young persons could go with one another for years without becoming increasingly familiar. The increased familiarity increases sex desires, and unless they are gratified both people are frustrated. Not realizing the true source of the frustration each blames the other for inadequacies that really do not exist, and they decide that they should find more suitable partners. This may, of course, have the advantage of providing experience and may make one a little more tolerant the next time he falls in love. If the couple decides to relieve the tension by having premarital intercourse the danger is perhaps increased. The back-seat-of-the-car or motel variety of coitus is simply an "outlet," marred by fear, hesitancy, and haste, and does not give a sample of the satisfactions of intercourse enjoyed by a couple acting in accord with the professed sanctions of society. Further, doubt does arise concerning the fidelity of the partner, doubt that may precipitate the parting of an otherwise admirable couple. Each goes his way, sadder, wiser, and less marriageable (Terman found that the happiness score of both men and women virgins was higher than those with sexual experience [307:325] and Kinsey found that women with premarital sexual experience were twice as likely to be unfaithful during marriage as were the virgins. [172:427])

Another disadvantage of the prolonged courtship is the reduction of chances to meet others of the opposite sex. Studies have been made that show that boys who have been seriously in love four or five times make better husbands than do those who have loved just the one and only.

It may be that it is not the long courtship that contributes to the happier marriage but a combination of other factors. A long courtship means that the couple is older and more mature. It means that they are willing to postpone the gratification of their desires and are hence fundamentally more stable than those who enter precipitously into marriage. It is likely that those who take the longer course are fundamentally more cautious and analytical about their problems.

If it were possible to use good sense about the matter of falling in love instead of subscribing to the fallacy of romantic love depicted on the screen, there are some words of wisdom that could be given to the adolescent. High school boys and girls should be advised to study the variety and types of attractive personalities. They might then see that it is quite important that they *be* the right person. They should be advised that friendships with several boys and girls will do more to build personality than will the limitation of experience. There is the possibility that unless planned decisions are made with regard to degree of intimacy, there is a danger of an amount of intimacy that would offset the advantages of longer courtship. The advice for those in college might be somewhat different. Waiting for post-college days will greatly restrict the marriage market. There is less need for prolonging courtship than in high school because of the greater maturity of the couples. This would mean that college people might well form their decisions on periods of acquaintance of less than a year, instead of waiting a year or two and then having to start all over again, or of then suddenly deciding that the match was about as good as could be hoped for.

Baber [10:134] asserts that if mistakes in the courtship period are to be avoided young people must use their heads early; he points out five potential sources of error: (1) Belief in the "one person" theory may lead to a fruitless search for the perfect mate. The truth is that there are probably many persons who could be the right person if the emphasis were on building a marriage rather than upon discovering a "perfect" union. (2) The falling in love misconception may lead an individual to mistake the response to the physical attractiveness of another for something more essential. The fact is that the flaming passion of youth should normally and desirably settle into the steady glow of mutual trust, companionship, and acceptance, which underlies the really successful marriage. (3) The misinterpretation of sex attractiveness for love may precipitate a risky marriage. Sex appeal before and after marriage is important, but divorce statistics show that sex is not able to span the chasm of personality inadequacy. Satisfactory sex relations (not sexual outlets) are dependent upon the daily compatability of personality. (4) Undue emphasis upon one personality trait of the loved one may lead to two errors. One is the overlooking of important character defects; and the other is the overlooking of strong points because of concentration upon a disliked quality. "He is two years younger than I," "He's too short for me," or "His jaw muscles grind when he chews," are examples. (5) Narrowing the field of search too early may be a factor that limits personality growth. Going with several friends will show that there is the possibility of learning to love several persons and will also help to develop necessary skills in getting along with others.

Husband-wife relationships

The difficulty of a problem is partially dependent upon the view taken of it. As is suggested by the foregoing material, the success of marriage is dependent upon many factors—not the least of which is maturity and stability of personality. This section deals with a very limited number of factors that function in marital satisfaction.

Making the marriage work

There can be no doubt that some marriages should be terminated for the mutual good of both spouses, and sometimes a divorce will result in improvement of a situation for one. On the other hand, the success of courts of domestic relations, which attempt to solve difficulties instead of permitting escape from them, indicates the enhancement of success when an effort is made. In short, it would be well if young people were advised not to jump hastily to the conclusion that their marriage is a failure but rather to take the attitude that they are going to make it work if effort and patience can make it work. As one divorcee put it, "When I found that I was not in a continued state of ecstasy, I thought I was miserable." Her rueful remark indicated not only intolerance for difficulty but adherence to an early adolescent concept of love.

Except in the Hollywood and Hans Christian Andersen version of wedded bliss it is probably quite normal for the newly married to wonder if they have not made a mistake, if it would not have been advisable to have married an earlier sweetheart, or if they could not find better mates on another try. Yet after a period of years characterized by conflict, anger, disappointment, and regret alternated with periods of joy and satisfaction they gradually realize that their thoughts have merged, their ideals have become similar, and their actions have become coordinated to such an extent that no conscious thought is given to we, us, and ours. One partner's thoughts of self are automatically inclusive of both.

The wife as a worker

Adolescent lack of realism about marriage is sometimes shared by the adult who wants his daughter supported in the manner to which she has become accustomed—forgetting that it took him some twenty or thirty years to build the custom. The young married couple sometimes attempts to achieve this by having the woman work. Especially is this true if the woman has been educated and has ambition for a career. The couple may plan to have the wife work only until they "get started," but they find that the woman's participation as an earner becomes essential. In fact, one-third of all employed workers in 1950 were women, and half of these were married—with the percentage of married workers increasing yearly. [354]

It must be admitted that there are sometimes reasons why women must work, but quite often the consideration is one of apparent convenience rather than necessity. If it is possible to get along without the woman's working (exceptions might include a husband's illness or injury or extended education) there are a number of disadvantages that can be said to accrue from the wife's employment. One is simply the matter of tradition—perhaps the man needs the satisfaction of feeling that he can support his family. Doing it alone builds his ego feelings and renders him more competent in the home and on the job. Added to this is the fact that a woman suffers no feelings of disgrace because she chooses to make her career that of homemaker. Second, it becomes easy to get used to living on an income that the husband alone cannot earn, thus it seems to be essential that the wife work. This may mean the postponement of having children; and while there is no guarantee that having children will prevent divorce, the fact is that there are fewer divorces among those who have children. (This, however, may simply be a matter of not yet having had time to have children since the peak incidence of divorces occurs within two years after marriage.) Third, it places quite a strain on a woman to carry on the double job of homemaking and a career with real competence. This strain may have the result of reducing satisfaction from marriage even though the lack of continuous contact may avert the extreme of divorce. Fourth, the effect of the mother's working is a poor influence on children. Of course, just bearing a child does not make a woman a good mother; but the usual occurrence with the working mother is a succession of nursemaids or baby-sitters, which has a poor psychological influence on the child. Any or all of the hired mother-substitutes may be good, but the frequency of change is a hazard. Fifth, progressively high tax rates on higher incomes may result in a very low net gain from the wife's working. It has been asserted by some that the wife's job is really an expensive luxury. [198]

If the young people could make definite plans about the wife's working and stick to them, there are some sound approaches to the problem: (1) Set a definite length of time that the wife will work — and decide on no exceptions "for the sake of convenience." (2) Decide upon certain articles that will be purchased with her income: refrigerator, stove, bedroom set, but not a rapidly depreciating article like a car. (3) Plan for the wife to work until the husband has completed his education.

Sex factors in marital adjustment

At some time in his education, either at home or in school, the adolescent needs to have instruction about the proper role of sex in family life. Sexual adjustment in marriage is admittedly the cornerstone to successful marriage, but it is not the entire structure. The report that sexual adjustment is so satisfactory that personality inadequacies of both parties can be overlooked does not accord with the findings of most authorities. [321:246] Edward J. Stieglitz confirms the importance of sex in marriage but goes on to say:

> But sex alone will not hold marriages together. Not today, when life expectancy far exceeds the normal termination of sexual vigor. Centuries ago, when the mores of marriage were first laid down, few partners survived beyond an age of active sexual hunger, or long beyond the time when their children needed both parents. Today we are faced with a much longer life expectancy.
>
> Lasting happiness in marriages is not fortuitous. It results from planned cultivation, persistent effort, and vigorous self-discipline. Mental companionship and mutual mental stimulation are the adhesive and the ferment which keep marriage a joy and an adventure forever. Mental companionship is predicated upon mutual esteem. If two people do not mature together, if one grows and one stands still, there develops a chasm between them, a chasm which becomes ever wider and deeper and which ultimately not even sex can bridge. To think is to grow and in growing we live.*

Alfred C. Kinsey [172:567] has provided some information that suggests the possibility of obtaining greater satisfaction from sex relations in marriage. There are differences in the response of male and female; but to a much greater extent than was formerly thought, there are many likenesses. Women, as do men, respond to cultural expectation; and in our culture it has been thought that a woman was unladylike to evince sexual interest, while for a man not to do so was an indication of lack of masculinity. It now seems that women are physiologically as capable of erotic arousal, as capable of rapid orgasm, as are men. However, the role of culture is not to be swept aside with a few words. The fact remains that women *are psychologically different* from men because of cultural conditioning. Hence it is only after years of experience that some women cast off the notion of shamefulness and show the interest in sex that men have shown ten or twelve years earlier. It is a difficult problem for women to have to prize their chastity for about twenty years and then, after the few spoken words of a minister or civil authority, to become markedly amorous.

---

* Edward J. Stieglitz, *The Second Forty Years* (Philadelphia: J. B. Lippincott Company; 1946), pp. 208–209.

Both man and wife would do well to consider the feelings and the satisfaction of the other. Concentration on this, during the sex act, would mean that men would less abruptly seek "release." They would spend the time in foreplay that would tend to make the wife seek the satisfaction of her husband instead of regarding coitus as a rather disgusting duty. If kind words have been spoken during the day, if the couple has worked together about the house, with the children, in the yard, the wife is more ready to respond and is more likely to experience orgasm. There are large individual differences in the speed with which orgasm is reached by males, but in general it is true that rapid ejaculation is a goal of males in the lower classes. While women are almost as capable of reaching speedy orgasm as are men [172:163] slower orgasm by men means that they are probably giving more thought to the woman's satisfaction; thus the chance is better that mutual orgasm will be achieved. These data indicate two lessons that should be learned: (1) men should practice the withholding of ejaculation and (2) more attention should be given to psychological factors.

Terman [307:272] has presented data to show that the man's frequency of "preferred" intercourse is higher than that of his "reported" intercourse while the woman's preferred and reported frequency of intercourse is about the same. This difference is probably due to age differences—the man usually being older, so that women have had insufficient time to throw off the inhibitions with which they have lived so many years. But whatever the cause, the man can learn an important lesson—he had better get used to the woman's setting the pattern for frequency of intercourse. Again we come back to the matter of concern for the partner's feelings. Incidentally, this mutual concern will result in greater satisfaction for both partners and has the possibility of resulting in increasing frequency of intercourse.

Let it be repeated that sex is not the *most* important factor in marriage though it is important and receives a great deal of attention in the literature on marriage. However, three things point to greater sex satisfaction: (1) the giving of sincere attention to personality factors, (2) the man's taking more time before and during the sex act, and (3) *graciously* permitting the wife to set the pattern of frequency—which, it seems, she will do anyway.

Factors in marital happiness

The foregoing discussion has dealt with sex factors in marital happiness; there are some additional considerations that should be taken into account. These are important because they point the way to the removal of certain misunderstandings and some inadequate understandings.

Happiness of parents

Terman states: "Our theory is that what comes out of a marriage depends upon what goes into it and among the most important things going into it are the attitudes, preferences, aversions, habit patterns, and emotional-response patterns which give or deny to one the aptitude for compatibility." * In the light of this statement it is not surprising to find that an important background factor in marriage is the happiness of parents. It is not that happiness is an inherited trait but that children have a chance to develop the habit of happiness if their parents set the pattern. Moreover, they have a chance to see and learn the important attitude of give-and-take which conditions happiness of parents or the younger generation. Those who would seek to use their brains as well as their hearts to create a satisfactory marriage might well look into the happiness of the loved one's parents. There is the chance, however, that unhappiness in parents could have the effect of making the young person be all the more determined to make his marriage work. Even so, it would be well to recognize and discuss the hazards of an unsatisfactory example.

In addition to the happiness of parents, Terman lists a number of other items that are closely associated: A happy childhood is indicative of the capacity to make marital happiness. This may be detected by the young person's watching to see if the reminiscences of the loved one are pleasant or are of a complaining nature. Lack of conflict with the mother and father is a background correlate of happiness in marriage. Home discipline that was firm but not harsh also points to satisfactory marriage. However, this is depend-

---

* By permission from *Psychological Factors in Marital Happiness*, by Lewis M. Terman. Copyright 1938, McGraw-Hill Book Company, Inc. P. 110.

ent both on personality stability and the situation involving discipline.

For those whose home background was unfavorable all hope need not be abandoned. Many learn from their parents what *not* to do. One girl of divorced parents said, "I'm all the more determined to make my marriage a successful one." But such persons need to be warned of their additional task so that they may place additional emphasis on a continuous program for developing in themselves the qualities for being a good mate.

Sex education as a background factor

There is a growing consensus that sex in our culture is as much a matter of psychology as it is of physiology. This realization is reflected in the fact that the amount of sex instruction by parents is steadily increasing, especially among the better educated. Adequate instruction tends to prevent some of the disgust and aversion toward sex that limit the probability of connubial bliss. Among the factors that are deemed to be helpful are the following:

1. Parents should be frank about matters of sex and information should be begun in early childhood. While the amount of detail that should be given will vary with age it should be realized that a preschool child can receive the information without emotional shock because sex and sex organs are no more, or no less, interesting than other parts of his anatomy.

2. All the child's questions should be answered fully. He will ask no more and absorb no more than he is capable of comprehending. But the main thing is to keep the way open to the discussion of progressively more intimate details.

3. During adolescence, if the questions are too difficult for the parent, he should admit his lack of information and suggest that they become learners together.

4. Sex instruction should include information about the organs and functions of both sexes regardless of the sex of the child. Both sexes should be taught to be proud of their sex. Among other things this would include refraining from teasing a boy about his first shaves and his changing voice. It will mean that mothers should avoid referring to the menstruation as the "sick time" or the "curse." Perhaps it is indicative of a trend in the right di-

rection that girls wear sweaters that reveal their womanly curves and that boys are proud of their physique and muscles.

5. Sex instruction should emphasize the institution of marriage and reference should be made to the love of man and woman. Discussion of marriage should be an integral part of the discussion of the fulfillment of sex desires. If this were done some of the difficulty of transition from virginity to sex relations in marriage might be diminished. It should be realized that ideally preparation for marriage should be a planned part of development at all stages of life.

The need for a balanced perspective regarding sex is revealed in the following:

> Attempting to shut sex out of one's life does not raise one to a higher plane of existence, as some people suppose. It only relegates one to a more incomplete and more arid existence. In the last analysis, sex cannot be shut out. Whether it finds natural expression or not, no matter where it is put from one extreme of manifestation to the other, it will play a part in affecting the individual's life and must be taken into account. If it is repressed or avoided, it is still not without its effect. One may as well try to rule out metabolism.*

The role of physical health

The importance of personality as a factor in successful marriage has been stressed repeatedly—H. A. Bowman goes so far as to devote three of sixteen chapters on marriage to personality factors, and his discussion of sex is under the heading of personality. [37:280–367] A too frequently neglected factor in personality is physical health. A person would not go so far as to pick a mate because of good health but it might be wise, in view of the number of potential mates, to avoid the intimacy that leads to love and marriage if poor health exists. Marriage at best involves many adjustments and the health that conduces to patience, tolerance, and confidence is an item worth considering.

The desirability of health has implications for the individual adolescent. He should take care to observe the simple rules of health that are taught in the elementary school. Attention to diet is impor-

---

* By permission from *Marriage for Moderns,* 2nd Edition, by Henry A. Bowman. Copyright 1948, McGraw-Hill Book Company, Inc. Pp. 343–344.

tant during that time of physical development when the appetite is particularly demanding. The young man or woman should avoid the intemperate indulgence in candy bars, hamburgers, and soft drinks that will interfere with the eating of regular meals. Young people should be advised to get a sufficient amount (this will vary somewhat with the individual) of sleep on a rather regular schedule. Some of the irritability of adolescents may be traced to ignoring the need for recuperation of physical energy. They must be led to examine their activity schedules (academic, part-time work, and recreation) to see that rest and sleep are provided for. Physical activity, especially in the open air, is to be recommended for all—not just the athletes. Girls particularly should appreciate the changed mores that make the wallflower type less attractive to boys than the outdoor girl. The effect of drugs and tobacco upon health and personality should be the subject of discussion by and with adolescents.

Education for family life

Family life and the secondary school

Education for family life is primarily a parental responsibility. Even if there is no mention of family the church plays an important role in education for marriage because of the values that are ordinarily stressed. The community as a whole is concerned—the kind of opportunities provided for the development of adolescents will have direct bearing upon marital adjustment. The nation is also involved since the confusing and conflicting marriage and divorce laws of the various states condition the stability of the family. The school is perhaps less directly involved in marriage than is any other of the social groups mentioned above; nevertheless, the school is in the most advantageous position to bring about an improvement of the family situation for all those who are concerned.

It should be admitted that the direct study of family and marriage is not the only approach to improvement. All that has been previously said in this book about improving the mental health, physical health, and social adjustment of the adolescent has bearing on the marital adjustment of the individual. Still further, citizenship, marriage, and vocational adjustment (the concerns of Part Four) are outcomes of all the things discussed in other chapters.

A suggested course in human relations and family life

The American Social Hygiene Association has outlined a series of topics that might be treated as aspects of other courses. These topics indicate the breadth and ramifications of the subject. [230:10–20] The headings are reproduced here to show how inclusive the problems of marriage are and to stress the importance of providing competent teachers.

EDUCATION FOR HUMAN RELATIONS AND FAMILY LIFE

Objectives of the course: A. To help adolescents make personal adjustments. B. To help adolescents make family adjustments. C. To help adolescents meet social demands.

I. The family in a democracy: A. Early history of families. B. Differing personalities within families. C. Contributions of members to family. D. Contributions of the family to members. E. Role of both sexes in family life. F. Results of adolescent cooperation. G. Value of family councils. H. Value of adopted families for neglected children. I. Family living as democracy in action.

II. Problems of the adolescent as a member of the family: A. Mental growth and changes. B. Physical development. C. Emotional and social growth.

III. Boy-girl relations: A. Respect for the opposite sex. B. Normality of sex yearnings. C. Dating. D. Petting—"Wise or unwise"? E. "Going steady"—a step between friendly companionship and marriage. F. Reproduction on various levels.

IV. Marriage: A. Courting is a preliminary to marriage. B. Marriage customs. C. Divorce.

V. Problems in homemaking: A. Place of normal family in its relation to the community. B. Economics of the home. C. Labor unions' and trade organizations' effects upon the family. D. Culture of the home. E. Management of the home is a vital factor in happiness of the home. F. Child care.

VI. Social problems involving individual, family, and community: A. Securing social acceptance in accord with standards of family, school, church, and community. B. Results of an individual's "bucking" social convention. C. Common difficulties involved when marriage involves different races, religions, and nationalities. D. Individual responsibility to the next generation.

VII. Governmental and international problems for the betterment of mankind: A. Better housing. B. Reduction of maternal and infant mortality. C. Well-planned care and correction of defectives, delinquents, and dependents. D. Recreational facilities for youth to aid normal development. E. Medical science and the betterment of human beings. F. International phases of social hygiene.

There are some who feel that marriage and family relations should be taught as an integral part of other courses rather than as a separate high school course. Facts and their interpretation should be correlated with other subjects as much as possible. It is the author's feeling that marriage and family relations constitute such an important area in the adolescent's present adjustment and has such profound implications for his future effectiveness that splitting up instruction may not be the best plan. There is the risk of missing some of the significant areas and the risk that some of the instructors may not be emotionally prepared to present the information.

Who should teach the course

There is, of course, the possibility that adequately prepared teachers, both academically and in terms of personal adjustment, will be difficult to find. Some of the problems to be considered in selecting the teacher include the following:

1. It might be better to have a man teach the course so that it would have more appeal for boys. The girls are perhaps looking forward to marriage as an integral part of their future, and they know that men are very much a part of the family.
2. It would seem better to have a successfully married person teach the course, though this should not rule out the possibility of a single person's having both the emotional and academic qualifications for effective teaching.
3. There is the possibility that an older person, though happily married, whose own youth was in the era of reticence in discussing sex may not be emotionally prepared to discuss freely all the problems that arise.

4. It can be said without equivocation that the teacher should have high rapport with young people. Such rapport is based upon personal adjustment, a genuine liking for young persons, a sensitivity to their ideas and questions, and patience with their prejudices.

5. Probably the ideal choice would be a person with several years of happy marital experience who has studied recent trends and has a wholesome modern viewpoint. The qualifications for the ideal teacher are the same as for an ideal marriage: proper education, wholesome experience, and good mental health.

Introducing the course

As should be the case with all curricular innovations, there should be time devoted to the preparation of the citizens of the community for acceptance of the course. A series of meetings with interested parents and leaders in the community should be devoted to the discussion of the problems and probable difficulties. It might be well to have as a participant in these meetings an outsider from some nearby university, college, or social hygiene agency. Equally important, there should be someone who knows the prevailing sentiment of the community and who is also aware of who the key figures in the community are. Finally, youth themselves should have representatives on the planning group.

Questions to be considered include these: When is the course to be taught? Is it to be elective or required? Is it to be credit or non-credit? Should it be experimentally tried on post-school individuals? The leaders of introductory meetings should have definite ideas and plans as to what should be included in the course; *but* this does not mean that the program should be adopted. Rather the plans are to give something concrete to work *from* so that the ultimate plan is genuinely a community product.

Summary

The study of an institution that profoundly and almost universally affects the lives of young people, as does marriage, must be an integral part of the study of adolescence. Marriage can be a vital factor in the enrichment and fulfillment of the human personality. Despite recognized hazards, marriage is becoming increasingly popular; more and more people are getting married at younger ages. Among the more important hazards are the changing mores and the inadequacies of the personalities involved. Proper preparation and instruction can enhance the values of marital unions and avert or modify the dangers.

Attention should be directed to *being the right mate*—though the problem of selection should still be considered. Major differences in religion and race are hazards, but enough people have successfully bridged the differences so that it cannot be said that such marriages are doomed to failure. Courtship periods should be long enough to provide opportunity to permit the couple to know one another but not so long as to stimulate tensions which arise from the almost inevitable increase in the degree of intimacy.

Those who do marry should be determined to make their marriage work rather than to adopt the orientation that they will see how they fit as partners. Family income and the wife's working are important conditioning factors in the success of marriage. There is no clear consensus as to what a minimum income should be or whether or not the wife should be a wage earner; but there is some evidence that the attitude taken toward money should be considered along with dollars and cents. Sex is a fundamental consideration, but basic aspects of sex are so commonly shared by all people that sex satisfaction is ultimately traced to personality considerations rather than anatomy and physiology.

Important background factors for marital satisfaction are happiness of the parents, healthy attitudes toward sex engendered by adequate and wholesome instruction, and good physical health. These are by no means all of the important factors but research proves them to be among the more important.

The secondary school can do much to point the way to better adjustment in marriage by giving comprehensive courses of instruction. These would include the study of personality development, boy-girl relationships, and broad social problems as well as the obvious topics of marriage, sex, and economics in the home. The broadness of the course indicates that, in the final analysis, helping to make better homes for today's adolescents is a responsibility that must be shared by the community, the school, the home, and the young person. Since adolescents are so profoundly effected by marriage, the combined efforts are eminently worthwhile.

1. Do you think that people in college should get married if the girl's parents are willing to continue her support until she completes college?

2. Would you favor more stringent or less stringent divorce laws? (Use the laws of your own state for a point of departure.)

3. List five characteristics that you would most want to have your mate possess. Compare the list with those found in texts on marriage.

4. Defend the proposition that emphasis on *being* the right mate is more constructive than emphasis on *finding* the right mate.

5. How far should you go with the attitude that the marriage *must* work?

6. What are some of the implications for marriage of the statement, "The pleasures of sex, though intense, are not lasting?"

7. How might a young person judge the marital happiness potential of a boy or girl friend's parents without an actual trial?

8. What would you consider to be the two or three *most* important points to be dealt with in a high school course in marriage and the family?

9. What merits and shortcomings do you have that would condition your success as a teacher of a high school course in marriage?

10. Evaluate Baber's statement, "Harsh pronouncement on the evils of divorce will have little effect."

RECOMMENDED SUPPLEMENTARY READING

Baber, Ray E. *Marriage and the Family,* 2nd Ed. (New York: McGraw-Hill Book Company, Inc.; 1953), 719 pp.
    This is a truly outstanding book. It is thorough in scholarship, and written with an occasional light touch not ordinarily found in textbooks.

Any chapter can be read with enjoyment. The last chapter, "The Conservation of Family Values," is particularly recommended. It is thoroughly indexed so that special topics can readily be found.

Bertocci, Peter A. *The Human Venture in Sex, Love, and Marriage* (New York: Association Press; 1951), 143 pp.

Petting during adolescence, sexual intercourse in human experience, the functioning of human personality, and the roots of creative marriage are the major divisions of this concise book. The treatment is directed to the personal problems of young people.

Duvall, Evelyn Millis. *Facts of Life and Love for Teen-Agers* (New York: Popular Library; 1953), 254 pp. (paper cover).

Mrs. Duvall, Consultant for the National Council on Family Relations, deals objectively with questions of pubertal changes, sex worries, dating, courtship, petting, and preparation for marriage. The advisers of adolescents and adolescents could profit from a reading of the book.

Lehner, G. F. J., and Kube, Ella. *The Dynamics of Personal Adjustment* (New York: Prentice-Hall, Inc.: 1955), pp. 327–353.

The authors show that sexual adjustment is intimately related to physiological and psychological factors in the total personality. Courtship and marriage problems are discussed. Sex adjustment is both a cause and result of other marital adjustments.

Wittels, Fritz. *Sex Habits of American Women* (New York: Avon Publications, Inc.; 1951), 189 pp. (paper cover).

The title of this book is probably designed to attract attention. The fact is that the book presents data from prominent researchers in the field of sex and marriage; for example, Lewis M. Terman, Alfred Kinsey and associates, R. L. Dickenson and others.

AUDIO-VISUAL MATERIAL

This Charming Couple (McGraw-Hill Book Company, Inc., 330 West 42nd St., New York 36) 19 min., so., b. and w.

This couple is very much in love with "love," but not with each other. They make no attempt to understand each other's shortcomings. Although they are wed at the end of the film, the audience knows the marriage is doomed.

NOTE: The above film is part of a series of five, on marriage, put out by McGraw-Hill Book Company.

Can the advantages of paid work experience and school attendance be combined? What is the changing nature of adaptation to the working world? How can we best prepare youth to develop saleable and satisfying skills?

CHAPTER SIXTEEN

Adjusting to the World of Work

"In the working life alone is to be found lasting satisfaction for the soul and the hope of salvation for mankind." This statement, made by one of the author's undergraduate professors, seems to have lasting merit. In a society where "what you do" is of more interest than "who you are" the significance of work is an important factor in the maturing processes. Approximately a third of the adult's time is spent at, or in preparation for, his work; so it is important that he view his work in such a way as to gain maximum satisfaction from it. If an occupation is regarded simply as a means of making a living, the way is open for it to be regarded as obligatory drudgery. If work is viewed as an integral part of a way of life, it is more likely that the creative opportunities in work can be capitalized upon. An aspect of life so pervasive and important deserves the careful study of every person interested in human development.

The role of work has been previously indicated at many points in this book. The delay of work opportunities and the lack of chores—which are less uniformly required today—have been cited as obstacles to the adjustment of adolescents. The earliest aims of secondary education included giving attention to vocational adjustment. The first of the "Imperative Needs of Youth" is stated thus: "All youth need to develop saleable skills and those understandings and attitudes that make the worker an intelligent and productive participant in economic life. To this end, most youth need supervised work experience as well as education in the skills and knowledge of their occupations." * Two of the "Developmental Tasks of Adolescence" (see Chapter Three)—achieving assurance of economic independence and selecting and preparing for an occupation—deal directly with work. The chapter "Adolescents and Their Schools" necessarily contained frequent references to the world of work. It is evident that constructive approaches to the adjustment of adolescents must include vocational orientation. This chapter centers about two aspects of this approach: (1) challenging some misconceptions about vocational selection and training and (2) suggesting some basic approaches.†

Opportunities in occupations

The personal values of work

Our dealings with young people might well include emphasis upon the creative opportunities of work. The fact that a man must work for a living (a means to an end) is well known—it is an obligation to himself and to society. The fact that work is *per se* a rich way of life (an end in itself) is not so well recognized. Since many persons may not get to do just the thing they would like to do, it is necessary to stress the possibility of getting satisfaction from what can be, or must be, done. Avocations can help but attitudes toward work may also contribute to satisfaction.

The working life affords an effective approach to the satisfaction of basic human needs. (1) A person gains the recognition of his fellow men for a job well done. Whether it be gardening, repairing an automobile, building dams, curing the sick, or teaching the young, a man's vocation provides a chance for the approval and approbation of his fellow men. (2) A wide-open opportunity for achievement is contained in work. Many of the so-called "blind

---

* National Association of Secondary-School Principals, National Education Association, *Planning for American Youth, Revised Edition* (Washington, D. C.: National Association of Secondary-School Principals; 1951), p. 9.

† Since the author's views on vocational selection and training are often at wide variance with much published material, this chapter will furnish the student with an unusual opportunity critically to evaluate what he reads.

alley" jobs have been changed or obliterated by some ingenious individual. (3) In our society, having a job is an important element in maintaining a feeling of security. The lack of a vocation is a contributing factor in many kinds of mental disorders. (4) An occupation affords an open door to the gaining of new experiences. Any work might be done more quickly, more effectively or more interestingly—as is attested to by the barber's sign, "Haircuts free if we cannot talk on your subject."

It has been said that "There is no such thing as an interesting book: there can only be interested readers." * This idea might be rephrased to say, "There are no blind-alley jobs; only blind workmen." This point is well illustrated by a story of a shoe salesman. The young man began his work in the store by selling after school and on Saturdays. He found that he could sell more shoes by knowing his product well, so he studied the shelves while he was not busy with customers. He found books about shoes and studied their history—discovering when sandals became shoes, when and where ankle-high shoes progressed to calf-high ones, why wooden shoes were worn, when heels began to be used, and the like. The consequence of his knowledge was that while he entertained customers with facts about shoes he sold more shoes per unit of time than others in the store. The boss raised his wages and tried to turn as many customers as possible to the young man. One year the boss was not able to go to Fall River, Massachusetts, on his annual buying trip so he sent the young salesman in his place. Knowing shoes and customers as he did, the young man made such appropriate purchases that at the end of the year more shoes had been sold and the inventory was correspondingly smaller. After this the boss took his annual trip to Florida and sent the salesman to do the buying at Fall River. In the meantime the man's interest had expanded to the study of leathers. He knew the comparative value of steerhide from Texas and from Argentine. The values and comparative advantages of alligator, snakeskin, kid, and kangaroo were learned. Facts about the curing and tanning of leathers were acquired. Because of his knowledge he attracted the attention of the manufacturers, who, as a group, asked him to be their leather buyer. In performing his

---

* A. B. Herr in Alfred Stefferud, *The Wonderful World of Books* (New York: The New American Library of World Literature, Inc.; 1953), p. 85.

duties he became a world traveler—adding still more to his knowledge through capitalizing on his creative opportunity. Today, twenty-five years after the author read this story, such specialization leading to world travel is much more common.

Work has therapeutic value. The idea that persons who have suffered mental breakdowns, as well as those who are physically ill or disabled, should have rest is gradually being replaced by the theory of work therapy. In hospitals for the mentally ill it is considered important to give the patients something to do. An important step in the rehabilitation of the physically maimed and in the utilization of handicapped persons is to help them to develop vocational skills. The therapy of work also has a place in the life of the ordinary individual when he meets a time of crisis. Having a job to do takes one's mind off his troubles, it provides for a release of tensions. Application to daily tasks keeps one from worrying; and, because something is done, work often resolves the conditions that lead to worry. These assertions are supported by what happened to individuals during the depression years of the 1930's. At first an individual was likely to think that unemployment was a temporary thing and he would soon get his job back or go to another. Then he began to think that he was not a good enough person for the kind of work he had done and perhaps he should seek a lower level job. Not finding one, he often became convinced that he was a worthless, unemployable person. The fact that the same thing was happening to others offered little solace. Finally, he was so sure that he was a complete misfit that his worth as a worker was actually undermined. Workers in the field of adolescent development must appreciate the fact that young persons might quite likely develop similar chronic feelings of inferiority. Just doing something is not enough. Work must have a purpose—it must have some significance—if it is to have therapeutic value. A job must be more than an anesthetic—it must be a tonic to sincere endeavor.

Work generates optimism. Optimism is a double-faceted state of mind which comes partially from the work a person does and in turn creates additional opportunity. However, it is not the person who plunges blindly into the performance of an obligatory task who becomes optimistic. It is the person who visualizes the end and meaning of his work, who sees the relation of his work to the total economy, who sees himself growing on the job, who becomes rationally optimistic. Lasting progress is a step-by-step process which takes much time and much energy. The statement of William James, made half a century ago, is most pertinent today:

> . . . As we become permanent drunkards by so many separate drinks, so we become saints in the moral, and authorities and experts in the practical and scientific spheres, by so many separate acts and hours of work. Let no youth have any anxiety about the upshot of his education, whatever the line of it may be. If he keep faithfully busy each hour of the working day, he may safely leave the final result to itself. He can with perfect certainty count on waking up some fine morning to find himself one of the competent ones of his generation, in whatever pursuit he may have singled out. Silently, between all the details of his business, the *power of judging* in all that class of matter will have built itself up within him as a possession that will never pass away. Young people should know this truth in advance. The ignorance of it has probably engendered more discouragement and faint-heartedness in youths embarking on arduous careers than all other causes put together.*

This does not mean that a man can succeed at anything or everything if he just works hard enough. It does mean that in the work a person is capable of doing, the individuals who assiduously apply themselves are the ones who become competent and prominent. Young people should be led to realize that realistic optimism is a matter of combining work with faith.

Distribution of vocational opportunities

From books on vocational guidance, and chapters on vocational preparation in texts dealing with adolescents, it is easy to gain the notion that choices should be made on the basis of abilities, including intelligence, and interest. This, it seems, is hardly a realistic approach to the important problem of vocational adaptation. Free choice of the individual is hardly in accord with the structure of society. This idea was strengthened by the author's work as a Navy classification officer in World War II. (It is admitted that the Navy is not society—but the trends are remarkably similar.)

A battery of nine basic tests was given to each recruit, with addi-

---

* William James, *Talks to Teachers on Psychology*, New Edition (New York: Henry Holt & Company; 1899), p. 78.

tional tests for some rates (classifications of work) and schools. Interviews with each recruit resulted in more data—education, interests, work experience, hobbies. On the basis of the test scores and other data each recruit was coded 1, 2, or 3 ("best," "good," and "use only if necessary") for one or two specific jobs or rates. In testing and interviewing a company of men the results might come out as follows:

RATE OR SCHOOL	CODE 1	CODE 2	CODE 3	IMMEDIATE SEA DUTY
Aviation machinist	5	10	15	
Signalman	2	15	15	Remainder of
Yeoman	3	5	0	company
Hospital corpsman	2	12	20	

This, however, did not mean that these men would be assigned to the school of their choice or that their civilian education, work experience, and interest could be utilized. Quotas for the various schools, projected by the study of probable needs, were published by the Bureau of Naval Personnel at Washington, D. C., and sent to the various training centers. Broken down into the number needed from one company the quota for a given period might be: Aviation machinist, one, Signalman, two, Yeoman, none, and Hospital Corpsman, twenty. The reader can anticipate the result. There was work to be done, jobs to be filled, and when possible they were filled with the best qualified men. When it was not possible to fill them with well-qualified men, quotas were filled anyway. Many recruits complained that no attention was paid to their qualifications or desires—that they were sent to schools they did not want to attend. Both complaints were justified, but the demands of the total situation had to be recognized. The large quota for Hospital Corpsmen was filled—with able men when possible and with less able men when necessary.

There is another and less discouraging aspect of the situation. These men had been warned that they might not get what they wanted and were qualified for. The imperative needs of the Navy were emphasized in indoctrination lectures, the need for corpsmen (or any other rate that was currently heavy) was especially stressed and the duties and opportunities were explained. Interviewers tried to "sell" men on the jobs that had to be done and would code heavily in the direction of getting the best possible men for the current demands. Even so, drafting was necessary. With that preparation and warning most of the men tried to do a good job when they went to the corpsmen's school. Some, at a later time, said: "I like it now," "There's more to it than I thought," "I'm learning a lot that can be of use to me." In short, they adapted themselves to the situation that was forced upon them.

The parallels to civilian life are probably more than superficial. In a community of 10,000 there are about 100 teachers, principals, or supervisors in the public schools, perhaps twelve to fifteen judges and lawyers, twelve to fifteen physicians, ten clergymen, and six dentists. [356:88] The choices of high school seniors will come closer to approximating this distribution than will the choices of high school freshmen, but it is still a long way from fitting the actual situation. The Michigan State College Social Research Service made a study of 12,000 high school seniors and found that while the professions actually occupied 16 per cent of the male population, 40 per cent of the boys wanted such vocations and 25 per cent expected to become professional workers. Eight per cent wanted and expected to be employed in sales and clerical work, but 24 per cent were so occupied. At the other end of the scale, 3 per cent of the boys expected to be unskilled workers (but did not aspire to the jobs) although 13 per cent of the adult population was so employed. [359:4] Nor does the over-choosing of professional careers mean that the needs for a given profession, teaching, will be filled with willing and able persons because relatively few high school pupils choose teaching—particularly is the choice low among boys. The percentage distribution of workers in the United States, in eleven groups of occupations, is shown in Table 9, page 508.

Vocational choice, opportunity, and ability

The vocational interests or choices of adolescents are influenced by several factors. The most important influence comes from parents (one-fifth considered this the most influential factor). Friends, professional acquaintances, relatives other than parents, and teach-

TABLE 9   **Per Cent Distribution of Experienced Workers by Major Occupation Groups: 1940 and 1949** *

MAJOR OCCUPATION GROUP	1949	1940
All experienced workers	100.0%	100.0%
Professional and semi-professional workers	6.7	7.0
Farmers and farm managers	7.9	10.4
Proprietors, managers, and officials, excluding farm	10.5	7.6
Clerical and kindred workers	12.7	10.0
Salesmen and saleswomen	6.3	6.3
Craftsmen, foremen, and kindred workers	13.5	11.7
Operatives and kindred workers	20.7	18.7
Domestice service workers	3.1	4.6
Service workers, except domestic	7.6	7.6
Farm laborers and foremen	4.8	7.0
Laborers, except farm and mine	6.3	9.1

* Source: U. S. Bureau of the Census, Annual Report on the Labor Force, 1949 (Series P.–50, No. 19), p. 4. Estimates are for April 1949 and March 1940.

ers each account for about one-tenth of the choices. Other factors include opportunity for study or quick employment, vocational tests, social recognition of the work, opportunity for advancement, hobbies, and advertisements. Some youngsters will gladly take any job they can get, hoping that it will be temporary, while they earn money to get married, buy a car, help the family—and then find themselves staying on that job. It can be seen that some of these reasons might not be particularly good ones, viewed from the standpoint of long-term personal satisfaction. Parents might sometimes tend to compensate through their children for their own felt lacks or to overestimate their sons' or daughters' abilities. It is possible that friends, acquaintances, and other relatives might be a little more realistic because their personal stake in the issue is negligible. Teachers, if they have studied individuals and vocational opportunities, might be in a better position to give guidance. Opportunity for employment is a valid reason and might be built into a conviction through guided study. Youth might profit from emphasis upon the idea of doing willingly the work that has to be done.

There is a developmental pattern in vocational interests. Figure 19 shows that the early interests of a child are unrealistic and tend toward the spectacular. R. G. Kuhlen shows that men teachers had high interests in railroad engineering from five to twelve years, wishing to be a pro ball player was high from eight to sixteen, ambition to be a doctor reached a peak at fifteen, being an engineer was high at eighteen and the idea was still entertained at twenty-three. Women teachers had a similar pattern in which the ideas of becom-

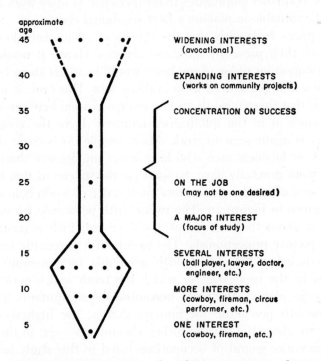

FIG. 19. Schematic representation of evolving occupational interests

It is possible that pressure to make an early occupational choice might result in (1) a weak foundation for the job one does in the middle years or (2) lack of varied interests that lay the background for expanded interests in maturity.

ing an actress or musician, nurse, librarian, and office worker were respectively predominant. [179:504] The latter developmental pattern suggests another factor of interest in the adolescent's vocational interest; that is, girls tend to become realistic about their vocational choices earlier than do boys. Howard M. Bell states in another study, "These comparisons suggest . . . that there is either less vaulting ambition among the young women, or else there is a good deal more realism in their understanding of themselves and the kind of world they are living in." * Fortunately, it is true that both boys and girls become more realistic in their choices as they become older. This developmental trend indicates that the idea of prompting youngsters to make an early vocational choice has some hazards. It further emphasizes that experience in *some* work activity would be valuable in making a later vocational choice.

It happens frequently that the choices of adolescents do not accord with their presently indicated abilities. Hence it would seem that an important phase of guidance would be to get them to assess their own abilities as well as to evaluate jobs. However, it must be observed that there is no sharp line of demarcation between various job families as to the intelligence required. Here the tyranny of averages is again seen to work. Many people do become doctors, teachers, or business men who have lower intelligence than others in that work generally have. Support for the statement that there is a great deal of overlapping in test intelligence of workers in various jobs is given in Figure 20. The twenty-fifth percentile for accountants is at about the same point as the seventy-fifth percentile for motion picture projectionists. The twenty-fifth percentile for bookkeepers is below the seventy-fifth for automotive electricians. In the two cases for which the tenth and ninetieth percentiles are plotted, the tenth percentile for accountants is below the ninetieth percentile for miners; that is, the highest scoring miners are above the lowest scoring accountants—yet, in these two jobs, the entire gamut of occupations listed in this study has been run. It is conceivable that, had circumstances been different, some of those who had been engaged in mining (the lowest of the occupations listed) might have been accountants.

---

* Howard M. Bell, *Youth Tell Their Story* (Washington, D. C.: American Council on Education; 1938), p. 134.

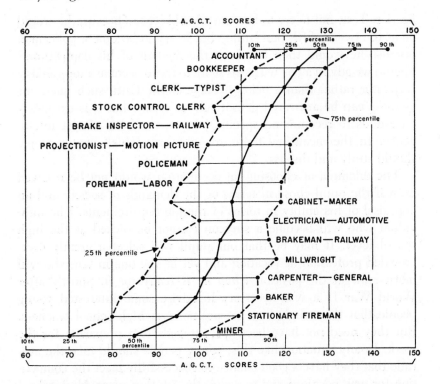

FIG. 20. **Army General Classification Test Scores grouped by occupations of enlisted men**

Data from Naomi Stewart, "A. G. C. T. Scores of Army Personnel Grouped by Occupations," *Occupations*, 26:5–41, 1947. Approximately every fifteenth occupation from a list of 227 is represented above. The range plotted is from the 25th to 75th percentile, except that the 10th and 90th percentile is shown for accountants and miners.

There are, however, some unanswered questions relating to work done, ability, and job satisfaction. Could it be that the highest ranking miner might be happier than the lowest ranking accountant—because for the miner he would find the competition easier to meet while the accountant would find the going hard? Could the high ranking miner be a dissatisfied worker because his abilities are not sufficiently challenged by the work he does? Is it safe to advise the high school boy, who would score 114 on the Army General Classification Test, not to try to become a bookkeeper (because he would be at the twenty-fifth percentile) but to try to become a policeman because he would then be above the median of his competitors? Should we advise a boy with this score to try to become a top-ranking carpenter rather than a below-average clerk? Until such questions as these can be answered definitively, it seems that it is extremely hazardous to recommend specific jobs on the basis of test intelligence. In the meantime these are questions which young people should study and discuss.

The dilemma of choosing an occupation would not be resolved even if the pupil chose in terms of the demands of society and an appraisal of his ability in terms of the job requirements. The individual who will become a surgeon cannot be picked at the high school level. It may be that our pupil will select a greatly overcrowded profession or vocation and yet be the one in ten who will merit and get the position *when he is ready for it.* Shortly after World War II it was necessary to advise some interested young people that they might not get positions as high school teachers. But they need not have been discouraged from preparing for the work. In any situation like this, young people should take the attitude that they have a good chance to successfully meet the competition for new positions and to secure the job they want. High school pupils can be advised to prepare for the things they choose—if they will, at the same time, *prepare themselves psychologically* for the possibility that it might ultimately be expedient to do something else.

Those who work with adolescents might well evaluate this proposition: The vocational dissatisfaction that is mentioned in books on guidance and adolescence might partially be due to the attitude that one takes toward the job he has to do, rather than being solely the result of a job that is incompatible with interest and ability. Hence, a job for vocational counselors is to prepare adolescents for doing well what they can find to do—building habits of work, attitudes of sincerity and personal adaptability that will render them better capable of *ultimately* doing the thing for which they are best suited.

Vocational orientation and the school

Vocational training

There is much argument as to whether or not there should be vocational training in high school. Some feel that if we are to meet the needs of all youth there should be specific training in jobs that young people will find available. In large high schools there are frequently a few courses designed to develop skills and knowledges for specific vocations. In large cities there are sometimes technical high schools where certain pupils gather from all parts of the community to take courses in automobile mechanics, carpentry, electricity, plumbing, and distributive education. Rural schools frequently offer courses in agriculture and animal husbandry. In contrast to this view, there are many who feel that a general education is the best preparation for any job. They argue that the necessarily large expense involved in giving training in specific vocations is not warranted in terms of the initial, but not necessarily long-term, advantage that the student of vocational courses enjoys. This argument is strengthened by the data indicating that only 10 per cent of American workmen need training that extends over a period of more than six months. Another 25 per cent of the jobs require from four days to six months preparation. The remaining 65 per cent can learn the job they have to do in less than four days. [79:31, 273]

The foregoing data do not mean that the needs of the 65 per cent should be ignored. There are indications that those who will earn their living at jobs not in the white-collar class can be rendered substantial service even without specific vocational training. The opportunity lies in the field of *occupational education* as contrasted to occupational training. Occupational education has the advantage of being less specific than training and hence is more likely to avoid the error of preparing young people for work in fields they will not find available.

Occupational education

Young people should be advised that their success in any line of work depends, to a very large extent, upon their ability to get along

with people. Even in the professions, where high degrees of technical skill are necessary, success depends to a marked extent on human
relations. It is estimated that nine-tenths of the teachers who fail do
so because they cannot get along with others. Vocational education
that emphasizes courtesy, cooperation, and consideration is realistic
and helpful.

Knowing how to take directions is an important skill at any level
of occupational endeavor. Pupils in school who complain about
assignments, who think it smart to ignore rules, who will only work
when they can do it in their own way, are building habits that will
make pay raises and promotions more difficult to secure. Those who
express the wish to be their own boss should be viewed carefully
by teachers to see if the expression is a resentment against authority
or is really an indication of healthy independence. The healthy person can take direction and still show independence and self-
determination.

Studies of the efficiency of workmen show that there is a marked
relation between marital satisfaction and/or good personal adjustment and productivity. Persons having marital or emotional problems are considerably more prone to have accidents than are happy
individuals. Hence, a big step toward better vocational adjustment
is time and study devoted to problems of personal adjustment.
Further, since a substantial part of a man's life is spent in his home
and with his family, it is important that vocational education for
all students include the consideration of marriage problems and
mental health problems.

Another problem relating to personal adjustment and efficiency
on the job has to do with leisure time. Most young people will have
to at least begin with jobs that require a low degree of skill and a
high amount of routine. To compensate for this monotony and
repetition it is important that one should really *re*-create himself
in his leisure time. Furthermore, there is a persistent tendency to
increase the amount of leisure time—a development made possible
through technological improvement and motivated by the ideal of
freedom.

J. E. Wallace Wallin states the problem in very strong language,

. . . a drastic reduction in the work load might create more mental-
health problems than it would solve. Long hours of idleness, in-

stead of conducing to mental health, might actually create serious hazards to its attainment and preservation. Boredom and idleness might indeed become a greater menace to the nation's mental and social health than is poverty.*

Obviously, occupational education must be concerned with preparation to use leisure time constructively.

A committee for the *World Book Encyclopedia* has taken the broad approach to occupational orientation, suggested by the foregoing, by asking questions of parents about the young person. [232] Adolescents might well become concerned with giving attention to the issues raised as realistic approaches to selecting and preparing for their life work.

1. How does your child get along with others? Does he prefer being alone? Does he enjoy people? Do people enjoy him? Does he study people? Would he enjoy working directly with people? How does he work in groups? Does he lead? How does he follow the leadership of others? How does he take responsibility? What does he do in a crisis? What does he do in competition? (Each of these questions has 10 to 20 suggested questions for checking.)
2. How does your child's mind work? Is he reflective? Does he concentrate? What does he do in mathematics? Is he artistic? Does he appreciate nature? Does he experiment? Does he plan?
3. What are your child's nervous reactions? Is he methodical? Is he accurate? What does he do with detail? Does he keep continuously on the go? How does he take routine? Does he enjoy danger? What results does he want? How does he work under pressure?
4. How does your child's body work? How healthy is he? How strong is he? Does he have manual skills? Is he mechanically inclined?
5. Other important considerations: Has your child settled on a definite occupation? Has the family any set preferences as to what they want the child to become? Has the child had genuine work experience to date? What opportunity has the child had

---

* By permission from *Personality Maladjustments and Mental Hygiene*, 2nd Edition, by J. E. Wallace Wallin. Copyright 1949, McGraw-Hill Book Company, Inc. P. 245.

for observing others at work? What education is required for the occupation tentatively selected? What training and experience would be required for the occupation selected? *

Examination of the foregoing questions will show that most of them deal with personality and social factors that have bearing on any occupation. It is only with question five that specific education and training appear to become important.

Career days

Some schools have taken a step toward occupational orientation through career days—two or three days given over to assemblies in which the place of work in life, the availability of jobs, and the kind of education needed for maximum efficiency are discussed. After the general talks the pupils, in small groups, go to hear visitors talk about their work. Each pupil is encouraged to listen to a number of talks instead of remaining in the group that is discussing the one field that he may now think will be his life work. Different groups of visiting lecturers come in on each of the two or three days devoted to this study. School officials encourage these individuals to present both the bright and dark side of their work; they are asked to describe the personal qualifications the worker must possess, the kind of preparation needed, the conditions of work, the chances of employment, the scale of pay and the chances for future progress in the work. Near the end of the day the pupils may again meet in general assembly to evaluate the work done.

A variation of career days is a vocational exhibit. Displays designed to convey to students information regarding local occupations are arranged by trade or professional organizations. Additional reading matter on the occupations is made available. An attempt is made to relate the work to the school work the pupil is presently doing. In charge of each display or booth there is a representative from the business or industry to answer questions. [171]

Another popular variation of the career days is college days. The plan is to have representatives of the colleges, to which the high school graduates typically go, come and talk with groups of students

* From *An Occupational Guidance Record,* copyrighted by Field Enterprises, Inc. Used by special permission.

who think they might be interested in certain colleges and certain courses. After introductory talks the representatives may do some individual counseling with the seniors who want advice.

Interests and aptitudes

A great deal has been written about the advisability of giving interest and aptitude tests to high school pupils so that they might be guided into suitable occupations in which they were likely to remain interested. Such approaches must be viewed with skepticism, for several reasons. The first has already been mentioned—being interested does not mean that jobs are available. Two decades ago there was some doubt that a young person could find any job. Today the prospects are brighter but there still remain the fluctuations of opportunity in terms of technology, including automation, and geographical availability. Table 9 indicates that opportunity and interest do not necessarily coincide.

The second reason why interests are not a reliable guide is that interests grow and develop—they are not something with which a person is born. Hence although an individual's present interests do grow out of those he once had, there is no assurance that still further development will not take place. Interest is the identification of an individual with some person, thing, or situation. There is a feeling that that person, thing, or situation has some significant meaning for the interested individual. This feeling evolves from familiarity, from knowledge, from the development of skill, and from the feeling of success that comes through accomplishment in the area of interest. Often the problem of vocational orientation is not to discover interests that already exist but to find ways in which new interests may be evolved. Many of the men who were drafted for hospital corps school in the Navy determined to make the best of it, and as a result healthy interests evolved. Many persons who were, as youngsters, forced to practice the piano finally became genuinely interested in their playing—it is probable that those who did not become interested despite the acquisition of skill were ones who had initially determined that "I'll be darned if I will like it." In view of the uncertain occupational future of youth, it might be well to spend more time emphasizing the evolution of interests and less on the "measurement" of those already existing. Is it not possible that the emphasis upon *finding* a job to suit present interests actually increases the probability of dissatisfaction?

A further reason for skepticism in viewing the occupational field from the standpoint of interest is that interests do not necessarily connote ability. Although there is a tendency for young people to choose occupations that seem to accord in general with their ability [56] many choose vocations for which they have little aptitude. R. F. Berdie concluded on the basis of published research that special interests have little relation to specialized ability or to intelligence. [19] Mechanical interest does not necessarily connote mechanical ability. Interest tests may, however, prove to be a very valuable approach to a counseling situation. The present interests may provide a "take-off" point for discussing the implications of developing interests.

The problem of predicting what, for an individual, will be a suitable occupation is complicated by the inadequacy of many of the common measuring instruments. This is particularly true in the realm of personality measurement. Varying degrees of validity and reliability are claimed for a variety of personality tests. Results are presented in terms of mathematically precise norms—percentile ranks in personal adequacy, self-sufficiency, home adjustment, and the like. However, in spite of widespread popularity, these devices are viewed critically by some psychologists. L. F. Shaffer levels a charge against personality inventories in general with the following words:

> Such devices vainly seek the pot of gold at the end of the rainbow; a simple, cheap, foolproof method for studying personality. Teachers, administrators and school counselors who are tempted to consider the use of such devices would be benefitted by a psychological insight into the fact that their own great need to do something about personality problems leads them to the delusion of accepting instruments of very low objective value.*

Each individual has aspects of his personality that he attempts to hide from all others. J. S. Plant has called this secret self an "envelope" of privacy. [246] Because of this secret self, G. G. Thompson states: "It is surprising (in the face of this preponderance of

---

* L. F. Shaffer, in Oscar K. Buros (Ed.), *The Third Mental Measurements Yearbook* (New Brunswick: Rutgers University Press; copyright 1949), p. 56.

negative research findings) that these personality questionnaires should continue to be so widely used in schools and youth-guidance organizations." *

Many of the so-called mechanical ability tests are in somewhat the same category as personality inventories. Some of the tests reflect knowledge that could have been acquired in various courses. Others, instead of indicating mechanical aptitude, are more an indication of general intelligence. (It must be admitted that intelligence will ordinarily be no handicap to a mechanic.) Some of the tests cover information that reflects experience as a mechanic—gear ratios, threads per inch, kinds of wrenches, gauges of taps, and uses of materials. Tests requiring manipulation are perhaps more dependable, but the problem of how to fit manipulative aptitudes to specific jobs has not yet been solved.

The vocational counselor is faced with three rather disturbing questions: Should youngsters be advised to select fields of work in which they are interested and seem to have the required level of intelligence to the exclusion of consideration of probability of employment? Are present interests mature enough to form the basis for a long-range prediction? Can interests and aptitudes be measured with enough accuracy to permit the making of definitive recommendations? The fact that rather reserved answers must be given to these questions need not mean that data on interests and aptitudes should be disregarded. Measures of these should be employed along with data regarding test intelligence, the personal knowledge of the teacher relative to the pupil's personality, and information regarding the pupil's leisure-time interests. The demands of society and industry, the probable opportunities for extended education, should also be taken into account. Counseling that uses a wide base of information will necessarily be tentative—and probably, in the long run, more helpful.

General education as an approach to vocational orientation

Work occupies a major portion of any individual's life and time; finding a job and developing skills are among the important needs and tasks of young persons. Difficulties in the way of successfully filling the vocational needs of youth include: (1) the multiplicity

---

* George G. Thompson, *Child Psychology* (Boston: Houghton Mifflin Company; 1952), p. 614.

of jobs performed in adult life (30,000 titles are listed in the *Dictionary of Occupation Titles*), (2) the discrepancy between what needs to be done and what workers want to do, (3) the difficulty of measuring both people and jobs in terms of capacities possessed and abilities needed. In spite of these difficulties, much can be done to facilitate youth's adjustment on the job through encouraging him to stick with his general education program. The broad base for vocational orientation that is thus built will, in the long run, prove to be the most profitable.

It was indicated in Chapter Seven, "Adolescents and Their Schools," that those who stayed in school until graduation had distinct advantages over the early school-leavers in their vocational adjustment. In one study the graduate was superior to the late drop-out and the late drop-out was superior to the early drop-out in each of the following: (a) number of promotions or raises, (b) holding on to one job, (c) fewer and shorter periods of unemployment, (d) higher job satisfaction, (e) more recreational pursuits, (f) more hobbies, and (g) greater frequency of additional training. The two main reasons why graduates leave jobs are to move on from a seasonal job and to take a better job. The four major reasons for early drop-outs to leave a job are the seasonal shift, dislike of job, personal reasons, and to take a better job. [58:6, 10] Since many drop-outs are as capable as those who stay in school and since the average difference in intelligence of the two groups is small, it seems reasonable to believe that *some* of the superiority of the person who stays in school is due to the kind of experiences he has acquired. Schools, as noted before, need to face the task of providing some gratifying experiences to *all* pupils.

Even at the higher levels of education concern over the early selection of and specific training for a job may be questioned. Recently the author was interviewed by "talent scouts" for an insurance company, who were seeking college graduates. When asked what preparation was desired they said, "It really doesn't make any difference." "Well, a background in economics and business courses would help, wouldn't it?" "Yes, but no more than courses in sociology, literature, and history. We just want college graduates —men with broad interests, skill in human relations, knowledge about the world in general. We can easily get business school graduates to do the routine work of an office. What we want are men who can handle people and coordinate the efforts of those who are under their supervision." This is not intended to imply that professional training for medicine, law, engineering, and education is undesirable or unnecessary. It is intended to emphasize the fact that many things are involved in valuable education besides specific vocational preparation.

There is no doubt that specific vocational education has merit in large high schools where enrollments will tend to justify special offerings. Vocational education may emphasize the values stressed in general education. Critical thinking, respect for order, clarity of expression, creativity, and the desire for increased knowledge can be emphasized by both the vocational and academic teacher. Furthermore, business courses in city schools are at the same time fitting a local situation and filling an adolescent interest—even those going on to college will profit from typing and shorthand. Agriculture courses can easily and economically be given in rural high schools—and since the bulk of high school graduates continue to reside in their community such courses will result in an enrichment of the community as a whole. Courses in personal hygiene, oral communication, writing, special classes for improving reading skill, and functional mathematics courses are emphases that will enhance employability. Because many girls will make their vocation that of homemaking and because boys will soon be spending a substantial portion of their time in their own homes, an essential of good general education will be some direct emphasis on marriage and family.

Judging from the post high school careers of young persons, it seems safe to say that substantial vocational benefits will accrue through general education. A CIO official stresses this point:

> There have been many quarrels among educators as to the merits of cultural vs. vocational education. This is unfortunate. . . . Labor hopes that out of our schools will come persons who are significant in themselves, who can make a real contribution to their communities, vocationally, and who are committed to the democratic ideal and willing to add their bit in the eternal struggle to keep it and improve it.*

* Orville C. Jones, "Labor's Concern for Education," *Phi Delta Kappan*, 34, 1953, 224.

Oral and written communication should be taught in such a way
that youngsters can develop both interest and skills. Heavy emphasis should be placed on the improvement of reading skills because
it will be through reading that continued and unusual progress will
be made in many vocations. Skill in the manipulation of number
concepts should be a continuing emphasis—not only for the sake of
the job but for the management of income and expenditures. The
study of history, literature, and science can make contributions to
full living that create a more productive workman as well as a happier, well-socialized individual.

Work-experience education

The meaning of work-experience education

A movement, rapidly gaining in popularity, which is designed to
fill the needs of youth more adequately is that known as work-
experience education. It consists fundamentally of a combination of
the usual high school education and actual work experience that
will provide, ". . . opportunities for young Americans to learn
about the world of work and to be occupationally competent . . ." *
The student pursuing this plan takes a part-time job, under the
supervision of some faculty member, and concurrently continues
his regular high school work (sometimes the academic load is reduced).

Work-experience education takes many forms, depending upon
local points of view and work opportunities. In general, it may be
defined as: student participation in the production of goods or the
performance of services in the usual setting, under the direction of
the school and with related instruction provided by the school.
[154:183 and 167:415] Some work-experience programs are contained within the walls of the school—students perform part-time
library work, secretarial functions, sales jobs, provide office services
and janitorial and teaching assistance. [258] Another common form
is the cooperative work plan, in which some local businessman or
manufacturer provides part-time work for students, paying them
an agreed-upon rate. The work is supervised by a faculty member

---

* U. S. Office of Education, *Report of the National Conference on Life Adjustment* (Washington, D. C.: U. S. Government Printing Office; 1950), p. 16.

and the employer. Emphasis is placed upon the educational value of the work (exploratory functions, development of good work habits, and exercise of vocationally valuable personality traits) and the work is coordinated with the student's academic program. Sometimes the supervision is done only by the employer and he and the student make reports to the school. This method is not favored by educators, who feel that the monetary aspects of the employment may then take precedence over the educational values.

Advantages of the work-experience program

Presuming that work-experience education consists of part-time, paid employment, under the supervision of a faculty member, the following are considered to be some of the advantages: This experience gives the adolescent a chance to earn some money and thus take a step toward the independence that he needs to have in order to make continued personality growth. It gives him an improved chance to develop an awareness of the meaning and function of money. It provides for a smoother transition from the school to the world of work. It strengthens the motivation of pupils for their school work by relating work responsibilities to educational opportunities. It promotes the socialization of youth by widening the circle of acquaintances and experiences and by demonstrating the need for the development of commendable personality characteristics. It gives a youth an opportunity to explore various vocations; even if he does not select one in which he has had experience, his wider background enhances his appreciation of the work of others. Finally, work experience widens the offerings of the school so that a better chance for meeting individual differences is provided.

Citizens of the community and employers may also profit from the organization of work-experience programs. Closer rapport between the school and the patrons, who must share the burden of financial support, is made possible by work-experience education. Employers have found that such programs lower rates of labor turnover because there is a better understanding of the nature and conditions of work. Employers have an opportunity to locate future workers who will be most valuable. It is felt that work-experience programs promote better citizenship by increasing mutual appreciation between worker and employer and between school and business. [167:418] It is possible that future studies may demonstrate that the self-esteem generated in adolescents by a part-time job is accompanied by lower delinquency rates.

Opportunities for work experience

When a few key figures in the community have been enlisted in the preliminary planning, or when some local fraternity or service club will sponsor a survey, it is usually possible to find places where students may simultaneously learn, earn, and serve. The young people can themselves do much of the planning and organizing. In Phoenix, Arizona, teen-agers established an employment agency and prospected for positions. After an original period of doubt on the part of adults, there was enthusiastic response both financially and in the finding of jobs. Jobs were found for baby-sitters, lawn workers, delivery boys, janitors, typists, and store clerks. [293] Some of these are not jobs that would be included in work-experience programs sponsored by the school, but the story shows that jobs are available and youngsters will work when they get a chance.

In larger population centers jobs are available in both service and manufacturing industries. Jobs may be open in such trades as auto mechanic, plumber, electrician, appliance repairman, metal worker, painter, carpenter, tinsmith, draftsman, and machinist. In placing boys in these occupations, it is necessary to see that legal requirements are observed. Smaller communities will not have such a diversity of opportunities, but work in the distributive occupations is usually available—salesman, store manager, stock clerk, office worker, receptionist, typist, bookkeeper, and business machine operator are jobs that can be found in any community. Retail establishments are a particularly rich area of possibilities.

If the general training aspects of the program—meeting people, developing a social personality, putting your "best foot forward," increasing skill in communication, and building good citizenship—are kept in mind specific training in occupations is probably less important. Work experience discussed and interpreted in the school can have important implications for the young worker regardless of the field he finally enters. If the following statement is deemed to be valid, then we need to be less concerned about specific work experience opportunities than about a variety of experiences which form a basis for future development.

The really serious problem is not employment but the need to upgrade whole segments of the population in a very short time. Automation requires trained and educated people in unprecedented numbers. The quantitative need alone will be so great . . . that the eight or ten million college students we can expect fifteen years hence will be barely sufficient. One large manufacturing company (now employing 150,000) figures that it will need *seven thousand* college graduates a year, once it is automated, just to keep going; today it hires three hundred annually.

But the need is above all qualitative—for *better educated* people. The "trained barbarian," the man who has acquired high gadgeteering skill, will not do. Even in routine jobs, Automation will require ability to think, a trained imagination, and good judgment, plus some skill in logical methods, some mathematical understanding, and some ability well above the elementary level to read and write— in a word, the normal equipment of educated people. Under Automation, a school could do a student no greater disservice than to prepare him, as so many do today, for his first job. If there is one thing certain under Automation it is that the job—even the bottom job—will change radically and often.*

The big opportunity in work-experience education lies in motivating the pupil to stay in school and to work hard at the school's offerings. There is some basis for the error of thinking of schools as the sole means of education, for the main function of the school is to promote learning and it provides the situation that is most conducive to economical learning.

Principles for the effective operation of work-experience education

An analysis of various work-experience programs reveals a number of underlying principles that should be observed in order to secure maximum beneficial results. The major principles are:

1. Since this is a community enterprise, citizens, prospective employers, pupils, parents, and teachers should participate in the initial planning.
2. A survey of the community should be made to find the type of experiences available and prevent superficial use of some opportunities and overloading of others.

---

* Peter F. Drucker, "The Promise of Automation: America's Next Twenty Years, Part II," *Harper's* 210, April, 1955, 45.

3. Rates of pay, school credit, distribution of the student's time, responsibilities of worker and employer, and the like, must be agreed upon in advance of placement.
4. Individual and group conferences should pave the way to fitting the students to the work that will be most meaningful to them as individuals.
5. The work program should be coordinated with the total and regular school curriculum so that the motivation provided by work experience may be capitalized upon.
6. The program should be continuously supervised by a faculty member (or members if the load is heavy) who gives his full time to the program so that he can visit with students and employers on the job.
7. All teachers must know their roles and be firmly behind the plan.
8. The primary aim is education, so the workers should be moved from one job to another as they approach the level of satisfactory performance.
9. There should be a continuous program of evaluation so that (1) students will get the maximum benefit from their experiences and (2) the rights of employers will be protected.
10. The program should not be one for academic or disciplinary misfits but rather an opportunity and privilege for any and all serious pupils.
11. The program must not degenerate into a "help the needy" situation. Students who do not need financial aid still need the confidence generated by earning their own money.

Vocations and the adolescent's future

The effect of military service

War and preparation for war has no uniform effect upon the adolescent's future vocation. Some boys are alarmed into early school leaving, earning a little money and having a good time before they are drafted. They promise themselves that they will continue their education after their period of service when they can get veterans' benefits. Others consider it wise to get the best academic preparation and training in skills that they possibly can so that when they are drafted they can find something to do besides become a deck hand or a buck private. Adults generally seem to agree with the idea of immediate continuance of school. The following advice to a young man seems to be representative,

> In the first place, by all means complete your high-school work. All of the military services are anxious that as many as possible of their personnel at all levels, possess a high-school background as a minimum educational qualification. . . . If you plan to go to work, to take some kind of trade or industrial training, or to attend an institution of higher education, go right ahead with these plans. . . . It is most unwise for you to anticipate your call and possibly find yourself waiting around a number of months before entering upon service. . . .*

Education that is good for the country is also good for the individual. Harold W. Dodds, in the following words, shows that continued education is advisable *and* that vocational preparation need not be highly specific even at the collegiate level.

> True, the work of a second lieutenant on active duty will not add to his specialized knowledge of a particular civilian vocation. But if he keeps his eyes open and determines to profit from his chances to mix and work with all sorts of people such as he never met in college, he will learn much that will make him a more successful lawyer, a more knowing banker, a more efficient businessman afterwards; a better teacher if this is the profession he intends to follow, or even a better clergyman.†

Dodds states that technical training is necessary, but he also emphasizes the necessity for a strong base upon which to build future success.

Building for the future

A study of the career patterns of adult workers has some important implications for the future of the adolescent. It was found that the worker holds from one to eleven jobs before he settles down in

---

* H. K. Newburn, *The Manpower Situation and the High School Student* (Eugene, Oregon: University of Oregon, School of Education; 1951), pp. 8–9.

† Harold W. Dodds, "Your Boy and the ROTC," *The Atlantic*, 191, 3, 1953, 27.

the one he considers his regular work. The average number of jobs held in a period of ten years is 3.6. [74:456] Furthermore, the jobs ultimately held are related to the jobs initially held; that is, unskilled workers originally held unskilled jobs, professional workers originally held sales or clerical jobs. Hence, changing jobs does not, in most cases, mean progress—in fact, although the average worker held 3.6 jobs his progress up the occupational hierarchy averaged only +.19 of a step. One other finding of interest is that, particularly on the lower rungs of the occupational ladder, progress was made largely on the basis of self-instruction—yet it is at these levels that there is the least upward mobility. These data seem to warrant the following advice for young workers who are concerned about both the present and the future: (1) The frequency of job changes indicates the desirability of broad approaches to vocational selection. Choose families of occupations as the focus of study rather than a program of specific skill development. (2) View your first job as you viewed your work experience education in the school—as an orientation to the world of work rather than as training for a single skill. (3) Lay a firm foundation now—in reading, mathematics, social studies, and the like—for the study that must be undertaken, but that few seem to be capable of carrying out, at a later time.

Summary

Work is a way of life as well as a means of making a living. From work a man gains recognition, satisfies his desire for achievement, and contributes to feelings of security. In terms of mental health, work has both prophylactic and therapeutic value. Hence, the problem of vocational orientation and adjustment is one of the more relevant topics in the study of adolescent development.

Some of the points that must be recognized in counseling with young people and preparing them for their future work include: Consideration of the distribution of probable occupational opportunities, the relationship of pupil's abilities to his choice, the probable availability of educational opportunity necessary in various job families, and the fluctuating interests of adolescents.

Vocational training has a definite place in the optimum adjustment of the adolescent but, since most jobs require so little specific training, it seems advisable to lay broad foundations that will permit flexibility in later selections. Occupational education, which stresses general habits, traits, and attitudes, seems to be highly advisable for any worker and has been found to be particularly advantageous to those who will hold the jobs lowest on the job hierarchy.

Aptitude testing is less dependable than many people seem to believe. It is difficult to measure aptitudes for specific jobs because such varied combinations of aptitudes will contribute to success on a particular job. Moreover, we do not know just what aptitudes are required on specified jobs. Interest tests are somewhat more helpful, and when used to guide into families of occupations have merit as supplementary data. It is important to remember that typically the interests of adolescents undergo developmental processes and that new interests may be developed by means of successful experience.

It seems valid to recommend that, along with vocational training and orientation activities, there be a strong emphasis on general education. This education should include emphasis on the tools of learning—reading, communication, and mathematics—and upon the development of healthy minded persons who view work as an opportunity for accomplishment and expression, who anticipate the necessity for doing some things that must be done even though there are other things they would rather do, and who seek to cultivate the leisure time activities that will help round out their total activities into a balanced program of work and play.

Work-experience education is an attempt to bridge the gap between school and the world of work. Its increasing popularity is probably due to the following advantages: It enlists the interest and help of the entire community, it provides excellent training at a lower cost than that involved in vocational classes, it gives youngsters a change to bolster their egos by permitting them to *earn their own* money, and it serves to motivate the regular work of the school more effectively.

The problem of vocational adjustment is a continuous one. Hence the prime aim of vocational education in the school should be to establish the basis for continued and later progress. Young people are building today for the kind of work that will give them and their fellows the maximum of satisfaction tomorrow.

1. Can you think of any personal values of work, besides those listed in the text, that should be described to adolescents?

2. Under what circumstances do you think young people would be most likely to choose a vocation in accord with their ability?

3. Knowing that there are few electricians in your community, when would you, and when would you not, advise a young man to prepare for that work?

4. How would you deal with a girl who is determined to be a nurse, but who, in comparison with other nurse candidates, has only a tenth percentile rank in intelligence?

5. What are some kinds of vocational training that you think should be included in a high school enrolling 250 pupils? in one enrolling 100 pupils?

6. How might the "Occupational Guidance Record" (World Book Encyclopedia) be used in a class in occupational education?

7. Tell why you agree or disagree with the view of aptitude testing presented in the text.

8. What do you think should be the ten major emphases in general education designed to promote vocational adaptation?

9. Do you believe that all pupils should participate in a work-experience education program? Should truants be placed in the work experience education program?

10. Do the attitudes of typical youth (not those in college) toward military service agree with those presented in the text?

11. What plans could the student in college lay now for continued learning after he secures a position?

Kitson, Harry D. *I Find My Vocation,* Rev. Ed. (New York: McGraw-Hill Book Company, Inc.; 1947), 278 pp.

This book, written for high school students, can be read with profit by parents and teachers—those who give the greatest amount of vocational advice. Among the points of emphasis are the growing nature of interests and aptitudes, the adaptability of most workers, and the dignity of all socially constructive work when it is conscientiously done.

Knapp, Robert H. *Practical Guidance Methods* (New York: McGraw-Hill Book Company, Inc.; 1953), pp. 86–131.

The chapter, "Helping Youth through Vocational Guidance" gives a balanced presentation of methods and aspects of vocational selection and preparation. An unusually helpful feature is a listing of government agencies from which vocational data may be secured, private publishers who have unique materials, and a list of films.

Kuhlen, Raymond G., and George G. Thompson (Eds.) *Psychological Studies of Human Development* (New York: Appleton-Century, Crofts, Inc.; 1952), pp. 442–478.

These readings, selected from various sources, deal with (1) development of vocational preferences, (2) adolescents' preferences *and* expectations, (3) the characteristics of career patterns, (4) the creative years in scientific and literary work, and (5) job satisfactions at various occupational levels.

Sanderson, Herbert. *Basic Concepts in Vocational Guidance* (New York: McGraw-Hill Book Company, Inc.; 1954), pp. 237–310.

These three chapters describe the characteristics of adolescents that must be considered in counseling with them. Sound principles of counseling and the cooperative role of parents and teachers are discussed.

Witmer, Helen L., and Ruth Kotinsky (Eds.) *Personality in the Making* (New York: Harper & Brothers; 1952), pp. 290–307.

This chapter deals with four fallacies: (1) you can't get anywhere without a college education, (2) white collar work is more desirable than trade or technical work, (3) vocational guidance and training should result in the selection of a specific lifetime occupational goal, and (4) aptitude testing is the answer to vocational problems.

AUDIO-VISUAL MATERIAL

How To Investigate Vocations (Coronet Films, Coronet Building, Chicago 1), 11 min., so., b. and w. or color.

The film is designed to help students investigate and select appropriate work. How to interpret tests, apply results to specific vocations, and how to gain and use actual job experience are clearly shown.

Personal Qualities for Job Success (Coronet Films), 11 min., so., b. and w. or color.

College as well as high school students will profit from this portrayal of personal qualities needed for job success. Covers initiative, appearance, work habits, taking criticism, getting along with others, etc.

Is delinquency or citizenship the typical adolescent behavior? How can adolescents be given more significant community roles? What factors contribute to delinquency? What influences the development of habits or participating citizenship?

CHAPTER SEVENTEEN

Adjusting to Society: Citizenship and Delinquency

The great majority of adolescents make admirable adjustments to society even in the face of an admittedly high number of contemporary hazards. All too frequently these relatively quiet, happy, and efficient youngsters escape recognition. Occasionally one of them gets newspaper notice for winning a prize in a county or state fair. Another is recognized for achieving scholastic honors. Another heroically saves a life and is lauded for it. But daily, the nation over, some one teen-ager out of a thousand is noted for assault, stealing, drinking excessively, or for some sex offense. Too often adults generalize from the latter type of incident and overlook the many who unobtrusively are in their own ways playing the role of effective citizens. It is for this reason that the author has chosen to put delinquency and citizenship in the same chapter; but even a fifty-fifty division is not a true representation of reality.

Another reason for treating these two problems in the same chapter is that, to the extent that citizenship training is effective, delinquency will be reduced. If delinquent activities are to be abated then some positive activities should be placed in their stead. It is increasingly being recognized that the prevention of delinquency, by providing constructive pursuits for youth, is much more effective

533

than are programs for the correction and/or punishment of the erring youth.

It is, furthermore, believed that if a positive, confident view of youth can replace the view that they are a despicable, decadent group that must somehow be held in check, then youth will respond by living up to the more optimistic view. The individual in adolescence reflects the view that others have of him no less than does the infant and the child. It is important that we adults have confidence in the ability and desire of youth to be good citizens.

Helping adolescents toward citizenship

The importance of citizenship

Our nation is founded on the premise that all individuals share responsibility for effective government and the preservation and improvement of living. Early settlers appreciated their responsibility and made assiduous efforts to preserve their rights and responsibilities. The establishment and improvement of public schools was justified in terms of helping the growing individual become a good citizen. Every statement of the aims of education, from the kindergarten level through higher education, stresses the factor of citizenship. But the efforts of functioning citizens and of teachers have not produced altogether satisfactory results.

Almost every election is followed by the comments of newspaper and magazine editors on the small number of eligible citizens who vote (see Figure 21). Many do not even bother to make themselves eligible by registering. Efforts to beat "the government" out of taxes, the carelessness of the smoker in national forest, the roadside "litter-bug," the despoiling of beaches, the exceeding of speed limits, the defacement of public buildings, are tiny samples of the failure to assume the individual responsibility of being a citizen. Similar failures to be citizens are seen in the school. Books are defaced, playgrounds are littered, rules are sometimes deliberately flaunted, poor sportsmanship is displayed at inter-school contests, and many fail to live up to what for them are appropriate aspirations. A disheartening attitude of "let the other guy do it" is much too noticeable.

Earlier it was stated that there was no one cause for neurosis—

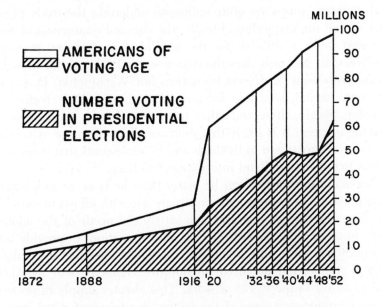

FIG. 21. **Tendencies to apathy on the part of American voters**
("Liberty is being lost by [millions of] lazy people 'who just don't vote.' ") See Citizens Education Project, *Political Parties and Presidential Elections* (New York: Bureau of Publications, Teachers College, Columbia University; 1952) p. 4.

or for suicide, broken homes, and the like—and it seems that there is no one cause for the failure to achieve optimum results in producing citizens. One factor might be the life of relative ease that is lived in our nation. There are many problems, certainly, but for the great majority there is the feeling that they are so much better off than their ancestors that it is easy to develop feelings of complacency. Another factor, noted in social class studies, is the feeling of discouragement that pervades minority racial and religious groups and the members of the lower socio-economic strata. They feel that others are trying to hold them down and that to struggle against the discrimination might very well make things worse. Their feeling is certainly not without justification.

The reason more commonly given for careless functioning as a citizen is that government has become so complex that special training is needed to understand the issues. Such training is necessary and pressure groups are quite willing to undertake the study to get that special understanding. Finally, the size and remoteness of government make it difficult for the individual to feel any personal involvement. Not only does the citizen see little chance for immediate improvement of defects he notices but Washington, D. C., or the state capital, seems so far away that there is little feeling of urgency. Singly, these and other factors are felt by individuals in varying degrees. It is likely that many of them converge as vectors to create the apathy in individuals and in adolescents that is the real threat to our national and international welfare.

No man's citizenship can be better than he is as an individual. Hence, efforts to improve citizenship are one with efforts to improve the home life of the youngster, to satisfy the needs of the adolescent, to reduce the hazards of class discrimination, to provide better conditions for health, to improve the schools, to effect the realization of intellectual potential, to improve character and morality, and to adjust to the world of work. This chapter simply raises to a level of prominence some of the factors in adolescent development that might otherwise receive only incidental treatment.

The meaning of citizenship

Citizenship means many different things, only one of which is the most commonly thought of—voting. The concept has been narrowed down by the Citizenship Education Project of Teachers College, Columbia University, to the more widely accepted elements. "Democracies have failed when people have ceased to exercise control over policy formation. Therefore the heart of citizenship may be viewed as the degree and quality of influence exercised by the people over their leaders and over policy formation." * In order to exercise this control *individuals must be informed and they must act.* Hence, the effective citizen is characterized by the following behaviors and attitudes.†

He *participates* in the life and the welfare of the community. He acts on the premise that the evils of one part of the nation or com-

---

* Willis Griffin and Allen Felix, "Citizenship Education Project," *Phi Delta Kappan*, 33, December, 1951, 165.
† Key words from Edwin T. Ingles, Regional Representative, Citizenship Education Project; Address, "The Teaching of Active Citizenship," Portland, Oregon, February 26, 1954.

munity have a bearing on the welfare of other parts. He gives his time and effort to the tasks that should and must be done.

He is *informed* about the problems involving his citizenship. He keeps in touch with affairs of health, safety, recreation, and welfare. He knows the issues and the candidates in political campaigns. Any ignorance is a challenge to become informed rather than an excuse to avoid action.

He is *religious*. He respects himself enough to seek the fulfillment of all the facets of his personality. He takes seriously the thought that he is his brother's keeper, and he recognizes that his reverence is reflected in his respect and concern for his fellow men.

He is *tolerant*. The word tolerant is perhaps not the best choice. A good citizen is *respectful* of the differences in people. If prejudices exist he feels that it is his duty to do what he can to reduce or eliminate them. He knows that in a democracy all persons have the right to freedom, equality, and justice. He is concerned about human problems even when he is not directly personally involved.

He is *friendly*. He is willing to lend a helping hand when and where it is needed. He respects the right of others to the privileges which are afforded by government and other democratic institutions. He seeks and encourages traits of leadership in others—being a good follower in those areas of his lesser competence.

He is *active in voting*. He takes his full load in the running of affairs of the government, school, church, and home. While he may not know a lot about all of these affairs he does feel responsibility for knowing what is going on. He maintains the scientific attitude of an open mind—being willing to change attitudes and opinions on the basis of additional evidence. He seeks the achievement of improved judgments.

He *manifests neighborliness*. He is not submissive to authority because he is afraid but because he sees in rules and regulations the operation cf principles of justice and freedom. He exercises the self-discipline that shows he respects the rights and privileges of others. His lack of selfishness reveals his social and emotional maturity.

He renders *service*. He takes pleasure in working for the things that he is convinced will make a better life for all. He knows that such service will not only bring about immediate improvement in the running of public affairs but is a means of stimulating his own personality development.

He works for the *conservation* of resources and values. This includes, but is more than, his attack upon the careless woodsman, the "litter-bug" and despoiler of public property. He also seeks to conserve the resources that inhere in the development of latent talents of individuals. He works for the conservation and improvement of the home, the school, the church, and his government.

He performs productive *work*. He develops some constructive vocation that contributes to the welfare of his community. He not only has the desire to be independent and hold down a real job but he wants to do that job in a manner that merits self-respect and the respect of his fellow men.

The values of the *family* are appreciated. Despite the inevitable conflicts that arise in the close association of vigorously active persons, he recognizes that the mutual welfare of all is involved in the solution of the conflicts. Progressively he comes to realize that perfection in family living is not an end product but a process involving continuous personality adjustment.

The above list of attitudes and behaviors shows that the present-day concept of citizenship includes, but goes far beyond, the teachings of civics and government classes. It goes further than stressing the importance of participation in student government. It includes the whole life and education of the growing person. The stress, in short, is that knowledge must be accompanied by *action*. [263] Citizenship education for adolescents must therefore provide experiences that involve practice in the exercise of activities of a citizen.

Community factors in adolescent citizenship

It has been emphasized throughout this book that the wholesome development of adolescents is dependent upon the convergence of many constructive factors. This generalization is of no less importance when it is focused upon one characteristic of adolescence—citizenship. Parents, as the prime molders of personality, are the most important factors in the community of the adolescent.

> . . . It is reasonable to expect that parents will teach and encourage their children to respect the rights of others in the home

and elsewhere. They should teach and encourage honesty, thrift, temperance, the importance and dignity of hard work, respect for law, respect for public and private property, courtesy, and love for country. Parents should give moral, spiritual, and health training. They should make efforts to help children understand the importance of getting along with others. They should strive to understand, and then to satisfy, the basic human needs of their children. They should let children help in making some of the decisions that have to be made in the home, but, by the same token, they need not let children make all the decisions. When parents rear their children in this manner they are teaching and promoting good citizenship . . .*

Those who seek to understand and work effectively with adolescents should appreciate the resources available to them in the form of churches, welfare and recreation departments of cities, juvenile courts, Boy and Girl Scout organizations, psychological clinics, libraries, and museums. These are more plentifully provided in the cities but in the rural communities there are 4-H groups, Future Farmers, the Grange, and agricultural extension services. Because of the variety of services provided and the interests met, these organizations must be part of the concerted effort to produce good citizens. Any groups or individuals failing to recognize the contributions that these varied organizations can provide are shortsightedly curtailing the efficiency of their own efforts.

Outstanding personalities are another resource of the community for providing opportunities for operational citizenship for adolescents. These persons may be influential because of wealth, previous community service, unique experiences, or because of high ideals and faith in the improvability of mankind. Successful business men have often spearheaded movements for playgrounds, swimming pools, youth programs, and have seen the wisdom involved in engaging the services of youth in the pursuit of the project. It is often the priest, minister, or rabbi who works with youth—either providing facilities for development or enlisting the participation of youth in projects that make for better communities for all age groups.

* American Association of School Administrators, *Thirty-second Yearbook, Educating for American Citizenship* (Washington, D. C.: The National Education Association; 1954), p. 77.

There are two ways of capitalizing on the services of such individuals. One of these is to follow their leadership in their attempts to implement their ideas. Too often such persons encounter the difficult obstacle of apathy on the part of the more ordinary citizen. The second use is to enlist their support in programs and projects that others have initiated. Often the primary reason for the prestige of individuals is outside the realm of interest in youth. Hence others must inform them on the merits of programs directly devoted to the interests of youth and seek their cooperation. In recent years, school administrators have increasingly come to realize that progress is hampered by failure to reach key individuals. The varied interests and beliefs of many people make it virtually impossible to reach decisions without the prestige and influence of power figures. [221:208]

The wider community will have its greatest positive impact on youth when it joins effort with the schools. It has been noted that one of the greatest developments in education is the growing integration of school and community. [200]

The schools and citizenship

Today, it has been noted, there is an apparent apathy on the part of a substantial portion of the population. If effective education for citizenship is to be afforded, schools must take the first step to supply the present lack of incentive.

An effort to improve citizenship training is participation in student government. Student councils, homerooms, activity clubs, class and classroom organizations, have been introduced to meet the needs of youth—including opportunities to exercise active citizenship. These activities have produced some encouraging results but there is also a large area of failure. An examination of the reasons for failure suggests some of the steps that should be taken to improve their efficacy.

1. Programs have too often been formulated without a definitive study of local needs and purposes. The result has been a breach between assumed, and often ambiguous, purposes and the activities and organizations planned to achieve them. Too many programs have been a matter of imitation. Thus they not only do

not fit the local needs but the educative opportunities involved in planning the activities are lost.

2. A lack of faith in youth is manifest. Class officers and student councilmen are often appointed by the faculty. Although self-government as a technique for developing citizenship has been professed the administrator retains veto power. Often there is a tendency to restrict student activities to routine, superficial, and unimportant tasks instead of dealing with really serious problems.

3. An outcome of the above two factors is that there is low participation. Low participation is also stimulated by socio-economic status of the pupil. Both prestige and costs are involved but the result is that pupils from the upper strata participate in the ratio of about 3 to 1 from the lower classes.

4. The hue and cry against high school sororities and fraternities indicate that control by privileged groups must be reckoned with. Even in schools where there are no fraternities, power often resides with athletes or students who have received the approbation of the faculty.

5. The student activities programs have often not been seriously considered as an integral part of the school. Eligibility requirements and the lack of faculty time devoted to planning are manifestations of this factor in failure.

6. Faculty interest and support are frequently lacking. This is caused by the fact that teachers are not involved in the planning and because the extra duties are not taken into account in the division of teacher load.

There are, on the other hand, some promising trends which indicate the probability of more rapid progress toward developing citizenship in the next few years.

1. There is an increasing tendency to involve pupils in planning both curricular and non-class activities. Pupils and teachers are cooperating in evolving plans for personal adjustment, school projects, and community participation. A part of this cooperation includes evaluation of the activities.

2. Headway is being made in the participation of pupils in policy

making for athletics—budgets, schedules, and student responsibilities are considered.

3. There is an increasing effort to join the activities programs with the program of studies. Core curriculum, student-teacher evaluation, teachers counseling *with* pupils are manifestations of this trend.

4. Greater effort is being made to make the community an integral part of the educational program. This is seen in work-experience education, the use of the community as a curriculum resource, and the efforts of pupils to improve the community. [106]

There need not be, and there should not be, a detailed description of what the secondary schools should do toward implementing the *action* part of citizenship programs. Local variations to meet specific needs is paramount, but it is not necessary to dream up programs. Already there are a few schools working successfully with many different kinds of programs and projects. Suggestions for local modification and introduction are contained in the things that have been done in other communities. The Citizenship Education Project of Teachers College has used this point of view by serving as a clearing house for ideas. Participating schools report the kind of activities they have practiced together with an evaluation of them. In turn they receive materials and additional ideas from others. Other projects such as the Civic Education Project of Cambridge, the Detroit Citizenship Study, the Kansas Study of Education for Citizenship, and the Citizenship Studies in Syracuse also act as clearing houses for ideas and the focus for distributing materials.

Some of the things that have been done for and by teen-agers, either independently or with the aid of such organizations as listed above, show a great deal of ingenuity and a very widespread distribution of interests. The illustrative list also indicates the inclusive nature of citizenship.

At Ferron, Utah, teacher Clarence Dahle and his pupils in agricultural classes transformed the life of the community. A study was made of the effects of fertilization of soil so that hay could be grown locally. Cattle could then be wintered and sold at higher prices in the spring. Good cattle wintered better and were more efficient "hay burners" than scrub cattle, so Purebred Herefords gradually replaced other less profitable livestock. Dahle's pupils are now mature citizens in the community where they practiced aspects of citizenship in the school. [262]

Among the activities that have been reported by the Citizenship Education Project are the following: In South Orange–Maplewood, New Jersey, students on a rotation basis are assigned to perform school services ranging from the care of gymnasium equipment to helping in the library. Eighth-graders in Steelton, Pennsylvania, prepared a citizens' handbook after first-hand inspection of governmental activities, law enforcement, and studies of sanitation. In Dubuque, Iowa, community welfare was studied in citizenship classes. Such things as safety education, youth welfare, and personal responsibility were considered. The Federal government was duplicated in miniature. Opportunities are found, in such studies, to become acquainted with the Constitution, the two-party system, Congress and the Supreme Court as living institutions rather than as words in a textbook. [290]

Each year some 300,000 high school youngsters travel by bus, train, or private cars to Washington, D. C., to gain an appreciation of the magnitude, tradition, and workings of our national government. They visit the White House, the Lincoln and Jefferson memorials, Mount Vernon, the Supreme Court, and see the original of the Declaration of Independence. The National Gallery of Art, the Library of Congress, the Federal Bureau of Investigation take on additional and personal meaning because of the first-hand experience the students have with them. [348]

In local communities, schools have enlivened the task of teaching for citizenship by stress on the community as a curriculum resource. It would require a book to describe ways in which students have gone even further than using the community as study material by participating in the solution of problems and projects.* Students have sometimes joined in, and sometimes initiated, local clean-up

* Examples of such books are Paul R. Hanna, *Youth Serves the Community* (New York: D. Appleton-Century Company, Inc.; 1936), I. James Quillen and Lavone A. Hanna, *Education for Social Competence* (Chicago: Scott, Foresman and Company; 1948), American Association of School Administrators, *Educating for American Citizenship* (Washington, D. C.: The National Education Association; 1954).

campaigns, "get-out-the-vote" movements, surveys of public opinion on health, education, better government, and the like. Other illustrative examples may be drawn from the participation of one school —Sequoia Union High School of Redwood City, California. In one year the students planned and participated in a scrap steel drive, working with civilian defense workers; joined with the city transportation officials in a movement to support the pooling of rides—a speaker's bureau of chosen students provided speakers for business, fraternal, and social groups; posters were prepared for various campaigns; participated in drives for the sale of stamps and bonds and for the support of the Red Cross and United Service Organizations; provided volunteer workers for nearby farms; and activated the Junior Red Cross. Back of all of these activities were the purposes of better citizenship: learning to work cooperatively, the pooling of opinion and information, helping others, and developing attitudes of responsibility to government. [252:310]

The adolescents' responsibility

The efforts of the community and of the school would be fruitless as far as producing better citizens is concerned without positive response on the part of the adolescents. Logically, we might be inclined to say that they should first prove themselves capable of conducting their personal and school affairs harmoniously before they are accorded serious roles in community affairs. Practically, we must admit that personal, school, and community affairs are but aspects of the same, integrally related, process. Sound psychology backs the notion that positive approaches are superior to negative approaches. For example, it is better to encourage citizenship activities in the place of delinquent behavior rather than to demand elimination of delinquency before youth will be granted responsibility in public affairs. Thus, in addition to attempts to impress the youngster with the present significance of keeping morally clean and mentally alive, of keeping the school neat and in good repair, of observing the rights of peers, there should be contemporaneous stress on the role each young person can play in his future government.

In class discussions Passaic, New Jersey, high school students became concerned at the apathetic attitude of citizens toward voting. They not only made house-to-house canvasses to see that voters were registered and intended to vote but they also campaigned by compiling and distributing information about candidates and issues. They acted as runners and watchers for their favorite candidates. Some students went as far as tutoring immigrants so they could become citizens. It is felt that the big gains lie in the appreciation that students develop of the privilege of voting. [71]

The development of such attitudes toward citizenship is by no means universal. In fact, a loud and frequent cry is that adolescents do not even know the pertinent facts about history and government that are purportedly taught in the school. It has apparently been assumed that the transfer from studying to action is automatic. Students of psychology know that, in general, high transfer from study to behavior is the result of specific planning for transfer. [21:176] Four measures would tend to enhance the development of sounder knowledge and more favorable attitudes: (1) Adults must set the example that will be either unconsciously absorbed or consciously imitated. (2) Formal studies of history and government must be amply illustrated and demonstrated by examples the student can see in his daily experiences. (3) Class study must consist partially in the discussion of personal, individual involvement in governmental activities—the provision of schools, civic welfare, safety, and the like. (4) Youngsters must have the opportunity to participate in the government of their own affairs, but they should also have planned roles to play in the government of their wider community.

Despite the fact that adolescents cannot vote in local and national elections, young persons cannot wait until the age of twenty-one to achieve the status of citizens. There are some things that they should progressively come to appreciate. They can begin to develop their ideas on government by studying its form and function. They can begin developing plans for personal participation by studying issues, keeping abreast of current affairs, and developing informed opinions. They can begin to make their choices of future personal action by studying party organizations and their relationship to personal objectives. There are certain things to remember as political idealism is formulated. A citizen must try his best to base his actions on clear thinking that is concerned with the future and with the welfare and interests of others. He must remember that *one* is an important number. There are many examples of individuals who have improved whole communities by the force and conviction of their actions. It must be remembered that politics is a continuous activity that goes on whether a citizen makes his own desires and interests felt or not. [214:45]

Voting and the teen-ager

President Eisenhower, on January 17, 1954, said: "For years our citizens between the ages of eighteen and twenty-one have, in time of peril, been summoned to fight for America. They should participate in the political process that produces this fateful summons." This belief is shared by many people. Most adolescents feel that military service without voting privileges is akin to taxation without representation. Even before the teen-age vote became an issue the feeling was expressed that youth needed more responsibility in government.

It is of the utmost importance that youth be given opportunities for experiencing and participating in governmental undertakings, for that is the best way in which they can come to appreciate government as part of their lives. It is also vital that young people develop an attitude of responsibility toward government and the duties of citizenship. . . .

One of the greatest needs of youth is not to be set apart from adults, but to participate with adults in the understanding and management of natural resources and human institutions. The lessons to be learned from the totalitarian states include the danger of separate youth movements, and the necessity of offering youth a chance to live and grow and achieve within a free society. Confining the energies of young people within the barriers of race or defective education or lack of employment opportunity or restricted opportunity for effective choices of association and vocation stultifies their personality and endangers the nation of which they are citizens and the world of which they are a part.*

There are several seemingly valid reasons why voting privileges should be extended to eighteen-year-old individuals. Not the least

---

* Katharine F. Lenroot, "Youth and Government," *The Annals of the American Academy of Political and Social Science*, 236, 1944, 165, 167.

of these reasons is that young men of this age are called on for service in time of military crisis. In these recurrent crises they have acquitted themselves admirably. It has been pointed out that youth quickly achieve more maturity when they have the obligation of military service thrust upon them. It would seem that a better way than armed service to help them mature would be to give them responsibility in the government that so intimately affects their lives.

Many young people, being in school and studying current issues, are better informed on election issues and candidates than are voting citizens. Having the privilege of voting, or being promised that privilege within the very near future, would add motivation that would make them be even more aggressive students of local and national affairs. Even those who are out of school live in a time much different from that in which our statutes were formed. Today radio, television, and abundant newspapers and magazines make information readily available to all, whereas formerly many persons (even older citizens) lacked a ready source of contemporary data.

The late teen years represent a period of psychological readiness for citizenship. It is during this period that idealism is shaping rapidly—building, of course, on foundations laid earlier. It is during this period that the adolescent is thinking of himself in relation to a role in the world. Hence, if he sees corruptness and bad government yet has no chance to do anything about them, he is likely to develop the *laissez-faire* attitude that so disturbs statesmen and serious minded citizens. The importance of this period of readiness is accentuated by the fact that in the next few years (the early twenties) youth are so busy with getting started in a career and laying the foundations for a smoothly functioning family life that their responsibilities as citizens are likely to suffer. R. J. Havighurst has pointed out that the arduous tasks of occupation and family are quite likely to postpone the assumption of civic responsibility. [136:263] It would seem wise to initiate the vital "developmental task" of citizenship during a period that is less likely to see strong competition from other developmental tasks.

It has been shown that the older a person becomes the more conservative he gets. Lifetime habits tend to favor that which is merely good as against that which is better. [63:261] With the population growing older because of increased longevity the pressure of youth is needed to insure vitality and to encourage innovations to meet the evolving conditions of the present. Some regard this as a danger, but where youth have been given a vote (Georgia) those in high positions have been gratified by the wisdom and fairness of youth. [280]

It is felt that earlier responsibility in governmental activities would result in youth having greater respect for laws. They would feel that they had a part in the making of the governmental situation that surrounds them. As it is, they lose the interest generated in school before they have a chance to exercise it.

If it be true that youth are maturing more rapidly today than they were formerly (some estimate a two-year superiority in psychological maturity by the late teens) due to improved education and better living conditions, the responsibility of citizenship would give them added incentive to act their age. Where they have been granted mature status (right to marry, own property, take a job, and the like) they have justified the faith placed in them. Someone might observe that they have not done well in the responsibility of driving a car. But when youth have been properly prepared for driving, through driver education programs, they have done an admirable job. It is a paradox that youth who do admirable jobs of piloting $500,000 planes cannot handle relatively slow, earth-bound four wheelers. It seems obvious that it is a matter of preparation rather than youth. Certainly, voting citizenship would be much more functional if it accompanied or followed closely after formal preparation for it.

There are arguments against the voting privilege. It might be better for the reader to evaluate them than for the author to record his evaluation of them. They may be stated as follows: (1) There is no similarity between fighting and voting. The judgment and skill needed by a soldier bear no relationship to the judgment and skill required of a citizen. (2) There are many eighteen-year-olds who are not mature—they have not worked, have not had the requisite experience. (3) The kinds of problems that face the modern voter require more, rather than less, preparation. (4) Relatively few countries in the world set the voting age as low as eighteen. (5) Young people are too easily swayed by propaganda and raucous leadership. They may go to extremes. [280]

Youth and the citizen of tomorrow

It has been the contention throughout this book that many of the difficulties of adolescents spring from lack of a feeling that what they are doing has significance and from lack of purpose. Technological and social changes have resulted in making them dependent for a period of time extending beyond their achievement of varying aspects and degrees of maturity. No single change is going to result in the eradication of contemporary hazards to growing up, but an area of great promise is present in making youth feel their importance as citizens—giving them feelings of significance and worth. Two possibilities are suggested. One is to give youth increasing autonomy in the conduct of their own affairs and the other is to grant them the privilege and responsibility of citizenship in the wider community. These changes promise to make of them better citizens today and more effective citizens tomorrow.

The symptom called delinquency

The author has a discouragingly large mass of material on and references to delinquency and a discouraging paucity of data on the making of adolescent citizens. Yet more adolescents become praiseworthy citizens than contribute to delinquency statistics. The imbalance in published material is probably due to the fact that the ordinary escapes notice and the unusual attracts attention. Then, too, delinquency is expensive in terms of life and property. It constitutes a threat to the well-being of the individual and society. It deserves the attention it gets because searching out the factors that contribute to failure in adolescence will sharpen our realization of what can and should be done to improve the lot of adolescents.

Nature and extent of delinquency

It is advisable to review some fundamental postulates of psychology. One of these is that behavior is caused. There are reasons why some youngsters make socially approved adjustments to society and there are reasons why some do not. Often these reasons occur in complicated contexts that are difficult to understand. Too frequently in individual cases the cause is never understood and the

TYPES OF ADJUDICATED DELINQUENCIES

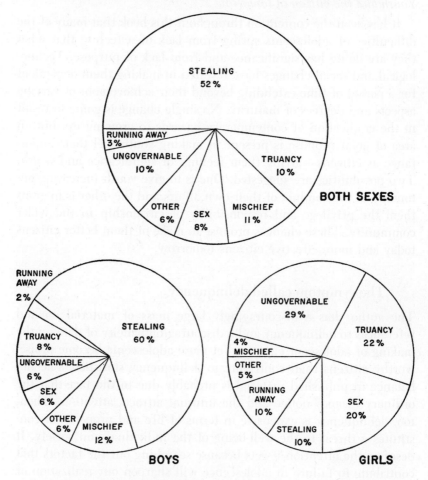

FIG. 22. **Types of delinquencies**
Delinquencies of boys and girls and of boys and girls combined. From *Partnership in Youth* (Albany: New York State Youth Commission, Bulletin No. 3, February, 1950), pp. 4–5.

delinquent behavior continues because the cause, or causes, remain unchanged. Another postulate in human psychology is the fact of multiple causation. Though simple explanatory factors are sought the basic explanation must usually be found in an intermeshing of forces. A third postulate is that all behavior is symptomatic. The recent emphasis on projective techniques as a means of understanding personality trends is a recognition of the fact that the way a person acts and feels is a revelation of his potentialities and motivations. Delinquency must be understood as an attempt on the part of the individual to adjust to his world. It is his way of seeking harmony with the world as he sees it and his way of relieving the tensions he feels. Delinquency, like other symptoms of failure to adjust, must be perceived as the individual's abortive attempt to tell others, "I need help. I hurt. Something is wrong and I can't tell what it is."

Delinquency is behavior that, in given circumstances, comes into conflict with the law. Psychologically it may be regarded as a nonadjustive "adjustive mechanism." Socially, delinquency is what the law says it is, as that law is interpreted in the local community—or by the judge. W. C. Kvaraceus gives a *clinical* definition of the delinquent but admits that this is often not the definition given by guardians of the law. "He is a youngster who habitually resolves his personal-social problems through overt aggressive behavior, which dominant society finds bothersome and contrary to its value-identifications. For the youngster this delinquency-aggression is purposive and adjustive; from the point of view of society, it constitutes an irritating maladaptation." * *Legally* the act of delinquency is defined by the various states according to the age of the person committing the act. In one state a transgressor might be classified as a delinquent while in another he would be treated as an adult offender. The conditions under which the act takes place may in various states be factors in determining whether or not it will be judged to be delinquent.

Statistics on the extent of delinquency might be quite different if there were a commonly-used definition and uniformity in court practices. The Children's Bureau of the U. S. Department of Health, Education, and Welfare reports as follows:

Juvenile delinquency is fast becoming America's No. 1 social problem!

---

* William C. Kvaraceus, *The Community and the Delinquent*, p. 57. Copyright 1954 by World Book Company.

At the present time the number of young people apprehended by the police for delinquent behavior is increasing at an alarming rate. The current rise began with the "cold war." It has received a big boost from the Korean War.

In the 3-year period from 1948 to 1951 the number of children appearing before juvenile courts reporting to the Children's Bureau *increased* a total of *17 per cent*.

In that same period the number of boys and girls in this age group from 10 to 17 increased only 5 per cent. In other words, juvenile delinquency is increasing at a faster rate than the child population.

Surprisingly enough, the less densely populated areas of the country seem to be experiencing even sharper increases than this 17 per cent average. Courts serving jurisdictions of less than 100,000 persons showed an average increase of 29 per cent—and a number of these "small" courts had increases in excess of 50 per cent!

This sudden increase in both the rate and volume of delinquency reminds us of World War II, when all-time records in juvenile misbehavior were established. The world was turned upside down then. Many families were separated. Fathers were away in the armed forces. Mothers on war jobs were sometimes unable to give their children proper care. Young boys and girls roamed the streets to all hours of the night. Home life suffered.

The present international situation seems to be having a similar effect. People feel anxious about the future. Home and community life have been greatly altered by the change in pace brought on by accelerated defense activities.

In this atmosphere of sudden change and a doubtful future, many parents have not been able to give their children the steady care and supervision necessary for normal social development. Children need a stable home life. Without it they can easily become delinquent.*

The statistical part of the quotation we must believe. Whether or not the increase in juvenile court cases reflects a general increase in delinquency due to upset world conditions, we cannot say. It may be

---

* *Helping Delinquent Children* (Washington, D. C.: U. S. Department of Health, Education, and Welfare, Children's Bureau; 1953), pp. 5–6.

that more young people are taken to court because of a sharpened awareness of delinquency and an accompanying rise in the rate of identification and treatment. In either case the problem needs understanding and the children need help.

There are those, including the author, who feel that attributing delinquency to the turmoil of world conditions is neither valid nor helpful. Anxiety of parents is conveyed to children through word and act, but upsetting conditions and complex problems have always been a part of man's history. It will be more constructive to attempt to define some of the specifics that seem to contribute to delinquency.

Fallacious notions about delinquency

An initial step in understanding delinquency might well be to question some of the existing beliefs. The following are recognized as being fallacies: Better playgrounds will result in the disappearance of delinquency. More education will cause delinquency to disappear. Alien groups in our population account for the high incidence of delinquency. Delinquents stem from inferior heredity potentialities. Delinquency is caused by broken homes. Poverty is the cause of delinquency. Poor methods of child rearing cause delinquency. [85] Delinquency is caused by low intelligence. Delinquency is caused by facial disfigurement and bodily malformation.

These fallacies are dangerous for two reasons. (1) Each of them contains an element of truth, hence some evidence points to its credibility; but no one of them is sufficiently inclusive to be considered *the* cause or *the* explanation. (2) These fallacies are often plausible enough to prevent continued thinking about the specific factors that are operative in individual cases and in given localities.

Factors contributing to delinquency

There is an increasing tendency for authorities to shun the placing of blame for delinquency on one or two factors. Instead of causes it is more accurate to speak of contributing factors. The evidence points to the participating of many converging forces which channel behavior into unacceptable forms. [124:281]

It has been popular to attribute delinquency to broken homes— and there is evidence that among delinquents the incidence of broken homes is higher than for the general population. Yet many children are delinquent whose homes are intact, and many are up-standing citizens whose homes are broken. Hence the contemporary investigator looks beyond the broken home, or the physically intact home, to the personalities who constitute the family. It is conceiv-able that some homes are improved by divorce or desertion—an unstable personality may cease to be a stimulus in the life of the child, leaving a parent who provides a better environment despite the fact that the environment is not bisexual. A delinquency precip-itating situation may be presented by virtue of parents' staying together despite a chronic inability to get along. It appears that it is not the broken home *per se* that contributes to delinquency but the inadequacy of the adults who cannot get along and manifest the symptom of divorce or desertion.

One of the earlier explanations of the causes of delinquency was living in a disorganized or impoverished neighborhood. The rate of waywardness is high in such areas, and attempts are made to bring about improvements. But providing playgrounds or improving hous-ing will not solve the problem—though such things might be the balancing factor that would prevent some individuals from becom-ing delinquent. Inadequacy of the parents, their inability to make good life adjustments, is conceivably a reason for their continued existence in a poor neighborhood. The Gluecks found that frequent change of residence seemed to be an important factor in explaining delinquency: ". . . we found that the delinquents had far less chance than the other boys to develop neighborhood ties. . . . One out of every three of the delinquents had changed residence eleven or more times, as compared with but one in ten of the nondelin-quents." *

The existence of racial minorities sometimes contributes to de-linquency. [245:27] Adolescent members of such groups may feel the insecurity of being poorly established financially. They are sub-ject to discrimination and prejudice on the part of the majority group and are often taunted and teased. Puerto Ricans, Negroes, and Mexicans are thus driven to the defensive mechanism of delin-quent acts; they group together in gangs and engage in warfare to

---

* Sheldon and Eleanor Glueck, *Delinquents in the Making* (New York: Harper & Brothers; 1952), p. 82.

relieve their hostility and are then pointed out as being morally depraved for their transgressions.

Closely related to, actually a part of, community disorganization is the contributing effect of low socio-economic status. Lower-class children constitute a disproportionately large part of the delinquent group for two reasons: (1) They have more than average difficulty in meeting their needs and in adjusting to the demands of the dominant and higher social groups. (2) They lack the parental and financial protection that often keeps the upper- and middle-class teen-age law breaker from being identified as a delinquent. They therefore contribute more generously to statistical delinquency.

Psychological factors within the home of low socio-economic status are often conducive to the development of delinquent patterns. Parents may quarrel quite openly; there are likely to be overt manifestations of infidelity; beatings, drunkenness, and desertion or separation are common. Irresponsibility, shiftlessness, incompetence, and financial and personal inadequacy (which has contributed to their low status and tends to perpetuate it) render the parents comparatively incapable of exercising adequate supervision of children and adolescents. [9:527] At school these youngsters are subjected to the slurs, taunts, and discrimination of upper-class students. [143:202] Teachers add to their burdens by awarding them grades that are in wide disagreement with their indicated ability. [75] There is evidence that a studied attempt is made to keep lower-class youngsters out of certain clubs, student activities, and leadership activities, with the exception of athletics. (Indeed, sports may serve as an opening wedge for acceptance for some.) Altogether there is an ugly picture of more fortunate individuals compounding the unhappy position of children and youth who have already encountered many frustrating conditions. It speaks well for youth that more of them do not become chronic delinquents.

Another disagreeable aspect of delinquency and socio-economic status is that many youngsters from the so-called better homes are also law-breakers but do not so frequently come to light as statistics. There is some question as to whether or not what might be called "white collar delinquency" is increasing more than the general trend, but the following words of Kvaraceus reflect a growing recognition of its existence:

There is little doubt that most delinquents, as children of lower status, have been confronted by many more problems of living, have undergone more frustrations, and have been given less help in their growth and development toward dominant middle-class virtues than the children of higher status. At the same time, the child of higher status is apt to be protected and screened off so that he does not come within the ken of the researcher, whereas the lower-status child is more apt to be referred to official agencies and courts. In some of the more recent studies there is the suggestion that more children of upper status are being met in delinquency situations. Whether this is due to a real increase in delinquency among families of higher status or whether it merely reflects an improvement in the referral procedures remains a matter for conjecture.*

Some studies present the disturbing conclusion that schools may be a factor in precipitating delinquency. W. W. Wattenberg found that for some children the freedom of vacations reduced the incidence of getting into trouble, while there was an increase during the school terms. Certain schools encourage the development of destructive aggression—although for most children, schools tend to prevent the formation of patterns of delinquency. [337]

It has long been noted that the average delinquent has more frequently failed to be promoted than the average non-delinquent. Delinquents as a group get proportionately fewer high grades and proportionately more low or failing grades than does the generality. In a society where success in school is so highly valued this becomes a source of disappointment and frustration for the individual. He is criticized by his parents, and teachers frequently are unable to cover their personal dissatisfaction. These feelings on the part of the child and adults prompt some young people to resort to the aggressive behavior that is called delinquent. Some seek escape through truancy—so many, in fact, that truancy has become one criterion of pre-delinquent behavior. Frequent moving, as noted above in the discussion of community factors, is a source of difficulty for some, since adjustments must be made to new companions, new teachers, and new curricular demands. [180:135] For some, school is made

---

* William C. Kvaraceus, *The Community and the Delinquent*, p. 37. Copyright 1954 by World Book Company.

unbearable by autocratic, prejudiced, or unsympathetic teachers. Some of the blame for the negative role of the school must be placed on the inadequacy of the curriculum to meet the needs of specific individuals. This is not simply a matter of not having the intelligence to do academic work because the average intelligence of delinquents is but slightly below that of non-delinquents. Of course, many delinquents have extraordinarily high intelligence. The failure of the school program lies in its not having been adapted to the felt needs of the individual. Many feel that the school has no relation to what they are doing now or will do in the future.

Personal characteristics of the delinquent

All the factors contributing to delinquency do not reside in the external environment. The personality of the individual is involved in the reaction the individual makes to environmental frustrations. Although a part of the personality response is due to previous conditioning, another part is due to congenital factors that seem to produce a predisposition to delinquency.

Low intelligence may contribute to a predisposition toward delinquency, though it certainly cannot be deemed a cause. Studies indicate that intelligence, as evaluated by present tests, of the delinquent averages ten IQ points lower than does the generality. Many, despite relatively high test intelligence, do not seem to possess the specific aptitudes required for academic success. Hence, in school systems where rigid academic standards prevail, there are some who suffer the frustration of comparison with peers who are typically more successful. Low intelligence may also contribute to the slow development of moral responsibility or the lack of discriminative judgment that would lead to more circumspect behavior. Some authorities feel that the greater proportion of below-average and low intelligence of delinquents as a group may lead to their more easily being caught in delinquent acts and thus becoming so identified. Some who have higher intelligence engage in what is technically delinquent behavior but escape detection by virtue of their ingenuity. Protection by parents in the higher socio-economic groups, where test intelligence averages somewhat higher, must also account for some of the statistics on the lower average intelligence of the delinquent. A study covering a period of seventeen years, reported by Ruth Fairbank, suggests that our ideals of delinquency and dependency for the mentally subnormal must be revised by taking into account the effect of a favorable environment. A large portion of a group of 166 subnormal children were found to be self-supporting, morally responsible, and law-abiding despite an earlier prognosis of prostitution, failure to be self-supporting, and delinquency. [104] Obviously, low intelligence constitutes a hazard when no attempts are made to prevent the realization of poor adjustment and when it is combined with other factors that contribute to illegal behavior.

Bodily malformation or facial disfigurement may be factors in some delinquency. These differences set some children off from the group and create justified feelings of being unwanted or unaccepted. However, the fact that many who have such handicaps do not become delinquent emphasizes the fact that problems are frequently less serious than the attitude taken toward them. It may be a long struggle to convince the individual with deformity that it is the inner self that is important after the first contact with another, but it is a struggle that has resulted in success for the individual who has good parents and wise teachers.

While sex cannot be said to contribute to delinquency certain relations of sex to delinquency should be noted. Four to seven times as many boys as girls become delinquent, though this disparity is decreasing in recent years. Boys become delinquent at an earlier age. [9:519] These differences are attributed to the greater freedom granted to boys in our culture and the more intimate supervision of girls. In view of the commonly held belief that girls have greater emotionality than do boys, this presents an optimistic hope for favorable outcomes of programs devoted to the welfare of boys. The greater part of the delinquency of girls consists of sex offenses. Part of this difference is due to the double standard, which condones the sowing of wild oats by boys but condemns girls for similar behavior. Kinsey has shown that although girls achieve anatomical maturity earlier than do boys their sexual appetites reach a peak at a later age. [172:143, 202] Hence sex delinquency must be attributed to something other than an overpowering urge.

L. K. Frank summarizes research data and the consensus of authorities in the following passage:

. . . From clinical records there are indications that some of the young girls who are involved in sex delinquencies and who have venereal infections are individuals who have never accepted, indeed have rejected, the female and feminine role. They are likely to be daughters from families where the mother has been of little importance, receiving little or no respect from her husband, often a cowed, submissive wife; moreover, these girls have never enjoyed approval or admiration from their fathers and so have never developed any feeling of being a woman with a sense of their own dignity or worth as a woman. Consequently they have no difficulty in playing the role of sex object, offering themselves freely to any casual male, calculatingly cool and deliberate. They have little sex interest and are passive if not frigid. To speak of them as victims of passion, or weak-willed individuals who could not resist sex temptation, is to misunderstand completely their conduct and their feelings. By exercising power over men, some are getting revenge for the years of humiliation they have suffered as girls under dominant fathers and contemptuous brothers.*

The foregoing well illustrates two fundamental facts about delinquency. One is that the real factors behind delinquency are not too readily discernible. The other relates to the pervasive influence of salutary home environments and mentally healthy parents.

The emotional instability of delinquents has been consistently noted in studies.

As a rule delinquents show more evidence of abnormalities. They tend to have a higher rate of instability, destructiveness, and dependency. . . . The offending groups all hold a large proportion of restless, impulsive, active, defiant, and extroverted youth . . . the delinquent is a daring, adventurous, egocentric type, yet he is often bothered by feelings of inferiority.†

It is recognized, however, that such traits are not possessed only by delinquents. Delinquency is but one of the symptoms that may spring from some pattern of such traits. Further, it must be recognized that the personality traits themselves are outcomes of situa-

---

* L. K. Frank in National Society for the Study of Education, *43rd Yearbook, Part I, Adolescence* (Chicago: The University of Chicago Press; 1944), p. 245.
† Kvaraceus, *op. cit.*, p. 95. Copyright 1954 by World Book Company.

tions and conditions the growing individual has encountered. In other words, the attack on delinquency must be through an attack on the factors that generate and perpetuate such traits. This is tantamount to saying that delinquency, like other problems of adolescence, can best be approached by the study of *all* the conditions that shape the lives of adolescents.

The problem of discipline permeates the problems of youth and delinquency. Unfortunately there are strong adherents to both of two extreme views. One group believes in stern, immediate, unequivocal, and decisive treatment of the resistant child and adolescent. Another believes that freedom to exercise self-control is the road to achieving the goals of effective discipline. It seems probable that the goal of discipline—self-directed but socially oriented behavior—can best be reached by a course midway between these two. Certainly the authoritarian approach does not achieve the goal of self-direction. Conformity is based on fear and non-conformity may break out wildly when fear is not sufficiently strong. On the other hand, too much freedom before the individual is prepared for self-direction has a bewildering effect. Children need the firm direction and counsel of adults; without it they are tense and uncertain. Improvement of the home and school will come when adults learn to steer this narrow middle path, giving direction when it is needed, establishing strong barriers in appropriate situations, and allowing freedom when the consequences of freedom are educative and not excessively dangerous. S. E. Burr points out that the misinterpretation of the theories of progressive education must bear some of the responsibility for the school's role in delinquency. Parents who believe that the child should never be admonished make a similar error. [53] On the other hand, authoritarian control in the police state manner is inimical to our democratic way of life. [111:18] While discipline is important, it must be remembered that it is only one factor. Love, acceptance, admiration, happy parents, effective teachers, interested citizens, are also factors in the personality development of adolescents.

Predicting juvenile delinquency

Like other personality characteristics, delinquency does not arise overnight. The tensions, frustrations, and personal inadequacies that lead to the breaking of law are persistent factors that have been at work a long time. Thus the term "pre-delinquent" behavior has been used for some time. This is a way of saying that certain traits and behaviors, if they continue to grow unchecked, will probably result in delinquency when the individual becomes older.

In the foregoing discussion of personal characteristics of the delinquent it was noted that there are differences in the average delinquent and average non-delinquent person.

. . . Various investigators have reported that those children who as a group, are delinquent, or who become delinquent, differ significantly from other children in such areas as the following: family relationships, home conditions, location of residence, social and economic status, truancy record, school retardation, academic aptitude, school marks, liking for school, immaturity, club membership, companionship, family mobility, etc. This is not meant to imply that every delinquent differs from every non-delinquent in these areas, since there is always in evidence considerable overlapping between the two groups on any one of the variables studied. However, it is true that many more delinquents, for example, receive lower marks in school, repeat their school grades, play truant, and entertain a fierce dislike for school than do children who are not delinquent or who do not become delinquent. Similarly, more delinquents than non-delinquents have unsatisfactory family and home situations. Still other differences have been observed in other areas.*

These average differences have given rise to the hope that the behaviors and situations that precede delinquency could be identified early enough to allow steps for the prevention of delinquency. Questionnaires, rating schedules, and check lists have been devised to help locate children who are vulnerable to, prone to, or in contact with the conditions contributing to, delinquency. It is recognized that differences between delinquents and non-delinquents are not mutually exclusive, but the average differences may be helpful in identifying the *potentially* delinquent. Thus the user of such devices is advised not to identify children as pre-delinquent but to use the results as supplements to sound clinical judgment. [123:205] It is important on those parts of the prediction schedule

* William C. Kvaraceus, *K D Proneness Scale and Check List, Manual of Directions* (Revised), p. 3. Copyright 1953 by World Book Company.

having to do with personality traits (questionnaires, projective techniques, or observations) to get back of the behavior to the cause. The schedules do not tell what to do, they simply indicate that difficulty exists. It is up to the parents and the school to institute proper remedial measures. The school is probably in the most advantageous position to note the difficulties and to initiate personality improvement programs or to remove some of the conditions that aggravate frustrations.

Preventing delinquency

The family, because of its profound influence in shaping the initial growth of personality, must receive foremost consideration. The Gluecks stress the following specifics that help or hamper wholesome adjustment: (1) Discipline by the father, (2) supervision by the mother, (3) affection of the father for his children, (4) affection of the mother for her children, and (5) cohesiveness of the family. [102] Both the delinquent and the conforming child must take what they get. Hence the approach must be through more effective education for family life.

The adult personalities that are the core of the family have been a long time in the making. Hence a more promising approach than attempting to change persons who have already reached maturity—though discouragingly slow—is through education of children and adolescents for more robust personality. Ruth Strang sums up the needed school emphases in the following ten points: (1) Providing a variety of crafts, art, music, athletics, as well as academic experiences for children, (2) understanding the unique capacities of individuals and encouraging their development, (3) providing flexible programs that meet the indicated needs of individuals, (4) helping children to build skills and gain knowledge without excessive experiences of failure, (5) guiding children in the building of appropriate individual goals and encouraging growth toward those goals, (6) helping children gain satisfaction from human relationships, (7) allowing opportunities for normal emotional response—avoiding judging these on adult standards, (8) handling classroom disturbances in an objective manner, (9) counseling with students to help them in the proper evaluation of difficulties, and (10) working with other agencies to improve the home and the community. [299:267]

The fact that some delinquency seems to stem from low intelligence or bodily malformation suggests that special agencies have a contribution to make to the prevention of delinquency. Special classes, guidance services, medical and psychiatric treatment, child guidance clinics, and school social workers can serve to avert some cases of incipient delinquency.

The fact of multiple causation of delinquency makes it obvious that community-wide and nation-wide approaches must be recognized and implemented. Community recreation facilities, planning for the part-time employment of youth, improving the holding power of the schools, special agencies for the study and therapy of children, improved police practices and improved and consistent court practices, and improvements of institutions for the treatment of delinquents must be among the areas studied.

The work of all persons and agencies comes to focus in the moral development of the child. If there has been a steady emphasis on the right and wrong of conduct, if the rights and privileges of others have been stressed, if responsibility has been accorded and expected, then the child will grow into adolescence with the feeling that he is most appreciated when he acts in socially approved ways —and he will know what these ways are. Moral responsibility is the outcome of mental maturity, successful social experience, and knowledge. Teachers, counselors, youth leaders, and parents must realize that moral development is not simply the result of maturation but depends on maturation plus appropriate experience. Direct instruction will capitalize on the criticism of improper conduct and commendation of varied manifestations of proper behavior.

It is easy to see that such emphases in the school depend upon the knowledge and maturity of teachers. Careful selection of properly trained teachers by administrators and school boards is an important step. But the greatest hope inheres in teachers who find satisfaction in their life and work and who have the deeply established habit of continued learning. Their knowledge must embrace an understanding of the needs of children and adolescents and ways of meeting those needs. They are more than mechanical dispensers of knowledge, they are dynamic interpersonal agents in educating the whole child. [168] The nature of the knowledges and attitudes required for meeting needs has been summarized in the following: (1) Teachers know that behavior is caused by identifiable factors,

564   *Continuation of the Maturing Processes*

(2) they can accept and respect every child, (3) they recognize the uniqueness of each child and seek ways to foster optimum development, (4) they are aware of the developmental tasks at the various phases of growth, (5) they know the general principles of growth and development, and (6) they know how to gather and use relevant information about individual development. [249:19] These are not easy functions to perform, but the reward of seeing more adolescents grow to healthy maturity is great.

Summary

Most adolescents are good citizens but there are enough failures and shortcomings to warrant giving more attention to direct study of and involvement in citizenship responsibilities. The complexity of our government demands early and continuing study of the responsibilities of citizenship. Effective citizenship begins with the wholesome and well rounded development of individuals.

Education for citizenship must aim at participation, information, religious orientation, tolerance and respect, friendliness, neighborliness, service, conservation, productive work, and the preservation of family, church, and community life. Such education must be the shared responsibility of the home, community agencies (church, welfare agencies, communication, recreation, and the like), and the schools. The schools might well be made the focal point of improved preparation for citizenship. More functional course work and efforts to improve student participation in government are imperatives. Many suggestive and representative programs for citizenship are in current operation. A most encouraging aspect of these programs is the extent to which adolescents actually enter into the workings of the government and community life. Adolescents have a responsibility for efficiently executing the opportunities accorded them. It is worth remembering that responsibility is a source of motivation for developing efficiency. One way to give this responsibility is to grant the teen-ager a vote while his primary life task still consists of learning.

The study of delinquency is highly important not only because of expense in life and property but because attention can be focused upon many of the hazards to development during adolescence.

Delinquency must be understood as a symptom of maladjustment created by many unfavorable factors. Recent statistics on the rate of delinquency indicate that the old explanations involving low socio-economic status, though still valid, are not sufficiently inclusive. Rather than causes of delinquency, it is helpful to think of contributing factors—such as broken homes, badly warped (though not broken) homes, disorganized neighborhoods, frequent change of residence, and discrimination against racial and religious minorities.

It is somewhat discouraging to find that schools must bear some blame for contributing to delinquency. Grade failures and low marks (aggravated by inflexible curriculums that do not allow for varied activities, needs, and motivations) and emotionally immature teachers are the prime school hazards. The delinquent himself must take some blame because many others, who do adjust, encounter problems just as difficult as his. However, low intelligence, poor opportunities, bodily malformations, and disfigurement must be regarded as mental health problems rather than causes for blame.

Knowledge of the traits, behaviors, and typical milieus of adolescents has led to the construction of delinquency prediction instruments. These devices *help* to locate those who are prone to become delinquent or who are exposed to unfavorable environments. Proper, individual therapy must then be instituted to prevent the realization of the unfavorable prognosis. Besides individual therapy, community-wide approaches (preparing young adults for parenthood, providing better teachers and better schools, improving legal practices, and strengthening all agencies for moral education) are important in the general problem of delinquency. Altogether, the reduction of delinquency depends on the program of improved preparation for youthful citizenship.

STUDY AND REVIEW ITEMS

1. What are some adult manifestations of the belief that training for citizenship is not entirely adequate?
2. Can you think of any qualities of a good citizen that are not mentioned in the chapter?

3. Describe some activities or projects, which you know from personal experience, that have engaged adolescents in the welfare of the community as a whole.
4. Describe some school practices with which you are acquainted that indicate "lip-service" only to the development of citizenship.
5. How would you explain the failure of many adolescents to develop good citizenship in areas where they have been given opportunity to do so?
6. What do you think would be the effect on the community and nation of giving eighteen-year-olds the right to vote?
7. How do you feel about the contention that world-wide unrest and tension explain recent rises in delinquency rates?
8. What are some of the shortcomings of the terminology, "causes of delinquency?"
9. Do you feel that it is justifiable to claim that the school sometimes contributes to delinquency?
10. If personality traits do not clearly distinguish the delinquent from the non-delinquent, what purposes can delinquency prediction devices serve?
11. What kind of discipline of children and adolescents do you think might be most effective in preventing delinquency?
12. What might you, as a student today, do to prevent any further rise in, or to reduce, delinquency rates?

RECOMMENDED SUPPLEMENTARY READING

American Association of School Administrators. *32nd Yearbook, Educating for American Citizenship* (Washington, D. C.: National Education Association; 1954), pp. 133–322.
   Part IV of this volume deals with the meaning of citizenship and how it is related to basic needs. This section describes some things that are being done to promote good citizenship and indicates some things that should be done. Bibliographies at the end of each chapter indicate the wide ramifications of citizenship education.

"Education for Citizenship," *Phi Delta Kappan,* 33, 1951, 161–224.
   The entire issue of this magazine is devoted to articles on citizenship. Many projects such as the Citizenship Education Project (Columbia), and the Detroit, Syracuse, and Kansas studies are described. Other articles deal with projects being conducted in various schools. A citizenship training inventory is reproduced.

Federal Security Agency. "Juvenile Delinquency: A Selected Bibliography" (Mimeographed). Washington, D. C.: Social Security Administration, Children's Bureau, March, 1953, 41 pp.

This indexed and annotated bibliography will help the student find references pertaining to his particular interest in the field of delinquency. Books, articles, and mimeographed materials are included. The divisions are General Considerations, Incidence, Causes, Prevention, Treatment, and Organizations for Control.

Gillespie, James M., and Allport, Gordon W. *Youth's Outlook on the Future* (Garden City, N. Y.: Doubleday and Company, Inc.; 1955), 61 pp.

This booklet contains brief descriptions of the attitudes youth in different countries take toward their personal lives and future careers. The American sample consists in a description of studies of Harvard, Radcliffe, and Miami University students. The aim is to increase international understanding through comparative study.

Kvaraceus, William C. *The Community and the Delinquent: Cooperative Approaches to Preventing and Controlling Delinquency* (Yonkers: World Book Company; 1954), 566 pp.

The author of this inclusive book recognizes that delinquency is created by many factors and must be prevented and treated through the cooperation of many individuals and agencies. He offers no ready-made solution; rather he shows how *each community* may work out its own unique approach.

AUDIO-VISUAL MATERIAL

Children in Trouble (March of Time, 369 Lexington Avenue, New York 17), 10 min., so., b. and w.

A widely acclaimed documentary film which forcibly portrays the factors leading to delinquency. The cooperative roles of home, church, school, and community in the wholesome development of children are emphasized.

Our Basic Civil Rights (Coronet Films, Coronet Building, Chicago 1), 14 min., so., b. and w. or color.

Civil rights are defined by courts and preserved by citizens. In this film basic concepts of civil rights are presented and attention is directed to the fundamental liberties of our society. The film was winner of the 1950 Freedoms Foundations Award.

What characteristics must parents, teachers, and counselors have in order to be of maximum help to adolescents? What are the next goals adolescents must pursue after passing through the teens? What traits must adolescents develop now in order to succeed in adult roles?

CHAPTER EIGHTEEN

The Adult and the Adolescent

An attempt has been made, throughout this book, to point out some of the implications for guidance of the facts, principles, and theories of development during adolescence. This chapter will summarize some of the more inclusive generalizations and recommendations that have been made earlier.

A further purpose of this chapter is to show that maturing processes continue after the teen years and the early twenties. It is easy to slip into the error of believing that the first twenty or so years of life are *the* years of preparation for the rest of life. The truth is that all that has preceded is a preparation for the present—whether that present be at age thirty, forty, or eighty. All of us are now preparing for the developmental tasks that will confront us at our next stage of development. We might even say that "Life is just one darn developmental task after another."

It has been emphasized repeatedly that the adolescent's perplexity may be reduced if he is prepared beforehand for the situations he is likely to face. Similarly, it is worth emphasizing that present development will show its greatest productivity when the problems of later life are anticipated and some preparation is made for them. Such study and preparation will result in adolescents' having happier, more stable, and more efficient adults around them. And when we stop to consider the number of times that the pervasive influence of adults affects the attitudes and behavior of adolescents, we realize that this study on the part of adults may have a great impact on the younger generation. Separating the study of childhood, adolescence, and adulthood is simply a matter of convenience in academic discussion. Each phase is shaped by what we wish (or others wish us) to become, and each phase is inescapably an outcome of what has gone on before. "Today is yesterday shaking hands with tomorrow."

Basic considerations in adolescent development

The importance of goals

Many psychologists view all behavior as goal seeking. Sometimes the individual does not know what it is he desires; he may be only dimly aware of the fact that urges, drives, and appetites are creating tensions which he feels as restlessness. The consequence is random, diffuse, sporadic, and often contradictory behavior. More highly motivated and better directed behavior is likely to stem from conscious realization or specific formulation of goals. The individual needs a destination as well as energy.

Most of the foregoing chapters have dealt with goals, immediate and future, which could profitably be realized by the adolescent and which must be realized by the adult who would be a beneficial influence. Some of the goals for adolescents have their roots in organic, psychological, and social needs. Concepts of goals were further developed through a discussion of the developmental tasks of adolescence. Many of these goals merited extended discussion under the headings of educational programs and aspirations, achieving more mature emotional control, preparation for marriage, occupational orientation, and preparation for and becoming effective citizens.

A clearer perception of these varied goals can be achieved if the individual has a philosophy to serve as an integrating force. It would be presumptuous to think that such a philosophy could be stated in a few paragraphs (or even a whole book) but the following words from a prominent leader can serve as an orientation. President Eisenhower, at the Evanston, Illinois, World Council of Churches Assembly, said:

. . . we know that there is no true and lasting cure for world tensions in guns and bombs. We know that only the spirit and mind of man, dedicated to justice and right, can in the long term enable us to live in the confident tranquillity that should be every man's heritage . . . Today the campaign for a just and lasting peace desperately needs the lifting and transforming power that comes from men and women, the world over, responding to their highest allegiances and to their best motives.

. . . The goal should be nothing short of inviting every single person in every single country in the world who believes in the power of a Supreme Being to join in a mighty, simultaneous, intense act of faith . . . a personal prayer [for] a just and lasting peace. If this mass dedication launched an unending campaign for peace, supported by prayer, I am certain wondrous results would ensue. It would change things, because it would change men. [It would serve as] a reminder to each of us that the cause of peace needs God.*

The basic factors needed for world peace are no different from the ones needed for harmonious social relations in peer groups, home, school, occupation, and citizenship. Love and respect for others, the merit of practiced brotherhood, the fact of personal responsibility, and the need for continuous striving toward more complete self-realization are basic factors in international relations AND in personal philosophy. Adolescents will be materially helped in many areas of their adjusting if they can be led to accept these teachings of great religions.

The importance of many approaches

In view of the age range of adolescence and the rapid changes that take place in the youngster from the age of thirteen to the age of twenty, it is obvious that generalizations are hazardous. Differences due to intelligence, physique, emotionality, and background complicate the problems of understanding adolescents even within a given age bracket. Many forces such as cultural expectation, technological changes, educational tradition, and community mores are vital factors in adolescent development. The adolescent must make contacts with many individuals—his peers, his parents, his teachers, his leaders in youth groups, and his part-time employers. Social

---

* "The Nation: Under God," *Time*, 64, August 30, 1954, 7.

class influences create wide differences in occupational orientation, educational expectation, and personal and social attitudes. It becomes obvious that no one approach to the problems of adolescence can be accepted as a panacea. Giving young persons a job, allowing them more freedom, extending their education, giving them a vote, providing more opportunities for organized recreation—no one of these can be accepted as a final solution, though each may be of considerable value in particular situations and for unique individuals. Better milieus for the development of adolescents must result from the cooperation of many individuals and organizations and from many approaches. Any one person can do only part of the job. "Counseling in school without joining forces with social agency, physician, church, or public health authority is as futile as doctoring a school child for an emotional disorder without taking the school into account." *

The difficulty of making specific and precise recommendations leads the faint-hearted to exclaim, "What's the use?" It would be helpful if the student of adolescence would respect the proposition widely held in the social sciences, that recommendations and approximations are helpful when they are stated in terms of probabilities. As approximations are tested, strength is added to the probability. [125:87–88] Thus, knowledge about adolescence (or marriage, delinquency, the functioning of intelligence) becomes more valuable as it becomes less specific regarding minute details. The factor of multiple causation must inevitably point to the need for many approaches.

The importance of leaders

With some truth it has been said, "As the teacher, so is the school." But it must be readily admitted that, important as the teacher is, equipment, building, educational tradition, administrative philosophy, and curriculum are also factors bearing on the vitality of the school. Having said this we can return to the proposition that well informed, mentally healthy, and sincerely confident adults can be tremendous assets in the life of the adolescent.

It is highly probable that most of the readers of this book have

---

* G. S. Stevenson, "Mental Hygiene Problems of Youth Today," *Mental Hygiene*, 25, 1941, 650.

had contact with at least one or two outstanding teachers who did much to instill love and respect for learning. Many of you (but, judging from the typical lack of interest in religion in the late teens and early twenties, not all) have had contact with some person who made church and religion quite meaningful. A few of you have been helped to grow beyond some delinquent tendencies by some competent and understanding adult. Parents, of course, exert a powerful influence on the behavior and attitudes of their offspring. Adults often, without meaning to, become models for the adolescent who is seeking to give direction to his development.

There is an alluring temptation to "pass the buck" for adolescent conduct from him to the parent; the teachers blame the parents, the parents in turn blame *their* education and *their* parents. At some point the chain of responsibility must be broken by someone's saying, "I will assume responsibility for doing what I can to initiate a new orientation." A good starting point is to consider the present readers of this book as future leaders of young people. Hence the remainder of this chapter is devoted to the personal problems of college students, the problems of young adults, and the problems of middle and old age. A really major contribution to the welfare of adolescents can be made by adults who are learning to live more productive, more harmonious, and generally happier lives.

Developmental tasks of college students

Developmental tasks are learning problems encountered at various stages of life. If one task is successfully achieved the next task is made less difficult and social approval is merited. If the task is failed, disapproval is shown and the attack on successive tasks becomes more hazardous. In this section, the tasks described are of primary concern to a select group—those who attend college. Their successful achievement of these tasks will strengthen the attack on tasks that are more universal.

Educational problems

There are many reasons for going to college. Some men and women attend in order to achieve competence in a profession. Some wish to get a general education—one that will point to happy, full, and harmonious living in general—and plan to gain their vocational knowledge *on the job* they finally obtain. Others attend because of the desire to make social contacts they feel will be enjoyable and profitable. Still others seek to develop a particular talent—athletic, musical, or dramatic, for example. Many, no doubt, attend because it is the thing to do, because their parents want them to—or because their friends are going and they want to go along.

Some of these purposes, obviously, are better than others. They are better in the sense of providing stronger motivation to achieve the purpose for which the colleges and universities are designed— acquainting the student with the accumulated experiences of our forebears. Statistical studies of the success of graduates do not indicate that attending college is any guarantee of financial or personal-living success. Such studies do indicate that there is a strong probability that those who apply themselves consistently and thereby develop good work habits are most likely to be among the successes. The borderline student, the social isolate, and the athlete who does not simultaneously achieve "rounded development" are most likely to be among those who fail to achieve the success that might be expected of them. A serious consideration of long-term purposes is highly recommended for all students. Adults who have considered the fundamental purposes of education will be better able to counsel wisely with adolescents.

Some may be perplexed by problems of choice of a course of study. There has been and there continues to be a debate between the proponents of specialized and technical education and those who support the superiority of general education.* The reader may be reassured by knowing that some who have specialized are well satisfied, while some wish they had taken a general course. A similar conclusion was reached by those who had taken liberal arts. It appears to the present author that there is a strong probability that those who were dissatisfied would still have been unhappy had they chosen otherwise. The important thing is probably not so much the kind of education but what kind of man took the education and

---

* Students who would like to investigate these arguments will find some representative ones in John Gerber and Kenneth Houp (Eds.) *The Writer's Resource Book* (Chicago: Scott, Foresman and Company; 1953). Pages 139–160 contain five articles on the subject of general *vs.* specialized education.

what the education did to him. There is no way of your knowing just how you will put your education to use. The present emphasis should be to get as much as possible out of present opportunity by assiduous application to present tasks. Certainly the immediate goal should be to develop the habits and attitudes, through serious work now, that will be of maximum value in the post-college years. It should be remembered that college is more than preparation for life —it is an important slice of life. Such considerations as these will help the adult counselor avoid anxiety about the adolescent who has not yet chosen a specific course; moreover, these items will give him the faith to encourage youth in their tentative educational choices.

The balanced use of time is a problem of vital present and future significance. Students with the highest test intelligence do not uniformly earn higher grades than their more average fellow-students. Part of this difference is attributable to the economical use of time. Each student should, if he has not already done so, draw a time schedule that will guide him in the use of his twenty-four hours per day. This schedule should include appropriate blocks of time for the following activities: (1) class and laboratory sessions, (2) study periods (including a definite place) for each class, (3) free study periods—to care for unexpected and unusual preparations, (4) adequate amounts of sleep, (5) part-time work and miscellaneous duties like cleaning and washing, (6) time for the leisurely consumption of meals, (7) personal responsibilities—letter writing, house duties, committee work, and (8) free time and recreation. [21:25–28] The fact that the student is under pressure makes following the schedule the more imperative. In this day of speed the student needs such a guide as surely as a pilot needs a plan of flight.

The need for balanced use of time is indicated by the fact of low correlations between aptitudes that individuals have. Musical ability, artistic talent, capacity for social adaptation, or athletic prowess cannot be accurately inferred from measures of general intelligence. Some will need more time for a given activity than will others. Furthermore, it is frequently advantageous for the student to allow time for the sampling of other activities without the total neglect of intellectual development. The opportunity for exploration of varied interests is typically rather rich in the college environment. Such explorations may result in finding an engrossing vocational field, but other advantages are more apparent. A student will probably find in such activities the variety that adds spice to life and hence makes him a more eager and energetic learner of the academic material. His curiosity and zest for learning are kept alive. Further, leisure-time pursuits may be initiated that will have enduring value for stimulating balance in later life activities. Many of today's college students will be leaders and models for adolescents in the near future. Those who have developed a catholicity of interests will be better able to devise projects and direct activities in sufficient variety to appeal to greater numbers of adolescents.

Serious consideration should be given to social participation. It must be admitted that there are differences in the desire and skill of individuals in this area, but a person must not too readily excuse himself from social contacts on the grounds of innate or acquired differences in social aptitude. Sound counsel can be inferred from the statement that no matter what line of work a man follows his success will in large measure be determined by his ability to get along with others. Not only does vocational efficiency depend on skill in human relations but enjoyment of life in general is intimately related to this skill. Unfortunately, it has been found that 10 per cent of a college student body tends to carry the major load of student activities. Half of the students are silent or inactive. Measures of the capacity for social adjustment are directly related to the number of activities in which students participate. Probably participation is a reflection of capacity as well as exercise of social skills. [7:495–496] In view of these data, college students would be wise to take advantage of opportunities for social participation. The social skills so developed will provide the basis for building better rapport with adolescents they will know and counsel.

In order to provide opportunities for academic, social, and cultural pursuits, savings of time should be sought. A plan (the time schedule) is a good first step. Another important step would be to improve study habits. Most college students are relatively inefficient readers—yet a major part of study involves reading. Usually there is no improvement from freshman to senior year in reading skill, for unless planned attention is devoted to betterment the student simply consolidates the habits he has acquired earlier. Yet, because the older a person grows the more meaning he attaches to the printed words, it has been found that more mature students make more rapid progress, when specific attention is devoted to improvement, than do younger persons. It is not unusual for a student to double his reading rate, under the stimulus of specific practice, in periods of six to ten weeks. A small daily investment of time early in the college career would effect a large saving in time for the full college course (see Chapter Eleven). Even in the senior year a student would profit immensely from practice in reading because the skill achieved would enable him to become more quickly acquainted with the requirements of his post-college vocation.

The adult who acquires superior skills in reading will find that his reading interests increase. It is probable that the skill does more to develop such interest than reading interest does to increase skill. Such interested adults will be able to prescribe specific books to adolescents in terms of their unique problems and ambitions. The adult's enthusiasm will, in some degree, be transmitted to adolescents, who will then be able to see their world more clearly.

A reader becomes a critical reader only after years of experience in reading, for the critical sense, that is, the ability to understand, analyze, evaluate, and to form judgments, comes only with intellectual maturity. . . .

. . . He explores the meanings of new words with zest, disciplines his mind to concentrate under distracting circumstances, acquires the habit of reflecting about what he reads, and responds creatively to the stimulus of an awakened imagination and to the challenge of new ideas. Through the medium of the printed page, he takes possession of his cultural heritage; because books exist, the competent reader is a citizen of all times and places; he has perspective on the past and a realistic vision of the future; he does not live a two-dimensional existence in the present moment.[*]

Efficient reading and the ability to see through an author's eyes are skills that can best be taught to young persons by those who have such abilities themselves.

When a person is exposed continuously to new ideas and data, as he is in the college environment, skill in taking notes is a big ad-

---

[*] Stella S. Center, *The Art of Book Reading* (New York: Charles Scribner's Sons; 1952), p. 1.

vantage. It has been found that when grades were checked with notebooks, the students who had compact, accurate, complete, and systematic notes earned the superior grades. [27:143–145] Suggestions for effective note-taking include these: (1) Read through the entire selection first. This method helps develop good reading skills and allows you to judge the importance of what is recorded. (2) Keep the writing brief both for book and lecture notes. You cannot listen while you write. (3) Use the lecturer's indication of numbered items (such as "Several factors . . ." or "Three items must be . . .") as suggestions for listing ideas. (4) Review notes just as soon as possible after making them. If you feel that the clues are somewhat too brief you can then fill in more details from your memory. (5) Some successful students take only clue words and phrases during a lecture and as soon as possible thereafter rewrite the notes more fully and neatly.

Those of you who will become teachers of adolescents can utilize note-making skill in two ways: (1) for your own advantage and (2) as the basis for helping your pupils become more efficient.

The student's approach to study and class activities will be more constructive if he has an interest in what is taking place. It would be well to get rid of the fallacious idea that interests are innate or accidental. Interest grows as knowledge and experience in a given area increase. The instructor cannot *make* a subject interesting, he can only set up the conditions that might make it easier for the student to *take* an interest. However, it would be well if the student would assume responsibility for developing an interest instead of blaming the instructor for being dull or suffering from boredom throughout a course. Suggestions for creating interests or strengthening weak ones are as follows:

1. Be an active participant in class. Listen attentively, respond to questions when the opportunity is available, participate in discussions, read actively. Anticipate ideas, practice the habit of disagreement, and evaluate that with which you agree.

2. Use the psychology of suggestion by acting as though you were interested from the very beginning. Instead of fulminating against a required course which you dislike, try to figure out some good reasons why the curriculum makers thought it was worthy of being required.

3. Arrange for the experience of success. Anyone tends to be more

interested in things he can do well. Therefore, make sound daily preparations for classes that will allow you to take an active and intelligent part—even though action be limited to critical listening. Make adequate preparations for examinations instead of depending on some last moment cramming. Do not judge success entirely in terms of being at the head of the class but more in terms of doing better than you have previously done.

4. Make your study as personal as possible. Seek to find relationships of the subject matter to your present life and to your future vocational, social, and family career. In some form or another ask yourself, "What can I get out of this book or course that will improve my lot in life?" and "How can I go about getting this maximum good?"

5. Formulate your goals for each course as clearly as you can. Some students are satisfied with the goal of passing the course and gaining the credit, but the higher motivation is provided by listing goals in terms of abilities and knowledges rather than the symbols (grades and credits) of improved skill and knowledge.

6. Acquire information—you cannot be interested in that about which you have no knowledge. Those who are interested in mathematics, literature, sociology, or psychology must have some knowledge about them. A lack of interest in them is likely to be a symptom of an intellectual gap. This does not mean that you must be interested in everything—it does mean that you should seek the knowledge that will create interest in the courses that lead to your particular educational objective.

7. Expand your present interests by relating them to the new experiences you are having. Figure out as many relationships between courses as you can. If you have an opportunity to take survey courses you will have a sound introduction to some of these relationships that expand and integrate interests.

8. Make use of what you learn by taking part in class discussions, by using the material in conversations with your classmates, by writing term papers incorporating your evaluation of the material, and by relating it to present and anticipated activities. [22:121–126] Knowing the factors that foster interests will enable parents, teachers, and counselors to make conscious use of the psychology of interests in the constructive guidance of youth.

Choosing and preparing for a career

One of the major developmental tasks of the college student is choosing, and making adequate preparation for, a career. Many readers of this book will have made their choice; others will have chosen tentatively; and still others will be relatively, or even wholly, undecided. There are advantages and disadvantages in each status. Those who plan for professional careers like medicine, law, teaching, or engineering will profit from an early choice, which will give them time to fulfill the many specific requirements for such vocations. Those who have chosen tentatively have the advantage of being able to fulfill requirements but they also have the psychological freedom to shift their goals in terms of current situations, trends, and opportunities. They will have a chance for wide range of employment—in jobs that are just as financially and personally rewarding and socially significant as are the professions. Many important positions in industry, insurance, trade, and service are available to college educated individuals. There is less emphasis in these careers on specific courses and majors than there is on being a broadly educated, socially effective individual who has a variety of interests—qualities that tend to make him an effective leader and organizer.

There is, in fact, no need for despair on the part of the college graduate who is still shopping around for a satisfying position. Many successful men and women did not focus upon their present lines of work until they were thirty, forty, or even fifty years of age. Some have found their enjoyable vocations at even later ages. These observations lead to the conclusion that occupational selection is less important than is preparation—including post-college experience. We need to remember these considerations in our evaluation of the problems of young persons.

The remarks made in Chapter Sixteen about the vocational orientation of adolescents are pertinent for those who are now in college. One point to recall is that developing a wholesome attitude toward work will help in the pursuit of any career. Work provides many satisfactions; among them are accomplishment, recognition, adventure, relief from worries, and the need for personal fulfillment. It is unfortunate, in view of the importance of work for personal integrity and social significance, that some people give such undue importance to leisure. The too-common attitude that "just getting by is good enough" must also be criticized. Verbal exhortations to respect the role of work are only a starting point. The student can begin now by formally stating the immediate and ultimate objectives of his present tasks. He can put enough time on present pursuits to achieve the success and develop the interests that will make good attitudes *and work habits* a part of his characteristic equipment. Another factor, closely related to the foregoing, is the need to place some emphasis on *being* the right person for the job along with finding the right job. An individual can do much to make himself the right person for the job if he will be skeptical of the belief that each must find the "just right" job. The fact is that many will have to do whatever work is available. It is distinctly possible that only the individual with very limited talents needs to find exactly the right work. [231] Those who have many talents—and this would include typical college students—are probably capable of filling many different kinds of positions effectively and happily. It is highly probable that the wide extent of dissatisfaction with jobs stems partially from the delusion that each one must find *the* occupation for which he is uniquely and innately endowed.

Vocational interest and aptitude tests may be of value in assessing a person's present status and *indicating areas* in which he will be best situated for the time being. Results on such tests should be used for raising further questions rather than being regarded as answers. It will be well to remember that both abilities and interests are built through practice and familiarity. The college graduate should therefore take what appears to him to be the best available opportunity (or perhaps the only one) and seek to develop his competence therein, instead of regarding this first job as a stepping stone or a temporary expedient until the "perfect position" is located. This does not mean that he should avoid any change of jobs just to show his determination and tenacity. It does mean that a creative attitude toward work is as important as the job itself. Vocational tests that are interpreted as proof that a man must work at one certain thing in order to be effective and happy may do more harm than good because of the negative attitude engendered.

There are other traits and attitudes that condition vocational success. While deficiency in any of these does not indicate certain failure, taken all together they make an exceedingly significant composite. A healthy self-regard (or concept of self) which stems from knowing and doing those things that are morally and ethically correct is a step toward both confidence and competence. Respect for others, both the manual worker and the top executive, will enable a man to take and give directions graciously. Personal cleanliness and neatness of dress do more than impress others; these habits give a feeling of assurance that comes from high self-regard. Punctuality, reliability, industry create good impressions on professors, and if they become habits they will later create good impressions on employers. These traits will *have* to be developed at some time; if they are developed now they will draw interest for a longer period of time as well as making the "principal" greater. The maintenance of good physical and mental health is a continuing problem. A man cannot work efficiently when he suffers from various ailments or is plagued by worries, resentments, jealousies, and insecurities. Both mental and physical health are outcomes of the application of knowledge about these areas.

Other traits might be mentioned—for example, fluency, carefulness, cooperation, enthusiasm, honesty, refinement. Perhaps more important is the continuously exercised habit of learning. The idea has often been expressed that a college education never hurt anyone who could continue to learn after he received his degree. The top persons in any line of activity are ones who did not settle into a simple routine. They are often the ones who brought their creativity to what had formerly been a monotonous or routine job. Such creativity is not necessarily the evidence of an innate capacity or aptitude. What appears to be high intelligence or creativity is often just a function of much knowledge. The habits of continuous learning will allow the individual to keep abreast of, and to go ahead with, rapid technological progress and business reorganization. Moreover, there is the great personal benefit of keeping, if not young, at least, vital. "There is experimental evidence to support the claim that those who continue to apply themselves to the learning of verbal materials all through life are able to maintain their efficiency as learners better than those who do not have such a history." [*]

---

[*] Oscar J. Kaplan, "Psychological Aspects of Aging," *The Annals of the American Academy of Political and Social Science*, 279, 1952, 35.

The major share of the college student's life is yet to be lived. Practically all of his vocational life remains before him. Application of the foregoing ideas is therefore of personal importance. Still more important is the application of these ideas to the vocational orientation of adolescents—who have a still greater portion of their lives to live. They must be advised by adults who have themselves achieved a balanced perspective of vocational selection and preparation as continuing tasks.

Courtship and marriage

As a group college students are most likely to be concerned with problems of courtship and marriage, since the average age of college students closely coincides with the average age at marriage. This is a fortunate situation since the college campus is an exceptionally good hunting ground for a life partner. To delay the selection of a mate until a person is better equipped financially, until a more suitable partner is located, until work experience has been acquired, can be more hazardous than undertaking marriage at an early age. There is a good chance that delay beyond the college years will so narrow the field of choice that ultimately a much less advantageous marriage will be contracted. Both the young man and young woman will find that the chances of meeting others are much smaller in the work world than they were on the campus. Often the ones whom the individual does meet have previously "taken the step." Baber relates the case of a young woman—college graduate, intelligent, now a bank clerk—who knew only three single men. She became engaged to one of them—middle aged, bald, and "generally impossible." He was of a different religious faith, and he was bewildered when the conversation became intellectual. Fortunately, the engagement was broken and she later met and married a man more similar in background, with whom she established many common interests. [10:140–141] The relative stability of marriages between college people indicates that it is probable that they have achieved the emotional, social, and intellectual maturity that would make further delay a doubtful benefit.

The really important factors in a satisfactory marriage are (1) being and selecting a partner who is psychologically mature and (2) entering the marriage contract with a firm determination that this is for a lifetime. It is quite possible to use intelligence as well as emotion in selecting a mate. But the use of intelligence must come in the early stages of courtship. The following criteria can be used for observing the qualities that will be assets in marriage: Does the person have friends of both sexes? If the answer is yes there is an indication that he or she has ability for warm social relations. Does the person have the same religion and possess some of your interests? If so, there is the possibility that some of the obstacles to harmonious relations will be smaller. Does the person come from the same socio-economic level? It must be remembered that the habits and ideals of individuals are intimately influenced by membership in a given social class. Does the prospective partner have good health? Chronic illness is often both a cause and a result of inadequate personality adjustment. Do negative personality traits tend to overbalance the positive characteristics? Jealousy, the lack of social graces, possessiveness, moodiness, habitual ignoring of ethical practices, and lack of a sense of humor increase the burden of adjustment—a burden that will, even in the best of situations, be heavy enough. Does the courted person belong to three or four organizations? Studies indicate that those who belong to several organizations establish marriages that are deemed to have the highest adjustment scores.

Some things a person can discover by conversations. Among the items to be discovered is whether or not there is agreement on the number and timing of children. The degree of self-centeredness can be judged on the basis of whether conversations are primarily about self or a substantial part of the talk is about other things and other people. Perhaps one of the more important items is to discover what a person feels about his family. If he likes his family, reminisces pleasantly on the events of childhood, and if his parents are happy and living together, it is likely that he has developed the habits of happiness which will make for a stable and satisfactory marriage. If, on the other hand, he talks of parental unfairness and sibling jealousies and complains of family hardships, a prospective partner might become wary of the possibility that marriage is sought as an escape from something unpleasant. It is well to remember that happiness is a habit the individual carries with him.

Finding a marriage partner is definitely only the first step in establishing a mutually gratifying relationship. At the very best, both partners must realize and anticipate the inevitable difficulties. For some these problems are devastating but for others the solution of problems is an avenue to strengthening the union. Among the problems that will need to be solved are the following: (1) Mutually satisfactory sex relations will have to be developed—these are created, not discovered. (2) The couple must live within their income—two cannot live so cheaply as one so the restriction of personal desires must be discussed and planned. (3) Having children will limit both the wife's and the husband's freedom; crying babies are annoying; and loss of sleep demands firm control of tendencies toward irascibility. (4) Each partner has work to do, so the one who complains is likely to find relatively little sympathy from the other —each must attempt to appreciate the fact that the partner has obligations. (5) New social relationships must be established—life cannot be lived in blissful isolation, so friends should be sought that are mutually enjoyable. (6) Each will have his own interests, which will be pursued independently—this desire for independence should be mutually respected. (7) The ultimate goals of marriage should be discussed—the wife's and husband's career, the place of children, owning a home, are things that should not be left to happenstance. Other problems could be mentioned but all of them can pretty well be indicated by the generalization that emotional maturity should be, or should be becoming, a habit. Solution of such problems will do much to provide the healthful family milieu which is so important in the rearing of adolescents who will themselves build stable homes.

Happiness in marriage is a symptom of good mental health, which, like physical health, results from the studied and steady application of basic rules. The major rules for mental health are summarized in the following:

To use one's abilities and skills effectively and with enthusiasm, without aiming only or chiefly for happiness. The mature individual does not aim always for happiness. There is a higher contentment and peace of mind that may involve unhappiness, effort, and even suffering that can be assimilated by the mature mind. There are stakes, goals, rewards, and values in the struggle of life that are higher than individual happiness or comfort. Many of our soldiers with high courage and in horrible experience knew this, and because many of them lived by such values we are enabled to be here tonight.

To work, do something worth-while, pull one's load unless one is sick. Many people have been deprived of one of the basic satisfactions in life because circumstances have prevented them from cultivating that habit of effort and achievement, however humble.

To do something because it needs to be done, has to be done by somebody, regardless of one's immediate feelings.

To get along and cooperate with others, to be able to work in an organization, even to work for a time under unfair and unpleasant authority.

To stand frustration, failure, mistakes, disappointment, and carry on—whether the frustration be of one's ambition or in one's personal relationship with others.

To stick to a job when it is difficult, to persist in effort, show tenacity—that is morale.

To take responsibility, show independent initiative, be self-decisive, self-moving, self-directing.

To absorb frustration and failure without developing handicapping, disintegrating tensions of fear, anger, depression, suspicion, blaming others, withdrawal, or undue bodily disturbances associated with intense emotion.

To show devotion, effort, and love to something beyond one's self.

Such are the qualities of emotional, mental, or personality health that we all—fathers, mothers, children, society—have to cultivate. And it is possible for all of us continually to improve our capacities in these regards.*

This is a large order but it must be admitted that satisfaction in an enterprise involving the intimate and complicated relationships that marriage does is not to be achieved by the application of some simple nostrum. Neither are the problems of adolescence to be solved by any one approach. However, better solutions by the pres-

---

* Kenneth E. Appel, in William B. Terhune (Ed.) *Living Wisely and Well* (New York: E. P. Dutton and Company, Inc.; 1949), pp. 78–79. Quoted by permission of the editor.

ent college generation will have three salutary results for adolescents: (1) providing sample, or model, approaches, (2) supplying a better kind of leadership for clubs, athletics, schools, and church, and (3) ultimately producing a better parental influence.

The developmental tasks of young adults

Despite the difficulty of the developmental tasks of adolescents and post-adolescents, it seems probable that those of early adulthood are the most difficult of a lifetime. This is not so much because the tasks are inherently trying but because there is so little help available. Many suggestions have been given in publications and through formal schooling for the earlier tasks of childhood and adolescence. Recently much attention has been given to the tasks of middle maturity and old age. There is much in current publications that can give substantial help in the approach to the tasks of the second half of life. But this is not the case with the tasks of people aged twenty-five to thirty-five. It has apparently been assumed that former schooling and family experience will have solved their problems. Yet the incidence of mental breakdown is great, the rate of crime is high, and marriage is highly vulnerable during these years. It is safe to recommend strongly that present attention be given to the anticipation of some of the problems of early adulthood.

Living with a marriage partner *

Successful living in the parental family provides good indoctrination for living with a marriage partner. The pleasures of sex compensate for the difficulties encountered in some of the other areas of marital relationships. Yet still the task is difficult. The relationships of a son or daughter and a parent are quite different from those of a husband and a wife. Parental guidance is no longer so quickly available in times of stress. The need for exercising independence is now more a matter of demand than of desirability. Difficulties must be solved to the mutual satisfaction of both, whereas formerly stubborn resistance or demand may have sufficed

---

* These headings and the ones in the following section are adapted from Robert J. Havighurst, *Human Development and Education* (New York: Longmans, Green and Company; 1953), pp. 268–283.

as a palliative to conflict. Anger, disgust, and resentment must now be disguised because a mate may not feel the obligation for tolerance that is characteristic in parental and sibling relationships. There is no readily available arbiter for the (more or less) objective solution of conflicting demands.

It is certain that no categorical answers can be given to marriage problems. It can safely be recommended that such problems be discussed in detail and with considered respect for the other's viewpoint. In the event of chronic difficulty a much more pertinent suggestion can be given: that the pair seek the counsel of expert advisers. The success of marriage counselors is such that it seems exceedingly unwise to make a decision for separation or divorce without this step. Reconciliation scores as high as 90 per cent have been recorded by some agencies. [10:140–141] The continued existence of problems and the fact that they can be solved point to two important considerations: (1) The help we give adolescents in solving their present problems provides them a cushion against the jolts of succeeding years. (2) There is an indication that it is rarely too late —adjustment is a continuous process.

Having and rearing children

Having children is a typical occurrence; nevertheless, it is at times difficult and women are often apprehensive for their safety and still more frequently concerned about the loss of their figures. Sex relations have to be curtailed; to some, intercourse during pregnancy is disgusting. Hence the compensatory function of sex is lost during a period of difficulty. New psychological orientations are forced on the young parents. Formerly they could be assured that others were concerned with pleasing them and their goodness was rewarded by reciprocal goodness on the part of others. An infant makes no such concession. He demands much and gives nothing (intentionally) for the services accorded him. The adult is forced to act selflessly. The expenses involved in bearing and rearing children are heavy, and there is no monetary return on the investment. In short, the responsibility that the young person incurs at the time of the first born child is the heaviest he has ever yet assumed.

Fortunately, the rewards for the successful assumption of these responsibilities are very great. Children provide a substantial impetus to the habit of continuing personality development. The self-denial that parents must practice is an avenue to the building of healthier, more stable personalities. Unintentionally, the infant provides an object of love for them that greatly enriches their lives. His smile, his health, and his progressive accomplishments are a sufficient reward, transcending the material, for the hazards of the undertaking.

The best approach to the successful achievement of, and gratification from, this task is wholesome and continuing personality growth. The feelings the parent has about his children are a rather direct reflection of the concept the parent has of himself. Those who are at peace and harmony with themselves will find it easier to enjoy their children and achieve success in rearing them. [159:232–235] The help that can be given through classes for parents and prospective parents, the counsel of the family doctor, the reassurance and advice given by a minister, should be actively sought. The most enduring help toward better future child rearing must, however, be that which becomes influential during the parents' childhood and adolescent years—that is, the kind of influences the readers of this book will (it is hoped) exert on the next generation.

Acquiring a home

After a child has been born the young people turn, if they have not already done so, to the task of establishing a rather permanent home. When the student of psychology studies the relationship of poor housing to illness, personality inadequacy, and delinquency he recognizes the seriousness of this task. Two things have taken place that are of significance in the successful achievement of this task. (1) The recent development of amortization plans for house payments has materially lessened the hazards of buying that were characteristic thirty-five or forty years ago. Small down payments and low interest rates have been a boon to struggling young couples. (2) The still more recent development of the "Do it yourself" idea has resulted in saving money and improved maintenance of homes. It is still too early to evaluate this movement but there are potentialities in it for stimulation to study, for creativeness, and for financial savings.

Bargains in homes are available but they are often difficult to locate. Paint and putty may cover defective workmanship. The size
of joists and rafters, which one cannot readily see, is more important
than the readily perceived smoothness of floors. From chimney top
to foundation there are details that profoundly affect values. Since
a loan may not be amortized for twenty or more years, it will be
well to study the matter of house construction and financing more
seriously and energetically than was the case with many "three
hour" college courses. The perfect home will not be found—another
bath will be needed, a closet should have sliding doors, the bedroom should be longer, an outlet should be on the south wall, and
so on and on. But gross errors can be avoided by spending some
time and intelligence on published materials. It seems that investment in a home, representing probably the largest single expendi-
ture in the lives of many families, might well be a part of the course
of study for adolescents that deals with home and family.

Achieving vocational proficiency

Since much of a college career is devoted to vocational preparation it is gratuitous to say that this task is important. In our culture,
where status depends so largely on what a person does, vocational
proficiency is unusually significant. There are other reasons why a
person cannot assume that getting a job is the significant step. One
of the reasons for emphasis on *achieving* efficiency is that rapid
technological and managerial progress demands continuous adaptation on the part of the worker and manager. An important personal
reason is that those who reach the top, in whatever line of work
they may have singled out, have shown unusual progress in the initial stages of their careers. Many workers of the plodding type who
hope to progress by virtue of seniority find themselves displaced by
more aggressive and progressive young persons. In fact, the older
worker is regarded with some suspicion because he has not progressed more rapidly. Young college-trained individuals do not typically need to be advised to work hard. They should be advised to
supplement their work with study and to live a balanced life.

There can be no prescription for living a balanced life, but some
typical errors can be indicated. Some devote so much time to the
performance of routine obligations that they do not read and study

enough to maintain a healthy perspective. Some work so hard that they neglect their marriage partner and their children. This in turn may cause difficulties that quickly and markedly affect proficiency on the job. The relative absence of young persons in civic affairs and in church activities indicates that excessive amounts of attention are being devoted to vocational proficiency. It would be well to stand off and develop long-term plans for attaining vocational success. It might be found that better balance of time, recognizing home, family, community, and church, would tend to build the robust personality that would contribute most to ultimate success. No better preparation for these tasks can be provided than to make these considerations a part of the habit patterns of the present generation of adolescents.

Forming new friendships

As a student progresses through school he typically will remain in contact with some of his former friends. There are many school and college activities that, being primarily social, provide easy opportunities for the development of new friendships as locales are changed. The need for finding new friends suddenly becomes acute when the individual takes a full time job and when he gets married. Many of the common grounds on which facile contacts are made are eliminated by marriage. The single young men and women, formerly friends, do not share the problems of the newlyweds. Sporadic attempts may be made to keep the contacts alive, but unless the single ones soon get married it is found to be a somewhat futile effort. Geographical factors will make a difference. When a man takes a job it is often, though not typically, in another city or state. Moving, even without the shift in marital and job status, would weaken former friendships. The new work situation and the new community do not ordinarily have a huge supply of lonesome individuals—as was the case in college. Hence there is usually little more than a sporadic effort to make the newcomer welcome. It is not because the established people are aloof or snobbish; it is simply a matter of their having already made the transition to intimate neighborliness.

Many young adults feel isolated and abandoned under such circumstances. They may become discouraged about their work and their location. This will contribute to inefficiency on the job and discouraging tensions in the home. Those who do not realize the source of their discouragement and anxiety have an additionally difficult problem because they do not know what approach to make. Some become so defeated that they will abandon the opportunities that are available and return to their familiar surroundings, taking whatever means to a living happen to be available. The following recommendations may prove to be of value: (1) Realize that it is not haughtiness that makes others act unfriendly. The newcomer should do what he can to go more than halfway in social overtures. (2) Make contact with the church and acquaint the minister, rabbi, or priest with the difficulty. The church, drawing from a wide geographical and occupational area, probably has other young people, not in the same business circle, who are faced with similar problems. (3) Join dance, card, and literary clubs. Take extension classes, join the hobby clubs sponsored by the local library or museum, if such activities are available. (4) Try to recognize that others are looking at you as adults—they do not provide the ready-made solutions that were characteristic during childhood and adolescence.

Developmental tasks of the middle years

Robert J. Havighurst makes the following comment about the years from thirty to fifty-five:

> In the middle years, from about thirty to about fifty-five, men and women reach the peak of their influence upon society, and at the same time the society makes its maximum demands upon them for social and civic responsibility. It is the period of life to which they have looked forward during their adolescence and early adulthood. And the time passes so quickly during these full and active middle years that most people arrive at the end of middle age and the beginning of later maturity with surprise and a sense of having finished the journey while they were still preparing to commence it.*

---

* Robert J. Havighurst, *Human Development and Education* (New York: Longmans, Green and Company; 1953), p. 268.

Assuming civic responsibility

One of the disappointing conclusions that must be drawn about the effectiveness of higher education is that too few graduates take an active part in civic affairs. There is much rationalization on the basis of "rotten politics" and "vested powers." Apparently the notion of government of, by, and for the people has not been deeply inculcated. The fact is that some persons must and do conduct the affairs of state, and these are typically individuals in their middle years.

The impetus to civic participation is great in these middle years because a citizen sees that in owning a home, having a position or investment in the community, and having children who are directly affected by community organizations, he has a large stake in the conduct of affairs. Although some are deeply engrossed in making a big splash in the financial world, many others find time to contribute to community betterment. They may have given up the idea that they will be the most important figures in their occupational area; they may see that a basic move toward further progress is spreading their roots; or they may be gratified with their success and still have the time and energy (characteristic of middle age) that allows them to participate wholeheartedly. Their experience and perspective are such that they do have a contribution to make.

This task would more effectively be done if individuals in their adolescence and early adulthood would look forward to it and make their presence felt before the middle years.

Living within an income

With few exceptions, the adolescent and the young adult dream of the time when their incomes will be sufficient to satisfy their wants without scratching, pinching, and borrowing. The college-educated individual will typically experience rather gratifying increases in income in the early stages of his career. But costs too rise rapidly as he assumes the duties of rearing children, buying and furnishing a home, and expanding his circle of friends and activities. Costs continue to rise even after income has become somewhat stabilized—incomes tend to reach a high point in the middle forties and level off or decline slightly after the middle fifties. [126:580]

Our economy, which has been characterized as a consumption oriented one, creates wants through advertising and emphasis on slight differences. [242] This, added to the factor of rising costs, makes it difficult to live within the family income.

There are three major aspects of this problem: (1) It is necessary to learn to balance the needed against the desirable and the desirable against the less desirable—choosing those things that will tend to bring satisfaction to the greatest number within the family for the longest period of time. (2) It is necessary to impress children with the limitations the budget places upon them. Parents attempt to teach this lesson by the early granting of an allowance with progressive increases with age—encouraging youngsters to supplement their finances with their own earnings. (3) Unless a paternalistic government takes over the financing of the increasing number of individuals who reach their seventies and eighties, it will be necessary for individuals to plan their later years so as to avoid being a burden to their offspring. Insurance, savings, and annuities will bite into the operating budget during the working years.

The achievement of this task of managing finances looks simpler than it is. It is necessary to make and stick to long-term plans for budgeting income and expenditures. Medical, casualty, and accident insurance plans reduce the hazards of such long-time planning by spreading the risk over greater numbers of persons. Such ability to plan expenditures justifies the recommendation made earlier that adolescents be given progressively larger autonomy in handling their own finances.

Living with adolescents

The reader has seen, from reading the foregoing chapters, that living with the teen-ager makes it necessary for the parent to establish a new kind of relationship. The acceptance of two major viewpoints may serve to reduce the complexity of the task. (1) It is quite normal and natural to encounter difficulties in the new relationship with adolescents. Because the adolescent must assert himself the parent cannot do the *right* thing. Too much permissiveness will bring the charge of not caring and too much authority merits the criticism of not giving the youngster a chance. Between these extremes the parent will be accused of being vacillating. (2) Some conflict is a symptom of healthy growth toward maturity. Despite the temporary irritation, parents would not want their children so dependent that they would not occasionally protest.

A substantial portion of this book has been devoted to suggestions for solving this task. It must suffice at this point to give the broad, but pertinent, panacea: Adults must continuously seek the maturing of personality that will permit them to be good examples and to have tolerance for the differences the span of years creates. (Many of the readers of this book can help themselves in a future problem and their parents in a present problem by seeking to accelerate the maturing processes in themselves.)

Developing appropriate leisure-time activities

It is foolhardy for persons in the middle years to assert, "You're only as old as you think you are." The years inevitably take a toll and limit the things a person can safely do as surely as the years add to his potentiality by encouraging development of new skills. As individuals grow the differences between them become greater. Hence, it would be futile to recommend a specific type of leisure-time activity. However, the following quotation makes a general suggestion that each one can manipulate to suit his own need and orientation:

> Certain things need to be said to people in their thirties and forties. They need to know that life offers fulfillment at every stage, that self-realization and pleasure are possible even in old age, that the imagination is always there for us to use. . . .
>
> I think it is a big mistake to present any particular art or craft as the one most desirable for people. There are hundreds and hundreds of arts and crafts, and what you will like, I won't, and vice versa. One man's art is another man's poison. That is why the problem of testing for artistic aptitudes, discovering latent interests, is so important. Painting is a most valuable and respectable art, and yet a woman of fifty may prefer to make original dresses for dolls. An older man may wish to do needle point. Another older woman may wish to build a miniature theater. A man may want to make plastic jewelry. . . .

Unsuccessful aging means withdrawal from life. We stop seeing, and begin to look and watch. We hear but no longer are aware.
We breathe but do not smell. We touch but do not feel. We dwell
deep within the dark well of our loneliness and isolation.*

Most authorities expressly state that the best preparation for creative leisure interests in the mature years resides in the activities
tried in childhood and youth. Parents and youth leaders who sample varied activities are investing in both their present and youth's
future.

Developing new relationships with the marriage partner

During the middle and later years of life the importance of sexual activity in marital relationships declines steadily and markedly.
[172:351] The husband's preoccupation with his vocation will
probably have declined as he has settled into competent and confident performance of his work. As children grow through adolescence and into adulthood the demands upon parental time and concern have greatly lessened. All these changes thrust upon the middle-aged person the necessity for making new adjustments to the
spouse. In order to achieve lasting satisfaction from marriage a community of interests other than sex, finances, and children must be
established. The problem is further complicated by physiological
and psychological changes, which are called the menopause and
climacteric.

Obviously this problem is more than a matter of continuing to
give attention to matters of personal grooming or of developing mutually satisfactory hobbies—though these are items of significance.
Like so many other developmental tasks of adolescence and adulthood this one demands attention to the total program for effective
living. The solution lies in over-all growth and continuous learning.
Dr. Stieglitz has summarized the recommendation in the words,
"To think is to grow and in growing we live." † Participation in
community affairs is an approach that can be highly recommended.
[233] This will have the double effect of taking the middle-aged

---

* George Lawton, "Aging Creatively," in Clark Tibbits (Ed.) *Living Through
the Older Years* (Ann Arbor: University of Michigan Press; 1949), pp. 114–116.
    † Edward J. Stieglitz, *The Second Forty Years* (Philadelphia: J. B. Lippincott
Company; 1946), p. 209.

person's mind off personal worries and providing the impetus for keeping up with rapid cultural change.

Adjusting to physical changes

Besides the decline in sexual vigor noted in the middle years, this is about the time when people begin to complain that the print in telephone directories is getting smaller and smaller. Some people avoid the use of bifocals, apparently under the delusion that their advancing years can be denied by refusing to wear one of the badges of middle age. Other changes include growth of hair on the lips of women and in the nose and ears of men. The skin becomes progressively more wrinkled and drier. Depressions in the flesh appear where formerly there were firm muscles. The "middle aged spread" may appear on the careless man or woman. The tendency is unfortunate but partially avoidable. The accumulation of fat is a threat to good health—and often is a symptom of poor mental health. The loss of interest in children and competition may result in seeking the compensation of excessive eating and drinking. The decline of physical vigor results in less exercise and the accumulating fat makes it more difficult to take exercise. Excessive weight causes, or at least aggravates, certain morbid conditions of the heart, circulatory, and digestive system.

Three recommendations for achieving success in this task may be recommended. (1) An attempt should be made to find the compensations of age: more time for contemplative activities, prestige achieved from proven competence, the satisfaction of having done a good job in raising children, the opportunity for exploring some areas that had to be neglected in the earlier years. (2) Regular physical examinations should be scheduled and the advice of the physician with regard to the amount and kind of exercise and the amount and kind of food should be taken. (3) The rules of health should be assiduously applied—especially such things as getting rest during illness and accepting slower rates of recovery from illness, getting regular sleep, avoiding overeating. (4) Probably the best preparation for acceptance of these changes is the fostering of satisfactory living at all ages—including the childhood and adolescent years.

Developmental tasks of old age

Detailed description of the developmental tasks of old age will typically have little interest for the reader of this book. Hence these tasks will be very briefly described by way of showing that all of life consists in continuing developmental processes. Furthermore, preparation for these tasks is best approached through the solution of the tasks that each person is presently occupied with solving.

Adjusting to physical decline

Inevitably as aging continues the efficiency of the circulatory, digestive, and muscular systems declines. The rate of decline can be slowed by the habit of healthful living. But, to a large extent, the adjustment is a psychological one of learning to adapt graciously to lessened physical energy and even to living with some degree of invalidism. No doubt as more people grow to older ages and as experience accumulates there will be more precise advice that will be pertinent for the individual in his later maturity.

Accepting retirement and lessened income

It is possible that the sheer force of large numbers of aged people will bring about changes in our attitudes toward retirement. More probably research findings will show the folly of an arbitrary retirement age. [1] These findings show that decline of physical skill and vigor is often compensated for by increased judgment and steadfastness. In the executive type of work the individual's efficiency may increase beyond the sixties. Yet on the whole there will be some decline, and both because of this and because of the tradition of retirement, individuals must expect to retire and must learn to live with lessened income.

Adjusting to the death of the marriage partner

Only rarely do the wife and husband die at approximately the same time. Some men and many women must learn how to live without the help and companionship to which they have been accustomed for some forty or fifty years. Since women live, on the average, somewhat longer than do men and because of the tradition of the man's marrying a younger woman, there are approximately twice as many widows as there are widowers in the later sixties. It is estimated that 85 per cent of women who are octogenarians are without husbands. [136:279]

Many solutions of the difficulties have been attempted—each with some merits. The widow (or widower) may move to a smaller house, live in an apartment, join up with a partner of the same sex, move in with the children, join an organized group of "old timers," or continue to get along in the accustomed residence. Each of these approaches involves some major adjustments of habitual patterns. Unless the individual has anticipated and prepared, by developing continuous habits of learning, the problems may be of traumatic dimensions.

Adjusting to an older age group

The glorifying of youth and youthfulness in our country leads some old people to attempt to maintain contact with middle-aged or younger individuals. Some such contacts are of benefit—people of all ages are stimulated by contacts with others of all ages. But if such contacts are maintained at the cost of repudiation of the old-age group, the pace is likely to become too rapid for the declining powers of the elderly man or woman. There are hazards, too, in having friends only among contemporaries. The death rate is high in the later years and the probability is strong that friends will die. The familiar, intimate circle becomes smaller and smaller. Emerson's words, "He who has a thousand friends has not a friend to spare," should be heeded by those of all ages. The habit of continuously forming new friendships is the best preparation for this developmental task of the later years.

Establishing satisfactory living arrangements

The lessened vigor and resilience characteristic of the later stages of aging make necessary a more cautious way of living. Steps and stairs must be treated as hazards. Proximity to shopping and entertainment centers becomes highly desirable. Nearness to relatives or some dependable friend or agency is essential during times of illness or accident. Living costs have to be cut down to match a lessened income. The desire for rest and a leisurely pace makes quiet increasingly attractive. It has been found that mild climates add much to the comfort of the aged. Retirement in Southern California or Florida can be recommended on physical as well as psychological grounds.

Young men and women may now think that they would just as soon die as grow so old as to live through the problems of the aged. This feeling is common. Many people say they would like to die when they are seventy-five or eighty. Most of them have a decided change of mind when they reach their seventy-fourth or seventy-ninth birthday. Longfellow's words (in *Morituri Salutamus*) are challenging:

> Shall we then sit us idly down and say
> The night hath come; it is no longer day?
> The night hath not yet come; we are not quite
> Cut off from labor by the failing light;
> Some work remains for us to do and dare;
> Even the oldest tree some fruit must bear;
> And as the evening twilight fades away
> The sky is filled with stars, invisible by day.

Summary

Whatever a person's age, all of the past and present is a preparation for developmental tasks yet to come. All of life is goal seeking and it is most advantageous to formulate and plan these goals on a conscious level—purposeful activity is superior to purposive behavior. Since individuals and situations differ, goals must be varied. The problems of adolescents can best be resolved through many approaches. Many problems the adolescent must solve himself, but the help and understanding of wise and well-balanced adults are often valuable aids.

College students can be of great help to new generations of adolescents. Professional study of adolescence is highly desirable. But the present achievement of developmental tasks in college is a kind of preparation that also has great value. Among these tasks are (1) choosing, and making maximum use of the choice of, an academic career—developing good study habits is an important first step—(2) choosing and preparing for a career—worrying less about the specific choice than about developing the traits that will promote success and satisfaction in all vocations—(3) choosing a mate and working to make the relationship a satisfactory one for the marriage partner.

Developmental tasks continue to be presented during the early adult years. It is necessary to adjust habits, desires, idiosyncracies, and ambitions to a wife or husband who also has habits, desires, idiosyncracies, and ambitions that must be recognized. Having and rearing children inevitably changes perspective and the nature of living patterns. Acquiring a home imposes a responsibility that for approximately twenty years others have carried without bothering the younger generation. The young adult must make his good impression in his vocation early and must maintain the impression through consistent effort. Yet some time must be reserved for the developmental task of forming new friends—who are not too readily available.

Persons in their middle years have reached or are reaching the peak of vocational success. There still remain for them various adjustments in the course of effective living. Additional civic responsibility may justifiably be assumed. More time, their stake in the community, and the wisdom they have accumulated make civic participation highly desirable. The age of peak earnings emphasizes the need for learning to live within the normal income. New problems appear with children who are asserting the desire for freedom so firmly expressed by adolescents. Leisure time must fill the gap left by completed responsibilities and by declining physical vigor. All these changes involve establishing new relations with the spouse.

Old age, too, involves developmental tasks: adjusting to physical decline, to lessened income, to the death of the spouse, to an older age group, and to new living arrangements.

Nature's greatest gift to mankind was making men and women less than perfect. Mankind's attempt, and the individual's attempt, to come closer to full realization of potentialities gives continuing purpose to life. The problems of adolescents, like everyone's problems, will never be solved. When unnecessary obstacles to achievement have been removed there will still remain the task of making that which is good still better.

STUDY AND REVIEW ITEMS

1. What do you feel should constitute some of the foremost goals of development for adolescents?

2. What are three or four suggestions of first importance in preparing leaders for adolescents?

3. Referring to the concept of "developmental tasks" described in Chapter Three, would you consider that educational problems are a "task" for college students?

4. What are some of the advantages of an early choice of career? of a delayed choice of career?

5. What formal steps do you feel might advantageously be taken to help young adults with their developmental tasks?

6. See how detailed a list you and your classmates can make of problems involved in buying a home.

7. What could be done in high school and college to make civic responsibility a more uniformly successful achievement of the middle years?

8. What evidence is there that achieving new relations with the spouse is a developmental task of the middle years?

9. What are some of the factors that would soften the task of living on a lessened income in the later years?

10. Cite reasons for agreeing or disagreeing with the statement that our greatest gift from nature is our incompleteness.

11. In what ways can the contemporary development of the habit of continuous learning bear upon the developmental tasks of old age?

RECOMMENDED SUPPLEMENTARY READING

Giles, Ray. *Begin Now—To Enjoy Tomorrow,* 2nd Ed. (Newark, New Jersey: The Mutual Benefit Life Insurance Company; 1951), 57 pp.
This booklet, which may be obtained free from the publisher, is devoted to anticipation of problems to be encountered in the later years of life. It is easy to read. The recommendations are psychologically sound.

Havighurst, R. J. *Human Development and Education* (New York: Longmans, Green and Company; 1953), pp. 257–283.
Part V of this book deals with the developmental tasks of early adulthood, the middle years, and later maturity. The author stresses the varying degrees of difficulty of tasks as they are encountered by people coming from different socio-economic strata.

Huxley, Julian. *Evolution in Action* (New York: Harper & Brothers; 1953), 182 pp.
Here is a challenge to mankind and to individual man. Huxley contends that biological evolution is completed but that evolution of the mind is merely beginning. If advantage is taken of the potential of pooled intellectual resources, evolution can take on much richer meanings.

Mursell, James L. *Using Your Mind Effectively* (New York: McGraw-Hill Book Company, Inc.; 1951), 264 pp.
Since learning is a lifelong job it is never too late to learn how to do it more effectively. This entertainingly written book incorporates the recommendations that have been found, through experiment and experience, to lead to success.

Wattenberg, William W. *The Adolescent Years* (New York: Harcourt, Brace & Company, Inc., 1955), pp. 393–406.
This selection deals with adults' reactions to teen-agers. Both derogatory and constructive views are described. Suggestions are given for the improvement of the lives of adults which will result in the wider acceptance of a wholesome attitude toward adolescents.

AUDIO-VISUAL MATERIAL

Planning for Success (Coronet Films, Coronet Building, Chicago 1), 11 min., so., b. and w. or color.
The emphasis in this film is on the relationship of success to personal adjustment. Suggestions for realistic and helpful goals are given.

Glossary

ability That which a person is capable of doing. See *capacity* and *aptitude*.

accident proneness The tendency of some individuals to manifest personal inadequacy or emotional instability by being involved in accidents with disproportionately high frequency.

adjustment Denoting conformity and adherence to demands and requirements. Harmony of inner desires and aptitudes. In this text the word is used not just to indicate submission to expectation but also refers to changing demands to bring them into more harmonious relation with other aspects of balanced living.

adolescence A process of growth from childhood to adulthood. May be thought of as the period of development during the teen years.

affective Relating to emotions.

amnesia Loss or partial loss of memory due to shock, illness, or repression of disturbing thoughts or experiences.

androgens The male sex hormones, produced in quantities by the pituitary and testes. Found in smaller quantities in the female.

aptitude That which a person is potentially capable of doing. Usually refers to a capacity that is somewhat above the average in relation to what is typically possessed by others.

attitude A mental predisposition that tends to cause an individual to think or act in a given manner.

authoritarianism Characterized by obedience to peremptory demand as contrasted to the exercise of individual autonomy and freedom.

axillary Pertaining to the armpit—the juncture between a limb and the body. Hence, axillary hair is hair that grows under the arm.

capacity That which an individual is potentially capable of learning to do. The basis upon which abilities are developed.

character A person's consistent pattern of reaction to ethical, moral, and religious situations.

climacteric A critical period of life, especially the middle years when marked decline in sexual adequacy and functioning often imposes grave psychological readjustments. See *menopause.*

clique   A small (four or five to a dozen) and rather exclusive set of individuals, bound together by similarity and contiguity.

coefficient of correlation   The numerical indication of the degree of relationship between measures of two sets of phenomena.

correlation   Parallel relation in the existence of different functions or structure.

compensation   Making up for lack or deficiency, or *felt* lack, in one aspect of personality by the achievement of superiority in some other trait. There is an erroneous belief that a person congenitally weak in one area will have counterbalancing talents.

compulsion   An irresistible motivation to do some act even though the act is completely illogical.

conflict   Emotional tension created by contradictory impulses or desires. Indecision caused by the need for choosing between two courses or having to do one thing when another course is preferred. Some conflict is normal but chronic conflict may become frustration.

crowd   The group of individuals of both sexes among whom the adolescent finds his casual friends and the associates with whom he ordinarily plays and congregates. A social group larger and less intimate and less exclusive than the clique. See *gang*.

crush   The devotion of a young person for an older person, usually of the same sex; may also refer to an ardent liking for an older person of the other sex.

defensive behavior   Patterns of conduct developed by the individual to protect himself from real and imaginary threats to security.

delinquency   Pertaining to aggressive behavior which society finds bothersome and which is, consequently, disapproved. The violation of law by an individual who has not attained the age of legal responsibility.

development   Change in character and quality, including improvement of function, which is a concomitant of total growth. See *growth*.

developmental tasks   Learnings that are requisite to effective contemporary processes of adjustment and that prepare the individual for the succeeding stages of development. Hence, they are learnings that should desirably be accomplished in a rather restricted period of time.

displacement   The venting of an emotion on some person or thing other than the person or thing that precipitated the feeling. (The adolescent may quarrel with his peers because of anger aroused by a parental demand. The anger is actually directed toward the parent, but the young person refrains from talking back to the parent.)

dogma A definite tenet or set of beliefs imposed by authority. The doctrine of a particular church or religion.

ectomorph Tall, fragile, flat-chested, delicate individual, typically with long, poorly-muscled extremities. Great surface area in proportion to mass, hence overly exposed to the world. (One of Sheldon's three "body types.")

endomorph Heavy body type. The digestive viscera predominate. Usually, though not always, this weak body type is fat. See *mesomorph*.

emotion A stirred-up state of the organism. Actually a rather vague word since it may vary from the mild state of being interested to the extreme state of rage and hate—also it refers to the pleasant and integrative feelings as well as to very unpleasant and disintegrative affective states. A condition influenced by an external situation and an internal feeling state.

empirical Based on experience or observation. Often contrasted to *experimental* because there are no consciously designed controls. Cautiously collected empirical data are highly valuable.

estrogens The female sex hormones, produced in quantities by the pituitary and the ovaries. Found in a smaller amount in the male.

experimental Characterized by the rigid control of variables while leaving one feature constant in order to determine contributing factors in the occurrence of a given phenomenon.

frustration A state of being baffled. Personality disorganization brought on by long continued, unresolved conflict involving goals or desires.

functional disorder A disturbance resulting in a change in the performance of a part of the body, but with no structural alteration of tissue noted.

gang A rather closely knit but large (see *clique*) group of individuals bound by some specific purpose, often, but not necessarily, criminal in nature. Sometimes composed of only one sex.

geriatrics   The branch of medicine that considers the physiological aspects of growing old. This term is also applied to study of the psychological aspects of aging.

gerontology   Study of the socio-economic conditions that have particular impact on the behavior and adjustment of persons in the later years of life.

gonads   The sex glands that produce the sperm of the male (the testes) and the ova of the female (the ovaries).

gonadatropic hormone   A secretion of the anterior lobe of the pituitary gland which stimulates growth of the sex organs and development of secondary sex characteristics.

growth   Increase in mass. Increased weight and length of the organism or parts of the organism. (This text, in common with many others, uses the word growth as an equivalent to development.)

heredity   In this text the word refers to the potential which the individual possesses at the time of conception, which is transmitted to him by his ancestors in terms of gene characteristics. A potential for development.

heterosexual   Pertaining to the relations between the sexes. These relations need not be considered as primarily sexual in nature; that is, visiting, conversing, dancing, playing, and the like, may be heterosexual without involving sex activity.

homosexuality   Retardation or arrest of sexual development at the level of attachment to individuals of the same own sex.

hormones   The substances secreted by the smooth, or internal glands —the thyroid, parathyroids, adrenals, and others. These substances enter directly into the blood stream and affect organs and functions that may be physically remote from the secreting gland.

hysteria   Physical dysfunction without organic cause; for example, loss of vision without disease or damage in the eye or in the central nervous system. A functional neurosis.

ideal   A standard of behavior. A concept for goal-seeking behavior or of a situation that approaches perfection.

intelligence   There are many concepts of intelligence. The one taken in this book is as follows: Intelligence is a function of capacity and experience which facilitates the making of manifold effective adjustments to the total environment.

interest   The feeling of identity which one has for some person, thing, or situation.

laissez-faire   Herein refers to social climates characterized by lack of external control. The "let-alone" attitude with respect to the conduct of the affairs of children and adolescents.

masturbation   Manipulation of the genitals or bodily movement that stimulates the genitals so that sexual excitation takes place. Masturbation may, or may not, result in orgasm. The old synonym of "self-abuse" is inaccurate and unjust in view of the normality of this behavior.

maturity   The state of adulthood, ripeness. But *appropriate* maturity may be conduct which is normal and expected for children and adolescents but which is still short of having achieved adult status.

menarche   The first menstruation.

mesomorph   Hard, firm, strong, and upright body. Blood vessels are large, skin is thick. Strength and sturdiness predominate. (See *ectomorph, endomorph.*)

menopause   The period at which there is a natural cessation of menstruation, usually at about age 45 to 50. Of significance in the study of adolescence because the psychological difficulties often involved for the mother occur at about the time children are becoming adolescents.

morals   The codes of conduct that have been derived from living in a particular society—the mores. Standards of conduct set by social groups.

mores   Customs and conventions of society which tend to shape the behavior of members of a given society. Folkways having ethical significance.

morphology   The study of body types and the manner and results of studying them according to build.

multiple causation   A principle of psychology emphasizing that explanations of behavior on the basis of one causative factor are overly simple. Behavior and growth are the result of many factors and influences.

needs   The lack of something requisite to existence or at least to effective or enjoyable existence.

neoplasms   Abnormal formations or growths. Tumors or cancers.

nephritis   Inflammation or disease of the kidneys. One form is Bright's disease.

neuroses   Mental or emotional disturbances less serious than psychoses. Conditions in which the individual chronically falters and stumbles in daily living.

nocturnal emission   Spontaneous discharge of semen during sleep— usually accompanied by dreams of a sexual nature.

organismic   Referring to the totality of growth processes. Organismic age, for instance, refers to the average or composite of chronological, mental, emotional, bone, dental, muscular, physiological, etc., age or growth toward maturity.

organogenic   Having origin in bodily or physiological functioning.

orgasm   The peak of sexual excitement at which point tension is released and relaxation immediately ensues. In the male this involves release of semen but in the female the relaxation is more general in nature.

ossification   The hardening of the bones that accompanies maturing.

pathological   Relating to the study and treatment of diseases. A condition of illness.

percentile   A means of showing a standard value in terms of relative rank or standing in a theoretical group of 100; that is, a score of 75 correct responses out of 100 questions *might* have a percentile value of 90—meaning that out of the group of 100 subjects, ten would exceed the score of 75.

personality   The totality and uniqueness of the individual, including physical, mental, moral, and emotional potentialities and achievements by which individuality in the eyes of others is achieved. The totality of the person, especially in terms of social behavior.

petting   Deep kissing and fondling designed to arouse sexual desires. Necking is sometimes defined as "from the neck up" and petting as "from the neck down."

phenomenon   Any occurrence. In psychology especially that which is common or characteristic.

phobias Abnormal fears of some harmless object or situation. Fears stemming from illogical connection of some result to a factor not involved in the real cause.

pre-pubertal Changes that appear and characteristics that exist just prior to the time at which the major degrees of physiological sex maturity are achieved.

projective technique Certain procedures by which inner personality trends are analyzed or feelings are released. Fundamentally, projective techniques consist in the subject's adding structure (or reading meaning into) unstructured situations—painting, playing with toys, finishing a story, or interpreting pictures, cloud formations, or ink blots.

psychogenic Having origin in mental functioning. Originating in the thinking processes.

psychological measurements Devices through which status or achievement in certain functions (intellectual ability, knowledge, emotional and social adjustment, and the like) is estimated or evaluated.

psychology of suggestion A condition that leads to the acceptance of an idea for reasons other than information or logic. Propaganda, repetition, use of prestige, clichés, being a "good fellow" are approaches to the psychology of suggestion.

psychoses Any of a number of more serious mental disturbances. Physical causes such as brain dysfunction or toxic conditions are often present. Some psychoses may be psychogenic in origin and lead to involve physical disabilities.

psychosomatic Having to do with the relationship of mind and body. A psychosomatic disorder is one that involves bodily impairment with no evident organic cause; the cause is presumed to be "mental." For example, ulcers attributed to nervous tension.

puberty Maturation of the sex organs to the level of adult functioning. The most noteworthy of the physiological changes that indicate the beginning of adolescence.

puppy love Transitory boy-girl friendships characteristic of the early teens. (The adolescent tends to regard these passing stages of development as being quite serious, and the adult should recognize the seriousness of this feeling.)

purposeful An action pursued because it has a definite purpose which is perceived by the individual.

purposive Action directed toward satisfaction of certain needs or desires, but these needs are not consciously realized and defined by the behaving individual. Unconscious striving for psychological equilibrium.

readiness   Mental, physical, social, and emotional maturation that is sufficient to produce a condition in which the individual will profit from exposure to a particular learning situation.

religion   A system of faith in and worship of a being higher than a mortal.

secondary sex characteristics   Physical features that develop as a result of primary changes in the sex organs at the time of puberty. For example: change of voice and appearance of pubic hair in boys and girls; receding of the hairline at the sides of the forehead, growth of hair on the face (boys); growth of the breasts and broadening of the hips (girls).

social class   A group of individuals similar in their possession of certain advantages, privileges, and a status that stems from membership in that particular group. (*Lack* of advantages, privileges, and status may also be the characteristic quality.)

social mobility   The movement of a person from one level of class status to another. Especially upward mobility, referring to the rise of a person from his present class to a higher one.

sociogram   A schematic representation of the friendship and/or work preferences of a group of individuals. A representation of cleavages in social groups.

sociometry   The study of interpersonal attractions and relationships through the schematic representation of friendship preferences.

somatotype   A class or category into which the body build of a person causes him to be placed; for example, endomorph, mesomorph, ectomorph.

somnambulism   Walking or executing other rather complex activities while sleeping. Often considered a manifestation of emotional instability.

Stanford-Binet test   A pioneer and still widely used American individual test of mental ability. The one most frequently used in standardization and establishment of the reliability and validity of group tests of mental ability.

validity   The extent to which a test properly evaluates that quality or ability which it is designed to evaluate.

work experience education   A plan whereby the adolescent supplements and correlates his formal education with actual work on the job, in the store, or in the field.

Bibliography

In the text, bibliographical citations, with the exception of direct quotations, refer to the numbered items in the following list. When only one number is given the item generally refers to an article or short pamphlet. When a number follows the colon, in the text reference, it indicates the page of the book referred to by the item number.

In this Bibliography, numbers in brackets refer to the page of the text on which the item is cited.

1. Abrams, Albert J. "Barriers to the Employment of Older Workers," *Annals of the American Academy of Political and Social Science,* 279:98–105, January, 1952. [598]
2. Alberty, Harold, in National Society for the Study of Education, 51st Yearbook, Part I, *Adapting the Secondary-School Program to the Needs of Youth* (Chicago: University of Chicago Press; 1953). [297]
3. Allport, Gordon W., in Carl Murchison (Ed.) *Handbook of Social Psychology* (Worcester: Clark University Press; 1935). [348]
4. American Association of School Administrators. *Educating for American Citizenship* (Washington, D. C.: National Education Association; 1954). [374]
5. American Council on Education. *The Relation of Religion to Public Education* (Washington, D. C.: American Council on Education; 1947). [390]
6. Anderson, Harold H., in P. A. Witty and C. E. Skinner (Eds.), *Mental Hygiene in Modern Education* (New York: Farrar and Rinehart, Inc.; 1939). [24, 108]
7. Anderson, John E. *The Psychology of Development and Personal Adjustment* (New York: Henry Holt & Company, Inc.; 1949). [576]
8. Ausubel, David P. *Ego Development and the Personality Disorders* (New York: Grune and Stratton; 1952). [424]
9. Ausubel, David P. *Theory and Problems of Adolescent Development* (New York: Grune and Stratton; 1954). [147, 316, 382, 457, 555, 558]

614

10. Baber, Ray E. *Marriage and the Family,* 2nd Ed. (New York: McGraw-Hill Book Company, Inc.; 1953). [22, 261, 461, 475, 478, 480, 484, 583, 588]

11. Bader, D. P., and E. V. Beach. "Wants of Adolescents: I. A Preliminary Study," *Journal of Psychology,* 3:505–511, 1937. [372]

12. Baker, Harry J. *Introduction to Exceptional Children,* Rev. Ed. (New York: The Macmillan Company; 1953). [58, 316]

13. Banning, Margaret Culkin. "The Case for Chastity," *The Reader's Digest 20th Anniversary Anthology* (Pleasantville, New York: The Reader's Digest Association; 1941). [461]

14. Barker, Roger G., Tamara Dembo, and Kurt Lewin, in Roger C. Barker and Others (Eds.) *Child Behavior and Development* (New York: McGraw-Hill Book Company, Inc.; 1943). [319]

15. Bayley, Nancy. "The Long and Short of It," *Educational Leadership,* 2:331–335, 1945. [140]

16. Benedict, Ruth. *Patterns of Culture* (New York: Mentor Books; 1934). [9]

17. Benedict, Ruth, in 13th Yearbook of the Department of Supervisors and Directors of Instruction, *Mental Health in the Classroom* (Washington, D. C.: National Education Association; 1940). [114]

18. Bennett, M. E. *College and Life,* 4th Ed. (New York: McGraw-Hill Book Company, Inc.; 1952). [359]

19. Berdie, R. F. "Factors Related to Vocational Interests," *Psychological Bulletin,* 41:137–157, 1944. [518]

20. Bernard, Harold W. *Mental Hygiene for Classroom Teachers* (New York: McGraw-Hill Book Company, Inc.; 1952). [19, 53, 110, 234]

21. Bernard, Harold W. *Psychology of Learning and Teaching* (New York: McGraw-Hill Book Company, Inc.; 1954). [545, 575]

22. Bernard, Harold W. *Toward Better Personal Adjustment* (New York: McGraw-Hill Book Company, Inc.; 1951). [235, 359, 481, 579]

23. Bernard, William. *Jailbait* (Garden City: Garden City Books; 1951). [460]

24. Bigelow, Maurice A. *Adolescence: Educational and Hygienic Problems* (New York: Funk and Wagnalls Company; 1924). [9, 17]

25. Binger, Carl. "What Is Maturity?" *Harper's,* 202:70–78, May, 1951. [20]

26. Bingham, June. *Do Cows Have Neuroses?* (White Plains, New York: The Westchester Mental Hygiene Association; 1948). [415]

27. Bird, Charles, and Dorothy M. Bird. *Learning More by Effective Study* (New York: D. Appleton-Century Company, Inc.; 1945). [359, 578]

28. Blair, Arthur W., and William H. Burton. *Growth and Development of the Preadolescent* (New York: Appleton-Century-Crofts, Inc.; 1951). [42, 150]

29. Blanchard, Phyllis, in J. McV. Hunt (Ed.) *Personality and the Behavior Disorders,* V. II, (New York: The Ronald Press Company; 1944). [424]

30. Bliven, Bruce, Jr. "The Learning Time of Your Life," *Redbook,* 102, No. 5:21ff., 1954. [285]

31. Block, Virginia Lee. "Conflicts of Adolescents with Their Mothers," *Journal of Abnormal and Social Psychology,* 32:192–206, 1937. [197]

32. Bogomolets, Alexander A. *The Prolongation of Life* (New York: Duell, Sloan and Pearce, Inc.; 1946). [23]

33. Bond, E. A. "The Yale-Harvard Freshman Speed-Reading Experiment," *School and Society,* 54:107–111, 1941. [357]

34. Bossard, James H. S. "Family Backgrounds of Wartime Adolescents," *Annals of the American Academy of Political and Social Science,* 236:39, 1944. [196]

35. Bossing, Nelson L. "Readjustments in the School Program for the Adolescent," *School Review,* 49:428–435, 1941. [27]

36. Bossing, Nelson L., and Robert R. Martin. *Youth Faces Its Problems* (Chicago: Laidlaw Brothers; 1950). [123]

37. Bowman, Henry A. *Marriage for Moderns,* 2nd Ed. (New York: McGraw-Hill Book Company, Inc.; 1948). [492]

38. Bradley, William A. "Correlates of Vocational Preferences," *Genetic Psychology Monographs,* 28:99–169, 1943. [294]

39. Breckenridge, M. E., and E. L. Vincent. *Child Development,* 2nd Ed. (Philadelphia: W. B. Saunders Company; 1949). [169, 402]

40. Bretsch, Howard S. "Social Skills and Activities of Socially Accepted and Unaccepted Adolescents," *Journal of Educational Psychology,* 43:449–458, 1952. [313]

41. Bridges, K. M. B. "Emotional Development in Early Infancy," *Child Development,* 3:324–341, 1932. [308]

42. Brink, William G. "Reading Interests of High-School Pupils," *School Review,* 47:613–621, 1939. [361]

43. Britten, R. H. "Illness and Accidents among Persons Living under Different Housing Conditions," U. S. Public Health Reports, 56:609–640, 1941. [401]

44. Britten, Rollo. "Physical Impairments and Socio-economic Factors," *The Milbank Memorial Fund Quarterly*, 26:391ff, 1948. [192]

45. Brock, John F. "The Red-Headed Africans," *Atlantic*, 192, No. 6:68–70, 1953. [169]

46. Bromley, Dorothy. "Education for College or for Life?" *Harper's*, 182:407–418, 1941. [54, 213, 236]

47. Brookover, W. B. "Teachers and the Stratification of American Society," *Harvard Educational Review*, 23:257–267, 1953. [265]

48. Brown, Carlton. "We Can Lick Alcoholism," *Science Illustrated*, 3:45, June, 1948. [429]

49. Bruch, H., "Obesity in Relation to Puberty," *Journal of Pediatrics*, 19:365–375, 1941. [402]

50. Bullis, H. E., and Emily E. O'Malley. *Human Relations in the Classroom* (Wilmington: The Delaware Society for Mental Hygiene, Course I, 1947; Course II, 1948; Course III, 1951). [311, 324]

51. Burck, Gilbert. "How Hard Do Americans Drink?" *Fortune*, 47:121–125, March, 1953. [428]

52. Burgess, Ernest W., and Leonard S. Cottrell, Jr. *Predicting Success or Failure in Marriage* (New York: Prentice-Hall, Inc.; 1939). [482]

53. Burr, Samuel Engle, Jr. "Behind Today's Delinquencies," *Phi Delta Kappan*, 35:231–236, 1954. [560]

54. Burton, William H. *The Guidance of Learning Activities* (New York: D. Appleton-Century Company, Inc.; 1944). [346]

55. Burton, William H. "Education and Social Class in the United States," *Harvard Educational Review*, 23:243–256, 1953. [268]

56. Byrns, Ruth. "Relation of Vocational Choice to Mental Ability and Occupational Opportunity," *School Review*, 47:101–109, 1939. [518]

57. Cameron, Norman, and Ann Magaret. *Behavior Pathology* (Boston: Houghton Mifflin Company; 1951). [399, 416]

58. Canadian Research Committee on Practical Education. *Better Schooling for Canadian Youth*, Toronto, 1951. [50, 520]

59. Cantril, H., and W. A. Hunt. "Emotional Effects Produced by the Injection of Adrenalin," *American Journal of Psychology*, 44:300–307, 1932. [306]

60. "Census of Population, 1950," Preliminary Reports, Series PC–7, No. 1, February 25, 1951. [476]
61. *City Workers Family Budget* (Washington, D. C.: U. S. Bureau of Labor Statistics; December, 1947). [192]
62. Clemmons, Anne M., and Harriet Williams. "Motivating Adolescents to Optimum Growth with the Wetzel Grid," *Journal of Home Economics,* 44:192–194, 1952. [401]
63. Cole, Lawrence E. *Human Behavior: Psychology as a Bio-Social Science* (Yonkers: World Book Company; 1953). [547]
64. Cole, Lawrence E., and William F. Bruce. *Educational Psychology* (Yonkers: World Book Company; 1950). [293]
65. Cole, Luella. *Psychology of Adolescence,* 4th Ed. (New York: Rinehart and Company, Inc.; 1954). [306, 362, 412, 418]
66. Conrad, Herbert S., Frank N. Freeman, Harold E. Jones, in National Society for the Study of Education, *43rd Yearbook,* Part I, *Adolescence* (Chicago: University of Chicago Press; 1944). [288]
67. Cooper, Courtney R. *Designs in Scarlet* (Boston: Little, Brown and Company; 1939). [123]
68. Cooper, R. C. "Improving the Technique of Reading in Service Schools," *Military Review,* Fort Leavenworth, 28:20–24, 1948. [357]
69. "The Cost of College," *Newsweek,* 45:98–100, May 9, 1955. [215]
70. Coronet Films, "15th Anniversary Issue," Chicago 1: Coronet Building, 1954–1955. [325]
71. Crandall, Robert, "The Kids are Campaigning, Too!" *American Magazine,* 154:31ff, October, 1952. [545]
72. Cubberley, Ellwood P. *Public Education in the United States* (Boston: Houghton Mifflin Company; 1919). [390]
73. Cureton, T. K. "The Unfitness of Young Men in Motor Fitness," *Journal of the American Medical Association,* 123:69–74, 1943. [263]
74. Davidson, Percy E., and H. Dewey Anderson, in Raymond G. Kuhlen and G. G. Thompson (Eds.) *Psychological Studies of Human Development* (New York: Appleton-Century-Crofts, Inc.; 1952). [528]
75. Davie, James S. "Social Class Factors and School Attendance," *Harvard Educational Review,* 23:175–185, 1953. [555]
76. Davis, Allison. "Poor People Have Brains, Too," *Phi Delta Kappan,* 30:294–295, 1949. [269]

77. Davis, Allison, and Kenneth Eells. *Davis-Eells Test of General Intelligence or Problem-Solving Ability* (Yonkers: World Book Company; 1953). [266, 283]

78. Davis, Allison, and Robert J. Havighurst. *Father of the Man* (Boston: Houghton Mifflin Company; 1947). [110]

79. Davis, Frank G. (Ed.) *Pupil Personnel Service* (Scranton: The International Textbook Company; 1948). [513]

80. Davis, Kingsley. "Adolescence and the Social Structure," *Annals of the American Academy of Political and Social Science*, 236:8–16, 1944. [20]

81. Davis, Kingsley. "The Sociology of Parent-Youth Conflict," *American Sociological Review*, 5:523–535, 1940. [127]

82. Deutscher, Max, and Isidor Chein. "The Psychological Effects of Enforced Segregation: A Survey of Social Science Opinion," *Journal of Psychology*, 26:259–287, 1948. [116]

83. Dewey, Richard, and W. J. Humber. *The Development of Human Behavior* (New York: The Macmillan Company; 1951). [115]

84. Dickenson, Frank G. "The Coming Class War—Old vs. Young," cited in *Harpers*, 205:81, July, 1952. [25]

85. Dienstein, William. "Facts and Fancies about Delinquency," *Phi Delta Kappan*, 35:227–230, 1954. [553]

86. Dillon, Harold J. *Early School Leavers* (New York: National Child Labor Committee; 1949). [211, 224]

87. Dimock, H. S. "A Research in Adolescence. I. Pubescence and Physical Growth," *Child Development*, 6:177–195, 1935. [45]

88. Dollard, John, L. W. Doob, N. E. Miller, O. H. Mower, and R. R. Sears. *Frustration and Aggression* (New Haven: Yale University Press; 1939). [191, 313, 422, 423]

89. Drucker, Peter F. "The Promise of Automation: America's Next Twenty Years, Part II," *Harper's*, 210:41–47, April, 1955. [23]

90. "Drug Addiction among Students," *The World Almanac* (New York: New York World-Telegram; 1952). [425]

91. Duvall, Evelyn Millis. *Facts of Life and Love for Teen-Agers* (New York: Popular Library; 1953). [458]

92. Duvall, Evelyn Millis. *Keeping Up with Teen-Agers* (New York: Public Affairs Committee, Inc.; 1947). [6]

93. Eberhart, W. "Evaluating the Leisure Reading of High School Pupils," *School Review*, 47:257–269, 1039. [361]

94. *Education—An Investment in People*, U. S. Chamber of Commerce, Committee on Education, 1945–46. [217]

95. Educational Policies Commission. *Moral and Spiritual Values in the Public Schools* (Washington, D. C.: The National Education Association, 1951). [377]

96. Edwards, Newton, in National Society for the Study of Education, *43rd Yearbook*, Part I, *Adolescence* (Chicago: University of Chicago Press, 1944). [112]

97. Elias, L. J. "Farm Youths' Appraisal of Their Adjustments Compared to Other Youths," *Washington Agricultural Experiment Station, Bulletin* 513, 1949. [111]

98. Elkin, Henry. "Aggressive and Erotic Tendencies in Army Life," *American Journal of Sociology*, 51:408–413, 1946. [118]

99. Ellis, Albert, and Robert M. Beechley. "A Comparison of Child Guidance Clinic Patients Coming from Large, Medium, and Small Families," *The Journal of Genetic Psychology*, 79:131–144, 1951. [193]

100. "Endocrinology in Male and Female Development" (Medical Division of Sharp and Dohme) *Seminar*, 14:No. 4:3–19, 1952. [149]

101. Espenschade, Anna. *Motor Performance in Adolescence*, Monograph of the Society for Research in Child Development, 5, No. 1:177–195, 1940. [140]

102. "Experiments for Spotting Future Delinquents Tried," United Press, New York, February 8, 1954. [562]

103. "Facts and Figures in Mental Health," *Understanding the Child*, 21:66, 1952. [403]

104. Fairbank, Ruth E. "The Subnormal Child—Seventeen Years After," *Mental Hygiene*, 17:177–208, 1933. [44, 558]

105. Farnham, Marynia F. *The Adolescent* (New York: Harper & Brothers; 1952). [53, 185, 188, 409, 411, 425]

106. Faunce, Roland C. "Schools for Adolescents: Nonclass Experiences," *Review of Educational Research*, 24:66–73, 1954. [542]

107. Fleming, Robert S. "Problems of Emotional Health in the Program of the High School," *The High School Journal*, 35:74–79, 1951. [314]

108. Foster, Roy A. "A Picture of Health," *National Education Association Journal*, 42:274–275, 1953. [173]

109. Frank, Lawrence K., in National Society for the Study of Education, *43rd Yearbook*, Part I, *Adolescence* (Chicago: University of Chicago Press, 1944). [419]

110. Frank, Lawrence K. "Needs and Problems of Adolescents in the Area of Emotional Health," *The High School Journal,* 35:66–74, 1951. [303]

111. Frank, Lawrence K. *Personality and Culture* (Danville, Illinois: The Interstate Printers and Publishers; 1948). [310, 380, 560]

112. Freud, Anna (translated by Cecil Baines). *The Ego and the Mechanism of Defense* (London: Hogarth Press and the Institute of Psychoanalysis; 1939). [11]

113. Fromm, Erich. *Man for Himself* (New York: Rinehart and Company, Inc., 1947). [375, 386]

114. Garrett, Henry E. "A Developmental Theory of Intelligence," *American Psychologist,* 1:373–378, 1946. [276]

115. Garrett, Henry E., A. I. Bryan, and R. Perl. "The Age Factor in Mental Organization," *Archives of Psychology,* No. 176, 1935. [288]

116. Gates, Arthur I. *What Research Says to the Teacher: Teaching Reading* (Washington, D. C.: Department of Classroom Teachers, American Educational Research Association of the National Education Association; 1953). [357]

117. Garrison, Karl. *Psychology of Adolescence,* 4th Ed. (New York: Prentice-Hall, Inc.; 1951). [362]

118. Garrison, Karl. *The Psychology of Exceptional Children,* Rev. Ed. (New York: Ronald Press Company; 1950). [312]

119. Gerrity, John. "The Truth about the Drug Menace," *Harper's Magazine,* 204:27–31, February, 1952. [426]

120. Gesell, A. "The Genesis of Behavior Form in Fetus and Infant: The Growth of the Mind from the Standpoint of Developmental Morphology," *Proceedings of the American Philosophical Society,* 84:471–488, 1941. [48]

121. Giles, Ray. *Begin Now—To Enjoy Tomorrow* (Newark, New Jersey: The Mutual Benefit Life Insurance Company; 1951). [200]

122. Glick, Paul C., and Emanuel Landau. "Age as a Factor in Marriage," *American Sociological Review,* 15:517–529, 1950. [479]

123. Glueck, Sheldon, and Eleanor Glueck. *Delinquents in the Making* (New York: Harper & Brothers; 1952). [561]

124. Glueck, Sheldon, and Eleanor Glueck, *Unraveling Juvenile Delinquency* (New York: The Commonwealth Fund; 1950). [356, 553]

125. Goode, William J., and Paul K. Hatt. *Methods in Social Research* (New York: McGraw-Hill Book Company, Inc.; 1952). [572]

126. Goodenough, Florence L. *Developmental Psychology*, 2nd Ed. (New York: Appleton-Century-Crofts, Inc.; 1945). [33, 109, 593]

127. Hall, G. S. *Adolescence: Its Psychology and Its Relations to Physiology, Anthropology, Sociology, Sex, Crime, Religion and Education* (New York: D. Appleton & Company; 1904). [8]

128. Hand, Harold C. *Principal Findings of the 1947–48 Basic Studies of the Illinois Secondary School Curriculum Program* (Curricular Series A. No. 51, Illinois Secondary School Curriculum Program, Bulletin No. 2, Springfield, Illinois, 1949). [225]

129. Handy, Robert T. "The Christianity of Main Street," *Crossroads*, 4:No. 3:20–22, 1954. [387]

130. Hankins, Dorothy. "The Psychology and Direct Treatment of Adolescents," *Mental Hygiene*, 27:238–247, 1943. [27]

131. Hanley, Charles. "Physique and Reputation of Junior High School Boys," *Child Development*, 22:247–60, December, 1951. [165]

132. Harris, Dale B., in National Society for the Study of Education, *49th Yearbook*, Part I, *Learning and Instruction* (Chicago: University of Chicago Press; 1950). [343]

133. Hartmann, George W., in C. E. Skinner (Ed.) *Educational Psychology*, 3rd Ed. (New York: Prentice-Hall, Inc.; 1951). [343]

134. Havemann, Ernest, and Patricia S. West. *They Went to College* (New York: Harcourt, Brace & Company, Inc.; 1952). [217]

135. Havighurst, Robert J. *Developmental Tasks and Education* (New York: Longmans, Green and Company, Inc.; 1952). [20, 79]

136. Havighurst, Robert J. *Human Development and Education* (New York: Longmans, Green and Company, Inc.; 1953). [29, 80, 86, 191, 200, 383, 547, 599]

137. Havighurst, Robert J., and Hilda Taba. *Adolescent Character and Personality* (New York: John Wiley and Sons, Inc.; 1949). [382]

138. Heaton, Margaret M. *Feelings Are Facts* (New York: The National Conference of Christians and Jews; 1952). [309]

139. "Helping Hands," *Time*, 61:102, March 16, 1953. [373]

140. *Higher Education for American Democracy, V. II. Factors in Attendance Establishing the Goals,* Report of the President's Commission on Higher Education (Washington, D. C.: U. S. Government Printing Office; 1947). [226]

141. Hightower, P. R. *Biblical Information in Relation to Character and Conduct,* Studies in Character III, No. 2 (University of Iowa, 1930). [384]

142. Hofstra Research Bureau, Psychological Division, Hofstra College. *Use of Alcoholic Beverages among High School Students* (New York: Mrs. John S. Sheppard Foundation, Inc.; 1953). [429, 430, 431]

143. Hollingshead, August B. *Elmtown's Youth: The Impact of Social Classes on Adolescence* (New York: John Wiley and Sons, Inc.; 1949). [244, 247, 250, 347, 447, 555]

144. Hollingworth, Leta S. *The Psychology of the Adolescent* (New York: D. Appleton & Company; 1928). [9]

145. Hoover, J. Edgar. "Highlights of Uniform Crime Reports for 1950," *The World Almanac* (New York: *New York World-Telegram;* 1952). [421]

146. Horney, Karen. *The Neurotic Personality of Our Time* (New York: W. W. Norton and Company, Inc.; 1937). [185, 410]

147. Horrocks, John E. *The Psychology of Adolescence* (Boston: Houghton Mifflin Company; 1951). [163, 165, 263]

148. Horrocks, John E., and Mae E. Buker. "A Study of the Friendship Fluctuations of Preadolescents," *The Journal of Genetic Psychology,* 78:131–144, 1951. [445]

149. Houseman, William, "Are U. S. Teenagers Rejecting Freedom?" *Look,* 18:25ff, February 26, 1952. [380]

150. "How Good ARE Our Public Schools?" *The Reader's Digest,* 65:34–36, September, 1954. [451]

151. Hurlock, Elizabeth B. *Adolescent Development* (New York: McGraw-Hill Book Company, Inc.; 1949). [383]

152. Huxley, Aldous. "Who Are You?" *Harper's,* 189:512–522, 1944. [51]

153. Ingraham, Norman R., Jr. "Health Problems of the Adolescent Period," *The Annals of the American Academy of Political and Social Science,* 236:117–127, 1944. [172]

154. Ivins, Wilson H., in National Society for the Study of Education, *52nd Yearbook,* Part I, *Adapting the Secondary-School Program to the Needs of Youth* (Chicago: University of Chicago Press; 1953). [522]

155. Ivins, Wilson H., William H. Fox, and David Segel. *A Study of the Secondary School Program in Light of Characteristics and Needs of Youth,* Bulletin of the School of Education, Indiana University, V. 25, No. 6, 1949. [228]

156. Jacobson, Paul B. (Ed.) *The American Secondary School* (New York: Prentice-Hall, Inc.; 1950). [225]

157. Jellinek, E. M., in Yale Summer School of Alcohol Studies, *Alcohol, Science and Society* (New Haven: Quarterly Journal of Studies on Alcohol; 1945). [428]

158. Jersild, Arthur T. *Child Development and the Curriculum* (New York: Bureau of Publications, Teachers College, Columbia University; 1946). [452]

159. Jersild, Arthur T. *Child Psychology,* 4th Ed. (New York: Prentice-Hall, Inc.; 1954). [589]

160. Jersild, Arthur T. *In Search of Self* (New York: Bureau of Publications, Teachers College, Columbia University; 1952). [442]

161. Jersild, Arthur T., in National Society for the Study of Education, *38th Yearbook,* Part I, *Child Development and the Curriculum* (Bloomington, Illinois: Public School Publishing Company; 1939). [166]

162. Jersild, Arthur T. "Self-Understanding in Childhood and Adolescence," in William E. Martin and Celia B. Stendler (Eds.) *Readings in Child Development* (New York: Harcourt, Brace & Company, Inc.; 1954). [18, 310, 324, 356]

163. Johnson, Granville B. "The Relationship Existing between Bilingual and Racial Attitude," *The Journal of Educational Psychology,* 42:357–365, 1951. [348]

164. Jones, H. E. *Motor Performance and Growth* (Berkeley: University of California Press; 1949). [166]

165. Jones, H. E. in National Society for the Study of Education, *43rd Yearbook,* Part I, *Adolescence* (Chicago: University of Chicago Press; 1944). [163]

166. Jones, H. E., and H. S. Conrad, in National Society for the Study of Education, *43rd Yearbook,* Part I, *Adolescence* (Chicago: University of Chicago Press; 1944). [279, 286, 288]

167. Jordon, Bernard A., and Harry B. Spencer, in Franklin R. Zeran (Ed.), *Life Adjustment Education in Action* (New York: Chartwell House, Inc.; 1953. [522, 524]

168. Kaminkow, Hyman B. "Basic School Approaches in Preventing Juvenile Delinquency," *Understanding the Child,* 22:73–78, 1953. [563]

169. Kaplan, Oscar J. "Psychological Aspects of Aging," *The Annals of the American Academy of Political and Social Science,* 279: 32–42, 1952. [43, 284]

170. "Keeping Abreast in Education," *Phi Delta Kappan,* 36:79, 1954. [407]

171. Kenyon, Lawrence B. "A Course in Occupations," *Bulletin of the National Association of Secondary School Principals,* 32:131–138, 1948. [516]

172. Kinsey, Alfred C., Wardell B. Pomeroy, Clyde E. Martin, and Paul H. Gebhard. *Sexual Behavior in the Human Female* (Philadelphia: W. B. Saunders Company; 1953). [424, 454, 459, 479, 483, 488, 489, 558, 596]

173. Kinsey, Alfred C., Wardell B. Pomeroy, and Clyde E. Martin, *Sexual Behavior in the Human Male* (Philadelphia: W. B. Saunders Company; 1948). [189, 424]

174. Kirkendall, Lester A., and Ruth Farnham Osborne. *Dating Days* (Chicago: Science Research Associates, Inc.; 1949). [457, 459, 460]

175. Klineberg, Otto, "Negro Intelligence and Urban Residence," in Guy E. Swanson and Others (Eds.) *Readings in Social Psychology,* Rev. Ed. (New York: Henry Holt and Company, Inc.; 1952). [281]

176. Knapp, Robert H. *Practical Guidance Methods* (New York: McGraw-Hill Book Company, Inc.; 1953). [328]

177. Kretschmer, E. *Physique and Character* (New York: Harcourt, Brace & Company, Inc.; 1925). [160]

178. Kuder, G. F., and B. B. Paulson. *Discovering Your Real Interests* (Chicago: Science Research Associates, Inc.; 1949). [356]

179. Kuhlen, Raymond H. *The Psychology of Adolescent Development* New York: Harper & Brothers; 1952). [19, 316, 317, 346, 373, 510]

180. Kvaraceus, William C. *Juvenile Delinquency and the School* (Yonkers: World Book Company; 1945). [556]

181. Kvaraceus, William C., in National Society for the Study of Education, *47th Yearbook,* Part I, *Juvenile Delinquency and the Schools* (Chicago: University of Chicago Press; 1948). [41]

182. Landis, Paul H. *Adolescence and Youth* (New York: McGraw-Hill Book Company, Inc.; 1947). [25]

183. Landis, Paul H. *Adolescence and Youth,* 2nd Ed. (New York: McGraw-Hill Book Company, Inc.; 1952). [260, 261, 419, 451]

184. Latham, A. J. "The Relationship between Pubertal Status and Leadership in Junior High School Boys," *The Journal of Genetic Psychology,* 78:185–194, 1951. [166]

185. Lee, J. J. "A Study of Certain Individual Differences Found among Crippled Children and of Certain Problems Involved in Their Education and Training," Doctoral Dissertation, Ohio State University, 1942. [60]

186. Lenrow, Elbert. *Reader's Guide to Prose Fiction,* New York: D. Appleton-Century Co., Inc.; 1940). [363]

187. Levy, John, and Ruth Monroe, in Jerome M. Seidman (Ed.), *The Adolescent, A Book of Readings* (New York: The Dryden Press; 1953). [354]

188. Lewis, Claudia. *Children of the Cumberland* (New York: Columbia University Press; 1946). [111, 259]

189. Lewin, Kurt. "Experiments in Social Space," *Harvard Educational Review,* 9:21–32, 1939. [323]

190. Lewin, Kurt, Ronald Lippitt, and Ralph K. White. "Patterns of Aggressive Behavior in Experimentally Created 'Social Climates,'" *The Journal of Social Psychology,* 10:271–299, 1939. [185, 321]

191. Lindgren, Henry C. *Mental Health in Education* (New York: Henry Holt and Company, Inc.; 1954). [329]

192. Los Angeles City Schools, "Moral and Spiritual Values in Education," School Publication #402, 1944–45. [325]

193. Lowman, C. L. "A Consideration of Teen-Age Athletics," *Journal of Health and Physical Education,* 12:398–399, 1941. [172]

194. Lund, Frederick H. "Adolescent Motivation: Sex Differences," *Pedagogical Seminary and Journal of Genetic Psychology,* 64:99–103, 1944. [172]

195. Lund, F. H., E. R. Yeomans, and E. A. Geiges, "Health Indices in Relation to Age, Sex, Race and Socio-economic Status," *Journal of Social Psychology,* 24:111–117, 1946. [401]

196. Maccoby, Eleanor E., and Patricia K. Gibbs, in William E. Martin and Celia B. Stendler (Eds.). *Readings in Child Development* (New York: Harcourt, Brace & Company, Inc.; 1954). [258]

197. McCreary, William H., and Donald E. Kitch. *Now Hear Youth,* Bulletin of the California State Department of Education, 22:7, October, 1953. [236, 238]

198. McFadden, Frances. "I Can't Afford My Wife's Job," *Harper's,* 205, No. 1228:62–65, 1952. [487]

199. McKenney, Ruth. "The Difficult Age," *Holiday Magazine,* 14:14–24, November, 1953. [446]

200. Mackenzie, Gordon N., and Gloria C. Cammarata. "Schools for Adolescents: Community Relations," *Review of Educational Research,* 24:91–100, 1954. [540]

201. McMillen, A. W. "Army of Boys on the Loose," *Survey,* 63:388–393, 1932. [191]

202. McNemar, Quinn. *The Revision of the Stanford Binet Scale* (Boston: Houghton Mifflin Company; 1942). [288]

203. McTeer, Wilson. "Observational Definitions of Emotions," *Psychological Review*, 60:172–179, 1953. [305]

204. Maier, N. R. F. "Studies of Abnormal Behavior in the Rat: XIV. Strain Differences in the Inheritance of Susceptibility to Convulsions," *Journal of Comparative Psychology*, 35:327–335, 1943. [40]

205. Malamud, W., and G. Palmer. "The Role Played by Masturbation in the Causation of Mental Disturbances," *Journal of Nervous and Mental Diseases*, 76:366–379, 1932. [49]

206. Malm, Marguerite, and Olis G. Jamison. *Adolescence* (New York: McGraw-Hill Book Company, Inc.; 1952). [26]

207. Mann, Erika. *School for Barbarians* (New York: Modern Age Books; 1938). [30]

208. Matsner, Sidonie, and Benjamin C. Gruenberg. "Crosscurrents in the Rearing of Youth," *The Annals of the American Academy of Political and Social Science*, 236:67–73, 1944. [109]

209. Mays, Benjamin E. "Progress in Race Relations," *Presbyterian Life*, 7, No. 3:8–9, 1954. [260]

210. Mead, Margaret. *Coming of Age in Samoa* (New York: William Morrow & Co., Inc.; 1928). [9]

211. Menninger, Karl. *Man against Himself* (New York: Harcourt, Brace & Company, Inc.; 1938). [419]

212. Menninger, Karl. *The Human Mind*, 3rd Ed. (New York: Alfred A. Knopf; 1953). [375]

213. Menninger, William C. "Things I Never Would Have Learned at Home," *Reader's Digest*, 65:129–132, November, 1954. [125]

214. Merriam, Robert E., and John W. Betha. *Understanding Politics* (Chicago: Science Research Associates, Inc.; 1952). [546]

215. Metropolitan Life Insurance Company, "Statistical Bulletin," V. 34, No. 8, August, 1953. [400, 403]

216. Midcentury White House Conference on Children and Youth. *Child and Youth at the Midcentury: A Chart Book* (Raleigh, North Carolina: Health Publications Institute; 1951). [192]

217. "Migratory Labor in American Agriculture," *Report of the President's Commission on Migratory Labor* (Washington, D. C.: 1951). [192]

218. Mikesell, William H., and Gordon Hanson. *Psychology of Adjustment* (New York: D. Van Nostrand Company, Inc.; 1952). [407]

219. Millard, Cecil V. *Child Growth and Development* (Boston: D. C. Heath and Company; 1951). [157]

220. Miller, H., and D. W. Baruch. "Psychosomatic Studies of Children with Allergic Manifestations," *Psychosomatic Medicine,* 10:275–279, 1948. [413]

221. Miller, Van, and Willard Spalding. *The Public Administration of American Schools* (Yonkers: World Book Company; 1952). [540]

222. "Minority of Drivers Cause Most Accidents," *Science News Letter,* 58:204; Sept. 23, 1950. [407]

223. Monroe, Dorothy. "Dallas Invests in Teen Agers," *American Home Magazine,* 42:26–28, June, 1949. [406]

224. Moreton, F. E. "Attitudes toward Religion among Adolescents and Adults," *British Journal of Educational Psychology,* 14:69–79, 1944. [376]

225. Morton, R. L. *Teaching Arithmetic* (Washington, D. C.: National Education Association; 1953). [52]

226. Montgomery, Ray. "John Dewey and the Egg-in-the-Bottle," *Phi Delta Kappan,* 34:95, 1952. [380]

227. Mowrer, O. Hobart. "Learning Theory: Historical Review and Re-interpretation," *Harvard Educational Review,* 24:37–48, 1954. [309]

228. Murray, H. A., and Clyde Kluckhohn, in Kluckhohn, Murray, and D. M. Schneider (Ed.) *Personality in Nature, Society and Culture,* 2nd Ed. (New York: Alfred A. Knopf, Inc.; 1953). [422]

229. Nelson, Henry B. "High School Drop-Outs and Stay-Ins," *The School Review,* 60:255, 1952. [223]

230. New Jersey Advisory Committee on Social Hygiene Education. *Education for Human Relations and Family Life on the Secondary School Level* (New York: The American Social Hygiene Association, Inc.; 1941). [494]

231. O'Connor, Johnson. "Redirecting Americans," *Atlantic Monthly,* 167:193–200, 1941. [581]

232. *An Occupational Guidance Record* (Chicago: The World Book Encyclopedia Reference Library; 1938). [515]
     A Career-Planning Guide (World Book Encyclopedia, 1956).

233. Ogden, Jean, and Jess Ogden. "Sharing Community Responsibility," *The Annals of the American Academy of Political and Social Science,* 279:98–105, 1952. [596]

234. Olson, Clara M. "The Adolescent: His Society," *Review of Educational Research,* 24:5–11, 1954. [332]

235. *The Oregonian*, 72:No. 16, April 19, 1953, p. 1. [374]
236. *The Oregonian*, 94:No. 29, April 26, 1954, p. 6. [374]
237. Parry, Douglas F. "Experimental Practice in Improving the Emotional Health of Secondary School Students," *The High School Journal*, 35:80–88, 1951. [326, 451]
238. Parsons, Talcott. "Age and Sex in the Social Structure of the United States," *American Sociological Review*, 7:604–616, 1942. [439]
239. Patterson, Don S., in Franklin R. Zeran (Ed.) *Life Adjustment Education in Action* (New York: Chartwell House, Inc.; 1953). [234]
240. Patty, William L., and Louise S. Johnson. *Personality and Adjustment* (New York: McGraw-Hill Book Company, Inc.; 1953). [416, 463]
241. Pennington, L. A., Irwin A. Berg, and George D. Stoddard. *An Introduction to Clinical Psychology* (New York: The Ronald Press Company; 1948). [419]
242. "The People" (The American Character), *Time:* 64:22–25, September 27, 1954. [594]
243. "Personal and Otherwise," *Harper's Magazine*, 204, No. 1221: 14–16, 1952. [427]
244. *Planning for American Youth*, Rev. Ed. (Washington, D. C.: National Association of Secondary School Principals; 1951). [86, 94]
245. Plant, J. S., in National Society for the Study of Education, *47th Yearbook*, Part I, *Juvenile Delinquency and the Schools* (Chicago: The University of Chicago Press; 1948). [554]
246. Plant, J. S. *The Envelope* (New York: The Commonwealth Fund; 1950). [329, 518]
247. Poole. Ernest. "Sons of the Wolf," *Harper's*, 175:460–469, 1937. [30]
248. Prescott, Daniel A. *Emotion and the Educative Process* (Washington, D. C.: The American Council on Education; 1938). [71]
249. Prescott, Daniel A., and Others. *Helping Teachers Understand Children* (Washington, D. C.: American Council on Education; 1945). [564]
250. Preston, George H. *The Substance of Mental Health* (New York: Farrar and Rinehart, Inc.; 1943). [375]
251. Preu, Paul W., in J. McV. Hunt (Ed.) *Personality and the Behavior Disorders*, V. II (New York: The Ronald Press Company; 1944). [418]

252. Quillen, I. James, and Lavone A. Hanna. *Education for Social Competence* (Chicago: Scott, Foresman and Company; 1948). [544]
253. "Raid Snares 13 Teenagers," *The Oregonian,* April 13, 1953. [6]
254. Rainey, Homer P., in National Society for the Study of Education, *38th Yearbook,* Part II, *General Education in the American College* (Bloomington, Illinois: Public School Publishing Company; 1939). [105]
255. Ramsey, G. V. "The Sexual Development of Boys," *American Journal of Psychology,* 56:217–233, 1943. [11]
256. Remmers, H. H., and C. G. Hackett. *Let's Listen to Youth* (Chicago: Science Research Associates, Inc.; 1950). [198, 219, 236, 292]
257. Remmers, H. H., and Lyle M. Spencer. "All Young People Have Problems," *National Education Association Journal,* 39:182–183, 1950. [107, 198]
258. Ridgway, John M. "A Work-Experience Program," *National Education Association Journal,* 41:166–167, 1952. [522]
259. Robinson, Thomas E. "His Teacher Improved, Too," *National Education Association Journal,* 41:54, 1952. [344]
260. Rorty, James. "Bread and the Stuff We Eat," *Harper's,* 200, No. 1198:42–48, 1950. [169]
261. Rorty, James. "The Thin Rats Bury the Fat Rats," *Harper's,* 198, No. 1188:28–32, 1949. [168]
262. Rummell, Frances V. "What Are Good Teachers Like?" *School Life,* 30, No. 9:4–9, 1948. [543]
263. Russell, William F. "Better Education for Citizenship," *Phi Delta Kappan,* 33:161–164, 1951. [538]
264. Ryan, W. Carson. "Facts and Figures in Mental Health," *Understanding the Child,* 21:66, 1953. [168]
265. Sadler, William S. *Adolescence Problems* (St. Louis: C. V. Mosby Company; 1948). [419]
266. Schneiders, Alexander A. *The Psychology of Adolescence* (Milwaukee: The Bruce Publishing Company; 1951). [29, 384]
267. Schneiders, Alexander A. "Emotional Development in Children," *Education,* 72:216–223, 1951. [306]
268. *Schools and the 1950 Census,* Research Bulletin of the National Education Association, 29:No. 4 (Washington, D. C.: National Education Association; 1951). [211]
269. Schukart, Janice. "Achieving a Better Understanding of Adoles-

cent Problems through Creative Writing," Unpublished master's thesis, Portland, Oregon, Reed College, 1950. [331]

270. Scoggin, Margaret C. "Teen-Agers Read for Fun," in Alfred Stefferud (Ed.) *The Wonderful World of Books* (New York: Mentor Books; 1952). [363]

271. "Senseless," *Time*, 64, No. 9:15, August 30, 1954. [422]

272. Seward, Georgene H. *Sex and the Social Order* (New York: McGraw-Hill Book Company, Inc.; 1946). [189, 424]

273. Shaffer, Laurance F., in Oscar K. Buros (Ed.) *The Third Mental Measurements Yearbook* (New Brunswick: Rutgers University Press; 1949). [328]

274. Shalott, Sidney, and H. C. McFadgen. "Our Youngsters Don't Have to be Killers," *Saturday Evening Post*, 222:81, December 17, 1949. [406]

275. Sheldon, William H., and S. S. Stevens. *The Varieties of Temperament* (New York: Harper & Brothers; 1942). [50]

276. Sherman, Mandel, and Cora B. Key. "The Intelligence of Isolated Mountain Children," in Wayne Dennis (Ed.) *Readings in Child Psychology* (New York: Prentice-Hall, Inc.; 1951). [282]

277. Shiebler, Howard A. "Half Our Audience Is Walking Out," *School Executive*, 70:40, June, 1951. [223]

278. Shock, Nathan W. "The Effect of Menarche on Basal Physiological Functions in Girls," *American Journal of Physiology*, 139:288–291, 1943. [158]

279. Shock, Nathan W., in National Society for the Study of Education, *43rd Yearbook*, Part I, *Adolescence* (Chicago: University of Chicago Press; 1944). [153]

280. "Should 18-Year-Olds Have a Vote?" *Current Events*, 53:No. 20, 154, February 22–26, 1954. [548]

281. Shuey, A. M. "Improvement in the Scores of the American Council Psychological Examination from Freshman to Senior Year," *Journal of Educational Psychology*, 39:417–428, 1948. [285]

282. Shuttleworth, F. K. *The Adolescent Period*, Society for Research in Child Development, Inc., V. 14, No. 49, No. 1, 1949. [11]

283. Sims, Verner M. "Some Correlates of Social-Class Identification among High School and College Students," *The School Review*, 60:160–163, 1952. [257]

284. Sisson, E. D. "Vocational Choices of Students from Cities, Towns, and Farms," *School and Society*, 54:94–96, 1941. [263]

285. "Six Reasons Marriages Fail," Philadelphia: United Press, February 23, 1954. [478]

286. Smith, Harry P. *Syracuse Youth Who Did Not Graduate* (Syracuse, New York: Board of Education; 1950). [225, 226, 227, 236]

287. Sorenson, Roy. "Wartime Recreation for Adolescents," *Annals of the American Academy of Political and Social Science,* 236: 145–151, 1944. [356]

288. Spalding, Willard B., and John R. Montague. *Alcohol and Human Affairs* (Yonkers: World Book Company; 1949). [430]

289. Spalding, Willard B., Personal interview, Portland, Oregon, November 10, 1953. [110]

290. Spencer, Lyle M. *Junior Guidance Newsletter,* Chicago: Science Research Associates, April, 1953. [543]

291. "Statistics of Insane," *The Encyclopedia Americana,* 15:152, 1949. [317]

292. Stendler, Celia B. "Social Class and the Curriculum," *Educational Leadership,* 7:371–375, 1950. [269]

293. Stocker, Joseph. "Yes, We Have Jobs for Kids," *Nation's Business,* 40:32–35, 1952. [524]

294. Stoddard, George D. in National Society for the Study of Education, *39th Yearbook,* Part I, *Intelligence: Its Nature and Nurture* (Chicago: University of Chicago Press; 1940). [39]

295. Stolz, Herbert R., and Lois M. Stolz. *Somatic Development of Adolescent Boys* (New York: The Macmillan Company; 1951). [139]

296. Stott, L. H. "Adolescents' Dislikes Regarding Parental Behavior, and Their Significance," *Journal of Genetic Psychology,* 57:393–414, 1940. [263]

297. Stott, L. H., and Minnie P. Berson. "Some Changes in Attitudes Resulting from a Preparental Education Program," *Journal of Social Psychology,* 34:191–202, 1951. [200]

298. Stowe, Leland. "Farewell to 'Home, Sweet Home'," *Reader's Digest,* 66: 156–160, June, 1955. [30]

299. Strang, Ruth, in National Society for the Study of Education, *47th Yearbook,* Part I, *Juvenile Delinquency and the Schools* (Chicago: University of Chicago Press; 1948). [562]

300. Straus, Robert, and Seldon D. Bacon. *Drinking in College* (New Haven: Yale University Press; 1953). [375, 429]

301. Strecker, E. A., F. G. Ebaugh, and Jack R. Ewalt. *Practical Clinical Psychiatry,* 6th Ed. (Philadelphia: The Blakiston Company; 1947). [418]

302. Symonds, P. M. "Human Drives," *Journal of Educational Psychology,* 25:694, 1934. [70]
303. Symonds, P. M. "Inventory of Themes in Adolescent Fantasy," *American Journal of Orthopsychiatry,* 15:318–328, 1945. [318]
304. Symonds, P. M. *The Psychology of Parent-Child Relationships* (New York: D. Appleton-Century Company, Inc.; 1939). [179]
305. Tait, J. W. "Race Prejudice and Personality," *School: Secondary Edition,* 34:795–798, 1946. [116]
306. Tarver, James D. "Age at Marriage and Duration of Marriages of Divorced Couples," *Sociology and Social Research,* 36:102–106, 1951. [476]
307. Terman, Lewis M. *Psychological Factors in Marital Happiness* (New York: McGraw-Hill Book Company, Inc.; 1938). [179, 483, 489]
308. Terman, Lewis M., and M. Lima. *Children's Reading* (New York: D. Appleton & Co., 1927). [45]
309. Terman, Lewis M., and Melita H. Oden. *The Gifted Child Grows Up* (Stanford, California: Stanford University Press; 1947). [58, 96, 164, 293]
310. Thomas, W. I. *The Unadjusted Girl* (Boston: Little, Brown and Company; 1923). [71]
311. Thompson, George C. *Child Psychology* (Boston: Houghton Mifflin Company; 1952). [329]
312. Thompson, Warren S. *Population Problems* (New York: McGraw-Hill Book Company, Inc.; 1942). [112]
313. Thorndike, R. L. *Children's Reading Interests: A Study Based on a Fictitious Annotated Titles Questionnaire* (New York: Teachers College, Columbia University; 1941). [346]
314. Thorndike, R. L. "Growth of Intelligence during Adolescence," *Journal of Genetic Psychology,* 72:11–15, 1948. [281]
315. Thrasher, F. M. *The Gang,* Rev. Ed. (Chicago: University of Chicago Press; 1936). [166]
316. Tibbitts, Clark, and Henry D. Sheldon. "Introduction: A Philosophy of Aging," *Annals of the American Academy of Political and Social Science,* 279:1–10, 1952. [25, 112]
317. *Time,* 64:65, July 26, 1954. [157]
318. Toepelman, W. C. "Veterans' Accomplishments and Attitudes in College," *Journal of Higher Education,* 3:9–10, 1946. [282]
319. Tooher, Walters. "A Car Is Their Classroom," *Parent's Magazine,* 24:28, August, 1949. [403]

320. Toops, Herbert A., in Oscar K. Buros (Ed.) *The Third Mental Measurements Yearbook* (New Brunswick: Rutgers University Press; 1949). [352]

321. Travis, Lee E., and Dorothy W. Baruch. *Personal Problems of Everyday Life* (New York: D. Appleton-Century Company; 1941). [488]

322. Trow, W. C. *Educational Psychology,* 2nd Ed. (Boston: Houghton Mifflin Company; 1950). [71]

323. *Two Years after School,* A Report of the Canadian Research Committee on Practical Education, Toronto, Canada, 1951. [227]

324. Tyler, Ralph W. "Educability and the Schools," *Elementary School Journal,* 49:200–212, 1948. [60]

325. Tyron, C. M. *U. S. Inventory I, Social and Emotional Adjustment* (University of California: Institute of Child Welfare; 1939). [196]

326. "The U. S. Negro, 1953," *Time,* 61:55–58, May 11, [116]

327. Van Waters, Miriam. *Youth in Conflict* (New York: Republic Publishing Company; 1925). [25]

328. Vogel, Victor H., and Virginia E. Vogel. *Facts about Narcotics* (Chicago: Science Research Associates; 1951). [425, 426]

329. Vorse, Mary H. "America's Submerged Class: The Migrants," *Harper's,* 206, No. 1233:93, 1953. [193]

330. Wallin, J. E. Wallace. *Personality Maladjustments and Mental Hygiene,* 2nd Ed. (New York: McGraw-Hill Book Company, Inc.; 1949). [194, 312, 409]

331. Warner, W. Lloyd. *American Life* (Chicago: University of Chicago Press; 1953). [111]

332. Warner, W. Lloyd, and Others. "Social Status in Education," *Phi Delta Kappan,* 30:113–119, 1948. [270]

333. Warner, W. Lloyd, and Mildred Hall Warner. *What You Should Know about Social Class,* Chicago: Science Research Associates, Inc.; 1953). [269]

334. Warner, W. Lloyd, Robert J. Havighurst, and Martin B. Loeb. *Who Shall Be Educated?* (New York: Harper & Brothers; 1944). [60, 246, 251, 257]

335. Warner, W. Lloyd, and P. S. Lunt. *The Social Life of a Modern Community* (New Haven: Yale University Press; 1941). [244]

336. Wattenberg, William. *The Adolescent Years* (New York: Harcourt, Brace & Company; 1955). [221]

337. Wattenberg, William. "Delinquency during Summer Months," *Journal of Educational Research,* 42:253–267, 1948. [556]

338. Weaver, Paul. "Youth and Religion," *Annals of the American Academy of Political and Social Science,* 236:152–160, 1944. [387, 388]

339. Weinrich, Ernest F. "How Can a School Increase Its Holding Power of Youth?" *The Bulletin of the National Association of Secondary School Principals,* 35:126, 1952. [211]

340. Wellman, Beth. "Mental Growth from Preschool to College," *Journal of Experimental Education,* 6:127–138, 1937–38. [281]

341. Wetzel, N. C. "Physical Fitness in Terms of Physique, Development, and Basal Metabolism with a Guide to Individual Progress from Infancy to Maturity," *Journal of the American Medical Association,* 116:1187–1195, 1941. [142]

342. "What to Do about the Drug Menace," *National Parent Teacher,* 46:30, March, 1952. [425]

343. White, Robert W. *The Abnormal Personality* (New York: The Ronald Press Company; 1948). [415, 416]

344. Whitney, F. L. *The Elements of Research,* 3rd Ed. (New York: Prentice-Hall, Inc.; 1950). [15]

345. Whyte, William F. "A Slum Sex Code," *American Journal of Sociology,* 49:24–31, 1943. [462]

346. Wilder, Thornton. "The Silent Generation," *Harper's,* 206:34–36, April, 1953. [15]

347. Wiles, Kimball. "Schools for Adolescents: Needed Research," *Review of Educational Research,* 24:100–102, 1954. [298]

348. Williams, Bill. "The Seniors Take Over D. C.," *Pathfinder,* May, 1953. [543]

349. Witmer, Helen L., and Ruth Kotinsky. *Personality in the Making* (New York: Harper & Brothers; 1952). [116]

350. Witty, Paul A. *The Gifted Child* (Boston: D. C. Heath and Company; 1951). [283]

351. Witty, Paul A. *Reading in Modern Education* (Boston: D. C. Heath and Company; 1949). [359]

352. Wolfenstein, Martha, in Harry L. Miller (Ed.) *The Ways of Mankind* (Chicago: The Center for the Study of Liberal Education for Adults; 1953). [389]

353. Wolfert, Ira. "I Saw Japan's Wings Clipped," *Coronet,* 14:3–7, 1943. [374]

354. Women's Bureau, U. S. Department of Labor, *Handbook of Facts on Women Workers,* Bulletin 237, 1950. [486]

355. Wood, Hugh B., in Franklin R. Zeran (Ed.) *Life Adjustment Education in Action* (New York: Chartwell House, Inc.; 1953). [381]
356. Woodring, Paul. *Let's Talk Sense about Our Schools* (New York: McGraw-Hill Book Company, Inc.; 1953). [507]
357. Woodworth, R. S., in Wayne Dennis (Ed.) *Readings in Child Psychology* (New York: Prentice-Hall, Inc.; 1951). [46]
358. Wylie, Philip. "They're Not Too Young to Marry," *The American Weekly*, March 7, 1954. [324]
359. *Youth and the World of Work*, Social Research Service, East Lansing, Michigan, Michigan State College, 1949. [507]
360. "Youth Research Institute," headed by Lester Rand, International News Service, June, 1953. [218]
361. Zachry, Caroline B., and Margaret Lighty. *Emotion and Conduct in Adolescence* (New York: D. Appleton-Century Company, Inc.; 1940). [150]
362. Zubek, John P., and P. A. Solberg, *Human Development* (New York: McGraw-Hill Book Company, Inc.; 1954). [289]

Index of Names

Index of Subject Matter